Visual Basic

.NET Unleashed

Paul Kimmel

Visual Basic .NET Unleashed

Copyright © 2002 by Sams Publishing

International Standard Book Number: 0-672-32234-x

Library of Congress Catalog Card Number: 2001089220

Printed in the United States of America

First Printing: January 2002

04   03   02   4   3   2

Trademarks

Warning and Disclaimer

ASSOCIATE PUBLISHER
Linda Engelman

ACQUISITIONS EDITOR
Sondra Scott

DEVELOPMENT EDITOR
Chris Haidri

MANAGING EDITOR
Charlotte Clapp

PROJECT EDITOR
Elizabeth Finney

COPY EDITOR
Margaret Berson

INDEXER
D&G Limited, LLC

PROOFREADER
D&G Limited, LLC

TECHNICAL EDITORS
John Cottrell
Eric Lett
Frank Arndt

TEAM COORDINATOR
Lynne Williams

MEDIA DEVELOPER
Dan Scherf

INTERIOR DESIGNER
Gary Adair

COVER DESIGNER
Aren Howell

PAGE LAYOUT
D&G Limited, LLC

Contents at a Glance

Contents

About the Author

Paul Kimmel is the founder of Software Conceptions, Inc. Paul provides Visual Basic consulting services to small, medium, and large corporations, having architected and implemented client/server, e-commerce, and Web applications throughout the United States and Canada.

Paul Kimmel is the author of several books on .NET, Visual Basic, VBA, Delphi, and C++ programming and has been programming professionally for 12 years and contributing to and authoring periodicals and books since 1992. Paul Kimmel is the author of the Visual Basic newsletter, *CodeGuru VB*, for Earthweb, Inc. Paul resides in Okemos, Michigan with his wife, Lori, and four children—Trevor, Douglas, Alex, and Noah—and various and sundry pets.

Dedication

Visual Basic .NET Unleashed is dedicated to my 7-year-old daughter Alex Marie. Precocious and beautiful, Alex is a shining light in my life, and I thank God for her every day.

Love, Daddy

Acknowledgments

Thank you for buying and reading *Visual Basic .NET Unleashed*. Sharon Cox and I envisioned this project almost three years ago. At that time, I mistakenly thought I would be writing *Visual Basic 7 Unleashed*. What a difference a year made! My good friend Sharon is no longer with Sams, and Visual Basic .NET is not just Visual Basic 7. Without a continued commitment from my agent Chris Van Buren at Waterside and from Sondra Scott at Sams, I would not have written this book. I appreciate the opportunity that Sams has given me to write this book for you. By taking a moment of your valuable time to read these acknowledgements, you will help me thank the people who made writing *Visual Basic .NET Unleashed* possible.

Special thanks to the professionals who reviewed the original outline and provided valuable feedback: David Jung, Senior Systems Architect, Mullin Consulting Inc.; Mike Amundsen, Consultant and Author; and Ari Bixhorn, Visual Basic Product Manager, Microsoft Corporation. Their feedback during the conception of this book was invaluable and greatly appreciated.

A bow of gratitude goes out to Rob Howard and Connie Sullivan at Microsoft for redirecting dozens of questions to the people with the answers. Special thanks to Bill Chiles for timely information on macros, add-ins, wizards, and the global assembly cache. Thanks to Ty Carson for dropping what he was doing to put me in touch with some multithreading guys. (Thanks to Peter Monadjemi, author at large, for letting me explain threads to him.) And, thanks to all of the folks at Microsoft behind the scenes working to chase down answers to dozens of questions. Visual Basic .NET is a welcome "first-class" language that is a pleasure to develop with and write about.

Thanks to Duke Power in Charlotte, NC, and Jim Roundtree at ComConTech. Mr. Roundtree is a consummate professional, and I appreciate the matchmaking he did between Duke Power and me. Working with Toni Johnson, Jackie Gooding, Jack Blanton, and Bill Jones was my pleasure and good fortune. Bill Jones is the founder of the Enterprise Developer's Guild in Charlotte and provides a top-notch service that is helping dozens of developers with Visual Basic .NET. Jack Blanton, through his insightful questions, reminded me that Visual Basic .NET will present some real challenges to professional Visual Basic developers. I kept Jack and others at the Enterprise Developer's Guild in mind when writing this book, and I hope my efforts will help make the transition to Visual Basic .NET less of a burden.

I would like to thank Dennis Courtney at the Washington Area Delphi Users Group for allowing me to address their remarkable group. Borland's Delphi and Visual Basic .NET now share an intermingled history because one of Delphi's key architects is responsible for bringing .NET to Visual Basic developers. Thank you, Dennis, for your gracious hospitality.

My good friend Frank Arndt has been helping me hash out ideas for over 10 years now. Frank is a good sounding board for ideas, and I greatly value our relationship. Frank helped edit chapters in this book, along with Eric Lett and John Cottrell, who spent countless hours pouring over the code and text to help assure the highest quality and most accurate book possible. Eric works for the Credit Union of Central Manitoba, Canada, and ran the code several times through the various versions of .NET to help ensure that all of the code listings worked. John is a Senior Client/Server Developer at ALLTEL Information Services in Atlanta, Georgia; John worked diligently to ensure that we provided you with the best facts.

To you, the readers, I express my gratitude for spending your time and your hard-earned dollars in supporting my efforts. I hope my efforts support yours. If you have any questions or comments, please contact me at pkimmel@softconcepts.com.

Finally, and most importantly, I would like to thank my wife, Lori, and children Trevor, Douglas, Alex, and Noah. Without their patient and loving support, writing and programming would only be time stolen from them. They remind me every day that I am doubly blessed for having a loving family and an opportunity to do the things I love.

Tell Us What You Think!

As the reader of this book, *you* are our most important critic and commentator. We value your opinion and want to know what we're doing right, what we could do better, what areas you'd like to see us publish in, and any other words of wisdom you're willing to pass our way.

As an Associate Publisher for Sams, I welcome your comments. You can fax, e-mail, or write me directly to let me know what you did or didn't like about this book—as well as what we can do to make our books stronger.

Please note that I cannot help you with technical problems related to the topic of this book, and that due to the high volume of mail I receive, I might not be able to reply to every message.

When you write, please be sure to include this book's title and author as well as your name and phone or fax number. I will carefully review your comments and share them with the author and editors who worked on the book.

Fax: 317-581-4770

E-mail: feedback@samspublishing.com

Mail: Linda Engelman
             Associate Publisher
             Sams Publishing
             201 West 103rd Street
             Indianapolis, IN 46290 USA

Introduction

Writing a book that is targeted at hundreds of pages is a big task. "A journey of a thousand miles begins with a single step." You and I together are embarking on similar journeys. Mine is a journey of producing pages and yours is learning a language that may seem like an insurmountable task to some. I assure you that we can and will make this journey together, successfully.

Overview

Visual Basic .NET is more than simply Visual Basic 7. Microsoft has almost completely revamped a language that millions of developers know and love, Visual Basic 6. Perhaps the reasons for changing VB so dramatically require a book of their own, but that is a story best left for Microsoft to tell. Some things were clearly missing in past versions of VB. These missing things may not seem apparent to those completely content with Visual Basic as it used to be, but deficits existed.

When you and I are finished, you will see the new power and beauty of Visual Basic .NET and I hope you will agree that it was time for a VB overhaul.

Visual Basic .NET Unleashed is a complete book on the fundamentals of programming in a fully object-oriented language filled with new idioms and capabilities like true inheritance and polymorphism, event handlers, structured exception handling, and Web services. In addition to presenting you with fundamentals, it is the charter of this book to give you extra insight and advice based on real-world experience to help you become more productive with Visual Basic .NET than you ever were able to be with Visual Basic 6.

Visual Basic .NET has everything, including the kitchen sink. Visual Basic .NET presents the reader with more power and potential than any other implementation of Basic ever has.

Who Should Read This Book

Visual Basic .NET Unleashed was written to help the new and professional programmer make the transition to a completely revamped language. This book will help you make the transition to Visual Basic .NET smoothly and completely, and provide you with a comprehensive source for all of your VB programming needs.

If you are a Visual Basic 6 (or earlier VB edition) programmer, a new programmer, or switching from another language to Visual Basic .NET, this book was written for you. You will find information ranging from the fundamentals of object-oriented programming (OOP) to topics and examples demonstrating some of the most advanced object-oriented idioms and sophisticated .NET programming.

From the outset I have carefully coded and organized examples, and those examples are provided for you on the www.samspublishing.com Web site and at www.softconcepts.com. I took the time to incorporate one of the best aspects of Extreme Programming (a.k.a. XP), *Refactoring*. As often as possible, I employed Refactoring in an effort to provide you with examples of high-quality, simple object-oriented code that you can reuse to help you solve problems. The code samples will not look like VB6 code; they will look like Visual Basic .NET code. My efforts are intended to help you make a departure from VB6 and employ Visual Basic .NET to the greatest degree possible.

I used Martin Fowler's *Refactoring: Improving the Design of Existing Code* as a reference for the refactoring. Any mistakes in misapplying refactoring techniques are my own. You will also note that I completely dropped the Hungarian notation with which most of you are probably familiar. The Hungarian notation was written for a different generation of programming languages and was helpful in its time. However, the object-oriented and strongly typed nature of Visual Basic .NET mitigates the notation's benefit, so it is not employed in this text.

When you are finished with just the first few chapters in this book, you will be able to successfully build Visual Basic .NET applications. When you have completed the book, you will be able to employ the most powerful aspects of Visual Basic .NET professionally and completely. If your goal is to write professional solutions in Visual Basic .NET, this book is definitely for you.

Visual Basic .NET Is a First-Class Language

When I attended the Microsoft authors' summit in November of 2000, key Microsoft people kept referring to Visual Basic .NET as a "first-class" language. This acknowledgment by Microsoft that there was room for improvement in the old VB was a big step. Visual Basic .NET is a first-class language.

Visual Basic .NET now includes things that have been available to C++, Java, and Delphi programmers for years. Those of us who have programmed in these other languages, yet loved VB, patiently awaited the changes that would enable us to get out of "DLL Hell" and would remove limitations that definitely exist in VB6. With the arrival of Visual Basic .NET, those limitations are gone. My job is to show you what those limitations were while showing you what is available in Visual Basic .NET. For new capabilities, I might or might not explicitly say, "You couldn't do that in VB6," but VB6 programmers will know.

Visual Basic .NET is a first-class language because it explicitly supports and contains things that are indicative of a first-class language, including inheritance, virtual methods, shared methods, event handling, structured exception handling, multithreading, and encapsulation at the namespace level. Inheritance in Visual Basic .NET means that you inherit methods and properties rather than just an interface. Event handling is implemented through delegates, special classes that allow you to write dynamic event handlers as well as being used to support forms. Shared methods—sometimes called class methods or static methods—support invoking behaviors at the metaclass level. Support also exists for multithreading, namespaces, and parameterized constructors. You will find that applications written in Visual Basic .NET are limited far more by your imagination than by the language itself and the .NET Framework.

In this book we will discover many things together. If you have only programmed in VB6, I suspect the new VB will seem astounding to you. If you have programmed in Java, C++, or Delphi, and love Visual Basic, you will sigh with recognition, and agree that finally VB is no longer the disadvantaged cousin that some other language programmers consider it to be.

On the surface, Visual Basic .NET is almost as easy to get started with as VB6. If you only scratch the surface you might be disappointed, and your code also will be disappointing. As with many things, what lies beneath the surface makes all of the difference in the world.

What Is the Common Language Runtime?

In marketing material, you can learn that the Common Language Runtime (CLR) is a replacement for stodgy COM, MTS, the VB runtime DLL, and some other technologies. In a practical sense, the CLR is the result of Microsoft doing what we all should be doing—finding a means of leveraging one body of code to the greatest benefit by making it reusable in many contexts.

The CLR is a common architecture of classes and code that is shared among all languages under the .NET Framework. This means that much of the core body of code that makes Visual Basic .NET work is shared between C# (C sharp), Visual C++, and other languages yet to be implemented for .NET.

The CLR is essential in making Visual Basic .NET an equal sibling of other .NET languages. Ultimately, you are afforded the same power as other languages and the CLR makes deploying your Visual Basic .NET applications much easier.

Compelling Reasons to Switch to Visual Basic .NET

The compelling reasons to upgrade to Visual Basic .NET are not easy to explain in a couple of paragraphs. Reasons to switch include WebForms, Web applications, Web Services, the CLR, structured exception handling, true object-oriented programming, and multithreading—just to name a few.

When you have read *Visual Basic .NET Unleashed*, the benefits of switching will be clearer to you than if I attempt to synthesize the benefits in one or two paragraphs here. What you should know up front is that the reasons to switch to VB .NET are real and tangible and have little or nothing to do with marketing hype. If I do my job well in this book, you will be able to provide clear evidence of those reasons to managers, peers, and customers in the form of expressive, powerful, extensible, and more robust applications than ever before possible.

Implications

The implications of switching to Visual Basic .NET are that you will have to completely rewrite your applications written in earlier versions of VB. It is worth noting that Microsoft has included an upgrade tool. When you open VB6 applications in Visual Basic .NET, the Upgrade Wizard runs automatically. How well this will work on real-world applications is the real question. Run against a simple HelloWorld application written in VB6, the wizard produced a lot of extra code to support compatibility. (The HelloWorld upgrade and the original application are available for download from www.samspublishing.com.)

Besides providing upgrade assistance from VB6, Microsoft has already made minor compatibility concessions to Visual Basic .NET to support modest backward compatibility, but this in and of itself does not mitigate the need for completely rewriting VB6 applications. The benefit of rewriting is that you will be able to do more with less, and take full advantage of Visual Basic .NET. The implications of not rewriting may include code that is significantly more complex than it needs to be and difficult to maintain, and you may still have to rewrite major portions of upgraded code to cobble it together.

The need to rewrite existing applications may protract adoption of Visual Basic .NET more than a simple upgrade would. However, the benefits will be tangible to all—customers and programmers alike—and ultimately, well worth the effort.

What You'll Find in This Book

Visual Basic .NET Unleashed covers the new Visual Basic .NET language, the unified Visual Studio IDE, Web programming with WebForms, ADO.NET, Web Services, GDI+, and much more.

Visual Studio .NET is an enterprise tool. To demonstrate the power of the tool in the context of Visual Basic .NET, you will encounter some coverage of macros and the Automation Extensibility Model for customizing your Visual Studio experience.

To help you derive the greatest benefit from programming in an object-oriented language, *Refactoring*, an aspect of *Extreme Programming (XP)*, is employed to provide you with code that is practicable in the real world.

Finally, all of the code listings from the trivial to the complex are available for download from www.samspublishing.com. The code examples are organized by chapter.

The New Visual Basic Language

Some of the keywords and statement-level aspects of Visual Basic remain in Visual Basic .NET, but this is where most of the similarities end.

Comprehensive coverage of the Visual Basic core language as implemented in Visual Basic .NET is presented in *Visual Basic .NET Unleashed*.

Advanced Object-Oriented Programming

Classes in Visual Basic 6 support interface, or COM, inheritance. Interface inheritance is orthogonal to object-oriented inheritance. With classes in VB6, you define public methods and attributes in a class, and then implement them in another class. This works moderately well but is not as powerful as the superclass and subclass relationship afforded in object-oriented inheritance.

In Visual Basic .NET, you get methods and attributes from the superclass, or parent class, and extend them in subclasses. The benefit is a greater degree of code reuse. The idioms for OOP in Visual Basic .NET and the grammar supporting them are different. You will find comprehensive coverage and examples of the revised object-oriented idioms contained in this text.

Besides fundamental OOP idioms, this book covers and demonstrates the effect OOP revisions have in Visual Basic .NET on interface design, using namespaces, defining classes, implementing delegates, inheritance, polymorphism, encapsulation, and shared methods. All theoretical discussions are backed by examples demonstrating the techniques.

After you have mastered new OOP idioms, *Visual Basic .NET Unleashed* goes on to demonstrate advanced concepts like reflection, attributes, multithreading, and Web programming.

Code examples will be refactored as the book progresses to demonstrate how to achieve optimum reuse and benefit from your code.

Common Language Runtime

Visual Basic .NET Unleashed will demonstrate a multitude of classes in the CLR, including the expanded `System.Diagnostics` class that affords you a greater measure of testing and debugging capabilities.

Other aspects of the CLR will be introduced where it is appropriate to do so. For example, when we are discussing interface design and forms, we will work with Windows Forms and GDI+.

Client/Server Development

Client/server programming is still a mainstay in programming. A moderate amount of ADO.NET programming can be found in Chapter 19, which discusses ASP.NET and Web applications.

Database programming needs a lot of coverage, and I am diligently working on a new book to provide you with more information on Web programming and ADO.NET. Check out the www.samspublishing.com Web site for more information about that book.

Programming for the Web

Visual Basic .NET is an excellent choice for programming for the Web. ASP.NET uses code-behind modules that can be implemented with the same Visual Basic .NET as used in Windows Applications. Chapter 18 demonstrates Web Services and Chapter 19 introduces ASP.NET Web applications and server controls. The topic of extensive control of programming for the Web really needs its own book. I am hopeful that by the time you have digested this book, I will have a comprehensive book on Web programming available for you.

Summary

As you probably have gathered, we have a tall order. A book of modest size would be hard pressed to cover new features of a language without introducing an entirely new language. This is not a modestly sized book. *Visual Basic .NET Unleashed* is a fairly comprehensive book covering a large gamut of topics in Visual Basic .NET programming. It is large and comprehensive out of necessity because there is much for you to discover in this new language.

My goal is to provide you with a comprehensive resource that you can read and return to as your experience and needs grow. Consequently I will begin ... well, ... at the beginning. The first chapter introduces the new unified Visual Studio IDE and progresses rapidly through fundamental and advanced programming, to illustration and explanation of the most powerful features of Visual Basic .NET programming.

Thank you for buying this book. I hope you enjoy and profit by the adventure.

Introducing Visual Basic .NET

IN THIS PART

Using the Unified Visual Studio IDE

CHAPTER 1

In the beginning, a new architecture was created. The architect held the model to the light and Bill Gates saw that it was good, and he said, behold, we shall call the architecture .NET. Then the economy imploded, e-commerce companies failed, and according to the news, many people lost a lot of money on tech stocks.

From a historical perspective of about a year from now, we will look back and this will look like a correction or hiccup. The new economy is based on information, just as the old economy was based on manufacturing. We are in the Information Age, or what Shoshana Zuboff refers to as the business of *informating*, the process that translates descriptions and measurements of activities, events, and objects into information (Zuboff, 1988).

Visual Basic .NET is a timely release of a newly architected product to address the need to make information ubiquitous, to "informate." Businesses need to track transactions and buying habits, and make goods and services accessible by various connected devices, including cellular phones.

I grew up on Basic: ROM-BASIC, BASICA, GW-Basic, Basic for DOS, Visual Basic for DOS, and half a dozen versions of Visual Basic for Windows. Visual Basic .NET owes something to its predecessors, but Visual Basic .NET is the most significantly and radically changed version of Basic to date. Everything—from a unified Integrated Development Environment (IDE) and tools to the Common Language Runtime (CLR) and the object-oriented grammar—has all changed. If you are an experienced VB6 programmer, you will find many familiar elements in VB.NET that will make you feel right at home and several new features that you can sink your teeth into.

For all these reasons, we are beginning at the street level with the IDE. In this chapter, you will see some of the best and most useful features of Visual Studio .NET, and tools in the .NET Framework. We will even create a few applications. (We do have to get back to making a living.)

User-Customizable Profiles

When you open Visual Studio .NET for the first time, the first thing you will notice is that there is no separate menu item to start Visual Basic. To create a Visual Basic application, you will need to choose Start, Programs, Microsoft Visual Studio .NET 7.0, and then Microsoft Visual Studio .NET 7.0. (Henceforth, I will refer to this as starting Studio or Visual Basic.)

When you run Studio for the first time, you will be presented with the Start Page, an HTML page that plays the role of IDE navigator. The menus are enabled, but before you start programming you will want to do a little housekeeping first. If you accidentally close the Start page, you can reopen it by choosing Help, Show Start Page in Studio.

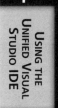

The Start Page is presented first because Microsoft has unified Visual Studio to be a single environment for all .NET development. A unified IDE is indicative of the interoperability between .NET languages.

Visual Studio .NET includes profile management. Selecting My Profile on the Start Page allows you to define a user profile, which basically means that you can make Visual Studio look and respond as close to what you might expect from a Visual Basic environment. Setting your profile to Visual Basic as a first step makes your environment behave as consistently with Visual Basic 6 as possible, allowing for the fact that there are significant changes in VB .NET.

To customize the user profile for Visual Basic users, perform the following steps:

1. If the Start Page isn't shown, choose Help, Show Start Page from the Studio Help menu.

2. In the left column beneath Get Start, select My Profile. (The Start Page is an HTML page, so work with it as such. Everything is point-and-click hyperlinks.)

3. In the Profile combo box, select Visual Basic Developer. (If the remaining combo boxes contain the values you want—references to a Visual Basic 6 style configuration—you can skip the remaining steps.)

4. In the Keyboard Scheme combo box, select Visual Basic 6.

5. In the Window Layout combo box, select Visual Basic 6.

6. In the Help Filter combo box, select Visual Basic and Related.

7. For the Show Help radio buttons, select whichever you prefer; I chose Internal Help.

8. For the At Startup Show combo box, select Show Start Page, or you may elect to have Studio open the New Project dialog box just as VB6 does.

At this point you can explore some of the other Start Page options, but you are ready to open your first project. Let's create a simple console application while we look at some of the project features.

Creating a Project

To pay homage to our forebears, we will examine the revised project management facilities and create the notorious "Hello World" application as a console application. (For more information on Project Templates, refer to the section later in this chapter, "An Overview of Project Templates.")

By now you will have configured your profile to using Visual Basic settings. At this point choose File, New, Project in Visual Studio .NET. The New Project window lists project types; select the Visual Basic Projects folder. On the right side of the New Project dialog box, select the Console Application template. (You may have to scroll the Templates window a little to find it.)

At this point, you will be presented with a default project name, most likely ConsoleApplication1, and a Location. The default location will be a subdirectory of where Visual Studio .NET was installed. Change the default name to HelloWorld, and select the location where you want the project to reside. It's important to note at this point that Visual Studio .NET uses a hierarchical source file structure; keep in mind that creating a new project will create several folders and files.

> **Tip**
>
> In Visual Studio .NET, you can close a solution without opening a new solution by choosing File, Close Solution. A *solution* is the term used to refer to your project.

After you've indicated the project name and location, click OK to create the console application. What Visual Studio .NET will do is create a solution, a .sln file, and other files that constitute a blank console project.

Project Files and Directories

A flat project topology isn't a very good way to organize project files, and all we have in software development is organization. Housekeeping is critical to managing intellectual property such as source code. Microsoft has acknowledged the value of organization by refining Studio to create a hierarchical solution structure for Visual Basic projects. (Refer to the "Solution Explorer" section later in this chapter for more information on managing project files.)

At the beginning of the section, we created the HelloWorld console solution. Visual Studio created a subfolder with the same name as the project, bin and obj subfolders, for storing the application files and intermediate files respectively, and the solution and source code files in the HelloWorld folder. If you look in the obj folder, you will see that Studio is distinguishing between DEBUG intermediate files and release files. (See "Adding Your Project to Source Control" for more on build management.)

In the HelloWorld folder, you will find AssemblyInfo.vb, HelloWorld.sln, HelloWorld.suo, HelloWorld.vbproj, HelloWorld.vbproj.user, and Module1.vb. See Table 1.1 for an overview of file extensions in the HelloWorld solution and their use.

TABLE 1.1 VB .NET File Extensions in Visual Studio

File Extension	Description
.sln	Solution file, which is similar to the VB6 group file and contains one or more projects
.suo	Contains user options for a solution
.vbproj	Represents a single project, or all of the files that are used to create an assembly
.user	Contains project-level user options
.vb	Contains source code

There are several other project types and each comes replete with incumbent file extensions. For example, your macros are stored in files with a .vsmacros extension (see Chapter 4).

All that remains in our console application is AssemblyInfo.vb and Module1.vb. The AssemblyInfo.vb file contains extra information, or metadata, about your application. For now, leave the AssemblyInfo.vb file alone. (For more on the AssemblyInfo.vb file and metadata, read Chapter 12, which explains metadata.)

Module1.vb (named so by default) is the primary file of interest for our console application. First you will note that module files no longer have a .bas extension. The module file for the console application contains some special text, as shown in Listing 1.1.

LISTING 1.1 A .vb File in the HelloWorld console application

```
Module Module1
Sub Main()
End Sub
End Module
```

The lines containing `Module Module1` and `End Module` define the boundary of the module source code. In .NET, more than one entity can be defined per file; therefore, types are delimited using a block statement indicating the beginning and ending of a new type. Because a console application was requested, an empty `SubMain` was added to the module. `Sub Main` is the entry point for a console application. The General view of the property pages indicates that `Module1` is the Startup object, as shown in Figure 1.1. To view the property pages, open the Solution Explorer by pressing Ctrl+Alt+L and click the HelloWorld project (or whichever project you are working on). Choose Project, Properties. (The Project menu is context-sensitive; the menu items change depending on the element selected in the Solution Explorer.)

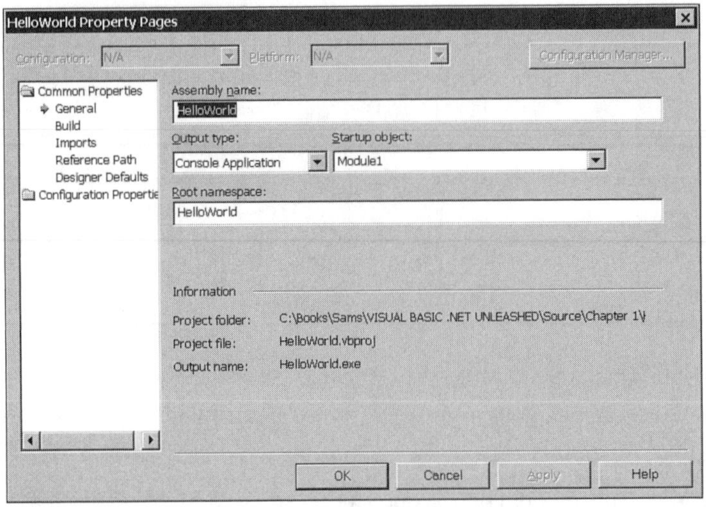

FIGURE **1.1**

The General view of the property pages, indicating that HelloWorld is a console application that starts with Module1.

This is our first application so we will keep it simple. Revise the code from Listing 1.1 to write "Hello World" to the console, as shown in Listing 1.2.

LISTING **1.2**   Homage to those who came before

```
Module Module1
Sub Main()
System.Console.WriteLine("Hello World!")
End Sub
End Module
```

The only revision from Listing 1.1 to Listing 1.2 is the addition of the System.Console.WriteLine("Hello World!") line. Press the shortcut key for the Debug, Step Into menu a couple of times to step through the demo. (If you are using the VB6 profile, as we will be in this book, the shortcut is F8; the default profile uses F10 for debug stepping.) You will notice a command window open that displays the text Hello World!.

This brief fragment introduces a lot of new things. First, notice that we are using parentheses without the Call keyword. In VB .NET we don't need the Call, but we do need parentheses. Also, notice the use of the System.Console namespace. Namespaces have to do with organizing classes to avoid global name conflicts. That is to help prevent you and me from naming two classes identically. Visual Basic .NET doesn't require you to indicate explicitly that you want to create an executable. If you step through the program or run it by pressing F5, Studio compiles an executable and places it in the bin folder. After you step through the code in Listing 1.2, HelloWorld.exe resides in the bin project subfolder. To run the console application outside the IDE, click Start, Run in Windows and type cmd in the Run dialog box (for Windows NT/2000). Change folders to the bin location containing your project's executable, type the name of the executable, and then press Enter.

Adding Your Project to Source Control

Creating intellectual property is what software development is about. Microsoft started with some handwritten notes on porting B.A.S.I.C. from a PDP-11 to a version for the Altair-MIPS. At one time or another, the handwritten notes were transcribed into a book. If anyone had known that this chicken-scratched version of Beginners All Purpose Symbolic Instruction Code (B.A.S.I.C.) would eventually be worth half a trillion dollars, they would have locked it in the vault at the intersection of Gold Vault Road and Bullion Boulevard at Fort Knox.

> **Note**
>
> All intellectual property should be archived. This includes manuscripts, graphic art, legal documents, and, of course, source code. Version control tools are easy and affordable enough for anyone to use.

When you are writing software, you are creating intellectual property that has value to someone, and as property it should be protected. Version control applications like Visual SourceSafe perform this task. Visual SourceSafe stores the code in a database and allows you and others to check files in and out between revisions. Visual SourceSafe tracks revisions, allowing you to access any version of the code at any time.

If you begin a project with source control, you will find it significantly easier to revise and customize your code with impunity. The source control tool allows you to restore your code easily to any prior state, if used properly. Using SourceSafe with Visual Studio .NET is easier than ever.

There are a few prerequisites to adding your solution to Visual SourceSafe. You will need Visual SourceSafe installed. You will need to create a database and have the administrator create a user name and password for you. If a SourceSafe database is configured, from Visual Studio .NET, choose File, Source Control, Add Solution to Source Control. You will be prompted to enter your user name, password, and the name of your SourceSafe database.

Note

You can add code to make your application an Automation controller for SourceSafe too. Suppose you are writing a program for designing marketing media. You want to allow the creative marketing people to archive their information. Instead of re-creating a source management tool, add some code to control SourceSafe and encourage your customers to buy SourceSafe.

Why does all this work so well? SourceSafe is accessible from Studio because someone had the foresight to make SourceSafe an Automation server application. This means that Automation controller applications can be written to manage SourceSafe externally. Visual Studio .NET is a SourceSafe automation controller.

Configuring SourceSafe

The Source Control view of the Options dialog box enables you to configure source control information. For example, I navigated to the SCC Provider subview, and Visual Studio .NET had already retrieved information, including my user name. When I actually checked in the HelloWorld solution, it also grabbed the information about the database to use and updated the Source Control view appropriately.

Default information, including your default SourceSafe database, is stored in configuration files and SourceSafe can obtain this information. Whatever SourceSafe makes available via its Automation interface can also be requested from Automation controllers. Hence Visual Studio .NET can obtain necessary configuration information from SourceSafe, and allow you to modify it via the Source Control view (see Figure 1.2).

In the General subview of the property pages, you can check the first two check boxes (see Figure 1.2). These two options will ensure that the most recent files are retrieved from source control when you open a solution and that everything is checked in when you close the solution.

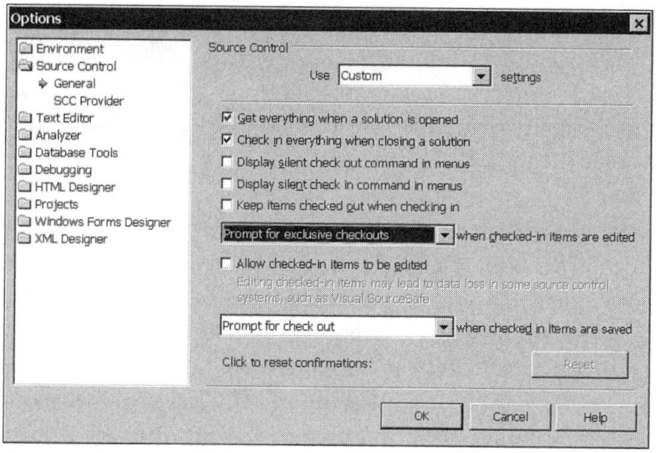

FIGURE 1.2
Configure source control to get everything when you open a solution and check in everything when you are finished coding by checking the options as shown.

Source Control Capabilities

After you incorporate Source Control into your solution, many of the options available directly from SourceSafe are incorporated into the Source Control submenu (File, Source Control). You can choose to get, share, check in, check out, or compare files, and view file histories.

SourceSafe is a separate product, so covering it in detail would require another book. However, there are some things that you can do to get the most out of SourceSafe or any Source Control product. First, use source control from day one. Second, don't controvert the role of source control. It's the tool's responsibility to track versions; making subprojects to track separate versions of source gets in the way of the tool. Don't do it. Finally, use sharing, branching, pinning, and labeling—available in many source control products—to manage your code effectively.

Appointing a librarian to manage the source product is a good idea. A librarian can ensure that source control is being used properly, help arrange training for novices, and facilitate build management. For very small teams, the librarian may also be assigned other duties.

Building Projects

There are several kinds of builds that you will want to make. When you are testing new code just added, verifying that refactoring didn't break anything, or if your code is being tested internally, you will want to perform a debug build.

> **Note**
>
> *Refactoring* is a change made to the internal structure of software to make it easier to understand and cheaper to modify without changing its observable behavior (Fowler, 2000).

When your code has been tested according to the application's needs and the qualitative standards determined—which should include unit, integration, and black-box testing and can include white-box testing and a thorough quality assurance review—you will want to perform a release build. *Black-box testing* refers to testing from the user's perspective without knowledge of the algorithms and types that describe how the solution was implemented. *White-box testing* refers to testing by stepping over the individual lines of code with knowledge of the algorithms and types. For a detailed discourse on testing, refer to the book *Software Testing* by Ron Patton from Sams.

Visual Studio .NET allows you to configure and manage options for debug, release, or custom builds.

Using the Configuration Manager

The Configuration Manager dialog box displays the active solution configuration and the project contexts for each project in your solution. (When you read "solution," think Visual Basic Group, or .VBG.) Open the Configuration Manager by choosing Build, Configuration Manager. To add a new solution configuration, select <New...> from the Active Solution Configuration drop-down list. To change the name of or delete an existing solution configuration, select <Edit...>.

The Project Contexts grid displays the list of configuration information for each project in your solution. The Project column contains the project name. The Configuration column displays the currently selected desired build configuration, and the Platform column indicates the platform for which the build is targeted. The Build column indicates whether the project will be compiled. A final Deploy column will be displayed for projects that are deployable. The Deploy column indicates whether a project will be deployed when the Run or Deploy command is invoked.

Common Properties

Project configuration settings can be viewed and modified by selecting the project from the Solution Explorer and choosing Project, Properties. The Common Properties folder in the property pages contains configuration information common to all configurations.

General Property Defaults

The General properties define the assembly name, the type of the target application, startup module, and the Root Namespace, as well as static text indicating the project folder, project filename, and target application name.

Compiler Defaults

Select the Build view from Common Properties, and you will see that Option Explicit is On and Option Strict is Off and Option Compare is set to Binary. In the Build view, you can select the project icon too. Change Option Strict to On. I will elaborate in a moment why this is the preferred setting.

As a refresher, Option Explicit On means that you must declare variables before using them. Option Strict On precludes late binding, which is demonstrated by assigning a specific type to a general type and invoking a method of the specific type. Option Strict On requires you to perform a specific type cast. Option Strict On also enforces narrowing type conversions where only implicit conversions of smaller types to larger types are allowed. See Listing 1.3 from the OptionStrict.vbproj example.

LISTING 1.3   Demonstrating an implication of the compiler setting Option Strict On

```
Sub Main()
Dim AnInt As Integer = 5
Dim ALong As Long = 7
ALong = AnInt
' causes compiler error when Option Strict On
AnInt = ALong
MsgBox(AnInt)
End Sub
```

In Listing 1.3, if Option Strict is On, AnInt = ALong causes a compiler error. If you assign a long to an integer, there is a possibility that information will be lost due to squeezing a 64-bit long into a 32-bit integer. However, the reverse isn't true; converting an integer to a long is okay. Thirty-two-bit integers fit nicely into 64-bit longs. If Option Strict is Off, the compiler will allow you to perform widening implicit type conversions.

The default comparison option is a case-sensitive compare, or Option Compare Binary.

Imports Property Defaults

The Imports statement allows you to import and remove namespaces, and the Import section of the project's Common Properties folder contains a list of the namespaces that are already imported. (A *namespace* consists of a logical grouping of types. Elements in the same namespace are found in the same assembly.)

Reference Path Properties

The References properties are used to define a list of folders that will be searched to resolve references in your application.

Designer Defaults

The Designer Properties page provides configuration information for the layout of the Web designer, the target browser schema, and Web scripting languages.

The Page Layout property indicates whether controls should be laid out linearly or using a two-dimensional grid layout. Target schema enables you to indicate what version and brand of Web browser your application is targeting, and client script language allows you to select VBScript or JScript as the default language for scripting.

Configuration Properties

The Configuration Properties folder contains pages for managing Debugging, Optimizations, Build, and Deployment options.

The Debugging page allows you to specify a Start Action and Start Options. A Start Action might be to load an external program. For example, you need to load a host application for a DLL. When you are creating an add-in, the Start external program would be VS .NET itself. Start Options provide fields for specifying a working directory and command-line arguments. (Refer to the section "Retrieving Command-Line Arguments" in Chapter 13 for more information on console applications and command-line arguments.)

The Optimizations page contains a few basic compiler optimization settings. The Build page allows you to specify an output path, generate debugger information, and define application constants. The Configuration page provides quick access to the Configuration Manager and enables you to specify the current configuration.

Debug Build

The default recommended configuration options are selected for a Debug build. As with Visual Basic 6, you can specify command-line arguments, specify a working directory, remove integer overflow checks, enable optimizations, tell the compiler to treat warnings as errors, specify an output path, and define compiler constants.

When you open the property pages and select the Configuration Properties folder, you are modifying values that will be saved to the configuration selected in the top left corner of the Configuration Properties view. By default the Debug configuration writes the application to the \bin folder, generates debug information, enables build warnings, and defines the constants DEBUG and TRACE. All these options are set for the Build view of the default Debug configuration.

I prefer not to compile or ship code with warnings, so I indicate that compiler warnings should be treated as errors.

Release Build

A release build is the build you are going to ship to your customers. The release build is similar to the debug build but doesn't generate debug information, nor does it define the DEBUG constant.

For the release build, you may be able to tolerate a slower compile for a more optimized application. To use the optimizing compiler, select Enable Optimizations in the Optimizations page of the Configuration properties pages.

Command-Line Builds and Make Files

Some development shops prefer to perform command-line builds, or more likely, use makefiles to automate the build process, and for good reason. A *makefile* allows you to automate checking out files by label, perform precise compilations on any complexity of source and target applications, and run automated scripts to build installation disks. (There are other things that you can do as well.)

If you need to perform a command-line build, here is an example.

```
"C:\Progam Files\Microsoft Visual Studio .Net\Common7\IDE\devenv"
➥ OptionStrict.sln /runexit
```

The preceding command will build the OptionStrict.sln solution and run the executable. The /runexit instructs devenv.exe to run the program and exit. Notice that you are running Visual Studio (devenv.exe) to perform the build.

The Code Behind the Form

One of the first things you are likely to do is to create a new Windows Application project. (A review of other project types is provided later in the section "An Overview of Project Templates.") When you create a new Windows Application project, Visual Studio—configured for Visual Basic 6 profiles—will appear as shown in Figure 1.3.

Although your view may be a little less crowded than the view captured in the low-resolution figure, the casual observer will quickly recognize Visual Basic. It's not until you switch to the code view of the form that you may get a sinking feeling that something is really, really different here.

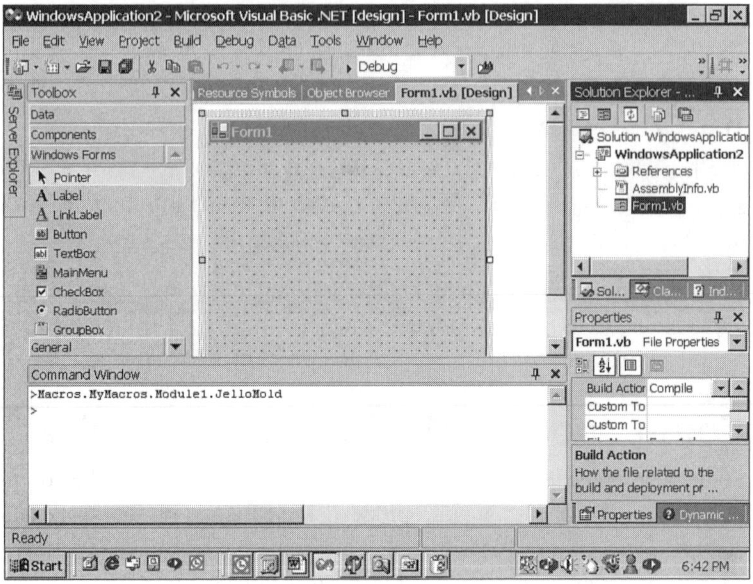

FIGURE **1.3**

*The VS .NET view,
with the Visual
Basic 6 profile
selected, of a
new Windows
Application
project.*

For this reason I want to take a few minutes here to help you get accustomed to the radical way VB .NET code looks. (If you have seen Java or C++ code, the VB code in the form won't seem so strange.) Listing 1.4 gives the complete listing of a blank form in a Windows Application project.

LISTING **1.4**   The code for a form with no controls in Visual Basic .NET

```
1:   Public Class Form1
2:       Inherits System.Windows.Forms.Form
3:
4:   #Region " Windows Form Designer generated code "
5:
6:       Public Sub New()
7:           MyBase.New()
8:
9:           'This call is required by the Windows Form Designer.
10:          InitializeComponent()
11:
12:          'Add any initialization after the InitializeComponent() call
13:
14:      End Sub
15:
16:      'Form overrides dispose to clean up the component list.
17:      Protected Overloads Overrides Sub Dispose(ByVal disposing As Boolean)
18:          If disposing Then
19:              If Not (components Is Nothing) Then
```

```
20:                    components.Dispose()
21:                End If
22:            End If
23:            MyBase.Dispose(disposing)
24:        End Sub
25:
26:        'Required by the Windows Form Designer
27:        Private components As System.ComponentModel.IContainer
28:
29:        'NOTE: The following procedure is required by the Windows Form Designer
30:        'It can be modified using the Windows Form Designer.
31:        'Do not modify it using the code editor.
32:        <System.Diagnostics.DebuggerStepThrough()>
➡ Private Sub InitializeComponent()

33:            '
34:            'Form1
35:            '
36:            Me.AutoScaleBaseSize = New System.Drawing.Size(6, 15)
37:            Me.ClientSize = New System.Drawing.Size(292, 268)
38:            Me.Name = "Form1"
39:            Me.Text = "Form1"
40:
41:        End Sub
42:
43: #End Region
44:
45:
46: End Class
```

The form code contains a lot of information that we never had to see before. The good news is that the code view uses Outlining indicated by the presence of [+] and [-] tags in the code view. A lot of the code between the initial #Region and #End Region is managed by the form. (See the section "The #Region Directive" for more information.) The region with the identifier string "Windows form designer generated code" is the object-oriented code that is working behind the scenes to construct and destruct the form and any controls added to the form.

Using the code-outlining feature of Studio, Listing 1.5 shows the same code with the Form Designer-generated code collapsed.

LISTING 1.5 Revision of the code from Listing 1.4, with generated code supporting the Form Designer collapsed using Studio's code outlining feature.

```
[-]Public Class Form1
Inherits System.Windows.Forms.Form
[+][Windows FormDesigner generated code]
End Class
```

In Listing 1.5, I added the code-outlining buttons to show you where the code editor places them. Click the [+] and you will see all the generated code.

Listing 1.5 (with the generated code collapsed) is a little easier to get a handle on, but it still doesn't look like VB6 form code. The first thing you will notice is that the forms are classes, not some hybrid cross between a class and a module. The Public Class Form1 and End Class lines define the class rather than the file that the class is in. The second thing you will notice is that the blank form inherits from the Form class defined in the System.Windows.Forms namespace. (We'll get back to form inheritance later in this chapter.) Next is the generated code. We won't worry about that for now. Finally, you'll notice the End Class statement.

When you define methods and properties for forms, you will write them between the Public Class Form and End Class statements. When you add controls and define event handlers, Visual Studio will add that code in the generated code section. That's really all there is to it. Simply get used to a class, module, or structure block defining the boundaries rather than the file.

Why is it important to make the distinction between the file as class container versus the class idiom as container? The answer is that Visual Basic .NET allows you to define more than one class per file. Listing 1.6 demonstrates a form containing an additional Foo class.

LISTING 1.6   Visual Basic .NET allows multiple class definitions per file

```
1:  Public Class Form1
2:      Inherits System.Windows.Forms.Form
3:
4:  [ Windows Form Designer generated code ]
5:
6:
7:    Private Sub Form1_Load(ByVal sender As System.Object, _
8:      ByVal e As System.EventArgs) Handles MyBase.Load
9:
10:   Dim F As New Foo()
11:   F.ShowName()
12:
13:   End Sub
14:
15: #End Region
16:
17: End Class
18:
19: Public Class Foo
20:
21:  Public Sub ShowName()
22:     MsgBox(Me.GetType().Name)
```

```
23:   End Sub
24:
25: End Class
```

Lines 1 through 17 define the class with an added event handler for the OnLoad event. Form1_Load was generated when I double-clicked the Form control. Because the Form OnLoad event handler generated the code, it was placed in the generated section. (Also note that I collapsed most of the generated code to keep the listing short. Lines 19 through 25 are in the same file as the form class definition. Lines 19 through 25 define a second class, Foo, with a single method, ShowName.)

The Form1_load event handler creates a new instance of Foo named F. The Dim statement should look familiar to VB6 programmers. Line 11 calls F.ShowName().

There is a lot of new stuff that I glossed over, such as the presence of arguments for the Form1_Load event handler, the use of the handles keyword at the end of the event handler, and the fact that none of the method calls use the word Call but clearly use parentheses. Listing 1.6 is correct as listed.

Tip

Event handlers are implemented as special classes called delegates, or multicast delegates. See Chapter 9, "Understanding Delegates," for more information.

This very brief listing shows some of the changes that might take some getting used to. We will cover them all in time, but for now we have to move on.

Now let's take a look at some of the features you will find in the IDE.

Switching from the Code View to the Object View

If you examine Figure 1.3, you will notice that there is a tab just above the form. These view tabs allow you to switch quickly between the Design view and the Code view. If you open other files or help, these views will be accessible by view tabs too.

Tip

Press Ctrl+Tab to cycle from left to right and Ctrl+Shift+Tab to cycle from right to left among all views in either Tabbed Documents or MDI Environment mode.

To switch from the Design view to the Code view, you can also use the F7 key. Press Shift+F7 to switch from Code view to Design view.

Tab views are selected by default in the General tab of the environment options. To change to a multiple document interface—no tabs, similar to Visual Basic 6—choose Tools, Options. In the General view of the Environment Options, change the settings to MDI environment to convert to the older style of form navigation. If you have forgotten how MDI applications work, the MDI environment will display all open views in the Windows menu.

Namespaces

Namespaces have been in use for a while in languages like C++ and Java. Namespaces support a higher classification system than classes. A group of classes can be contained in a namespace, making classes in that namespace distinct from classes with the same name in another namespace. The more code that is shared globally, the more value is derived from namespaces.

Visual Basic .NET uses namespaces. You will see namespaces used in `Imports` statements or in the Property Pages, Common Properties Imports view. Think of namespaces as a means of adding references to other projects and applications.

> **Note**
>
> A *singleton* object is a class instantiated only once in a system. The `Debug` object is an example of a singleton.

For example, the `Debug` singleton object resides in the `System.Diagnostics` namespace. You can write the fully qualified name, including the namespace each time you refer to the `Debug` object, or a better alternative is to add a reference to the namespace. Here is an example of a code fragment written in a click event handler that demonstrates writing some text to the Output window. The first example uses the fully qualified name and the second example requires that the `System.Diagnostics` namespace be imported.

```
System.Diagnostics.Debug.WriteLine( _
"Welcome to Valhalla Tower Material Defender!")
Debug.WriteLine("This is a test of the emergency broadcast system")
```

Both examples work because the `System.Diagnostics` namespace is added as a project `Import` by default. Of course, the shorter version and importing the namespace is preferable unless there is a conflict between two entities.

The `Imports` statement takes the following form:

```
Imports namespace
```

where `Imports System.Diagnostics` is an example of importing the `Diagnostics` namespace. `Imports` statements must precede other declarations but can follow `Option` statements. I generally place `Imports` statements at the beginning of a file, immediately after any `Option` statements.

An even better way to import namespaces is to use the property pages. To add a namespace to the Imports view of the property pages, select the project in the Solution Explorer and select Properties from the right-click context menu (or by choosing Project, Properties). Select the Common Properties folder and the Imports item. Type the name of the namespace you want to import in the Namespace field and click Add Import. The imported namespace should appear in the Project Imports list.

> **Caution**
>
> You can enter gibberish for the namespace, and you won't know you have a bad name until you attempt to compile your application.

Code Outlining

Code outlining provides you with a convenient means of collapsing and expanding parts of code. You can expand areas of current interest and collapse others depending on the section of code you are focusing on. Figure 1.4 shows the code in an empty form after choosing Edit, Outlining, Collapse to Definitions.

FIGURE 1.4

The view of an empty form after choosing Edit, Outlining, Collapse to Definitions.

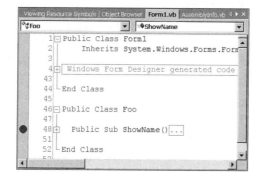

The most direct means of collapsing part of an outline is by clicking the collapse [-] button. To expand an outlined section of code, click the expand [+] button. The outline buttons are added automatically as you add and remove code.

Other outlining features include Hide Selection, Toggle Outlining Expansion, Toggle All Outlining, Stop Outlining, and Stop Hiding Current.

> **Tip**
>
> You don't have to expand a hidden block of code to view the contents. Placing the mouse pointer over the [...] hidden block of code will cause the IDE to display a popup hint containing a formatted view of the collapsed code.

Hide Selection allows you to hide a block of selected code. The selection can span part or all of more than one outlined section. Hide Selection compresses the code to the expand button and an ellipsis in a box. A hidden selection appears roughly as a boxed ellipsis [...]. To unhide a selection, use the Stop Hiding Current menu item.

Toggle Outlining Expansion reverses the current state of the innermost outlined section wherever the cursor is located. Stop Outlining removes the Outlining indicators from the code view, and Collapse to Definitions shows just definitions. For example, if you had a subroutine named Foo, Collapse to Definitions would result in just the subroutine definition being visible, followed by the [. . .] where the subroutine body is collapsed.

The Edit, Outlining, Toggle All Outlining menu item toggles all code outlining. If code is collapsed, this menu item expands it and vice versa.

The #Region Directive

The #Region directive facilitates code outlining. Regions are useful for organizing your code by regions of importance. For example, you could add a region directive around private members of a class and collapse that region to make it easier to find public methods. The basic format of this directive is as follows:

```
#Region " identifier string "
#End Region
```

The region can be expanded and collapsed and will have an identifier string to indicate what is in that region. The extra spaces are included to pad the text inside the box in which the text is displayed.

Be thoughtful when you modify code in a #Region directive. This is especially true of the code in a form with the directive

```
#Region " Windows Form Designer generated code "
```

This region contains some code that must be defined in the form for it to work correctly, including the New, Dispose, and InitializeComponent subroutines. Generally, code you aren't supposed to modify is preceded by a comment indicating its required status.

Regions can't begin or end inside methods, but you can wrap entire classes or chunks of code within a class in a region.

Code Editing and Documentation Features

The Visual Studio IDE contains several useful features for documenting your code. The IDE supports task lists, the legacy code-commenting features of ' and Rem—short for remark—a Comment and Uncomment toolbutton that allows you to comment or uncomment multiple lines of code at once, line numbering, and automatic word wrap. Let's go over each of these features to see how to employ them and where they are useful.

TODO Comments and the Task List

Visual Studio provides a Task List feature. The Task List capabilities are summarized in Table 1.1. One of my favorite features is the ' TODO comment tag. Enter a comment using the apostrophe or Rem comment token and precede the text of the comment with the TODO tag; that comment will be added as an item in the Task List. To view TODO comments in the Task List, choose View, Show Tasks, All.

You may add custom tags that are added as prioritized tasks in the Options dialog box. Choose Tools, Options. From the Environment folder, select the Task List view and add a custom token in the Comment Tokens section. Refer to Figure 1.5 for a pictorial guide. In Figure 1.5, I added an EXTRACT_METHOD Comment Token. I use this Comment Token to mark code that needs the Refactoring, Extract Method.

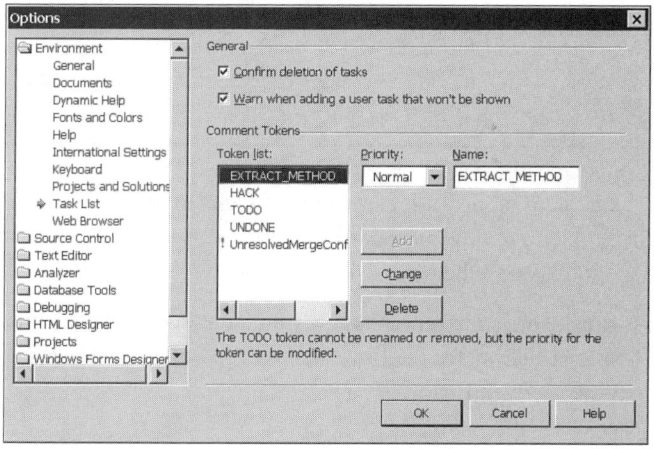

FIGURE 1.5

Add custom Comment Tokens for task management from the Task List view of the Options dialog box. Choose Tools, Options, Environment to open the view as shown.

Table 1.2 contains a view of other useful task management capabilities in Visual Studio .NET.

TABLE 1.2 Task List Management Tools from the Show Tasks Menu Item

Task Name	Description
Previous View	Restores the previous Task List view.
All	Displays all Task List entries for all open files.
Next Task	Navigates to the next task in the Task List.
Previous Task	Navigates to the previous task in the list.
Comment	Filters the Task List to show Comment tasks; for example, a 'TODO item would show up in the list if the Comment filter were selected.
Build Errors	Shows problems as you write or compile your application. If you solve the problem, the task is automatically removed from the Task List.
User	Tasks entered directly into the Task List. Click "Click Here to Add a New Task" and type the description for your task. User-entered tasks can be checked off when completed and deleted from the Task List context menu.
Shortcut	Place the cursor at the line of the code where you want to enter a shortcut. Choose Edit, Bookmarks, Add Task List Shortcut. You can double-click the Shortcut in the Task List to return to that line of code. (Shortcut bookmarks are represented by a blue graphic arrow in the left margin of the code editor.)
Current File	Shows tasks in the currently selected file only.
Policy	If an Enterprise Template is applied to the project, the problems detected by the Template Description Language (TDL) will be displayed (and filtered) by this menu item. (This option is available in the Enterprise version of VS .NET.)
Checked	Filters tasks that are checked, indicating that they are completed.
Unchecked	Filters the Task List showing only tasks that are unchecked.

Double-click an item in the Task List to move focus to that location in your code. Resolve the problem, remove or modify the comment to indicate that it has been resolved, and move on to the next task in the list.

The Task List categories are represented by an icon. You can check the help documentation for "Task List Views" for the list of icons. You will become accustomed to Task List icons as you use the Task List.

Built-in intelligence includes IntelliSense to figure out which tasks should be displayed as you move from context to context in the Visual Studio IDE. IntelliSense technology includes member lists, parameter information, quick info complete word, and automatic brace matching in the IDE. Choose Edit, IntelliSense to explicitly invoke IntelliSense features. (See the section "IntelliSense" later in this chapter for an overview of these features.)

Comments

From earlier versions of Basic, we inherited the ' and Rem comment tokens. To add a comment in Visual Basic .NET, simply precede some text in the code editor with either the apostrophe or the Rem token.

Many programmers comment out blocks of code that they have written for testing purposes, no longer need, or perhaps haven't quite finished but want ignored in order to compile. Visual Basic .NET includes the Comment Out Selected Lines and Uncomment the Selected Lines toolbuttons. Comment and Uncomment are available on the Text Editor toolbar or the Advanced submenu on the Edit menu.

To comment several lines of code, click and drag the mouse, highlighting all the code you want to comment. Click the Comment Out Selected Lines toolbutton. Each line in the selection should now have an apostrophe as the first character in the line.

It's probably okay to leave blocks of code commented out temporarily. An easy way of blocking out code and ensuring that it gets cleaned up eventually is to use a conditional compiler directive and a TODO comment task reminder. Listing 1.7 demonstrates the technique.

LISTING 1.7   Using compiler conditional code to remove commented code

```
 1:  Private Sub Form1_Load(ByVal sender As System.Object, _
 2:    ByVal e As System.EventArgs) Handles MyBase.Load
 3:    ' TODO: Demonstrates code removed by a compiler directive
 4:    ' that always evaluates to False
 5:  #If False Then
 6:    Dim I As Integer
 7:    For I = 1 To 100
 8:      Debug.WriteLine(I)
 9:    Next I
10:  #End If
11:
12:  End Sub
```

The #If False Then conditionally compiled code has a test that is always False, hence the code in lines 6 through 9 is effectively commented out. The TODO task will remind you to clean this code up if it remains commented out.

Editor Options

The Visual Studio IDE adds a couple of new editing features. From the General view, which you access by choosing Tools, Options, Text Editor, Basic, you can instruct the IDE to add line numbers in the left margin of the code editor and to automatically wrap text if it exceeds the virtual edge of the code editor page. See Figure 1.6 for a pictorial view of the Word Wrap option in the foreground; you can see the line numbers added in the background.

FIGURE 1.6

General text editor options include line numbering and word wrap features, turned on by making the selections shown here.

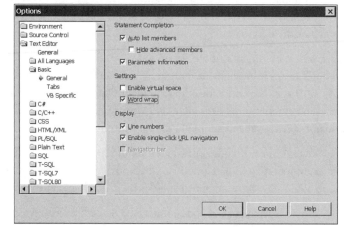

The presence of line numbers has no effect on the code or its compilation. Word wrap is automatic. If you resize the code editor, wrapped code and comments are adjusted accordingly. You don't need the remark token for wrapped comments; nor do you need the code continuation character, the underscore (_), for automatically wrapped code.

Wrapped code is indented on the first line but begins in column one on subsequent lines. This can make reading the wrapped text a bit difficult.

Configuring IDE Options

Spending a lot of time customizing the IDE has never borne much fruit. Generally, barring a few specific changes, the default settings for the IDE work reasonably well. When you identify a specific need, look it up and make the change.

In this section, I will briefly cover configuration options and point out a few interesting ones. Later in the book, if we need a specific setting, I will tell you about it and how to modify it.

All configuration settings discussed in this section refer to the values in the Options dialog box. The Options dialog box uses the folder metaphor for navigating views.

Environment Options

The Environment options contain general configuration and IDE settings organized by the following subviews: General, Documents, Dynamic Help, Fonts and Colors, Help, International Settings, Keyboard, Project and Solutions, Task List, and Web Browser.

Many of these configuration items are options that you can set once and forget. A few interesting General options include the At Startup combo box on the General tab. You can instruct the IDE to start up showing the start page, the last loaded solution, the Open Project dialog box, New Project dialog box, or an empty environment each time you start Visual Studio. Selecting the Show New Project dialog box at startup provides the behavior most similar to the default VB6 behavior.

From the earlier section on TODO Comments and the Task List, you know that you can add comment tokens in the Task List subview. Comment tokens, like TODO, instruct the IDE to add that item as a task to the Task List.

You may also find it useful on occasion to modify your Internet Explorer options while developing in .NET. From the Web Browser subview, click the Internet Explorer Options button to open the same configuration dialog box displayed when you select Tools, Options in Internet Explorer.

Source Control Options

The Source Control folder contains General and SCC Provider subviews. This tab contains information about the source control you are using. For example, if you are using Visual SourceSafe 6, this view will contain login information and describe source control-related behaviors relative to Visual Studio.

If you choose Options, Source Control, General, and then select Get Everything When a Solution Is Opened, this setting ensures that you have current files from source control. Selecting Check In Everything When Closing a Solution will ensure that source control is updated with your latest changes.

Text Editor Options

The Text Editor folder contains several subviews, many of them language-specific. Select the Basic subview to turn on automatic word wrapping and reference line numbers in your code.

When Word Wrap is checked, any text that exceeds the virtual edge of the page represented by the screen real estate available to the code editor is automatically wrapped. You won't need to add the line continuation character for code, and you won't need to add a remark token for wrapped comments.

Windows Forms Designer Options

The Windows Forms Designer page has options for the number of pixels between dots shown on a form at design time, Show Grid, and the Snap to Grid option, checked by default.

GridSize indicates the pixel spacing between dots on designers if the Show Grid option is True. Snap to Grid indicates whether the designer should move controls to the nearest grid position or not.

Analyzer Options

Visual Studio Analyzer—available in the Enterprise Edition—provides users with a visual view of distributed, multitier applications. Analyzer is a profiler, as well, helping you find and resolve performance bottlenecks and find out what is going on inside and outside of your application. The Analyzer view allows you to configure options related to Visual Studio Analyzer.

Database Tools Options

The Database Tools view allows you to configure general options for the Database Designer as well as specific options for SQL Server and Oracle.

Debugging Options

The Debugging options contain general information for managing integrated debugger behavior.

In the Debugging, General subview, the Use IntelliSense to Verify Breakpoints option is checked. This feature ensures that breakpoints are valid. If a break is invalid, the IDE places a question mark inside a red dot in the left margin and adds an item indicating there is a problem in the Task List.

The General view also contains a Confirm Correct File Was Found When Finding Source option. This option is unchecked by default. If checked, it will display a dialog box asking you to confirm that the correct source file was found when debugging.

The Debugging, Edit, and Continue subview has several options all checked by default. The Enable Edit and Continue option is designed to allow you to modify code while debugging and continue debugging after you have modified the code; unfortunately this feature is currently only available in Visual C++.

HTML Designer Options

HTML Designer options contain choices indicating which view you want the Designer to open in, Code or Design view, and horizontal spacing and grid settings.

Projects Options

The Projects subview contains configuration options related to Visual C++ for the most part. You can, however, access your Internet Connection Settings from the Web Settings subview.

XML Designer Options

The Schema Designer view contains one setting. You can elect whether to start the schema pages in schema or XML view.

Debugging in the New IDE

Integrated debugging occurs in the Visual Studio IDE. There are also some external tools for debugging. DbgUrt.exe is a Common Language Runtime debugger, and Cordbg.exe is a CLR test debugger shell, a command-line debugging utility.

The CLR includes a suite of extended debugging capabilities defined in the System.Diagnostics namespace. Diagnostics includes the Singleton Debug object, which includes Assert, and Writeline, which replaces Print. (Refer to Listing 1.2 for an example of the Writeline statement.) There are new methods in the Debug object for Tracing and much more.

To give you a taste of the new power you will find in System.Diagnostics, Listing 1.8 provides a brief example of an attribute tag that instructs the debugger to disallow stepping into a method marked with this attribute.

LISTING 1.8   Using System.Diagnostics and a compiler attribute to disable stepping into a particular method

```
1:  Public Class Form1
2:    Inherits System.Windows.Forms.Form
3:
4:  #Region " Windows Form Designer generated code "
5:    [ Windows Form Designer generated code here ]
```

continues

LISTING **1.8** continued

```
16:    Private Sub Form1_Load(ByVal sender As System.Object, _
7:       ByVal e As System.EventArgs) Handles MyBase.Load
8:       SteppedOverCode()
9:    End Sub
10:
11: #End Region
12:
13:    #Region " My Stepped Over Code "
14:    ' TODO: Add the discussion on attribute block delimiter
15:    ' and system.diagnostics to chapter 12 on debugging.
16:    <System.Diagnostics.DebuggerHidden()> Private Sub SteppedOverCode()
17:      MsgBox("The debugger won't trace this subroutine")
18:    End Sub
19;   #End Region
20:
21: End Class
```

Listing 1.8 conceals the Windows Form Designer-generated code except for the
Form_Load event handler. OnLoad calls SteppedOverCode, which is in a user-defined
region to facilitate outlining for this region of code. The SteppedOverCode subroutine is
prefixed with a compiler attribute: <System.Diagnostics.DebuggerHidden()>. The
effect of this attribute is that users won't be able to step into SteppedOverCode when
debugging, demonstrating some of the new power extended to Visual Basic .NET developers. Chapter 12, "Defining Attributes," covers attributes in detail.

Basic Debugging Shortcuts

Here are a few salient debugging shortcuts, including the location of stack frame information. To Step Over code, press the Shift+F8 keys. To Step Into code, press F8, and to
Step Out again, press Ctrl+Shift+F8. Step Out is a useful feature when you find yourself
tracing a bunch of methods you really don't need to see. Press Shift+F11, and you will
immediately be taken outside of the current procedure back to the calling procedure.

The F9 key toggles a breakpoint, F5 starts the application in the IDE, and Shift+F5
restarts debugging. Use Ctrl+F5 to start the application without debugging it. All features
described thus far are available on the Debug menu using the Visual Basic 6 profile.

If you want to step into the disassembled code, using the F8 key will step into procedures as well as into disassembled code.

I find the Stack Frame view useful for debugging. The Stack Frame view has been
moved to the Debug Location toolbar; the Debug Location toolbar is displayed when you
are debugging. The Stack Frame view is implemented as a drop-down list. The Stack

Frame shows the methods called in order of most recent to least recent. You use the Stack Frame to view the path your code took to get to its current location.

Debug, Disable All Breakpoints and Debug, and Enable All Breakpoints are the same menu item. When you disable a breakpoint, you turn it off without removing it; enabling all breakpoints has the opposite effect. This feature allows you to toggle breakpoints without finding and removing them.

One of my favorite features is that breakpoints are maintained between sessions. This means that when you set a breakpoint in your code and close the solution, the breakpoint information is still set when you reopen the solution. Very nice.

Structured Exception Handling

Probably the single most important tool for building robust applications is the addition of structured exception handling. Visual Basic .NET includes the `Try...Catch...End Try` and `Try...Finally...End Try` idioms for defining a structured exception-handling block and a resource protection block respectively.

An exception-handling block is called when an error occurs and is used to write code to resolve the error. `Try...Catch...End Try` replaces the `On Error...Goto` from VB6. `Try...Finally...End Try` is for protecting resources, like file handles. The `Finally` clause of an exception handler is always called, ensuring that things like open files are closed properly.

You can still use `On Error...Goto` in VB .NET, but its use is deprecated and is likely to be removed in the near future. You cannot use exception handling and `On Error...Goto` in the same procedure.

Structured exception handling is a welcome addition to Visual Basic .NET. You will encounter examples throughout this book.

An Overview of Project Templates

You can choose from several kinds of project templates when creating a new Visual Basic .NET project. This section introduces each briefly and indicates where you can find examples of these kinds of projects in this book.

Windows Application

The Windows Application Project Template is the basic template for Windows applications. This project is created containing a single blank WinForm. Examples of Windows applications are provided throughout this book. Many are small applications demonstrating isolated topics. For more in-depth material on building Windows applications, see Chapter 15, "Using Windows Forms," and Chapter 16, "Designing User Interfaces."

The EmptyForm.sln described earlier in the chapter illustrates what the Studio IDE will provide for you when you begin a Windows Application project.

Class Library

A class library project creates a DLL containing .NET classes. Class libraries in Visual Studio .NET are created similarly to COM libraries in Visual Basic 6 but aren't COM libraries. Rather, a class library in .NET is an assembly designed to work with the .NET Framework.

> **Tip**
>
> Set the project name when you create a new class library project. This ensures that the project, root assembly, and namespace are all set correctly.

Refer to the solution `ClassLibraryDemo`, which contains a trivial Windows application and a class library. The class library is defined in the namespace `ClassLibraryDemo`, which can be determined from the general view of the Common Properties in the Property Page dialog box. The `TestClassLibraryDemo` Windows application contains a reference to the class library. From there we can instantiate objects defined in the class library. (Refer to Chapter 7, "Creating Classes," for an example of a class library.)

Creating a Class Library

The basic steps for creating a class library begin with selecting the Class Library Project Template from the New Project dialog box. Implement classes in the class library as you would anywhere else. Build the library. When you add a reference to it from another application, you can create instances of classes in the library as if they were classes defined in the application.

Adding a Reference to and Using a Class Library

These are the steps you will need to take when using a class library:

1. In the Solution Explorer view of the application that wants to use the class library, right-click over the project name.
2. From the context menu, select Add Reference. Select the Projects tab of the Add Reference dialog box.

3. If the library is in the current solution, the project name will be listed; otherwise, click Browse and navigate to the class library application.

4. Click Open to add the class library reference.

5. When you have returned to the Add Reference dialog box, select the reference and click Select.

Your application now has a reference to that class library. All these steps are very similar to the process in Visual Basic 6.

Having the reference to the library, you can create instances of classes in the library with the Dim statement and the fully qualified namespace and class path, or you can import the namespace and then refer directly to the class. Here is an example of both:

```
Imports ClassLibraryDemo
```

The imports statement is placed at the top of the source file. When you want to create a class from the ClassLibraryDemo, the following example works:

```
Dim MyVar As New LibraryClass()
```

Notice that the namespace isn't prefixed to the name of the class, LibraryClass. Also notice the parentheses at the end of the class, LibraryClass(). This is consistent with the constructor-calling convention used in other languages.

Alternatively, you can use the fully qualified namespace and class name to declare variables in a class library.

```
Dim MyVar As New ClassLibraryDemo.LibraryClass()
```

There are some similarities in syntax for variable declaration and object creation, and there are some revisions that reflect changes in the underlying language.

If you want to create custom components, define a class library project and add the following statement to the class definition.

```
Inherits System.ComponentModel.Component
```

Windows Control Library

The Control Library template contains a UserControl, an empty container control for creating visual components. UserControl is the original container control class carried over from Visual Basic 6.

ASP.NET Web Applications

Web applications allow you to create applications for the Web using WebForms, consistent with how you build applications for Windows.

Web applications are one of the keys to .NET. Use Web Application projects where you would have used the sluggish Visual Interdev and ASP in the past.

Web applications take care of the complexities of defining the application server, the aspx files, and the HTML. When you are defining a Web application, the design-time environment is almost identical to the environment for Windows applications. This results in a much simpler and more consistent Web application development experience.

Web Application Development Preparation

To create, test, and debug Web applications, you will need to do a little preparation. You will need Internet Information Server (IIS) installed on your workstation or on your network. This is a prerequisite to installing VS .NET if you plan to build Web applications on that PC. You will also need to be in the Debug Users or Administrators group to debug your application. (If you are stuck on the Internet settings, how to configure user permissions, or some other problem, check with your system administrator.)

Creating a Demo Web Application

In Visual Studio .NET, choose File, Project, Web Application. The location for your application will be the URL of your Web server (IIS). Provide a name for the Web application, and click OK. By default you should get a blank application with one WebForm named WebForm1.aspx. The toolbox should have a Web Forms tab. These are controls imported from `System.Web.UI.WebControls` namespace.

Drag and drop a text box and button onto the WebForm (shown in Figure 1.7), and change the text property of the button to `GoTo`. (All of this works identically to making the same modifications on a WinForm.) Double-click the button. The IDE will generate an `OnClick` handler and open the WebForm1.aspx.vb source code in the editor. Add the code as shown in Listing 1.9 to redirect the user to the URL typed into the `TextBox.Text` property.

LISTING 1.9   Using the `Response` class to redirect a Web application to another URL

```
1:  Protected Sub Button1_Click(ByVal sender As System.Object, _
2:     ByVal e As System.EventArgs) Handles Button1.Click
3:
4:     Response().Redirect(TextBox1().Text)
5:
6:  End Sub
```

FIGURE 1.7

The design-time view of a Web application in Visual Studio .NET.

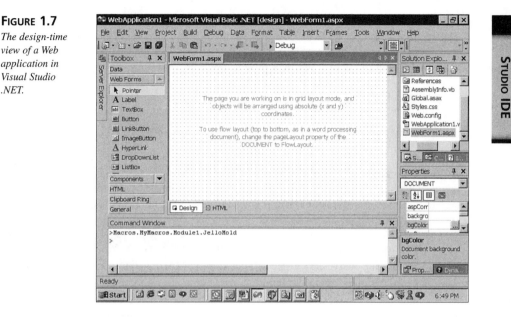

Press F5 to run the application. (Place a breakpoint on line 4 if you want to step into the code when the user presses the GoTo button.) When you press F5, the application will compile into a DLL and Internet Explorer will open with the WebForm. Enter a URL into the text box and click GoTo. You should be redirected to the Web site represented by the URL text.

What I hope you gather from this demo application is that Microsoft has made significant improvements to the process of developing Web-enabled applications. By writing VB code and presenting a design-time environment almost identical to that of standard Windows applications, programmers can leverage their VB programming skills when building Web applications.

ASP.NET Web Service

If Visual Basic .NET only brought us a whole object-oriented language and Web applications built with WebForms and ASP.NET, Visual Basic .NET would be a marvel indeed. But wait, there is much more.

There has been a general march toward a microkernel operating system for many years now. A microkernel operating system theoretically is an operating system where most of the services of the system are centrally located, and there is just enough of the operating system to boot the workstation. Theoretically, this cuts down on distribution, configuration, maintenance, and possibly other kinds of costs associated with owning computers.

Web services may or may not be intentionally designed as another step toward a micro-kernel, but Steve Balmer, CEO of Microsoft, was recently quoted as saying that client applications will probably be browser-based. Considering Balmer's position, this statement is more akin to goal setting than prognostication.

If the client is a browser and browsers are connected to the Internet and Internet server applications, we are already moving toward a time and place where computer resources may reside anywhere in the world.

This is what Web Services do for us. Web Services are a technology based on SOAP and XML technology. The basic idea behind a Web Service application is that the Web Service can reside anywhere and be used by any client application anywhere. Using a standard protocol like XML is a hedge to increase the likelihood that any and all software tool vendors can jump on board.

The Web Service Project Template creates an empty Web Service. Although VS .NET makes programming Web Services possible and easier, there is enough here that I will refer you to the chapters related to building Web Services. Chapter 18, "Using and Implementing Web Services," introduces Web Services and provides a first-look example. Chapter 19, "ASP.NET Web Programming," discusses the technologies that Web Services depend on to work. Chapter 20, "Writing to the Event Log," covers Disco (the Web Services Discovery Tool) and how to find and use existing Web Services.

Web Control Library

The Web Control Library Project Template is the basic project for building controls that can be used on WebForms with Web Applications.

Empty Project

The Empty Project Template creates a solution with a single Windows Application project containing no forms, modules, or references.

Empty Web Project

The Empty Web Project Template creates an empty Web solution and project.

New Project in Existing Folder

The New Project in Existing Folder Template creates a blank Windows Application project without creating a new folder, named after the project.

Enterprise Edition Projects

There are several project template types available only in the Enterprise Edition of VS .NET. Each is covered briefly in the subsections that follow.

Database Project

Create a Database Project by choosing File, New, Project, Other Projects, Database Project. The database project stores references to the database and allows you to run scripts and queries.

The Database Project allows you to manage and create queries, triggers, stored procedures, modify the database, database references, and contains a visual query designer. If you have used Access, the views in the Database project will look superficially familiar.

Visual Basic Simple Distributed Application

The Visual Basic Simple Distributed Application template creates a Windows Application project that includes empty classes for all the various aspects of distributed applications that you might include.

The basic template includes a WebForm, a WinForm, a class for managing database access, another class for managing business rules, and a few other empty classes.

You can use all these features in a distributed application, but more than likely you will use one presentation layer, perhaps a business layer, and a persistence layer. Thus you more than likely will use either WebForms or WinForms but probably not both.

We won't cover a project specifically started from Simple Distributed Application template, but we will cover all the various aspects included in a distributed application, including WebForms, WinForms, class libraries, and database programming.

Visual Basic Distributed Application

The Visual Basic Distributed Application template creates a blank project anticipating the potential that an advanced distributed enterprise system may need several applications or components in a given category.

The kinds of projects added to the project template are defined by a policy file. The purpose of the policy file is to describe the application types and components that describe the technology that will be used for a given application type and act as a technology guide.

Analyzer Project

The Analyzer Project creates a solution for managing a Visual Analyzer session and resultant profiling data. Effectively using the Visual Analyzer and profiling is an important subject but beyond the scope of this book.

Visual Studio .NET Add-In

You can select from the Visual Studio .NET Add-In or Shared Add-In. These project templates are defined under the Extensibility Projects subfolder in the New Projects dialog box.

Visual Studio .NET has added macros and an Automation Extensibility Model for customizing and extending Visual Studio itself. One of the characteristics of a first-class tool is that the tool can be used to extend itself. Visual Studio fits that bill.

Refer to Chapter 4, "Macros and Visual Studio Extensibility," for more information on add-ins.

Shared Add-In

The Shared Add-In project allows you to select from a wide variety of application hosts, including Word, Visual Studio, Visual Studio Macro IDE, Visio, Project, PowerPoint, Outlook, FrontPage, Excel, and Access.

Shared Add-Ins can be used in any of the hosts you select during the wizard creation phase.

IntelliSense

When you are prompted to enter data into a text field in Internet Explorer and you are provided with a list of choices based on previous input, this is the AutoComplete feature. AutoComplete is part of the *intelligence input that makes sense* technology, or *IntelliSense*.

Visual Studio enhances IntelliSense technology to provide class member lists, procedure parameter information, quick info, complete word, and VB-specific features.

List Members

When you are typing the name of an object reference and type the member-of operator— the period—the List Member feature of IntelliSense displays a list of members of that object that you can choose from to complete your code. To manually list members, choose Edit, IntelliSense, List Members, or press Ctrl+J.

Parameter Info

Parameter Info provides you with the names and types of parameters required by procedures, templates, or attributes. After you type the opening parentheses, the parameters list is displayed. When you are typing the parameters, the current parameter is displayed with a bold font.

Parameter Info can be invoked manually by choosing Edit, IntelliSense, Parameter Info. The best thing about IntelliSense features is that they are context-aware. IntelliSense responds with a behavior that depends on what you are currently doing. For example, if you are typing a procedure call, IntelliSense will display parameter information when you need it.

Quick Info

Quick Info is represented by the tooltips that appear when you move the cursor over code in the editor. You can manually invoke Quick Info tips from the IntelliSense menu, but generally you don't have to.

Complete Word

The Complete Word feature displays a list of possible choices based on partial text entry. For example, if you can't remember the `System.Diagnostics.DebuggerHidden` attribute that prevents code from being stepped into, you could type the Debug part and press Ctrl+Space, and a list of possible matches based on what you could remember would be shown in the Complete Word list. Press Enter to select the one that matches what you are looking for.

VB-Specific IntelliSense

IntelliSense in Visual Basic provides some specific features for VB only. IntelliSense in VB recognizes specific keywords and will provide you a drop-down list of possible choices based on code context.

Keywords like `Goto`, `Exit`, `Implements`, `Option`, and `Declare` when followed by a space will cause a drop-down list to be displayed with possible choices. For example, typing `Exit` followed by a space in a subroutine will result in a single item list containing the word `Sub` to be displayed. Select the item you want from the list and press Enter.

IntelliSense will display a list of choices for enumerations and a list containing True and False for Boolean types.

Using Views

Several views are available in Visual Studio to help you manage what is going on in the development process. Some of these views will be familiar to Visual Basic 6 developers and others are unique to .NET.

Let's take a moment to go over some of the Visual Studio View menu items.

Solution Explorer

Visual Studio is an enterprise development tool. The Solution Explorer contains a solution-level view. When you are developing in Visual Basic .NET, a *solution* is similar to a .VBG, Visual Basic group.

A solution can contain one or more projects (see Figure 1.8). The Solution Explorer shows the solution at the top of the view and each project grouped within the solution. Each element in the solution view has a different context menu, accessed by selecting the element and right-clicking, with appropriate menu choices for that element. For example, when you create an add-in, the wizard will create a Visual Studio Deployment Project (.vdproj) as part of the solution. The Deployment Project will contain menu items for building, deploying, running Windows Installer to install and uninstall the AddIn, and options for managing related information such as the Registry settings.

FIGURE 1.8

A view of the Solution Explorer containing the HelloWorld.sln solution.

From Figure 1.8, we see the HelloWorld solution containing the HelloWorld project. The HelloWorld project is a console application containing References, AssemblyInfo.vb, and Module1.vb. Module1 contains the source code. The References section contains references to external components, projects, and COM objects.

Database, Visual Modeler, and Visual Analyzer projects are contained in solutions (.SLN files) and will therefore be managed in the Solution Explorer.

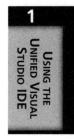

Class View

The Class view contains information similar to the Solution view except that the Class view organizes data from the object-oriented perspective of the data.

Using Figure 1.9 as a guide, you are looking at the Class view of the HelloWorld solution, the HelloWorld project, the Module, and the members of that module. The only member of module1 is Main, shown in the figure.

FIGURE 1.9

The Class view of HelloWorld.

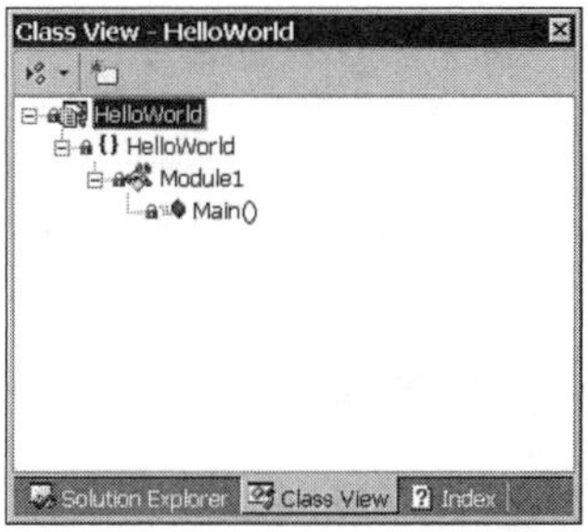

```
Class View - HelloWorld
HelloWorld
  () HelloWorld
    Module1
      Main()

Solution Explorer | Class View | Index
```

The module is most closely related to a class that contains all Shared members. The Class view will be helpful because Visual Basic .NET allows you to define multiple modules and classes per file. When you are looking at the Class view in Figure 1.9, remember that the unit of encapsulation is no longer the file. The relationship in Visual Basic 6 was one module or one class per one .bas file or .cls file respectively. Both classes and modules are contained in .vb files, and the relationship is one file to many definitions.

For more information on object-oriented topics, like the class idiom, refer to Part II. Shared members are covered in Chapter 11, "Shared Members."

Server Explorer

The Server Explorer view allows you to manage several kinds of server applications that are accessible from your network.

Open the Server Explorer to browse or interact with database servers, Web Services, and Windows services. You can drag and drop elements from the Server Explorer to your applications, and Visual Studio .NET will add the related components to your application and complete the correct connectivity information.

Resource View

Manage .rc Windows resource files in your project from the Resource View window. Refer to the help section on Creating a New Resource Script file in the VS .NET help for more information on this subject.

Properties Window

Press F4 to open the Properties window. The Properties window is a context-based view of the design-time properties of components. The selected component is displayed in the drop-down list box and properties for the selected component are displayed and modifiable beneath the selected object.

Toolbox

The toolbox has a substantial number of components that you can drag and drop onto your applications. The kind of application you are working on will affect the tools shown in the box. If you are working on a Windows application, the toolbox will contain WinForm components. On the other hand, if you are working on a Web application, WebForm components will be available in the toolbox.

Read the chapters in Part II for more on programming with components, including programming with GDI+.

Pending Check-ins

Source Control is tightly integrated into Visual Studio. The Pending Check-ins view contains modified files in the current solution. Use Source Control at project inception to protect your intellectual property.

The Source Control view allows you to customize the default behavior of source control for Visual Studio.

Web Browser

The View menu contains a Web Browser startup menu for convenience. This is illustrative of the tightly integrated relationship between Visual Studio .NET and Internet development.

The Web Browser view of the General folder (under Tools, Options) contains such information as the Home Page and Search Page. By default the Home Page is `vs:/default.htm` and the Search Page is `http://msdn.microsoft.com`. If you choose View, Web Browser, Show Browser, by default you get the Visual Studio Start Page, which is the `vs://default.htm` page.

When the browser is started from Visual Studio, it's displayed as an integrated browser.

Other Windows

Several miscellaneous views can help you resolve development issues and manage your projects in Visual Studio. These views are mentioned here briefly and will be mentioned in this book when they are beneficial to our discussion.

Task List

The Task List is context-based. Different views, like the code editor or compiler, place elements in the Task List. Use the Task List, as mentioned earlier, to help track and resolve outstanding issues.

Document Outline

The Document Outline feature is similar to the Class view feature. Class view provides you with a hierarchical view of elements in your Windows applications; the Document Outline provides you with a hierarchical view of elements in your HTML and WebForms. (Refer to Figure 1.10 for an example.)

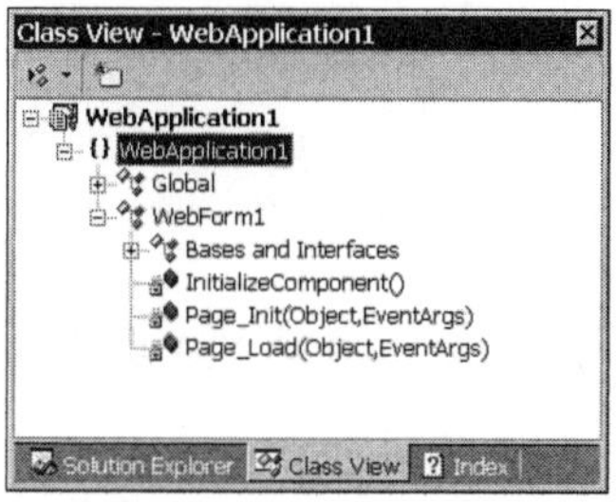

FIGURE 1.10
Document Outline view displays a control and HTML tag-based view of your Web form.

Click an element in the Document Outline view and Visual Studio will navigate you to that element on your Web form.

Command or Immediate Window

The Immediate window performs double duty as the Immediate window, similar to its VB6 role and the Command window, which is a new role devised for VB .NET.

To open the Command window, select View, Other Windows, Command Window in Visual Studio. By default the window is opened in command mode. The command mode is used to issue commands directly to Visual Studio .NET.

To switch from command mode to immediate mode, type `immed` at the > prompt in the Command window. Immediate mode plays the same role as it did in VB6; the Immediate window is for debugging. Switch back to command mode by typing `>cmd` in the Command window while in Immediate mode. For a list of commands, refer to the Help Topic "Visual Studio Commands with Arguments."

An example of a Visual Studio command you can execute in the Command window is

```
? MyVar
```

where `MyVar` is a variable defined in the current procedure. You can also issue more complex commands like

```
Debug.QuickWatch(MyVar)
```

The previous command will display the QuickWatch dialog box with the variable `MyVar` and its value displayed.

Output Window

The Output window displays output from compilation as well as text written using the Debug object. For example, if you write `System.Diagnostics.Debug.WriteLine("This is a test!")`, the text "This is a test!" (without the quotes) will be written to the Output window.

Debug text is written to the Immediate window in VB6. In VB .NET, debug information is written to the Output window.

Macro Explorer

The Macro Explorer contains macros defined for use with Visual Studio .NET. The Macro Explorer allows you to manage macros.

When you create a macro, the Macro Designer runs, and you can modify and test the macro in the designer. You will be surprised at how much implementing macros in Visual Studio .NET is like writing Visual Basic code. Follow these steps to create a spoof macro named `JelloMold`.

1. Choose View, Other Windows, Macro Explorer.
2. Right-click MyMacros in the Macro Explorer and select New Module.
3. Visual Studio will run the Macro Designer and create a new module. Add the following code to the module:
   ```
   Sub JelloMold()
   MsgBox("Jello Mold")
   End Sub
   ```
4. Close the Macro Designer, saving the macro.
5. Back in Visual Studio, open the Command window.
6. In the Command window, type
   ```
   Macros.MyMacros.Module1.JelloMold
   ```

When you run the macro, you should get a simple dialog box with the text `Jello Mold` displayed. The way macros are stored and behave is consistent with the way Visual Basic namespaces, classes, modules, and methods behave.

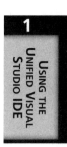

This example was a trivial one, just to keep things moving. You will find macros and the Automation Extensibility Model useful over time for automating development tasks. We will look at some practical uses for macros in Chapter 4.

Object Browser

The Object Browser view is very similar to the VB6 Object Browser. The biggest difference is one of semantics. You have to keep in mind that you are looking at namespaces, and although namespaces are similar to reference libraries, the underlying technology is different.

Figure 1.11 contains a shot of the Object Browser focused on the `TextBoxBase` class, the superclass for `TextBox`. The Visual Studio .NET Object Browser is used in the same manner as the VB6 Object Browser; that is, to get a handle on the architecture, including an accessible view of the methods, properties, and events defined for a class.

FIGURE 1.11

The Object Browser showing the methods, properties, and events of the TextBoxBase *class.*

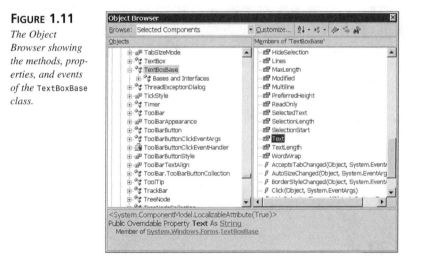

Documentation

A great feature of Visual Studio is the Code Comment Web Report. Visual Studio will examine a solution and create a cross-referenced Web document—a professional-looking HTML document, might I add—automatically for the benefit of the developers or consumers of your source code. (Figure 1.12 shows the Code Comment Web Report focused on the `Form1` class from the `EmptyForm` project.)

FIGURE 1.12

Public members of
EmptyForm.Form1
shown in an auto-matically gener-ated Code Comment Web Report.

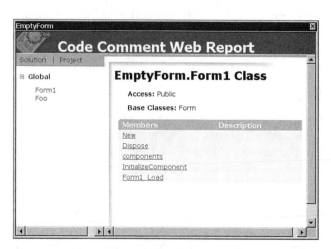

Note

C# supports the automatic inclusion of code comments. If you add an extra hash mark, using three hash marks (/ / /) instead of two, C# will add those comments to your Code Comment Web Report. Currently the code comment feature isn't supported in Visual Basic .NET, but we can hope.

In anticipation of your comments being included in Web documentation, it might be a good time to start practicing writing complete sentence comments.

Create HTML documentation for your solution by choosing Tools, Build Comment Web Pages. Click OK and the rest is done automatically.

Summary

Although it's impossible to introduce every feature in a tool as comprehensive as Visual Studio, Chapter 1 demonstrated a few of them and introduced you to many.

You should now be aware of several key features supported by .NET and have a good idea where to find comprehensive material on those subjects.

Visual Basic is a first-class language, supporting real object-oriented programming. WebForms and Web applications make Internet programming as fun and productive as Windows programming. Web Services support building and using solutions across the Internet and around the world. Visual Studio .NET supports macros and the Automation

Extensibility Model, allowing you to fully customize and extend your development environment.

If all Visual Basic .NET did was to give us a complete object-oriented architecture, the upgrade would be worth the price and learning curve. Keep in mind, though, that besides all the great technologies described in the last section, you get Visual Analyzer and an extensive suite of tools for building, testing, debugging, and deploying everything from simple Windows applications to complex distributed applications. (You will have to buy the Enterprise Edition to get all of the tools and capabilities mentioned. Refer to the documentation for your specific edition of VS .NET for a list of included features.)

In Chapter 2, you will get to see some of the differences between Visual Basic 6 and Visual Basic .NET programming before we jump into full-blown code and object-oriented programming.

CHAPTER 2

Out with the Old, In with the New

Visual Basic .NET introduces a lot of changes. These changes may seem like a needle scratching across a 12-inch vinyl album and make you feel you've lost your groove. Chapter 2 will help you find your groove by introducing the basic changes in data types, operators, variable declaration, and fundamental syntax from Visual Basic 6 to Visual Basic .NET.

File Extensions

The clearest signal that things have changed is that the file extensions in Visual Basic .NET have been changed.

Visual Basic Group Files Are Solutions

File extensions changed in Visual Basic .NET to accommodate the way in which files are managed in the unified Visual Studio IDE. The concept of a whole system is referred to as a solution. In Visual Basic 6 when you add a second, third, or more projects, a Visual Basic Group, or .VBG, file is created.

The same convenience of working with multiple projects exists in Visual Basic .NET. The VBG equivalent is the solution, or .SLN, file.

Source Files Have a New Extension

A second big change is that no distinction is made between files containing classes, forms, or just code. All Visual Basic source code is written in files having a .VB extension, including user controls, components, forms, classes, modules, assemblies, and source for Web Forms.

Several additional new file extensions, however, are related to other kinds of files. For example, model files have an .MDX extension.

Note

Visual Basic .NET supports the class idiom and the module idiom. Think of a module as a special class where all members of the module are shared—sometimes called static or class members in other languages.

Shared members exist at the metaclass level, that is, you don't need an instance of an object to access shared methods. The Module idiom is supported to make Visual Basic .NET seem a little less foreign.

The new .VB file extension is indicative of the source file being a container for code in general. New syntactical idioms were defined to make the distinction between kinds of entities, such as classes and modules, allowing for multiple entities being defined in a single file (see Listing 2.1).

LISTING 2.1   Multiple modules defined in a single file

```
Module Module1

  Sub Test()
    MsgBox("Module1")
  End Sub
End Module

Module Module2

  Sub Test()
    MsgBox("Module2")
  End Sub

End Module
```

The code in Listing 2.1 is defined in a single file named Module1.vb. You might expect that only Module1 would exist in the Module1.vb file. There is no enforced correlation between the filename and the module name in VB .NET. A new convention you can adopt is to name the module file the same as the dominant—the most important—module in the file; this will help you find your code handily.

As you can see from Listing 2.1, two methods have identical names: Test. The `Module` statement defines a separate entity. We could say that `Module1` and `Module2` encapsulate a method `Test`. If you are unfamiliar with the idea of encapsulation, see Chapter 7, "Creating Classes," for greater detail on this subject.

Back to our understanding of modules: Modules are classes with all shared members. The `Shared` idiom is covered in Chapter 11, "Shared Members," but for now you can just remember that prefixing the Module name and a period to the member will indicate which module and member you're referring to.

If you wrote the following line

```
Module1.Test()
```

a message box with the text "Module1" would be displayed, and the next line

```
Module2.Test()
```

would display the text "Module2." Because Test is defined in two modules, calling Test without the module name would result in an ambiguous declaration error at compile time. Generally you don't have to specify a module when accessing members of the module. You can simply think of module code as global code, but if you get an ambiguous declaration error, the cause is probably related to code similar to that in Listing 2.1.

A vanilla Windows application containing forms would also include an options file with a .suo extension and a .vbproj file for each project in the solution. Run the application and you might find resource files for your forms with a .resx extension. There are several other file types, but we can defer the discussion of those file types until we talk about those aspects of Visual Studio.

Namespaces

Another noticeable change is the use of namespaces. Chapter 6, "Reflections," provides thorough coverage of namespaces. For now, you can think of a namespace as a means of organizing classes.

As software becomes increasingly complex, we will need higher levels of abstraction to organize code. Types were defined to collect data. Procedures were defined to organize and manage lines of code. Classes were invented to organize procedures and data, and now we have namespaces to organize classes.

When you create a VB .NET project, a default namespace with the same name as your project is defined for you. In our vanilla Windows module example in Listing 2.1, I chose the default name. The project ended up with this name as the namespace; the default name is WindowsApplication1. The namespace for a project can be viewed on the General view of the project's Property Pages.

For practical purposes you can complete one of two tasks when trying to use classes, procedures, or objects defined in a namespace. Type the fully qualified namespace path of the entity or add an Imports statement to the Imports list, also in the Property Pages.

Note

When you look up information in the help file, part of the information provided is the namespace containing the entity you're inquiring about. For example, if you look up the Debug.Writeline method, you will get information about the System.Diagnostics namespace. To use the code in diagnostics, add an Imports statement at the top of the module or in the Property Pages.

Here is an example of an Imports statement for system.diagnostics:

```
Imports System.Diagnostics
```

In Chapter 1, you learned that several of the basic namespaces are added based on project type. For example, our Windows application imports the `System.Windows.Forms`. `System.Windows.Forms` is what is commonly referred to as WinForms.

References

If you open the Solution Explorer, you will find a References section. Semantically this is identical to the Visual Basic 6 References. The steps for adding a Reference in VB .NET are pretty similar to the steps for adding a Reference in VB6.

Here are the steps to add a reference to your project:

1. Open the Solution Explorer.
2. Find the References section of the project.
3. Right-click to display the References context menu and click Add Reference.

You can add .NET assemblies, COM objects, or references to dependent projects in the current solution. (Adding a project reference was done in ClassLibraryDemo.sln in Chapter 1. A test application for the class library needed a reference to the class library while it was under development. Use the Add Reference dialog box to make interdependent applications under simultaneous development accessible to each other.)

Option Statements

Visual Basic 6 supported several `Option` statements:

*   `Option Explicit` required the programmer to declare all variables.
*   `Option Base [0|1]` redesignated the lower bound index of arrays.
*   `Option Compare [Binary|Text|Database]` indicated the default behavior of string comparisons.
*   `Option Private` indicated that module code was private to the hosting application.

A few of these option statements made it to Visual Basic .NET, but `Option Base` didn't.

Option Explicit

`Option Explicit` was carried over into Visual Basic .NET. You can set the project level `Option Explicit` mode to `On` or `Off` for the project in the Build view of the Property Pages and override it locally in the module.

The default value at the project level is `Option Explicit On`. This is true for a reason. It's bad to have ambiguous variable declarations.

Scope boundaries are defined by blocks of code such as procedures, modules, classes, and applications. It's possible in the same application to have two variables or procedures with the same name. Without scope rules, we would run into name conflicts.

`Option Explicit On` helps you avoid the case where you implicitly declare a variable, or so you think, but a variable with an identical name exists in a broader scope. Your code ends up modifying that variable unintentionally.

A second problem existed in VB6: implicit variables were variants. `Variant` data types aren't very efficient, and were intended to support COM rather than as a general programming tool.

Explicit variable declaration means that the variable is declared using the `Dim` statement and expressing a data type. Implicit variable declaration is when you introduce a variable without a `Dim` statement. (Refer to the section "Variable Declarations" for more details.) When `Option Explicit On` is set, you have to declare all variables with the `Dim` keyword before you use them. By modifying `Module1` from Listing 2.1, we can demonstrate in Listing 2.2 the behavior of `Option Explicit` in either mode.

LISTING 2.2 Demonstrating `Option Explicit`

```
 1: Option Explicit Off
 2:
 3: Module Module1
 4:
 5:    Sub Test()
 6:       Message = "Module1"
 7:       MsgBox(Message)
 8:    End Sub
 9:
10: End Module
```

Tip

You want as much of your code as possible to exhibit any errors it contains at compile time. `Option Explicit On` supports this notion.

The code in Listing 2.2 works as you might expect. The `Message` variable is declared implicitly and initialized to the string "Module1." If line 1 is changed to Option Explicit

On, the code in Listing 2.2 will cause a compiler error. To declare the `Message` variable as a string and initialize it, redefine line 6 as follows:

```
Dim Message As String = "Module1"
```

The statement now explicitly declares `Message` as a string and initializes the string. (Single statement declaration and initialization is new in Visual Basic .NET. See the section on "Variable Declarations" for details.)

Visual Basic .NET doesn't support the `Variant` data type. Instead you get an `Object` type with implicit declarations. This is never what you want. You always want to declare a specific type, allowing the compiler to help you as much as possible. If you actually need a generic type, declare a variable of type `Object`. (See the section "Data Types" for more on `Object` types.)

2

OUT WITH THE
OLD, IN WITH
THE NEW

> **Note**
>
> Much of the available literature indicates that implicitly declared variables will be `Object` types. In Visual Basic .NET everything is an object; however, in actuality, it does appear that the compiler is performing some type conversion based on the value assigned to the implicitly declared variable. Revise Listing 2.2, line 7 to MsgBox(Message.GetType().Name) with `Option Explicit Off`, and the application will report that `Message` is a `String`.
>
> If you initialized `Message` to an integer value, for example `Message = 1`, and requested type information with `Option Explicit Off`, the reported type would be an `Int32` type. `GetType` reports type information based on the contents of the variable at the time `GetType` is called.

Option Compare

The default comparison is `Option Compare Binary`. A `Binary` comparison is also referred to as a case-sensitive comparison. The alternate choice is `Option Compare Text`. This statement is set to `Binary` at the project level; it can be changed at the project level and overridden at the module level.

`Option Compare Database` is no longer supported in VB .NET.

Option Strict

`Option Strict` is a new compiler directive. `Option Strict Off` is the default mode. The preferred setting is `Option Strict On`, but this setting has some implications for the behavior of code. We'll cover the recommended `Option Strict On` state first, followed by a demonstration of the kinds of problems you might encounter if you leave it off. To set `Option Strict On`, open the project's Property Pages, select the Build page, and change Compiler Defaults Option Strict to On.

When `Option Strict` is on, no implicit type conversion is allowed by the compiler. Again, this is what you want. Listing 2.3 demonstrates a subroutine that tries to implicitly convert a long to an integer.

LISTING 2.3 Code that tries to implicitly convert a long to an integer

```
1: Sub TestStrictMode()
2:   Dim I As Integer = 5
3:   Dim L As Long = 100
4:   I = L
5: End Sub
```

If `Option Strict On` is true, the code in Listing 2.3 will report `Option Strict disallows implicit conversions from Long to Integer` because the code tries to convert the variable L, a long, to an integer.

What would happen if the long L contained a number bigger than the integer could hold and `Option Strict Off` were true? The answer is that the compiler wouldn't catch the possibility of the extra bits in the long potentially overflowing the available bits in the integer, resulting in the possibility of an unhandled exception at runtime rather than an error at compile time. Modifying line 3 of Listing 2.3 to initialize L to 100 billion—100,000,000,000—and running with `Option Strict Off` compiles, but raises the unhandled exception shown in Figure 2.1.

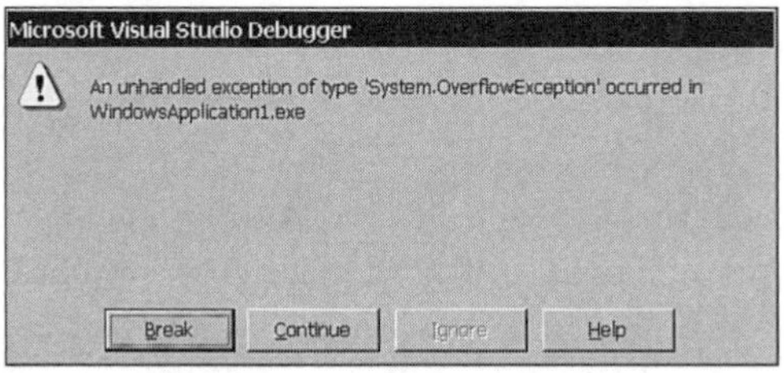

FIGURE 2.1

An unhandled
OverflowException
caused acciden-
tally when a
number too big
to fit in an integer
was assigned
from a long.

> **Note**
>
> It's your personal choice whether you like to drive without a seatbelt or not. The same is true for how you operate when you're programming. If you like implicit variable declaration and find yourself looking for a pernicious bug, try turning on `Option Explicit` and `Option Strict` and rebuilding. These two options may help you bubble defects up to compile time.

`Option Strict` only allows widening type conversions. With `Option Strict On` you can assign an integer to a long, which is fine because the long has a sufficient number of bits to hold the integer value, but the reverse is not true. With `Option Strict On`, you may not assign a long to an integer—a narrowing type conversion—without an explicit type cast. A cast is your way of programmatically indicating that you're aware of the overflow risk, but you believe that the value of the long in this situation will fit into the number of bits available in an Integer. (See the section later in this chapter on "Type Conversion Functions" for more information.)

`Option Strict On` prohibits late binding, operations on the Object type other than equality, inequality, `TypeOf...Is` and `Is` tests. You are required to declare the type of a variable using the `As` clause with `Option Strict On`, too.

Option Private Module

`Option Private` is no longer supported in Visual Basic .NET. `Option Private` kept other code from using code in your VB6 modules, but VB .NET doesn't need it.

Visual Basic .NET supports access specifiers. You can add the private access specifier to members of a module to keep outside code from using those members. (Refer to Chapter 7, "Creating Classes," for more on information hiding and access specifiers.)

Option Base

`Option Base` is no longer supported. `Option Base` in VB6 allowed you to indicate whether arrays started at 0 or 1. For example,

```
Dim MyArray(10) As Integer
```

in VB6 allocated a 10-element array of integers if `Option Base 1` were set and an 11-element array—indexed from 0 to 10—if `Option Base 0` were set.

Visual Basic .NET, for all intents and purposes, uses an `Option Base` of 0.

It's worth pointing out that things like the number of array elements will cause minor but annoying stumbling blocks for developers initially. VB .NET beta 1 and early beta 2 supported 0 to n-1 element arrays, where n was expressed as the number of elements. In April 2001, Microsoft made some concessions to VB6 developers; returning arrays to behave like `Option Base 0` with indexes 0 to n, or having n+1 elements, was one such concession.

Further confusion might exist because books were written based on the beta software and published before these concessions were made. Fortunately the authors of those beta books added disclaimers that should be taken to heart. Read the section on arrays later in this chapter for examples of VB .NET arrays.

Data Types

Part of the Common Language Runtime is the Common Type System (CTS). To provide cross-language support, .NET defines a type system that describes how types are stored and the allowable values for a type to ensure that the data can be used across languages. For languages to work in the .NET Framework, they need to implement types in accordance with the CTS.

CTS types encompass classes, interfaces, and value types. Types in .NET can have methods, properties, fields, and events, which we will come back to in a minute. What all this means to Visual Basic .NET is that types and acceptable values for those types that you've become familiar with have changed to support .NET. This section describes changes to existing types and the introduction of new types. (For a comprehensive discussion of the .NET Framework, see Chapter 14.)

Table 2.1 names the various data types, the namespace in which they are defined, and the acceptable range of values for each type.

TABLE 2.1   CTS Data Types That Supplant VB6 Data Types

Name	*Namespace*	*Bytes*	*Range*
Boolean	System.Boolean	2	True or False
Byte	System.Byte	1	0 to 255 unsigned
Char	System.Char	2	0 to 65535 unsigned
Date	System.DateTime	8	January 1, 1 CE to December 31, 9999
Decimal	System.Decimal	16	Approximately $\pm 7.9 \times 10^{28}$ with no decimal point; to ± 7.9 with 28 decimal points to the right of the decimal; the smallest non-zero number is $\pm 1 \times 10^{-29}$ (see the section on decimals for specific values)
Double	System.Double	8	Approximately -1.7E308 to -4.9E-324 for negative values; 4.9E-324 to 1.7E308 for positive values (see section on double floating-point numbers for more information)

TABLE 2.1 continued

Name	Namespace	Bytes	Range
Integer	System.Int32	4	-2,147,483,648 to 2,147,483,647
Long	System.Int64	8	-9,223,372,036,854,775,808 to 9,223,372,036,854,775,807
Object	System.Object	4	Stores any type; replaces Variant
Short	System.Int16	2	-32,768 to 32,768
Single	System.Single	4	Approximately -3.4E38 to -1.4E-45 for negative values; 1.4E-45 to 3.4E38 for positive values (see section on floating-point numbers for more information)
String	System.String	Platform-Dependent	0 to approximately 2 billion Unicode characters
User-	System.ValueType Sum	Platform-Dependent	Sum of the size of the data types defined in the user type

Getting used to the new values of the data types will be much easier than thinking of data types as objects. As stated in the opening paragraph, data types in VB .NET can contain methods, fields, properties, and events. (Fields are private data members, usually containing an underlying value of a property. Refer to Chapter 7, "Creating Classes," for more on fields.)

For example, the following code writes the maximum value of an integer to the Output window:

```
Debug.WriteLine(Integer.MaxValue)
```

Integer is the type and MaxValue is a shared attribute of Integer types. Shared members are equivalent to C++ static members or Pascal class members. (Refer to Chapter 11, "Shared Members," for more on this new idiom.) The important thing to note is that Integer is an aggregate type; although it's used like a primitive type, it's a structure and has members.

In the subsections that follow we will cover the new data types, implemented per the requirements of the Common Language Runtime, and the capabilities provided by these types.

Object Types

The Variant type originally was implemented to support COM programming. Variant types add a lot of unseen overhead to an application and sometimes lead to ambiguous code. The Variant has been replaced with the Object class in VB .NET.

Object is the name of the root class for all classes and structures in the Common Language Runtime. (The Structure construct replaces the Type construct. For more information refer to Chapter 5, "Subroutines, Functions, and Structures.") The end result is that all classes in .NET have common, basic behaviors introduced at the lowest level, and you still have a generic type if you need it. Table 2.2 contains the methods introduced in the Object class.

> **Note**
>
> If you are at all familiar with Delphi—implemented in Object Pascal—a common ancestor named Object will sound familiar to you. This is almost exactly the name of the Object Pascal common ancestor. In Object Pascal the common ancestor is TObject.
>
> Even though naming a class Object probably won't lend itself to clarifying the difference between an object and a class for some, having a common ancestry lends itself to implementing some pretty useful things in a development tool. Read Chapters 8, "Adding Events," and 9, "Understanding Delegates," for examples of how a common ancestry is employed in a Windows object-oriented framework.

TABLE 2.2 Members of the Object Class Inherited by All Classes and Structures

Member	Description
Equals	Tests hash code to determine equality
GetHashCode	Returns mathematically derived hash code representing the object's value
GetType	Returns class of type (exists to support polymorphic behavior for arguments passed as Object, as demonstrated by event handlers)
ReferenceEquals	Returns a Boolean indicating whether or not two object references refer to the same object
ToString	Returns a string representation of the object

> **Note**
>
> It's important to note that all these member methods in no way suggest that common operators, such as =, have been supplanted by verbose methods. Common operators still exist, and you will use those operators for everyday operations. (Refer to the section on operators later in this chapter for more information.)

All the methods listed in Table 2.2 are instance methods, except the `ReferenceEquals` method. You need an instance of a class to invoke instance methods. `ReferenceEquals` is a shared method, which can be invoked using the class or an instance.

Equals

The `Equals` member returns a Boolean indicating whether the value of the calling instance is equivalent to the value of the argument instance. The `Equals` method is used to test hash code values to determine object equality. Using the prior code fragment, `J.Equals(I)` is True.

GetHashCode

`GetHashCode` is introduced at the `Object` level and returns a mathematically derived number. A hash function must return the same value for disparate objects if two objects of the same type represent the same value. Hash codes are used to facilitate storing data in an abstract data type referred to as a *hash table*. By ensuring a random distribution of values, the hash code can be used to index elements in the hash table very quickly.

> **Note**
>
> Another interesting feature in .NET is the `GetHashCode` method. What is that all about? I haven't found a specific reference to explain it completely, but my guess is that an equality test based on a hash code is much faster than writing all those member-wise comparisons.
>
> ```
> Object1.Field1 = Object2.Field2
> Object1.Field2 = Object2.Field2
> ```
>
> Member-wise equality testing becomes tedious to write. But hashing algorithms could be written generically, relying on all objects to have a `GetHashCode` method.
>
> The help documentation suggests that hash codes should be based on a constant, immutable field in a class. Thus all objects of the same type producing the same hash code are equal.

GetType

GetType returns the Type class, or *metaclass*, of the invoking type. The following example illustrates.

```
Dim I As Integer
MsgBox(I.GetType.Name)
```

I.GetType returns the metaclass of the Integer type, which is an Int32 type. The Name property is of the Type class. In the example the message box would display Int32, the CLR type of an integer.

A metaclass is an instance of the class itself. This is essential to supporting Run Time Type Information (RTTI). RTTI is the name of the capability of an object-oriented framework to be able to determine the class of objects at runtime. This gives us tremendous flexibility. (An excellent example afforded by a dynamic type system is demonstrated in Chapter 6, "Reflection.")

GetTypeCode

GetTypeCode returns the type code for an object. I.GetTypeCode, where I is an Integer, returns the value 9, which is the enumerated constant TypeCode.Int32.

ToString

The ToString method returns a string representation of an object. (Calling ToString on an Integer would yield the string equivalent of that integer's value.) This method at the lowest level of the class hierarchy is useful because it ensures that all types can be represented as string values. This makes it especially easy to implement procedures such as MsgBox, passing in any type for the message.

Integral Types

There are four integral types in VB .NET: Short, Integer, Long, and Byte. Byte, Integer, and Long existed in VB6, and Short has been introduced in VB .NET. The number of bytes used to store integers and longs has been doubled in VB .NET from 16 to 32 and 32 to 64, respectively. The number of acceptable values for a type is a function of permutating the number of bits. Thus a 32-bit integer is capable of storing 2^{32} possible values; split the number of possible values between negative and positive values, allow for zero, and you get a range of values from -2,147,483,648 to 2,147,483,647.

Integral types represent whole numbers only. Integers are useful for whole-number operations and indexing operations, such as those found in For...Next loops. Integer types are ValueType classes, a direct descendant of the Object type. All types are classes in

.NET, although `ValueType` looks and feels like a native data type. Types descended from `ValueType` are generically referred to as *value types*, implying a difference between types like integer and *reference types* like a `Button` control.

The difference between reference types and value types is that reference types carry runtime type information around with them at runtime and value types do not. `ValueType` runtime type information is available in the metadata of the assembly (refer to Chapters 6 and 12 for more information on assemblies and metadata). When the CLR needs to treat a value type as a reference type, such as when you request type information for a value type, an operation known as *boxing* occurs. Boxing, named after the Intermediate Language (IL) instruction performed behind the scenes, is the process of creating a heap object and copying the value of the value type into the heap object. This allows the CLR to treat the value type as a reference type. When the reference type is no longer needed, the reverse process, called *unboxing*, is performed.

The differences between value types and reference types exist to support types that seem as easy to use as native types but have the benefit of objects. Fortunately all of the boxing and unboxing occurs behind the scenes seamlessly. (You can get a bird's-eye view of how .NET works by examining an executable in the ildasm.exe—IL Disassembler—utility.)

> **Note**
>
> *Public* members are members that are accessible to code outside the class or structure. *Protected* members are accessible to the containing class or subclasses. Refer to Chapter 7, "Creating Classes," for more on public and protected access specifiers. Access specifiers have to do with the concepts of encapsulation and information hiding.

To determine the members of an `Integer`, look up the CTS type `Int32` and its ancestor classes in the help files. The `Public` shared Fields of an `Integer` type are the aforementioned `MaxValue` and `MinValue`. The `Public` shared method of an `Integer` is the `Parse` method. Public instance methods are those inherited from `Object`, and you can extend two protected methods, `Finalize` and `MemberwiseClone`, by deriving a new type from `Object`.

MinValue and MaxValue

`MinValue` and `MaxValue` in integral types are shared fields and thus are accessible without creating an instance of the type. For example, the following code refers to both shared members using the `Integer` type:

```
Dim Test As Boolean
Test = ( Integer.MinValue < 100000 ) and (100000 < Integer.MaxValue)
```

Test evaluates to True. The test would be False in VB6, but in VB .NET 100,000 is between the minimum and maximum values for Integer types.

> **Note**
>
> The appearance of methods in a specific section does not imply that these methods may not exist in other classes too. Methods such as MinValue, MaxValue, and Parse are not limited to integral classes.

Shared Method: Parse

Parse is a shared method that converts the string representation of a number to its integral equivalent.

```
Dim Number As String
Number = "4"
Debug.WriteLine(Integer.Parse(Number))
```

This example declares a variable, Number, as a String type. The string "4" is assigned to the variable, Integer.Parse(Number)—uses Parse—returning the string as an Integer.

Non-Integral Types

Non-integral types are floating-point numbers, including the Single, Double, and Decimal types.

Floating-point numbers support storing a wider range of values and are useful for math operations that result in fractional numbers. The Single and Double types support a greater range of values than the decimal type, but Single and Double are subject to rounding errors. The Decimal type is better suited for financial calculations that are less tolerant of decimal rounding errors.

You can use floating-point or exponential notation when assigning values to Single or Double variables. Floating-point notation is *whole.part* format, for example, 3.14159. Exponential, or scientific, notation uses the *mantissaEexponent* format. For example, 3e2 is equivalent to 300. (Mantissa is the value part, usually normalized for a single significant digit, and the exponent is also referred to as the power multiplier.)

If you initialize a Decimal number with a value greater than the largest Long integer value, you must add the suffix D at the end of the initial value. For example, Dim Number

As Decimal = 9223372036854775808D assigns roughly 9 quintillion to the variable Number (or, roughly the size of Bill Gate's fortune before the most recent stock decline).

Floating-Point Division

Floating-point numbers were modified to conform to the Institute of Electrical and Electronics Engineers (IEEE) standard for floating-precision numbers. The result is that you get some new behaviors when performing floating-point arithmetic.

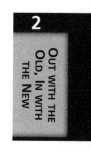

> **Caution**
>
> The equivalent of 1/0 returns Infinity and math.Sqrt(-1) returns Not a Number (NaN) for floating-point numbers. The equivalent Integer divisions (1\0 and -1\0) would cause a DivideByZeroException.

Dividing a number by 0 results in the value Infinity being returned. For example, the following code displays a message box containing the word Infinity:

```
Dim D As Double = 0
MsgBox( 5 / D )
```

Trying to evaluate the square root of -1 yields the value NaN (Not a Number). The following code gives an example:

```
MsgBox( Math.Sqrt(-1))
```

Visual Basic 6 required that you write an error handler to catch problems like division by zero. In Visual Basic .NET, you can use non-integral type instance methods or operators to test for these values.

Non-Integral Type Members

There are several members for non-integral types. Table 2.3 lists and describes the members of the Single and Double types.

TABLE 2.3 Floating-Point Type Members

Name	Description
	Shared Field
Epsilon	Smallest positive constant value greater than zero. (Refer to the section "Size of Types.")
MaxValue	Largest possible value
MinValue	Smallest possible value

TABLE 2.3 continued

Name	Description
NaN	Symbolic constant representing a value that's Not-a-Number (NaN)
NegativeInfinity	Symbolic value (*-Infinity*) representing negative infinity
PositiveInfinity	Symbolic value (*Infinity*) representing positive infinity
Shared Method	
IsInfinity	Returns a Boolean indicating whether the argument represents Infinity (for example, Double.IsInfinity(D/0) is True)
IsNaN	Returns a Boolean indicating whether the argument represents NaN
IsNegativeInfinity	Test for negative infinity (for example, -1/0)
IsPositiveInfinity	Test for positive infinity (for example, 1/0)
Parse	Converts string argument to type of class
Instance Method	
CompareTo	Compares instance to argument reference, returns less than 0 if instance is less than argument; 0 if instance equals reference argument; and greater than 0 if instance is greater than reference argument

All members listed in Table 2.3 are public members of the Single and Double types.

Non-Integral Decimal Type

Decimal numbers replace the role previously played by the Currency type. Currency no longer exists in Visual Basic .NET. Members of the Decimal type are listed in Table 2.4. The list is huge, but so much effort was paid to support Decimal values (to help track Chairman Bill's fortune) that I thought the least we could do was provide a reference listing.

TABLE 2.4 Decimal Type Members

Name	Description
Shared Field	
MaxValue	Largest maximum Decimal value
MinusOne	Represents the number negative 1
MinValue	Largest negative value

TABLE 2.4 continued

Name	Description
	Shared Field
One	Represents the number 1
Zero	Represents the number 0
	Shared Method
Add	Add to `Decimal` values
Compare	Compares two `Decimal` arguments, for example `Decimal.Compare(D1, D2)`.
	`D1 < D2` returns `< 0`;
	`D1 = D2` returns `0`, and
	`D1 > D2` returns `> 1`.
Divide	Returns `Decimal` result of D1 divided by D2 (for example, `Decimal.Divide(D1, D2)`, where `D1` and `D2` are `Decimal` values)
Equals	Determines whether two values are equal using Hash code
Floor	Rounds a `Decimal` to next lower number (for example, `Decimal.Floor(5.7) = 5`
FromOACurrency	Converts Office Automation Currency type to `Decimal`
GetBits	Decimal represented as binary array of `Int32` elements (for example, `Decimal.GetBits(3).GetValue(0) = 3`)
Multiply	Performs decimal arithmetic on two arguments
Negate	Negates the value of the `Decimal` argument
Parse	Converts a string to a decimal (see Listing 2.4)
Round	Rounds `Decimal` argument to the number of the decimal places indicated (for example, `Decimal.Round( 10.347, 2 ) = 10.35D`)
Subtract	Subtracts two `Decimal` arguments returning `Decimal` difference
ToByte	Converts `Decimal` to 8-bit equivalent; if value is greater, `Byte.MaxValue` throws an exception (refer to section on Structured Exception Handling in this chapter)
ToDouble	Converts `Decimal` to `Double` (see `ToByte`)
ToInt16	Converts `Decimal` to 16-bit `Integer` (see `ToByte`)
ToInt32	Converts `Decimal` to 32-bit `Integer` (see `ToByte`)
ToInt64	Converts `Decimal` to 64-bit `Integer`

TABLE 2.4 continued

Name	Description
	Shared Method
ToOACurrency	Converts a `Decimal` value to Office Automation Currency type (currency types are still supported in Microsoft Office)
ToSByte	Converts `Decimal` to signed `Byte` (see ToByte)
ToSingle	Converts `Decimal` to `Single` (see ToByte)
ToUInt16	Converts `Decimal` to 16-bit unsigned integer (see ToByte)
ToUInt32	Converts `Decimal` to 32-bit unsigned integer (see ToByte)
ToUInt64	Converts `Decimal` to 64-bit unsigned integer (See ToByte)
Truncate	Returns `Decimal` without the fractional part
	Constructor
Decimal	Initializes a new `Decimal` constructor
	Instance Method
CompareTo	Compares instance to argument; returns -1, 0, and 1 if instance is less than argument, equal to argument, or greater than argument, respectively

Money is important to our culture, and the many `Decimal` members provide us with a lot of power in managing `Decimal` data. As promised, Listing 2.4 demonstrates how the `Parse` method can be used to convert a formatted string to its `Decimal` equivalent.

LISTING 2.4 Calling `Decimal.Parse` on a string containing a comma-delimited numeric value converts that string to a `Decimal`.

```
Dim Number As String
Number = "100,000,005"
Debug.WriteLine(Decimal.Parse(Number))
```

Listing 2.4 writes 100000005 (one hundred million five) to the Output window. Many of the methods like `Parse` are commonly used in a polymorphic way. That is, you call `Parse` and it behaves in a meaningful way based on the type of the class. Using the same name for methods that perform semantically the same operation makes it easier to remember those method names. Just imagine if you had to memorize a unique name for the Parse–behavior for every data type. (For more on polymorphism, see Chapter 7, "Creating Classes.")

Double Types and `DateTime` Variables

Visual Basic .NET doesn't store date and time variables as `Double` precision numbers. The Common Language Specification defines a `DateTime` type distinct from the `Double` type.

Visual Basic 6 supported the following coding practice:

```
Dim D As Double
D = Now
```

After the line `D = Now`, D would contain a double precision number. The whole part of the number represented the date and the fractional part of the number represented the time. Visual Basic .NET will return the error `Use the ToOADate method on a Date to convert a Date type to a Double`. (See the section on `DateTime` data types for more information.)

Char Data Type

`Char` is defined in `System.Char`. The `Char` type has been widened to 16 bits to support Unicode characters. The 128 ASCII characters are sufficient to support the English alphabet, but Unicode was defined to support all characters in all other languages, including the 5,000 or so Japanese Kanji characters.

The concept of a character type doesn't exist in VB6. In addition, Visual Basic .NET doesn't support the fixed-length String notation:

```
Dim S As String * 1   ' no longer supported in VB.NET
```

Hence a `Char` type fills the void nicely. Table 2.5 defines the members of the `Char` type.

TABLE 2.5   Members of the New `Char` Structure

Name	Description
Shared Field	
MaxValue	Constant that represents largest char value
MinValue	Constant representing smallest char value
Shared Method	
CompareTo	Compares instance to argument; returns -1, 0, or 1 indicating that instance is less than argument, equal to argument, or greater than argument, respectively
GetNumericValue	Returns the numeric value of the Unicode character

TABLE 2.5 continued

Name	Description
	Shared Method
GetUnicodeCategory UnicodeCategory constant	Category of Unicode character grouped by enumerated
IsControl	Boolean indicating whether the character is a control character
IsDigit	Tests for Unicode digit category
IsLetterOrDigit	Tests for Unicode letter or digit category
IsLower	Tests for Unicode lowercase letter category
IsNumber	Tests for Unicode decimal or hexadecimal digit category
IsPunctuation	Tests for Unicode punctuation mark category
IsSeparator	Tests for Unicode separator category
IsSurrogate	Tests for Unicode surrogate character category
IsSymbol	Tests for Unicode symbol category
IsUpper	Tests for uppercase Unicode category
IsWhiteSpace	Tests for whitespace category
Parse	Converts value of string argument to Unicode character
ToLower	Converts the Unicode character to lowercase
ToUpper	Converts the Unicode character to uppercase

Declaring Char variables has the same basic syntax as declaring other types of variables. The basic syntax is

```
Dim C As Char
```

Refer to the upcoming section on "Variable Declarations" for more details. Shared fields and methods can be called with an instance or a class reference. The following example displays the uppercase A character in a message box:

```
MsgBox( Char.ToUpper("a"))
```

String Type

The String type has undergone some transformations. Strings are classes like other types in Visual Basic .NET. You may no longer declare fixed-length strings as you did in VB6, but we picked up some extra goodies in return.

Strings can be about 2 billion characters long (and we now have PCs capable of storing strings that big), and strings have a tremendous number of members that make string management significantly easier.

Thus far the chapter doesn't contain a lot of code snippets for other types, but strings are so common that I have included several examples of code statements to demonstrate some of the new string capabilities listed in Table 2.6. (You will see the other examples used throughout this book. For additional examples of data types in use, refer to the sections "Variable Declarations" and "Operators" later in this chapter.)

TABLE 2.6   Visual Basic .NET String Class Members

Name	Description
Shared Field	
Empty	Constant representing an empty string
Shared Method	
Compare	Compares two string argument objects
CompareOrdinal	Compares two string arguments without considering local national language or culture
Concat	Returns a new string created by appending one or more strings together
Copy	Returns a new string copy of the argument string
Format	Similar to C's `printf`; replaces format specifiers in format string with arguments provided to method
Intern	Returns a reference to the string instance
IsInterned	Retrieves string reference
Join	Inserts separator string between each string in an array
Instance Property	
Chars	Returns character at position
Length	Returns the string length
Instance Method	
Clone	Clones this string
CompareTo	Compares this string to argument string
CopyTo	Copies specified number of characters at offset to target index in array of Unicode characters
EndsWith	Returns a `Boolean` indicating if this string ends with argument string

TABLE 2.6 continued

Name	Description
	Instance Method
GetEnumerator	Returns a CharEnumerator enabling you to iterate over string
IndexOf	Returns index of substring
IndexofAny	Returns the index of the first occurrence of any character in the argument array of characters
Insert	Inserts specified string into this string at index
LastIndexOf	Returns index of last instance of substring or character
LastIndexOfAny	Returns the last index of any of the characters specified in the argument array
PadLeft	Right-aligns string padding characters on left with spaces or specified character
PadRight	Left-aligns string padding spaces or indicated character on the right
Remove	Removes indicated number of characters, starting at index
Replace	Replaces all occurrences of substring
Split	Splits string elements into an array at delimiter; opposite of join
StartsWith	Boolean indicating if this string is prefixed with argument string
SubString	Copies substring from instance string
ToCharArray	Copies characters in string into Unicode character array
ToLower	Returns lowercase copy of instance string
ToUpper	Returns uppercase copy of instance string
Trim	Trims specified characters from instance string
TrimEnd	Trims specified characters from end of instance string
TrimStart	Trims specified characters from start of instance string

Listing 2.5 contains various unrelated code fragments that demonstrate some of the string methods.

LISTING 2.5 Examples of `String` class members

```
1:   Sub TestStringMethods()
2:
3:       Dim S As String = _
4:       "Welcome to Valhalla Tower Material Defender"
5:       Dim T As String = S.Clone()
6:
7:       Debug.WriteLine(S.ToLower())
8:       Debug.WriteLine(S.ToUpper())
9:       Debug.WriteLine(T.EndsWith("Defender"))
10:      Debug.WriteLine(S.Chars(5))
11:      Debug.WriteLine(String.Concat("Hello", " ", "World"))
12:      Debug.WriteLine(S.Substring(5, 10))
13:
14:      Debug.WriteLine(String.Format( _
15:        "Abraham Lincoln was born {0:s}", "February 12"))
16:
17:      Dim Enumerator As CharEnumerator = S.GetEnumerator
18:
19:      While (Enumerator.MoveNext())
20:        Debug.WriteLine(Enumerator.Current())
21:      End While
22:
23:      Dim R() As String = {"2", "12", "1966"}
24:      MsgBox(S.Join("/", R))
26:   End Sub
```

Most of the code will make immediate sense to you. Lines 3 and 4 demonstrate the new form of combined variable declaration and initialization in VB .NET. (See the section on "Variable Declarations" for more information.) The form of member access may be a little confusing; just remember that the sequence is *object.member* for instance members and *class.member* for shared members.

Lines 17 through 21 demonstrate an `Enumerator`. If you've worked with iterators before, for example in C++, this code will make sense to you. Instead of subscripting the string directly, a class was written to manage iterating over the elements. The benefit of an enumerator is that the code is identical for enumerating over any type that supports working with the `Enumerator` class.

Line 23 may seem a little odd, too. It declares and initializes an array of strings. (Again, see the section "Variable Declarations" for more information.) You will see examples of string members used in code throughout this book.

Boolean Type

The Boolean type has gone through a couple of gyrations to get to its present state. In VB6, Boolean values used 0 for False and -1 for True as the underlying integral values. Originally VB .NET was designed to use 0 and 1 for False and True respectively.

0 and 1 are supported by the CLR, but in concession to VB6 developers, the underlying values of Booleans were converted back to 0 and -1. If you used beta 1 but skipped beta 2 of .NET, you may have missed this transmogrification. To work properly with the CLR Boolean values have to be converted internally to 0 and 1, but when—or perhaps if—you evaluate Booleans as integers, you will get the 0 and -1 value.

To further complicate matters, Boolean operators were going to be converted to logical rather than logical and bitwise operators, and Boolean evaluations were going to be short-circuited. All these planned changes were repealed in or around April 2001. What we ended up with is Boolean behavior very similar to the behavior in VB6.

The end result is that if you always use Boolean True or False, the underlying value will have no adverse impact on your code, and Boolean values have a greater semantic meaning than do integer-as-Boolean values.

Boolean Operators

Boolean operators include And, Or, Not, and Xor. AndAlso and OrElse were added to support short-circuit evaluations in VB .NET. (See the next section for a discussion of AndAlso and OrElse operators and short circuit evaluations.)

Visual Basic .NET performs the same logical and bitwise operations with And, Or, Not, and XOR as does VB6. If the types of the operands are Boolean, the Boolean operators perform a logical evaluation. If the operands are integral, a bitwise evaluation is performed. Listing 2.6 demonstrates various logical and bitwise evaluations with the result of the operation referenced by line number in the paragraph following the code listing.

LISTING 2.6 Logical and bitwise operations in VB .NET

```
 1: Sub TestBooleans()
 2:
 3:   Dim B As Boolean
 4:   B = False Or True
 5:   Debug.WriteLine(B)
 6:
 7:   B = False Xor False
 8:   Debug.WriteLine(B)
 9:
10:   B = False And True
```

LISTING 2.6 continued

```
11:    Debug.WriteLine(B)
12:
13:    B = Not True
14:    Debug.WriteLine(B)
15:
16:    Dim I As Integer
17:
18:    I = 3 Or 4
19:    Debug.WriteLine(I)
20:
21:    I = 2 And 4
22:    Debug.WriteLine(I)
23:
24:    I = 3 Xor 3
25:    Debug.WriteLine(I)
26:
27:    I = Not 5
28:    Debug.WriteLine(I)
29:
30: End Sub
```

Line 5 writes True to the Output window. Line 8 writes False to the Output window; logical Xor evaluations are only True when the operands don't match. The logical test on line 10 yields False because False And anything is False. The negation of True is False; line 14 writes False to the Output window. Because line 18 is evaluating two integers, the operation will be bitwise. The last four bits for 3 are 0011, and the last four bits for 4 are 0100. 0100 Or'd with 0011 is 0111 or 7. Line 19 writes 7 to the Output window. 2 and 4 have no bits in common, so line 22 writes 0. All bits are equal on line 24. Xoring bits is exactly the way to get 0 in a bitwise evaluation. Negating 5 (having all 0s except the last four bits are 0101) yields all 1 bits in the topmost 28 bits and 1010 in the last four bits. (Remember that integers are 32 bits in VB .NET.)

Boolean Evaluations Aren't Short-Circuited

Visual Basic .NET performs complete Boolean evaluations unless you use the AndAlso and OrElse operators. A complete Boolean evaluation means that all operands are evaluated to determine the result of the statement.

Consider the statement False And *anything*. False And *anything* will always yield False. There is no practical reason to evaluate the right-hand-side (rhs) operand. Not evaluating the other operand in this context is referred to as short-circuiting evaluation. But what happens if the rhs operand is the result of a function? Further, what happens if that function does something like updating a database? The answer is that in the False

And scenario, short-circuited evaluations would never update the database. The fragment that follows illustrates the scenario.

```
Function UpdateDatabase() AS Boolean
  ' update database
  return Passed
End Function


If( BoolVal And UpdateDatabase()) Then
```

The fragment tests the `BoolVal` Anded with the return value of `UpdateDatabase`. If `BoolVal` is False and Boolean evaluations were short-circuited, `UpdateDatabase` would never be called. Consider another example:

```
Function LogIn() As Boolean
  ' Login  and return connected state
  return IsConnected()
End Function


If( LoggedIn() Or LogIn() ) Then
  ' Process
```

In the first example, the `UpdateDatabase` method is always called in VB .NET. In the second example, if `LoggedIn` is True, an `Or` operator will yield True. If the loop short-circuited, `LogIn()` wouldn't get called. Because VB .NET was switched back to complete Boolean evaluation, `LogIn()` will always be called.

Writing code that depends on short-circuit or complete Boolean evaluations can lead to side effects. You can write some clever code like the `LoggedIn() Or LogIn()` statement, but it's best not to write too much clever code. Avoid writing code that depends on side effects related to the kind of Boolean evaluation employed, and you will sleep better.

If you intentionally want to write code that uses short-circuited evaluations in VB .NET, you can use the `AndAlso` and `OrElse` operators. `AndAlso` short-circuits `And` operations and `OrElse` short-circuits `Or` operations. For example, to short-circuit the `LoggedIn()` or `LogIn()` if conditional, replace the `Or` with `OrElse` and the statement is interpreted to mean *if not logged in, then log in.*

DateTime Type

`Date` and `Time` variables have been overhauled. Instead of the underlying value of a date and time variable being stored as a `Double`, `DateTime` is a type in its own right. VB6 stored the date as the whole number part and the time as the fractional part of a `Double`. For example, .5 was equivalent to #12:00:00 PM# in VB6.

When you want to manage date and time data in VB .NET, you will need to declare variables as `DateTime` types. A few methods exist for backward compatibility, but `DateTime` types in VB .NET are subclassed from the `ValueType` class and have all new methods and attributes of their own. Table 2.7 lists the public members of the `DateTime` type. Listing 2.7 offers some sample statements that demonstrate some of the new capabilities of `DateTime` types.

> **Note**
>
> The .NET Framework supports overloaded operators for types, like `DateTime`. Operator overloading isn't supported in Visual Basic .NET; hence the help related to overloaded operators isn't applicable to VB .NET. Operator overloading is one of those idioms, along with parameterized or template methods, that give the impression of C++ being more difficult to program in.

TABLE 2.7 `DateTime` Types Are `ValueType` Objects in VB .NET, Not Doubles

Name	Description
	Shared Field
MaxValue	Largest possible date; December 31, 9999 (the Y10K bug)
MinValue	Smallest possible date; January 1, 1 CE (Common Era)
	Shared Property
Now	Current date and time
Today	Today's date
UTCNow	Current time on this computer expressed as UTC (Universal Coordinated Time or Greenwich Mean Time [GMT])
	Shared Method
Compare	Compares two date arguments; t1 < t2 returns -1; t1 = t2 returns 0; t1 > t2 returns 1
DaysInMonth	Takes the year and month and returns the number of days in that month and year; year is used to account for leap year and February
FromFileTime	Returns `DateTime` equal to operating system file timestamp
FromOADate	Converts VB6, or OLE Automation Date to `DateTime` (for example, `DateTime.FromOADate(0.5)` is 12:00:00 PM)
IsLeapYear	Boolean indicating whether argument year is a leap year

TABLE 2.7 continued

Name	Description
	Shared Method
Parse	Converts string date to DateTime
ParseExact	Converts string argument to a DateTime using an IFormatProvider.System.Globalization. DateTimeFormatInfo implements the IFormatProvider interface
	Constructor
DateTime	Initializes a DateTime instance
	Instance Property
Date	Returns the Date value of instance
Day	Returns day of month of instance
DayOfWeek	Instance day of the week
DayOfYear	Returns the numeric day of year
Hour	Returns hour value of instance
Millisecond	Returns millisecond value of instance
Minute	Returns minute value of instance
Month	Returns month value of instance
Second	Returns second value of instance
Ticks	Returns number of 100-nanosecond ticks representing ticks since 1/1/0001 CE
TimeOfDay	Time value for instance
Year	Year value of instance
	Instance Method
Add	Adds TimeSpan argument to instance value
AddDays	Adds specified days to instance
AddHours	Adds hours to instance
AddMilliseconds	Adds milliseconds to instance
AddMinutes	Adds minutes to instance
AddMonths	Adds months to instance
AddSeconds	Adds seconds to instance
AddTicks	Adds ticks to instance
AddYears	Adds years to instance

TABLE 2.7   continued

Name	Description
Instance Method	
GetDateTimeFormats	Returns `DateTime` format String
Subtract	Subtracts time of duration from instance
ToFileTime	Converts `DateTime` to local system file time
ToLocalTime	Converts UTC to local time
ToLongDateTime	Converts instance date value to string
ToLongTimeString	Converts instance time to `String`
ToOADate	Converts instance to OLE Automation compatible date (`Double`)
ToShortDateString	Converts instance date to `String`
ToShortTimeString	Converts instance time to `String`
ToString	Converts date and time to `String`
ToUniversalTime	Converts instance to UTC `DateTime`

Note

Prior to 1582, time was tracked using the Julian calendar. In 1582, Pope Gregory XIII created the Gregorian calendar. In later centuries the Gregorian calendar was adopted by European countries, India, China, and the American colonies.

The Gregorian calendar tracks two eras: the time before Christ (BC, or before Christ) and the time after Christ (AD, or anno Domini (Latin for "year of our Lord"). The generic initialization for these two eras is BCE (before common era) and CE (common era).

`DateTime` types track time as the number of ticks, where a tick is 100 nanoseconds, since 12:00 AM January 1, 1 CE (or AD).

The Gregorian calendar introduced leap years, 12 months per year, and the number of days per month, including the 28 days in February and 29 in a leap year.

The new `DateTime` type measures time from 12:00 AM January 1, 1 CE from the Gregorian calendar in 100-nanosecond ticks. (It's interesting to note how much more closely we track time as computing power grows.) Listing 2.7 demonstrates some basic capabilities of the new `DateTime` class. You will see many more examples throughout the rest of the book.

LISTING 2.7   Using the new `DateTime` type

```
 1: Sub TestDateTime()
 2:
 3:   Debug.WriteLine(DateTime.FromOADate(0.5))
 4:   Debug.WriteLine(DateTime.Parse("12:00:00 PM"))
 5:   Dim Provider As New System.Globalization.DateTimeFormatInfo()
 6:   Debug.WriteLine(Provider.AMDesignator())
 7:   Debug.WriteLine(DateTime.ParseExact("12:42", "hh:mm", Provider))
 8:
 9:   Dim D As DateTime
10:   D = Now()
11:
12:   Debug.WriteLine(D.ToUniversalTime())
13:
14:   Debug.WriteLine("UTC-LocalTime=" + D.ToUniversalTime(). _
15:     Subtract.ToString())
16:
17:   Debug.WriteLine("Ticks since 12:00AM January 1, 1 CE=" _
18:     + Now().Ticks())
19:
20: End Sub
```

Line 3 converts the Double 0.5 to noon writing 12:00:00 PM. Office XP still uses VBA and consequently uses `Doubles` to store date and time values. On line 3, `FromOADate` converts an OLE Automation date to a `DateTime`. Line 4 converts the string to a `DateTime`; keep in mind that `DateTime` is a class rather than an instance. Line 4 demonstrates using a shared method. Line 5 creates an instance of `DateTimeFormatInfo` that implements the `IFormatProvider` interface. Line 6 uses the provider to get the `AMDesignator`, printing AM. Line 7 uses the `Provider` object as an argument to `ParseExact`.

Line 9 declares a `DateTime` variable `D` and line 10 initializes it to `Now`. You can declare and initialize variables on the same line in VB .NET (see the next section for more details.) Line 12 converts the current local time to Universal Coordinated Time (UTC). I reside in Michigan; UTC time is four hours ahead of Michigan (or EDT) time, which is demonstrated on line 14 using the `Subtract` method. Line 17 returns the number of ticks until the present date and time. When I ran the code the first time, the number of ticks was 631,244,136,636,562,500, or about 631 quadrillion.

Variable Declarations

Variable declarations have undergone some changes that will make them more convenient to use in VB .NET.

In VB6 you couldn't declare multiple variables of a specific type. If you declared a list of variables in VB6, all variables except the last variable in the list were variants. VB6 didn't support variable declaration and initialization in the same statement either. Each of the subsections describes the different styles of VB .NET variable declaration. The comparisons to the old style are included to help you find your bearings.

Declaring and Initializing a Single Variable

VB6 required that you declare and initialize a variable in two separate statements (assuming that `Option Explicit` was On). VB .NET supports doing both in a single statement. Listing 2.8 contains several VB6 variable declarations and initialization statements, followed by the VB .NET equivalent.

LISTING 2.8   VB6 variable declaration and initialization statements

```
 1: Private Sub Command1_Click()
 2:
 3:    Dim I As Integer
 4:    I = 5
 5:    Dim S As String
 6:    S = "Jello Mold"
 7:
 8:    Dim D As Date
 9:    D = Now
10:
11:    Dim F As Double
12:    F = D
13:
14:    Dim S1 As String: S1 = "Some More Text"
15:
16:    Debug.Print S1
17:
18: End Sub
```

As you can determine from Listing 2.8, each of the variables are declared in `Dim` statements and initialized after that. (Note on line 12 that a `Double` is initialized with a `Date`; that's a no-no in VB .NET.) You may also declare and initialize a variable on the same line in VB6, as line 14 demonstrates, but this constitutes two separate statements. Listing 2.9 demonstrates the more concise VB .NET equivalent code.

LISTING 2.9   The VB6 code from Listing 2.8, revised for VB .NET

```
 1: Private Sub button4_Click(ByVal sender As System.Object, _
 2:     ByVal e As System.EventArgs) Handles button4.Click
 3:
```

LISTING 2.9 continued

```
 4:    Dim I As Integer = 5
 5:    Dim S As String = "Jello Mold"
 6:    Dim D As Date = Now()
 7:    Dim F As Double = D.ToOADate()
 8:    Dim S1 As String = "Some More Text"
 9:    Debug.WriteLine(S1)
10:
11: End Sub
```

Line 1 demonstrates the button-click event handler. Event handlers are covered in detail in Chapter 8, "Adding Events." For now, suffice it to say that Command controls are Button controls in VB .NET, event handlers get a reference to the invoking object, and argument parameters passed in the System.EventArgs reference. Handles is a new keyword, also discussed in more detail in Chapter 8.

> **Tip**
>
> As a good, general programming practice, always provide an initial value for variables. Initial values provide you with a reliable reference point.

The code on lines 4 through 9 of Listing 2.9 performs precisely the same tasks as Listing 2.8 from VB6 does. Note that declarations and initializations are contained in a single statement, and initial values can be derived from functions. Of course, you can split declaration and initialization, but unless you have a very good reason not to, provide an initial value when you declare a variable.

Multivariable Declaration

Declaring multiple variables in the same statement in VB6 resulted in one typed variable and everything else was a Variant. In addition to variant types not being supported in VB .NET, this is seldom if ever what you want. Listing 2.10 demonstrates multiple variable declarations in VB6 code followed by the VB .NET code. A brief synopsis follows each listing.

LISTING 2.10 VB6 code declaring multiple variables in a single statement

```
1: Private Sub Command2_Click()
2:
3:    ' VB6 Multiple Variable Declaration
4:    Dim I, J, K As Integer
5:
```

LISTING 2.10   continued

```
 6:    I = 5
 7:    J = "Ooops!"
 8:    K = 15
 9:
10: End Sub
```

In Listing 2.10, I and J look as if they might be integers, but they are actually variants. Only K is an integer. Hence we can assign J a string as demonstrated in line 7. This is never what you want. If you tried to assign a string to K, you would get a compiler error. You want the compiler to check for data misuse as does VB .NET. Listing 2.11 demonstrates the VB .NET equivalent.

LISTING 2.11   Declaring multiple variables in VB .NET

```
 1:    Option Strict On
 2:
 3:    Module Module3
 4:
 5:      Sub MultipleVariables()
 6:
 7:        ' VB6 Multiple Variable Declaration
 8:        Dim I, J, K As Integer
 9:
10:        I = 5
11:        J = "Ooops!" ' Causes compiler error
12:        K = 15
13:
14:      End Sub
15:
16: End Module
```

Caution

The code in Listing 2.11 intentionally doesn't compile. The compiler will indicate that Option Strict doesn't allow an implicit conversion from string to integer. The implication is that each of I, J, and K are integer types, whereas only K is an Integer in the VB6 code in Listing 2.10.

Listing 2.11 is identical to Listing 2.10, except the code is written in a vanilla procedure in Listing 2.11 and an event handler in Listing 2.10. Listing 2.11 also demonstrates the placement of the procedure in a module and the Option Strict On statement.

> **Note**
>
> Always write all code with `Option Explicit On` and `Option Strict On`. (I imagine that future versions of VB .NET will remove these options entirely, ensuring strict and explicit code.) You always want the compiler to catch as many errors as it can, followed by handled exceptions at runtime (see the section on exception handling later in this chapter). The compiler is very good at detecting and helping you resolve errors; by writing explicit code, you're enabling the compiler to do a lot of work for you.

Keep in mind that `Option Strict On` must be true for the compiler to catch the assignment of a string to an integer as demonstrated in Listing 2.11. With `Option Strict Off`, the error will manifest itself as an `InvalidCastException` at runtime.

Multiple Initializers Not Allowed

Visual Basic .NET supports multiple variable declarations and ensures that they are all the type specified in the `As` clause. However, when you use multiple declarators you may not include initialization. For example, the code fragment

```
Dim I , J , K As Integer = 3, 4, 5
```

represents invalid code even in VB .NET. Remove the initial values and the code is correct.

Declarator is the term used to describe a variable declaration and initialization statement. For example, `Dim D As Datetime = Now()` is a declarative statement, or a declarator.

Defining Constants

Constant declarations must include the data type with `Option Strict On` in Visual Basic .NET. In VB6 the data type was determined by the initial value; VB .NET will determine the data type if it's not explicitly included in an `As` clause and `Option Strict Off` is `True`. The first fragment demonstrates a VB6 constant declaration and the second demonstrates the same declaration in VB .NET using the data type.

```
' VB6 Code
Const ADate = #12:00:00 AM#
Debug.Print ADate
```

Here is the VB .NET equivalent:

```
' VB.NET Code
Const ADate As DateTime = #12:00:00 AM#
Debug.WriteLine(ADate)
```

Notice that the biggest difference is the presence of the `DataType` in VB .NET. Both VB6 and VB .NET require that you use a constant value to initialize a constant; the value may not be derived from a function.

Instantiating Objects

Refer to Chapter 7, "Creating Classes," for an extensive discussion of object-oriented principles. In this section I will present a brief introduction, so you can progress with the examples between now and Chapter 7. Let's examine a few simple concepts before we look at creating objects.

A class is a description of an entity. Classes indicate what methods, properties, and fields you will find in instances of a kind. A *metaclass* is a variable of the class type. Metaclasses are returned by the `GetType()` polymorphic method introduced in the `Object` class. When you're using a class as if it were an object, at that time the class is referred to as a metaclass. Instance and object are synonyms. An instance, or object, is when you declare a variable whose type is a class and allocate memory to it. This process is referred to as instantiating an object, or creating an instance of an object.

Objects are instantiated using the `New` keyword. This is similar to how you created objects in VB6; however, classes in VB .NET have constructors. A constructor is a method whose job it is to initialize objects. Objects are created in VB .NET with code similar to the following:

```
Dim List As New Collection()
```

The code fragment declares and initializes an instance of the `Collection` class. The class is `Collection` and the object is `List`. The type of the object `List` is `Collection`. Note the addition of the parentheses in VB .NET.

Parameterized constructors are constructor methods that can accept arguments. In many languages the constructor method has the same name as the class, and in others a special name is used for the constructor by convention. In VB .NET constructors are named `New`, but the parameters are passed to constructors between the parentheses following the class name. For example, a `DateTime` type is a `ValueType` which in turn is a subclass of the `Object` class. Hence you may use the more verbose version of construction for `DateTime` objects as demonstrated next.

```
Dim MyDate As New DateTime(1966, 2, 12)
Debug.WriteLine(MyDate)
```

The verbose form of the `DateTime` declaration shows the `New` keyword and the parameters passed to the `DateTime` constructor. In the case of `DateTime` types there are actually seven overloaded constructors. An *overloaded constructor* is like any overloaded method.

An *overloaded method* is a method or methods in the same class that have identical names but distinguishing parameter signatures.

Method overloading wasn't supported in VB6 but is supported in VB .NET. Read Chapter 7, "Creating Classes," for more on advanced object-oriented idioms supported in VB .NET.

Initializer Lists

The admonition to provide initial values to variables applies to complex data types too. In the case of classes the initialization is accomplished by the constructor. Structures can have constructors too, so we can easily supply initial values to structures. What about arrays?

Array declaration and initialization is slightly more complex than declaring Integer types, but you can declare and initialize arrays in a single statement in VB .NET. The following statement declares and initializes an array demonstrating an initializer list.

```
Dim MyArray() As Integer = {1, 2, 3, 4}
```

The array is declared as an unbound array of type `Integer`. The initializer list (`{}`) constructs the array with four elements: 1, 2, 3, 4. You may not provide initializer lists for arrays declared with a specific size. For example, the following is an invalid statement:

```
Dim MyArray(4) As Integer = {1, 2, 3, 4}
```

Arrays are classes defined in the `System.Array` namespace. For more information on arrays and array methods, see the section "Arrays and Collections" later in this chapter.

Operators

To review, operators are the special symbols, such as `+`, `/`, `Mod`, and `AndOr`, that allow you to perform arithmetic, bitwise, comparison, concatenation, and logical operations in statements. Each operator takes a prescribed number and type of operands, or data.

Several new operators have been added to Visual Basic .NET. Some of these operators are designed to support bitwise logic and others have been defined to provide an abbreviated form of standard arithmetic. Several new assignment operators have been borrowed from C++. Look over Table 2.8 for a review of VB .NET operators.

TABLE 2.8   Visual Basic .NET Operators

Action	Symbol	Description
	Binary Operands	
Exponentiation	^	Written x^y; raises x to power y
Subtraction	-	x-y; performs subtraction and as an unary operator, negation
Multiplication	*	x*y; performs multiplication
Floating-point Division	/	x/y; floating-point division returns `Double`, except returns `Single` if both operands are `Byte`, `Integer`, or `Single`; returns `Decimal` if either operand is a `Decimal`
Integer Division	\	x\y; integer division
Modulo Division	Mod	x `Mod` y; returns remainder of division of x by y
Addition	+	x + y; sum of x and y
Assignment	=	x = y; assigns value of y to x
Exponentiation Assignment	^=	x ^= y; raises x to the power y and assigns the result to x
Multiplication Assignment	*=	x *= y; multiplication of x and y and assignment to x
Floating-point Division and Assignment	/=	x /= y; floating-point division of x by y and assignment to x
Integer Division and Assignment	\=	x \= y; integer division of x by y and assignment to x
Addition and Assignment	+=	x += y; sum of x and y and assignment to x
Subtraction and Assignment	-=	x -= y; subtraction of y from x and assignment to x
Concatenation and Assignment	&=	x &= y, where x and y are strings; concatenation of x and y and assignment to x
Equality	=	x = y; tests for equality
Inequality	<>	x <> y; tests for inequality

2

OUT WITH THE OLD, IN WITH THE NEW

TABLE 2.8 continued

Action	Symbol	Description
Binary Operands		
Less Than	<	x < y; tests for x less than y
Greater Than	>	x > y; tests for x greater than y
Less Than or Equal to	<=	x <= y; tests for x less than or equal to y
Greater Than Or Equal to	>=	x >= y; tests for x greater than or equal to y
Like	Like	*string* Like *pattern*; compares *string* argument to *pattern* argument.
Is	Is	*object1* is *object2*; tests to determine if *object1* and *object2* refer to the same object
Concatenation	&	*string1* & *any_expression*; converts right-hand-side argument to string and concatenates to left-hand-side argument
Concatenation	+	*string1* + *string2*; concatenates two strings; may cause error if one of the left or right operands isn't a string
And	And	Bool1 And bool2 or x And y; logical And for Booleans and bitwise And for integrals
Or	Or	Applies to bool1 Or bool2 and x Or y; logical Or on Booleans and bitwise Or on integrals
Xor	Xor	Bool1 Xor bool2 or x Xor y; logical exclusive-Or for Booleans and bitwise exclusive Oring of integrals
AndAlso	AndAlso	Short-circuited And operation
OrElse	OrElse	Short-circuited Or operation
Unary Operands		
AddressOf	AddressOf	Returns address of procedure; used extensively for delegates in VB .NET
GetType	GetType	GetType(*any*); returns runtime type of argument
Not	Unary	Not bool or Not x; logical negation for Booleans and bitwise negation for integrals

Many of these operators you've seen before. We won't rehash those. A few others are new and `AddressOf` has taken on new importance. Let's take a moment to cover new or changed operators.

All operators of the form *token=* perform two operations. For example, I += 5 is expanded to I = I + 5. These combined operators have been around in C++ for about 12 years or so.

`AddressOf` has taken on new importance in VB .NET. In VB6 you could use the `AddressOf` operator to pass the address of a procedure to APIs that needed a callback procedure. (A *callback* is simply a procedure invoked by its address.) In VB .NET you can create your own callbacks and use them in your program. Callbacks are supported directly with the delegate idiom. Read Chapter 9, "Understanding Delegates," for more on this advanced topic.

Type Conversion Functions

Earlier in the chapter, I recommended that you use `Option Strict On` and `Option Explicit On`. These settings will let the compiler help you catch errors at compile-time because they preclude a lot of implicit type conversions. You still need a good way to convert data from one type to another. To this end Visual Basic .NET includes dozens of type conversion capabilities.

Also noted throughout this chapter is the introduction of the `ToString` method in the `Object` class. Because every class and structure is an `Object`, every type contains a `ToString` conversion method. Many types also contain a method that takes a string argument and converts it to a specific type. For example, in the `DateTime` type, the `Shared` `Parse` method converts a string to a `DateTime`. The two statements below demonstrate converting a string to a `DateTime` and a `DateTime` back to a string, respectively.

```
Dim ADate As DateTime = DateTime.Parse("12:00:00 AM")
Dim AString As String = ADate.ToString()
```

Many of the VB6 conversions have been carried over to VB .NET; a few have been replaced to support new types. In VB6, the conversion functions took an expression of a specific type or variant. In VB .NET the argument type is an `Object`, which means that you can pass any subclass of an `Object` that makes sense for the specific kind of conversion. Table 2.9 lists the VB6 conversion functions and their VB .NET replacements.

TABLE 2.9 VB6 Conversion Functions and Their VB .NET Replacements

VB6	VB .NET	Description	Range
CBool	CBool	Converts Object to Boolean Type	Valid string or numeric expression
CByte	CByte	Converts Object To Byte	0 to 255
None	CChar	Converts Object to Char	0 to 65535
CCur	CDec	Converts Object to Decimal	See VB6's CDec below
CDate	CDate	Converts Object to DateTime	Any valid date or time value
CDbl	CDbl	Converts Object to Double	Any valid Double value (see Table 2.3)
CDec	CDec	Converts Object to Decimal	Any valid Decimal value (see Table 2.3)
CInt	CInt	Converts Object To Integer	Any valid Integer value (see Table 2.3)
CLng	CLng	Converts Object to Long	Any valid Long value (see Table 2.3)
CSng	CSng	Converts Object to Single	Any valid Single value
CStr	CStr	Converts Object to String	Any valid String
CVar	CObj	Converts Object to Object	Any value
None	CShort	Converts Object to Short	Any valid Short (see Table 2.3)

As you can determine from Table 2.9, most conversion functions were carried over to VB .NET. Where the VB6 column contains None, no VB6 conversion function exists.

For reference, see Appendix A, "VB 6 Programming Element Changes in VB .NET."

Variable Scope Changes in VB .NET

Visual Basic .NET supports block-level scope. Generally, it's best to declare variables in as narrow a scope as possible; this rule directly supports the "don't-use-global-variables" rule.

VB6 variables within a `For...Next` loop are accessible in the scope containing the `For...Next` loop. Visual Basic .NET variables in a `For...Next` loop aren't accessible in the outer scope. Listing 2.12 demonstrates VB6 scope and Listing 2.13 demonstrates the block scope revision in VB .NET.

LISTING 2.12 VB6 scope is limited to procedure scope

```
1: Private Sub Command6_Click()
2:   Dim I As Integer
3:   For I = 1 To 100
4:     Dim D As Integer
5:     D = D + 1
6:   Next I
7:   MsgBox D
8: End Sub
```

In VB6, line 7 displays 100. `D` has procedure scope even though it was defined in the `For...Next` loop. In VB .NET, `D` has block scope and line 7 causes the error `The name D is not defined` (see Listing 2.13 for a revision).

LISTING 2.13 VB .NET supports block scope

```
Sub BlockScope()

    Dim I, D As Integer
    For I = 1 To 100
      D = D + 1
    Next I

    MsgBox
End Sub
```

For `D` to be accessible outside the `For...Next` statement, the variable must be defined outside the `For...Next` loop; that is, `D` must be defined in the scope in which it's used.

Any variable defined in an outer scope is visible to narrower scopes but not broader scopes. For example, a procedure variable, like D, is visible to the For...Next block's scope, which is narrower than the procedure but not accessible outside of the procedure.

Flow Control Statements

Several flow control statements have been revised in Visual Basic .NET. GoSub is no longer supported. The Call keyword is supported but no longer required for function and subroutine calls and will probably disappear in future versions of VB .NET.

On Goto and On Gosub computed branching is no longer supported. Replace computed branch statements with the Select Case statement. On Error Goto is supported for backward compatibility but should be replaced with structured exception handling (see the section "Structured Exception Handling" for details).

The While...Wend statement block still exists, but Wend has been replaced with End While. Listing 2.14 demonstrates While...End While.

LISTING 2.14   While...End While replaces While...Wend

```
1:  Sub WhileEndWhileTest()
2:
3:      Dim I As Integer = 1
4:      While (I < 10)
5:        I += 1
6:        Debug.WriteLine(I)
7:      End While
8:
9:  End Sub
```

The fundamental behavior of the loop hasn't changed. A While...End While loop processes zero or more times and when you type While, the End While is added automatically for you, completing the block. Use While...End While exactly as you would the VB6 While Wend loop.

Arrays and Collections

Arrays have undergone a couple of changes in VB .NET. Originally (beta 1) arrays were designed to contain n elements with indexes from 0 to n-1, where n represents the number of elements in the array. The Option Base statement is no longer supported. In beta 2, arrays were reverted back to VB6 Option Base 0 arrays. An array declared as follows

```
Dim A(10) As Type
```

contains $n + 1$ elements indexable from 0 to n. The sample array contains 11 elements. You can still use `LBound` and `UBound` to manage the array bounds, use the `Array.GetLowerBound` and `Array.GetUpperBound` methods, or always use the lower bound limit of 0.

In addition to changes in arrays, new abstract data types (ADTs), including `ArrayList`, `BitArray`, `Dictionary`, `HashTable`, `Queue`, `SortedList`, `Stack`, and `StringCollection` have been added to the `System` namespace. The `Stack` class is demonstrated at the end of this section, in the subsection "Abstract Data Types."

`Collection` is defined in the `Microsoft.VisualBasic` namespace for backward compatibility. (Refer to the section "Abstract Data Types" for more information on Collections.)

Range Arrays Not Supported in VB .NET

Range arrays aren't supported in VB .NET. VB6 allowed you to define an arbitrary lower and upper bound for arrays, as in the following:

```
Dim I(3 To 5) As Integer
```

The fixed range array notation isn't supported in VB .NET.

N-Dimensional Arrays Are Supported

Multidimensional arrays are supported in VB .NET. To declare an *n*-dimensional array, express each dimension as a comma-delimited number indicating the size of each dimension of the array. Keep in mind that each dimension contains $n+1$ elements.

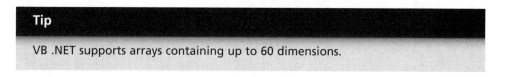

Tip

VB .NET supports arrays containing up to 60 dimensions.

```
Dim Doubles(10, 10) As Double
```

The statement declares an 11×11 dimension array of doubles. Arrays are subclassed from `System.Array`, affording some new capabilities that make array management easier (see "Arrays Are Subclassed from `System.Array`"). Listing 2.15 demonstrates indexing a two-dimensional array.

LISTING 2.15 Indexing an *n*-dimensional array

```
 1: Sub TestArray()
 2:     Dim Doubles(10, 10) As Double
 3:
 4:     Dim I, J As Integer
 5:     For I = Doubles.GetLowerBound(0) To Doubles.GetUpperBound(0)
 6:
 7:       For J = Doubles.GetLowerBound(1) To Doubles.GetUpperBound(1)
 8:
 9:         Doubles(I, J) = I * J
10:         Debug.WriteLine(Doubles(I, J))
11:
12:       Next
13:     Next
14:
15: End Sub
```

The two-dimensional array in Listing 2.15 is indexed in a nested for loop using new methods GetLowerBound and GetUpperBound (lines 5 and 7) on each dimension of the array to make determining arrays bounds much easier. It's preferable to use the new capabilities of the Array class than using older functions like LBound and UBound. Refer to the section "Arrays Are Subclassed from System.Array" for more information.

Resizing Arrays

As in VB6, arrays can be resized dynamically using the ReDim statement. To preserve existing elements of the array, include the Preserve keyword. The following statement represents resizing the 10×10 array in Listing 2.15:

```
ReDim Doubles(10, 100)
```

Add the Preserve keyword after ReDim and the rightmost dimension values will be saved. If you use Preserve and change any dimension other than the rightmost one, you will get an ArrayTypeMismatchException at runtime. For example, you could write

```
ReDim Preserve Doubles(10, 105)
```

but

```
ReDim Preserve Doubles(5, 100)
```

would raise an ArrayTypeMismatchException at runtime. The code is trying to change the dimension of the array and preserve a dimension that isn't the rightmost dimension. The dimension sized 100 is the rightmost dimension in the example.

Returning Arrays from Functions

You can return arrays from functions in VB .NET. (This is also supported in VB6.) To return an array, define the return type of the function as an array of type and assign the array variable in the Return statement. (Function results are returned using the Return keyword, as demonstrated in VB .NET.) Listing 2.16 demonstrates returning an array of bytes from the function GetArray.

LISTING 2.16   Returning an array from a function in VB .NET

```
 1: Function GetArray() As Byte()
 2:
 3:     Dim Bytes() As Byte = {0, 1, 2, 3, 4, 5}
 4:     Return Bytes
 5:
 6: End Function
 7:
 8:  Sub TestArray()
 9:     Dim I As Integer
10:     Dim Bytes() As Byte = GetArray()
11:
12:     For I = Bytes.GetLowerBound(0) To Bytes.GetUpperBound(0)
13:        Debug.WriteLine(Bytes(I))
14:     Next
15:  End Sub
```

TestArray calls GetArray on line 10 and the return value of GetArray is used to initialize the local array Bytes on line 10. The GetLowerBound and GetUpperBound methods are used to dynamically determine the upper and lower bounds of the array. (A couple of other new features are demonstrated here: the declarator on line 3 of GetArray demonstrates initialization of the Byte array and line 4 demonstrates how to use the Return keyword. To return the value of a function, simply place the Return keyword where you would have assigned the return value to the function name in VB6.)

Arrays come with new capabilities as described in the next section. If you need a dynamically changing array, use the new System.ArrayList ADT. ArrayList allows you to dynamically resize the array by changing the Capacity property.

Arrays Are Subclassed from System.Array

Arrays are subclassed from System.Array in Visual Basic .NET. Table 2.10 lists the members inherited by Arrays and describes each member.

TABLE 2.10   Members of the `Array` class Inherited by Arrays

Name	Description
Shared Methods	
BinarySearch	Uses binary search to find element of one-dimensional sorted array
Clear	Sets a range of elements to Nothing
Copy	Copies range of elements from one array to another
CreateInstance	Creates an array of the specified type and size
IndexOf	Searches a one-dimensional array, returning index of first matching value
LastIndexOf	Finds last index of matching Value
Reverse	Reverses the order of array elements; can be applied to some or all of the array
Sort	Arranges the elements in sorted order
Instance Properties	
IsFixedSize	Always returns False unless overridden by subclass
IsReadOnly	Always returns False unless overridden by subclass; indicates ReadOnly status of Array
IsSynchronized	Indicates if array is thread-safe; Always returns False unless overridden by subclass
Length	Returns the number of elements in the array
Rank	Returns the number of dimensions of the array
SynchRoot	Returns a synchronized version of the array for thread-safe access
Instance Methods	
Clone	Returns a shallow copy of the array; contained objects are referenced, not copied
CopyTo	Copies elements of one-dimensional array to specified index of target array
GetEnumerator	Returns an IEnumerator (see Listing 2.5 for an example of an enumerator)
GetLength	Returns the number of elements in the specified dimension
GetLowerBound	Returns the lower bound of the specified dimension
GetUpperBound	Returns the upper bound of the specified dimension
GetValue	Returns the value indicated by index arguments

TABLE 2.10   continued

Name	Description
	Instance Methods
Initialize	Initializes elements of the array by calling the default constructor; only performs action on ValueType arrays
SetValue	Sets value of array indicated by index arguments

Protected methods and methods inherited from Object aren't listed here. They exist and you can look them up in the help. The most important thing to note is that VB .NET arrays are as easy to use as VB6 arrays, but they come loaded with many additional capabilities.

Listing 2.5 demonstrates how to use enumerators (which provide a consistent interface for iterating over elements), and Listings 2.15 and 2.16 demonstrate some of the new capabilities of arrays.

Arrays contain one more element than the upperbound value because they are zero-based in .NET. An array Dim A(5) As Integer contains six elements indexed from 0 to 5. It is a good idea to use GetLowerBound and GetUpperBound methods or enumerators to avoid confusion over array boundaries. You will see more array examples in later chapters.

Abstract Data Types

Visual Basic .NET defines (via the CLR) abstract data types that provide you with a wide variety of storage options for data. VB includes a new ArrayList, BitArray, Dictionary, HashTable, Queue, SortedList, Stack, and StringCollection.

Although these ADTs are too numerous to squeeze into this chapter, I will incorporate them in code examples in later chapters where appropriate. Here are some brief definitions:

- Collection is not part of the CLR but was incorporated into the Microsoft.VisualBasic namespace on behalf of VB developers.
- The Collection is defined in the Microsoft.VisualBasic namespace.
- The ArrayList is a smarter array that has built-in dynamic capacity management.
- BitArray represents bits as indexable True and False values indicating the state of the bits.
- A Dictionary provides an abstract class for key and value pairs; the Registry is a physical example of a Dictionary, as are INI files.

- `HashTable` stores elements by a computed index that makes accessing elements of a `HashTable` fast and convenient.

- A `Queue` is a first-in, first-out ADT, or a FIFO, data storage type. `SortedList` is an ordered list of data.

- A `Stack` is a last in first out, or LIFO, storage type, and `StringCollection` is a collection specifically for storing string data.

Listing 2.17 demonstrates the basic capabilities of a stack. Stacks are defined to store data and contain simple operations like `Push` and `Pop`. Add an element to the top of the stack with `Push` and take an element from the top of the stack with `Pop`.

LISTING 2.17   Demonstration of the basic capabilities of a `Stack`

```
 1: Sub DemoStack()
 2:     Dim MyStack As New Stack()
 3:
 4:     Dim I As Integer
 5:     For I = 102 To 65 Step -1
 6:       MyStack.Push(I)
 7:     Next
 8:
 9:     While (MyStack.Count > 0)
10:       Debug.WriteLine(MyStack.Pop())
11:     End While
12:
13: End Sub
```

Line 2 instantiates an instance of `Stack`, defined in `System.Collections`. The `For` loop pushes the numbers 102 to 65 onto the stack. The `Push` operation takes an `Object` argument, so anything can be placed into the stack. The `While` loop `Pops` elements from the stack. If you run the sample code, you will see that the elements come out of the stack from 65 to 102, in reverse of the order in which they were put into the stack. All the collection data types are roughly based on an array of elements; it's the semantic operations that make them convenient for solving one kind of a problem over another.

> **Note**
>
> Functions and subroutines have changed some in VB .NET. There is enough information on writing procedures that this topic is covered in its own chapter. Refer to Chapter 5, "Subroutines, Functions, and Structures" for more information on this subject. Chapter 5 also covers enumerations.

Structured Exception Handling

Visual Basic .NET still supports `On Error Goto` error handling, but you should replace the old VB6 style `On Error Goto` statements with structured exception handling. (It's also likely that `On Error Goto` will be removed in future versions of VB; Microsoft is giving us a chance to get used to exceptions.)

Structured exceptions are one aspect of VB .NET that promote VB to a first-class language. Exceptions are subclassed from `Objects` and exception handling is more robust and precise than `On Error Goto`.

Exception handling was invented as a means of replacing the error-prone error code return value and supports writing more robust applications. Exception handling in VB .NET supports `Try...Catch` exception blocks and `Try...Finally` resource protection blocks. This topic requires more than a few paragraphs, so considerable coverage is provided in Chapter 3, "Basic Programming in VB .NET."

Visual Basic .NET Handling of Reserved Words

Visual Basic .NET allows you to use reserved words in code. If you accidentally use a reserved word, such as `Enum`, as a variable, the IDE will place square brackets around the word. You can then use the reserved word in a non-reserved way as long as every occurrence has the brackets around the reserved word.

Using reserved words in this way probably isn't a good idea because it may lead to confusing, unsightly code. It's also a safe bet that this quirk won't survive for long.

Unfortunately, there are times when you may not be able to avoid using keywords, especially when they define a type. The `System.Reflection` namespace defines the type `Assembly`. `Assembly` is both a type and a keyword. When you declare `Assembly` variables, the code editor will add the brackets around the `Assembly` type declaration but may not always add the brackets, especially when a reserved word is used as a variable name.

Compatibility Between VB6 and VB .NET

Experienced users of Visual Basic 6 will find that once they understand key differences between VB6 and VB .NET, it's possible to easily migrate VB6 code to the VB .NET environment.

Microsoft.VisualBasic

The Microsoft.VisualBasic compatibility namespace includes elements relevant to VB6 compatibility. If you open a VB6 project in VB .NET, the migration wizard will run. Migrating code from VB6 to VB .NET uses things from the compatibility namespace. For new code, I would suggest you use the new types, idioms, collections, and other features of VB .NET because elements of the Microsoft.VisualBasic compatibility namespace will probably find their way into the circular file soon.

Programming Elements Not in Visual Basic .NET

Many elements of VB6 didn't make it into VB .NET. Some aspects of VB6 were replaced and others are no longer supported. To provide you with a comprehensive table of VB6 elements, the elements that were left out of VB .NET are described in a table in Appendix A. Refer to Appendix A for a complete list of features that were revised or removed in VB .NET. (Many are covered in this chapter, but the table in Appendix A will provide you with one location for reference.)

Summary

The size of this chapter alone should indicate how extensive the changes to VB .NET are. Some people may try to play down the changes to VB .NET. In some ways, VB .NET is still VB, but if that's all anyone sees, they are missing the bigger picture.

In this chapter, you learned that VB .NET is an object-oriented system, having a root class of Object. All classes and structures inherit from the root Object class. You also learned that the Type idiom was replaced with the more powerful Structure idiom. Simple data types actually have lineage descending from Object and ValueType, making primitive types more advanced but just as easy to use as VB6 primitives.

If you find yourself feeling a little lost as you proceed with your study of VB .NET, return to this chapter for the basic information on fundamental changes to VB. Also check out Appendix A for resource information on migrating to VB .NET, more compatibility issues, and basic revisions to Visual Basic for .NET. Enumerations, structures, functions, and subroutine changes are explained in Chapter 5 in the form of what we can do in VB .NET.

Chapter 2 was written to provide you with a reference for programming changes at a general level. Now that you are aware of the differences between VB6 and VB .NET, Chapter 3 begins our focus on the powerful things we can do with .NET.

Basic Programming in Visual Basic .NET

CHAPTER 3

In this chapter, you'll get your first chance to write Visual Basic .NET code unencumbered with the coding practices and idioms of yesterday. We will use Visual Basic .NET code and only Visual Basic .NET code. Chapter 3 provides you with an opportunity to experiment and explore the basic programming concepts that are the molecules of every program.

This chapter looks at variable declaration and initialization, block scope, static variables, and more on arrays and abstract data types. I will also introduce you to the concept of shadow variables, and provide you with some more examples on defining procedures and structures. Near the end of this chapter, we will look at the new garbage collector and the impact it has on using objects. Finally, this chapter wraps up with comprehensive coverage of exception handling. Because you will use exception handling in all of the code you write—though perhaps not all procedures—you need to master the concepts of exception handling early.

Declaring and Initializing Variables

There is one significant difference in the way you write declarations for simple types and object types. That difference is the use of the keyword New. (We'll look at New more in the section "Using Objects.")

Variables can be declared and initialized in Visual Basic .NET on a single line. In addition to resulting in fewer lines of code, this new feature can be applied with some simple rules to make code more robust.

Before we look at several declarative statements, here is an overview of the best practices regarding variables that we will follow throughout this book:

- Always provide an initial value for variables.
- Declare and initialize variables in a single statement.
- Declare variables immediately before they are used.
- Declare variables in the narrowest scope possible.
- Use the refactoring "Replace Temp with Query" to keep the number of temporary variables to an absolute minimum.

In each of the subsections, I will demonstrate several declarators supporting each of these best practices. In the final subsection, I will demonstrate the concept of refactoring, and illustrate benefits derived from refactored code.

Initialize Variables

In programming, so many things can go wrong that we need to hedge as often as possible to make things go right. These hedges, like splitting aces in blackjack, are good practices that help us progress deliberately without sweating details. By providing an initial value for variables, we are providing a reference point, or known state, that we can use to evaluate a variable. Essentially, by providing an initial state and controlling the value of variables, we can always evaluate a variable to determine whether its value is within an acceptable range. However, if we never expressed what an acceptable initial value was, we can't test the initial state.

The desirability of a variable having an initial state is exactly why object-oriented languages have constructors and parameterized constructors (the section "Using Objects" in this chapter covers these more). It's so that we can initialize even objects.

The general form of a variable declaration is as follows:

```
Dim varname As datatype = expression
```

> **Note**
>
> Although VB6 code often was encumbered with a pseudo-Hungarian notation prefix for variables, we will not use the Hungarian notation in this book. The first reason is that no single notation existed, resulting in many inconsistencies. A second reason is that we are working with a strongly typed, object-oriented language, which mitigates the need for prefixes. Consequently, a notation would only increase our labor.
>
> We will use a very simple notation in this book (you can adopt it or not). Fields will be prefixed with an F and properties will have an identical name, without the F, as their underlying field values. This convention was borrowed from Object Pascal and helps us name fields and properties consistently and quickly and makes the job of matching fields to properties trivial.

varname is replaced with a suitable variable name. Generally, whole words, no non-standard abbreviations, and no prefixes are used for variable names (see the note). *datatype* is the name of a class, structure, or ValueType like Double. *Expression* is a suitable expression for the data type. (The syntax changes slightly for objects and events. See the section "Using Objects" for object declarations and Chapter 8 for an example of WithEvents statements.) Listing 3.1 demonstrates several declarations, including suitable initial values.

LISTING 3.1 Several declaration and initialization statements.

```
 1: Module Module1
 2:
 3:   Sub AHandler(ByVal o As Object, ByVal e As System.EventArgs)
 4:     Debug.WriteLine("Read chapter 9")
 5:   End Sub
 6:
 7:
 8:   Sub Main()
 9:
10:    Dim S As String = Command()
11:    Debug.WriteLine(S)
12:
13:    Dim TodayDate As DateTime = Today()
14:    Debug.WriteLine(TodayDate)
15:
16:    Dim MyArray() As Double = {3.14159, System.Math.Sqrt(2)}
17:    Debug.WriteLine(MyArray(1))
18:
19:    Dim MyHandler As EventHandler = AddressOf AHandler
20:    MyHandler(Nothing, Nothing)
21:
22:    Try
23:      Dim MyException As Exception = New Exception("Raise an exception!")
24:      Throw MyException
25:    Catch e As Exception
26:      Debug.WriteLine(e.StackTrace())
27:    End Try
28:
29:
30:   End Sub
31:
32: End Module
```

Tip

If you are debugging in the IDE, you set the command-line arguments by opening the project's properties pages. Choose Project, Properties, Configuration Properties, Debugging to open the view. Modify the command-line argument's value to set the command-line argument.

Listing 3.1 defines some spurious declarators. The examples typify some of the declarations you are likely to encounter in everyday code. Line 10 demonstrates declaring a string and initializing it to the command-line arguments. The value of Command will include all of the arguments that follow the /cmd switch.

Line 13 demonstrates how to initialize a DateTime to today's date. Line 16 demonstrates initializing an array of doubles; MyArray is initialized to contain an approximate value for π and the square root of 2, returned from System.Math.Sqrt.

Line 19 declares MyHandler as the Delegate type EventHandler and initializes it to the address of the subroutine AHandler. Lines 19 and 20 illustrate that Visual Basic .NET can work with function pointers and introduce the subject of delegates. Delegates are special classes that support function pointers and are used to implement event handling in Visual Basic .NET. Chapter 9, "Understanding Delegates," gives more information on this subject. (For now, suffice it to say that when MyHandler is called on line 20, the subroutine on lines 3 through 5 is actually called.)

Lines 22 to 27 demonstrate declaring and initializing the root exception object. Line 24 demonstrates throwing an exception, which is similar to raising an error in VB6. Lines 25 through 27 demonstrate a Catch block. The last section of this chapter covers exception handling.

Declare and Initialize Variables in a Single Statement

The biggest problem with uninitialized variables is related to pointers in C and C++. Because C/C++ pointers can point to any memory location, an uninitialized C/C++ pointer might be pointing to BIOS memory. Visual Basic .NET has limited support for pointers, so we are able to get away with the default initialization of variables to the null equivalent more often.

> **Tip**
>
> By default VB .NET initializes numeric types to 0, strings to empty strings, and objects to Nothing.

However, Visual Basic .NET does support delegates and dynamic object creation. It is preferable that these types have an initial value; otherwise, your code will be littered with checks for Nothing or an equivalent. Calling an uninitialized Delegate results in a NullReferenceException, which is cleaner than crashing because of a pointer trashing BIOS memory, but still annoying.

As a convenience, it is easier to have one rule for all cases than to make exceptions to the rule. Thus it is easier to always declare and initialize variables in a single statement.

Declare Variables Immediately Before First Use

There is no compelling reason to declare variables at the top of a procedure. Declaring them immediately before first use makes it easy to track the type and purpose of a local variable.

As an added benefit, if you are able to apply the refactoring "Replace Temp with Query," having the temporary variable close to its point of use makes getting rid of the temporary variable easier too. (See the section "Employ Refactoring: Replace Temp with Query" for more information on refactoring.)

Declare Variables in the Narrowest Scope Possible

Global variables are bad. The reason global variables are bad is because the opportunity for misuse is greatest. The opportunity for misuse of data should be reduced as much as possible; or, simply put, the narrower the scope, the better.

You are familiar with module, class, structure, and procedure scope. You may also use accessibility specifiers to further reduce opportunity for misuse. Accessibility specifiers like `Public`, `Private`, `Protected`, `Friend`, and `Protected Friend` are discussed in Chapter 7. Block-level scope has been added to Visual Basic .NET. Block-level scope is the narrowest scope of all. Refer to the section "Working with Block-Level Scope" for more information.

Employ Refactoring: Replace Temp with Query

This book does not cover all the details of refactoring. A great book on refactoring is Martin Fowler's *Refactoring: Improving the Design of Existing Code*, published by Addison-Wesley. However, where it is suitable to mention refactoring, I will do so.

What Is Refactoring?

Refactoring is an outgrowth of XP (Extreme Programming), which has been popularized by Kent Beck and others. XP includes concepts like pair programming and resolving problems in the structure of code with refactoring. Refactoring stems from a dissertation by William Opdike.

My definition of refactoring is "factoring out common code." The real benefit of refactoring is that it provides a language, or a frame of reference, for talking about improving code, and offers a set of almost algebraic rules to make refactoring an orderly process.

We can't summarize Martin Fowler's book here, so for now, just accept that refactoring is a good thing. Refactoring helps move towards the fewest occurrences of repetitive code and helps achieve greater opportunity for reuse. Refactoring may also lead to a means of measuring the qualitative value of code. Good code is refactored code; bad code often is not.

Replace Temp with Query

"The problem with temps is that they are temporary and local. Because they can be seen only in the context of the method in which they are used, temps tend to encourage longer methods" (Fowler, p. 120). Long methods are less desirable than short methods.

By replacing a temporary variable with a query—a function that returns the value previously maintained by the temporary variable—we shorten the procedure and increase the likelihood that other fragments of code can use the query method instead of reconstructing the temporary variable.

Assume that we have two properties: `Sale` and `TaxRate`. `TotalSale` is defined as the sale plus the cost of taxes. Also, suppose that we have a fragment of code that declares a local temporary variable to store `TotalSale`:

```
Dim TotalSale As Decimal = Sale * (1 + TaxRate)
Debug.WriteLine(TotalSale)
```

The `Debug.WriteLine` statement plays the role of using the temporary variable.

To replace temporary variables with a query method, first look for temporary variables that are assigned a value just once, as is `TotalSale`. (If it is assigned values more than once in a procedure, you may need to simplify the procedure or keep the temporary.) Having identified the temporary, perform the following steps to complete the refactoring:

1. Define a function, adding a `Get` to the temporary variable name. Define the function to return the calculated value of the two fields. (In the example, `Sale` and `TaxRate` represent the two fields.)
   ```
   Function GetTotalSale() As Decimal
     Return Sale * (1 + TaxRate)
   End Function
   ```

2. Replace the initialization of the temporary with the function call.
   ```
   Dim TotalSale As Decimal = GetTotalSale
   Debug.WriteLine(TotalSale)
   ```

3. Compile and test the modification to ensure that the code behaves identically and yields the same results.

4. Having confirmed identical behavior, remove the temporary variable and replace the use of the temporary with the call to the query method.

```
Debug.WriteLine(GetTotalSale())
```

5. Compile and test.

The purpose of refactoring is to get the same result with simpler code. Testing after each phase of the refactoring makes it easier to roll back changes if the code behaves differently.

Critical to Extreme Programming and refactoring is the testing process. The benefit of the refactoring "Replace Temp with Query" is that long procedures become shorter, while performing the same operations, and the frequency of debugging the local temporary calculation decreases to one time, in the query method.

The benefit of such refactoring often rises over time. The more times you would have written the calculation for the temporary again, the more savings you achieve.

Working with Block-Level Scope

Scope relates to opportunity for use. When a name is in scope, you can use it; when a name is not in scope, you cannot use it.

There are several layers of scope in Visual Basic .NET. From the broadest to narrowest scope, there is namespace, type (applies equally to class, module, and structure), procedure, and block scope. Things declared in a broader scope are accessible to narrower, subordinate scopes directly. For example, a private class field is accessible to a procedure in the same class and will not cause a name conflict with a field with the same name in another class.

Additionally, narrower-scoped names are accessible to other areas of code using the member-of operator (.). For example, the `ToString` method is defined as a public method of `Object`. Because `ToString` is public, it is accessible outside the `Object` class, but you have to precede the call to `ToString` with a class reference and the member-of operator, `class.ToString()`.

Variables declared in a procedure or block have procedure-level or block-level scope, respectively. A block in a procedure is narrower than the containing procedure, so procedure variables are accessible in a block, but block variables are not accessible in the containing procedure. As mentioned in Chapter 2, block scope is new in Visual Basic .NET.

Block-scoped variables are those variables introduced for the first time in a `For Next`, `For Each`, `While End While`, or `If Then` construct. Any variables introduced with a `Dim` statement in a block construct are accessible only in that block when `Option Explicit` is `On`. Consider the following code fragment, using an arbitrary block to demonstrate block scope behavior:

```
If ( True ) Then
  Dim I As Integer
  I = 10
End If
I = 5
```

If `Option Explicit` is `On`, you will get a "name is not declared" error reported by the compiler at the last line, assuming that `I` is not defined in the containing procedure. If `Option Explicit` is `Off`, the compiler will report a "block-level variable hides variable in enclosing block error" because the implicit `I` in the statement `I = 5` hides the explicit `I` in the `If Then` block. Further, when `Option Explicit` is `Off`, if `I` were first used in the block, then `I` would be accessible outside the block.

Consider another example:

```
Option Explicit Off
If (True) Then
  I = 10
End If
Debug.WriteLine(I)
```

This code writes 10 to the Output window.

If you want a variable to be accessible in an outer scope, move the declaration of the variable to the outer scope, as in this final example:

```
Option Explicit On
Dim I As Integer
If(True) Then
  I = 10
End If
Debug.WriteLine(I)
```

The variable `I` is defined outside the block and consequently is accessible in both the scope where it is defined and the narrower scope of the `If Then` block.

A second detail to watch out for is that block variables have to be initialized between trips in and out of block scope to prevent unexpected results. When working with block scope, establish a consistent set of rules to prevent problems related to block scope. The following rules, if applied consistently, should preclude any problems:

- Always set `Option Explicit On`.
- Define variables in the narrowest scope possible.

- Apply the "Replace Temp with Query" refactoring discussed earlier, reducing the number of temporary variables and limiting potential scope-related problems.
- Always initialize variables, especially variables declared in a block-level scope.

Static Variables

The Static keyword is used to indicate that a variable will maintain its value between successive calls to a procedure. VB6 supported making all procedure variables static by adding the Static keyword to the procedure header. Visual Basic .NET does not support procedure-header use of Static.

Using Static Variables

The mechanics for declaring static variables require that you replace Dim with Static as demonstrated in the following function:

```
Function GetCounter() As Integer
  Static Counter As Integer = 0
  Counter += 1
  Return Counter
End Function
```

Each time GetCounter is called, Counter will be incremented by 1. The first time GetCounter is called it will return 1, and each subsequent call to GetCounter will return Counter + 1. (Note the use of the new addition and assignment operator, +=.)

> **Caution**
>
> You cannot use the compound operators, like +=, in an initialization statement for a variable. For example, Static Counter As Integer += 1 will cause a compiler error.

A function like GetCounter is a good way to get a unique value during the program's run.

Static Variables and Memory

Procedure variables are created in stack memory. The stack memory is temporary memory. Items are added to the stack as local variables are declared in a procedure and removed when the procedure ends. Static variables are actually created in the data segment. The memory for static variables is allocated and remains as long as your program is running, just as variables declared outside of a procedure in a module are.

Using Arrays

Since about 1990, when C++ began gaining popularity, it has been a recommended practice to encapsulate arrays of memory in a class. Storing arrays of data in a class allows the array to perform memory and bounds checking in conjunction with the class and behind the scenes.

Using an unadorned array requires that you manage bounds checking and reallocation of memory (using ReDim). On occasion you may want to use the new array class, but for most new code you will probably find ArrayList easier to use and less error-prone. ArrayList is covered in the section "Working with New Abstract Data Types."

Arrays Are Instances of System.Array

All arrays are instances of System.Array. All members of System.Array were listed in the last chapter in Table 2.10, so we won't repeat that information here. Keep in mind that even simple arrays are classes in Visual Basic .NET.

For additional reference, arrays implement the ICloneable, IList, ICollection, and IEnumerable interfaces.

Declaring Arrays

There are a couple of basic kinds of array declarations. You may declare an array without a fixed number of elements, represented by the empty parentheses (), and optionally include an initializer list. Or, you may declare an array with a fixed number of elements. However, an array with a fixed number of elements specified cannot also have an initializer list.

```
Dim StringArray() As String = {"This", "is", "a", "test"}
Dim FixedArray(3) As Double
```

The size of StringArray is not specified but is indicated by the initializer list {} containing the words This, is, a, and test. StringArray will have four elements indexed from 0 to 3. (Remember that Option Base is not supported, so the first element of a Visual Basic .NET array is 0.)

> **Note**
>
> Remember that Visual Basic .NET does not support the range array using the following syntax:
>
> ```
> Dim A(low To high) As datatype
> ```

`FixedArray` contains four elements. In Visual Basic .NET, the number of elements is always *n*+1. `FixedArray` is declared as `FixedArray(3)`, resulting in four indexable elements from 0 to 3.

Much of the work we used to have to handcraft in VB6 is already implemented in Visual Basic .NET. The next section demonstrates some of the new capabilities of arrays.

Using Array Methods

In addition to array initializer lists, there are many methods that you can take advantage of that make sorting, copying, and finding elements of an array much easier. Many of these methods are `Shared` methods (refer to Table 2.10 for details). Listing 3.2 demonstrates several array methods.

LISTING 3.2 Demonstration of array methods.

```
 1: Sub Main()
 2:
 3:     Dim StringArray() As String = {"This", "is", "a", "test"}
 4:     Dim FixedArray(3) As Double
 5:
 6:     Array.Sort(StringArray)
 7:
 8:     Dim E As IEnumerator = StringArray.GetEnumerator()
 9:
10:     While (E.MoveNext())
11:       Debug.WriteLine(E.Current())
12:     End While
13:
14:     Array.Reverse(StringArray)
15:
16:     E.Reset()
17:
18:     While (E.MoveNext())
19:       Debug.WriteLine(E.Current())
20:     End While
21:
22:     Debug.WriteLine(Array.IndexOf(StringArray, "test"))
23:
```

LISTING 3.2 continued

```
24:     Dim NewArray(StringArray.Length) As String
25:     Array.Copy(StringArray, NewArray, StringArray.Length)
26:
27:     Debug.WriteLine(Array.IndexOf(NewArray, "a"))
28:
29:
30: End Sub
```

Lines 3 and 4 repeat the declaration of StringArray and FixedArray from the last section. Line 6 calls the Shared method Sort, passing StringArray as the array to be sorted. After line 6 the strings are ordered as a, is, test, and This. Line 8 declares an IEnumerator interface variable and the enumerator for StringArray is returned. Using enumerators allows you to work with a common interface for enumerating many kinds of data.

The enumerator is positioned before the first element, which makes it convenient to start iterating with MoveNext (see lines 10 and 18). MoveNext returns a Boolean indicating whether or not there is a value at that position. E.Current returns the current element. (Of course you can still use a For loop and an index to iterate over elements of an array, if desired.)

Line 14 sorts the array in descending order with the Reverse method. Again, Reverse is a Shared method, so we pass the array we want reversed as an argument to the method. Line 16 resets the enumerator because we left it pointing past the last element on line 12. Line 22 demonstrates finding an element of an array with the IndexOf method. Line 25 demonstrates copying an array. The number of elements of the source and target arrays must be identical; on line 24 I used the length of StringArray to allocate NewArray. You can also use the ReDim command to resize the target array before copying the array.

Resizing arrays was covered in the section "Resizing Arrays" in Chapter 2.

Multidimensional Arrays

Visual Basic .NET supports multidimensional arrays and nested arrays. A *multidimensional array* is an array containing a comma-delimited list of array dimensions. A two-dimensional array, for instance, contains two numbers indicating the size of each dimension. Multidimensional arrays are also referred to as *matrices*.

Chapter 2 demonstrated multidimensional arrays. We won't repeat that information here, but will demonstrate an array of arrays.

We can add any object to the Array type. If we store heterogeneous objects in an array, we can rely on late binding to determine what an element of the array is, or we can perform dynamic type checking and conversion. Because the recommended Option Strict On setting prohibits late binding, I will demonstrate how to convert the elements of the nested arrays to a specific type at runtime. (You also need to know how to perform dynamic type conversions to work with multicast delegates in Chapter 9.)

Note

Late binding refers to the compiler determining the type of an object at runtime. For example, in VB6 we might have defined a variable as a variant and then assigned an object to it with CreateObject. The following Visual Basic .NET code demonstrates a late bound reference to MS Excel with Option Strict Off and replacing the Variant required in VB6 with the Object required in Visual Basic .NET.

```
Module Module1

    Private Excel As Object
        Sub Main()

        Excel = CreateObject("Excel.Application")
        Excel.Visible = True

        MsgBox("Stop")
        End Sub

    End Module
```

Early binding is indicated when we add a reference to the object we want to create and declare a variable of that type. An early bound object is an object whose type is known by the compiler at compile time.

Option Strict forces the compiler to do more work and is a recommended setting; thus we give up late bound objects for the benefit of stronger compiler type checking.

To declare an Array object, use the same syntax as any other array and declare the type as Array. Listing 3.3 demonstrates an example with an array defined to contain six elements. To insert a nested array into each indexed position of the array, assign the array object to an indexed position of the containing array. Nested array elements are accessed by indexing the containing array or using an enumerator. To access an element of the nested array, you need to convert the nested array object to a specific type.

LISTING 3.3 Nested arrays and dynamic type conversion.

```
1: Sub Main()
2:
3:   Dim StringArray() As String = {"This", "is", "a", "test"}
4:   Dim AnArray(5) As Array
5:
6:   AnArray(0) = StringArray
7:   Debug.WriteLine(CType(AnArray(0), String())(0))
8: End Sub
```

From the listing, you can easily determine that declaring the outer, generic array (line 4) is no different than declaring an array of any type. Assigning `StringArray` to `AnArray(0)` nests `StringArray` into the first element of `AnArray`. Line 7 demonstrates using dynamic type conversion to get the nested array back to a usable form. The code is packed tightly into a single statement; the next fragment breaks line 7 into a more verbose listing.

```
Dim Elem As Object
Elem = AnArray(0)
Dim Temp() As String
Temp = CType(Elem, String())
Dim S As String
S = Temp(0)
Debug.WriteLine(S)
```

Line 7 from Listing 3.3 translates into the very verbose seven lines of code in the preceding fragment. `AnArray(0)` returns an object. `CType` converts the `Object` to a string array. Having the string array, we can access elements of the string array, and finally write the value of the string.

Listing 3.3 demonstrates that it is possible to write convoluted, terse code in Visual Basic .NET. However, the code demonstrates what is possible but not necessarily prudent. Sometimes the data structure can make it very easy to store and manage specific kinds of data. If you find yourself coding nested arrays, hide the complexities of managing the data in a class. As a better alternative, consider using one of the new abstract data types rather than a `System.Array`.

Working with New Abstract Data Types

A revised `Collection` class similar to the VB6 `Collection` is defined in the `Microsoft.VisualBasic` namespace. Visual Basic .NET has added several new Abstract Data Types (ADTs) to ultimately replace the `Collection` class. The names of the new classes were enumerated in Chapter 2, including an example of using the `Stack` class. The subsections that follow demonstrate `ArrayList`, `HashTable`, `SortedList`, and `Queue`.

Members of `ArrayList`

The `ArrayList` class is a designed replacement for an unadorned array. Although arrays in Visual Basic .NET are classes, they are designed to work similarly to VB6 arrays. This means you have to resize the arrays and preserve elements manually, which is likely to yield code that is littered with `ReDim` statements.

Dynamic array sizing is semantical behavior that belongs to an array. In an object-oriented programming language, you would expect that such behavior is defined as part of an array class. Combining storage and capacity management in a single class is what `ArrayList` has to offer. You will find `ArrayList` easier to use than a `System.Array` or the VB6-style collection.

Table 3.1 lists the members of `ArrayList`.

TABLE 3.1 `ArrayList` Members

Name	*Description*
	Shared Method
Adapter	Wraps an `ArrayList` around an object that implements `IList`
FixedSize	Returns a fixed-size wrapper, allowing elements to be modified but not added or removed
ReadOnly	Returns a read-only wrapper around an `ArrayList`
Repeat	Returns an `ArrayList` containing multiple copies of the argument value
Synchronized	Returns a thread-safe list wrapper
	Instance Property
Capacity	Used to get or change the capacity of an `ArrayList`
Count	Returns number of elements in the list; capacity may be greater than or equal to count
IsFixedSize	Returns a Boolean indicating whether or not the `ArrayList` has a fixed size
IsReadOnly	Returns a Boolean indicating whether or not the `ArrayList` is read-only
IsSynchronized	Returns a Boolean indicating whether or not access to the `ArrayList` is synchronized
Item	Used to index elements of the `ArrayList`
SyncRoot	Returns an object used to synchronize `ArrayList` access

TABLE 3.1 continued

Name	Description
	Instance Method
Add	Appends an element to the `ArrayList`, increasing the capacity if necessary
AddRange	Appends elements from an `ICollection`
BinarySearch	Searches for element using binary algorithm
Clear	Removes all elements
Clone	Performs shallow copy of all elements
Contains	Returns a Boolean indicating whether or not the element is in the `ArrayList`
CopyTo	Copies all or part of the `ArrayList` to a one-dimensional `System.Array`
Equals	Determines whether the argument array references the calling array
GetEnumerator	Returns `ArrayList` enumerator
GetHashCode	Hashing function inherited from `Object`
GetRange	Copies range of elements to a new `ArrayList`
GetType	Returns metaclass of `ArrayList`; inherited from `Object`
IndexOf	Returns the index of a particular element of the array list
Insert	Inserts an element into the list at specified index
InsertRange	Inserts a range of elements at specified index
LastIndexOf	Returns the index of the last occurrence of object
Remove	Removes the first instance of argument object
RemoveAt	Removes element at specified index
RemoveRange	Removes a range of elements at specified index
Reverse	Sorts the array in reverse order
SetRange	Copies range of elements over the elements in the `ArrayList`
Sort	Reorders the data in ascending order
ToArray	Copies elements to `System.Array`
ToString	Returns name of object
TrimToSize	Sets capacity to number of elements

3

BASIC
PROGRAMMING IN
VISUAL BASIC .NET

The next section demonstrates some of the characteristics of `ArrayList`.

Using ArrayList

The biggest benefit of ArrayList over System.Array is that ArrayList has dynamic capacity management built in. When you use System.Array, you have to make sure there is enough room for an element. If not, you have to add capacity to the array with ReDim. On the other hand, if you use the ArrayList Add, AddRange, Insert, or InsertRange methods, the capacity is adjusted as needed.

ArrayList has significant advantages over VB6 arrays but fewer advantages over Visual Basic .NET System.Array; however, capacity management is enough of a reason to prefer ArrayList over System.Array. Many of the methods in ArrayList are similar to methods in Array (see "Using Array Methods"); therefore, we will not repeat examples of those methods here. Capacity management and adding and managing a range of elements are additional features offered in ArrayList. Let's take a look at examples of using these behaviors. Listing 3.4 demonstrates behaviors of ArrayList that are not found in System.Array.

LISTING **3.4**   Behaviors of ArrayList not found in System.Array.

```
 1: Sub DemoSetRange()
 2:
 3:    Dim MyArray As New ArrayList()
 4:
 5:    Dim Array1() As Integer = {0, 1, 2, 3, 4, 5}
 6:
 7:    MyArray.InsertRange(0, Array1)
 8:
 9:    Dim I As Integer
10:
11:    For I = 0 To MyArray.Count - 1
12:       Debug.WriteLine(MyArray(I))
13:    Next
14:
15:    Debug.WriteLine("Contains 3? " & MyArray.Contains(3))
16:
17: End Sub
```

The example declares an ArrayList named MyArray using one of three possible constructors. The constructor on line 3 takes no parameters. Line 5 allocates a System.Array and initializes the members to the integers 0 through 5. Line 7 demonstrates ArrayList.InsertRange. InsertRange takes a start index and an ICollection object. System.Array implements the ICollection interface, so System.Array is a suitable argument for InsertRange. In fact, any class that implements ICollection (HashTable, Stack, Queue, and SortedList are other examples) is a suitable argument for

InsertRange. Lines 11 through 13 demonstrate that elements of an `ArrayList` can be accessed as if it were a simple array. (Of course you can use the new `Enumerator` behavior that you saw in Listing 3.2, as well.)

Line 15 demonstrates the `Contains` method. `Contains` takes an object, which can be a literal integer like 3, and returns a Boolean indicating whether or not the object is in the `ArrayList`. In the example, `Option Strict` is `On` so the Boolean returned by `Contains` is printed using the `ToString` method of the Boolean type.

HashTable

Hash tables use key and value pairs. The key is processed through a hashing function that is designed to generate a unique value that is then used as an index into the hash table to the location containing the value. Hash tables strike a balance between resource usage and speed.

Instead of probing each element for equality to determine whether objects are equal, simply processing the key provides an index to the location that contains the associated value. There is a significant amount of research on hash tables, hashing functions, and key-collision avoidance. (You may have studied some of them in college if you were a computer science major, but the .NET Framework provides a `HashTable` implemented for you.)

The `System.Collections.HashTable` class implements a hash table available for you to use. `HashTable` works externally much like a data dictionary. Provide a unique key and an associated value, and the `HashTable` takes care of the rest.

Suppose you were storing personnel records in memory for quick access. You might key each record on the Social Security number, and the value would be the personnel record. (For the demonstration, we will simply store a person's name to represent the personnel record.)

Listing 3.5 declares a new instance of a hash table and adds some unique elements to the hash table keyed on pseudo-Social Security numbers. The values stored in the hash table represent the data associated with the keys. (The key is the first argument and the value is the second argument of the `Add` method.)

LISTING 3.5   Storing items in a hash table.

```
1: Sub DemoHashTable()
2:   Dim Hash As New Hashtable()
3:   Hash.Add("555-55-5555", "Frank Arndt")
4:   Hash.Add("555-55-5556", "Mary Bonnici")
5:   Hash.Add("555-55-5557", "Paul Kimmel")
```

LISTING 3.5   continued

```
 6:
 7:    Dim Enumerator As IDictionaryEnumerator = Hash.GetEnumerator
 8:
 9:    While (Enumerator.MoveNext())
10:      Debug.WriteLine(Enumerator.Key & "=" & _
11:        Enumerator.Value)
12:    End While
13:
14: End Sub
```

Tip

Enumerator objects are read-only. To modify elements of a collection like a HashTable, you can use a For Next loop, indexing the elements of the collection directly.

HashTable uses an IDictionaryEnumerator object to iterate over elements. Line 7 declares an enumerator and lines 9 through 12 iterate over each element displaying the key and value pairs. (.Key and .Value were not defined in the IEnumerator interface; they were added in the IDictionaryEnumerator.)

SortedList

The SortedList ADT is based on the dictionary interface. Recall from the last section that a dictionary is a collection of key (or name) and value pairs. SortedList maintains two internal arrays. One keeps track of keys and the second keeps track of values. As with a hash table, the key values of a sorted list must be unique.

SortedList has methods similar to ArrayList, in addition to the key and value pairs introduced with HashTable. SortedList is defined in the System.Collections namespace. For more information on SortedList, look in the MSDN help files.

Queue

Queue data structures are also referred to as First In First Out (FIFO) data structures. Think of a queue as a line. There is a first in line, a last in line, and everything in between.

Just as Stacks have a language for adding elements to the collection—Push and Pop—to denote adding and removing elements to a Stack, Queue uses the notion of *enqueuing* and *dequeuing*. All of the collection-based ADTs work with Objects; hence to enqueue means to add an Object to the queue and to dequeue means to remove an Object from the queue.

Queues are a natural choice when you want the first item put into a collection to be the first item out. Listing 3.6 demonstrates basic queue behavior.

LISTING 3.6   Basic queue behavior.

```
 1: Sub DemoQueue()
 2:
 3:   Dim Q As New Queue()
 4:   Q.Enqueue("One")
 5:   Q.Enqueue("Two")
 6:
 7:   While (Q.Count > 0)
 8:     Debug.WriteLine(Q.Dequeue)
 9:   End While
10:
11: End Sub
```

The output from Listing 3.6 is One and Two. The elements are dequeued in exactly the same order in which they were enqueued.

Queues implement several of the same COM interfaces as other ADTs defined in the System.Collections namespace, like ICollection, IEnumerable, and ICloneable. For this reason queues have many of the same operations by name as other ADTs.

Assessing the ADTs

For general purpose in-memory storage, ArrayList will suffice. For key and value pairs, use HashTable or SortedList. If you want objects stored and retrieved in the same order, use Queue, and if you want the last element put into a collection to be the first one out, use Stack. The fundamental behaviors of the collection classes are identical. The semantic operations are consistent with the type of data structure.

Shadow Variables

Variables can exist in several places and in broader or narrower scopes. Sometimes this causes problems because it may be unclear to the compiler what the code means. For example, when a variable is defined at the procedure level and a variable with the same name exists in a block within the procedure, the variable in the block hides the variable with the same name in the outer scope. In Visual Basic .NET, this is referred to as *shadowing*. That is, the narrow scope variable *shadows* the outer scope variable.

At the block level, the compiler will report an error: "Block-level variable hides a variable in an enclosing block." An example of causation follows:

```
Sub Main()

  Dim V As Object

  If True Then
    Dim V As Object
    V = Nothing
  End If

End Sub
```

V in the inner block hides the variable outside of the If...Then block. To resolve this problem, simply rename or remove the block-level variable. However, if the problem exists at the module, class, or structure level, you can use a variety of techniques to clarify your intent.

Suppose Module1 declares a module-level Integer I, and suppose Sub Main declares a local variable I. Within Main all references to I will shadow the variable in the outer, module scope. This scenario is demonstrated by the next code fragment:

```
Module Module1

  Dim I As Integer

  Sub Main()

    Dim I As Integer
    I = 10
    Debug.WriteLine(Module1.I)
  End Sub

End Module
```

All references to I in Main refer to the I defined in Main. What if you wanted to modify the outer scope's I variable? In the case of a module, you would simply prefix the reference to I with the module name. Based on this fragment, if we wanted to refer to I in the outer scope, Module1.I would clearly indicate our intent to the compiler.

If the containing entity were a class, we would use the Me (reference to self) object, as in Me.I. The reason we can use the module name is that modules are for all intents and purposes classes with all shared members. The reason we cannot reliably use the class name and have to use Me is that classes are instantiated many times, and each object will have a different name.

Visual Basic .NET also introduces the Shadows keyword. Shadows is used when a sub-class reintroduces a name in a superclass, hiding the name in the superclass and that is what you want to happen. I will defer the discussion of Shadows until Chapter 7, "Creating Classes," because it will be beneficial if inheritance and overloading methods are covered before we continue talking about the Shadows qualifier.

Functions and Subroutines

If you are familiar with VB6 functions and subroutines, you have the basics for now. There are some additional changes that you need to familiarize yourself with, including the revision allowing function results to be assigned with the Return keyword.

Chapter 5 provides you ample opportunity to experiment with functions, subroutines, and the new Structure idiom. Chapter 5 also includes some function qualifiers that you may have forgotten about, including Optional and ParamArrays.

Defining Structures

The Type idiom has been replaced with the Structure idiom. Structures are significantly more advanced than types. In addition to the ability to define aggregate data types, Structures allow you to define parameterized constructor, property, and method members.

Chapter 5 combines coverage of functions and subroutines with coverage of the new Structure idiom and examples of defining and using enumerations.

Using Objects

We have talked a lot about objects. If you have programmed in C++, many of the idioms related to object-oriented programming will seem familiar to you, but in this book, we make no assumptions about your experience with object-oriented programming. Although Chapter 7 discusses defining classes in detail, including coverage of inheritance, polymorphism, and encapsulation, this section briefly introduces a few basic concepts, so you will have no trouble working with objects for now.

Visual Basic .NET supports true object-oriented programming. Critical to this is the idea of inheritance and constructors. We'll defer our discussion of inheritance until Chapter 7, but you need to know about constructors now.

What Is a Constructor?

A *constructor* is a member of a class that has a special role—to initialize the class. In VB6 this role was satisfied by the `Class_Initialize` method, which was called implicitly when you created an object.

`Class_Initialize` took no arguments, which meant you were unable to initialize an object with externally passed-in values. Visual Basic .NET replaces `Class_Initialize` with the constructor `New()`. `New` is the constructor subroutine that is responsible for initializing objects. Every object has one constructor that takes no arguments, but `New` can be overloaded to take one or more arguments depending on the needs of the class.

`New` is invoked, when you use the `New` keyword when creating an instance of an object, as in the following:

```
Dim Button As New Button()
```

This example creates an instance of a `Button` component—which replaces the `Command` control from VB6. Tracing into the `Button` class would show that the preceding statement traces right into a subroutine named `New`, the constructor in Visual Basic .NET. Every class can have many constructors and inherits at least one from the `Object` class. Listing 3.7 demonstrates a constructor call that dynamically adds a button to a form at runtime.

LISTING 3.7 A `Button` component is dynamically constructed with `New Button`.

```
 1:    Private Sub Button1_Click(ByVal sender As System.Object, _
 2:       ByVal e As System.EventArgs) Handles Button1.Click
 3:
 4:       Static NextTop As Integer = 0
 5:       Dim Button As New Button()
 6:       Button.Text = "Button" & Controls().Count
 7:       Button.Top = NextTop
 8:       Controls().Add(Button)
 9:       NextTop = Button.Bottom
10:
11:    End Sub
```

When the `Click` event is invoked the event handler in Listing 3.7 is called. Line 4 declares a static variable that tracks the last bottom location of the most recently created control on line 9. Line 5 constructs a new `Button` component. Line 6 provides a unique caption for the button, line 7 positions the button, and line 8 adds the button to the form's `Controls` list.

In addition to demonstrating construction, Listing 3.7 demonstrates dynamic component creation. Refer to Chapter 16, "Designing User Interfaces," for more information on dynamic component creation as a means to create flexible UIs.

Parameterized Constructors

Now that you know a constructor is the term used to refer to the New method, you might ask what a parameterized constructor is. Quite simply, a parameterized constructor is a constructor that takes arguments. Because New is essentially a method, adding arguments to New is the same as adding arguments to any method.

The slight difference in passing arguments to regular methods versus the New constructor method is that the arguments are passed in the parentheses following the data type rather than the New keyword. Here's an example:

```
Dim MyException As Exception = New Exception("Raise an exception!")
```

The statement constructs a new Exception object passing the string "Raise an exception!" to the constructor. From the code fragment you might assume that there is a subroutine Exception that takes a String argument, but in reality the New method is getting the argument.

> **Note**
>
> In C++ and Java the constructor has the same name as the class. Object Pascal, by convention, uses Create for a constructor. These languages pass the arguments to the constructor in parentheses after the constructor name. If Visual Basic .NET were to follow this convention, the construction of the Exception would look like this:
>
> ```
> Dim MyException As Exception = New("Raise an exception!") Exception
> ```
>
> That seems a little strange. Just remember that New is the constructor and parameters are being passed to New even though it doesn't look as if this is the case.

Destructors

A destructor is a special method that is used to deinitialize an object. In VB6 the Class_Terminate method was called implicitly when an object was destroyed. Visual Basic .NET implements a garbage collector (GC) rather than explicit object destruction. The GC is a subprogram that runs in the background returning memory assigned to objects back to the memory pool.

> **Caution**
>
> You can explicitly run the GC, but it isn't recommended that you do so. To force the GC to run, type `System.GC.Collect`.
>
> The GC is designed to run efficiently during times when your program is idle. Running the GC manually contradicts its intended use.

You cannot tell when the garbage collector will actually run and release your objects, and no equivalent of `Class_Terminate` is called in Visual Basic .NET.

By convention, a method named `Dispose` can be implemented to perform any cleanup you may need in your classes, for example, closing an open file. Chapter 7 will demonstrate how to implement and use `Dispose`; you may encounter examples of it in code between now and Chapter 7.

Exception Handling

Exception handling is a new feature in Visual Basic .NET. Exception handlers are intended to ultimately replace the `On Error Goto` construct. Exception handlers provide a more robust means of communicating and managing errors and have been available in more advanced languages like C++ and Object Pascal for several years now.

All exception classes are subclassed from the `System.Exception` class. The basic exception class contains information similar to that found in the VB6 `Err` object. The differences are that there is no global exception object always available—exception objects are created and raised when needed—and in Visual Basic .NET you can subclass and define your own exception classes.

Try...Catch

The `Try...Catch` block is used to catch and handle errors for which you can provide a resolution. The basic `Try...Catch` block takes the following form:

```
Try
    ' some protected code
Catch
    ' resolution on error
End Catch
```

The protected code goes in the `Try` part of the block and the resolution part is written in the `Catch` block. The `Try` code is always executed and the `Catch` block is executed only in the event of an error.

VB6 simply shuts down on an unhandled error. In some circumstances it may be okay to shut down the application, but most of the time, it is another aggravation users don't need. Visual Basic .NET shuts down the application and makes an attempt to run a Just-In-Time debugger.

If an error is important enough to shut down your application, exceptions will at least provide you with an opportunity to do so in an organized manner. For example, the unavailability of a database may be a sufficient reason to shut down the application. However, when possible, if you can program a resolution to the problem and retry the code, exception handlers allow you to do that. If the problem doesn't need a resolution, you might simply want to show the error to the user and keep on trucking.

There are two kinds of exception handling. The first is referred to as the exception handling block, and the second is referred to as the resource protection block. Both are exception-handling blocks, with the difference being the keywords used to define the blocks, and their intended uses. The exception handler designed to handle errors uses the `Try...Catch...End Try` block and the resource protection exception handler uses the `Try...Finally...End Try` block. These types are demonstrated in the following subsections. Listing 3.8 demonstrates a generic `Try...Catch` block used to protect against division by zero.

3

BASIC
PROGRAMMING IN
VISUAL BASIC .NET

> **Note**
>
> Recall that division-by-zero for `Doubles` yields a return value `Infinity`. Integer division-by-zero raises a `DivideByZeroException`.

LISTING 3.8 Generic exception handler that catches all exceptions.

```
 1: Public Sub TestGenericException()
 2:
 3:     Dim I As Integer
 4:     Dim Numerator As Integer = 5
 5:     Dim Denominator As Integer = 0
 6:
 7:     Try
 8:         I = Numerator \ Denominator
 9:         Debug.WriteLine(I)
10:     Catch
11:     End Try
12: End Sub
```

Lines 7 through 11 demonstrate a generic `Try...Catch` exception-handling block. This code can be used where you would have written an `On Error Resume Next` in VB6. A `Catch` statement with no code is referred to as a *silent exception*. (Basically, a silent exception works similarly to `Resume Next`. The reason the demonstration code contains more than `I = 1/0` is because the Visual Basic .NET compiler can catch direct integer division by zero, whereas the VB6 compiler cannot.)

The `Try` part of the exception handler is simple enough that if we want to report the division-by-zero error, we might write a literal message that indicates what went wrong. To implement notification behavior, add something like `MsgBox("Division by zero error")` between the `Catch` and `End Try` lines of code.

Catching Specific Exceptions

Except when you prefer a silent exception, you will probably want to catch and respond to specific kinds of exceptions. Catching specific exceptions is supported with a slightly modified syntax.

In Listing 3.8 we know that we are anticipating a potential division-by-zero error. If we want to catch that error specifically, we need to make a minor modification to the `Catch` block to indicate our intentions. Listing 3.9 demonstrates catching a specific type of exception, the `DivideByZeroException`.

LISTING 3.9 A `Catch` block for a specific exception.

```
 1: Public Sub TestGenericException()
 2:
 3:     Dim I As Integer
 4:     Dim Numerator As Integer = 5
 5:     Dim Denominator As Integer = 0
 6:
 7:     Try
 8:         I = Numerator \ Denominator
 9:         Debug.WriteLine(I)
10:     Catch e As System.DivideByZeroException
11:         MsgBox(e.Message)
12:     End Try
13:
14: End Sub
```

The revision from Listing 3.8 to 3.9 is constrained to lines 10 and 11. The `Catch` statement is a declarator. Thus the revision to the `Catch` statement as demonstrated on line 10 declares an object of type `System.DivideByZeroException` and initializes it with a caught exception. The `Message` property of the exception object is displayed in a message dialog box.

Based on the revised definition of this Catch block, all other exceptions would be ignored. If you want to catch all exceptions, use Catch without an exception type. If you want to catch specific exceptions, list each type of exception you would like to handle with an additional Catch statement. Listing 3.10 demonstrates catching multiple exceptions.

LISTING 3.10 Multiple Catch clauses.

```
 1: Public Sub BackupFile(ByVal FileName As String)
 2:   Dim F As System.IO.File
 3:   Try
 4:     F.Delete(FileName + ".bak")
 5:     F.Copy(FileName, FileName + ".bak")
 6:
 7:   Catch e As System.UnauthorizedAccessException
 8:     MsgBox(e.Message)
 9:   Catch e As System.IO.FileNotFoundException
10:     MsgBox(e.Message)
11:   End Try
12: End Sub
```

Listing 3.10 demonstrates two Catch clauses. Line 7 catches the UnauthorizedAccessException that might occur when you attempt to delete or modify a read-only file. Line 9 catches the FileNotFoundException that might occur when you try to copy a file that doesn't exist.

It is impossible to include all possible ways in which the preceding code might be written. For example, you could check to see if the files existed before trying to delete and copy them. As a general rule, if an If...Then conditional check can preclude the problem, use the conditional check. However, the exception handler will catch errors you might not have thought of. In the listing you could check to see if the file exists before attempting to delete the file, but what if the file exists and is write-protected? You would still get an UnauthorizedAccessException.

Think of exception handlers as safety nets for high-wire walkers and an If...Then conditional similar to deciding whether or not you should be on the wire in the first place. If you have to be up on the wire, it's a good idea to have a net. All of the second-guessing in the world won't catch you if you fall off the wire but have decided to forego the net.

From Bjarne Stroustrup (Stroustrup 1994), the inventor of C++ and father of object-oriented languages for the PC, we know the following things about the aim of an exception handler:

3

BASIC PROGRAMMING IN VISUAL BASIC .NET

- "An exception handler isn't intended as simply an alternative return mechanism ... but specifically as a mechanism for supporting the construction of fault-tolerant systems."

- "An exception handler isn't intended to turn every function into a fault-tolerant entity, but rather as a mechanism by which a subsystem can be given a large measure of fault tolerance even if its individual functions are written without regard for overall error-handling strategies."

- And most importantly, "An exception handler isn't meant to constrain designers to a single 'correct' notion of error-handling, but to make the language more expressive."

Summarized, this means that the application of exception handling, like many things in programming, requires a subjective measure of good taste and experience.

Throughout this book I often include a statement or rationale indicating why an exception handler was used for each unique occurrence, or rationale for an exception block in code.

Raising Exceptions

Exceptions are objects. If you elect to raise an exception to indicate an error condition that a procedure is not going to handle, you create an exception object like any other object and throw it.

To create an exception instance and throw it, write code as demonstrated in the following example:

```
Throw New Exception("message text")
```

Throw is a Visual Basic .NET keyword used similarly to the Raise method in VB6. New invokes the constructor for the exception class, and Exception represents any valid exception class subclassed from System.Exception.

If you want to rethrow an exception in an exception block, you can add the Throw statement all by itself in the Catch block. Throw without an explicit exception object raises the last caught exception.

Exception Filters

Catch clauses can have a filter applied that enables you to refine the Catch statement. Consider the example in Listing 3.10. Suppose we only wanted to catch the exception UnauthorizedAccessException if the file exists. We could accomplish this goal by adding a when predicate to the Catch statement:

```
Catch e As System.UnauthorizedAccessException when F.Exists(FileName + ".bak")
```

Due to the addition of when, this Catch clause will only catch an
UnauthorizedAccessException if the backup file exists (perhaps the file exists
but is read-only).

Try...Finally

Try...Finally blocks are referred to as *resource protection blocks*. Although Catch
blocks are only invoked upon an exception of the type indicated in the Catch clause—
keeping in mind that Catch without an exception predicate catches all exceptions—
Finally clauses are always invoked whether there is an exception or not.

Try...Finally blocks are used to ensure that allocated resources are cleaned up. The
general order of the Try...Finally statement is illustrated in this algorithmic example:

```
Allocate resource (for example, open a file)
Try
  Use the resource (for example, add some text to the file)
Finally
  Clean up the resource
End Try
```

In this example, only Try, Finally, and End Try are literals. Demonstrating the
Try...Finally block using the StreamWriter class, we could create a StreamWriter,
try to write some text, and close the writer in the Finally block. Listing 3.11 demonstrates both StreamWriter and the Try...Finally statement.

LISTING 3.11 A resource protection block protecting a file managed by the
StreamWriter object

```
 1: Public Sub WriteText(ByVal FileName As String, ByVal SomeText As String)
 2:
 3:    Dim W As New System.IO.StreamWriter(FileName, True)
 4:    Try
 5:       W.WriteLine(SomeText)
 6:    Finally
 7:       W.Close()
 8:    End Try
 9:
10: End Sub
```

As described in the algorithm, the StreamWriter is allocated on line 3. Line 5 uses the
protected resource to write SomeText, and the Finally block ensures that the file represented by the StreamWriter object is closed.

Try...Catch and Try...Finally blocks may be combined to protect against exceptions
and resource corruption. To this end, you may nest or combine exception-handling

blocks as needed for the desired effect. Consider Listing 3.11 again. What if you want to catch the `UnauthorizedAccessException` and ensure that opened streams were actually closed? We can combine an exception block with a resource protection block as demonstrated in Listing 3.12.

LISTING 3.12   A `Try...Finally` block nested inside a `Try...Catch` block

```
 1: Public Sub WriteText(ByVal FileName As String, ByVal SomeText As String)
 2:
 3:   Try
 4:     Dim W As New System.IO.StreamWriter("sample.txt", True)
 5:
 6:     Try
 7:       W.WriteLine("Add some text")
 8:     Finally
 9:       W.Close()
10:     End Try
11:
12:   Catch e As System.UnauthorizedAccessException
13:     MsgBox(e.Message, MsgBoxStyle.Critical)
14:   End Try
15:
16: End Sub
```

The outer `Try...Catch` block catches `UnauthorizedAccessException` for all of the code in between lines 3 and 12. If we get past line 4, the `Try...Finally` block will ensure that the open `StreamWriter` is closed on line 9.

You will see many examples of `Try...Catch` and `Try...Finally` blocks throughout this book. As with exception-handling blocks, I will elaborate on the rationale behind `Try...Finally` blocks where it is useful and not redundant to do so.

Summary

Chapter 3 provided you with an opportunity to experiment with some of the new features in Visual Basic .NET. You will use structured exception handling and create objects in every substantial program you write in Visual Basic .NET.

In addition to demonstrating how to use exception-handling blocks, create objects, and pass parameters to constructors, this chapter demonstrated how to declare and initialize variables and use several of the new Abstract Data Types defined in `System.Collections`.

Chapter 4 will look at how to get more mileage out of your development experience by using macros and the Automation Extensibility Model to customize and extend the Visual Studio IDE.

Macros and Visual Studio Extensibility

IN THIS CHAPTER

The purpose of this chapter is to introduce the idea of automating repetitive tasks in your development environment. Macros are pretty common and many nonprogrammers are familiar with them. Most programmers know what macros are for and can figure out how to use them fairly easily.

Extensibility, however, is another subject. Extending an IDE like Visual Studio generally falls into the advanced camp. Visual Studio .NET, meaning Visual Basic .NET too, has purposefully introduced an extensibility model that provides you with access to the IDE, allowing you to extend and customize more easily as you see fit.

Unfortunately, if you fall into the beginner-programmer camp, extensibility might seem out of your grasp for now. I assure you it is not impossible, although if you are a new programmer, you might understand extensibility better after you have read the first 10 chapters of this book. However, macros are readily available even to moderately skilled programmers.

What is the motivation for this chapter being introduced so early, then? This chapter is intentionally introduced early in the book to get you to begin thinking about automating repetitive tasks, so that before you even finish the book, you will be able to put automation into action. You will probably find macros familiar and easy, but you might find extensibility and writing add-ins a bit more challenging. If that is the case, skim through the second half of this chapter on extending the Visual Studio .NET IDE, and return to it when you have finished the first 10 chapters or when you have an automation task to perform.

On the other hand, if you are an experienced programmer, you will find automation approachable and very useful. It is unlikely that you will spend a considerable amount of time writing macros and add-ins, but when you do, those customizations should make your life easier. Anything that might make life easier is something we want to know about. After reading this chapter, you will have a better idea of the kinds of automation that are available and how you can exploit them.

Automating Repetitive Tasks

Macros have existed for quite some time now in applications for PCs. If recollection serves, macros were available in early versions of Quattro Pro and Lotus 1-2-3, perhaps as early as 1987. Historically macros were implemented as a token-based language with a simple grammar and keywords that represented actions in an application. More recently macros were implemented and supported by applications in Microsoft Office through programming in Visual Basic for Applications (VBA).

With the introduction of .NET, macros are available and are written using Visual Basic

.NET. The same language that you write your VB .NET applications with can be used to automate repetitive tasks. Macros still use commands to represent tasks in the IDE, but when you write customizations to these macros, you can write them in the same VB .NET code you use to write applications.

You gain two advantages in VS .NET. Macros can be written in VB, and more of the Visual Studio .NET IDE has been exposed in the extensibility model, making it easier to access aspects of the IDE for customization.

Demo: Recording a Macro

The easiest way to automate a task is to record a series of steps in the IDE and then play them back when you need that series of steps performed again.

In production code that I am building for a customer, I always include a brief comment and copyright block indicating ownership and authorship of the code. This code is tedious to write but beneficial to have. The code block varies only slightly between projects, so it is one of the first things I automate when I sit down to begin a new project. A sample of the copyright block follows.

```
' filename.vb - Raison d'etre
' Copyright  2001. All Rights Reserved.
' Software Conceptions, Inc. www.softconcepts.com
' Written by Paul Kimmel. pkimmel@softconcepts.com
```

Although you will not see these blocks much in this book (because listings in this book already are protected by copyright), they are added to production code. Perhaps this copyright block is not perfectly legal, but it is functional. (Check with your company's legal department or an attorney specializing in copyright law if you adopt this strategy.)

Every time a new source code file is added to a project, the block is added to the code. If I turn the macro recorder on the first time I manually type the copyright block, I can play back the block of text for each successive file added to the project. To record the copyright block macro, follow these steps:

1. In Visual Studio .NET, choose Tools, Macros, Record TemporaryMacro (or press Ctrl+Shift+R) to start recording.
2. Type the block of text as you would like it to appear at the top of a source code .vb module.
3. Choose Tools, Macros, Stop Recording (or press Ctrl+Shift+R) to stop recording.

The macro will be recorded as a temporary macro named `TemporaryMacro` in a module named `RecordingModule`. We will come back to this in a minute. For now you should know that you can press Ctrl+Shift+P to play the macro back, which is the shortcut for the Tools, Macros, Run TemporaryMacro menu item in the Visual Studio .NET IDE (hereafter just called IDE).

Keep in mind that if you record another macro, the current temporary macro will be overwritten. To protect your macro from being overwritten, you need to save a copy of it outside of `TemporaryMacro`. First, let's take a moment to view the macro code generated by the recording.

Viewing a Recorded Macro

You can view a recorded macro by opening the Macro Explorer. To open the Macro Explorer, choose Tools, Macros, Macro Explorer or press Alt+F8 (see Figure 4.1). From the Macro Explorer, double-click on the `RecordingModule` to look at the generated code.

FIGURE 4.1

Macro Explorer view.

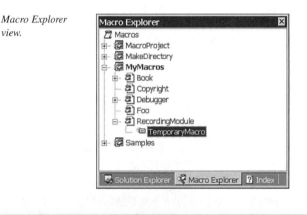

> ### Tip
>
> You can export macro modules from the Microsoft Visual Studio Macros IDE, which you can run by choosing Tools, Macros IDE.

By default the recorded macros are stored in MyMacros.vsmacros. (You can use the Windows Explorer to find the physical file location of MyMacros.vsmacros on your PC.) In Figure 4.1 you can see the expanded RecordingModule in MyMacros. For all intents and purposes, RecordingModule is a VB .NET module within the .vsmacros file, and macros consist of procedures with an individual procedure entry point. Listing 4.1 shows the complete listing, including the temporary macro created after recording the copyright block.

LISTING 4.1 The `TemporaryMacro` created from recording the copyright block.

```
 1: Option Strict Off
 2: Option Explicit Off
 3: Imports EnvDTE
 4: Imports System.Diagnostics
 5:
 6: Public Module RecordingModule
 7:
 8:     Sub TemporaryMacro()
 9:         DTE.ActiveDocument.Selection.Text = _
10:             "' filename.vb - Raison d'etre"
11:         DTE.ActiveDocument.Selection.NewLine()
12:         DTE.ActiveDocument.Selection.Text = _
13:             "' Copyright (c) 2001. All Rights Reserved."
14:         DTE.ActiveDocument.Selection.NewLine()
15:         DTE.ActiveDocument.Selection.Text = _
16:             "' Software Conceptions, Inc. www.softconcepts.com"
17:         DTE.ActiveDocument.Selection.NewLine()
18:         DTE.ActiveDocument.Selection.Text = _
19:             "' Written by Paul Kimmel. pkimmel@softconcepts.com"
20:         DTE.ActiveDocument.Selection.NewLine()
21:     End Sub
22: End Module
```

The macro is straightforward; when the macro is run, a line of text is added, followed by a new line, until all of the lines of text are added. More importantly, this simple macro introduces some of the key features of the extensibility model, including a key feature—the DTE.

The `Imports EnvDTE` adds the common environment object model namespace to the macro project. `EnvDTE` implements the object model for extensibility.

The `DTE`—Development Tools Extensibility or Development Tools Environment, depending on the source of information—object represents a handle to the IDE. `DTE.ActiveDocument` represents the document, or module, that has the focus. We will come back to these subjects later. For now let's examine the practical aspects of making the temporary macro more efficient and saving it to prevent the next recorded macro from overwriting this one.

Editing a Temporary Macro

`TemporaryMacro` is a little verbose. We will shorten it to demonstrate how we can edit recorded macros to extend capabilities.

From Listing 4.1 we know that `filename.vb` needs to be changed to reflect the actual filename. The description needs to be something specific and the date might not accurately reflect the actual year. Additionally, the temporary macro will be overwritten if a new macro is recorded; to improve the utility of the macro and prevent it from being overwritten, we will tackle these issues one by one.

Refactoring the Macro Code

Macros, like any other code, can benefit from refactoring. For string values you might consider replacing literals with constants. If the strings are contrived with code, you might combine replacing literals with constants and query methods; adding a query method is a refactoring.

Listing 4.2 demonstrates a basic refactoring that replaces the literals created by the macro with query methods. The actual macro is much simpler, and just as with production code, the query methods could be used in another context.

LISTING 4.2   A refactored macro.

```
1:  Option Strict Off
2:  Option Explicit Off
3:  Imports EnvDTE
4:  Imports System.Diagnostics
5:
6:  Public Module RecordingModule
7:
8:    Const sDescription As String = _
9:      "' filename.vb = Raison d'etre"
10:   Const sCopyright As String = _
11:     "' Copyright (c) 2001. All Rights Reserved."
12:   Const sOwner As String = _
13:     "' Software Conceptions, Inc. www.softconcepts.com"
14:   Const sAuthor As String = _
15:     "' Written by Paul Kimmel. pkimmel@softconcepts.com"
16:
17:
18:   Private ReadOnly Property Description() As String
19:     Get
20:       Return sDescription
21:     End Get
22:   End Property
23:
24:   Private ReadOnly Property Copyright() As String
25:     Get
26:       Return sCopyright
27:     End Get
28:   End Property
29:
30:   Private ReadOnly Property Owner() As String
31:     Get
```

LISTING 4.2 continued

```
32:        Return sOwner
33:      End Get
34:    End Property
35:
36:    Private ReadOnly Property Author() As String
37:      Get
38:        Return sAuthor
39:      End Get
40:    End Property
41:
42:    Private Function GetCopyrightBlock() As String
43:      Return _
44:        Description & vbCrLf & Copyright & vbCrLf & _
45:        Owner & vbCrLf & Author & vbCrLf
46:    End Function
47:
48:    Sub TemporaryMacro()
49:      DTE.ActiveDocument.Selection.StartOfDocument()
50:      DTE.ActiveDocument.Selection.Text = GetCopyrightBlock()
51:    End Sub
52:
53: End Module
```

Because the constants are treated like resource strings, a simple convention—prefixing the resource with an s—enables the properties to be closely associated by name with the resource strings. The refactored solution assembles the copyright block by concatenating the resource strings returned by the query methods; the end result is a much simpler macro and potentially reusable query methods. To convey meaning, the properties—playing the role of query methods—are implemented as read-only properties.

Writing code and macros this way requires a little extra effort but the end result is short, concise, well-named code that is genuinely flexible.

Dynamically Retrieving the `ActiveDocument` Name

Thus far our demonstration macro simply adds some text to our modules. For the macro to be more effective, it would be helpful if the macro added the correct filename to the copyright block. This will be useful, especially when we print the code for documentation purposes.

Now that the code is refactored, we can focus on one problem at a time. The first problem is retrieving the name of the module we are commenting and adding that information to the `Description` block.

Conveniently we can modify the literal to contain a string parameter, as follows:

```
Const sDescription = "' {0} - Raison d'etre"
```

Next we can modify the read-only property method to fill in the `ActiveDocument` name.

```
Private ReadOnly Property Description() As String
   Get
      Return String.Format(sDescription, DTE.ActiveDocument.Name)
   End Get
End Property
```

`DTE.ActiveDocument.Name` returns the document's name. The end result is a copyright block with the filename we are actually adding the copyright block to.

Adding a Dynamic Description Block

What about the comment? As it stands, the comment `Raison d'etre` is not very helpful. It would be useful if the documentor could add a comment, replacing the generic text with something particular to a given program.

Again we could modify the constant string and add a string parameter. At the time the user wants to add the block, we can display an `InputBox` and elicit a response. The modified string and `Description` property follow.

```
Const sDescription As String = "' {0} = {1}"

Private Function GetReason() As String
  Dim Reason As String = "Raison d'etre"
  Return _
  InputBox("Enter description:", "Description", Reason)
End Function

Private ReadOnly Property Description() As String
  Get
    Return _
      String.Format(sDescription, DTE.ActiveDocument.Name, GetReason())
    End Get
End Property
```

> **Note**
>
> Notice that a refactored style of programming tends to introduce more methods but those new methods are very short. This style is elected by the author for very specific reasons. To reiterate, these reasons are: Singular methods are easier to debug; reuse is a good thing; therefore methods can be reused, and lines of code cannot.

> In the short term, singular methods tend to produce more code. In a system, singular methods tend to be more extensible and reusable and result in significantly smaller and simpler systems.

The modified `sDescription` string contains two string-replaceable parameters. The modified `Description` property fills in both parameters. The first comes from the `DTE.ActiveDocument` object and the second comes as a return result from an `InputBox` dialog. Notice that instead of adding the code to solicit feedback from the user directly in the property, we used a query method; this eliminates a temporary variable and keeps the property method succinct.

Displaying the Correct Year

We can employ the same technique for updating the filename to update the copyright year. That is, by modifying the constant sCopyright string and replacing it with a parameter, we can fill in the calendar year within the property method.

```
Const sCopyright As String = _
    "' Copyright (c) {0}. All Rights Reserved."

Private ReadOnly Property Copyright() As String
  Get
    Return String.Format(sCopyright, Now.Year)
  End Get
End Property
```

As in the previous section, the constant string now contains a replaceable parameter, represented by {0}, and the property method dynamically fills in that parameter upon request.

The benefit of this style of code is that each aspect of it in and of itself is very simple. You can extend, customize, and maintain it with very little effort. Writing like this takes some practice, but you end up with good code the first time and revising it to get great code is much easier.

Our motivation for refactoring macros is the same as that for refactoring consumer code: We want less code, and we want that code to be more maintainable.

Saving a Temporary Macro

Saving macros is easy whether you have refactored code or not. The easiest way to preserve a macro is to save the module it is in, `RecordingModule`, to have a new module name. It is a good idea to save the macro—the procedure—too, giving it a better name. Follow these steps to rename the macro and the module.

1. To rename `TemporaryMacro`, in the Visual Studio .NET IDE (not the Macros IDE), choose Tools, Macros, Save TemporaryMacro.

2. Step 1 opens the Macro Explorer and highlights the macro name as if you had selected Rename from the Macro Explorer context menu. Enter a new name for the macro. For our example, rename the macro `InsertCopyrightTag`.

Now that we have the procedure that is the entry point for our macro, we can save the `RecordingModule` itself. Follow these steps to rename the `RecordModule` to `Copyright`.

1. Right-click on `RecordingModule` in the Macro Explorer opened when we renamed the macro.

2. From the context menu, choose Rename. Rename the `RecordingModule` to `Copyright`.

When you start recording a new macro, the IDE will create a new module named `RecordingModule` and add the `TemporaryMacro` automatically.

Running the Macro

There are a couple of ways that we can invoke our macro. While it is the temporary macro, we can run it with the menu commands Tools, Macros, Run TemporaryMacro. We can also run the `TemporaryMacro` (or any macro) by opening the Macro Explorer and selecting Run from the macro's context menu.

> **Tip**
>
> Macros can be run from the command line. Open a command window and type **devenv /command** *macroname,* where *macroname* is the qualified name of your macro, and you can run macros from the command line.

Finally, we can open the Command window (Ctrl+Alt+A) by choosing View, Other Windows, Command Window and enter the fully qualified name of the macro. To run the macro from the Command window, enter **Macros.MyMacros.Copyright. InsertCopyrightTag.**

Clearly, manually entering the `Macros.`*root namespace.module.macroname* would quickly become tedious if you use the macro more than a couple of times. If the macro will be used frequently, you might want to add a toolbar button or menu shortcut to invoke the macro. The next two subsections look at how you can incorporate or remove a shortcut to make invoking custom macros easier.

Mapping Macros to a Keyboard Shortcut

Frequently used macros can be mapped to keystrokes or toolbars for convenience. To map the `InsertCopyrightTag` macro—or any macro—to a keyboard shortcut, choose Tools, Options, Environment, Keyboard in the IDE (see Figure 4.2). Type **copyright** into the Show Commands Containing field. Select the `InsertCopyrightTag` macro (as shown in the figure), and select the Press Shortcut Key(s) text box. Press Ctrl+Alt+C, reflecting the shortcut key combination you want to map to the copyright macro.

FIGURE 4.2

Use the Options page to map a shortcut to your frequently used macros.

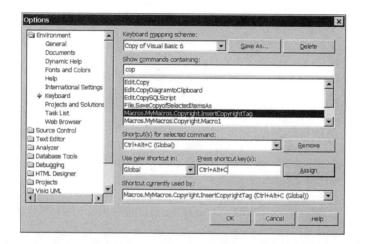

> **Tip**
>
> To run a macro without using a keyboard shortcut, open the Macro Explorer and double-click on a macro name.

When you have the macro shortcut keys selected, click the Assign button. Close the Options dialog box and return to the code editor. Press the shortcut keys to test your new macro shortcut.

Mapping Macros to the Toolbar

Macros can also be added as toolbuttons in the IDE. Right-click on the IDE toolbar and select the Customize context menu item. The Commands tab of the Customize dialog box (shown in Figure 4.3) enables you to add, modify, and delete toolbuttons.

4

MACROS AND
VISUAL STUDIO
EXTENSIBILITY

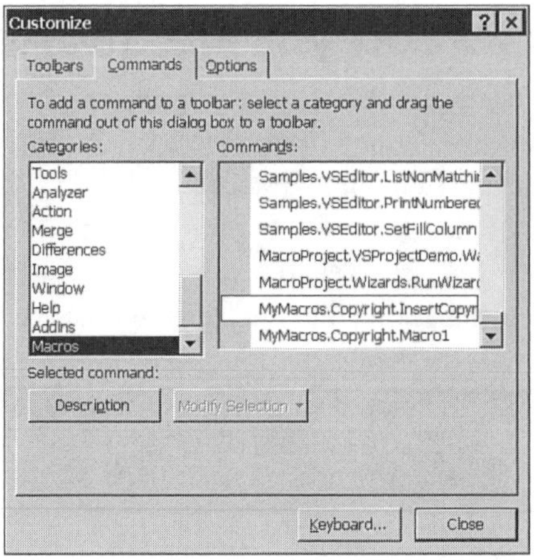

FIGURE 4.3

*Use the
Commands tab of
the Customize dia-
log box to manage
custom toolbutton
commands.*

Select Macros from the Categories list. By default, if you drag a macro from the
Customize dialog to the toolbar, a button with the name of the macro will be added to
the toolbar. For example, dragging MyMacros.Copyright.InsertCopyrightTag to the
Standard toolbar will insert a toolbutton with the caption MyMacros.Copyright.
InsertCopyrightTag to that toolbar.

Modifying the Macro Toolbutton Description

A long caption will take up too much toolbar real estate. To decrease the amount of room
used by the custom toolbutton, we can modify the name of the toolbutton.

> **Tip**
>
> You can add a keyboard shortcut from the Customize dialog box by clicking the
> Keyboard button. Clicking the Keyboard button opens the Options dialog box
> focused to the Keyboard tab.

Because the copyright macro inserts a copyright, we will modify the caption to display
the copyright symbol (©). To modify the button, leave the Customize dialog box open.
Right-click over the toolbutton to display the toolbutton context menu—or click Modify
Selection in the Customize dialog box—and modify the Name context menu item to contain the literal text. Alternatively, you could choose the Change Button Image menu item
and pick an appropriate icon (see Figure 4.4).

FIGURE 4.4

Pick an icon to associate with your toolbutton.

Using the Macro Explorer

The Macro Explorer (shown in Figure 4.1) provides quick access to available macros, and allows you to access the Macro IDE.

If you right-click the Macros root in the Macro Explorer, you can select from loading or creating a new macro project or opening the Macros IDE. Select individual macro modules to rename or unload the module, add a new module, or designate a particular module as the recording module. Select a macro procedure in a module to run, edit, rename, or delete an individual macro.

Exporting the Macro

If you want to share macros, you can export a macro from your IDE and another developer can import that macro into their IDE. This section introduces a pair of macros that allow you to enable or disable all breakpoints with a single macro command; these macros will be used to demonstrate exporting and importing macros. First let's introduce and review the new macros.

Macros for Enabling and Disabling Breakpoints

You can set breakpoints by clicking in the left margin of the code editor. You can right-click a breakpoint to modify its properties (see Figure 4.5) and set break conditions or modify the hit count. The hit count determines whether the breakpoint suspends execution every time or breaks based on some other rule (for example, Figure 4.6 shows the specification of a breakpoint setting that will break when the hit count is a multiple of 5).

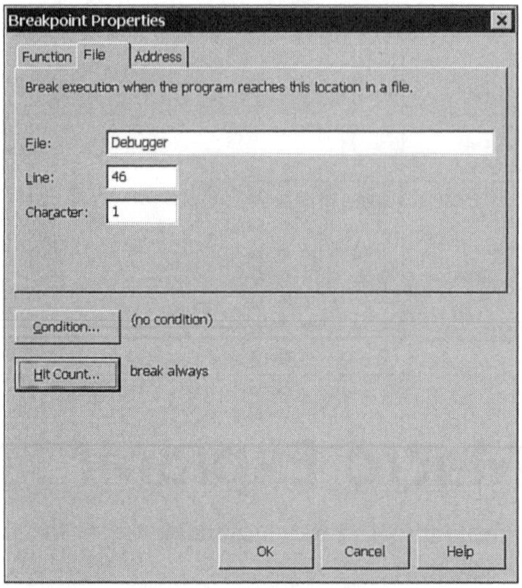

FIGURE 4.5

Breakpoint properties can be used to customize the behavior of break conditions.

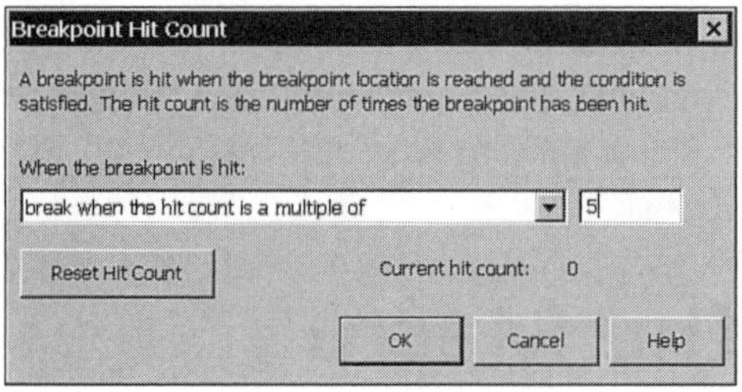

FIGURE 4.6

Customizing the breakpoint hit count.

When you spend the effort to create breakpoints, you might want to disable them without losing the effort expended in creating those breakpoints. The IDE allows you to disable breakpoints without removing them. To leave a breakpoint in place but disable it, right-click the breakpoint and select Disable Breakpoint from the context menu. Repeat the operation, selecting Enable Breakpoint to turn the breakpoint back on. However, if you have multiple breakpoints, it might be easier to enable or disable all breakpoints with a single macro command rather than enabling or disabling the breakpoints in the break-points window manually.

All of the breakpoints are accessible in the `EnvDTE.DTE.Debugger.Breakpoints` collection. (You would only know this if you have read this passage or explored the Extensibility object model.) To disable all breakpoints, we need to create a new macro. This can be accomplished by choosing Tools, Macros, New Macro Command in the VS .NET IDE. The following code would enable all breakpoints.

```
Sub EnableAllBreakpoints()
  Dim Breakpoint As Breakpoint
  For Each Breakpoint In DTE.Debugger.Breakpoints
    Breakpoint.Enabled = True
  Next
End Sub
```

Copying the macro to a new macro named `DisableAllBreakpoints` and rewriting
`Breakpoint.Enabled = True` as `Breakpoint.Enabled = False` would disable all
breakpoints. However, duplicating the code by copying and pasting is not something
we want to do even with macros; we need to abstract common behavior into a single
procedure. Abstracting common behavior for enabling and disabling yields the following
revision:

```
Private Sub SetBreakpointState(ByVal Enabled As Boolean)

  Dim Breakpoint As Breakpoint
  For Each Breakpoint In DTE.Debugger.Breakpoints
    Breakpoint.Enabled = Enabled
  Next

End Sub
```

In this version of Visual Studio Macros, we can only pass string arguments to macros. If
supporting procedures need arguments, you can pass these arguments as strings and convert them to the type the procedure needs or define a parameterless macro that passes a
specific value to the supporting procedure. Applying the second technique to the
`SetBreakpointState` macro yields the code in Listing 4.3.

LISTING 4.3 Two macros that are implemented in terms of a common behavior in
the macro module

```
 1: Private Sub SetBreakpointState(ByVal Enabled As Boolean)
 2:    Dim Breakpoint As Breakpoint
 3:    For Each Breakpoint In DTE.Debugger.Breakpoints
 4:       Breakpoint.Enabled = Enabled
 5:    Next
 6: End Sub
 7:
 8: Sub EnableBreakpoints()
 9:    SetBreakpointState(True)
10: End Sub
11:
12: Sub DisableBreakpoints()
13:    SetBreakpointState(False)
14: End Sub
```

Either `EnableBreakpoints` or `DisableBreakpoints` can be invoked in any of the usual ways that macros can be invoked, including from the IDE Command window, the Macro Explorer, the Macro IDE, or a keyboard or toolbar shortcut.

Practical Considerations

You can enable or disable all breakpoints from the Command window. If you open the Command window and type `Debug.DisableAllBreakpoints` or `Debug.EnableAllBreakpoints`, the IDE will perform these operations for you.

The example in this section was written to demonstrate the process of implementing macros and some of the capabilities of the DTE object. Because the capability of managing breakpoints already exists, we will add some additional behavior to our custom breakpoint management to make it a worthwhile endeavor.

Sending Information to the Output Window

In addition to the `DTE.Debugger` object, the `DTE` object contains a Windows collection. The Windows collection contains a reference to all of the windows in the IDE; therefore to send information to the Output window, all we need to do is request a reference to that window and invoke behaviors it has defined.

The revision in Listing 4.4 demonstrates how to get a reference to the Output window and send status information to it as we are enabling or disabling breakpoints automatically.

LISTING 4.4 Enabling and disabling breakpoints with logging information sent to the IDE's Output window

```
1:  Option Strict Off
2:  Option Explicit Off
3:
4:  Imports EnvDTE
5:  Imports System.Diagnostics
6:
7:  Public Module Debugger
8:
9:    Function GetOutputWindow() As OutputWindow
10:     Return _
11:       DTE.Windows.Item( _
12:       Constants.vsWindowKindOutput).Object
13:   End Function
14:
15:   Function GetActivePane() As OutputWindowPane
16:     Return GetOutputWindow.ActivePane
17:   End Function
```

LISTING 4.4 continued

```
18:
19:    Private Sub WriteState(ByVal BreakPoint As Breakpoint)
20:      GetActivePane.OutputString( _
21:        String.Format("Breakpoint ({0}) enabled={1}", _
22:        BreakPoint.Name, BreakPoint.Enabled) & vbCrLf)
23:    End Sub
24:
25:    Private Sub SetBreakpointState(ByVal Enabled _
26:      As Boolean)
27:
28:      Dim Breakpoint As Breakpoint
29:      For Each Breakpoint In DTE.Debugger.Breakpoints
30:        Breakpoint.Enabled = Enabled
31:        WriteState(Breakpoint)
32:      Next
33:
34:    End Sub
35:
36:    Sub EnableBreakPoints()
37:      SetBreakpointState(True)
38:    End Sub
39:
40:    Sub DisableBreakpoints()
41:      SetBreakpointState(False)
42:    End Sub
43:
44:    Sub EnableAllBreakpoints()
45:      Dim Breakpoint As Breakpoint
46:      For Each Breakpoint In _
47:        DTE.Debugger.Breakpoints
48:        Breakpoint.Enabled = True
49:      Next
50:    End Sub
51: End Module
```

The procedures EnableBreakpoints, DisableBreakpoints, and EnableAllBreakpoints you have seen already. Line 31 introduces a call to WriteState in the private SetBreakpointState method. WriteState references an object GetActivePane, which returns DTE.Windows.Item(Constants.vsWindowKindOutput).Object cast to an OutputWindowPane on line 16 by using it as a return argument for the GetActivePane function. An OutputWindowPane has a method OutputString that allows us to send text to the Output window. Lines 19 through 23 get the Output window pane and send formatted output to it indicating the name and state of the Breakpoint whose state was modified.

Query methods—`GetOutputWindow` and `GetActivePane`—were written to preclude writing a monolithic statement to access, type cast, and invoke a method on the Output window. This is a good technique for shortening and clarifying long statements.

Exporting Macro Modules

The complete set of macros in the `Debugger` module represent code that you might reasonably want to share with other developers. To do so, we need to export the module.

To export a macro module, open the Macros IDE from the Tools, Macros menu in the VS .NET IDE. Select the macro module that you want to export in the Macros IDE and choose File, Export *modulename*, where *modulename* is `Debugger` in this example. The Macros IDE will display an Export File dialog box that will allow you to select the location where the file will be exported.

Importing Macro Modules

To import a macro module, choose File, Add Existing Item from the Macros IDE. Public subroutines with no arguments or an `Optional` string argument with an initial value will be displayed in the Macro Explorer as macro entry points that can be invoked from VS .NET IDE or run from the Macros IDE.

Using the Macro IDE

By now you are familiar with IDEs in general, so we will just take a quick tour of the Macros IDE to point out some highlights.

> **Tip**
>
> You can change keyboard mappings in the Macros IDE by selecting Tools, Options, Keyboard. Selecting the Visual Basic 6 keyboard mapping scheme will make keyboard mappings in the Macros IDE consistent with VB6 mappings.

You can start the Macros IDE from the VS .NET IDE by choosing Tools, Macros, Macros IDE. The Macros IDE is project-centric; by default projects are stored in `C:\My Documents\Visual Studio Projects\VSMacros`. Every time you create a macro project, a new subfolder is created using the project name. By default the macro project name is the same as the namespace for the project and has a .vsmacros extension.

A module—exported to a .vb file—is stored internally in the .vsmacros file. Subroutines in the module are the actual macros. By default EnvDTE is imported using Imports EnvDTE added automatically to the top of the modules in a macro project.

You can use the same VB and coding techniques in macro modules as you would use in application modules. You can import other namespaces from the CLR as well as COM components by choosing Projects, Add Reference, although COM components will need to use TLBIMP.EXE on the COM component you want to import. Macro projects consist of modules and classes, but not forms.

Macro Security

Macros are stored as text in modules. Because macros are not compiled when you distribute them, anyone can look at your macro source code. If you want to protect macro code, you will need to place the macro code into an add-in and compile and distribute the add-in. (Refer to the section "Creating Add-Ins" later in this chapter for more information.)

Macro code is secure to the extent that it does not run when you open the macro. You must explicitly run a macro after it is loaded. If there are EnvironmentEvents defined, for example, OnStartupComplete, you will be warned about loading macro projects that contain event-handling code. By default Disable Event Handling Code is checked (see Figure 4.7); if you leave this option checked, potentially harmful macros that are run based on event code will not be started in the event-handling procedure.

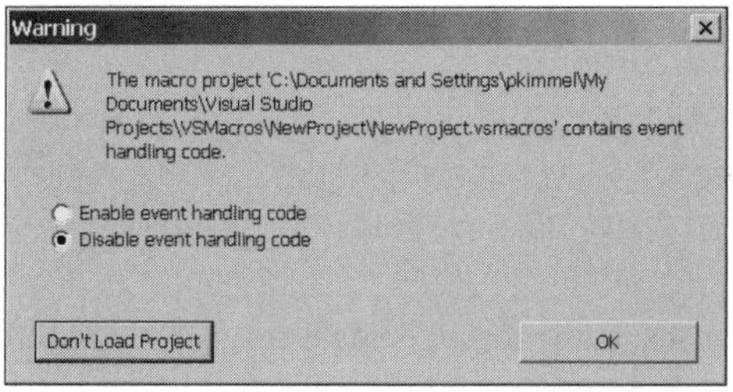

FIGURE 4.7

If a macro project has event-handling code defined, you are notified and can leave the Disable feature checked to prevent potentially harmful macros from running.

Warning	
⚠	The macro project 'C:\Documents and Settings\pkimmel\My Documents\Visual Studio Projects\VSMacros\NewProject\NewProject.vsmacros' contains event handling code.
	○ Enable event handling code
	● Disable event handling code
Don't Load Project	OK

4

MACROS AND VISUAL STUDIO EXTENSIBILITY

As long as you leave the Disable option selected, no macro code will start when a macro project is loaded, allowing you to safely share macro projects.

Macro Sharing

Macro code can be shared in a binary format by providing other users with the .vsmacros file or as text by exporting the individual .vb modules, which are exported as plain text files.

Creating a Macro Project

You can create a new macro project by selecting Tools, Macros, New Macro Project in the VS .NET IDE or by selecting New Macro Project from the Macros Explorer context menu. When you're in the Macros IDE, you cannot create a new macro project.

Follow the numbered steps and refer to the listing to create a macro that creates subfolders. (The example creates a subfolder for managing sample projects for this book.)

1. In the VS .NET IDE, choose Tools, Macros, New Macro Project.

2. Browse to the location where you would like to store the macro and type **MakeDirectory** for the Name of the macro project.

3. By default the module will be named Module1. Rename the module to Directory.

4. Double-click on the Directory module to open the Macros IDE with focus set on this new module.

5. Add the code shown in Listing 4.5 to complete the macro.

LISTING 4.5 A utility macro that creates project folders for new chapter examples

```
 1:  Option Strict On
 2:  Option Explicit On
 3:  Imports EnvDTE
 4:  Imports System.IO
 5:
 6:  Public Module Directory
 7:
 8:    Private Function GetSourceDirectory() As String
 9:      Return _
10:        "C:\Books\Sams\Visual Basic .NET Unleashed\Source\"
11:    End Function
12:
13:    Private Sub GetPath(ByRef Directory As String)
14:      Directory = _
15:        InputBox("Enter subfolder name:", _
16:        "Create Sub-Folder", Directory)
17:    End Sub
18:
19:    Private Function GetFullPath( _
```

LISTING 4.5   continued

```
20:     ByVal Directory As String) As String
21:
22:     If (Directory = "") Then GetPath(Directory)
23:     Return GetSourceDirectory() & Directory
24:  End Function
25:
26:  Private Sub DoMakeChapterDirectory( _
27:     ByVal Path As String)
28:     Try
29:        MkDir(Path)
30:     Catch
31:        MsgBox(Path & " alread exists", _
32:           MsgBoxStyle.Exclamation)
33:     End Try
34:  End Sub
35:
36:  Public Sub MakeChapterDirectory( _
37:     Optional ByVal Directory As String = "")
38:     DoMakeChapterDirectory(GetFullPath(Directory))
39:  End Sub
40:
41: End Module
```

The sample listing employs Option Strict On and Option Explicit On settings for the same reason as we use them for applications.

The listing also imports System.IO, demonstrating the use of other CLR namespaces within a macro. The query function GetSourceDirectory is a hard-coded method rather than a literal or string by choice. GetPath prompts the user for an input path. The motivation for this decision is that you cannot pass arguments to macros. Macros either have to be parameterless subroutines or all parameters have to have optional parameters with default values. In the sample listing, the macro is MakeChapterDirectory with an Optional parameter, Directory, with a default value of "". If the code is used in some other context, we can pass an argument to the macro procedure.

GetPath prompts the user for a subfolder and concatenates the subfolder to the book's path. DoMakeDirectory attempts to create the subfolder. If the subfolder already exists, the Catch block beginning on line 30 handles the error by telling the operator that the subfolder already exists.

4

MACROS AND
VISUAL STUDIO
EXTENSIBILITY

Managing Visual Studio from the Command Window

Visual Studio .NET has an extensive Automation Model that you can access through the Command window, macros, or by writing add-ins. There is a lot of information in the VS .NET Automation Model that you can access through the Command window, including the macros you write. (We will talk more about the Automation Model in the second part of the chapter, beginning after this section.)

To run a macro you will need to open the Command window and access your macros via the `Macros` collection. For example, to run the macro created in the previous section, open the Command window in the VS .NET IDE and in command mode, type the complete path to the macro, **Macros.MakeDirectory.Directory.MakeChapterDirectory** (see Figure 4.8).

FIGURE 4.8

Invoke macros using the Command window as shown, by typing the name of the macro.

You can use other aspects of the Automation Model in the same way. For example, to open the breakpoints window, type `Debug.Breakpoints`. IntelliSense works in the Command window, too, providing you with assistance in finding and invoking macros and using other Automation objects like the `Debug` object.

Responding to IDE Events

The DTE has exposed several categories of events for which you can write event handlers, enabling you to write code that fires when something in the VS .NET IDE occurs rather than requiring the user to explicitly start a macro.

Categories of events include `DTEEvents`, `DocumentEvents`, `WindowEvents`, `TaskListEvents`, `FindEvents`, `OutputWindowEvents`, `SelectionEvents`, `BuildEvents`, `SolutionEvents`, `SolutionItemEvents`, `MiscFilesEvents`, and `DebuggerEvents`. For example, `DTEEvents` has an `OnStartupComplete` event that fires when a macro project is loaded. `WindowEvents` passes a reference to a closing `EnvDTE.Window` object when you close a window in the VS .NET IDE. `BuildEvents` will notify your macro code when a build has begun and finished.

The subject of macros is probably one that can benefit from a book of its own. The number of event objects and associated member events available to macro authors is huge. If you think you need to respond to a macro event, filter the help engine on Visual Studio Macros and begin your search based on the event objects listed in the second paragraph of this section.

The mechanism for implementing event handlers in the Macros IDE is that you select your macro project in the macro Project Explorer and find the `EnvironmentEvents` module; double-click to open it. In the code editor view for the `EnvironmentEvents` module, select a Class Name from the left combo box and the event you want to implement from the Method Name, or right combo box. Write the code interacting with parameters and available objects similar to what you would do if you were implementing a VB .NET application. The fragment that follows implements the `DTEEvents OnStartupComplete` event.

```
Public Sub DTEEvents_OnStartupComplete() _
  Handles DTEEvents.OnStartupComplete
  MsgBox("Custom Event Handler: Macro Project Loaded")
End Sub
```

The `OnStartupComplete` event displays a message box indicating that the event project containing this `EnvironmentEvents` module has finished loading. The four procedures in Listing 4.6 demonstrate code that responds to an application build.

LISTING 4.6 Code that responds when you build your application

```
1:  Private Const Started As String = _
2:       "Build {0} started at {1}"
3:  Private Const Ended As String = _
4:       "Build {0} finished at {1}"
5:
6:  Private Function GetBuildStarted()
7:    Return String.Format(Started, _
8:       DTE.Solution.FullName, Now)
9:  End Function
10:
11: Private Function GetBuildEnded()
12:   Return String.Format(Ended, _
13:      DTE.Solution.FullName, Now)
14: End Function
15:
16: Public Sub BuildEvents_OnBuildBegin( _
17:   ByVal Scope As EnvDTE.vsBuildScope, _
18:   ByVal Action As EnvDTE.vsBuildAction) _
19:   Handles BuildEvents.OnBuildBegin
20:
21:   EventLog.WriteEntry("application", GetBuildStarted())
```

LISTING 4.6   continued

```
22:
23: End Sub
24:
25: Public Sub BuildEvents_OnBuildDone( _
26:    ByVal Scope As EnvDTE.vsBuildScope, _
27:    ByVal Action As EnvDTE.vsBuildAction) _
28:    Handles BuildEvents.OnBuildDone
29:
30:    EventLog.WriteEntry("application", GetBuildEnded())
31: End Sub
```

Implement OnBuildBegin and OnBuildDone events for the BuildEvents object and you could add an event log entry as demonstrated on lines 21 and 30, logging the start and finish time of a build using the shared method EventLog.WriteEntry.

As mentioned, you can respond to a lot of events. You probably will not write a significant number of IDE events, but they may be especially helpful on occasion. For now let's proceed to the subject of extensibility.

Customizing Visual Studio

The Visual Studio .NET Automation Model is extensive. As with macros it is unlikely that you will extend the IDE regularly unless you are in the business of writing tools and add-ins, but when you have a manual, repetitive task, extending the VS .NET IDE may be just the ticket. (It is also likely that, just as new component vendors emerged to create third-party components, new vendors to build IDE extensions are likely to emerge, too.)

Macro code is reasonably safe to run because you can disable events when you load a macro project and then you have an opportunity to examine the macro code before running it explicitly. (The event macros in the last section ran because I enabled macros when the prompt—refer to Figure 4.7—was displayed.) Unfortunately, macros can also be viewed by others. If you want the source code that is your macro to be concealed from third parties, you can create an Add-In project and ship the compiled add-in, instead of the uncompiled macro.

In this section we will take a look at the Visual Studio Extensibility model first and then I will demonstrate how to create add-ins.

Reviewing the Language-Specific Extensibility Object Model

Visual Studio .NET includes two extensibility object models. One is a project-neutral object model that provides access to the IDE, and the second is a programmable object model that provides access to projects and items in projects for Visual Basic .NET and Visual C# specifically. This section covers the objects on the latter object model.

The objects in the programmable object model are accessible by referencing VSLangProj.dll. The VSLangProj namespace includes the top-level object VSProject, which provides access to References, Imports, Project, ProjectItem, Configuration, and BuildManager objects.

This section briefly discusses the services or information these objects provide access to. You can use objects in VSLangProj in an automation or extensibility project by adding a reference to VSLangProj.dll. As a reminder to add the reference to a specific project, open the Solution Explorer, right-click on the Reference item, and in the .NET tab of the Add Reference dialog box (see Figure 4.9), select vsLangProj.dll. Click Select to add the DLL to the Selected Components list and click OK. When you have added a reference to VSLangProj.dll, add the VSLangProj namespace to the list of project imports on the Imports page of the project's Property Pages.

FIGURE 4.9

Adding the VSLangProj.dll reference to a project.

Component Name	Version	Path
System.Runtime.Remoting	1.0.2411.0	C:\WINNT\Microsoft.NET\Fra...
System.Runtime.Serialization....	1.0.2411.0	C:\WINNT\Microsoft.NET\Fra...
System.Security	1.0.2411.0	C:\WINNT\Microsoft.NET\Fra...
System.ServiceProcess.dll	1.0.2411.0	C:\WINNT\Microsoft.NET\Fra...
System.Web.dll	1.0.2411.0	C:\WINNT\Microsoft.NET\Fra...
System.Web.RegularExpressI...	1.0.2411.0	C:\WINNT\Microsoft.NET\Fra...
System.Web.Services.dll	1.0.2411.0	C:\WINNT\Microsoft.NET\Fra...
System.Windows.Forms.dll	1.0.2411.0	C:\WINNT\Microsoft.NET\Fra...
System.Xml.dll	1.0.2411.0	C:\WINNT\Microsoft.NET\Fra...
TlbExpCode	1.0.2411.0	C:\WINNT\Microsoft.NET\Fra...
TlbImpCode	1.0.2411.0	C:\WINNT\Microsoft.NET\Fra...
vslangproj	7.0.0.0	C:\Program Files\Microsoft.N...

Selected Components:

Component Name	Type	Source
vslangproj	.NET	C:\Program Files\Microsoft.NE...

4

MACROS AND
VISUAL STUDIO
EXTENSIBILITY

A graphic view of the programmable object model is available in VS .NET by browsing to the help URL `ms-help://MS.VSCC/MS.MSDNVS/vbcon/html/vblrfvslangprojhierarchychart.htm`. The help URL can be entered in the URL combo box on the Web toolbar.

VSProject

`VSProject` provides access to other objects in the programmable object model. Getting a reference to a `VSProject` object is a bit convoluted but can be easily demonstrated using the Macros IDE to quickly create the code.

The DTE (Development Tools for Extensibility) object represents the highest level of the development environment. The `DTE.Solution` property refers to all of the projects in the current instance of the environment. `DTE.Solution.Projects` is the collection containing a reference to all of the projects in the solution. `DTE.Solution.Projects.Item` allows you to index individual projects in the solution. For example, `DTE.Solution.Projects.Item(1)` returns the first project in the solution. `DTE.Solution.Projects.Item(1).Object` returns an `Object` property whose reference may be a VB project.

Listing 4.6 tests to determine whether the project `Object` property refers to a VB project and typecast the `Object` to the extensibility type `VSProject`, which in turn allows us to access specific project items, references, project imports, and configuration information.

LISTING 4.6 Working with the extensibility model begins by getting a reference to the `VSProject` object.

```
1:  Public Sub Verbose()
2:
3:    Dim Project As Project = _
4:      DTE.Solution.Projects.Item(1)
5:
6:    If (Project.Kind = PrjKind.prjKindVBProject) Then
7:
8:      Dim VSProject As VSProject
9:      VSProject = CType(Project.Object, VSProject)
10:
11:     Const sMessage As String = _
12:       "Project {0}'s first namespace is {1}"
13:
14:     MsgBox(String.Format(sMessage, _
15:       VSProject.Project.Name, _
16:       VSProject.Imports.Item(1).ToString))
17:
18:   End If
19:
20: End Sub
```

As mentioned, working with the extensibility model requires a little extra effort. Lines 3 and 4 get a reference to the first project in the current solution. Lines 6, 8, and 9 test to determine whether the `Project.Kind` is a Visual Basic project, and if it is, converts the `Project.Object` reference to the `VSProject` extensibility reference. `Project.Object` is defined as an `Object` type, but the type of the object assigned to it is a specific object like an instance of `VSProject`.

When we have the appropriately cast `VSProject` reference, we can access the members of `VSProject`. For example, as demonstrated in the listing, we can determine the project name and discover or modify the namespaces that the project imports.

VSProjectItem

The `VSProjectItem` object refers to a specific element in a project. A module is an example of a `VSProjectItem`. Continuing our previous example from the preceding section, we can request a `ProjectItem` from the currently selected project. (From Listing 4.6 we know that we have a reference to the first project in the solution.) The `VSProject.Project.ProjectItems` collection contains the `ProjectItem` objects in the project.

```
MsgBox(VSProject.Project.ProjectItems.Item(1).Document.FullName())
```

The example refers to the first `ProjectItem` object's `Document.FullName` property. The sample code displayed the `assemblyinfo.vb` project item in a message box.

As discussed in the previous example, each of these objects provides specific capabilities. For example, you can add modules to the project by adding a module to the `ProjectItems` collection. `Document` defines capabilities for managing documents like activating a window or saving the document.

References and Reference Objects

The `VSProject.References` collection supports programmatically managing references in a project. Because the `References` property is a collection, knowing how to use a collection in general means that you know how to use the `References` collection.

Assuming we have used code to get a reference to the `VSProject` object for a specific project, we can programmatically examine, add, or remove references at the project level. Listing 4.7 (macro code defined in `MacroProject.vsmacros` on this book's Web site) adds a reference to `VSLangProj` to the project referred to by the `VSProject` object.

4

MACROS AND VISUAL STUDIO EXTENSIBILITY

Listing 4.7 Adding a reference to a project programmatically

```
1:     Public Sub AddReference()
2:       VSProject.References.Add("VSLangProj")
3:     End Sub
4:
5:     Private Function VSProject() As VSProject
6:       Const sMessage As String = _
7:         "Project is not a Visual Basic project."
8:
9:       If (Project.Kind = PrjKind.prjKindVBProject) Then
10:         Return CType(Project.Object, VSProject)
11:       Else
12:         Throw New System.Exception(sMessage)
13:       End If
14:     End Function
15:
16:     Private Function Project(Optional ByVal Index _
17:       As Integer = 1) As Project
18:       ' By default return the first project!
19:       Return DTE.Solution.Projects.Item(Index)
20:     End Function
```

Tip

Flatten complicated object models with query methods, as demonstrated in Listing 4.7.

In the example, the macro AddReference relies on the VSProject—lines 5 through 14—and Project—lines 16 through 20—query methods to obtain a reference to a project.

Imports Object

The Imports collection works in a manner identical to the References collection. If you have a reference to the VSProject object, you can programmatically examine, add, and remove individually imported namespaces at the project level.

BuildManager Object

The BuildManager object is available to third-party vendors to facilitate integrating portable executable files. BuildManager was implemented to support developers who want to build custom extensions to the Visual Studio .NET IDE. (This is one of those subjects that demonstrates how big and complex the .NET Framework is; it could justifiably fill a book of its own. For this reason, I am not going to explore the subject here.)

Project Object

The `Project` object represents a single project in a solution. The `Project` query method on lines 16 through 20 of Listing 4.7 demonstrates how to get a reference to a single `Project` object.

Configuration Object

A `Configuration` object belongs to a `Project` object and allows you to programmatically access configuration information about a project. The macro demonstrates retrieving and displaying the configuration name of the active configuration.

```
Public Sub ConfigurationDemo()
  Dim Config As Configuration
  Config = _
    Project.ConfigurationManager.ActiveConfiguration
  MsgBox(Config.ConfigurationName())
End Sub
```

Note that the code fragment example depends on the `Project` query method in Listing 4.7.

ProjectItem Object

A `ProjectItem` represents an individual element in a project. Refer to the example in the earlier section "VSProjectItem."

Reviewing the Project—Neutral Extensibility Object Model

The project-neutral object model provides access to non-language-specific elements that can be manipulated programmatically, like windows, command bars, add-ins, documents, and debugger elements. You can view the complete model in the Automation Object Model Chart by entering the following URL in the VS .NET IDE:

```
ms-help://MS.VSCC/MS.MSDNVS/vsintro7/html/vxgrfAutomationObjectModelChart.htm
```

The whole object model is too big to cover in one chapter, but this subsection covers some of the highlights of the project-neutral, or Automation Object, model.

CodeModel Object

The `CodeModel` provides you with programmatic access to specific constructs in a source code file. `CodeModel` objects allow you to programmatically access constructs in a source code file.

4

MACROS AND
VISUAL STUDIO
EXTENSIBILITY

You can programmatically add constructs using a `CodeModel` object. The methods that allow you to add constructs are prefixed with `Add` followed by the construct type. For example, the method to add a structure is `AddStruct`.

The `CodeModel.CodeElements` collection property contains `CodeElement` objects. Generally there is a `CodeElement` for each declarative statement in a source code file. Listing 4.8 uses recursive descent to walk a `CodeModel`.

LISTING 4.8 Recursively walking through all of the elements of a `CodeModel`

```
1:  Option Explicit On
2:  Option Strict Off
3:
4:  Imports EnvDTE
5:  Imports System.Diagnostics
6:  Imports VSLangProj
7:  Imports System.Reflection
8:
9:  Public Module VSProjectDemo
10:
11: [ General Extensibility Object Model Demos ]
12:
13: #Region " Project Neutral Extensibility Object Model "
14:
15: #Region " Macro Entry Points "
16:    'Assumes an open project and module
17:    Public Sub WriteDocument()
18:      Dim Doc As Document
19:      Doc = Project.ProjectItems.Item(1).Document
20:      GetActivePane.OutputString(Doc.FullName)
21:    End Sub
22:
23:    Public Sub WalkSourceCode()
24:      WalkCodeElements( _
25:        ActiveDocument.ProjectItem.FileCodeModel.CodeElements)
26:    End Sub
27: #End Region
28:
29: #Region " Private Implementation Details "
30:
31:    Private Sub WalkCodeElements(ByVal Elements As CodeElements)
32:
33:      Dim Element As CodeElement
34:      For Each Element In Elements
35:        DisplayElement(Element)
36:        If (HasChildren(Element)) Then
37:          WalkCodeElements(Element.Members)
38:        End If
39:      Next
```

LISTING 4.8   continued

```
40:    End Sub
41:
42:    Private Function HasChildren(ByVal Element As CodeElement) As Boolean
43:       Return ((Element.IsCodeType()) And _
44:          (Element.Kind <> EnvDTE.vsCMElement.vsCMElementDelegate)) Or _
45:          (Element.Kind = EnvDTE.vsCMElement.vsCMElementNamespace)
46:    End Function
47:
48:    Private Sub DisplayElement(ByVal CodeElement As CodeElement)
49:       GetActivePane.OutputString(Formatted(CodeElement))
50:    End Sub
51:
52:    Private Function Formatted( _
53:       ByVal CodeElement As CodeElement) As String
54:
55:       Const Text As String = _
56:          "{0} element {1} found in {2}." & vbCrLf
57:
58:       Return _
59:          String.Format(Text, CodeElement.Name, _
60:             CodeElement.Kind.ToString, _
61:                CodeElement.ProjectItem.Name)
62:    End Function
63:
64:    Private Function GetOutputWindow() As OutputWindow
65:       Return _
66:          DTE.Windows.Item( _
67:             Constants.vsWindowKindOutput).Object
68:    End Function
69:
70:    Private Function GetActivePane() As OutputWindowPane
71:       Return GetOutputWindow.ActivePane
72:    End Function
73:
74: #End Region
75:
76: #End Region
77:
78: End Module
```

4

MACROS AND
VISUAL STUDIO
EXTENSIBILITY

Note

When you see code enclosed in brackets ([. . .]) in a printed code listing, it's a placeholder representing condensed code; for the full uncondensed version, you can refer to the complete source listing on the Web site for this book.

> **Caution**
>
> IntelliSense will not display the Members property of a CodeElement used on line 33. Uncheck Hide Advanced Members on the General page in the dialog box that you access by choosing Tools, Options, Text Editor, All Languages Options in both the Macros IDE and VS .NET IDE to see advanced options. Members will still not show up in this instance, but other advanced members will.

WalkSourceCode beginning on line 23 and ending on line 26 is the entry point for the macro. WalkCodeElements from lines 31 through 40 uses recursion to walk through the code elements of a project. GetActivePane and GetOutputWindow were introduced in Listing 4.4 and return the IDE's Output window. DisplayElement and Formatted produce a nicely formatted output.

The biggest benefit of the CodeModel object is the capability of manipulating code without writing a parser. Find the CodeElement you need and manipulate it through the properties of the CodeElement object.

Document **Object**

The Document object is the reference to a physical document in a Project. (Refer to the section on the VSProjectItem earlier in the chapter for an example using a Document object.)

Debugger **Object Model**

The Debugger object model provides access to breakpoints, debugger events, expressions, the language object, processes, programs, the stack frame, and threads. (Refer to the section "Macros for Enabling and Disabling Breakpoints" for an example using the Debugger object.)

Creating Add-Ins

As you might have gathered by now, a lot of information is available in the general and project-neutral extensibility models. What are all of these automation objects for? They are there to help language extenders—people like you—create Add-Ins among other things.

Because the object model is so vast, you will have to rely heavily on the help files to begin scratching the surface of extensibility; more than likely, several tool vendors will develop in-house expertise, and a developer from one of these shops will write an entire book on this subject.

In this section we will look at the necessary, basic considerations for creating VS .NET add-ins and will create some simple add-ins. Of course any add-in could potentially be a complex application by itself—consider Visual SourceSafe.

Creating an Add-In Project

Macros extend the IDE by providing automated solutions that can be run in the IDE. The biggest difference between an add-in and a macro is that add-ins are compiled into a separate .DLL and macros are not. The tasks you automate with macros or add-ins can be identical. The reason you would choose an add-in over a macro is one of distribution. If you write an extension that you want to sell, and you want to prevent customers from pillaging your source code, you will create an add-in project; otherwise a macro project will suffice.

The essential ingredients necessary to create add-ins are a DLL or class library, a project, and a class that implements the IDTExtensibility2 interface. There are other interfaces you can implement that will make your add-in more useful, but IDTExtensibility2 is the primary interface that an add-in must implement.

Fortunately, there is an add-in wizard that automates the basic steps necessary to create an add-in. Granted, the add-in created by the wizard is a do-nothing add-in, but it will get you jump-started. Follow the numbered steps listed following to create an add-in project that will compile and run.

1. Start a new project by choosing File, New Project, Other Projects Extensibility Projects, Visual Studio.Net Add-In. Click OK. Click Next at the Welcome screen.
2. On Page 1 of 6, select Create an Add-In Using Visual Basic. Click Next.
3. Page 2 of 6 uses the defaults, which define the Macros IDE and Visual Studio .NET as hosts for the add-in. Click Next.
4. On Page 3 of 6 name the add-in MyAddin and enter a description; for example, **My First Add-In.** Click Next.
5. On Page 4 of 6 we want to indicate that the add-in can be invoked from the Tools menu, the add-in should load when the host loads, and the add-in should be available to all users. (Check all check boxes except My Add-In Will Never Put Up a Modal UI.) Click Next.
6. On Page 5 of 6, check the check box if you want to add About box information. (If you do, modify the About box information accordingly.) Click Next.
7. On Page 6 of 6, review the Summary information, and if it is correct, click Finish.

The wizard will create an add-in project—in our example named MyAddIn—and a Windows Installer project named MyAddInSetup (using the *AddInName*Setup naming convention). The add-in project will have references, an assemblyinfo.vb module, and a module named connect.vb that contains the add-in class, `Connect`. `Connect` implements the `IDTExtensibility2` interface and, because we indicated that we wanted integration with the IDE's Tools menu, the `IDTCommandTarget` interface.

The add-in will compile and run as is, but it performs no real task at the present time. If you run the add-in from the IDE, it will compile and package the setup file MyAddInSetup.msi. (Creating the setup file takes a while, so be patient.) When the add-in project runs, it starts a new instance of the IDE with—in our case—the add-in added as a menu operation in the Tools menu. Go ahead and try it.

> **Caution**
>
> The add-in menu item may stop appearing in the Tools menu after you test the add-in to debug it. If this happens, close all instances of the IDE and double-click ReCreateCommands.reg in your Add-In directory. This step reloads the registry settings and the menu should reappear when you restart VS .NET.

Our vanilla add-in implements the `IDTExtensibility2` and `IDTCommandTarget` interfaces resulting in the code in Listing 4.9.

LISTING 4.9 The add-in module created by the Visual Studio .NET Add-In Wizard (repaginated to fit this page)

```
 1: Imports Microsoft.Office.Core
 2: Imports EnvDTE
 3: Imports System.Runtime.InteropServices
 4:
 5: #Region " Read me for Add-in installation and setup information. "
 6: ' When run, the Add-in wizard prepared the registry for the Add-in.
 7: ' At a later time, if the Add-in becomes unavailable for reasons such as:
 8: '    1) You moved this project to a computer other than which it was
➥originally created on.
 9: '    2) You chose 'Yes' when presented with a message asking if you wish
➥to remove the Add-in.
10: '    3) Registry corruption.
11: ' you will need to re-register the Add-in by building the
➥MyAddinSetup project
12: ' by right clicking the project in the Solution Explorer, then
➥choosing install.
13: #End Region
14:
```

LISTING 4.9   continued

```
15: <GuidAttribute("F61C62A7-A0F2-4660-87C7-67BCE5C0BF96"), _
16:   ProgIdAttribute("MyAddin.Connect")> _
17: Public Class Connect
18:
19:   Implements IDTExtensibility2
20:   Implements IDTCommandTarget
21:
22:   Dim applicationObject As EnvDTE.DTE
23:   Dim addInInstance As EnvDTE.AddIn
24:
25:   Public Sub OnBeginShutdown(ByRef custom() As Object) _
26:     Implements IDTExtensibility2.OnBeginShutdown
27:
28:   End Sub
29:
30:   Public Sub OnAddInsUpdate(ByRef custom() As Object) _
31:     Implements IDTExtensibility2.OnAddInsUpdate
32:
33:   End Sub
34:
35:   Public Sub OnStartupComplete(ByRef custom() As Object) _
36:     Implements IDTExtensibility2.OnStartupComplete
37:
38:   End Sub
39:
40:   Public Sub OnDisconnection( _
41:     ByVal RemoveMode As ext_DisconnectMode, _
42:     ByRef custom() As Object) _
43:     Implements IDTExtensibility2.OnDisconnection
44:
45:   End Sub
46:
47:   Public Sub OnConnection(ByVal application As Object, _
48:     ByVal connectMode As ext_ConnectMode, _
49:     ByVal addInInst As Object, ByRef custom() As Object) _
50:     Implements IDTExtensibility2.OnConnection
51:
52:     applicationObject = CType(application, EnvDTE.DTE)
53:     addInInstance = CType(addInInst, EnvDTE.AddIn)
54:     If connectMode = ext_ConnectMode.ext_cm_UISetup Then
55:       Dim objAddIn As AddIn = CType(addInInst, AddIn)
56:       Dim CommandObj As Command
57:
58:       'IMPORTANT!
59:       'If your command no longer appears on the appropriate
60:       ' command bar, you add a new or modify an existing command,
61:       ' or if you would like to re-create the command, close
62:       ' all instances of Visual Studio .NET and double click
63:       ' the(file) 'ReCreateCommands.reg' in the folder
```

LISTING 4.9 continued

```
64:        ' holding the source code to your Add-in.
65:        'IMPORTANT!
66:        Try
67:          CommandObj = _
68:            applicationObject.Commands.AddNamedCommand(objAddIn, _
69:              "MyAddin", "MyAddin", "Executes the command for MyAddin",
➥True, 59, Nothing, _
70:                1 + 2)
71:            '1+2 == vsCommandStatusSupported+vsCommandStatusEnabled
72:
73:          CommandObj.AddControl( _
74:            applicationObject.CommandBars.Item("Tools"))
75:        Catch e As System.Exception
76:        End Try
77:      End If
78:    End Sub
79:
80:    Public Sub Exec(ByVal cmdName As String, _
81:      ByVal executeOption As vsCommandExecOption, _
82:      ByRef varIn As Object, ByRef varOut As Object, _
83:      ByRef handled As Boolean) Implements IDTCommandTarget.Exec
84:
85:      handled = False
86:      If (executeOption = _
87:        vsCommandExecOption.vsCommandExecOptionDoDefault) Then
88:
89:        If cmdName = "MyAddin.Connect.MyAddin" Then
90:          handled = True
91:          Exit Sub
92:        End If
93:      End If
94:    End Sub
95:
96:    Public Sub QueryStatus(ByVal cmdName As String, _
97:      ByVal neededText As vsCommandStatusTextWanted, _
98:      ByRef statusOption As vsCommandStatus, _
99:      ByRef commandText As Object) _
100:       Implements IDTCommandTarget.QueryStatus
101:
102:      If neededText = _
103:        EnvDTE.vsCommandStatusTextWanted.vsCommandStatusTextWantedNone _
104:        Then
105:
106:        If cmdName = "MyAddin.Connect.MyAddin" Then
107:          statusOption = _
108:            CType(vsCommandStatus.vsCommandStatusEnabled + _
109:              vsCommandStatus.vsCommandStatusSupported, _
110:              vsCommandStatus)
111:        Else
```

LISTING 4.9 continued

```
112:          statusOption = vsCommandStatus.vsCommandStatusUnsupported
113:        End If
114:      End If
115:    End Sub
116: End Class
```

> **Note**
>
> Keep in mind that GUIDs will always be unique. Thus, the value of
> GuidAttribute on line 15 on your computer will vary.

As is immediately apparent from the listing, a few of these procedures are a little murky
and all of the statements are long, but when you evaluate each one they are pretty
straightforward. All of the code implements the two interfaces previously mentioned.
The IDTExtensibility2 methods are implemented as empty methods, and the
IDTCommandTarget methods have the necessary code needed to place a menu item in the
Tools menu and respond when it is clicked. The next two subsections discuss the
IDTCommandTarget and IDTExtensibility2 interfaces.

Implementing the IDTExtensibility2 Interface

IDTExtensibility2 is the basic add-in interface. There are five methods that you must
implement—although they can be empty methods—to define an add-in. These are
described in Table 4.1.

TABLE 4.1 IDTExtensibility2 Interface Methods That Have To Be Implemented To
Create an Add-In

Interface Method	Description
OnAddInsUpdate	Called when the Add-In Manager list changes
OnBeginShutDown	Called when the IDE is shut down before OnDisconnection
OnConnection	Called when an add-in is loaded
OnDisconnection	Called when an add-in is unloaded
OnStartupComplete	Called when the IDE has completed startup

From the descriptions, it is apparent that these methods are provided to allow you an
opportunity to initialize and release resources at opportunistic points during your add-
in's lifecycle. If you need some processing to occur before your add-in is run, implement

4

MACROS AND
VISUAL STUDIO
EXTENSIBILITY

`OnConnection` or `OnStartupComplete`. If you need processing to occur before your add-in or the IDE is shut down, implement `OnDisconnection` or `OnBeginShutDown`. Otherwise, leave the implementation of these interface methods blank, as demonstrated in Listing 4.9.

`OnConnection` is implemented to create the (named) Command object on lines 67 through 70, allowing the command to be invoked from the Command window, and adds the command to the Tools menu—in the example, on lines 73 and 74.

Implementing the `IDTCommandTarget` Interface

The `IDTCommandTarget` interface implements the menu item for the add-in. The `Exec` method is called when the menu item is clicked and `QueryStatus` returns the status of the command specified in the arguments, indicating whether the command is available.

The code implementing the `IDTCommandTarget` is very specific, suggesting that it is easiest if you let the wizard generate the add-in initially. You could, however, use the wizard-generated code as a template for creating add-ins manually.

Registering Add-Ins

To register your VB .NET add-in, open a command prompt window and run the Regasm.exe application with the `/codebase` switch, passing it the name of your add-in DLL.

Regasm.exe is installed in the \Winnt\Microsoft.Net\Framework\ directory by default. Because we indicated that the add-in should be available to all users in step 5 in the section "Creating an Add-In Project," the add-in keys are added to the registry in `HKEY_LOCAL_MACHINE\SOFTWARE\Microsoft\VisualStudio\7.0\AddIns\MyAddIn.` `Connect`.

The help topic `ms-help://MS.VSCC/MS.MSDNVS/vsintro7/html/vxconAdd-InRegistration.htm` titled "Add-In Registration" provides additional details on the keys that are added to the registry and appropriate values for those keys.

Here is an example demonstrating the proper registration of an add-in named MyAddIn.dll. (The example assumes that the current directory contains the add-in .DLL.)

```
C:\WINNT\Microsoft.NET\Framework\v1.0.3215\Regasm.exe myaddin.dll /codebase
```

(The specific location of Regasm.exe may vary by computer and version of the .NET Framework.)

> **Tip**
>
> The best way to ensure that add-ins are properly registered and installed is to run the Add-In setup project when you are finished testing and debugging your add-in.

Regasm.exe assigns a .NET assembly a `ClassID` and adds a registry entry. The reason for all of this has to do with the Add-Ins Manager. The Add-Ins Manager is an Automation server. Yes, that's right—old COM technology still lingers in a few places.

The `/codebase` switch puts the full path to the Add-In into the registry.

Implementing the `IDTToolsOptionsPage` Interface

Implement the `IDTToolsOptionsPage` interface when you want to define a custom Tools Options Page for your add-in. You will have to implement the following interface methods to create the Options page: `GetProperties`, `OnAfterCreated`, `OnCancel`, `OnHelp`, and `OnOK`.

`GetProperties` needs to return a `DTE.Properties` collection containing all of the properties on the custom page. `OnAfterCreated` is called after the page is created. `OnCancel`, `OnHelp`, and `OnOK` are called in response to the user clicking those buttons, respectively.

Adding Behaviors to the Add-In

Now that we have created an empty add-in, we need to add some code to define a behavior. Our add-in behavior is invoked when the user clicks the Tools, MyAddIn menu item or when the user types `MyAddin.Connect.MyAddIn` in the Command window. Either of these methods yields control to the `Exec` method we implemented, hence our new behavior needs to be initiated in the Exec method.

Building on the behavior we contrived in an earlier section, we can insert code to run the copyright-insertion behavior from the Add-In menu. That is, our add-in will insert a copyright tag.

To modify the `MyAddIn` add-in to use the `InsertCopyrightTag` macro, we will need to ensure that the macro project containing that macro is loaded. Alternatively, we can copy the macro code into the MyAddIn project and avoid a dependency on the macro. Listing 4.10 demonstrates the former approach; it is assumed that the macro project is loaded and we will execute the macro to actually perform the add-in behavior for us.

LISTING 4.10   Excerpt from Listing 4.9 showing the modifications to the add-in created by the wizard.

```
80:    Public Sub Exec(ByVal cmdName As String, _
81:      ByVal executeOption As vsCommandExecOption, _
82:      ByRef varIn As Object, ByRef varOut As Object, _
83:      ByRef handled As Boolean) Implements IDTCommandTarget.Exec
84:
85:      handled = False
86:      If (executeOption = _
87:        vsCommandExecOption.vsCommandExecOptionDoDefault) Then
88:
89:        If cmdName = "MyAddIn.Connect.MyAddIn" Then
90:
91:          DoExecute()
92:
93:          handled = True
94:          Exit Sub
95:        End If
96:      End If
97:    End Sub
...
120:   Private Sub DoExecute()
121:     ' Need to ensure the Copyright macro project is defined.
122:     applicationObject.ExecuteCommand( _
123:       "Macros.MyMacros.Copyright.InsertCopyrightTag")
124:   End Sub
```

Listing 4.10 is excerpted from Listing 4.9. Replace the Exec implementation and add the DoExecute method to complete the add-in MyAddIn. Line 91 invokes the DoExecute behavior when the Exec method is called. DoExecute is implemented in terms of the InsertCopyrightTag defined earlier in this chapter. Line 122 of DoExecute uses the EnvDTE.DTE.ExecuteCommand method to run the macro. ExecuteCommand works as if you had typed the statement in the Command window.

Because macros are implemented with VB .NET, you could literally cut and paste the macro code into the add-in as an alternative to invoking the macro.

Creating Wizards

Wizards are applications that help users perform some task. Generally the task represented by a wizard requires a sequence of specific operations; the point of the wizard is to alleviate tedium or simplify a multistep task into a linear sequence in which all responses yield a functional result.

From experience you probably know that Microsoft implements wizards as a sequence of dialog boxes with a graphic, some text providing instruction, and a simple input field or multiple choice selection. These wizards appear to be an integrated part of the application that uses them.

Creating wizards in Visual Basic .NET—and for VS .NET—is easier than creating an add-in. Ironically, there is no wizard that creates wizards. The general steps for creating a wizard for VS .NET are as follows:

1. Create a Class Library project.

2. Implement the `IDTWizard` interface and the one method defined by that interface, `Execute`. When the wizard is invoked, the `Execute` method is called.

3. Implement the wizard behavior, usually a sequence of dialog boxes and an end result.

4. Add a reference to the EnvDTE library.

5. Compile and register the wizard using Regasm.exe.

6. Create a text file with the same name as the wizard and a .vsz extension. For example, MyWizard.Dll needs a text file MyWizard.vsz. (We'll talk more about what is in the text file in a moment.)

7. Copy the text file in a folder depending on how you want it invoked. For instance, if you want the wizard to be available when a user selects File, Add New Item in a VB project, copy the .vsz file to the directory containing the Add New Item elements; the default location for the example is `C:\Program Files\Microsoft Visual Studio.NET\Vb7\VBProjectItems\Local Project Items\`.

As you can see, the number of steps is roughly equivalent to the number of steps for add-ins, but the actual amount of work is much less. The basic technique is to create a class library that implements `IDTWizard`, compile the library, and register it. Essentially, you implement one method. (Of course, there is all of the work the wizard will perform, too.)

4

MACROS AND
VISUAL STUDIO
EXTENSIBILITY

Note

Even if you have implemented interfaces in VB6, the syntax has changed between VB6 and VB .NET. You can skip ahead to Chapter 7, "Creating Classes," to learn more about interfaces and then return to this section, or take everything on faith for now.

The code in Listing 4.11 demonstrates a wizard that pops up a message box.

LISTING 4.11 A wizard that displays a message box provides a good template for creating wizards in general.

```
1:  Imports EnvDTE
2:
3:  Public Class Class1
4:      Implements IDTWizard
5:
6:      Public Sub Execute(ByVal Application As Object, _
7:          ByVal hwndOwner As Integer, _
8:          ByRef ContextParams() As Object, _
9:          ByRef CustomParams() As Object, _
10:         ByRef RetVal As wizardResult) Implements EnvDTE.IDTWizard.Execute
11:
12:         MsgBox("Hello World!")
13:         RetVal = wizardResult.wizardResultCancel
14:
15:     End Sub
16:
17: End Class
```

The `Execute` method gets several parameters. `Application` is a reference to the environment the wizard is running in. `hwndOwner` is the handle of the parent application. `ContextParams` contains information indicating the context in which the wizard was started; for example, File, Add New Items versus File, New Project. `CustomParams` are values you can pass to the wizard via the .vsz file in the form of `Param=Value` statements. `RetVal` is an enumerated value indicating whether the wizard succeeded or failed.

Creating the Wizard Launching File

A wizard launching file by convention has the same name as its associated wizard and .vsz extension. The wizard launching file is a simplified file similar to an .ini file, used to pass information to an application; in this instance a class library.

The basic format of the .vsz file is a text file with no sections and name and value pairs. For our sample wizard, all we need is a text file containing the following:

```
VSWIZARD 7.0
Wizard=Wizard1.Class1
Param=<Nothing>
```

If you need to pass parameters, pass them in the form `Param=value` as demonstrated in the sample file.

Having written the wizard launching file, copy it to the appropriate directories. As previously mentioned, copy the .vsz file to `C:\Program Files\Microsoft Visual Studio .NET\Vb7\VBProjectItems\Local Project Items\` to make the wizard available from the File, Add New Item submenu.

You can test wizards using macros to launch the wizard. I will demonstrate this technique after we register the wizard.

Registering the Wizard Class Library

Wizards are basically add-ins. Consequently, you use the same process to register wizards as you did for add-ins earlier in the chapter.

To register a wizard, type the full path to the regasm.exe application, the full path to your wizard, and make sure that you use the `/codebase` switch or the Add-Ins Manager will not be able to find your add-in. Assuming we have the same version of .NET, the following code will register a wizard named mywizard.dll that exists in the current directory.

```
C:\WINNT\Microsoft.NET\Framework\v1.0.3215\Regasm.exe mywizard.dll /codebase
```

To unregister the wizard use the `/unregister` switch with regasm.exe.

```
C:\WINNT\Microsoft.NET\Framework\v1.0.3215\Regasm.exe myaddin.dll /unregister
```

Testing the Wizard

The wizard is created and registered. The wizard launch file has been copied to the directories that contain other templates. You are now ready to test the wizard.

There are two ways you can quickly test the wizard. You can select File, Add New Item (or select the operation based on where you placed the launch file), or you can use a macro to launch the wizard. Listing 4.12 demonstrates a macro that will exercise the wizard.

LISTING 4.12 Use the Development Tools Environment (DTE) object and a macro to test your wizard

```
1:  Const Path As String = _
2:      "C:\Program Files\Microsoft Visual " & _
3:      "Studio .NET\Vb7\VBProjectItems\Local " & _
4:      "Project Items\Wizard1.vsz"
5:
6:  Public Sub RunWizard()
7:      Dim Guid As New _
8:        System.Guid("{164B10B9-B200-11D0-8C61-00A0C91E29D5}")
9:      Dim ContextParams(1) As Object
```

LISTING 4.12   continued

```
10:    ContextParams(0) = Guid
11:    ContextParams(1) = Nothing
12:    MsgBox("Launching")
13:    DTE.LaunchWizard(Path, ContextParams)
14: End Sub
```

The macro RunWizard creates a new GUID, using the GUID constructor and the globally unique identifier that indicates the template repository. (This information was taken from the registry, but doesn't seem to be a very robust way to write code.) The path to the wizard launch file and the array of objects, named ContextParams, are passed to the wizard.

Visual Studio Integration Program (VSIP)

A small percentage of developers may foray into the tools arena and build extensions for more than the challenge of building cool extensions. Macros, add-ins, and wizards will allow the average developer to build custom extensions to Visual Studio .NET. The fact that these tools exist and are implemented in a purposeful way indicates Microsoft's commitment to encouraging third parties to build extensions to Visual Studio .NET. Then, there is a very small group of vendors that will be intentionally building serious software for Visual Studio. For these folks Microsoft has implemented Visual Studio Integration.

Visual Studio Integration (VSI, also known as VSIP) is a license program that is designed to provide extenders an opportunity to integrate their products into Visual Studio .NET. For more information, refer to the "Visual Studio Integration Technical Guide" available from Microsoft.

To be brief, participating in this program costs a small chunk of change, and for your participation you get a Visual Studio Integration SDK and Visual Studio for Applications among other perquisites. Visual Studio for Applications itself is a pretty nifty product for writing custom extensions to applications without modifying the source code.

If you are an extender—companies like Turbo Power, Rational Software, Starbase, and IBM come to mind—you will want to look into the VSIP program.

Summary

The key to writing any software is in part understanding the grammar of a language, but more importantly it is understanding the context. Understanding what you are trying to accomplish and the tools at your disposal is the real battle.

Chapter 4 has introduced automation and extensibility fairly early in the book. If you are an accomplished VB6 programmer, you probably understand most of the concepts in this chapter. If you are a new programmer, you might be a little confused. Read further in the book and return to this chapter if necessary. The crux of this chapter is to get you thinking about automating repetitive tasks, even if you do not completely understand classes or interfaces. You will. After you have the grammar nuts and bolts worked out, you will be ready and able to tackle automation.

In this chapter macros, add-ins, and wizards were demonstrated. If you find yourself performing the same tedious task several times, consider writing a macro to automate the task. If you think others on your team or in the global community can benefit from your solution, make a custom add-in. Finally, any task that requires a fairly precise series of steps and might be difficult to understand is probably an excellent candidate for wizardry. You might not create these things every day, but when you do they should help alleviate tedious or problematic tasks.

4

MACROS AND
VISUAL STUDIO
EXTENSIBILITY

Subroutines, Functions, and Structures

IN THIS CHAPTER

Keywords and tokens are the atoms of computer languages. Visual Basic .NET's grammar is the equivalent of the physical laws that govern the interactions between these atoms. Statements are the molecules, and the procedures are the basic building blocks of every program.

Every object-oriented program contains classes made up of procedures that describe the behavior of the classes. The classes and the interaction of those classes define what a particular system is and does.

Chapter 5 covers functions and subroutines in depth. Because the next building block of aggregation is the structure, the `Structure` construct is covered in detail. Understanding how to declare, define, and implement procedures and their affiliated arguments and structures is the final precursor to advanced programming topics.

This chapter demonstrates how to define procedures and how to use the `ByVal`, `ByRef`, `Optional`, and `ParamArray` argument specifiers. The latter part of the chapter examines the `Structure` construct, which replaces the VB6 `Type`. `Structure` supports additional behaviors that `Type` doesn't support, including structure methods, constructors, and properties.

Writing Procedures

Basic procedure declarations haven't changed dramatically between VB6 and Visual Basic .NET. Procedures that do not have a return value are still defined with the keyword `Sub` and procedures that return a value are still defined with the keyword `Function`.

You will notice a few subtle changes when implementing and using subroutines and functions. The first such change is the use of parentheses for calling subroutines and functions. Always use parentheses when calling a function or a subroutine, but you don't need to add the `Call` keyword. We will cover additional changes to procedures in the subsections that follow.

Writing Subroutines

A subroutine is defined by typing the keyword `Sub` followed by a name and parentheses. The bounds of the procedure are constrained by the `End Sub` statement. Together the `Sub` *Name* and `End Sub` statements define the *procedure block*, or the extent of a particular sub.

```
Sub MySub()
End Sub
```

Any temporary variables defined in a procedure block have procedure scope. That is, variables with procedure scope are only accessible when the program's execution point is within the subroutine. Except for `Static` variables, procedurally scoped variables don't maintain their values between successive calls to the procedure.

> **Tip**
>
> VB6 supported adding the `Static` modifier to a procedure heading if you wanted all variables in that procedure to be static. Visual Basic .NET does not support this modifier in the procedure heading. If you want every variable in a procedure to be static, you must use the `Static` modifier on each variable.

In recent years, best practices have been identified and innovations have evolved from these best practices. The section "Defining Procedure Arguments" covers further specific implementation details regarding subroutines and functions. For now, let's examine the subroutine from the perspective of constraining procedure complexity. (The discussions in the next two sections, "Best Practices" and "Innovations in Programming," apply equally to subroutines and functions.)

Best Practices

For many years there have been several well-reasoned best practices that describe what constitutes a good procedure. Unfortunately these best practices haven't been adopted universally. With innovations in programming, specifically refactoring, it's possible that we will have a forum and a language for demonstrating and teaching these best practices to new and experienced developers.

The strategies described here can be reduced to several common maxims about software development. I will introduce each maxim in a separate statement followed by my comments about the problem presented by the maxim.

- Maxim 1: Systems grow exponentially in complexity.

  Advances in software development languages, such as the broad adoption of object-oriented languages, allow us to problem-solve at a much higher level of abstraction. Yet, software demand still outpaces the ability of people to implement increasingly complex solutions.

- Maxim 2: Programming is the hardest thing people try to do.

  I have heard many disagreements to this assertion, but there are few if any other endeavors that touch every other industry and combine engineering, mathematics, aesthetics, psychology, art, intercommunication skills, and raw creative talent.

- Maxim 3: Short-term memory is limited to juggling very few similar but related concepts at a given time.

  Short-term memory keeps us from juggling more than a couple of pieces of information at a time. Without strategies for limiting what must be considered and resolved at a single moment, our capacity to solve problems diminishes to the point of overwhelming frustration.

- Maxim 4: Software development projects have a high failure rate.

  Software projects fail because software is difficult to build. As a group, programmers are still working in environments where few of the necessary roles are fulfilled by trained and experienced professionals, and programmers are doing the bulk of the work with little formal process or design.

- Maxim 5: The greatest cost of ownership is incurred during the maintenance of a system, after it has been developed and put into initial production.

  It has been estimated that 60% of the cost of ownership of software is incurred after a system has gone into production. Cost of ownership represents a significant risk to any software endeavor and should be considered when choosing an implementation strategy.

- Maxim 6: Long procedures are bad. Short procedures are good.

  (This maxim focuses on procedures—the first five maxims were related to software in general.) Long procedures don't take into account limited short-term memory capacity, are likely to be significantly more difficult than short procedures, and are less likely to be reused.

The high incidence of failure in our industry is evidence that the way in which developers as a group are currently building software has shortcomings. Further, it seems to be apparent that we have discovered better ways of building software but haven't widely adopted many of them. The following bulleted list describes best practices to implement Maxim 6.

- Provide procedure names using whole words (or at a minimum, standardized abbreviations), combining a noun and verb to indicate the behavior of the procedure and what the procedure acts on.

- Keep procedures short. A predominant number of procedures should be less than five lines of code. If procedures are long, they are less likely to be reusable and more likely to be difficult to understand. (Use the refactoring extract method described in Chapter 8.)

- Keep parameter lists short. A long parameter list may indicate the absence of a key element in the problem domain. That is, a class is probably missing in the solution domain.

- Limit the use of temporary variables. Temporary variables make procedures longer and add to the clutter and confusion. Use the refactoring "Replace Temp with Query" introduced in Chapter 3. Optimizing compilers may place simple functions inline, but bear in mind that complexity costs more than the overhead of a function call.

- Declare variables, if needed, immediately before first use, limiting the number of explanatory comments.

- Use access specifiers to promote encapsulating implementation details, limiting the number of methods a consumer of classes has to consider at any point during development. (Refer to Chapter 7 for more on encapsulation.)

Employing the best practices described in this list will help keep you out of trouble at the procedural level. There are additional strategies to address other problems related to developing complex systems, which will be introduced in later chapters as appropriate.

Innovations in Programming

Apparently the term *best practices* wasn't catchy enough. Writers like Grady Booch were talking about best practices as early as the 1990s (Booch, 1994). Recently Kent Beck's Extreme Programming (XP) and William Opdike's Refactoring—which are catchier—are gaining a following. Specifically, refactoring, an aspect of XP, describes programming best practices in the context of all code. Instead of prescribing the things you should do to proactively prevent code from becoming obtuse, refactoring describes curatives that can be employed in a systematic manner to recondition code into a condition closer to an ideal. Possibly the best benefit of refactoring is that it introduces a forum in which code quality can be discussed and taught in a constructive and consistent manner.

As mentioned in the introduction, refactorings are introduced in this book where appropriate.

Writing Functions

All of the guidelines for writing good subroutines apply to functions. The only difference between a function and a subroutine is that a function is designed to return a value. VB6 return values were assigned to the function name. In Visual Basic .NET, the `Return` statement is used to return the value from a function. The basic syntax of a function is

```
Function Name() As DataType
   Return Value
End Function
```

For example, a function that returns an integer would be implemented as follows:

```
Function GetInteger() As Integer
  Return 1
End Function
```

> **Note**
>
> The precedence for introducing the Return statement is that it is close to the
> actual Ret instruction found at the machine-language level, and other lan-
> guages have employed a Return statement (or similar construct) successfully
> for years.

Use functions when you need to return a value, but in general avoid using functions simply to return an error code. Error codes are used much less frequently since the adoption
of exception handlers. Where you would have employed a function with a return error
code in VB6, use a subroutine and throw an exception in VB .NET.

Using the Return Statement

To demonstrate the Return statement, Listing 5.1 defines a recursive factorial algorithm.
Calculating *N*-factorial means returning the multiplicative value of all the digits from 1
to *N*. For example, 5 factorial (written in mathematics as 5!) is the value of 1 * 2 * 3 * 4
* 5, or 120.

LISTING 5.1   Calculating *N*-factorial using the Return statement

```
 1: Public Class Form1
 2:     Inherits System.Windows.Forms.Form
 3:
 4: [ Windows Form Designer generated code ]
 5:
 6:     Public Sub Check(ByVal Value As Long)
 7:         If (Value > 0) Then Exit Sub
 8:         Const Msg = "Factorial value must be greater than 0"
 9:         Throw New Exception(Msg)
10:     End Sub
11:
12:     Public Function Factorial(ByVal Value As Long) As Long
13:         Debug.Assert(Value > 0)
14:         Check(Value)
15:
16:         If (Value > 1) Then
17:             Return Value * Factorial(Value - 1)
```

LISTING 5.1   continued

```
18:          Else
19:              Return Value
20:          End If
21:
22:      End Function
23:
24:      Private Sub Button1_Click(ByVal sender As System.Object, _
25:          ByVal e As System.EventArgs) Handles Button1.Click
26:
27:          TextBox1.Text = Factorial(CLng(TextBox1.Text))
28:
29:      End Sub
30: End Class
```

Listing 5.1 defines a recursive `Factorial` function that calls itself when needed to aid in solving *N*-factorial. (Refer to the section "Working with Recursion" for more about recursive algorithms.) Lines 13 and 14 combine an `Assert` with a `Check` subroutine. The `Assert` is used to alert the developer to problems with the algorithm. In this instance, the assertion will let the programmer know if a consumer of the `Factorial` class is passing bad data. When you build the release version, all `Assert` statements are disabled. Assertions are written for the benefit of the developer. In addition to an assertion, you usually need to write runtime error-checking code. The `Check` method plays the role of runtime error handler.

> **Note**
>
> Line 13 uses an assertion to ensure that callers are passing values greater than 0 to the `Factorial` function. Using assertions to encourage callers to pass appropriate values to procedures is referred to as a *contract program*. The test value of the `Assert` method constitutes the contract. In Listing 5.1, the contract is `Value > 0`.
>
> Contract programming is an excellent way to ensure that consumers use methods in ways consistent with the needs of the algorithm.

The `Check` subroutine doesn't return an error code. Instead it throws an exception—line 9—if the value passed to the `Factorial` function is less than 1. Notice on the other hand that `Button1_Click` doesn't throw an exception when converting the value of `TextBox1` to a Long. If `CLng(TextBox1.Text)` fails, an `InvalidCastException` is thrown. The default behavior—raising an `InvalidCastException` (see Figure 5.1)—is the behavior we want, so no pre-type checking is necessary.

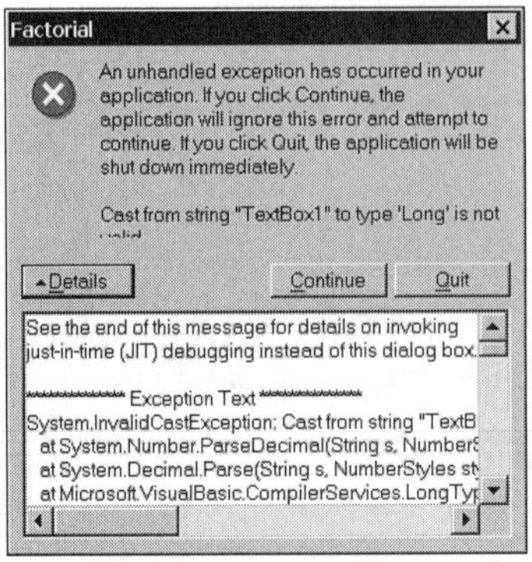

FIGURE 5.1

InvalidCast Exception can be raised when we try to convert from one data type to another as shown (running the executable outside of the IDE).

The recursive Factorial **function returns** Value **if** Value **is equal to 1. If** Value **is greater than 1, the current** Value **is multiplied by** Factorial(Value-1)**.**

The recursive Factorial function returns Value if Value is equal to 1. If Value is greater than 1, the current Value is multiplied by Factorial(Value-1). Figure 5.2 shows the stack frame when 5 is passed to the Factorial procedure. The stack shows successive calls to Factorial with the value of the parameter being decreased by one each time Factorial is called.

FIGURE 5.2

Stack memory showing recursive calls to the Factorial *function.*

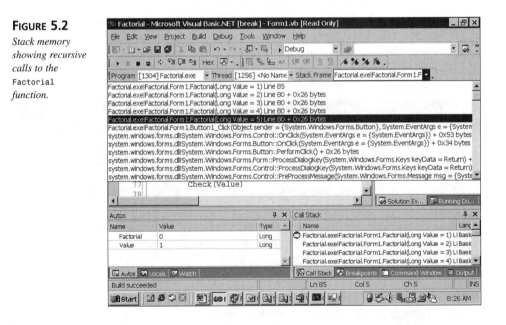

Throw an Exception Instead of Returning an Error

We could have returned a Boolean value in the Check subroutine. For example, Check could have been implemented as a function returning a Boolean as the result of Return

`Value < 1`. However, this would require every user to check the return value and implement a response to the return value. Unfortunately, programmers can and sometimes do ignore return error codes or Booleans.

Unlike error codes, exceptions can't be ignored, but the exception only needs to be checked when an error condition actually exists. Chapter 3 covers the fundamentals of exceptions. Line 9 demonstrates how we can throw an exception to indicate an error state in our code. As far as the `Check` subroutine is concerned, we are defining what constitutes an error, although if the code itself will cause an exception, we need do nothing.

Defining Procedure Arguments

Subroutines and functions generally need additional information to perform their roles correctly. However, passing too many arguments is considered bad form. Reducing the number of arguments can be accomplished by introducing a parameter object; refer to the section "Refactoring: Introduce Parameter Object" for an explanation of this refactoring.

You are trying to achieve multiple objectives when defining procedure arguments:

- The specifier you use should constrain the argument in a manner appropriate for its intended use. For example, immutable arguments should be passed by value with `ByVal`.

- The names of arguments should use whole words or standard abbreviations. Arguments are generally nouns representing data.

- The data type of an argument should constrain the possible values, such that inappropriate values for arguments are difficult to pass. Simply put, argument types should be as specific as possible. For example, if a limited range of integral values is appropriate, consider using an enumerated type to ensure data-type appropriate values.

- The number of arguments generally should be less than three. (Although this is a general guideline, you might want to consider further refinement of the solution if you have long parameter lists.)

The subsections that follow demonstrate how to use various argument specifiers to convey more meaning about your arguments and ensure their proper use.

Default Parameter Passing

Default parameter passing has changed in Visual Basic .NET. If you didn't use a parameter specifier in VB6, by default parameters were passed `ByRef`. Visual Basic .NET passes

parameters `ByVal` by default. A good programming practice is to be verbose; in other words, to explicitly indicate the intent of the code by typing the parameter specifier.

Passing Arguments `ByVal`

Changes to parameters passed by value using the `ByVal` specifier aren't reflected in the calling subprogram. When you want to ensure that a procedure doesn't change the value of the parameter, pass the parameter `ByVal`.

From the caller's perspective, the value pass is constant. The called subprogram can modify the value, but the modification is temporary to the called subprogram. Listing 5.2 demonstrates `ByVal` parameters.

LISTING 5.2 Changes to arguments passed `ByVal` aren't reflected in the calling subprogram

```
 1: Private Sub Increment(ByVal Value As Long)
 2:    Value += 1
 3: End Sub
 4:
 5: Private Sub Button1_Click(ByVal sender As System.Object, _
 6:    ByVal e As System.EventArgs) Handles Button1.Click
 7:
 8:    Dim Val As Long
 9:    Val = CLng(TextBox1.Text)
10:    Increment(Val)
11:    TextBox1.Text = CStr(Val)
12: End Sub
```

The example passes a long integer to `Increment`. `Increment` adds 1 to the `Value`. If you type 5 in TextBox1, `Value` will be incremented to 6 after line 2 runs, but when the procedure returns, the value of `Val` is still 5.

Keep in mind that assignments to aggregate types, like classes and structures, passed by value can be assigned to new instances of that type but the caller will still refer to the original object. However, you can change the value reference type members passed `ByVal` and those changes are reflected in the calling program. Changes to aggregate value types passed by value aren't reflected in the calling subprogram. A structure is an example of a value type, and a class is an example of a reference type. (The upcoming section "Value Types Versus Reference Types" provides more information.)

Passing Arguments `ByRef`

If you have a subroutine that needs to change multiple values, you can pass these arguments `ByRef`. The `ByRef` specifier indicates to the caller that arguments will be changed by the called subprogram.

To make the example in Listing 5.2 work as you might expect—Increment changes the value of the argument on behalf of the caller—modify the declaration of Increment, swapping ByVal for ByRef:

```
Private Sub Increment(ByRef Value As Long)
```

With this single revision, let's repeat the example given earlier. Call Increment with the value 5 and Val is incremented to 6. The incremented value is reflected in the calling subprogram and TextBox1 is updated to contain the new value.

When you pass a reference type ByRef, what you are indicating to a reader is that the object referred to by the argument may change and refer to a completely new object. Pass a reference type ByVal and you may modify the properties of the reference type. Pass a reference type ByRef and you may modify the actual object referred to.

Value Types Versus Reference Types

Memory is assigned to variables in two intrinsic ways: value types and reference types. *Value types* are variables that are created in stack memory, and *reference types* are variables that are created in heap memory.

Reference types can be assigned to the equivalent of a null value, which is the value Nothing. When you assign variables to reference types, you are getting a copy of the reference to the data. When you assign a variable to the value of a value type, you get a copy of the data. When a value type is destroyed, the data is destroyed with the variable. When a reference type is destroyed, the reference is destroyed, but the object referred to may still exist because other objects may refer to the actual data.

A class is an example of reference type and a structure is an example of value type. Hence, when you pass a structure ByVal, you are essentially assigning the structure to a variable and you get a copy. Consequently, any changes made to the ByVal Structure argument are reflected in the copy only, and the calling subprogram doesn't get the modified values. When you pass an instance of a class, you are passing a reference. Because both variables—the one in the calling subprogram and the argument—refer to the same physical object, changes to that object in the called subprogram are reflected in the caller.

What does ByVal mean where reference objects are concerned? ByVal means that you can't assign a new object to the argument and have the caller get the reference to the new object, but you can modify the object because you have a reference to the same object as the caller.

5

SUBROUTINES,
FUNCTIONS, AND
STRUCTURES

The following table shows the breakdown of components into reference types and value types.

Reference Types	Value Types
Classes	Enumerations
Arrays	Structures
Delegates	Primitive types
Interfaces	
Modules	

Listing 5.3 demonstrates the difference between value types and reference types.

LISTING 5.3 Changes to members of reference types are reflected in calling programs even when the reference types are passed ByVal, as demonstrated

```
 1: Public Class Form1
 2:     Inherits System.Windows.Forms.Form
 3:
 4: [ Windows Form Designer generated code ]
 5:
 6:     Private Sub Increment(ByRef Value As Long)[...]
 7:
 8:     Private Sub ModifyData(ByVal Arg As Data)
 9:       Arg.Str = "Modified"
10:     End Sub
11:
12:     Private Sub ModifyClass(ByVal Arg As ClassData)
13:       Arg.Str = "Modified"
14:     End Sub
15:
16:     Private Sub Button1_Click(ByVal sender As System.Object, _[...]
17:
18:     Private Sub Button2_Click(ByVal sender As System.Object, _
19:       ByVal e As System.EventArgs) Handles Button2.Click
20:
21:       Dim C As New ClassData()
22:       C.Str = Button2.Text
23:       ModifyClass(c)
24:       Button2.Text = C.Str
25:
26:       Dim D As Data
27:       D.Str = TextBox1.Text
28:       ModifyData(d)
29:       TextBox1.Text = D.Str
30:     End Sub
```

LISTING 5.3   continued

```
31:
32: End Class
33:
34: Public Structure Data
35:    Public Str As String
36: End Structure
37:
38: Public Class ClassData
39:    Public Str As String
40: End Class
```

Listing 5.3 defines the value type, Data, on line 34 and the reference type, ClassData, on line 38. When Button2_Click is called, an instance of ClassData, C, is created and passed ByVal to ModifyClass on line 23. When line 24 is run, C.Str now contains the value assigned to it on line 13. Comparing C on line 21 with Arg on line 12 using the test C Is Arg yields True whether the test is performed before or after the assignment to Arg. The keyword Is tests reference equality, and both C and Arg refer to the same object.

You can't test two value types with Is, but you can use the Equals method. Equals for structures performs memberwise comparisons. Arg.Equals would be True before the assignment to Arg on line 9 and False after the assignment. This is because the two objects refer to different memory locations and the value of Arg isn't the same as the value of D.

Reference types refer to the same memory location when reference assignment is performed, and value types refer to separate memory addresses after assignment. Figure 5.3 shows the different views of memory after assignment of two value types versus two reference types.

FIGURE 5.3

Comparing value type assignment to reference type assignment.

Value Type memory
after assignment B = A

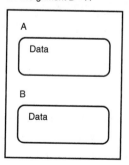

Reference Type memory
after assignment B = A

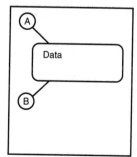

Although you can initialize variables of value types with the New keyword, doing so doesn't make them reference types. A reference type without the New keyword refers to Nothing. The only valid operation on such a reference type is assignment or an operation involving a Shared member.

Using Optional Parameters

When you use the Optional specifier, you are indicating that a parameter doesn't need to have an argument supplied for it. The Optional parameter must include a default value that will be used if the procedure consumer doesn't supply an argument for the Optional parameter.

Optional parameters must be the last parameters in the parameter list. If a procedure has optional parameters, you can indicate that you are skipping a parameter by placing a comma in the location where an argument and comma would normally go. Listing 5.4 demonstrates the syntax for an optional parameter.

> **Tip**
>
> When you are reading the help documentation, optional parameters are usually indicated by the parameter name being displayed in square brackets, as in Foo([*arg1*]).

LISTING 5.4 An optional parameter

```
 1: Private Sub HasOptionalParam(Optional ByVal Str _
 2:     As String = "Hello World!")
 3:     MsgBox(Str)
 4: End Sub
 5:
 6: Private Sub Button3_Click(ByVal sender As System.Object, _
 7:     ByVal e As System.EventArgs) Handles Button3.Click
 8:
 9:     HasOptionalParam()
10:     HasOptionalParam("New Value")
11:
12: End Sub
```

When you begin typing HasOptionalParam on line 9, IntelliSense shows the signature as HasOptionalParam([Str As String = "Hello World!"]). The square brackets around the Str parameter indicate that Str is Optional. If you do not supply an argument, as demonstrated on line 9, Str is given the value "Hello World!". When HasOptionalParam is called on line 10, Str is given the value "New Value".

What is the benefit of optional parameters? Optional parameters are a form of method overloading, explained further in the following section.

Overloading and Optional Arguments

Visual Basic .NET supports overloading procedures and property methods. To *overload* simply means to define more than one procedure with the same name but with differing parameter lists. Chapter 7 goes into overloading in more detail. The reasons for overloading simply have to do with minimizing the number of names and using identical names for semantically similar operations with different implementations.

Optional arguments are similar to overloading because you can invoke a procedure in different ways, with or without the optional parameters. Overloaded methods actually have different parameter lists. When you call an overloaded procedure, you are calling one of various different procedures based on the arguments you pass during the procedure invocation. When you call a procedure with optional parameters, you are always calling the same procedure, but the parameter list can be different during different invocations.

The rule for determining whether you need an optional parameter versus an overloaded procedure is straightforward. If the behavior is always the same—that is, the code is always the same—and much of the time you will be passing the same value, you need an optional parameter. If the implementation of the behavior changes based on the argument passed, you need an overloaded procedure. Applying this logic to the Increment procedure from Listing 5.2, we can decide that most of the time we want to increment a value by 1, but sometimes we want to increment by some other value. Because we are still talking about addition here, we need an optional parameter with a default value of 1. Listing 5.5 demonstrates the revised Increment procedure.

LISTING 5.5 Using optional parameters to create an overloaded invocation list

```
1: Private Sub Increment(ByRef Value As Long, _
2:     Optional ByVal Inc As Long = 1)
3:     Value += Inc
4: End Sub
```

Listing 5.5 represents the best implementation of the Increment procedure. The modified value is returned to the caller and most of the time we will increment by 1, but if we need to, we can pass an alternate increment value as the argument for Inc.

Passing Arguments by Name

Visual Basic .NET supports passing arguments by name. To pass an argument by name, use the *name:=value* syntax for identifying and supplying a named argument. You can change the order of named arguments, although it may add to confusion to do so, but you must supply all non-optional arguments when using named arguments. The following method demonstrates an arbitrary procedure and a statement passing arguments by name. (Note the reverse order of the arguments.)

```
Public Sub NamedArguments(ByVal I As Integer, ByVal S As String)

    MsgBox(String.Format("S={0} and I={1}", S, I), _
      MsgBoxStyle.Information, "Named Arguments")

  End Sub

NamedArguments(S:=5, I:=10)
```

The most useful application of named parameters is to use the pass-by-name technique to supply arguments to optional parameters as opposed to comma counting when you skip optional parameters.

Passing Optional Arguments by Name

As an alternative to using a comma to skip optional parameters, you pass optional arguments by name. Passing arguments by name allows you to pass parameters in any order, too. Listing 5.6 demonstrates a subroutine with a couple of optional parameters and demonstrates examples of passing parameters using space-comma to skip parameters and using the by-name convention as a convenient alternative.

LISTING 5.6   An example of optional parameters and passing arguments by name

```
 1: Public Sub TakesSeveralParams(Optional ByVal Val As Integer = 5, _
 2:     Optional ByVal Str As String = "String Data", _
 3:     Optional ByVal ADate As Date = #12:00:00 AM#)
 4:
 5:     Debug.WriteLine(Val)
 6:     Debug.WriteLine(Str)
 7:     Debug.WriteLine(ADate)
 8: End Sub
 9:
10: Private Sub Button4_Click(ByVal sender As System.Object, _
11:   ByVal e As System.EventArgs) Handles Button4.Click
12:
13:     TakesSeveralParams()
14:     TakesSeveralParams(10, , Today)
15:     TakesSeveralParams(, "Text", )
```

LISTING 5.6 continued

```
16:     TakesSeveralParams(Val:=-3, ADate:=Now)
17:     TakesSeveralParams(ADate:=Today, Str:="Some More Text")
18:
19: End Sub
```

The output from Listing 5.6 is shown in Figure 5.4. Each set of three lines represents one call to `TakesSeveralParams`.

FIGURE 5.4

The output from Listing 5.6 shown in the Output window.

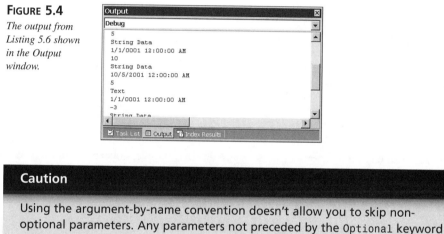

> **Caution**
>
> Using the argument-by-name convention doesn't allow you to skip non-optional parameters. Any parameters not preceded by the `Optional` keyword must have an argument supplied by the consumer.

Defining `ParamArray` Arguments

The equivalent of a parameter array has been around for a long time. Languages such as C and C++ have used parameter arrays to define standard input and output and formatting functions for 20 or so years.

Visual Basic .NET supports the `ParamArray` specifier. Preceding a parameter by the `ParamArray` keyword indicates to consumers that they may pass a varying number of arguments of the type specified in the `ParamArray` clause. Listing 5.7 demonstrates the syntax for defining a `ParamArray` parameter and passing and managing arguments passed to a `ParamArray`.

LISTING 5.7 Using `ParamArray` arguments

```
1: Private Sub ParamArrayDemo(ByVal ParamArray Values() As String)
2:     Dim Enumerator As IEnumerator = Values.GetEnumerator
3:
```

LISTING 5.7   continued

```
 4:     Dim Output As String
 5:     While (Enumerator.MoveNext)
 6:        Output = Output & Enumerator.Current & vbCrLf
 7:     End While
 8:
 9:     MessageBox.Show(Output, "Formatted Output", _
10:        MessageBoxButtons.OK, MessageBoxIcon.Information, _
11:        MessageBoxDefaultButton.Button1, _
12:        MessageBoxOptions.DefaultDesktopOnly)
13: End Sub
14:
15: Private Sub Button1_Click(ByVal sender As System.Object, _
16:     ByVal e As System.EventArgs) Handles Button1.Click
17:
18:     ParamArrayDemo("ParamArrayDemo.Exe", _
19:        "Copyright  2001. All Rights Reserved.", _
20:        "Written by Paul Kimmel. pkimmel@softconcepts.com")
21:
22: End Sub
```

ParamArrayDemo takes a ParamArray of Strings. In the example, copyright information is passed to the ParamArrayDemo subroutine and formatted by tacking on a carriage-return, line-feed pair. The carriage return and line feed are added on line 6 using the vbCrLf constant. Notice that an Enumerator was used to iterate over the parameter data and the MessageBox.Show method was used to display the message box. MsgBox is maintained for backward compatibility with VB6, but the CLR implements the MessageBox class in the System.Windows.Forms namespace.

ParamArrays are treated like an infinitely overloaded procedure taking zero, one, two, and so on, arguments of the same type. All arguments of the ParamArray must be of the same type. What this means in a technical sense is that if you define a ParamArray of a very generic type, like Object, you can pass an array of heterogeneous objects.

Reducing the Number of Parameters

Occasionally you will be coding and find out that you have a procedure that needs a huge number of parameters. Generally, this may imply that a useful entity in the problem domain doesn't have an implemented equivalent in the solution domain. In simpler terms, something that is part of the problem the code is designed to solve isn't defined as a class in the code.

You can simplify commonly grouped parameters or long parameter lists by moving the method to the class that contains most of the parameters as fields or by applying the

Refactoring "Introduce Parameter Object." A *parameter class* is a class whose members are fields and properties that are passed as arguments to a procedure. Consider the subroutine in Listing 5.8 that takes a value and determines whether the value is between the low and high range values.

LISTING 5.8   Determines whether the target value is between a low and high value, inclusively

```
 1: Function WithinRange(ByVal Target As Integer, ByVal Low As Integer, _
 2:   ByVal High As Integer) As Boolean
 3:     Return (Low <= Target) And (Target <= High)
 4: End Function
 5:
 6: Private Sub Button1_Click(ByVal sender As System.Object, _
 7:     ByVal e As System.EventArgs) Handles Button1.Click
 8:
 9:     MsgBox("0 <= " & TextBox1.Text & " <= 100 is " & _
10:       WithinRange(TextBox1.Text, 0, 100))
11:
12: End Sub
```

The function `WithinRange` takes a target value and low and high range values, returning True if `Target` is greater than or equal to `Low` and is also less than or equal to `High`. These kinds of functions often result in long parameter lists. By applying "Introduce Parameter Object," we can simplify the parameter list and get more mileage out of our code.

Refactoring: Introduce Parameter Object

The motivation for "Introduce Parameter Object" is to shorten complicated, long parameter lists—often you get a derived benefit from consolidating code. Because our minds are better at working with fewer elements of information, by consolidating several pieces of data into higher levels of abstraction, we are able to make further refinements.

The basic mechanics of "Introduce Parameter Object," as applied to our example in Listing 5.8, are as follows:

1. Define a new class whose members are the parameters that you want to replace.
2. Replace the parameters with an instance of the new class.
3. Compile and test.

Keep in mind that an objective when refactoring is to support the existing behavior in a new way. In Listing 5.8, we defined low and high integer values as our range and a target was the comparison value. What the parameters are used for provides us with a clue for a

good name. Low and High represent a range, so we will name our new class `Range`. Listing 5.9 shows the new `Range` class.

LISTING 5.9 The new class used to implement our parameter object

```
 1: Public Class Range
 2:    Private FLow, FHigh As Integer
 3:
 4:    Public Property Low() As Integer
 5:      Get
 6:        Return FLow
 7:      End Get
 8:      Set(ByVal Value As Integer)
 9:        FLow = Value
10:      End Set
11:    End Property
12:
13:    Public Property High() As Integer
14:      Get
15:        Return FHigh
16:      End Get
17:      Set(ByVal Value As Integer)
18:        FHigh = Value
19:      End Set
20:    End Property
21:
22:    Public Sub New(ByVal ALow As Integer, ByVal AHigh As Integer)
23:      FLow = ALow
24:      FHigh = AHigh
25:    End Sub
26: End Class
```

If classes are completely foreign to you, Chapter 7 will fill in the blanks nicely. Without too much explanation, `Range` defines a class that has two fields, `FLow` and `FHigh`. The fields are accessed through the properties `Low` and `High`. The `Sub New` defines a parameterized constructor that allows us to initialize the low and high values when the object is created. Now we can implement `WithinRange` using an instance of the `Range` class, as shown in Listing 5.10.

LISTING 5.10 Using the `Range` parameter object

```
1: Function WithinRange2(ByVal Target As Integer, ByVal ARange As Range)
2:    Return (ARange.Low <= Target) And (Target<= ARange.High)
3: End Function
4:
5: Private Sub Button1_Click(ByVal sender As System.Object, _
6:    ByVal e As System.EventArgs) Handles Button1.Click
```

LISTING 5.10   continued

```
 7:
 8:    MsgBox("0 <= " & TextBox1.Text & " <= 100 is " & _
 9:       WithinRange2(TextBox1.Text, New Range(0, 100)))
10:
11: End Sub
```

Notice that WithinRange2 takes the target value and an instance of the new Range class defined in Listing 5.9. A Range object is created as it is passed to the new implementation, WithinRange2, on line 9. We have satisfied the first motivation for this refactoring; we have shortened the parameter list.

The second motivation is that our new entity may suggest further refinements. In fact, if you think about it, you could easily infer that a range should know whether a value is within the Low and High bounds, suggesting that WithinRange should be a method of Range. Listing 5.11 demonstrates the refinement and the result on the code.

LISTING 5.11   Range revised to include the WithinRange method.

```
 1: Public Class Range
 2:    Private FLow, FHigh As Integer
 3:
 4:    Public Property Low() As Integer
 5:       Get
 6:          Return FLow
 7:       End Get
 8:       Set(ByVal Value As Integer)
 9:          FLow = Value
10:       End Set
11:    End Property
12:
13:    Public Property High() As Integer
14:       Get
15:          Return FHigh
16:       End Get
17:       Set(ByVal Value As Integer)
18:          FHigh = Value
19:       End Set
20:    End Property
21:
22:    Public Sub New(ByVal ALow As Integer, ByVal AHigh As Integer)
23:       FLow = ALow
24:       FHigh = AHigh
25:    End Sub
26:
27:    Public Function WithinRange(ByVal Target As Integer) As Boolean
28:       Return Low <= Target <= High
```

LISTING 5.11   continued

```
29:    End Function
30:
31: End Class
```

The only revision to the class Range is the addition of the WithinRange method. Notice that WithinRange now only has one parameter, Target. This is the idea behind the notion that object-oriented applications have shorter methods and fewer parameters. As demonstrated in the Range class, the parameter list of WithinRange was shortened by two-thirds. The revision had the following impact on the event handler that tests the Range class:

```
Private Sub Button1_Click(ByVal sender As System.Object, _
   ByVal e As System.EventArgs) Handles Button1.Click

   Dim ARange As New Range(0, 100)

   MsgBox("0 <= " & TextBox1.Text & " <= 100 is " & _
     ARange.WithinRange(TextBox1.Text))
End Sub
```

Notice that we only have to pass the target value to the WithinRange method.

A reasonable person might pause at this point and say, "Hey, I thought objects were supposed to make applications shorter?" This very short example certainly doesn't illustrate a shortening of the implementation. In fact, the listing almost doubled in size. That's true. The Range class added 31 lines of code to the application. The benefit received accumulates over time. The benefits of all the revisions are as follows:

- The code is more understandable.
- The parameter list is shortened.
- We only have to write and test this code one time and then we can use it forever.
- The Range class is portable, and can be used repeatedly in other applications.

The more times we need the Range behavior, or any behavior captured in a class, the greater our leverage will be over time and the greater increase in productivity and decrease in lines of code we will achieve. Hyperproductive programmers know these things. A hyperproductive programmer knows that a little extra effort up front will yield dividends now and in the future.

Many programmers won't stop to create classes out of types as simple as a Range type. There is still a lot of cutting and pasting going on. Cutting and pasting and structured programming are some of the reasons software projects are still failing at a phenomenal rate. The faulty reasoning is that the changes individually are so trivial that they couldn't possibly matter. This faulty reasoning usually holds true in the very short term, but as development progresses, poor programming practices add to the complexity and confusion until it's too late. The code becomes unmanageable. An objective of XP and refactoring is to get code under control and keep it that way.

Using Concise Argument Types

Strongly typed languages allow you to force the compiler to do a lot of work for you. By being as explicit as possible with your argument types, the compiler can help you make sure that you are passing good data to your procedures.

How does this work? Well, replacing two random integers with a Range type makes the code more expressive and constrains the way in which the code was written and used. Suppose you have a function that takes a name, phone number, and address. By defining a function that takes these three parameters, you've created an environment where any string data would technically satisfy the arguments. But, if you wanted to convey more meaning and ensure that the data passed were more likely to be the correct values, you could define a structure containing the three elements and pass the structure to the function. The structure (or class) can contain property methods that could encourage the consumer to initialize the members with suitable data, perhaps by validating the format of the phone number or ensuring that the city, state, and zip code of the address were appropriate.

Using concise types applies to even simpler kinds of data. Suppose you have a procedure that works on a subset of possible values of a simpler type, like an Integer. By defining an enumerated type containing named values representing the suitable Integers, you could define the procedure to take an argument of the Enumerated type. Now, the enumeration helps to ensure that only suitable arguments are passed.

Many times, modeling the data correctly alleviates the need for a lot of extra validation code. Consider the code in Listings 5.14 and 5.15. The first function sets an eye color using an arbitrary integer value (perhaps representing a field in a driver's license application for the Department of Motor Vehicles). The second, more expressive, version of the function uses an enumerated type to make the code more meaningful.

LISTING 5.12 Using an arbitrary integer to represent a value

```
1: Private FEyeColorInteger As Integer
2:
3: Public Sub SetEyeColor(ByVal Color As Integer)
4:   If (Color > 0) And (Color <= 2) Then
5:     FEyeColorInteger = Color
6:   End If
7: End Sub
```

5

SUBROUTINES,
FUNCTIONS, AND
STRUCTURES

LISTING 5.13   Using an enumerated type, making the code more expressive and deliberate.

```
 1: Private FEyeColorEnum As EyeColor
 2:
 3: Public Enum EyeColor
 4:    Blue
 5:    Brown
 6:    Green
 7: End Enum
 8:
 9: Public Sub SetEyeColor2(ByVal Color As EyeColor)
10:    FEyeColorEnum = Color
11: End Sub
```

Listing 5.12 uses an integer that could have four billion possible values, but only three are valid for a certain purpose. Listing 5.13 indicates to the reader that only Blue, Brown, and Green make sense by introducing a new enumerated type named appropriately for this particular scenario and containing the appropriately named values. (See the section "Using Enumerated Types" at the end of this chapter for more on the capabilities of enumerated types.)

Working with Recursion

Recursion refers to procedures calling themselves. An example of a recursive function was introduced in Listing 5.1; the `Factorial` function was implemented as a recursive function. Each time `Factorial` was called, one step of the equation was solved.

Recursive procedures call themselves before exiting until all recursions are complete. Using recursion as shown in the `Factorial` function can be problematic because this function will be called recursively n - 1 times where n is the initial value of the `Value` parameter. If `Value` were very large in the call to `Factorial`, you could end up running out of memory before all the recursive calls to `Factorial` could be handled.

Visual Basic .NET allows you to define very large procedural variables; I was able to declare an array of one hundred million 32-bit integers on my PC with 256MB of RAM.

To compare VB6 to Visual Basic .NET stack memory, I wrote two identical programs. Both programs called a subroutine `BlowStack`, which recursed infinitely, incrementing a static counter and updating the form's `Caption` (`Text` in Visual Basic .NET) property. The VB6 application recursed about 6,000 times before running out of stack space. The Visual Basic .NET application recursed 25,000 times before going into limbo. It appears as though the VB6 application ran out of stack space, and the Visual Basic .NET application just consumed all available memory. Keep in mind, though, that 25,000 anything isn't very much in a computer.

The integrated help doesn't cover the topic of stack memory in any detail, and unlike other languages, the amount of memory allocated to the stack isn't user-configurable. It appears as though Visual Basic .NET just uses whatever memory is available.

Defining Recursive Procedures

Another example of recursive procedures is given in the "Quick Sort" section in Chapter 9.

The number of times a quick sort will recur is relatively low. Thus the quick sort works very well using recursion and recursion helps simplify the implementation of the quick sort.

Removing Recursion

Recursive algorithms use the procedure as a looping mechanism. Think of the procedure as the loop control mechanism and the implementation of the procedure as the code in the loop. Generally, then, to remove recursion, you replace the call to the recursive procedure with a loop.

Applying this technique to the recursive factorial algorithm, Listing 5.14 demonstrates the Factorial function as a non-recursive function.

LISTING 5.14   Calculating *N*-Factorial non-recursively

```
 1: Public Function Factorial2(ByVal Value As Long) As Long
 2:    Debug.Assert(Value > 0)
 3:    Check(Value)
 4:    Dim I As Long
 5:    Dim Sum As Long = 1
 6:
 7:    For I = Value To 2 Step -1
 8:      Sum *= I
 9:    Next
10:
11:    Return Sum
12: End Function
```

Listing 5.1 called Factorial(Value-1) as long as Value was greater than 1. In Listing 5.14, the upper bound of the For loop represents the Value part of the call to the recursive Factorial algorithm and Step -1 represents subtracting 1 from Value for each recursive call. Looping down to 2 replaces the If (Value > 1) Then test in Listing 5.1.

(The Check subroutine implementation is shown in Listing 5.1.) The loop also could have been implemented using a While End While statement:

```
While (Value > 1)
  Sum *= Value
  Value -= 1
End While
```

Here we see the loop control as Value > 1, mirroring line 16 of Listing 5.1 exactly, and the decrement of Value as is done in the recursive call on line 17 of Listing 5.1.

Generally, recursion can be removed by using the recursive test and terminate condition as the bounding mechanism for a loop. The test and terminate condition of the recursive factorial algorithm in Listing 5.1 is Value > 1. To create the termination circumstance, Value is decremented after each pass of the recursive call or the loop.

> **Tip**
>
> Recursive algorithms are sometimes easier to implement and often more efficient, but replacing recursive algorithms with loops usually results in more readable code.

Defining Structures

Chapter 2 introduced the structure as the replacement for the Type construct. Types only supported the aggregation of data; the Structure construct is more closely related to the class construct than the Type construct.

Structures support fields, properties, events, and methods. This section will demonstrate how to define structures and how to implement each of the new capabilities of structures. The last subsection discusses features that are not supported in Structure constructs, which comprise the differences between structures and classes.

Use the Structure construct where you would have used a Type in VB6, keeping in mind all the additional capabilities afforded by the new construct.

Defining Fields and Properties

Fields are data members of aggregate types. Generally fields are Private members representing the underlying value of a property. Properties are generally used to represent the public means of referencing a field.

The distinction between field and property exists because it was decided years ago that the most reliable way to constrain data use was to access data through methods. Properties are really methods that look like data.

You will learn more about the `Private` and `Public` keywords in Chapter 7. For now, suffice to say that members of a structure (or class) can have an access specifier, including `Private` or `Public`, and these keywords constrain how consumers can use these members, or if consumers can even use members.

Private members can't be used by consumers of a structure, but public members can be. Listing 5.15 demonstrates defining a private field in a structure and allowing access to that field using a public property.

LISTING 5.15 Private fields and public properties

```
 1: Public Structure Description
 2:
 3:    Private FEyeColor As EyeColor
 4:
 5:    Public Property EyeColor() As EyeColor
 6:       Get
 7:          Return FEyeColor
 8:       End Get
 9:
10:       Set(ByVal Value As EyeColor)
11:          FEyeColor = Value
12:       End Set
13:    End Property
14:
15: End Structure
```

Line 3 defines the field `FEyeColor`. The F-prefix identifies the name as a field, and more importantly, dropping the F yields a perfect name for the associated property, `EyeColor`. This pairing of fields and properties makes it very easy and convenient to choose field and property names and keep the associations simple. This convention allows us to program quickly and concisely.

Lines 5 through 13 demonstrate the basic syntax of a property statement. Notice that a single property statement, containing a getter and setter, is distinct from the two individual property statements employed in VB6. Read Chapter 7 for complete coverage of the property idiom.

Listing 5.15 demonstrates a basic use of fields and properties. Although `EyeColor` can be used just like data, the `Get` and `Set` blocks work just like procedures—you can write any validation code (or other code) that helps you constrain the way the data is used.

Adding Structure Methods

The Structure construct supports methods too. Thus you can add functions and subroutines to your structures, associating behaviors with your aggregate, structure data types.

Suppose we add two more fields and their associated properties to our Description to support storing a first and last name with the description. We might want to implement a function to return a formatted full name rather than requiring the user to enter a full name. Also, we decide that we might want the full name displayed in first-name-first or first-name-last order. Listing 5.16 demonstrates one complete possible revision, adding the fields, properties, and new method.

LISTING 5.16   Adding methods to structures

```
 1: Public Structure Description
 2:
 3:    Private FEyeColor As EyeColor
 4:    Private FFirstName, FLastName As String
 5:
 6:    Public Property EyeColor() As EyeColor
 7:      Get
 8:        Return FEyeColor
 9:      End Get
10:
11:      Set(ByVal Value As EyeColor)
12:        FEyeColor = Value
13:      End Set
14:    End Property
15:
16:    Public Property FirstName() As String
17:      Get
18:        Return FFirstName
19:      End Get
20:      Set(ByVal Value As String)
21:        FFirstName = Value
22:      End Set
23:    End Property
24:
25:    Public Property LastName() As String
26:      Get
27:        Return FLastName
28:      End Get
29:      Set(ByVal Value As String)
30:        FLastName = Value
31:      End Set
32:    End Property
33:
34:    Private Function FirstNameOrder() As String
```

LISTING 5.16   continued

```
35:      Return FirstName & " " & LastName
36:    End Function
37:
38:    Private Function LastNameOrder() As String
39:      Return LastName & ", " & FirstName
40:    End Function
41:
42:    Public Function FullName(Optional ByVal UseFirstNameOrder _
43:      As Boolean = True) As String
44:      If (UseFirstNameOrder) Then
45:        Return FirstNameOrder()
46:      Else
47:        Return LastNameOrder()
48:      End If
49:    End Function
50:
51: End Structure
```

The revisions include the fields FFirstName and FLastName on line 4, the FirstName
and LastName properties on lines 16 to 32, and the three methods, FirstNameOrder,
LastNameOrder, and FullName from lines 34 through 49. The public method is a
function that returns the formatted full name based on the Optional parameter
UseFirstNameOrder. FirstNameOrder and LastNameOrder are Private methods because
they present partial implementation of the function FullName. Making FirstNameOrder
and LastNameOrder private simply keeps consumers from having to worry about two
methods. All a consumer needs to worry about is the FullName method and the order
desired. This constitutes a subjective implementation choice; a reasonable person could
have made FirstNameOrder and LastNameOrder public and dispensed with the FullName
method altogether. Generally, I try to keep public methods to a minimum, but that is a
preference rather than a rule.

As you can see from Listing 5.16, structures can become quite complex.

Implementing Constructors

As you learned in Chapter 2, all structures are System.ValueType entities. All value
types implicitly have a default, parameterless constructor.

Structure variables can be declared the same way as intrinsic types, like Integers, without the New keyword, or, you can declare Structures with the New keyword if you've
defined a constructor that takes parameters and want to define an instance of the structure using the parameterized constructor. Whether you use the New keyword or not when
declaring structure instances, structures are still value types as opposed to reference

types. Keep in mind that the distinction between a value type and reference type is copy-by-value versus copy-by-reference when instances are assigned, as depicted earlier in Figure 5.3.

Default Constructor

From Chapter 2, you know that a constructor is a special method responsible for initializing new instances. In Visual Basic .NET, constructors are defined as the subroutine `New()`. Constructors may or may not have parameters and can be overloaded. For example, in the following declaration, the variable *varname* represents any valid variable name and *type* represents any valid data type, including user-defined types:

```
Dim varname As New type()
```

This example explicitly invokes the `New()` constructor, although it may look as if you are calling a procedure *type()*.

You can't inherit from structures. All structures get a single default constructor—`Sub New()`—from their common ancestor `ValueType`, and you can define parameterized constructors. You can't overload the default constructor, as all `Structures` are implicitly declared with the `NotInheritable` keyword. Refer to Chapter 7 for more on classes and declaration attributes like `NotInheritable`, and refer to the section "Unsupported Structure Features" for more information on features that aren't supported when working with structures.

When you declare a structure variable, you are implicitly calling the empty constructor `Sub New()`; you can also explicitly construct a `Structure` by typing `Dim MyStructure As New StructureType()`, where `StructureType` is a user-defined structure. You must use the `New` keyword to invoke parameterized constructors.

Parameterized Constructors

Suppose we want to define a constructor for the `Description` structure that takes a first and last name. The facts that we want to initialize two fields and that they are both strings determine what the parameters for the constructor will be:

```
Public Sub New(ByVal AFirstName As String, ByVal ALastName As String)
  FFirstName = AFirstName
  FLastName = ALastName
End Sub
```

By convention, I matched the parameter names to the fields they will initialize by using the same root name with an A-prefix for the parameters and simply assigning the parameters to the associated field names.

To construct `Description` structures using the new constructor, you will have to use the

Form of the `Dim` statement that uses the `New` keyword.

> **Note**
>
> Constructor calls in Visual Basic .NET are a little confusing. The way `New` is used makes `New` look like a modifier on the type and the type actually look like the method call. For example, `New Description("Noah", "Kimmel")` looks like we are invoking a method `Description` with the modifier `New`. The C++ language treats `New` as an operator and constructors always have the same name as the class (or struct, in C++). Hence, if `Description` were defined as a type in C++, `Description` would actually be the constructor.
>
> Just keep in mind that in Visual Basic .NET, `New` is actually the constructor but the parameters are placed in parentheses after the type. Only Microsoft knows why `New` is used this way.

```
Dim MyDescription As New Description("Paul", "Kimmel")
```

The preceding statement actually calls the `New` subroutine defined at the beginning of this subsection.

Defining Structure Events

You can define events for structures, but you can't associate an event with a procedure using the `WithEvents` statement and the `Handles` clause. To define events for structures and associate them with an event handler, you need to complete several specific steps; we'll use the `Description` structure as a frame of reference to demonstrate:

1. Add an event statement to the `Description` structure. Whenever an attribute of a description changes, we will raise a `Changed` event passing the instance of the initiating structure. (Add the following statement to the definition of `Description`: `Public Event Changed(ByVal ADescription As Description)`. Because we can't subclass structures, we will use the specific type rather than the base class `Object` type for the `Changed` event.)

2. In each of the setters for `Description`, write a `RaiseEvent` statement, `RaiseEvent Changed(Me)`, passing the reference to itself. (Refer to Chapters 8 and 9 for much more information on events and delegates.)

3. In the class that will handle Changed events, define a subroutine with the same signature and, by convention, the same name as the event. (The example simply shows the FullName of the changed Description.)

```
Public Sub Changed(ByVal ADescription As Description)
  MsgBox(ADescription.FullName & " changed")
End Sub
```

4. After a Description structure is created, use the AddHandler method to associate the event handler with the event.

```
AddHandler FDescription.Changed, AddressOf Changed
```

Assuming that we used the same name of the event as the name of the handler and we have a variable FDescription defined, the preceding code is sufficient.

Listing 5.17 shows all the revisions to a data entry form and the Description structure necessary to implement and respond to Description.Changed events. Code not involved in the revision was hidden using code outlining to keep the listing from getting out of hand.

LISTING 5.17 Defining and responding to Structure events

```
 1: Public Class Form1
 2:
 3: [...]
 4:
 5:   Private FDescription As Description
 6: [...]
 7:
 8:   Private Sub Assign()[...]
 9:
10:   Private Sub Button1_Click(ByVal sender As System.Object, _ [...]
11:
12:   Private Sub InitializeEyeColors()[...]
13:
14:   Private Sub Changed(ByVal ADescription As Description)
15:     MsgBox(ADescription.FullName & " changed")
16:   End Sub
17:
18:   Private Sub Initialize()
19:     AddHandler FDescription.Changed, AddressOf Changed
20:     InitializeEyeColors()
21:   End Sub
22:
23:   Private Sub Form1_Load(ByVal sender As System.Object, _
24:     ByVal e As System.EventArgs) Handles MyBase.Load
25:
26:     Dim D As New Description()
27:     Initialize()
```

LISTING 5.17 continued

```
28:
29:    End Sub
30:
31:    Private Sub Button2_Click(ByVal sender As System.Object, _[...]
32:
33: End Class
34:
35: Public Enum EyeColor[...]
36:
37: Public Structure Description
38:
39: [...]
40:    Public Event Changed(ByVal ADescription As Description)
41:
42:    Public Property EyeColor() As EyeColor
43:       [...]
44:
45:       Set(ByVal Value As EyeColor)
46:         FEyeColor = Value
47:         RaiseEvent Changed(Me)
48:       End Set
49:    End Property
50:
51:    Public Property FirstName() As String
52:       [...]
53:
54:       Set(ByVal Value As String)
55:         FFirstName = Value
56:         RaiseEvent Changed(Me)
57:       End Set
58:    End Property
59:
60:    Public Property LastName() As String
61:       [...]
62:
63:       Set(ByVal Value As String)
64:         FLastName = Value
65:         RaiseEvent Changed(Me)
66:       End Set
67:    End Property
68:
69: [...]
70:
71: End Structure
```

You've seen a lot of this code in previous listings in this section, so those parts not related to the topic of this section were hidden with code outlining (introduced in

Chapter 1). All of the lines specifically part of the declaration, raising, or handling of the event are in boldface for your convenience.

Beginning at the top of the listing, each aspect of incorporating the Structure event is defined. Line 5 declares a Description variable named FDescription. Lines 14 through 16 define the event handler in the Form1 class using the same name as the event in the Description structure on line 40. Line 19 adds the handler Form1.Changed to the Description.Changed invocation list. Line 27 calls the Initialize method to initialize various aspects of the form. (This strategy is employed by convention.) Line 40 defines the event for the Description structure; this syntax is identical to the syntax used for event definitions in any entity. Lines 47, 56, and 65 raise the event in the setters (property Set methods) for the EyeColor, FirstName, and LastName properties, respectively.

As you can determine from Listing 5.17, defining events and event handlers for structures is identical to defining them for classes and modules. The biggest difference is that only classes support the WithEvents statement and Handles clause. Events in structures and modules are associated with handlers using the AddHandler statement.

Declaring Structure Variables

Events are value types, so they are declared like intrinsic types with the access specifier or Dim, followed by a name for the structure, the keyword As, and the structure name. As demonstrated in the previous section, you can also create an instance of a structure using the New keyword. To initialize a structure using a parameterized New constructor, you must use the New keyword. By default, the non-parameterized constructor defined in the ValueType class is invoked when you declare a structure.

ValueType is the immediate ancestor of structures. Structures aren't inheritable and you can't override the constructor defined in ValueType. More information on structure-related features that are not supported is upcoming in the "Unsupported Structure Features" section.

Information Hiding

Information hiding is an aspect of object-oriented programming. The premise is based on the idea that too much information is a bad thing when trying to solve problems. The affirmative principle is *divide et impera*, or divide and conquer.

The access specifiers Public and Private are supported for structures. Public members can be referenced by consumers; private members can only be referenced internally. (The Protected and Protected Friend access specifiers aren't supported because they relate to inheritance, which isn't supported for structures.)

Structure Arguments and Return Types

VB6 limits passing and returning structure types. You may only define structures as private members in VB6, and only pass and return structures between private members in VB6. These limitations severely inhibit the utility of UDTs in VB6.

Visual Basic .NET supports passing and returning structures in both public and private methods, and you can define nested structures (that is, types in classes) or standalone structures.

Using the Description structure introduced in Listing 5.15, the following subroutine and function are legal Visual Basic .NET code but would cause a compiler error in VB6 unless both the structure and the procedures were defined in a module or declared private in a form or class:

```
Public Structure Description[...]
Private FDescription As Description
Public Function GetDescription() As Description
  Return FDescription
End
Public Sub SetDescription(ByVal Value As Description)
  FDescription = Value
End Sub
```

The first statement represents the definition of our structure from Listing 5.15, Description. The second statement defines a variable of type Description. Both the function and subroutine are public. GetDescription returns a public structure and SetDescription accepts a public structure. The equivalent code isn't supported in VB6. Public UDTs in Visual Basic .NET make the structure much more powerful than the Type capabilities from VB6.

Unsupported Structure Features

Structures are not classes. Although the Visual Basic .NET structure is more closely related to the C++ `struct` idiom and the Visual Basic .NET class, there are some aspects of classes not supported in structures.

You may use a structure in new code for several reasons. Probably the most common example is to support legacy code, like the Windows API. However, structures aren't classes, and aside from a minor convenience in their declaration, you should consider using a class instead of a structure for new code. In fact, there is even a refactoring technique named "Replace Record with Data Class" that discusses the motivation for replacing classes with structures. The biggest reason to use structures is if some conjoined aspect of your program requires them, but in most cases new aggregate types should be defined as classes.

The following features are not supported by structures:

- Structures implicitly inherit from `System.ValueType` but can't inherit from any other type.
- Structures implicitly use the attribute `NotInheritable`; structures can't inherit from other structures.
- You can't define a parameterless constructor; you can define a parameterized constructor.
- You can't define a destructor for structures; destructors are represented by the `Dispose` method.
- Data members of structures can't have initializers, nor can they use the `New` keyword. You have to define a parameterized constructor to initialize objects or you have to initialize objects after a structure variable is declared, external to the structure.
- Members of a structure are public by default.

Structures are value types. When you assign structures, the code actually performs a memberwise copy of the members of the structure. Object assignment performs a reference assignment. Consequently, passing and returning structure variables will incur more overhead than using instances of classes.

Using Enumerated Types

Types defined using the `Enum` keyword are implicitly derived from `ValueType` just as structures are. Enumerated types provide a convenient notation for defining a list of values semantically associated to a named value. As demonstrated earlier, for example, you could use an enumeration `EyeColor` to constrain valid values for eye colors to realistic colors. In contrast, if you used the `Color` type, you might end up with indications that someone has mauve or cyan-colored eyes.

Table 5.1 lists the shared members of `System.Enum` types and provides a brief description for each. You will see these capabilities used where it's appropriate to do so, throughout this book.

TABLE 5.1   `System.Enum` Members

Member	*Description*
`Format`	Converts enumerated type to its string representation
`GetName`	Returns the string name of the constant specified
`GetNames`	Returns a string array of all the names in the enumeration
`GetUnderlyingType`	Returns the intrinsic underlying type of the enumeration
`GetValues`	Returns an array of the values of the enumeration
`IsDefined`	Returns a Boolean indicating whether the argument is a member of the enumeration

Table 5.1 introduces the public members of enumerated types, not including the members introduced from the ancestor type `Object`. The public members defined in every class—inherited from the `Object` class—were shown in Table 2.1 in Chapter 2.

Summary

Chapter 5 demonstrated revisions to functions and subroutines in Visual Basic .NET and discussed the extended utility of `Structure`, which has replaced the `Type` construct.

Functions and subroutines are called methods when they are defined as members of a class or structure. Collectively called procedures, they are the basic building blocks of all code. A complete understanding of the capabilities supported by procedures is essential for achieving the most expressive and appropriate code in every application.

5

SUBROUTINES,
FUNCTIONS, AND
STRUCTURES

Advanced Object-Oriented Programming

Reflection

An *assembly* is an application plus its self-describing information. The inclusion of self-describing information, or *metadata*, was designed to resolve the problem of "DLL Hell." "DLL Hell" is the moniker ascribed to the current versioning problems related to registering applications in the registry. Assemblies contain information about an application in addition to the Intermediate Language (IL) code that is considered to be the application. *Reflection* is the capability to dynamically discover and use information in assemblies.

Reflection allows developers to discover information about an assembly and dynamically create types and invoke capabilities on those types at runtime. Additionally, reflection allows developers to dynamically define new types at runtime.

The capability to discover information about types at runtime is not completely new. COM provided the `QueryInterface` method, which enabled developers to determine whether an object supported a specific interface. Reflection is an evolution of this capability on a larger scale. The `System.Reflection` namespace allows developers to discover information about assemblies, files, modules, methods, types, and much more. Additionally, reflection supports dynamic localization of code—the ability to modify code for a specific locale, also referred to as internationalization—plus the capability to emit code dynamically, and it directly addresses certain security issues raised by such dynamic activity.

Chapter 6 provides an overview of the `System.Reflection` namespace and explores some specific aspects of reflection in the Common Language Runtime (CLR).

Reflection Namespace

The `Reflection` namespace contains classes that support constructive access and management of assemblies. The `Assembly` class refers to an assembly, which includes the application and its metadata. There are classes representing modules, files, types, fields, global variables, attributes, parameter information, and much more.

`Reflection` is a big namespace that contains a lot of information. We will not be able to cover all of the capabilities of the `Reflection` namespace in this chapter, but it will act as a good starting point and provide you with a good foundation for further exploration of the `Reflection` capabilities.

Assemblies

Assemblies are represented in the CLR by the `Assembly` class. For practical purposes, an assembly is your application. In reality an assembly is your application and the metadata that describes the things that your application is made up of.

> **Note**
>
> *Manifest information* is information that makes an assembly self-describing. Refer to the later section "Manifest Resource Information."

The `Assembly` class is a root class in the `Reflection` namespace that is a starting point for obtaining manifest information and identifying and obtaining references to objects in an assembly, like modules, files, methods, and entry points. When you have these objects, you can dynamically invoke behaviors defined by elements in an assembly.

Assembly Class

The `Assembly` class implements getter methods that represent the objects in a module. The `System.Reflection.GetAssembly` method is a shared method that returns a reference to the assembly object containing the specified argument class.

> **Note**
>
> To use the capabilities of the `Reflection` namespace, add an `Imports System.Reflection` statement in the module that will use reflection, or add the `System.Reflection` namespace to the project imports.

By calling the `Reflection.Assembly.GetAssembly` method, passing the `System.Type` information to the method, you get a reference object to the assembly containing that object. For example, `Reflection.Assembly.GetAssembly(Me.GetType)` returns the assembly object containing the object represented by `Me`. If `Me` is a form's reference to self, a reference to the assembly containing that form will be returned. (An alternative to `GetAssembly` is `GetCallingAssembly`, which requires no parameters and returns a reference to the assembly containing the statement `GetCallingAssembly`.)

From the `Assembly` object you can obtain references to the modules, files, manifest information, entry point, and types defined in a specific assembly.

Assembly Members

Table 6.1 provides an overview of the members of the `Assembly` class.

TABLE 6.1   Members of the Assembly Class

Name	Description
Shared Methods	
CreateQualifiedName	Creates the name of a type
GetAssembly	Returns an assembly object containing the argument class
GetCallingAssembly	Returns the assembly containing the method call
GetEntryAssembly	Returns the first executable that was run
GetExecutingAssembly	Returns the assembly containing the currently running code
Load	Loads the named assembly
LoadFrom	Loads the assembly by path
Instance Properties	
CodeBase	Returns the location of the assembly in URN format
EntryPoint	Returns the starting point MethodInfo object for an assembly
Evidence	Returns security policy information
FullName	Returns the complete name of the assembly, including version and public key information
GlobalAssemblyCache	Returns a Boolean indicating whether the assembly was loaded from the Global Assembly Cache (GAC)
Location	Returns the URN of the loaded file
Instance Methods	
CreateInstance	Creates an instance of the argument type contained in the assembly
GetCustomAttributes	Returns the assembly's custom attributes
GetExportedTypes	Returns exported types defined in the assembly
GetFile	Returns a FileStream object representing a specified file from the manifest, which includes a list of files in the assembly
GetFiles	Returns an array of FileStream objects representing the files listed in an assembly's manifest
GetLoadedModules	Returns the loaded modules that are in the assembly
GetManifestResourceInfo	Returns information describing how a resource was persisted
GetManifestResourceNames	Returns the names of the assembly's resources
GetManifestResourceStream	Loads the manifest resource

TABLE 6.1 continued

Name	Description
	Instance Methods
GetModule	Returns the specified module
GetModules	Gets all of an assembly's modules
GetName	Returns the assembly's name
GetObjectData	Returns serialization information needed to instantiate the assembly
GetReferencedAssemblies	Returns all referenced assemblies
GetSatelliteAssembly	Returns a satellite assembly containing culture-specific information
GetType	Returns the type information for the specified type
GetTypes	Returns the types defined in the assembly
IsDefined	Returns a Boolean indicating if a custom attribute is defined
LoadModule	Loads a module in the assembly
	Instance Event
ModuleResolve	Raised when the CLR cannot load a module

Refer to the sections that follow for individual code examples demonstrating some of the capabilities of the `Assembly` class.

Manifest Resource Information

Manifests contain data that describes how the elements of an assembly relate to each other. Manifests contain assembly name, culture, strong name, files in the assembly, type reference, and information indicating referenced assemblies. The assembly name, version number, culture information, and string information describe the assembly's identity, allowing assemblies with the same filename to coexist in the Global Assembly Cache (GAC).

Note

Culture information includes such things as language and country to support multinational application development.

You can change manifest information using attributes (see Chapter 12), including trademark, copyright, product, company, and version information.

The `ManifestResourceInfo` defines `FileName`, `ResourceLocation`, and `ReferencedAssembly` properties. The `FileName` property defines the resource containing the manifest information. `ResourceLocation` defines the location of the manifest resource file, and `ReferencedAssembly` returns a reference to the assembly containing this manifest.

Module Object

`Assembly.GetModule` returns a named module in an assembly. *Module* in this context does not refer to the `Module` construct. An assembly's module is equivalent to an application, like an executable or DLL module.

> ### Tip
>
> You can use keywords in code if you wrap the use of those keywords in square brackets. For example, `Assembly` is a reserved word. To declare a type as an `Assembly` type, you can prefix the `Reflection` namespace to the type or declare the type using brackets as follows: `Dim A As [Assembly]`.
>
> IntelliSense will automatically place the `Assembly` keyword in brackets when it is selected from a member list.

When you obtain a reference to a `Module` object, you can request information about `Type` objects, like classes and structures, and information contained in those types.

When we are referring to an assembly's module and reflection, we are referring to an application. When you have a specific application (module), you can obtain information about types, like the forms and classes in the module, and from those objects you can derive information about methods, fields, properties, events, and parameters. Listing 6.1 contains code that walks the methods and fields of a single type in a module.

LISTING 6.1 Walking the fields and methods of a class in a module

```
1:    Private Function GetAssembly() As Reflection.Assembly
2:      'Return Reflection.Assembly.GetAssembly(Me.GetType())
3:      Return Reflection.Assembly.GetCallingAssembly
4:    End Function
5:
6:    Private Sub InsertText(ByVal Text As String)
7:      TextBox1.Text &= Text & vbCrLf
```

LISTING 6.1   continued

```
8:    End Sub
9:
10:   Private Sub InsertModuleElements(ByVal AType As Type)
11:     Dim Enumerator As IEnumerator = _
12:       AType.GetMethods.GetEnumerator
13:
14:     InsertText("Methods:")
15:     While (Enumerator.MoveNext)
16:       InsertText(CType(Enumerator.Current, MethodInfo).Name)
17:     End While
18:
19:     InsertText("Fields:")
20:     Enumerator = AType.GetFields.GetEnumerator()
21:     While (Enumerator.MoveNext)
22:       InsertText(CType(Enumerator.Current, FieldInfo).Name)
23:     End While
24:
25:   End Sub
26:
27:
28:   Private Sub WalkModule()
29:     InsertText(GetAssembly.GetModules()(0).Name)
30:     InsertText(GetAssembly.GetTypes()(0).Name)
31:     InsertModuleElements(GetAssembly.GetTypes()(0))
32:   End Sub
33:
34:   Private Sub MenuItem10_Click(ByVal sender As System.Object, _
35:     ByVal e As System.EventArgs) Handles MenuItem10.Click
36:     WalkModule()
37:   End Sub
```

> **Note**
>
> To run the sample code, open ReflectionDemo.sln and choose Demo, Assembly, GetModule. To run the code separately, create a new Windows application, include `Imports System.Reflection`, add a multiline `TextBox`, and define a new way to invoke `WalkModule`.

GetAssembly, defined on lines 1 through 4, is a query method that simplifies referring to an Assembly object. WalkModule uses GetAssembly to return the assembly containing the code in the listing.

The Assembly object is used to get the array of Modules on line 29 and the array of Types on line 30. The name from the 0th element of the modules is displayed and the name of the 0th element of the Types array is displayed.

InsertModuleElements on line 31 uses the Type at index 0 as the target type to walk. The sample code retrieves type Form1, which is a class, and passes that type to the InsertModuleElements procedure. The sample code gets Form1's methods and fields arrays on lines 11–12 and 20 and uses the enumerator implemented by those arrays to walk each method and field defined in Form1.

You have seen verbose code that uses arrays and enumerators in earlier chapters, but I will repeat it here for clarity by elaborating on the code that examines each method. (The preceding code example is closer to the code we might like to deploy, but may be a little ambiguous.)

From Listing 6.1 we have the code on lines 11 through 17 that displays all of the methods in the type represented by AType.

```
11:    Dim Enumerator As IEnumerator = _
12:       AType.GetMethods.GetEnumerator
13:
14:    InsertText("Methods:")
15:    While (Enumerator.MoveNext)
16:      InsertText(CType(Enumerator.Current, MethodInfo).Name)
17:    End While
```

A verbose form of the same code follows.

```
Dim MethodInfos() As MethodInfo
MethodInfos = AType.GetMethods
Dim Enumerator As IEnumerator
Enumerator = MethodInfos.GetEnumerator()
TextBox1.Text &= "Methods:" & vbCrLf
Dim AMethodInfo As MethodInfo
While (Enumerator.MoveNext)
  AMethodInfo = CType(Enumerator.Current, MethodInfo)
  TextBox1.Text &= AMethodInfo.Name & vbCrLf
End While
```

The revised verbose code performs singular operations on each line of code. Note, however, that it requires almost twice as many lines of code. The first revised line declares an array of MethodInfo types. The second line initializes that array by calling Type.GetMethods. The third and fourth lines declare and initialize an IEnumerator (introduced in Chapter 2 and explored further in Chapter 3). `IEnumerator` is an interface that defines two methods, `MoveNext` and `Reset`, and a property `Current`, providing you with a consistent interface for iterating elements of a `System.Array`. The fifth line adds some text to a `TextBox` indicating that the text that follows consists of method names. The sixth line declares a temporary variable used to store each `MethodInfo` object, and the loop appends the name of each method—`AMethodInfo.Name`—to the `TextBox` control.

Production systems should have concise rather than verbose code. A method named `DisplayMethodNames` that walks through the `MethodInfo` objects of a `Type` without creating several temporaries would yield clear and concise code.

File Object

The `Assembly` class contains `GetFile` and `GetFiles` methods. These methods return a `FileStream` object and an array of `FileStream` objects, respectively. The `FileStream` objects returned by the `Assembly` class are no different than any other `FileStream` object derived in any other manner; the methods and attributes are identical, only the state is different.

Listing 6.2 demonstrates how to load the bytes representing a file. `Assembly.GetFile` returns a `FileStream` representing the bytes of a module in an assembly.

Listing 6.2   Displaying some of the bytes in a module file as hexadecimal bytes using the `ThreadPool` and the `FileStream` returned by `GetFiles()(0)`

```
1:    Private Contents As String
2:
3:    Private Sub WriteFileAsHex(ByVal state As Object)
4:
5:      Dim Stream As IO.FileStream = _
6:        GetAssembly.GetFiles()(0)
7:
8:      Dim B(Stream.Length) As Byte
9:      Stream.Read(B, 0, Stream.Length)
10:
11:     Dim I As Integer
12:
13:     SyncLock GetType(Form1)
14:       For I = 0 To B.Length() - 1
15:         If (I Mod 8 = 0 And I > 0) Then Contents &= " "
16:         If (I Mod 16 = 0 And I > 0) Then Contents &= vbCrLf
17:         Contents &= Hex(B(I)).PadLeft(2, "0")
18:
19:         ' Remove if you want the whole file!
20:         If (I > 50000) Then Exit For
```

LISTING 6.2   continued

```
21:          Next
22:        End SyncLock
23:
24:        Invoke(CType(AddressOf UpdateText, MethodInvoker))
25:
26:    End Sub
27:
28:    Private Sub UpdateText()
29:      TextBox1.Text = Contents
30:      StatusBar1.Text = "Loaded"
31:    End Sub
32:
33:    Private Sub MenuItem11_Click(ByVal sender As System.Object, _
34:      ByVal e As System.EventArgs) Handles MenuItem11.Click
35:
36:      StatusBar1.Text = "Loading File..."
37:      TextBox1.Clear()
38:
39:      Threading.ThreadPool.QueueUserWorkItem( _
40:          AddressOf WriteFileAsHex)
41:    End Sub
```

Note

To avoid repeating a complete Windows application listing, the code in Listing 6.2 is an excerpt from ReflectionDemo.sln. To make the code a standalone example, create a new Windows application, add the `Imports System.Reflection` statement, copy `GetAssembly` from Listing 6.1, and replace the Windows Forms controls and events with the controls and events in your application.

When the user chooses Demo, Assembly, GetFile in ReflectionDemo.sln, the `Click` event handler on line 33 is invoked. The `StatusBar.Text` is updated, the `TextBox` is cleared, and something happens with the `ThreadPool`. We will come back to line 39 in a minute. Let's take a look at `WriteFileAsHex`.

Regardless of how `WriteFileAsHex` is invoked, what `WriteFileAsHex` does is request the `FileStream` represented by the `Reflection.File` object returned by indexing the 0th element of the array returned by `Assembly.GetFiles`. All of the bytes in the `FileStream` are read into the array of bytes B. Lines 14 through 21 convert all of the bytes to hexadecimal, formatting the bytes in two columns of eight bytes each.

Let's return to line 29 now. What is `Threading.ThreadPool.QueueUserWorkItem`? As you know, Visual Basic .NET supports free threading. There is a pool manager called the `ThreadPool` that contains some threads waiting around for you to give them some work to do. The `ThreadPool` manages the creation and allocation of threads; all you have to do is give them work by queuing a work item. Work items are represented by callback functions, also known as delegates.

There are several new topics here, including delegates, threads, thread pools, and how to safely use threads with controls. For now, you will have to take on faith that the code works correctly and safely. In summary, the `ThreadPool` is a pool of available threads, a delegate is a class representing a pointer to a function, and Windows Forms controls must be manipulated on the same thread as the one that owns them. The last point explains why the code uses the `Invoke` method on line 24 to update the `TextBox`.

Chapters 8 and 9 provide more information on delegates, and using the `ThreadPool` safely with Windows Forms controls is described in Chapter 15's section titled "Using the `ThreadPool`." The motivation for using threads in the example is to give you a first look at an advanced subject, multithreading, and to offload a potentially process-heavy task to a background thread, allowing the graphical user interface to remain responsive. Pushing big processes onto a different thread to allow our GUI to remain responsive reflects an actual reason we might want to use threads. More information about multi-threaded applications can be found in Chapter 14, "Multithreaded Applications."

`Location` Property

The `Assembly.Location` object returns the complete path information of the assembly containing the manifest for the assembly represented by the `Assembly` object.

`EntryPoint` Property

`Assembly.EntryPoint` returns the `MethodInfo` object representing the method that is the entry point for an assembly. For example, a console application would return the `shared sub main` procedure where your console application begins executing. (Refer to the section on `MethodInfo` for more information on the type returned by the `EntryPoint` method.)

`GlobalAssemblyCache` Property

The `Assembly.GlobalAssemblyCache` property returns a Boolean value. If the property returns True, the assembly is registered in the GAC and is a public assembly; otherwise, the assembly is a private assembly.

Type

The System.Type object is an object that describes a type. When you invoke GetType or index one of the types in the array of types returned by GetTypes, you have an object that describes the interfaces, classes, structures, modules, and enumerations in an assembly. GetTypes returns nested types, too, like nested classes or structures.

The System.Type object is critical to obtaining and managing objects using Runtime Type Information (RTTI) and consequently central to reflection. Type objects allow you to query the object to determine whether the type represents a class or COM object, whether the type is nested, and the access modifiers that were applied to the type.

Reflection is used implicitly during certain types of operations. In VB6 you could declare a variable as a variant, assign a specific object to that variant, and call methods of the specific object without performing any type conversions. (Refer to the following example.)

```
'VB6 Example
Dim V As Variant
Set V = New Collection
V.Add "Foo"
```

This type of code implicitly performs a call to QueryInterface. If the actual object—in this instance a Collection—does not support the interface, VB6 raises a runtime error. The preceding operation demonstrates late binding, or runtime binding. Late binding is supported in VB .NET by employing reflection. Unfortunately, this kind of lazy code defers a possible error until runtime. We want errors to manifest themselves as early as possible. For this reason, Chapter 2 suggested that Option Strict On be used to prevent late binding.

Refer to the help information for a complete reference of the Type members.

Binder

Binder objects are responsible for performing type conversions between arguments presented and the actual argument type needed.

Individual programming languages load and bind methods in a module individually. You can load assemblies and invoke methods on those assemblies using late binding through reflection. This is referred to as *custom binding*.

The most common scenario where this might be employed is by tools that allow users to explicitly invoke operations. Because the developer of such an application would not know in advance what a user may want to do, operations could not be associated with a visual metaphor in advance, such as a button or menu. For example, a user might pick from a selection of a thousand operations residing in any number of assemblies. Instead of trying to write static code for dynamic behavior, reflection and custom binding would allow you to load an assembly and invoke behaviors on that assembly as needed.

The subsections that follow demonstrate some of the ways in which assemblies can be loaded dynamically using reflection.

Loading Assemblies

Assemblies can be loaded at runtime without an application knowing what that assembly is in advance. Loading assemblies dynamically is probably not something you will do in the run-of-the-mill application, but just recently a developer from a local software company called me and asked me how to do this identical operation in a Delphi application. My response was "Oh, you're talking about reflection!" Unfortunately for that developer, the mechanics are not as thoroughly supported in Delphi as they are in the CLR. The call reminded me that dynamic type determination can be useful, especially for general tools builders. I am not sure, but it is a reasonable bet that reflection was designed for vendors building tools, and perhaps for Visual Studio .NET as a tool, too.

An assembly is an application containing metadata, which makes the assembly more than an application. Assemblies are self-contained files that look like applications on the outside but contain additional information like manifests and string name, public key data.

To load an assembly on the fly, you will need the name of an application containing assembly manifest information. From that application you can create an instance of the assembly returned by the Shared Assembly.Load function. And, of course, as we have been talking about, after you have loaded the assembly you can find out information about that assembly and invoke methods on types defined in the assembly. The end result is completely dynamic interaction with assemblies, or, applications, whichever you prefer.

The following fragment demonstrates loading an assembly:

```
Dim AName As String = _
  "C:\Temp\ReflectionEventDemo.exe""
Dim App As [Assembly] = [Assembly].LoadFrom(AName)
```

The assembly MyLibrary.dll is a Class Library project.

The example demonstrates a hard-coded path, but you could just as easily return a dynamic path from the OpenFileDialog or a list of assemblies. The first statement declares a constant representing the filename, AName. The application name is used to initialize the assembly via the Assembly.LoadFrom method.

After this code fragment is executed, you have roughly the equivalent of `LoadLibrary` from the Win32 API days, or a late-bound COM object. (Remember this is a rough equivalence to `LoadLibrary` or late-bound COM objects.) `Assembly` is a keyword and a class; wrapping the word `Assembly` in brackets indicates that we are using the class name rather than the keyword associated with assembly attributes (see Chapter 12).

Now that we have a loaded assembly, we can use reflection and the `Type.InvokeMethod` operation to dynamically invoke behaviors on that assembly.

Invoking Members on Dynamic Assemblies

Earlier in the chapter, I mentioned that `System.Type` was essential to RTTI and reflection. One of those essential features is the ability to use a type rather than an instance to invoke members defined by a type.

Continuing with the example from the preceding section, we now have an assembly. We can use techniques from early sections of this chapter to discover what types are defined by that assembly and invoke behaviors defined by those types. For our example, we will use known information to keep the example simple (see Listing 6.3).

LISTING 6.3   The listing for MyLibrary.dll and CustomBinding.vproj, both in CustomBinding.sln

```
1:  ' MyLibrary.dll - Class1.vb
2:  Public Class Class1
3:
4:     Public Sub Echo(ByVal Message As String)
5:       MsgBox(Message)
6:     End Sub
7:
8:  End Class
9:
10:
11: ' CustomBinding.exe - Form1.vb
12:
13: Imports System.Reflection
14:
15: Public Class Form1
16:    Inherits System.Windows.Forms.Form
17:
18: [ Windows Form Designer generated code ]
19:
20:    Private Sub LoadAndInvoke()
21:      ' Modify to point to location of DLL on your PC
22:      Const FileName As String = "C:\temp\MyLibrary.dll"
23:
24:
```

LISTING 6.3 continued

```
25:     Dim AName As String = FileName
26:         27:
28:     Dim MyAssembly As [Assembly] = [Assembly].LoadFrom(AName)
29:
30:     Dim Arguments() As Object = {"Custom Binding Demo"}
31:
32:     Dim AType As Type = MyAssembly.GetTypes()(0)
33:     Dim O As Object = MyAssembly.CreateInstance(AType.FullName)
34:
35:     AType.InvokeMember("Echo", BindingFlags.Default Or _
36:         BindingFlags.InvokeMethod, _
37:         Nothing, O, Arguments)
38:   End Sub
39:
40:
41:   Private Sub Button1_Click(ByVal sender As System.Object, _
42:     ByVal e As System.EventArgs) Handles Button1.Click
43:     LoadAndInvoke()
44:   End Sub
45: End Class
```

The first section of Listing 6.3 implements the class library MyLibrary.dll as a class library that contains a single class with a single method, Echo. Beginning on line 10, the second section of the listing contains a simple application with a single form, Form1. Form1 contains a button. When the button is clicked (see lines 41 to 44), Form1.LoadAndInvoke is called. (Keep in mind that you could easily pick assemblies using dialogs or manually enter them by selecting an assembly from the GAC.)

LoadAndInvoke declares the path to the application containing the assembly manifest information and uses that object to LoadFrom the assembly with which the application is associated. (This is the code we covered in the prior section.) For the sake of brevity, line 30 picks up by creating an array of objects. The array of objects plays the role of arguments passed to the dynamically invoked method. On line 32 we arbitrarily retrieve the first type defined in the assembly. We know that MyLibrary.dll only defines one type, Class1. We could just as easily have displayed a list of types and let the user pick one. Line 33 uses type information contained in the type object to create an instance of the type with Assembly.CreateInstance. CreateInstance uses the default constructor that every type possesses to create an uninitialized instance of the type.

Finally, Type.InvokeMethod passes a string naming the method we want to call, Echo. The second argument indicates the BindingFlags; we want to invoke a method, so we pass the BindingFlags.Default or'd with BindingFlags.InvokeMethod, indicating the kind of invocation we are making. The third parameter is Binder; we will come back to the `Binder` parameter in a minute. The fourth parameter is the object that will be used to invoke the method, and the final parameter, `Arguments`, is the array of arguments to pass to the method. From the listing we know `Echo` takes a single string argument, which is what `Arguments` was initialized with.

The net result is that we invoked a method in an assembly that the user could have supplied, with a name that the user could have picked from a list of available names, and passed methods that we could have expressed to the user by displaying the `ParameterInfo` names for any particular method. As a result we have completely dynamic code.

Where Does Binder Fit In?

`Binder` is an abstract class that we must inherit from. `Binder` is defined with the `MustInherit` modifier. `MustInherit` means that we must declare an instance of a class that inherits from `Binder` and implement all of the methods labeled `MustOverride`.

What `Binder` is designed to do is describe a transposition between actual argument types to formal argument types based on the type of member invoked, binding arguments, and specific parameters. Chapter 7, "Creating Classes," covers inheritance in detail. Listing 6.4 implements a do-nothing binder subclass demonstrating the syntactical mechanics of inheriting from an abstract class and implementing virtual methods; that is, methods modified with `MustOverride`.

LISTING 6.4 A do-nothing binder demonstrating the syntactical mechanics of inheriting an implementing `MustOverride Binder` method

```
1:  Imports System.Globalization
2:
3:  Public Class MyBinder
4:    Inherits Binder
5:
6:    Public Overrides Function ChangeType( _
7:      ByVal value As Object, _
8:      ByVal type As Type, _
9:      ByVal culture As CultureInfo _
10:   ) As Object
11:
12:     Return value
13:
14:   End Function
15:
16:   Public Overrides Function SelectProperty( _
17:     ByVal bindingAttr As BindingFlags, _
18:     ByVal match() As PropertyInfo, _
19:     ByVal returnType As Type, _
```

LISTING 6.4 continued

```
20:        ByVal indexes() As Type, _
21:        ByVal modifiers() As ParameterModifier _
22:    ) As PropertyInfo
23:
24:    End Function
25:
26:    Public Overrides Function BindToMethod( _
27:        ByVal bindingAttr As BindingFlags, _
28:        ByVal match() As MethodBase, _
29:        ByRef args() As Object, _
30:        ByVal modifiers() As ParameterModifier, _
31:        ByVal culture As CultureInfo, _
32:        ByVal names() As String, _
33:        ByRef state As Object _
34:    ) As MethodBase
35:
36:    End Function
37:
38:    Public Overrides Function BindToField( _
39:        ByVal bindingAttr As BindingFlags, _
40:        ByVal match() As FieldInfo, _
41:        ByVal value As Object, _
42:        ByVal culture As CultureInfo _
43:    ) As FieldInfo
44:
45:    End Function
46:
47:
48:    Public Overrides Sub ReorderArgumentArray( _
49:        ByRef args() As Object, _
50:        ByVal state As Object _
51:    )
52:
53:    End Sub
54:
55:    Public Overrides Function SelectMethod( _
56:        ByVal bindingAttr As BindingFlags, _
57:        ByVal match() As MethodBase, _
58:        ByVal types() As Type, _
59:        ByVal modifiers() As ParameterModifier _
60:    ) As MethodBase
61:
62:    End Function
63:
64: End Class
```

As you can glean from the listing, the Binder methods use a relatively high number of arguments and many of those are array arguments. (System.Globalization contains the CultureInfo class used in the parameter for ChangeType.)

ChangeType

ChangeType is used to implement changing the type represented by the value parameter to the type argument.

SelectProperty

SelectProperty returns a property from the available properties based on the selection criteria arguments.

BindToMethod

BindToMethod picks a specific method based on the argument information provided.

BindToField

BindToField selects one of the available fields based on the argument values specified.

ReorderArgumentArray

ReorderArgumentArray allows you to reorganize the array of arguments passed to InvokeMethod (see Listing 6.4).

SelectMethod

SelectMethod provides the Binder with a chance to select a method based on the arguments passed.

When you invoke a method using historical technology, keep in mind that method invocation and parameter passing are constrained by the name, types, and order prescribed by the language that the application was implemented in. The .NET Framework replaces problems caused by language implementations and calling orders with classes in the Reflection namespace that allow the user to describe how method invocations are bound.

Listing 6.3 passes Nothing for the Binder object because we are working with languages that are core languages implemented by Microsoft. Custom binding objects will probably come into play when third-party vendors begin implementing tools in other languages that will be integrated into Visual Studio .NET.

Activator Class

The `Activator` class is defined in the `System` namespace. `Activator` contains methods for creating object instances locally or remotely or obtaining instances of existing objects.

When you call `Type.CreateInstance`—see Listing 6.3, line 33—an instance of an `Activator` is created by the `Type` class to create the instance.

MethodInfo Class

`MethodInfo` objects are instances of classes that represent a method of a type. `MethodInfo` allows you to discover return types, modifiers, and attributes applied to the method, and a list of parameters used by the method.

As demonstrated throughout this chapter, discovery of method names and arguments allows the dynamic invocation of methods.

`InsertModuleElements` from Listing 6.1 demonstrates dynamic discovery of method names. Combine dynamic name discovery with dynamic parameter discovery, and you can invoke methods through the `Type.InvokeMember` method.

ParameterInfo Class

`ParameterInfo` objects represent the arguments associated with methods. `ParameterInfo` has properties that enable you to determine the name and type of the parameter, whether the parameter is optional, whether it has default values, and whether it is an input or output parameter.

FieldInfo Class

`FieldInfo` objects represent fields defined as members of a type. `FieldInfo` objects allow you to discover attributes, modifiers, names, and types at runtime.

PropertyInfo Class

By convention, fields contain private data represented by public property methods. It is intuitive that reflection supports all aspects of dynamic discovery and invocation, including property information.

EventInfo Class

The concept of the function pointer is new to Visual Basic .NET. In Chapters 8 and 9 you will learn that function pointers are types that point to the address of a function and those functions can be invoked via their addresses. Additionally, function pointers in .NET are wrapped in classes called Delegates.

Reflection supports the dynamic discovery of types, methods, fields, and events. This illustrates just how much Visual Basic has changed under .NET. In addition to having support for inheritance (refer to Chapter 7) and function pointers, the CLR supports the dynamic discovery of those function pointers, and subsequently, the dynamic assignment of event handlers to delegates.

Listing 6.5 demonstrates an application that loads a second executable assembly, creates an instance of the main form in that assembly, and assigns an event handler in the first application to an event in the second application.

LISTING 6.5   Dynamic event handling using reflection

```
1:    Private Sub AssignEvent()
2:
3:        Dim AName As String = "C:\TEMP\ReflectionEventDemo.exe"
4:
5:        Dim App As [Assembly] = [Assembly].LoadFrom(AName)
6:        Dim AType As Type = App.GetTypes()(0)
7:
8:      Dim AForm As Form = App.CreateInstance(AType.FullName)
9:      AForm.Show()
10:
11:       Dim Events() As EventInfo = AType.GetEvents
12:       Dim D As EventHandler = AddressOf Handler
13:
14:       Dim I As Integer
15:       For I = 0 To Events.Length - 1
16:         If (Events(I).Name = "Click") Then
17:           Events(I).AddEventHandler(AForm, D)
18:           Exit For
19:         End If
20:       Next
21:
22:    End Sub
23:
24:    Private Sub Handler(ByVal sender As System.Object, _
25:      ByVal e As System.EventArgs)
26:      MsgBox("Called from " & Application.ProductName)
27:    End Sub
```

> **Caution**
>
> Listing 6.5 demonstrates dynamic event handler assignment across assembly boundaries using reflection. This is not the recommended way to assign event handlers. Read Chapters 8 and 9 for normal event-handling operations.

Listing 6.5 creates an assembly object containing a simple Windows application. Line 8 creates the assembly with the `Assembly.Load` method. Line 9 gets the first type in the assembly. We know there is only one, the main form; in a practical example we would want to perform some sanity checking on the `Type` returned as `AType` on line 9. Lines 14 through 23 get all of the events defined for the `Form` type, searching for the `Click` event. When the `Click` event is found, a handler defined in the first assembly is assigned to a delegate in the second assembly.

> **Note**
>
> To test the dynamic event assignment using reflection, you will need to choose Demo, Dynamic Event Reflection in the ReflectionDemo.exe to assign the event handler and click on the main form in the second application, ReflectionEventDemo.exe.

When you compile and run both of the assemblies in `ReflectionDemo.sln`, you will see that clicking on the second assembly—after the event handler is assigned—runs code in the first assembly. You can verify this operation by placing a breakpoint on line 29 from the listing.

Emitting Types at Runtime Using Reflection

The `System.Reflection.Emit` namespace allows developers to emit types at runtime.

Part of the interest in writing books like this one is to try to understand what motivated Microsoft developers when they defined and implemented these capabilities. Sometimes it is obvious or guessable, and other times I have to ask and am fortunate enough to get answers from those in the know.

You are likely to use some of these new capabilities as the implementers intended, and more than likely many of you will contrive new uses for them. Reflection seems to be a replacement for COM Automation. The `Emit` namespace seems to be intended for code generators, perhaps for tools like Rational Rose that reverse-engineer UML models to generate code.

The `Reflection.Emit` namespace supports generating types at runtime using `Builder` classes. These `Builder` classes—like `AssemblyBuilder` and `MethodBuilder`—work by emitting IL (Intermediate Language) code. General information about classes capable of emitting code to the ILGenerator can be found by searching the help documentation topic `ms-help://MS.VSCC/MS.MSDNVS/cpref/html/frlrfSystemReflectionEmit.htm` in Visual Studio .NET.

There are many excellent examples of .NET code defined in the Visual Basic QuickStarts and Other Samples help topics. If you search the QuickStarts topics, you will find several solutions demonstrating various aspects of Visual Basic .NET programming. The example in Listing 6.6 is loosely based on the ReflectionEmitVB.vbproj example installed in the Microsoft.Net\FrameworkSDK folder when you installed the .NET Framework.

LISTING 6.6   Emitting a dynamic class as IL code

```
1:  Option Strict On
2:  Option Explicit On
3:
4:  Imports System.Threading
5:  Imports System.Reflection
6:  Imports System.Reflection.Emit
7:
8:  Public Class Form1
9:    Inherits System.Windows.Forms.Form
10:
11: [ Windows Form Designer generated code ]
12:
13:   Private Sub Button1_Click(ByVal sender As System.Object, _
14:     ByVal e As System.EventArgs) Handles Button1.Click
15:
16:     DynamicType.Test()
17:   End Sub
18:
19: End Class
20:
21:
22: Public Class DynamicType
23:
24:   Public Shared Sub Test()
25:     Dim AClass As Type = _
26:       CreateType(Thread.GetDomain, AssemblyBuilderAccess.Run)
```

LISTING 6.6   continued

```
27:
28:        Dim Obj As Object = _
29:          Activator.CreateInstance(AClass, _
30:          New Object() {"It's a brave new world!"})
31:        ' Reuse Obj reference here!
32:        Obj = AClass.InvokeMember("Text", _
33:         BindingFlags.GetField, Nothing, Obj, Nothing)
34:
35:        MsgBox(Obj)
36:     End Sub
37:
38:     Public Shared Function CreateType(ByVal Domain As AppDomain, _
39:       ByVal Access As AssemblyBuilderAccess) As Type
40:
41:        Dim AName As New AssemblyName()
42:        AName.Name = "EmitAssembly"
43:        Dim AnAssembly As AssemblyBuilder = _
44:          Domain.DefineDynamicAssembly(AName, Access)
45:
46:        Dim AModule As ModuleBuilder
47:        AModule = AnAssembly.DefineDynamicModule("EmitModule")
48:
49:        Dim AClass As TypeBuilder = _
50:          AModule.DefineType("AClass", TypeAttributes.Public)
51:
52:        Dim AField As FieldBuilder = _
53:          AClass.DefineField("Text", GetType(String), _
54:          FieldAttributes.Public)
55:
56:        Dim Args As Type() = {GetType(String)}
57:        Dim Constructor As ConstructorBuilder = _
58:          AClass.DefineConstructor(MethodAttributes.Public, _
59:          CallingConventions.Standard, Args)
60:
61:        Dim IL As ILGenerator = Constructor.GetILGenerator
62:        IL.Emit(OpCodes.Ldarg_0)
63:        Dim Super As ConstructorInfo = _
64:          GetType(Object).GetConstructor(Type.EmptyTypes)
65:        IL.Emit(OpCodes.Call, Super)
66:        IL.Emit(OpCodes.Ldarg_0)
67:        IL.Emit(OpCodes.Ldarg_1)
68:        IL.Emit(OpCodes.Stfld, AField)
69:        IL.Emit(OpCodes.Ret)
70:
71:        Return AClass.CreateType
72:
73:     End Function
74:
75: End Class
```

The shared method `Test` is called, which starts the process of creating the dynamic type. `CreateType` returns a `Type` object. `Activator.CreateInstance` is used directly to create an instance of the new type on line 28. (We used the `Activator` object implicitly in Listing 6.3 when `Type.CreateInstance` was called.) The `Obj` reference is reused on line 32 when we call `AClass.InvokeMember` to get the value of the field named `Text`. After lines 32–33 `Obj` refers to the `String` member `Text`. Clearly this is not an efficient way to write code in general, but is a powerful way to create types on the fly.

The `CreateType` method may seem a bit confusing to less experienced developers. After you have read the first 10 chapters or so of this book, the code itself should be comprehensible. Clearly, emitting IL is an advanced subject.

In summary, `CreateType` uses builder classes to create the various pieces of code. An `AssemblyName` and `AssemblyBuilder` are created first to create an assembly. On lines 46 and 47 a `Module` is created, using the `ModuleBuilder` class, and added to the assembly. Lines 49 and 50 define a single statement that creates the new class type. The statements on lines 52 to 54 add a single public, string field to the type. (Thus far, these are all steps that a programmer would perform manually by creating a project and defining a class in that assembly.) The `ConstructorBuilder` is used to define a parameterized constructor for our new type; the new constructor takes a single string argument. Lines 61 through 69 use an `ILGenerator` object to emit the IL code. Line 71 returns the new type.

Lines 65 through 69 represent generic, low-level code in IL that will be converted to machine-specific code by the JITter. These five strange-looking statements using OpCodes represent the IL form of code that defines a constructor. Line 65 calls the base constructor. Lines 66 and 67 manage arguments passed to the constructor, including the hidden reference to self, `Me` and the string parameter. Line 68 initializes the field, and line 69 emits the equivalent of the `Ret` instruction. Basically, the code is the IL version of statements you might write: `MyBase.New` and `Text = Value`.

Emitting code using reflection is one of those subjects that will probably be explored in its own book, after the dust from absorbing the core changes to Visual Basic .NET.

Other Places Reflection Is Used

Reflection is used in a variety of places in Visual Studio .NET, and you are likely to see it used as tool vendors begin developing extensions to Visual Studio .NET.

The `System.Runtime.Serialization` namespace defines classes for serializing and deserializing objects into linear bytes for persisting or transmitting those bytes. Serialization classes employ reflection to figure out what to persist.

`System.Runtime.Remoting` is used with distributed applications. The `Remoting` classes use `Serialization` to intercommunicate between client and server.

Localization

For the most part, localization is the process of converting text and visually displayed elements of an application to text and visuals that are suitable for a specific locale.

Jerry Hirshberg, the founder of Nissan Design International, in *The Creative Priority*, relates a story about a presentation of a minor change to the 280ZX sports car. Preparing for the presentation, the American Hirshberg wondered whether he should open with a joke when presenting to his Japanese audience. A Japanese peer encouraged him that if this is his usual style—to offer some humor—then he should do it. Hirshberg opened with the joke and received no discernible response. "As I paused and scanned the group, waiting for some cue, something off which I might at least bounce a saver ... ," Hirshberg sensed failure at his attempt at levity.

After the presentation, a senior Nissan official remarks that they especially enjoyed Hirshberg's humor. Hirshberg asks where he should look on a Japanese person to detect laughter, and the Nissan official replies, "We'd never be so personal as to show our teeth during something as important as your first presentation." Clearly, the manners of the locale suggested a behavior different than anticipated.

The same misleading information and response can occur when a programmer is designing a user interface, including text and graphics, with an ethnocentric perspective. Common language idioms or graphics may be offensive, inflammatory, or confusing in a different societal context.

The `System.Globalization` namespace contains classes for managing culturally based presentation. As you can glean from Listing 6.4, the `Reflection` namespace anticipates that even dynamically discovered or created types may have to take cultural information into account.

Summary

Building complex systems is a huge undertaking. Perhaps there is not enough time when implementing a framework as complex as the .NET Framework to build much more than what is deemed to be essential.

When you are trying to understand the vast amount of information that .NET consists of, ask yourself, "What is its purpose?" The answer regarding the `Reflection` namespace is that its purpose is to provide a revised, enhanced, and evolutionary approach to dynamically discovering and invoking code between applications. In the past this role was satisfied by automation. In the near future, at least, this role will be played by reflection.

The `Reflection` namespace is a big namespace and perhaps one we could categorize as advanced. This chapter will get you started on those infrequent occasions when you need to employ reflection. It is likely that in the near future there will be entire books devoted solely to this topic.

Creating Classes

The ability to define a class and create instances of classes is one of the most important capabilities of any object-oriented language. Until recently Visual Basic didn't really support object-oriented classes. Though VB6 modules were called *class modules*, they were really *interfaces* in the Common Object Model (COM) sense of the word. This means that VB6 didn't support the class idiom and didn't support inheritance, another powerful benefit of object-oriented languages.

The key difference between interfaces and classes is inheritance. Each implementation of a VB6 interface (class module) required that you implement all of the public methods for that interface. Classes, as opposed to interfaces, support inheritance. Inheritance means that subclasses include the fields, properties, methods, and events of the parent class. By building classes as extensions to existing classes, you can extend and expand existing code bases.

Both object-oriented classes and COM interfaces afford developers powerful idioms for writing and managing advanced solutions. Both interfaces and classes have beneficial uses, and now that both are implemented in Visual Basic .NET, Microsoft has made revisions to the interface and class idiom to prevent ambiguity. Both interfaces and classes have distinct grammar rules.

This chapter introduces the revised grammar for interfaces and the powerful features of the new class idiom, including inheritance, polymorphism, overloading, and overriding methods. In addition, this chapter provides more examples of exception handling and multithreading in Visual Basic .NET.

Defining Classes

A Visual Basic .NET class isn't a VB6 class. VB6 classes are declared and defined using the `interface` keyword in Visual Basic .NET. Classes in Visual Basic .NET are user-defined aggregate types that support inheritance and are distinct from COM interfaces, which is exactly what a VB6 class module is.

All classes in Visual Basic .NET are defined in a .VB file (as opposed to a .CLS file), and a .VB file may contain one or more classes. (Source files can mix and match classes, structures, and modules in the same file.) The basic syntax of a class is as follows:

```
Class classname
End Class
```

> **Tip**
>
> If you accidentally mistype the declaration of a class, the Visual Studio .NET IDE will use a squiggly underline to indicate the location of the error (see Figure 7.1).

FIGURE 7.1

The Visual Studio .NET IDE uses a squiggly line to underscore problem areas in your code.

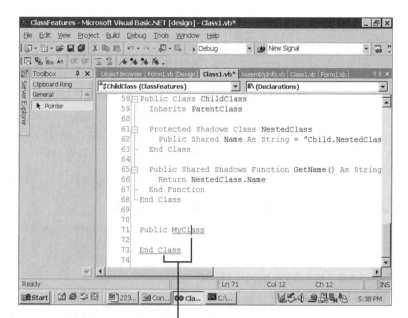

The IDE points out incorrect or incomplete syntax

Generally, classes are preceded by the `Public` access specifier, but can use other access specifiers. Refer to the section "Using Class Access Specifiers" for more on using access specifiers with classes.

The `Class` and `End Class` statements form the unit of encapsulation for the class idiom. All the members of the class are placed between these statements.

You can add any number of fields, properties, methods, and events to define an abstraction that suits the needs of a particular solution domain. Although you can add any number of members to a class, in most cases the following generic guidelines will help make your decisions easier.

- Classes should have approximately a half dozen or so public members, including both properties and methods. The number and variety of nonpublic members is more flexible simply because nonpublic members don't make classes harder for consumers to use.

- Any nonpublic members should be protected and virtual—having the `overridable` modifier—as a general rule.

Fields, properties, events, and methods can all be referred to as *members*. The term *member* simply refers to something being defined as part of a class.

As with all rules, there are exceptions. There is the *"Good Enough"* principle introduced by Grady Booch, which suggests that a reasonable and sufficient number and variety of members is good enough. There are advanced idioms introduced by James Coplien in *Advanced C++* that violate the general rules. A further example is represented by classes with all Shared members, like the Math class in the Common Language Runtime.

As I mentioned, the basic guidelines for defining classes are a reasonable starting point, but there are other rules and other motivations for creating classes. For example, the refactoring "Introduce Parameter Object" that yields efficiency in parameter passing can require the creation of extra classes.

Using Class Access Specifiers

There are five access specifiers in Visual Basic .NET, defined in the subsections that follow.

Public Access Specifier

The Public class specifier applied at the class level is the most common specifier. Public classes are classes that are intended to be used by any consumer. The Public access specifier follows any attributes and is placed immediately before the Class keyword. (Refer to Chapter 12 for more information on attributes.)

```
Public Class MyClass
End Class
```

Protected Access Specifier

The Protected access specifier can only be applied to nested classes. Protected nested classes are only accessible within the class and within child classes. You cannot define instance members of nested classes with higher visibility than the class definition.

A Protected nested class definition takes the following form:

```
Public Class HasProtected
  Protected Class ProtectedClass
  End Class
End Class
```

The class HasProtected has a nested class ProtectedClass. HasProtected can implement instances of ProtectedClass, and classes that inherit from HasProtected can declare and create instances of the nested class ProtectedClass.

Friend Access Specifier

Friend classes are accessible only within the program in which they are defined. If you add the Friend access specifier to a class definition, instances of that class can only be created from within the same program.

Assume we have a class library with a Friend class named FriendClass. We could create instances of FriendClass in the class library but not from within any consumer of the class library. We might say that FriendClass is for internal consumption only. Here's an example:

```
Friend Class FriendClass
  Public Shared Sub PublicMethod()
    MsgBox("FriendClass.PublicMethod()")
  End Sub
End Class
```

Use the Friend specifier to make a class part of the implementation details of a class library or some other application, precluding consumers of the application from using the Friend class.

Protected Friend Access Specifier

Protected Friend classes represent a union of the Protected and Friend specifiers. Protected classes must be nested classes; thus Protected Friend classes must be nested classes too. The following example shows a nested Protected Friend class:

```
Public Class HasProtectedFriend

  Protected Friend Class ProtectedFriend
    Public Shared Sub Test()
      MsgBox("Test")
    End Sub
  End Class

End Class
```

Protected Friend classes are nested classes. They generally are used as implementation classes of the class that contains them. Methods defined in nested classes can be called indirectly through proxy methods of the containing class. You can't return an instance of a Protected Friend class. Given the preceding example, the following code would be illegal:

```
Public Class HasProtectedFriend

  Protected Friend Class ProtectedFriend
    Public Shared Sub Test()
      MsgBox("Test")
```

```
      End Sub
   End Class

   Public Shared Function Factory() As ProtectedFriend

   End Function

End Class
```

The `ProtectedFriend` that appears in bold here would be underlined with a squiggly line, and the task list would contain a notice that `'Factory'` illegally exposes a `Protected Friend` type outside of the `Public Class 'HasProtectedFriend'`.

Private Access Specifier

The `Private` access specifier can only be applied to a nested class. A `Private` nested class represents implementation details of a class. When you have an internal problem that requires more problem-solving horsepower than simple methods can provide, define a nested private class that implements the abstraction. Here's how the syntax looks:

```
Public Class HasPrivate
   Private Class PrivateClass
   End Class
End Class
```

Instances of `PrivateClass` can only be created in instances of `HasPrivate`. A motivation for using a private class exists when you have a grouping of methods and properties, and you might need to store multiple instances of state for each of these objects. The distinction is that you don't want to expose the nested private class to external consumers.

You will seldom employ nested protected and private classes. However, the idiom exists and if you can contrive a useful purpose for it, go ahead.

Encapsulation and Information Hiding

Encapsulation and information hiding are object-oriented terms you might have encountered before. They are terms that have to do with strategy. *Encapsulation* literally means adding members—fields, properties, methods, and events—to classes or structures. As a general rule, members are added where they are most advantageous; that is, where they will promote the greatest reuse or an optimal refinement of your implementation.

A class *consumer* is a programmer that will create instances of the class. The producer (the person who creates the class) might be the ultimate consumer too.

A *generalizer* is a consumer that will inherit from your class.

Information hiding has to do with the partitioning of members between private, protected, public, and friend access to alleviate the burden of consumers or generalizers from learning about all members of your classes or structures. By limiting the number of members that consumers and generalizers have to learn about—that is, by selectively hiding information—your classes will be easier to consume.

Access Specifiers

The access specifiers Private, Protected, Public, Friend, and Shadows (we'll look at Shadows later in this chapter) are used to support information hiding.

Code in a class that you want to make available for general consumption is specified as having Public access. We say that a public interface is made up of Public members. Public members are implemented for the benefit of class consumers. Implement Protected members when you want to hide information from public consumers, but want to facilitate consumption by generalizers. Private members are for internal consumption only. We refer to members with Private access as implementation details. Only the producer needs to be concerned with the implementation details of a class.

Finally, Friend and Protected Friend are used to indicate that classes are consumable by entities in the same application. Friend access means intra-application access only. For example, if you define a class library and external consumers don't need or shouldn't have access to some classes in your class library, make those classes Friend classes.

As a general rule, make all methods Protected unless they have to be public. Reveal class members judiciously and deliberately.

Working with Scope

Scope has been extended in Visual Basic .NET to include block scope. New scope rules in Visual Basic .NET were introduced in Chapter 3. In addition to existing and new block-level scope rules, there is another aspect of scope that applies to Visual Basic .NET—support for inheritance introduces additional scope considerations.

When you inherit from an existing class, your new class has all of the inherited Protected, Friend, and Public members in the new class's scope. Fortunately, Visual Basic .NET won't allow you to create name confusion; the compiler will warn you of name conflicts. You can either rename conflicting members to create two disparate entities, or use the Shadows keyword to clarify name conflicts. (Refer to the section on "Using the Shadows Modifier" later in this chapter.)

Adding Field and Property Members

A *field* is a data member of a class. Fields can be ValueType members, like Integers or Dates, or can be aggregate types, like structures, enumerations, or classes. A *property* is a special member construct that is used like a field, but acts like a method. Properties are special kinds of methods that generally are used to provide constrained access to fields.

As a general rule, fields are private elements of a class. If access is provided to a field, the access is provided using a property. For this reason, fields are generally private and properties are generally public. However, sometimes fields aren't exposed through properties or at all. Properties don't always represent a field, either. Sometimes properties represent data persisted in a database, a registry or INI file, or some other underlying value, not a field.

The motivation for making fields private is that unrestrained access to data is inherently risk-inducing. Consider the steps for making Hollandaise sauce. Cook the yolks too quickly and you have scrambled eggs. However, by slowly introducing heat—the dial on the stove being analogous to a property for raising or lowering heat—you get a nice sauce consistency.

The dial on the stove is a metaphor for the property method. The field would be heat, and the dial represents the property for modifying the heat. The operator of the stove isn't allowed to increase fuel beyond a specific point. Listings 7.1 and 7.2 demonstrate two partial classes representing the stove and the throttle setting for a fuel system.

LISTING 7.1 A class representing the field and property for a stove temperature setting

```
1: Public Class Stove
2:
3:   Private FTemperature As Double
4:
5:   Public Property Temperature() As Double
6:
7:     Get
8:       Return FTemperature
9:     End Get
```

LISTING 7.1 continued

```
10:
11:        Set(ByVal Value As Double)
12:          Debug.Assert(Value < 400 And Value >= 0)
13:          If (FTemperature >= 400) Then Exit Property
14:          FTemperature = Value
15:          Debug.WriteLine(FTemperature)
16:        End Set
17:
18:    End Property
19:
20: End Class
```

Listing 7.1 introduces the field FTemperature as a Double. The FTemperature field is exposed through the Temperature property. The property Get method returns the underlying field value, and the property Set method assigns the new value to the underlying field value. Line 13 uses an assertion to ensure that no inappropriate temperature settings get past you, the developer, while you are building the system. When you deploy the class, the Debug.Assert method will be disabled by the compiler. If Stove were being used to control an actual stove, you would absolutely not want a temperature setting beyond the safe operating limit of the physical stove. In addition, we never ship a class without sanity checking for deployment. To make sure the temperature setting is safe when we ship the stove, we use a mirrored If-condition check to keep the temperature setting within safe operating limits.

Let's return to our discussion of grammar. You will note that I used an F-prefix for the field and dropped the F to contrive the property name. Notice also that the declaration for properties has changed. In Visual Basic .NET, the property statement is written as a single block structure. The Get method and Set method are nested blocks between the Property and End Property statements, defining the property block. (Recall that in VB6 the property getter and setter methods were defined as two separate and distinct blocks.)

Listing 7.2 demonstrates a new class named FuelSystem, which uses a different technique for ensuring that the throttle settings are within an acceptable range.

LISTING 7.2 Using an enumeration to constrain the field setting, combined with the property methods

```
1: Public Class FuelSystem
2:
3:    Public Enum ThrottleSetting
4:      Idle
5:      Cruise
6:      Accelerate
```

7

CREATING CLASSES

LISTING 7.2 continued

```
 7:   End Enum
 8:
 9:   Private FThrottle As ThrottleSetting
10:
11:   Public Property Throttle() As ThrottleSetting
12:
13:     Get
14:       Return FThrottle
15:     End Get
16:
17:     Set(ByVal Value As ThrottleSetting)
18:       FThrottle = Value
19:       Debug.WriteLine(Value)
20:     End Set
21:
22:   End Property
23:
24: End Class
```

The enumeration `ThrottleSetting` defines three valid settings for our throttle: `Idle`, `Cruise`, and `Accelerate`. If you combine the `Option Strict` setting with the enumeration, clients won't be able to set an inappropriate `Throttle` setting. `Option Strict` will ensure that all values passed to the `Property` setter is a `ThrottleSetting` value, and is consequently one of `Idle`, `Cruise`, or `Accelerate`.

Encapsulation and Properties

Access specifiers can be applied to any member of a class. Most often properties will be declared as `Public` members of a class or structure. You aren't precluded from defining properties with any other access specifier, however.

One strategy where `Protected` properties are employed is in classes that you intend for consumers to generalize. By declaring a class with `Protected` properties, you are allowing generalizers to decide whether or not to promote those properties to `Public` access.

The access specifier is placed before the `Property` keyword. If you don't explicitly add an access specifier, members will have `Public` access. Refer to Listings 7.2 and 7.3 for examples of the placement of the access specifier.

Tip

Explicitly type all access specifiers. The result will be code that reads as precise and intentional.

Defining Indexed Properties

Indexed properties are simply property methods that have a mandatory parameter. The mandatory parameter is semantically treated like an index, but after your code is in the property method, you can do anything you want to with the parameter. Let's quickly review properties and contrast basic properties with indexed properties.

A basic vanilla property statement has a getter and setter method. The getter method behaves like a function and is implicitly called when the property is used as a right-hand value. The setter acts like data used as a left-hand value, and sets the underlying value of the property. In its simplest incarnation, a property's value is stored in an underlying field. Both the property and the field have the same data type. Listing 7.2 demonstrates a basic property, including a getter, setter, and field value. Notice the property statement on line 11 of Listing 7.2. The property statement indicates a return type but takes no parameters.

In contrast, an indexed property has an argument between the parentheses. This argument doesn't represent the field value; rather, it represents an index to an underlying field value. The implication of the presence of an index is that the underlying field must be an array or collection. This is usually the case, too. However, the index can be used for anything, and the index parameter doesn't have to be a numeric value.

The fundamental idea behind indexed properties is that you can wrap arrays and other kinds of collections of data safely behind property methods. The motivation for doing so is the same as the motivation for wrapping singular data in property methods: You want to protect the data from abuse. Listing 7.3 demonstrates two indexed properties. Both actually refer to the same underlying array, but interact with the array in two different ways.

LISTING 7.3 Indexed properties

```
 1: Public Class Indexed
 2:
 3:   Private FStrings() As String = {"One", "Two", "Three"}
 4:
 5:   Public Property Strings(ByVal Index As Integer) As String
 6:     Get
 7:       Return FStrings(Index)
 8:     End Get
 9:     Set(ByVal Value As String)
10:       FStrings(Index) = Value
11:     End Set
12:   End Property
13:
14:   Private Sub Swap(ByVal OldIndex As Integer, _
```

Listing 7.3 continued

```
15:     ByVal NewIndex As Integer)
16:
17:     Dim Temp As String = FStrings(NewIndex)
18:     FStrings(NewIndex) = FStrings(OldIndex)
19:     FStrings(OldIndex) = Temp
20:   End Sub
21:
22:   Public Property Names(ByVal Name As String) As Integer
23:     Get
24:       Return Array.IndexOf(FStrings, Name)
25:     End Get
26:
27:     Set(ByVal Value As Integer)
28:       Swap(Names(Name), Value)
29:     End Set
30:   End Property
31:
32: End Class
```

There are two indexed properties in the class `Indexed`. The first begins on line 5, is named `Strings`, and takes an `Integer` argument. The parameter is named `Index` and literally acts like an index into the array of strings field, `FStrings`. Notice how the index is used to index the array in both the getter on lines 6 to 8 and the setter on lines 9 to 11. Lines 7 and 11 demonstrate an intuitive use of an index and an array. The getter is called when an instance of `Indexed` and the `Strings` property is used as an r-value, as in `MsgBox(Indexed.Strings(1))`. The setter is used when the `Indexed.Strings` property is used as a l-value, as in `Indexed.Strings(0) = "One"`.

Compare the `Strings` property with the `Names` property. As with the `Strings` property, the argument to the `Names` property plays the role of index. The type in the return type position—`As String` on line 5 and `As Integer` on line 22—represents the data type of the property. Hence `Strings` is an indexed `String` property and `Names` is an indexed `Integer` property. `Names` takes a string argument, `Name`, and returns the indexed position of that string in the underlying array.

Line 24 uses the `Shared` method `System.Array.IndexOf`, passing the array and the object to search for, and returns the index of the item in the array. Line 28 calls `Swap` using the current index of the existing element (found using the getter) and the new index presented by `Value`. The array element is swapped from the old position to the new position. The following statements demonstrate how you might find the `Names` property used in code:

```
Dim MyIndexed As New Indexed
MyIndexed.Names("One") = 1
```

After the code on the second line runs, the underlying field—the array FStrings—is equivalent to {"Two", "One", "Three"}. The value at the position represented by the name index of "One" is moved to index 1 by swapping with the value at index 1.

Benefits of Indexed Properties

The benefits of using indexed properties are multifold. An obvious benefit is that data should be protected by methods and easy to use like data. Just because the data happens to be an array or collection doesn't mean that it should be unprotected against abuse. Perhaps a not-so-obvious benefit is that more complex collections of data can be made easier to use by indicating that an indexed property is a default property. (More on indexed properties in a moment.)

Listing 7.3 doesn't demonstrate protecting the data from abuse. In an application we would need to provide some sanity checking to make sure that bad indexes or names weren't being used in our sample program. Let's look at some revisions we might make to make the code more robust. We'll begin with the Indexed.Names getter.

What would happen if I were to request Indexed.Names("Four")? Based on the existing implementation, I would get a -1 from the Array.IndexOf method. This is suitable, so we will leave the Names Get method as is. Alternatively, we could raise an exception if a name wasn't found, but anyone trying to use an invalid index will get an exception already. As a result, our choice is good enough.

Next, let's look at the Names property Set method. There is no sanity checking here. I can test the code to verify what the default behavior is. If a bad name-index is used, I should get an exception. In fact, Indexed.Names("Six") = 5 raises a System.IndexOutofRangeException. The caller probably needs to know that the statement failed; consequently, the exception is reasonable. On the other hand, we might decide that the code provides overly general information when the default exception occurs (see Figure 7.2).

7

CREATING CLASSES

> **Tip**
>
> For practical purposes, use the default exception if it provides reasonable feedback. You can always layer in extended behavior if you really need to.

For demonstration purposes, we will suppose that the default exception behavior isn't sufficient. We will implement extended behavior to provide more precise feedback to consumers of the Indexed class.

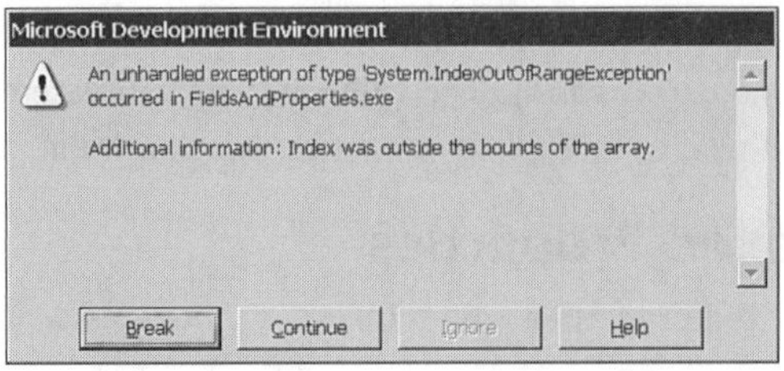

FIGURE 7.2

The default excep-tion raised when an invalid index is used with a `System.Array` *object.*

Revising the Names Property Set Method

The practical revision assumes that we want to revise our indexed `Set` property method to specifically tell the consumer that the index is invalid. Listing 7.4 shows just the revisions to the `Indexed` class from Listing 7.3.

LISTING 7.4 Adding custom revisions to invalid index-handling behavior

```
 1: Private Function ValidIndex(ByVal Index As Integer) As Boolean
 2:   Return (Index >= FStrings.GetLowerBound(0)) And _
 3:     (Index <= FStrings.GetUpperBound(0))
 4: End Function
 5:
 6: Private Overloads Sub Validate(ByVal Name As String)
 7:   Validate(Names(Name))
 8: End Sub
 9:
10: Private Overloads Sub Validate(ByVal Index As Integer)
11:   If (Not ValidIndex(Index)) Then
12:     Throw New ApplicationException(Index & " is an invalid index")
13:   End If
14: End Sub
15:
16: Public Property Names(ByVal Name As String) As Integer
17:   Get
18:     Return Array.IndexOf(FStrings, Name)
19:   End Get
20:
21:   Set(ByVal Value As Integer)
22:     Validate(Name)
23:     Swap(Names(Name), Value)
24:   End Set
25: End Property
```

The revision to the `Names` setter property method includes a call to a `Validate` function. We already know that we could write validation inline, but in earlier chapters, we dis-cussed the motivation for the refactoring "Extract Method." Essentially, we factored out the `Validate` behavior to keep the setter property method simple and to create reusable behavior in the form of a `Validate` procedure. The code introduces two forms of `Validate` using the `Overloads` modifier. One form of `Validate` takes a name and is implemented in terms of the other version, which takes an index. (Thinking ahead, we might need to validate the `Strings` property that uses an integer index.) To make the code more readable, we implement the actual index validation in a well-named method, `ValidIndex` (lines 1 through 4). Line 12 throws an exception if the index is invalid.

Notice that there are no comments. We substituted small, singular, well-named methods for comments that would be superfluous. If the `Indexed` class represented a significant abstraction, we might make an additional revision.

Subclassing an Exception Class

Suppose for the sake of argument that we want to use the exception-throwing behavior on line 12 of Listing 7.4 in several places and perhaps several classes. Also, suppose that the `Indexed` class represents a significant or important abstraction in our system.

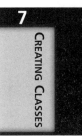

> **Note**
>
> You can find more details on exception handling in Chapter 5 and more on inheritance in Chapter 10.

We could introduce a new exception class that neatly encapsulates managing the invalid index. This is accomplished by subclassing an existing exception class and extending the behavior. This is perfectly acceptable to do, and developers have been extending exception classes in other languages for years.

We have established for our purposes that the `Indexed` class is important and that we need to reuse the abstraction, representing bad-index exceptions. The Visual Studio .NET help suggests that if we want to create our own application exceptions, we should subclass the `System.ApplicationException` class, so that's what we will do.

Our error condition occurs when a bad index is passed to the `Indexed` class's `Names` property `Set` method. The exception is raised on line 12 of Listing 7.4 when validation fails. This behavior is functional, so we won't change the orchestration of the code. We will, however, change the objects involved. The revision is demonstrated in Listing 7.5.

LISTING 7.5 The complete listing of the `Indexed` class, including a new exception class

```
1: Public Class IndexedException
2:   Inherits ApplicationException
3:
```

LISTING 7.5 continued

```
 4:    Public Sub New(ByVal Str As String)
 5:       MyBase.New(Str)
 6:    End Sub
 7:
 8:    Public Shared Sub ThrowException(ByVal Index As Integer)
 9:       Throw New IndexedException(Index & " is an invalid index")
10:    End Sub
11:
12: End Class
13:
14: Public Class Indexed
15:
16:    Private FStrings() As String = {"One", "Two", "Three"}
17:
18:    Public Property Strings(ByVal Index As Integer) As String
19:       Get
20:          Return FStrings(Index)
21:       End Get
22:
23:       Set(ByVal Value As String)
24:          FStrings(Index) = Value
25:       End Set
26:    End Property
27:
28:    Private Sub Swap(ByVal OldIndex As Integer, _
29:       ByVal NewIndex As Integer)
30:
31:       Dim Temp As String = FStrings(NewIndex)
32:       FStrings(NewIndex) = FStrings(OldIndex)
33:       FStrings(OldIndex) = Temp
34:    End Sub
35:
36:    Private Function ValidIndex(ByVal Index As Integer) As Boolean
37:       Return (Index >= FStrings.GetLowerBound(0)) And _
38:          (Index <= FStrings.GetUpperBound(0))
39:    End Function
40:
41:    Private Overloads Sub Validate(ByVal Name As String)
42:       Validate(Names(Name))
43:    End Sub
44:
45:    Private Overloads Sub Validate(ByVal Index As Integer)
46:       If (Not ValidIndex(Index)) Then
47:          'Throw New ApplicationException(Index & " is an invalid index")
48:          IndexedException.ThrowException(Index)
49:       End If
50:    End Sub
51:
52:    Public Property Names(ByVal Name As String) As Integer
```

LISTING 7.5 continued

```
53:     Get
54:        Return Array.IndexOf(FStrings, Name)
55:     End Get
56:
57:     Set(ByVal Value As Integer)
58:        Validate(Name)
59:        Swap(Names(Name), Value)
60:     End Set
61:   End Property
62:
63: End Class
```

The new exception class is defined on lines 1 through 12. Line 2 indicates that IndexedException inherits from System.ApplicationException. In object-oriented parlance, this is referred to as an *IsA* relationship. The *Unified Modeling Language* (UML) refers to inheritance as a generalization. We say that IndexedException is an ApplicationException.

IndexedException introduces an overloaded constructor that takes a string argument. The string argument to the constructor—line 4—will become part of the message of our exception. Line 5 uses the MyBase variable, which references the base class. MyBase is available just as the reference-to-self variable Me is. Line 8 introduces a Shared method. A Shared method that creates an instance of an object is referred to as a factory method. A factory method allows you to localize the construction and initialization of an object, mitigating the need to duplicate object construction code. Finally, the Validate procedure replaces the old statement from line 12 of Listing 7.4 with a call to the new factory method that creates and throws our new exception. (The original statement and the new statement are on lines 47 and 48, respectively, of Listing 7.5.)

Now you know the mechanics of defining indexed properties, adding validation code to the property methods, and how to introduce new exception-handling classes. If inheritance is a little confusing, you will find an elaboration on the subjects of inheritance and polymorphism in Chapter 10.

Using Default Properties

Visual Basic .NET supports Default properties, but unlike properties in VB6, only indexed properties can be Default properties in Visual Basic .NET. The reason is straightforward.

In VB6, we used the Set method when assigning an object reference to an object variable. Again, in VB6, if the assignee in a statement were an object and no Set were present, VB6 could infer that the coder intended to use the Default property. Hence, VB6

`Default` properties don't have to be indexed properties. The `Set` keyword provided the necessary compiler clue.

Visual Basic .NET doesn't use `Set` for object assignment. Thus the presence of an object and the absence of `Set` aren't sufficient to convey your intent to the compiler. In Visual Basic .NET, it's the presence of parentheses used with an object that provides the compiler hint indicating that a `Default` property is being requested. Consequently, all `Default` properties must be indexed properties in Visual Basic .NET, and you might have only one default property.

> **Note**
>
> Only indexed properties can be the `Default` property in Object Pascal too. The presence of *object*[] in Object Pascal provides a similar compiler hint that an indexed property rather than object assignment is being requested.
>
> It's possible—and very probable—that the revision to default properties is due in part to the influence of Anders Hejlsberg. Hejlsberg, now a Distinguished Engineer at Microsoft, was a principal architect at Borland, instrumental in the implementation of Delphi, which is built in Object Pascal. There are many such influences in Visual Basic .NET from Object Pascal. This isn't to say that Visual Basic .NET is Pascal-like; rather, Visual Basic .NET is an evolving language and Microsoft has the good sense to improve Visual Basic with a heterogeneous mixture of aspects from other languages.
>
> Granted, it might take some getting used to—I heard some developers referring to Visual Basic .NET as "Visual Fred" at Tech Ed—Visual Basic .NET is a radically improved product, but it's still Visual Basic.

To indicate that a property is the default property, place the `Default` keyword on the line of text that starts the `Property` statement, preceding the access specifier. An excerpt from Listing 7.5 shows the placement of the `Default` keyword, making the `Strings` property the default property:

```
Default Public Property Strings(ByVal Index As Integer) As String
  Get
    Return FStrings(Index)
  End Get

  Set(ByVal Value As String)
    FStrings(Index) = Value
  End Set
End Property
```

Assuming we declare an instance of `Indexed` using `Dim IndexedObject As New Indexed`, we can access the `Strings` property in the original verbose manner:

```
MsgBox(IndexedObject.Strings(1))
```

Or we can access it in the shorthand manner, relying on the `Default` modifier:

```
MsgBox(IndexedObject(1))
```

To recap, default properties must be indexed properties, you can only have one default property per class, and you can invoke property setter and getter methods on a default property using the verbose or shorthand form. The compiler will reconcile the code as needed.

Using Property Modifiers

In addition to the access specifiers, there are special property modifiers that are particular to properties only. These include the `ReadOnly` and `WriteOnly` modifiers.

A read-only property is a property that can be used as an r-value only. That is, a property statement that includes a `ReadOnly` modifier will generate a getter block only and users can evaluate the property but not modify it. Consumers of a class can think of `ReadOnly` properties as constants or immutable data, but keep in mind that a mechanism internal to the object can change the underlying value even though the consumer can't.

A write-only property is a property that a consumer can modify but can't view. Write-only properties implement a property setter only.

The outer property block is identical for `ReadOnly` or `WriteOnly` properties, except for the presence of the modifier. Internally, `ReadOnly` properties have a getter and no setter, and `WriteOnly` properties have a setter and no getter.

Implementing Read-Only Properties

An example of a read-only property might be one that returns a datetime stamp when an object is created. Because an object can only be created once—although you can have multiple instances of a class, any given instance will be created only once—it doesn't make sense to allow consumers to modify the creation time of an object.

If you need to track how long an object has been alive and want to make sure that consumers cannot change the creation time stamp, you can define a read-only `CreateTime` property and initialize it in the constructor:

```
Public Sub New()
  MyBase.New()
  FCreateTime = Now
End Sub
```

7

```
Private FCreateTime As Date

Public ReadOnly Property CreateTime() As Date
  Get
    Return FCreateTime
  End Get
End Property
```

Note the location of the `ReadOnly` modifier. The `Public` property `CreateTime` is defined as a `ReadOnly` property, hence it only has a `Get` block. The constructor—`Sub New`—initializes the underlying field, `FCreateTime`, when the constructor is called.

Another example where you might elect to employ a read-only property is a calculated field. If a property has no underlying field value and its value is derived, it makes no sense to implement a set property method. Consider the symmetric `ElapsedTime` property. If we wanted to determine the elapsed application runtime, we could return the elapsed time as the current time minus the `CreateTime`:

```
Public ReadOnly Property ElapsedTime() As TimeSpan
  Get
    Return Date.op_Subtraction(Now, FCreateTime)
  End Get
End Property
```

The `ElapsedTime` property is modified `ReadOnly` because it's dynamically derived each time it's called. The `ElapsedTime` property also demonstrates the new `TimeSpan` class, which was implemented to allow for very close time measurements. Another peculiarity is the `Shared` method `Date.op_Subtraction` invocation. Visual Basic .NET doesn't yet support operator overloading, so specially named methods with an `op_` prefix were implemented where the behavior represents an overloaded operator that might exist in C# for example.

`ElapsedTime` returns the difference between `Now` and the containing object's creation time. You can test the two properties with a couple of lines of code:

```
Dim O As New PropertyModifiers()
System.Threading.Thread.Sleep(1000)
MsgBox(O.ElapsedTime.ToString)
```

The first statement creates an instance of the `PropertyModifers` class containing the two predefined properties we have been discussing. The constructor initializes the field `FCreateTime`. The second statement uses the `Shared Sleep` method, which puts the current `Thread` to sleep. In the example, the thread is put to sleep for 1000 milliseconds, or 1 second. The third statement invokes the `ElapsedTime` property method, which returns a `TimeSpan` object. The `ToString` method is actually being called using the implicit reference to the `TimeSpan` object.

FIGURE 7.3

Shows the granu-
larity of the
TimeSpan *class in*
Visual Basic .NET.

FieldsAndProperties	☒

00:00:01.0014400

OK

The three sample statements culminate in displaying a message box as shown in Figure 7.3. According to the message box, it looks as if Visual Basic .NET required about 1.4 milliseconds after the thread woke up and the Now function was called.

Implementing WriteOnly Properties

WriteOnly properties are implemented less frequently, but you will encounter some good reasons for using them on occasion. One occasion is a password property.

Suppose you have a user-validation class that accepts a user name and masked password. It might be perfectly acceptable to answer a client object's query, "Who is the user?" But it would probably be a riskier proposition to answer "What is the password?" In such an instance, you might want to allow the user to enter the password but prevent any client objects from obtaining this information. You could implement a WriteOnly password property:

```
Private FPassword As String

Public WriteOnly Property Password() As String
  Set(ByVal Value As String)
    FPassword = Value
  End Set
End Property
```

Note that the code editor only creates a Set block, and the value assigned to the property is stored in an underlying field.

For practical reasons, you can modify the code to be even more secure. For example, you could implement a WriteOnly property that immediately validated the password, in the property setter, and then flushed the variable and only stored whether a valid property was presented but didn't actually store the password. Such a revision might prevent memory sniffer programs from displaying properties stored in the class's memory space.

Other property modifiers, like Shadows, can be used with properties as well as methods. To avoid presenting a significant amount of redundant information in your code, assume that modifiers can be applied to any class member unless the text indicates otherwise. WriteOnly and ReadOnly apply to properties only.

Defining Shared Properties

A comprehensive discussion on `Shared` members is presented in Chapter 11. Read Chapter 11 for a long discussion of `Shared` members with examples. For now, suffice it to say, properties can be `Shared` or instance members. `Shared` members mean that you can invoke the property on the class, and the property is defined with the `Shared` keyword. `Shared` members can also be invoked using instances, but instance members can only be invoked using an instance of the class. Here's an example:

```
Public Shared ReadOnly Property Name() As String
  Get
    Return "PropertyModifiers"
  End Get
End Property
```

The example defines a `Public`, `Shared`, `ReadOnly` property named `Name`. Because the class name never changes, unless changed in the editor, the method can be read-only. Making the property public means that consumers can query the call name, and using the `Shared` modifier means that we don't need an object (a class instance) to ask the class "What is your name?" If the class is named `PropertyModifiers`, we could invoke the getter by writing `PropertyModifiers.Name`.

The `Name` property in the fragment demonstrates very specific changes between Visual Basic .NET and VB6. The `Name` property is very precise in its intent. The difference is that Visual Basic .NET allows us to express intent and enforce it using very precise grammar. We could define a read-only property in VB6 by defining a `Let Property` statement only, but its read-only status was implicit. However, we couldn't define `Shared` members.

There may be debate among some developers whether these minor semantics really make a big difference. The answer is that they absolutely do. Programming is almost mathematically precise, and the languages we program in should be explicitly expressive to avoid ambiguous, obtuse, and excessive code. Nuance and subtlety should be left to the language of lovers and statesmen.

Adding Property Attributes

Attributes aren't completely new in Visual Basic .NET. You could actually use a text editor and modify attributes in VB6. To try this, open a VB6 class module—a .CLS file—modify the value of the `Attribute VB_PredeclaredId = False` attribute statement to `Attribute VB_PredeclaredId = True` and you will have an autocreated class. Supposing the class name is `Class1` with a method `Foo`: After modifying the attribute statement and importing the text-editor revised class, you could write `Class1.Foo` and the code would run. This works because the `VB_PredeclaredID` attribute is the mechanism that makes forms autocreated.

Okay, so why is this point important in a Visual Basic .NET book? Attributes are important because they are a full-fledged aspect of Visual Basic .NET development. Attributes are right out in the open, and they are a hundred times more powerful in Visual Basic .NET. Try the following code revision using the `Name` property from the last section:

```
Public Shared ReadOnly Property Name() As String
  <System.Diagnostics.DebuggerHidden()> Get
    Return "PropertyModifiers"
  End Get
End Property
```

Notice the use of the attribute on the getter. (The `DebuggerHidden` attribute was introduced in Chapter 1.) This attribute prevents the debugger from stepping into this property method. The fragment demonstrates an attribute class defined in the `System.Diagnostics` namespace.

Attributes can be used for a lot of things in Visual Basic .NET. For example, you use an attribute tag to convert a method into a WebMethod. Attributes are one of the reasons why this isn't your father's Visual Basic. Perhaps attributes may end up being like fast sports cars with adolescent drivers, but they are brand new in Visual Basic .NET and there is enough information that they need their own chapter. (And, of course a fast sports car is a tremendous amount of fun if tempered with experience and diminished testosterone levels.) For now, when you see a *<name>* tag in Visual Basic .NET code, remember that you are looking at an attribute. Chapter 12 covers attributes in detail.

Adding Methods to Classes

Methods are functions and subroutines that just happen to belong to a class or structure. We covered structures in Chapter 5, so all of our examples will be demonstrated using classes in this chapter.

Anything you can do with a procedure in a module, you can do with a procedure in a class. The only rule when it comes to methods is *subjective measure* of good taste. Personally, I like Beethoven and the rock band Creed, so my tastes are probably different than yours. Does this mean that all bets are off when it comes to implementing methods? The answer is both yes and no.

If you are the designer and programmer, you can do whatever you want. If you don't have to get paid for the code you write, you can go nuts. There are several good books on stylistic issues and rules of thumb. A recent book is Martin Fowler's refactoring book.

Grady Booch, James Coplien, and Bjarne Stroustrup have written excellent books on object-oriented programming. You can find references to some of these in this book's bibliography. And, you can use the examples in this book.

Most of the examples in this book are refactored to some extent, but more importantly, this is the way I have been writing code for about 12 years now. I write the style of code presented in this book for a very good reason: After 10-plus years, a half dozen languages, and millions of lines of code, my particular style allows me to write very small amounts of highly reusable, maintainable code and do it very fast. Here are a few basic guidelines I follow when implementing methods.

- Keep the public interface small. To paraphrase Booch (1995), implement a handful of public methods and properties.

- Provide a good name for methods, avoid nonstandard abbreviations, and use a good verb in the method name. (If you have a noun, you are probably referring to a property.)

- Implement methods so that they perform only the action stated in the method name; that is, define singular rather than plural methods.

- Limit methods to approximately three to five lines of code, never more than what can be viewed on a screen at one time.

- Use the refactoring "Extract Method" and give the new method a good name rather than write a long comment.

- Consider implementing all nonpublic methods as protected and virtual—you never know who will want to use them in the future.

These lessons weren't employed from day one. They were acquired from the masters of our time, over a period of time. Some of them, however—like short, singular methods—just always seemed to make sense. Finally, the guideline can be illustrated with a quick story.

Note

I purchased my first car for $325 when I was 15, the day I received my learner's permit. The term is *rolling wreck*. There was nothing beautiful about this car except for the idea of autonomy. It had four different-sized tires, a hole in the radiator the size of a football, the wrong transmission, and the front seat adjustment didn't lock. When the car stopped, the bench seat slid all the way forward; when the car accelerated, the seat slid all the way back.

Shortly after buying the car, I decided to start refurbishments. I chose to begin with the fan belt. I borrowed my dad's tools and began to try to remove the fan, followed by the water pump, and probably would have disassembled the engine block if I knew how, all to change the belt. After a couple of hours I gave up, put the few screws from the fan I was able to get out back in, and drove the car to a garage. The mechanic loosened the alternator, which eased the tension on the old belt. He slipped the belt off the alternator and over the fan, and placed the new belt on in reverse order. Finally, he increased the tension by adjusting the alternator and tightened the alternator bolts. The charge for about five minutes' labor was $35 bucks. Pretty steep for five minutes' work. He got 35 bucks, but not for the difficulty of the task—rather, he got paid because he knew how to perform the task. (Okay, I borrowed a little from an age-old fable.)

The moral is that knowing how and why is the only justification you need for making up your own reasons for deviating from general guidelines. Of course, if there is no justification, someone will challenge you or change your code when you aren't looking. Code is about as personal as any other creative activity. Following good rules for the general case will help your productivity; deviating will aid your genius.

Implementing Constructors and Destructors

There are two special methods you will need to implement. They are referred to as the constructor and destructor. A constructor is called to initialize a class, and a destructor is called to deinitialize, or finalize, a class. Visual Basic .NET implements the constructor as Sub New and the destructor as protected method Sub Finalize.

Every class gets at least one constructor inherited from the base class Object. Object defines a parameterless Sub New procedure that is called when you write code like the following:

```
Dim objectvariable As New classname
```

objectvariable represents any valid variable name and *classname* represents any valid reference type. From the statement, you might infer that New seems to be an operator, but if you step through a few examples, you will see that the statement proceeds directly to the Sub New() method. The New method—the constructor—is called when you create new instances of classes.

When an object is released from memory, the garbage collector calls the Sub Finalize method, the destructor. You can implement a destructor to deinitialize your objects by adding a Finalize method to your classes:

```
Protected Overrides Sub Finalize()
End Sub
```

> **Note**
>
> The garbage collection mechanism, or the garbage collector, is shortened to GC. GC is the namespace containing the garbage collector.

Traditionally, the purpose of a constructor is to release memory allocated to objects contained in a class. Because Visual Basic .NET employs a GC, you cannot be sure when the GC will actually call your destructor. You can still use a destructor to clean up objects contained in your classes, but if you have time-critical resources that need to be released, add a public Dispose method. By convention, we use a Public Sub Dispose() method to perform cleanup like closing files or recordsets.

Defining Constructors

Aggregation refers to adding members to a class. When your class has members that are themselves classes, and the class takes responsibility for creating and destroying instances of those members, we call this an *aggregation* relationship. When a class has members that are classes but some external entity creates and destroys those classes, we refer to this as an *association* relationship. When you define aggregation relationships in your class, you need to create a constructor for your class.

You can create a constructor for any reason, but you will need to create a constructor if you want to instantiate—or, create an instance of a class—aggregate members. The default constructor is represented by Sub New with no parameters. To demonstrate, I defined a LoaderClass that uses the System.IO.TextReader class to load a text file into an ArrayList.

```
Public Sub New()
  MyBase.New()
  FArrayList = New ArrayList()
End Sub
```

> **Note**
>
> The code will run correctly even if the `MyBase.New()` statement is removed. Semantically, all derived classes must call the parent constructor, but Visual Basic .NET seems to do it for you in most instances. Rather than trying to guess when and why Visual Basic .NET might call the base class's constructor, always place `MyBase.New()` as the first statement in your constructor. If you want to call a parameterized constructor in your child class, replace the empty-parameter constructor call with a parameterized constructor call.

The parameterless `Sub New()` calls the base class constructor using `MyBase.New()`. `MyBase` is a reserved word that allows you to refer to members in a class's *base class*, also called its *parent class*. The internal storage for the `LoaderClass` is an `ArrayList`. Because the `LoaderClass`—whose constructor is shown—owns the `ArrayList`, the constructor instantiates the `ArrayList` before anything else happens.

Defining Overloaded Parameterized Constructors

If you need to pass external data into your class to ensure proper initialization, you can define a parameterized constructor.

The `LoaderClass` is designed to load a text file into an `ArrayList`. Thus it makes sense to initialize `LoaderClass` objects with a filename. By having two constructors we can create instances before we know the filename, or we can initialize loaders with a filename:

```
Public Sub New(ByVal AFileName As String)
  Me.New()
  FileName = AFileName
End Sub
```

To avoid replicating code, we delegate part of the responsibility for class construction to the parameterless constructor with `Me.New()` and cache the filename parameter.

Having two `Sub New` methods in the same class means that you have overloaded the constructor. Constructors don't allow the use of the `Overloads` keyword. This is a special rule applied by the Visual Basic .NET engineers for constructors. (Refer to the section "Using Modifiers" later in this chapter for more on overloading methods.)

Implementing Destructors

If you allocate memory in a constructor, you need to implement a destructor to deallocate the memory. Sub New is used similarly to Class_Initialize from VB6, and Sub Finalize is used similarly to Class_Terminate from VB6. Objects created in a constructor need to be disposed of in the destructor.

Generally, if your class doesn't define a constructor, you probably don't need a destructor. Here is the basic form of the Finalize destructor, as implemented in the LoaderClass example class:

```
Protected Overrides Sub Finalize()
  Dispose()
End Sub
```

By implementing the destructor in terms of the Dispose method, you can call the Dispose method explicitly to release objects in advance of the GC. There are special considerations for cleaning up contained resources; refer to the next section for more on implementing a Dispose method.

The Finalize destructor is Protected; therefore, you cannot call it directly. The destructor is called by the GC. Here is a basic list of guidelines for implementing a destructor:

- Finalize methods incur some overhead, so don't define an overloaded Finalize method unless you have expensive resources to clean up that were allocated in a constructor.
- Don't promote access of the Finalize method to Public.
- Release owned objects in your Dispose method; implement Finalize by calling Dispose.
- Don't clean up references in your destructor; if your code didn't create an object, it is a reference, not an aggregate.
- Don't create objects or use other referenced objects in the Finalize method; destructors are for cleanup only.
- Call MyBase.Finalize as the first statement in your Finalize method.

Because you don't know when the GC will release your objects, you can implement a Public Dispose method and call it explicitly in a Finally block of a resource protection block if you want deterministic finalization for things like file streams and threads.

Implementing a Dispose Method

Destructors are protected. Consumers cannot and shouldn't call the Finalize method directly. You can run the garbage collector explicitly by writing System.GC.Collect, but doing so isn't a recommended practice and incurs significant overhead.

If you want to clean up expensive objects, implement a `Public Dispose` method and call that. Here are some recommended practices for implementing a `Dispose` method:

- Add a `Dispose` method by implementing the `IDisposable` interface. (`IDisposable` has one method, `Dispose`, and you can look up `IDisposable` in the help file to see some examples of classes that have implemented the interface.)

- Provide a public `Dispose` method if you have expensive resources, like Windows handles, recordsets, or file streams, that need to be released back to the system as soon as you are finished with them.

- Devise a mechanism to suppress disposal after a user calls `Dispose` directly.

- Call a base class's `Dispose` method if the base class implements `IDisposable`.

- Implement a `Finalize` method that calls `Dispose`. This will ensure that `Dispose` is always called.

- Release owned objects in your `Dispose` method.

- Consider throwing an `ObjectDisposedException` if your `Dispose` method has been called previously and a consumer tries to use the object.

- Call `GC.SuppressFinalize(Me)` in your `Dispose` method to tell the GC that it does not need to call the `Finalize` method.

- Allow object `Dispose` to be called more than one time. Second and successive calls should perform no operation.

Employing these guidelines, here is the `Dispose` method for the `LoaderClass`:

```
Public Sub Dispose() Implements IDisposable.Dispose
  Static FDisposed As Boolean = False
  If (FDisposed) Then Exit Sub
  FDisposed = True
  Close()
  FArrayList = Nothing
  GC.SuppressFinalize(Me)
End Sub
```

The `Dispose` method implements `IDisposable.Dispose` (thus we know that `Implements IDisposable` is included in our `LoaderClass`). The static local variable is used to make `Dispose` safe to call more than once. The second statement toggles the Boolean, indicating that we have called `Dispose`. The `LoaderClass.Close` method is called to close the `TextReader`, not shown yet, and the `ArrayList` is assigned to `Nothing`. Finally, `GC.SuppressFinalize` tells the GC that it does not need to call `Finalize` for this object.

Special Keywords

There are two keywords you will encounter when working with classes, `MyBase` and `MyClass`. `MyBase`—so you have already seen—allows you to invoke methods in your class's base class that may be overloaded in your class, resolving any name ambiguity.

`MyClass` is roughly equivalent to the `Me` reference to self. `MyClass` assumes that any methods called with `MyClass` are declared as `NotOverridable`. `MyClass` calls a method without regard for the runtime type of the object, effectively bypassing polymorphic behavior. Because `MyClass` is a reference to an object, you can't use `MyClass` in `Shared` methods.

The reference to self `Me` was carried over in Visual Basic .NET. `Me` requires an instance to use. `MyClass` invokes a method in the same class, but `Me` invokes a method in the object actually referred to by `Me`, that is, in a polymorphic way. Consider the following classes.

```
Public Class Class1
  Public Overridable Sub Proc()
  End Sub
  Public Sub New()
    Me.Proc()
  End Sub
End Class

Public Class Class2
  Inherits Class1
  Public Overrides Sub Proc()
  End Sub
End Class
```

When an object of type `Class2` is created, the constructor in `Class1` invokes `Class2.Proc`. If `Me.Proc` is revised to `MyClass.Proc`, then `Class1.Proc` is invoked.

Adding Function and Subroutine Methods

Methods are simply functions and subroutines that are defined within the confines of a class (or `Structure`) construct. The only challenge in implementing methods is picking the right methods for your problem, keeping them simple, and determining the kind of access or modifiers that make sense for each method.

Unfortunately, how methods are defined is a subjective matter of style. The best way to learn to implement methods is to read and write a lot of code, and select a style that proves to work reliably for you. Don't hesitate to experiment and revise. Listing 7.6 contains the complete listing for `LoaderClass`.

LISTING 7.6   The complete listing of the `LoaderClass`

```
 1: Imports System.IO
 2:
 3: Public Class LoaderClass
 4:    Implements IDisposable
 5:
 6:    Private FFileName As String
 7:    Private FReader As TextReader
 8:    Private FArrayList As ArrayList
 9:    Public Event OnText(ByVal Text As String)
10:
11:    Private Sub DoText(ByVal Text As String)
12:       RaiseEvent OnText(Text)
13:    End Sub
14:
15:    Public Property FileName() As String
16:      Get
17:         Return FFileName
18:      End Get
19:      Set(ByVal Value As String)
20:         FFileName = Value
21:      End Set
22:    End Property
23:
24:    Public Overloads Sub Open()
25:       If (FReader Is Nothing) Then
26:          FReader = File.OpenText(FFileName)
27:       Else
28:          Throw New ApplicationException("file is already open")
29:       End If
30:    End Sub
31:
32:    Public Overloads Sub Open(ByVal AFileName As String)
33:       FileName = AFileName
34:       Open()
35:    End Sub
36:
37:    Public Sub Close()
38:       If (FReader Is Nothing) Then Exit Sub
39:       FReader.Close()
40:       FReader = Nothing
41:    End Sub
42:
43:    Private Function Add(ByVal Text As String) As Boolean
44:       If (Text = "") Then Return False
45:       DoText(Text)
46:       FArrayList.Add(Text)
47:       Return True
48:    End Function
49:
```

7

CREATING CLASSES

LISTING 7.6   continued

```
50:  Private Function Reading() As Boolean
51:    Return Not FDisposed AndAlso Add(FReader.ReadLine())
52:  End Function
53:
54:  Public Sub Load()
55:    While (Reading())
56:      Application.DoEvents()
57:    End While
58:  End Sub
59:
60:  Public Sub New()
61:    MyBase.New()
62:    FArrayList = New ArrayList()
63:  End Sub
64:
65:  Public Sub New(ByVal AFileName As String)
66:    Me.New()
67:    FileName = AFileName
68:  End Sub
69:
70:  Private FDisposed As Boolean = False
71:
72:  Public Sub Dispose() Implements IDisposable.Dispose
73:    If (FDisposed) Then Exit Sub
74:    FDisposed = True
75:    Close()
76:    FArrayList = Nothing
77:  End Sub
78:
79:  Protected Overrides Sub Finalize()
80:    Dispose()
81:    MyBase.Finalize()
82:  End Sub
83:
84:  Public Shared Function Load(ByVal AFileName _
85:    As String) As LoaderClass
86:
87:    Dim ALoader As New LoaderClass(AFileName)
88:    ALoader.Open()
89:    ALoader.Load()
90:    Return ALoader
91:
92:  End Function
93: End Class
```

The LoaderClass defines a DoText method, two Open methods, Close, Add, Reading, and Load methods. DoText was implemented as a Private method; all it does is raise the event to notify any objects that might want to eavesdrop on the loading process. The

Open methods are both `Public`; they were defined with the `Overloads` modifier to allow consumers to open a file with a passed filename argument, or, without, assuming that the filename was already assigned in the constructor call or by modifying the property value. (The `FileName` property is defined on lines 15 through 22.) The `Add` method eliminates the need for a temporary. We can pass the result of the `TextReader.ReadLine` method as a parameter to `Add` and return a Boolean indicating whether we want the value or not. The `Reading` function returns a Boolean indicating that we were able to add the text and we haven't called the `Dispose` method (see lines 50 to 52). Line 51 demonstrates how to use the short-circuiting `AndAlso` operator. If `Dispose` has been called, `Reading` short circuits on `Not Disposed`. Otherwise, the next line of text is read. If `FReader.ReadLine` has read the entire file, the `ReadLine` method returns an empty string (`""`) and `Reading` returns False. Because we separated the `Reading` and `Add` behavior out, the `Load` method is a very simple `while` loop (lines 54 to 58).

Open, Close, and Load are the only public methods keeping the `LoaderClass` pretty easy to use for consumers. Everything else supports the three public methods and wouldn't make sense for consumers to call directly, so all the other methods are `Private`.

> **Note**
>
> Consider a single musician versus an orchestra. If you have one musician and one instrument, the kind of music and the orchestration of that instrument are severely limited. If you have an entire orchestra with dozens of musicians and instruments, the orchestration and subsequently the variety of music you can play are significantly increased.
>
> Monolithic methods are like the lone musician: enjoyable, but not very diverse. Many singular methods—think of overloaded constructors as an entire wind section—mean that each method can specialize and be reorchestrated in a greater variety.

In this particular example, we probably won't get a lot of code reuse out of `Add`, `Reading`, and `DoText`. What you will get are singular functions that are very easy to implement, and it's very unlikely that they will introduce errors. One more benefit that might not be obvious is that methods can be overridden in subclasses. (The private methods in `LoaderClass` would need to be made protected if we decided to extend them in a subclass, but we could do so with very little effort.) If you use a small number of monolithic methods, you have fewer opportunities for overriding and extending behavior.

Using Method Modifiers

Method modifiers enable us to exercise a greater, more verbose control over our method implementations.

Overloading Methods

The `Overloads` modifier is used to indicate that two or more methods in the same class are overloaded. The `LoaderClass.Open` methods demonstrate method overloading.

The benefit of method overloading is that it allows you to implement methods that support the same semantic operation but differ by argument number or type. Consider a method that writes text to the console, named `Print`. Without method overloading, you would have to implement a uniquely named method for printing any data type, for example, `PrintInteger`, `PrintString`, `PrintDate`. Such an approach would require that users learn the names of many methods that perform the same behavior. With overloading you could name all of the `Print` methods and let the compiler resolve which method to call based on the data type; offload tedious work to the compiler and let the programmer think about important things.

The procedure heading, number and type of arguments, and return type (if the procedure is a function) comprise the procedure's signature.

Tip

Properties can be overloaded too.

Here are the basic rules for using the `Overloads` modifier:

- You must use the `Overloads` keyword to indicate that two or more methods are overloaded (see Listing 7.6 for placement of the modifier).
- Overloaded methods must have a distinct type or numbers of parameters (Visual Basic .NET supports overloading methods on types that are very close, like `Integer` and `Long` parameters).
- You may not overload methods based on modifiers such as `Shared`.
- You may not overload methods based on the argument-calling conventions `ByVal` or `ByRef`.
- You may not overload methods based solely on the names of the parameters.

- You may not overload methods based on return type, although two overloaded methods may include different return types. For example, a subroutine and function with the same name and arguments may not be overloaded nor may two functions with the same arguments and only differing return types.

If you find yourself implementing operations because the data type is different but the kind of operation is the same, you do need overloaded methods. If you find yourself implementing two methods with the same code, but differing only by the value of one or more parameters, you need one method with an `Optional` parameter.

Overriding Methods

The `Overrides` modifier supports polymorphism. You use the `Overrides` modifier when you want to extend or change the behavior of a method in a base class. The base class method must have the same signature as the method overriding it.

We will revisit the `Overrides` modifier in Chapter 10.

`Overridable`, `MustOverride`, and `NotOverridable` Modifiers

The `Overridable`, `MustOverride`, and `NotOverridable` modifiers are used to manage which methods *can* be overridden and which *must* be overridden.

The `Overridable` and `NotOverridable` modifiers are mutually exclusive. The `Overridable` modifier indicates that a method can be overridden. The `NotOverridable` modifier indicates that you cannot override a method. The `MustOverride` modifier indicates that a method is abstract, and child classes must implement the `MustOverride` methods in a parent class. `MustOverride` implies that a method is overridable, so you don't need the `Overridable` modifier and `NotOverridable` doesn't make sense for `MustOverride` methods.

`MustOverride` methods have no implementation in the class where they are declared with this modifier. `MustOverride` methods are equivalent to purely virtual methods in C++ and virtual abstract methods in Object Pascal; descendants must implement these methods.

Using the `Shadows` Modifier

If you want a child class to use a name previously introduced in a parent class, use the `Shadows` keyword to do so. Shadowed names aren't removed from the parent class; the `Shadows` keyword simply allows you to reintroduce a previously used name in the child class without a compiler error.

The member in the child class doesn't have to be the same type as the shadowed member; the two members only need identical names. Any kind of member in a child class can shadow any kind of member in a parent class. A method in a child class can shadow a field, property, method, or event in a parent class. The following fragment demonstrates using the Shadows modifier to reintroduce a method in a child class with the same name as a method in the parent class.

```
Public Class A
  Public Sub Foo()
  End Sub
End Class

Public Class B
  Inherits A
  Public Shadows Sub Foo()
  End Sub
End Class
```

The listing shows two classes, A and B. B is subclassed from A; that is, A is B's parent. Both A and B have a method Foo. The introduction of the Shadows keyword on B.Foo means that B.Foo hides A.Foo. If you have identical names in two classes related by inheritance, you must use either the Shadows or Overrides modifier. (Refer to Chapter 10, "Inheritance and Polymorphism," for more details on using Shadows and Overrides.)

Shared Modifier

Shared members are accessible without creating instances of reference types or value types—classes or structures, respectively. Chapter 11 discusses shared members in detail.

Using Access Specifiers

Classes support the sage advice *divide et impera*, divide and conquer. A class allows you to think like a producer when defining a class and focus only on the implementation of the class. When you are using the class, you become a consumer of the class. Your only considerations as a class consumer are the public members, and both the public and protected members if you are implementing a child class.

The benefit of access modifiers is that as a consumer you don't ever have to worry about the private members and usually don't have to worry about the protected members. If you follow the general guideline to keep public members to a half dozen or so, as a class consumer you have effectively offloaded most of the implementation details—the private and protected members—of the class. That is to say, you have divided the problem into a simpler problem: understanding the class as a producer when you are writing the class and concerning yourself with only the public members as a consumer. This division of focus facilitates managing the complexity of a growing body of code. By aggressively managing code, using access specifiers to limit what consumers must comprehend, you can make your code easier to manage.

You can use `Public`, `Protected`, `Private`, `Friend`, and `Protected Friend` access specifiers on methods. Refer to "Using Class Access Specifiers" at the beginning of the chapter for a description of how each access specifier affects entities. The following list briefly reviews the impact of access specifiers on methods:

- `Public` methods can be called by any consumer or internally.
- `Protected` methods can be called by a generalizer (child class) or internally.
- `Private` methods can only be called internally.
- `Friend` methods can only be called within the same application.
- `Protected Friend` members can be called internally and by children within the same application.

Hundreds of examples are demonstrated throughout this book, including several in this chapter. Refer to the first section of this chapter, "Defining Classes," for general guidelines covering the number of methods and the employment of access specifiers.

Adding Class Events

When you want to notify a consumer of your class that something has happened inside your class, you can expose the occurrence as an event:

```
Public Event OnText(ByVal Text As String)

Private Sub DoText(ByVal Text As String)
  RaiseEvent OnText(Text)
End Sub
```

The `LoaderClass` (refer to Listing 7.6) raises an `OnText` event for each line of text read from the input file. The benefit of using events is that the class doesn't need to know which consumers are interested in receiving notification when the event occurs. The `LoaderClass` code doesn't change regardless of whether any consumer is handling the event.

The statement `Public Event OnText(ByVal Text As String)` creates a `Delegate` type implicitly. Any consumer that wants to handle the `OnText` event raised by the `LoaderClass` can use a `WithEvents` statement or an `AddHandler` statement. Here is an example of an `AddHandler` statement:

```
AddHandler FLoader.OnText, AddressOf OnText
```

The object that contains the `OnText` method (in the preceding statement) is added to the `Delegate` invocation list of the `FLoader.OnText Delegate`.

Events aren't polymorphic. That means that we cannot explicitly overload events in child classes. As a general implementation strategy, we can wrap `RaiseEvent` statements in a method and use the method (see `DoText`) as a proxy to raise the event. By using a proxy to raise events, we can override the proxy in child classes if we want to change the event-raising behavior.

Event handling has changed significantly in Visual Basic .NET, including the introduction of the `Delegate` and `MulticastDelegate` classes that make event handling more powerful. Chapters 8, "Adding Events," and 9 "Understanding Delegates," provide a comprehensive discussion of event handling and delegates.

Defining Nested Classes

A *nested class* is quite simply a class defined within a class. Nested classes can be defined with all of the elements of any other class. Here's the skeletal code for a nested class:

```
Public Class Outer
  Public Class Nested
  End Class
End Class
```

Your motivation for creating nested classes is to collect a group of elements that make sense together and only within the containing class. For example, if you have a class and some fields, properties, and methods that define a concept separate but a part of the containing class and you want to store multiple variations of state, you might implement a nested class.

In general you won't need to implement nested classes. Any implementation that can be done with nested classes can be done without nested classes. If you are interested, you can look into the advanced idioms, including the letter-envelope idiom, discussed by James Coplien in *Advanced C++*. Listing 7.7 provides an example of nested classes, demonstrating the grammatical technique.

LISTING 7.7   Multiple nested classes, inheritance, and multithreading in the TrafficLight.sln demo program

```
1: Public Class Signal
2: #Region " Public Members "
3:   Public Event OnChange(ByVal sender As System.Object, _
```

LISTING 7.7   continued

```
4:          ByVal e As System.EventArgs)
5:
6:      Public Sub Draw(ByVal Graphic As Graphics)
7:          Graphic.FillRectangle(Brushes.Brown, Rect)
8:          DrawLights(Graphic)
9:      End Sub
10:
11:     Public Sub New(ByVal Rect As Rectangle)
12:         FRect = Rect
13:         PositionLights()
14:         TurnOnGreen()
15:         CreateThread()
16:     End Sub
17:
18:     Public Sub Dispose()
19:         Static Done As Boolean = False
20:         If (Done) Then Exit Sub
21:         Done = True
22:         KillThread()
23:         GC.SuppressFinalize(Me)
24:     End Sub
25:
26:     Public Sub NextSignal()
27:         While (FThread.IsAlive)
28:           FThread.Sleep(SleepTime())
29:           ChangeState()
30:           DoChange()
31:         End While
32:     End Sub
33:
34: #End Region
35:
36: #Region " Protected Members "
37:
38:     ' Destructor
39:     Protected Overrides Sub Finalize()
40:         Dispose()
41:     End Sub
42:
43:     Protected Sub CreateThread()
44:         FThread = New Threading.Thread(AddressOf NextSignal)
45:         FThread.IsBackground = True
46:         StartSignal()
47:     End Sub
48:
49:     Protected Sub StartSignal()
50:         FThread.Start()
51:     End Sub
52:
```

LISTING 7.7   continued

```
53:    Protected Sub StopSignal()
54:      FThread.Abort()
55:      FThread.Join()
56:    End Sub
57:
58:    Protected Sub KillThread()
59:      StopSignal()
60:      FThread = Nothing
61:    End Sub
62:
63:    Protected Sub DrawLights(ByVal Graphic As Graphics)
64:      Dim I As Integer
65:      For I = 0 To FLights.GetUpperBound(0)
66:        FLights(I).Draw(Graphic)
67:      Next
68:    End Sub
69:
70: #End Region
71:
72: #Region " Private Members "
73:    Private FLights() As Light = _
74:      {New GreenLight(), New YellowLight(), New RedLight()}
75:    Private FRect As Rectangle
76:    Private FThread As Threading.Thread
77:
78:    Private ReadOnly Property Green() As Light
79:      Get
80:        Return FLights(0)
81:      End Get
82:    End Property
83:
84:    Private ReadOnly Property Yellow() As Light
85:      Get
86:        Return FLights(1)
87:      End Get
88:    End Property
89:
90:    Private ReadOnly Property Red() As Light
91:      Get
92:        Return FLights(2)
93:      End Get
94:    End Property
95:
96:    Private ReadOnly Property Rect() As Rectangle
97:      Get
98:        Return FRect
99:      End Get
100:   End Property
101:
```

LISTING 7.7   continued

```
102:    Private Sub PositionLights()
103:
104:      Dim I As Integer
105:      For I = 0 To FLights.GetUpperBound(0)
106:        FLights(I).Rect = GetRect(I)
107:      Next
108:
109:    End Sub
110:
111:    Private Sub TurnOnGreen()
112:      Green.State = True
113:    End Sub
114:
115:    Private Sub DoChange()
116:      RaiseEvent OnChange(Me, Nothing)
117:    End Sub
118:
119:
120:    Private Function GetRect(ByVal Index As Integer) As Rectangle
121:      Return New Rectangle(Rect.Left + 10, _
122:        Rect.Top + 10 + CInt(Math.Round((2 - Index) / 3 * Rect.Height)), _
123:        Rect.Width - 20, CInt(Math.Round(Rect.Height / 3)) - 20)
124:    End Function
125:
126:    Private Sub ChangeState()
127:      Static Current As Integer = 0
128:      Current = (Current + 1) Mod 3
129:      Dim I As Integer
130:
131:      For I = FLights.GetLowerBound(0) To _
132:        FLights.GetUpperBound(0)
133:        FLights(I).State = I = Current
134:      Next
135:    End Sub
136:
137:    Private Function SleepTime() As Integer
138:      Static T() As Integer = {1000, 5000}
139:      If (Yellow.State) Then
140:        Return T(0)
141:      Else
142:        Return T(1)
143:      End If
144:    End Function
145:
146: #End Region
147:
148:
149: #Region " Nested Members "
150:
```

LISTING 7.7   continued

```
151:    ' Virtual Abstract Nested Light Class
152:    ' Base class for the signal light classes
153:
154:    Private MustInherit Class Light
155:      Public State As Boolean = False
156:      Public Rect As Rectangle
157:
158:      Protected MustOverride ReadOnly Property _
159:        BrushArray() As Brush()
160:
161:      Protected Function GetBrush() As Brush
162:        If (State) Then
163:          Return BrushArray(1)
164:        Else
165:          Return BrushArray(0)
166:        End If
167:      End Function
168:
169:      Public Sub Draw(ByVal Graphic As Graphics)
170:        Graphic.FillEllipse(GetBrush(), Rect)
171:      End Sub
172:
173:      Protected Overrides Sub Finalize()
174:        Rect = Nothing
175:      End Sub
176:    End Class
177:
178:    ' RedLight nested class, inherits from Light
179:    Private Class RedLight
180:      Inherits Light
181:
182:      Protected Overrides ReadOnly Property BrushArray() As Brush()
183:        Get
184:          Static Brush() As Brush = {Brushes.Gray, _
185:            Brushes.Red}
186:          Return Brush
187:        End Get
188:      End Property
189:    End Class
190:
191:    ' YellowLight nested class, inherits from Light
192:    Private Class YellowLight
193:      Inherits Light
194:
195:      Protected Overrides ReadOnly Property BrushArray() As Brush()
196:        Get
197:          Static Brush() As Brush = {Brushes.Gray, _
198:            Brushes.Yellow}
199:          Return Brush
```

Listing 7.7   continued

```
200:       End Get
201:    End Property
202:
203:  End Class
204:
205:  ' GreenLight nested class, inherits from Light
206:  Private Class GreenLight
207:    Inherits Light
208:    Protected Overrides ReadOnly Property BrushArray() As Brush()
209:      Get
210:        Static Brush() As Brush = {Brushes.Gray, _
211:          Brushes.Green}
212:        Return Brush
213:      End Get
214:    End Property
215:  End Class
216: #End Region
217:
218: End Class
```

Because the listing is very long, the elaboration is subdivided into individual subsections. Each of the following subsections elaborates on a specific aspect of Listing 7.7.

Understanding the Motivation for Nested Classes

The motivation for using nested classes at all is questionable, because any class that can be nested could technically be implemented as a non-nested class. There might be some strategic reasons for implementing nested classes, but you will find them few and far between.

To demonstrate the technical aspects of implementing nested classes, the TrafficSignal.sln sample program was contrived. As a suggestion, the traffic signal lights—red on top, yellow in the middle, and green on the bottom—might make sense as nested classes. You are unlikely to encounter a need for a single-signal light that maintains state relative to other lights without the other lights. (You could have a single blinking yellow light, but you could implement that as an element of a different traffic signal. However, this does illustrate what you are likely to encounter when using nested classes: Each time you implement a nested class, you are likely to find an exception that suggests the class might be better off not nested.)

The Signal contains three instances of a Light class. Because the Lights only make sense in the context of the entire signal—or so we assume for our purposes—and we need more than one light, we implement the light as a nested class and create three instances of the light.

Defining the `Signal` Class

The `Signal` class represents a three-state, red-yellow-green traffic light. The signal will be defined to maintain its state and draw itself on a device context, in a Visual Basic .NET `Graphics` object.

The `Signal` class will have an array of three `Light` objects and a means of changing state in an ordered way from Green to Yellow to Red. Two signals at different signal-states are shown in Figure 7.4.

FIGURE 7.4

Two instances of the `Signal` *class from TrafficSignal. sln.*

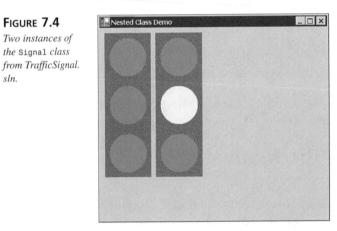

All of the members of the `Signal` class are defined on lines 1 through 146 of Listing 7.7. The subsections that follow elaborate on the different aspects of the `Signal` class.

Using Code Outlining to Organize

The first thing you will notice about Listing 7.7 is that it employs code outlining using the `#Region` pragma. A long, complicated class listing like the `Signal` class will benefit from a little extra housekeeping. The top half of the class contains the members of the `Signal` class, and the bottom half, starting on line 149, contains the nested classes. By adding `#Region` pragmas, you can collapse and expand whole subsections of your code to make development easier.

A reasonable practice to employ is to list members by priority. Consumers will only be interested in `Public` members, so `Public` members are listed first. Generalizers will be interested in `Protected` members too, so those are listed after the `Public` members.

Finally, `Private` members are only of interest to a producer—the person who implements the class; thus `Private` members are listed last.

> **Tip**
>
> A little housekeeping helps, but if the class is relatively simple, the members are added as they evolve, in no particular order.

By their sheer existence, nested members are the least significant members of a class. If the nested classes were significant to consumers, they wouldn't be nested; consequently, nested classes are listed last.

Defining the Constructor and Destructor

The `Signal` class has three instances of the `Light` class and a `Thread` object. For this reason, a constructor, destructor, and `Dispose` methods were added to the `Signal` class. The constructor and the `Dispose` method are defined on lines 11 to 16 and 18 to 24, respectively. The excerpt from Listing 7.7 is shown in Listing 7.8 for convenience. The `Protected Finalize` method simply calls the `Dispose` method—lines 39 to 41—and isn't repeated here.

LISTING 7.8 The constructor and `Dispose` methods of the `Signal` class

```
11:    Public Sub New(ByVal Rect As Rectangle)
12:       FRect = Rect
13:       PositionLights()
14:       TurnOnGreen()
15:       CreateThread()
16:    End Sub
17:
18:    Public Sub Dispose()
19:       Static Done As Boolean = False
20:       If (Done) Then Exit Sub
21:       Done = True
22:       KillThread()
23:       GC.SuppressFinalize(Me)
24:    End Sub
```

The constructor `Sub New` delegates all of its tasks to well-named methods. The names of the methods tell you what is happening. Another strategy is to add an `Initialize` method and delegate all initialization code to that method; this technique allows you to reinitialize an object without constructing a new object. The constructor clearly indicates

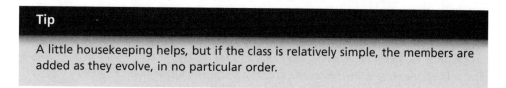

that the bounding `Rectangle` is being cached to a `Field`, the `Lights` are positioned, the green light is turned on, and the `Thread` is created. (Perhaps `RunThread` would more clearly indicate that the thread is created and running after line 15 runs.)

The `Dispose` method uses a static local variable to act as a sentinel. After `Dispose` is called one time, this method becomes a noop method. All `Dispose` does is kill the thread that controls the light states and suppress garbage collection. The lights themselves aren't released because they were created outside of the constructor on lines 73 and 74 with an array initializer.

Creating the Signal Thread

Line 15 (see Listing 7.7 or 7.8) calls the `CreateThread` method. All of the thread-management methods are shown in Listing 7.9, which is an excerpt from Listing 7.7.

LISTING 7.9 The thread-management methods of the `Signal` class

```
43:    Protected Sub CreateThread()
44:      FThread = New Threading.Thread(AddressOf NextSignal)
45:      FThread.IsBackground = True
46:      StartSignal()
47:    End Sub
48:
49:    Protected Sub StartSignal()
50:      FThread.Start()
51:    End Sub
52:
53:    Protected Sub StopSignal()
54:      FThread.Abort()
55:      FThread.Join()
56:    End Sub
57:
58:    Protected Sub KillThread()
59:      StopSignal()
60:      FThread = Nothing
61:    End Sub
```

Line 44 creates an instance of the `System.Threading.Thread` class. The `Thread` class constructor takes the `AddressOf` of a procedure; this procedure is where the thread will fork when the thread is started. Line 45 indicates that the thread is a background thread, allowing the application to quit and stop the signal threads. Line 46 calls `StartSignal`, which turns the traffic signal on by starting the subroutine on line 49. When `Dispose` is called, `Dispose` calls `KillThread`. From the listing you can determine that `KillThread` calls `StopSignal` and releases the thread object by assigning it to `Nothing`.

StopSignal calls the `FThread.Abort` method and `FThread.Join` waits for the thread to actually stop executing. `FThread.Abort` kills the thread by raising an uncatchable `ThreadAbortException`; the exception allows all of the `Finally` blocks in the thread to execute, so you need to call `Join` to ensure that the thread has completed.

Multithreading is brand new in Visual Basic .NET. If you haven't programmed in a multithreaded language before, threads might be a challenge to you. The `Thread` class and multithreaded programming in Visual Basic .NET are covered in detail in Chapter 14, "Multithreaded Applications."

Drawing the Signal Using an Event

`Signal` objects are drawn on whatever control passes its `Graphics` object to the `Signal.Draw` method. (In reality the signal should be a control, but we would have to digress too far from our discussion of nested classes to get there from here.) Consider these code excerpts:

```
6:    Public Sub Draw(ByVal Graphic As Graphics)
7:       Graphic.FillRectangle(Brushes.BurlyWood, Rect)
8:       DrawLights(Graphic)
9:    End Sub
...
63:   Protected Sub DrawLights(ByVal Graphic As Graphics)
64:      Dim I As Integer
65:      For I = 0 To FLights.GetUpperBound(0)
66:         FLights(I).Draw(Graphic)
67:      Next
68:   End Sub
...
161:      Protected Function GetBrush() As Brush
162:         If (State) Then
163:            Return BrushArray(1)
164:         Else
165:            Return BrushArray(0)
166:         End If
167:      End Function
168:
169:      Public Sub Draw(ByVal Graphic As Graphics)
170:         Graphic.FillEllipse(GetBrush(), Rect)
171:      End Sub
```

Drawing is performed in three methods. `Signal.Draw` on lines 6 to 9 simply draws the `Signal` as a `Rectangle`, and calls `Signal.DrawLights` to draw each of the contained lights. `DrawLights` iterates over each light and calls the light's draw methods, demonstrating the division of labor offered by classes and nested classes in this instance.

`Light.Draw` simply calls `Graphics.FillEllipses` (using the argument `Graphic`), using each object's cached `Rect` as the bounding region of the light and the `Light.GetBrush` method to determine the brush based on the state of the light. When the drawing method is invoked it only cares about `Ellipses`, `Brushes`, and `Rects`, not states and calculating bounding regions.

Line 163 and 165 (see Listing 7.7 or 7.9) uses the polymorphic property `BrushArray` to return the correct array of brush objects based on the instance of the lamp. If `State` = False, the off brush is returned; if `State` = True, the on brush is returned.

Chapter 10 offers an extended discussion on inheritance relationships and how polymorphic behavior like the `BrushArray()` property works, as well as a discussion on defining and implementing interfaces.

Defining the Abstract Base Class, `Light`

`Light`, `GreenLight`, `YellowLight`, and `RedLight` are all nested classes. `Light` uses the `MustInherit` class modifier. The `Light` class demonstrates abstract base classes in Visual Basic .NET, which means that `Light` is intended to be descended from but never directly created. `Light` has to use `MustInherit` because it declares an abstract property:

```
Protected MustOverride ReadOnly Property BrushArray() As Brush()
```

Notice that `BrushArray` from lines 158 and 159 of Listing 7.7 has no procedure block; it's a declaration only. Statements with `MustOverride` refer to virtual and abstract members, which means they must be implemented in a descendant class.

Virtual, abstract members are analogous to interface declarations in COM classes. `GreenLight`, `YellowLight`, and `RedLight` must each implement the property `BrushArray` or they will be virtual and abstract.

Declarative statements are used to guide the implementation of descendant classes. The way `Light` is implemented, its `Draw` method depends on `GetBrush`, and `GetBrush`, in turn, depends on being able to get the correct brush and color based on the state of a specific light. In structured languages, or incorrectly in object-oriented languages, this kind of behavior was implemented using a `case` statement.

Implementing the Signal Lights

The signal light classes themselves are easy to implement. Each specific light need only inherit from `Light` and implement the read-only property `BrushArray`. Listing 7.10 demonstrates the `RedLight` class only. (All of the lights are identical except for the values used to initialize the `BrushArray`.)

Listing 7.10   Implementation of one of the signal lights

```
178:    ' RedLight nested class, inherits from Light
179:    Private Class RedLight
180:        Inherits Light
181:
182:        Protected Overrides ReadOnly Property BrushArray() As Brush()
183:            Get
184:                Static Brush() As Brush = {Brushes.Gray, _
185:                    Brushes.Red}
186:                Return Brush
187:            End Get
188:        End Property
189:    End Class
```

Line 182 implements a protected, overridden, read-only property named BrushArray. A Static array of brushes is initialized to global brushes defined in the Brushes object. The RedLight class uses gray- and red-colored brushes.

There are several ways we could have implemented the colored signal lights. We could have used one Light class and a factory method that initializes the brush values based on the kind of light; kind could have been implemented using an enumeration. In software, as in all things, you eventually have to pick a direction and run with it. I specifically picked this implementation strategy to demonstrate nested classes, but I do like the way it turned out.

A Final Word on the Demo Program

In a production system, the traffic signal sample program would better serve an application as a component. If you were modeling a city's traffic lights, you would want to rethink the threads, too. In a city the size of Okemos, you might have 30 threads, but in Chicago you would blow up the computer switching all of the necessary threads. Additionally, the signal lights would need to be coordinated. A better implementation might be one threaded manager that coordinates lights at opposing intersections and manages the timing from block to block.

Finally, use better graphics if you are going to simulate the visual aspects of traffic management, or anything else for that matter.

Creating Instances of a Class

By now you have had many examples demonstrating how to create instances of classes. However, this is the first chapter exclusively addressing the topic of classes, so let's take a moment to review the syntax for object creation.

Classes are referred to as reference types. Reference types, as opposed to value types, are created by declaring a variable and using the New keyword followed by the name of the class and parentheses:

```
Dim reference As New Class()
```

The example looks as if you are calling a procedure named Class. This is the form of constructing an object. In actuality, this code calls the constructor Sub New defined in class Class. If you have parameters to pass to your constructor, they are passed between the parentheses, but you are still calling an overloaded version of Sub New. This might be a little confusing. Here is an example creating an instance of the Signal class from the previous section:

```
Dim ASignal As New Signal(New Rectangle(10, 10, 100, 300))
```

> **Tip**
>
> If a procedure takes an object, consider constructing the object—as with New Rectangle(10, 10, 100, 300)—during the call to the procedure. This technique will help you clean up those unsightly temporaries.

The statement declares and initializes an instance of the Signal class. The preceding statement still calls Signal.New(), passing an instance of a new rectangle to satisfy the Rectangle parameter (see line 11 of Listing 7.7). This form of the call is strange, but it's the one chosen by Microsoft.

Other languages use slightly different forms for constructors and destructors. C++ uses an operator new, which can be overloaded, and a C++ constructor has the same name as the class and the destructor is the class name with the ~ (tilde) token. Object Pascal uses Create and Destroy methods by convention, but really denotes constructors and destructors by introducing the keywords constructor and destructor.

Summary

Classes are different in Visual Basic .NET than in VB6. VB6 classes are now interfaces and literally use the interface keyword. Visual Basic .NET classes use the Class keyword and support inheritance, something not found in VB6. Chapter 7 is a precursor to these more advanced subjects.

This chapter demonstrated the nuts and bolts of defining classes, including adding fields, properties, events, and methods; how to manage complexity with access specifiers; and how to employ modifiers. This chapter introduced revisions to interfaces and how to implement interface methods, how to implement nested classes, use multithreading, and inheritance.

Chapters 8 and 9 expand on the discussion of events and delegates introduced in this chapter, and Chapter 10 continues the discussion of inheritance and polymorphism in Visual Basic .NET. Chapter 12 spends more time on the powerful concept of attributes.

Adding Events

CHAPTER 8

Your programs receive feedback from users via events. Events are an important aspect of Windows programming. On the object-oriented side of the fence are classes that contain properties and methods. Without events, Windows applications would have no way to respond to external occurrences such as key presses and mouse clicks, or to repaint the screen. Events can be supported in structured languages, but all Windows programming languages need events to respond to inputs from users and from Windows.

Objects can work effectively without events but are better equipped to respond to inputs with events. For controls, like the `Button` component, events are essential because they provide the key to responsive behavior.

Methods, properties, and events form a triad of capability that makes object-oriented languages work effectively in an event-driven operating system such as Windows. Because events are important to effectively implement responsiveness in Windows applications, they have taken on greater significance in Visual Basic .NET than in VB6. Events are not new in Visual Basic .NET, but greater control over their use makes Visual Basic. NET a first-class language.

The event idiom has an enhanced role in Visual Basic .NET. This chapter demonstrates how you can effectively use events in all aspects of Windows programming, including an introduction to delegates. Chapter 9 complements Chapter 8 by providing thorough coverage of delegates, and Chapter 23 demonstrates using events in WebForms. In this chapter, you will learn about the new keywords and capabilities that are available as improvements in event programming in Visual Basic .NET.

Understanding Events and Event Handlers

Windows is a message-based, event-driven operating system. Events are simply occurrences that can be almost anything; basic occurrences are things like someone moving a window on the desktop. The movement of a form is an occurrence after which other forms need to be notified, so they can repaint their visible client regions. We refer to such occurrences as events.

At the OS level, an event is usually caused by an interrupt request. When you hit a key on your keyboard, special subprograms called *interrupts* (in the case of the keyboard, interrupts 9 and 16) are fired internally. The Windows OS detects the interrupt and packages up all the information necessary to describe the interrupt. The package describing what occurred is a message. At the Windows level, messages are generic structures that contain information. In the case of the keyboard interrupt, the message would contain a type identifier and keyboard state information, including Shift and Ctrl key states and which other keys were pressed. In early Windows programming, programmers had to write message crackers that deciphered all the generic message information and figured out what to do with it. Raw messages were a little hard to work with because the data was very generic.

In a program, the receipt of a message is an event. At another level of abstraction, Windows receives messages and does the unpacking of each message, converting generic detail to message-type specific detail. For example, a keystroke could be converted to a well-named constant instead of a raw value. A program can pass the address of a procedure to the Windows OS that can be called in response to a particular action. Procedure addresses when used in this manner are referred to as *callbacks*. Procedure addresses used to respond to Windows events are called *event handlers*.

Passing procedure pointers is still a pretty low level of abstraction. What we want in software development is increasingly higher levels of abstraction, allowing us to work at general, high levels, rather than arcane low levels.

This is where VB6 comes in. Having all this complexity hidden from VB programmers was one of the things that made VB6 easy to program in. VB6 programmers simply clicked on a Command control and wrote some code. The specifics of working with procedure addresses, callbacks, events, interrupts, and messages were concealed from VB6 programmers. (Again, it's important to note that other languages, like C++ and Object Pascal, supported working at any of these levels of abstraction.) As a matter of fact, unless you programmed heavily with the Windows API, you might never have encountered a callback in VB6. This brings us to the present day.

Support for writing dynamic event handlers and callbacks has historically made other languages more expressive than Visual Basic 6. Hence, significantly more programmer support for writing event handlers was added to Visual Basic .NET. However, you will immediately notice a couple of things in Visual Basic .NET. You can still click on a button (equivalent to a VB6 Command control) and generate an event handler for that button, and you will notice that the code implementing this behavior has changed. The result is that event handling is still easy in Visual Basic .NET. What might not be readily apparent is that you can do a lot more than simply write event-handling code at design time.

A *dynamic event handler* is an event handler that is reassigned or managed programmatically while a program is running.

Visual Basic .NET supports writing static event handlers at design time, just like VB6. In addition to static event handlers, Visual Basic .NET supports writing and using procedural parameters—callbacks—at runtime, assigning multiple object events to a single

8

ADDING EVENTS

event handler, parameter passing to event handlers, multicasting events, defining procedural types, implementing Shared events, and declaring and raising events in structures, modules, and classes.

Most of the behavior described in the last paragraph is supported by the new, special class referred to as a delegate. We can use events in the same way we used them in VB6—click and code—and we can use them in a more advanced way by understanding how delegates work. In this chapter, we will look at delegates simply as a means of writing responsive code. Because delegates introduce some new concepts, we will cover more advanced techniques supported by delegates in Chapter 9.

Before we begin working with Visual Basic .NET event handlers, let's take a moment to examine some of the basics.

Basic Delegate: `EventHandler`

The basic event handler now has the following signature:

```
Sub EventHandler(ByVal sender as System.Object, ByVal e As System.EventArgs)
```

This is the signature of the delegate named `EventHandler`.

When you encounter code like the following example of an event handler for a button-click event, you can now readily identify it as code compatible with the `EventHandler` delegate:

```
Private Sub button1_Click(ByVal sender As System.Object, ByVal e As _
   System.EventArgs) Handles button1.Click
```

Notice that an `EventHandler` delegate is associated with subroutines, as opposed to functions. The *name* in this instance is `button1_Click`. As in VB6, the name by convention indicates the object name attached to the event name by an underscore (_). Also notice the two matching parameters, `sender` and `e`, and their respective data types. What's new about this code from the delegate definition is the `Handles` clause, which tells you very clearly what object and event this subroutine responds to. An event handler supports handling events for multiple objects. This is a departure from VB6 and is the reason the `Handles` clause exists. The `Handles` clause lists all the objects this event handles events for (the upcoming section "Connecting Multiple Events to a Single Event Handler" has more information on its use).

Basically, the event handler statement is designed to indicate its primary purpose. When `Button1` is clicked, `button1_Click` is called. Keep in mind, too, that an event-handling subroutine can be called directly just like any other subroutine.

A departure from VB6, as mentioned, is the inclusion of event arguments. These arguments provide some extra capability if used correctly.

Event Handler `Object` Argument

The `sender` argument is the usual invoking object. As you might recall, all Visual Basic .NET objects are derivatives of the `Object` class. This means that any object can be passed as the value of the event handler's `sender` argument.

Using a root object makes the general purpose event handler very flexible. For example, if you click `button1` (from the fragment) the value of `sender` will be `button1`. You might handily jump to the conclusion that this is no big deal. You created the handler using `button1`, so of course the `sender` is `button1`. When the event handler is invoked, you can simply refer to `button1` directly. Well, that's what we used to do in VB6 because we had few alternatives. And, you can still refer to a known object when you write the code, but you will be missing an advantage of the handler's `sender` argument.

If we use the `sender` argument and cast it to the right type, our event handler doesn't need to be revised if, for example, the name of the button changes. Making an event handler generic takes a little extra work but is worth the effort. Consider the two event handlers shown in Listings 8.1 and 8.2.

LISTING 8.1   Using an event handler in a VB6 way.

```
1: Private Sub button1_Click(ByVal sender As System.Object, _
2:     ByVal e As System.EventArgs) Handles button1.Click
3:
4:     MsgBox(button1.Text)
5:
6: End Sub
```

The first listing refers directly to `button1` because the code assumes that `button1` will always be the only object handled by this event. This is functional, but if `button1` changes or the event handler needs to be flexible in any way, the code is too rigid. Furthermore, if `button1` doesn't reside in the same code as the event handler, we would be breaching module or class boundaries. Breaching boundaries goes against good practices relative to supporting encapsulation. A preferable way to write the preceding code is demonstrated in Listing 8.2.

LISTING 8.2   A flexible way of handling the event handler sender argument in Visual Basic .NET.

```
1: Private Sub button1_Click(ByVal sender As System.Object, _
2:     ByVal e As System.EventArgs) Handles button1.Click
3:
4:     If (TypeOf sender Is Button) Then
5:        MsgBox(CType(sender, Button).Text)
```

8

ADDING EVENTS

LISTING 8.2   continued

```
6:     End If
7:
8: End Sub
```

As mentioned, the code is slightly more complex. Line 4 uses the `TypeOf` operator to determine if `sender` is a button. If `sender` is a button, the `CType` procedure is used to safely cast the object `sender` as a `Button`. `CType` returns a reference to the first argument dynamically cast as a type of the second argument. That is, `Object.ReferenceEquals(` `sender, CType(sender, Button))` is True. In the example, `CType` is returning a reference to sender cast as a `Button`. The `.Text` property returns the text property of the button.

Listing 8.2 works under more conditions than Listing 8.1. If `sender` isn't a button, the code is still correct. If `sender` is some other button, the code works correctly. If `button1` is renamed, the code in Listing 8.2 still works correctly. Listing 8.1 only works under one precise set of circumstances, when `button1` exists.

Because we are passing a generic base object and Visual Basic .NET supports dynamic type checking and casting, more kinds of classes can use the generic `EventHandler` effectively. `EventHandler` supports writing code related to a specific kind of object without knowing the actual name or location of the object. The `sender` argument represents what we know about the world from the inside of the `button1_Click` event handler. If we stick to using the `sender` argument rather than a specific known object, we are less likely to write brittle code.

Event Handler `EventArgs` Argument

In addition to passing the invoking object, there are specific kinds of events where it's useful to know more information about what was going on when the event was invoked. For example, it's enough to know that the sender was a button when the `button1_Click` event is invoked, but this might not be sufficient information if a mouse event occurred.

If the user clicked the mouse button, you might want to know the location of the mouse and which button was clicked. Clicking a mouse button raises an `OnMouseDown` event, and the actual event handler signature includes an `Object` and a `MouseEventArgs` parameter. Listing 8.3 demonstrates an event handler for `MouseDown` for a form.

LISTING 8.3   `MouseDown` event handler.

```
1: Private Sub Form1_MouseDown(ByVal sender As Object, ByVal e As _
2:     System.Windows.Forms.MouseEventArgs) Handles MyBase.MouseDown
3:
```

LISTING 8.3   continued

```
4:    MsgBox(String.Format("X={0:d}, Y={0:d}", e.X, e.Y))
5:    MsgBox(TypeOf e Is System.EventArgs)
6:
7: End Sub
```

The type of the second argument, e, is MouseEventArgs. From line 5 you will learn that MouseEventArgs IsA EventArgs, that is, MouseEventArgs is subclassed from EventArgs. Line 4 demonstrates some of the parameters of MouseEventArgs, including the X and Y position of the mouse. IntelliSense will help you discover the parameters of a subclass of EventArgs, or you can reference the help whenever a new EventArgs objects is passed to your event handler.

Listings 8.1 through 8.3 aren't intended to suggest that all delegates will have the same signature, including Object and EventArgs arguments. It just happens to be convenient for event handlers to share a common signature, especially where controls are concerned because many controls will have similar parameter needs, like Paint, Keypress, Load, or MouseDown. It's easier to use a generic signature that works for many cases than it is to implement a new handler for each type of control. (A less general approach would require a lot of additional coding on Microsoft's part and ours.)

Chapter 9 will demonstrate other kinds of delegates with additional parameters and no parameters. Throughout this book we will use standard delegates where it makes sense to do so, and implement custom delegates otherwise. Listing 8.4 demonstrates how we might combine these basic events in an application.

FIGURE 8.1

SimpleDraw.exe demonstrates using event handlers to respond to user inputs.

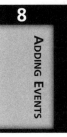

LISTING 8.4   The SimpleDraw.exe listing.

```
 1: Public Class Form1
 2:    Inherits System.Windows.Forms.Form
 3:
 4: #Region " Windows Form Designer generated code "
 5:
 6:    Private APen As Pen
 7:    Private OldX, OldY As Integer
 8:
 9:    Public Sub New()
10:      [...]
11:      APen = New Pen(Color.Black)
12:    End Sub
13:
14:    [...]
15: #End Region
16:
17: Private Sub DrawPoint(ByVal X As Integer, ByVal Y As Integer)
18:    CreateGraphics().DrawLine(APen, X, Y, OldX, OldY)
19: End Sub
20:
21: Private Sub ResetOffset(ByVal X As Integer, ByVal Y As Integer, _
22:    Optional ByVal Reset As Boolean = False)
23:
24:    OldX = X + CInt(Reset)
25:    OldY = Y + CInt(Reset)
26:
27: End Sub
28:
29: Private Sub Form1_MouseMove(ByVal sender As Object, _
30:    ByVal e As System.Windows.Forms.MouseEventArgs) Handles MyBase.MouseMove
31:
32:    statusBar1().Text = String.Format("X:{0:d}, Y:{0:d}", e.X, e.Y)
33:    If (e.Button = MouseButtons().Left) Then
34:      DrawPoint(e.X, e.Y)
35:    End If
36:
37:    ResetOffset(e.X, e.Y, e.Button = MouseButtons().None)
38:
39: End Sub
40:
41: Private Sub Form1_MouseDown(ByVal sender As Object, _
42:    ByVal e As System.Windows.Forms.MouseEventArgs) Handles MyBase.MouseDown
43:
44:    DrawPoint(e.X, e.Y)
45: End Sub
46:
47: End Class
```

The code listing defines a simple drawing program using a couple of mouse events and a few of the capabilities of GDI+. (For more on GDI+, refer to Chapter 17, "Programming with GDI+.") The application is trivial. It will allow basic line drawing as shown in Figure 8.1, but doesn't store the image nor does it handle repainting.

Code outlining was used to hide text that was generated by the IDE. The hidden outlined selections are represented by the [. . .] portions of the code. To create the sample program, declare a `Pen` and `OldX` and `OldY` integers. The `Pen` is defined in `System.Drawing` and is used for many of the graphics methods. `OldX` and `OldY` are used to follow the mouse movement. To complete the SimpleDraw application, perform the following steps:

1. Ensure that the `System.Drawing` namespace is imported into a blank Windows application.

2. Declare the aforementioned `Pen`, `OldX`, and `OldY` integer fields at the top of the `Form` class.

3. Define the subroutines `ResetOffset` and `DrawPoint` as shown in Listing 8.4.

4. From the toolbox, add a status bar control to the bottom of `Form1`.

5. To create the event handlers, `MouseMove` and `MouseDown`, switch to the Code designer view (if you aren't there already).

6. In the Objects list (in the same position as VB6, the Object list is the combo box at the top left side of the code editor), select (`Base Class Events`) for `Form1`.

7. From the Procedures list (also in the same position as VB6, the Procedures list is the combo box at the top right side of the code editor), select `MouseDown` and `MouseMove` in turn to generate the event handlers for these two events. (Refer to the section "Creating Event Handlers in the Windows Form Designer" for alternative ways to generate event handlers)

8. Add the code between each event handler as shown in Listing 8.4.

9. Change the background color of the form to White.

10. Press F5 to test the application.

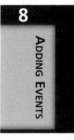

To create simple line drawings, click the mouse in the client region of the form and drag the mouse cursor around. You should see some rudimentary drawing.

I would like to point out a few details here. `ResetOffset` was written differently to begin with. `ResetOffset` is the result of a refactoring, explained in the next subsection. The `Pen` object is declared at the class level and created in the `New` constructor. This was done so that I would only have to create the `Pen` object one time. `CreateGraphics()` actually creates a graphics object. The constructor for a graphics object is protected, so the only way to get one is to call `CreateGraphics()`. `CreateGraphics()` is an example of

Microsoft programmers using Replace Constructor with Factory Method (whether they thought about it or not). One reason to use factory methods is to consolidate some specific steps that must be taken to ensure property initialization of an object; MS programmers were kind enough to hide the complexity of initializing graphics objects from us. Notice that I am creating a graphics object each time `DrawPoint` is called. This was done because the graphics object clips to the current client region. If the graphics object were created one time when the form was constructed, the next time the form was resized, drawing wouldn't work outside of the client region of the original form size. Creating the graphics object each time seems to incur no additional performance penalties and works correctly when the form is resized.

Refactoring: "Extract Method"

`MouseMove` from lines 29 to 39 from Listing 8.4 was originally defined as follows:

```
Private Sub Form1_MouseMove(ByVal sender As Object, _
  ByVal e As System.Windows.Forms.MouseEventArgs) Handles MyBase.MouseMove

  statusBar1().Text = String.Format("X:{0:d}, Y:{0:d}", e.X, e.Y)

  If (e.Button = MouseButtons().Left) Then
    DrawPoint(e.X, e.Y)
    OldX = e.X
    OldY = e.Y
  Else
    OldX = e.X + 1
    OldY = e.Y + 1
  End If

End Sub
```

Notice the `If...Then...Else` statement in the preceding listing. It's not immediately clear what the `OldX` and `OldY` code is doing and the listing is about 15 lines long, a bit too long. The motivation for refactoring this code is to shorten and clarify this method, make behaviors reusable as they will be in a separate method, and use a well-named method to articulate meaning.

What the code in the fragment does (as well as the same code in Listing 8.4) is update the status bar, draw the point if the left mouse button is down, and then adjust the `OldX` and `OldY` points.

The refactoring "Extract Method" is performed in the following prescribed manner:

1. Create a method with a name indicating what the method will do.

2. Extract the relevant code from the original method to the new method.

3. Add parameters to the new method to pass data used in the old method to the new

method.

4. Pass the data necessary to ensure proper operation from the old method to the new method.

5. Compile and test the changes.

For Step 1, I chose `ResetOffset` as the method name. Step 2 indicates that relevant code should be extracted from the old method. I removed the references to `OldX` and `OldY` from the `MouseMove` event handler and placed them into the `ResetOffset` method, sending the `e.X` and `e.Y` values as arguments to the new method. The last value I needed was a Boolean indicating when the offset values should be reset. For this implementation, when there was no button clicked, `OldX` and `OldY` values needed to be reset. The revised code is contained in Listing 8.4 from lines 21 through 39.

The complete mechanics and motivation for "Extract Method" can be found in Fowler, page 110. Other mechanics—to use Fowler's term—might be involved to complete the "Extract Method" refactoring. If temporary variables are used with the extracted code, you will need to relocate them to the new method. You might also want to perform the "Replace Temporary with Query" refactoring (introduced in Chapter 3). Finally, if any variables in the original method are modified by the new, refactored method, you might need to return that value as a `ByRef` argument or make the new method a function.

"Extract Method" is an easy refactoring technique to employ. It's one that will most likely be commonly used. By extracting code and making methods from that code, your procedures will stay smaller, be self-documenting, and you will have more atomic procedures that will have a greater incidence of reuse.

Connecting Multiple Events to a Single Event Handler

Visual Basic 6 allowed you to write one handler procedure to handle a single event type for multiple controls, but the controls had to be in a control array. An event handler for multiple controls was implemented to accept an index into the control array of the actual control raising the event. This is a structured solution; it involves arrays and indexes instead of polymorphism. The following VB6 code fragment demonstrates a control array, `Command1()`, associated with one event handler:

```
Private Sub Command1_Click(Index As Integer)
  MsgBox Command1(Index).Caption
End Sub
```

In the VB6 solution, `Command1` isn't even a control any more, it's an array of controls.

When I created the `Command1` control, I only created one `Command` button. To create the control array, I copied and pasted `Command1`. Instead of giving me similar properties and a separate control, VB6 changed the nature of the first `Command` control from a single control to an array of controls. Converting a control to an array of controls in order to assign a single event handler to multiple controls is not intuitive behavior. Controls and event relationships should work without an array (However, single event handlers for multiple controls were supported this way because VB6 doesn't support object-oriented inheritance.)

Intuitively, this isn't what you might expect: create a control, copy it, and you get a control array. What you might intuitively expect is a separate control with a very similar state. Visual Basic .NET supports copying the control. When you drop a control on a form, select the control. Press Ctrl+C to copy the control and Ctrl+V to paste the copy to the form. In Visual Basic .NET, you will get a second control with almost identical properties. The control name will be different and the actual object will be a separate object from the copied one: no control array.

To experiment with the revised copy-and-paste-control behavior in Visual Basic .NET, we'll use a button control. Using a button control, paint a button on a blank form. Copy the button and paste the copy to the form. Select both buttons—`button1` and `button2`, named by default—and double-click to generate an event handler. This step will create two separate event handlers, one for each button. Listing 8.5 shows the procedure body generated for each event handler.

Listing 8.5 Two empty event handlers for two separate button controls.

```
1: Private Sub button2_Click(ByVal sender As System.Object, _
2:    ByVal e As System.EventArgs) Handles button2.Click
3:
4: End Sub
5:
6: Private Sub button1_Click(ByVal sender As System.Object, _
7:    ByVal e As System.EventArgs) Handles button1.Click
8:
9: End Sub
```

When you click `button1`, the `button1_Click` event handler is called. When you click `button2`, the `button2_Click` event handler is called. Note the `Handles` clause at the end of each event handler indicating to which control and event the event handler will respond. To have a single event handler respond to more than one control, add a comma-delimited list of objects and events at the end of the `Handles` clause:

```
Private Sub button2_Click(ByVal sender As System.Object, _
```

```
ByVal e As System.EventArgs) Handles button2.Click, button1.Click
```

With the revision (shown in the fragment), `button2_Click` also handles `button1_Click` events. You can type the `Handles` clause manually or use the designer to indicate multi-control event handling. I will return to this topic after we look at some of the other ways of defining and using event handlers.

There are two other issues we need to take a moment to discuss. The first issue is why we would want one procedure to handle events for more than one control. The second issue is what happens in the preceding scenario where there are now two event handlers for one control, namely `button1`. Let's look at each issue in turn.

Multiple-Control Event Handlers

Event handlers most often respond to interaction from the user. It's common for multiple control metaphors to exist for a single operation. For example, in MS Word, I can click File, Open or the folder on the toolbar to open a file. The File, Open menu and the folder on the toolbar are both metaphors for the file open operation. Invoking this operation should run the same code, whether I use the toolbar button or menu command to invoke it. Because the operation is identical, the code also should be identical.

Allowing a single event to support multiple metaphors for invoking that behavior is supported by VB.NET. Additionally, because Visual Basic .NET supports object-oriented inheritance and polymorphism, we can use a single event handler and code to perform different operations based on different objects. Using the code from Listing 8.5, here is a demonstration in Listing 8.6.

LISTING 8.6 Two event handlers for one control.

```
 1: Private Sub WhoAmI(ByVal Value As Button)
 2:   MsgBox("I am " & Value.Text)
 3: End Sub
 4:
 5: Private Sub button2_Click(ByVal sender As System.Object, _
 6:   ByVal e As System.EventArgs) Handles button2.Click, button1.Click
 7:
 8:   WhoAmI(CType(sender, Button))
 9:
10: End Sub
```

The code on line 8 indicates who the sender was. (Notice the refactored `WhoAmI` procedure.) Yes, these are trivial examples, but the code demonstrates two techniques clearly: one handler and one set of code can respond to more than one control, and extracted methods with good names make code clearer.

Multiple Event Handlers for a Control

Visual Basic .NET supports assigning multiple procedures to one or more event handlers. This means that several procedures could each implement part of the solution. In Listing 8.5, if we modified line 2 to indicate that we wanted button2_click to handle the Click event for button1 and button2 and we left button1_Click intact, both the button1 and button2 handlers would be called when button1 is clicked.

Calling more than one procedure per event is an aspect of multicast delegates. Delegates keep a list of callbacks and invoke all procedures maintained in a list internal to the delegate. Multicast delegates are an interesting and powerful feature of Visual Basic .NET that we will explore more in Chapter 9.

Creating Event Handlers in the Windows Form Designer

Visual Basic 6 required that you switch to the code view to add event handlers for controls. This modality still exists in Visual Basic .NET.

> **Note**
>
> Beta versions of Visual Basic .NET also occasionally support managing events from the Properties view. Unfortunately, the Event button (see Figure 8.2) showed up in the Properties window in beta versions of Visual Basic .NET, although it was not supposed to. The Event button supports listing events in the Properties window and generating event handlers from the Properties window. Currently this behavior is only intentionally supported in C#.

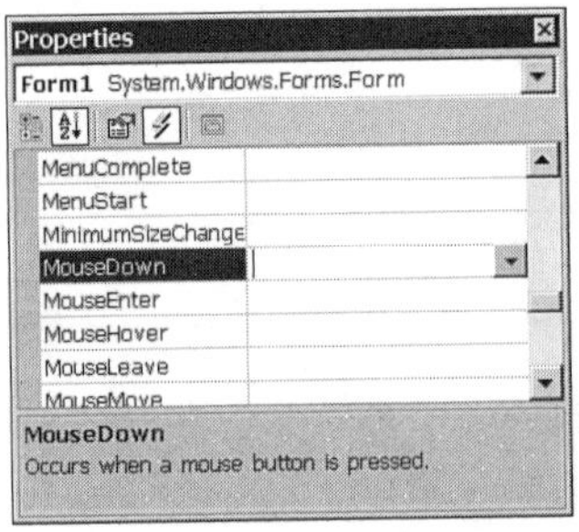

FIGURE 8.2

Generate event handlers from the Event list in the Properties window.

Use the left two buttons in the Properties window to order the events by category or alphabetically, respectively, depending on your tastes. Find the property that you want to implement a handler for and double-click in the Properties window adjacent to the event name. The Form Designer will generate the event-handling procedure, including the appropriate WithEvents statement (discussed later in this chapter).

Let's combine the MouseMove and Paint events with GDI+ to display the location of the mouse directly on the form. Complete the following steps to create the example:

1. Create a new Windows Application template and name it FormEvents.
2. Click on the blank form, Form1 by default.
3. Press F4 to display the Properties window.
4. Click on the Events button and the alphabetically ordered listing button.
5. Find the MouseMove event and double-click next to the event name to generate the empty MouseMove event. (The complete code is shown in Listing 8.7.)
6. All we want the form to do is repaint so that the mouse position text is updated on the form. Call the Form method Invalidate as demonstrated in listing 8.7.
7. Repeat step 5 to generate a Paint event handler for the form.
8. The argument e is a PaintEventArgs object. PaintEventArgs contains an instance of the Graphics object that we can use instead of calling CreateGraphics, as demonstrated in Listing 8.4. Draw the mouse position using the Graphics. DrawString method as demonstrated in Listing 8.7.
9. Compile and run the example.

The code displays the formatted X, Y coordinate of the mouse relative to the screen {0, 0} position, which is the upper-left corner of your monitor. Listing 8.7 is followed by a brief overview of some of the code in the listing you might not be familiar with.

LISTING 8.7 Using event handlers and GDI+ to track the mouse's movement.

```
1: Private Sub Form1_MouseMove(ByVal sender As Object, _
2:    ByVal e As System.Windows.Forms.MouseEventArgs) Handles MyBase.MouseMove
3:
4:    Invalidate()
5: End Sub
6:
7: Private Sub Form1_Paint(ByVal sender As Object, _
8:    ByVal e As System.Windows.Forms.PaintEventArgs) Handles MyBase.Paint
9:
10:    e.Graphics.DrawString(MousePosition().ToString(), Me.Font, _
11:       Brushes.Black, 10, 10)
12: End Sub
```

Lines 1 through 5 demonstrate the `MouseMove` event handler. `Invalidate` is a method of the `Form`; line 4 could also be written as `Me.Invalidate()`. `Invalidate` causes the form to be repainted. Line 10 uses the graphics object that is a member of `PaintEventArgs`—in Listing 8.4 we used a factory method, `CreateGraphics`, to get an instance of a graphics object. The `Graphics.DrawString` method is called. Forms also have a `MousePosition` method, introduced in the `Control` class. `DrawString` writes to the *device context* of the owning object. In the listing, the device context is the form's DC. The `Me` in `Me.Font` was used for clarity; we are passing the form's `Font` property, a global `Brushes` object, and constant X, Y offsets (both 10) to write the position of the mouse.

Device context is the conceptual representation of the drawing surface in Windows. The Win32 API refers to this as DC, and a handle to a device context is usually hDC. For example, in VB6 we might declare the API procedure `TextOut`, which takes a device context argument to determine the virtual surface to draw on, to perform a similar operation. (See Chapter 17, "Programming with GDI+," for more on the `Graphics` object and device contexts.)

> **Tip**
>
> `Invalidate` is introduced in the `Control` class. All controls have an `Invalidate` method, which sends a paint message to a control.

Recall that `ToString` prints a representation of the instance. `MousePosition` is a `Point` object. `ToString` for `Point` objects represents the `Point` object as a formatted X and Y offset, {X=10, Y=10}. (Interestingly enough, the various implementations of `ToString` serve as a good demonstration of polymorphic behavior. Recall, for instance, that `DateTime.ToString` prints a date and time value.)

All event handlers can be created from the Properties view. You can also manually write the code to define event handlers or create event handlers in the Code designer in a manner identical to the way event handlers were created in VB6.

Creating Event Handlers in the Code Editor

At the top of the Code editor, there is an Objects drop-down list on the left and an Events drop-down list—called Procedure list in VB6. The `Objects` and `Procedures` (or `Events`) controls existed in the Code editor in VB6, too (see Figure 8.3). To create an event handler in VB6 as well as Visual Basic .NET, select an object from the list on the left and the event from the list on the right. The Code editor generates the event procedure for you automatically.

FIGURE 8.3

Create an event handler in the Code editor by selecting the class and method names.

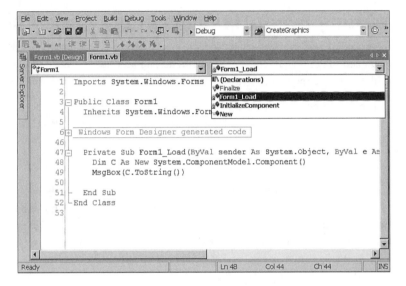

In VB6, the mechanism for wiring event procedures to events was implied. However, in VB 6, if you manually typed

```
Private Sub Form_Load()
End Sub
```

the event procedure was automatically associated with the event. In VB6 it was simply a matter of naming the procedure correctly, but the mechanism for associating the event procedure with the object was implicit.

Visual Basic .NET allows you to create events the same way—select an object and an event and the code is generated. Or, you can type the event procedure manually, but you have to associate the procedure with the event with code. Event procedures cannot be implicitly associated with the event simply by typing a correct procedure name. This added code requires a little more effort, but offers significantly greater advantage.

Visual Basic .NET allows you to associate event procedures with events in four advantageous ways: use the Form designer and create the event handler with the Properties view; use the Code editor's Objects and Procedures drop-down list; manually type the WithEvents statement and define the event procedure with a Handles clause; or define the procedure at design time and use the AddHandler method to associate the event handler at runtime. VB6 did not support creating events with the Properties view, nor

8

ADDING EVENTS

did it support passing events as procedural type arguments. In the next two subsections, I will demonstrate how to write the `WithEvents` statement and the event procedure and how to invoke the event handler with code.

Writing Event Handlers in the Code Editor

You need to perform two related operations to define event handlers at design time. First, you need to define a `WithEvents` statement, and second, you need to define a procedure with the correct signature and add a `Handles` clause at the end of the procedure.

For the example, let's declare a `WithEvents` statement for a form and define a `Click` event handler. A Form class is defined in `System.WinForms.Forms`. The `WithEvents` statement is as follows:

```
Private WithEvents Form1 As System.Winforms.Forms.Form
```

`Form1` is the object and `System.WinForms.Forms.Form` is the fully qualified path of the class. To define an event handler that automatically handles click events for `Form1`, we need a procedure with the correct signature and a `Handles` clause. The `Click` event handler is defined as an `EventHandler` delegate, a procedural type that is specifically a subroutine that has `Objects` and `System.EventArgs` arguments, so we need a procedure that takes those types of arguments:

```
Private Sub Form1_Click(ByVal Sender As Object, _
   ByVal e As System.EventArgs) Handles MyBase.Click
End Sub
```

Listing 8.8 demonstrates both parts of the manually typed `Click` event handler (the rest of the Form code is hidden using code outlining).

LISTING 8.8 Manually defining event handlers.

```
 1: Public Class Form1
 2:    Inherits System.Windows.Forms.Form
 3:    Private WithEvents Form1 As System.Windows.Forms.Form
 4:
 5:    [...]
 6:
 7:    Private Sub Form1_Click(ByVal Sender As Object, _
 8:      ByVal e As System.EventArgs) Handles MyBase.Click
 9:
10:      MsgBox("Manually Typed")
11:
12:    End Sub
13:
14: End Class
```

When you click the form having the code shown in Listing 8.8, the `Form1_Click` event handler on line 7 is called. The manually typed code is identical to the code generated by selecting (`Base Class Events`) from the Objects list and `Click` from the Procedures list.

Typing the code manually is not something you'll want to do all the time. However, it's necessary to understand how event handlers are wired together to use more advanced delegate techniques.

Associating Event Handlers at Runtime

Listing 8.8 defines a `Click` event handler. We could have named the `Click` event handler anything; I named it `Form1_Click` out of habit but `ClickEvent` would have worked. The `Handles MyBase.Click` clause is the part of the procedural statement that indicates that the procedure `Form1_Click` is an event handler.

`Form1_Click` is also a procedure that we can invoke directly and can be treated as a procedural type and assigned to an instance of a delegate. To invoke the procedure, simply call the procedure with two suitable arguments. `Form1_Click(Nothing, Nothing)` will call `Form1_Click`, passing `Nothing` as the value of the `Objects` and `System.EventArgs` parameters.

In Visual Basic .NET, you can assign the address of the procedure as the value of a `Delegate` variable:

```
Dim ClickEvent As EventHandler = AddressOf Form1_Click
ClickEvent(Nothing, Nothing)
```

`EventHandler` is a predefined `Delegate`, as mentioned. The first statement of the fragment declares `ClickEvent` as an `EventHandler` delegate and assigns the address of `Form1_Click` to `ClickEvent`. The second statement invokes the procedure through the delegate. The second statement in the fragment calls the `Form1_Click` subroutine.

Creating Runtime Event Handlers

You can define multiple responses to a single event. Like a symphony conductor orchestrating several musicians playing simultaneously, you can have a single event invoke multiple, orchestrated event handlers.

If you define more than one procedure with the same `Handles` clause, each procedure is called for a single event. For example, two separate procedures with `Handles MyBase.Click` clauses will each be invoked when the `Click` event occurs. This is related to the subject of multicast delegates (see Chapter 9). Suppose you have the `Form1_Click` event handler defined in Listing 8.8. If you defined a second procedure, arbitrarily named Form1_ClickToo with the Handles MyBase.Click clause, when Form1 was clicked, both procedures would be called. This works because delegates store a list of procedure addresses and invoke every procedure in the list when the event occurs.

You can also change the behavior of an event or layer behaviors at runtime with the AddHandler and RemoveHandler methods, which have the following syntax:

```
AddHandler object.event, AddressOf object.eventhandler
RemoveHandler object.event, AddressOf object.eventhandler
```

object.event is the instance and event type whose invocation list we want to modify. *object.eventhandler* is the object and event procedure that we want to add to or remove from the invocation list. The second argument of AddHandler and RemoveHandler is a delegate. Recall that AddressOf returns a delegate, satisfying the second argument requirement.

A common situation in which you need to manage event handlers dynamically is when you are dynamically creating and removing things, namely controls, that use event handlers. Listing 8.9 demonstrates code that adds buttons to a form at runtime. A button would be of little use without a Click handler, so the code demonstrates using AddHandler to define a response for the button. The code in Listing 8.9 displays the name of the button that invoked the Click event.

LISTING 8.9   Adding button controls and adding Click event handlers at runtime.

```
 1: Private Sub ButtonClick(ByVal Sender As System.Object, _
 2:   ByVal e As System.EventArgs)
 3:
 4:   MsgBox(CType(Sender, Button).Text)
 5: End Sub
 6:
 7: Private Sub button1_Click(ByVal sender As System.Object, _
 8:   ByVal e As System.EventArgs) Handles button1.Click
 9:
10:   Dim Button As New Button()
11:   Controls().Add(Button)
12:   Button.Text = "Button" & Controls().Count
13:   Button.Top = Controls().Count * Button.Height
14:   AddHandler Button.Click, AddressOf ButtonClick
15: End Sub
```

The Windows application project contains a single button, button1. When button1 is clicked, it creates a new instance of a button control. The button control is added to the

`ControlCollection`, `Controls`; `Controls` is a member of the `Form` class. The button text is "button" with the number of controls appended to the text to create a unique caption. Line 13 positions the button to ensure it's not covered by other buttons, and line 14 adds the handler `ButtonClick` to the button's `Click` event invocation list. When the button is clicked, lines 1 through 5 are executed.

You might use a technique similar to the one in Listing 8.9 if you are adding menu items, toolbar buttons, or creating forms or controls at runtime. Refer to Chapter 15, "Using Windows Forms," for more on dynamic control creation.

Creating Event Handlers in the WebForms Designer

WebForms are part of Visual Basic .NET. WebForms allow you to define ASP.NET-based applications similar to the way in which you would design Windows applications. The Form and Code designers for WebForms look and feel a lot like programming a Windows application. You create the application, paint controls on forms, and write VB code. When the application runs, users are served ASP.NET pages. From the developer's perspective, it's VB programming. From the user's perspective, it's a great Web experience.

Because creating Web applications in .NET is similar to creating Windows applications, the metaphors for creating event handlers are identical to those for creating event handlers for Windows applications. You can create event handlers from the Properties view, in the Code editor from the Objects and Procedures list, and manually with code.

The namespaces for WebForms are different because the infrastructure is different. And, fewer events are available because events on a WebForm have to make a roundtrip to the server. A Web application would suffer if all the events available in a Windows application were available in a Web application. Chapter 23, "WebForms," demonstrates how to implement a WebForms-based application and define suitable event handlers for a WebForm.

Declaring and Raising Events

Events are supported for classes, modules, and structures in Visual Basic .NET. You can also define shared events (refer to Chapter 11 for more on `Shared` methods).

8

ADDING EVENTS

The event model is designed so that you can define entities in such a way as to ensure that interactions are sustained at the interface level. (Keep in mind that the term interface is defined as the public properties, methods, and events of an *entity*, an instance of a class, module, or structure.)

Consider the following generic scenario. A grid control paints data in cells. When each cell paints, it needs to get data for each cell from the data provider. If the grid were implemented in such a way as to know what the cell data provider was and iterated over each cell, asking the provider for cell data, that grid would only be useful with that kind of data provider. The following algorithm demonstrates this:

```
For All Grid Cells
 Grid.Cell(index).Text = Provider(index).Text
Next
```

This can work in a polymorphic way. For example, if `Provider` were an interface and any control that wanted to work with a specific grid supported that interface, the generic algorithm works with anything that is a suitable provider. Such an implementation works with COM interfaces or object-oriented, inherited interfaces. For example, if `Provider` were any OLEDB provider, the grid would work with any OLEDB provider.

As an alternative, the algorithm could be supported with an event as follows:

```
For All Grid Cells
   RaiseEvent GridData(index, ByRef Data As String)
Next
```

Now the grid is generic and will work with any code that responds to the `GridData` event. A common implementation is to combine a general to specific approach to implementing classes. That is, classes at a lower level support a generic interface, like using an event, and as a class becomes more specific, the event is used to implement behavior for a specific kind of interaction. Using our grid example, an original grid class might support providing cell data via an event, and a specific subclass of the grid can provide the data from a `Recordset`.

A good general rule of object-oriented programming is that all entity interactions should occur through a property, method, or event. This rule doesn't apply to aggregate relationships. For example, if a combo box owns a list, internal interactions can occur with the specific list it owns. On the other hand, if a combo box needed a list of items but didn't maintain a list internally, it might expose a public property that allowed a consumer to associate a list with the combo box using a public property.

A violation of the entity interaction rule is commonly seen in code of the following form:

```
Form1.StatusBar1.Text = "Some Text"
```

From the fragment it's obvious that we are outside `Form1` because we wouldn't need the `Form1` reference from within `Form1`, and it would be dangerous to use an object name internally. What if the object weren't `Form1`? The result would be the dreaded access violation. At most we might use `Me.StatusBar.Text` to be verbose, but internally all we would need is `StatusBar.Text`. Having established that we are referencing the `Text` property of the status bar externally, we are presented with several problems. If status is implemented in some alternative fashion, all the external code referring to the `StatusBar1` control would break. If the implementation of `StatusBar` changed, so that the property was renamed to `Caption` (a plausible example, as demonstrated by Visual Basic .NET forms using a `Text` instead of `Caption` property), again, all the code referring to `Form1.StatusBar` would be broken. In fact, code that generally daisy-chains *object.member* references together is demonstrative of *tightly coupled* code that violates the entity interaction rule.

To support loosely coupled entity interactions, we might support the status updating behavior with a property `StatusText`. Consequently, the consumer could call `Form1.StatusText = "Some Text"` and the provider could implement the status in any desired manner without breaking dependent code.

Supporting entity interactions with an event is preferable to a producer calling a specific method of a consumer. Consider the paint behavior of any Windows form. It's impossible for Windows to know in advance what all the forms will be from here to eternity. The arrangement is such that when any forms are rearranged or hidden and revealed, Windows raises a `Paint` event. Any form that needs to respond to `Paint` events can tap into this raised event and know when some external factor has made it necessary for it to repaint itself. Each form isn't specifically aware of the other forms or applications when it responds to a `Paint` event. Neither does Windows know about all possible instances of a form. What Windows does know is that its responsibility to displayed forms is to notify them when they need to repaint.

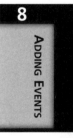

Events are critical to programming in Windows because events allow us to define specific interaction behaviors without indicating specific instances of objects.

Declaring Events

The purpose of a property is to maintain state information. The purpose of a method is to define behavior. The purpose of an event is to support response behaviors. A producer raises an event and a consumer responds; the interchange between producer and consumer is complete.

When you define an entity, you will add events for those occurrences that you want to provide an opportunity to which consumers can respond. Events are often coupled with behaviors. For example, a form knows how to perform basic painting. A form responds to a paint event and raises the paint event for form consumers to provide additional responses. An example was demonstrated in Listing 8.7. MouseMove is an event that occurs when a person physically moves the mouse pointing device. Windows applications already know how to respond to MouseMove. In Listing 8.7, an additional response was defined: The cursor position of the mouse was displayed on the form. This position of the mouse was displayed in concert with an additional event, Paint. Many predefined responses exist; as mentioned, MouseMove and Paint are two such events. You can add events for any occurrence you think necessary when defining classes, structures, and modules.

Events are always subroutines. Events don't return data to producers. Hence the form of an event statement is always Event *subname([args])*. The keyword Event is always required. The event name can be any meaningful name you'd like. And, because handlers are subroutines, you can define any number and type of arguments deemed necessary. Event arguments are completely optional just as subroutine arguments are.

Events also support access specifiers, allowing for public and nonpublic events. Prefix an event with the appropriate access specifier—for example, Private to make the event an internal event or Public to allow consumers to respond to the event—as you would any other member.

Raising Events

Raising an event is similar to a function call. In essence what you are doing is invoking a procedure-calling mechanism when you raise an event, but you are invoking the procedure through the event name rather than the procedure name.

Events are always subroutines with zero or more arguments. To raise an event, write the keyword RaiseEvent followed by what looks like a subroutine call, passing the necessary arguments as defined by the event statement.

Consider a class with a Public Event OnTest(). Event handlers for OnTest events are subroutines that take no arguments. To raise an OnTest event, you would write RaiseEvent OnTest at the point in your code where you want the OnTest event to occur. Listing 8.10 demonstrates a class with the event OnTest.

> **Note**
>
> The On prefix for event names was borrowed from Object Pascal. I will use it by convention for events throughout the rest of this book. The preposition On, as defined by www.dictionary.com, is "used to indicate occurrence at a given time," which clearly conveys what an event is. An event is an occurrence at a given time when a program is running.

LISTING 8.10   A class containing one member, an event named `OnTest`.

```
1: Class TestClass
2:    Public Event OnTest()
3:
4:    Public Sub DoTest()
5:      RaiseEvent OnTest()
6:    End Sub
7:
8: End Class
```

`TestClass` defines a single event, `OnTest`. Another borrowed convention from Object Pascal is to raise an event in a procedure prefixed with `Do`. Hence, `OnTest` would be raised in `DoTest`. Wherever in your code an `OnTest` event needs to be raised, you would call `DoTest`.

You can elect to use `Do` and `On` or not; just be consistent with whichever conventions you adopt.

Suppose we wanted to pass the object of the invoking entity in an event, as the `EventHandler` delegate does. We could modify `OnTest` to require an argument defined as `ByVal sender As Object`. The revision applied to the `Event` statement would appear as `Event OnTest(ByVal sender As Object)`. Revising Listing 8.10, line 5 to send the instance to the event consumer would be written as `RaiseEvent OnTest(Me)`.

The reference to self, `Me`, is suitable as an `Object` reference because `Me` refers to the instance of the containing object and every object in Visual Basic .NET is subclassed from the `Object` class.

8

ADDING EVENTS

Implementing Class Event Handlers

A *class event* is an event defined as a member of a class. Listing 8.10 demonstrates a class event.

Often events are occurrences for which you want to support an external response. For this reason events are commonly defined as `Public` members. You can define class events as `Protected`, `Private`, `Shared`, and `Friend Protected`. These access specifiers have the same meaning when applied to events as they do when applied to other members.

`Public` events can be handled by event handlers in other entities. `Protected` and `Protected Friend` events are handled by friends and child classes, and private events are internal events. However, the purpose of an event is to define an opportunity for an as-yet undefined external entity to respond to an occurrence. Within the same entity, all the members are accessible and child classes have access to parent members, thus mitigating the general, widespread use of nonpublic events.

Implementing Shared Event Handlers

Property, method, and event members support the Shared specifier. Shared members are accessible without an instance. To declare a shared event, follow the access specifier with the keyword Shared and the event name and arguments. For more on implementing shared events, read Chapter 11, "Shared Members."

Implementing Module Event Handlers

You can define and raise events in modules. The Module construct was ported to Visual Basic .NET for reasons of familiarity. From Chapter 2, you know that the Module construct is fundamentally a class with all shared members.

Consequently we can guess that if shared members are supported, and shared events are supported, module events are likely to be supported. In fact they are. You don't need to use the Shared specifier for module events. Another difference between class events and module events is that module events aren't supported by the WithEvents statement and procedures with the Handles clause. You must use AddHandler to assign a delegate—that is, the address of a procedure—to an event defined in a module. Consider the code in Listing 8.11, which defines a module event, and Listing 8.12, which defines the event handler.

LISTING 8.11   Implementing a module event.

```
1: Module Module1
2:
3:    Public Event OnEvent(ByVal Name As String)
4:
5:    Sub DoEvent()
6:       RaiseEvent OnEvent("Module1")
7:    End Sub
8:
9: End Module
```

LISTING 8.12   Implementing a module event handler.

```
1: Public Class Form1
2:     Inherits System.Windows.Forms.Form
3:
4: [...]
5:
```

LISTING 8.12   continued

```
 6:    Private Sub OnEvent(ByVal Name As String)
 7:       MsgBox(Name)
 8:    End Sub
 9:
10:    Private Sub button2_Click(ByVal sender As System.Object, _
11:       ByVal e As System.EventArgs) Handles button2.Click
12:
13:       AddHandler Module1.OnEvent, AddressOf OnEvent
14:       Module1.DoEvent()
15:
16:    End Sub
17:
18: [...]
19:
20: End Class
```

Listing 8.11 defines the OnEvent event and the DoEvent method, which we are implementing by convention, used to raise the event. Note that the event declaration is the
same whether the event is defined in a class or module. Listing 8.12 demonstrates the
definition of the handler OnEvent bearing the same signature as the OnEvent event
defined in Module1. (Another convention I often employ is to name my handlers the
same as my events; this makes for an easier pairing between events and handlers.
Because the event and the event handler are defined in separate entities, there is no name
conflict in doing so.) The button2_Click event demonstrates defining the event handler
OnEvent as the handler for Module1.OnEvent. The statement Module1.DoEvent on line
14 of Listing 8.12 simulates some fragment of code invoking the event handler.

As a general rule, it's the responsibility of the entity containing the event to raise the
event. For example, a form raises the Paint event in response to the Invalidate method.

Implementing Structure Event Handlers

Structures support event members too. Structures, like modules, don't support the
WithEvents statement and the Handles clause. You need to declare the structure and use
AddHandler to associate an event handler with a structure. The motivation for defining a
structure event is identical to defining an event for a module: you want to provide an
external entity an opportunity to respond to an occurrence in the structure. Listings 8.13
and 8.14 demonstrate a structure with an event and an example of some handling code.

LISTING 8.13   An event defined in a structure.

```
1: Structure Structure1
2:    Public Event OnEvent(ByVal sender As Object)
```

8

ADDING EVENTS

LISTING 8.13   continued

```
3:
4:    Sub DoEvent()
5:       RaiseEvent OnEvent(Me)
6:    End Sub
7:
8: End Structure
```

LISTING 8.14   An event handler for a structure.

```
 1: Public Class Form1
 2:      Inherits System.Windows.Forms.Form
 3: [...]
 4:
 5:    Private Sub OnEvent(ByVal sender As Object)
 6:       MsgBox(sender.GetType().Name)
 7:    End Sub
 8:
 9:    Private Sub button1_Click(ByVal sender As System.Object, _
10:       ByVal e As System.EventArgs) Handles button1.Click
11:
12:       Dim S As Structure1
13:       AddHandler S.OnEvent, AddressOf OnEvent
14:       S.DoEvent()
15:
16:    End Sub
17:
18: [...]
19:
20: End Class
```

Listing 8.13 defines an event, OnEvent, for a structure named Structure1. By our adopted convention, the event is raised in a Do subroutine. If the event were named OnStatusChange, by convention we would raise the event in a method named DoStatusChange. Structure1.OnEvent takes a single argument, which is satisfied by sending a reference to self. Listing 8.14 uses code outlining to hide extraneous form code not relevant to this discussion. Line 12 of Listing 8.14 declares an instance of Structure1. Line 13 associates the handler OnEvent with the Structure1.OnEvent event.

Unsupported Event Capabilities

Some general capabilities aren't supported for events. Events can't be overloaded or overridden in subclasses. However, if you implement a Do procedure that raises an event, you can override and overload that procedure, changing the way an event is invoked or even which event is called. Suppose you have an event `OnEvent` and you implement a subroutine `DoEvent`. Every time your code needs to raise `OnEvent`, you call `DoEvent`. Because `DoEvent` is a regular procedure, you can override or overload it.

Event signatures can contain `ByRef` or `ByVal` arguments but cannot use the `Optional` keyword and have optional arguments. The `ParamArray` specifier, which effectively allows you to include or not include arguments, is also precluded in the context of event statements.

Summary

Chapter 8 demonstrated the fundamental concepts of declaring, raising, and handling events. You can declare event members in classes, structures, and modules in Visual Basic .NET. Event handlers for structures and modules must be assigned with the `AddHandler` statement, whereas `WithEvents` and `Handles` or `AddHandler` can be used to associate event handlers with class events.

Event handlers are basically procedural types. Visual Basic .NET implements and supports procedural types and event handling as a special class, `Delegate`. Chapter 8 touched briefly on the concept of delegates and multicast delegates, and Chapter 9 will provide more information and advanced techniques for employing delegates.

Understanding Delegates

CHAPTER 9

Visual Basic 6 provided an opportunity for us to become familiar with events as a dynamic aspect of Windows programming. From Chapter 8, you know that an event is an occurrence in your program, and an event handler is a procedure defined to respond to that occurrence.

To review, the event-handling mechanism works because procedures are effectively addresses. If we know the arguments that are passed to a procedure and have a procedure's address, we can invoke a procedure because this is how procedure invocation works internally. VB6 allowed us to pass the address of a procedure to Windows for API calls that needed a callback address, but didn't support callbacks within VB6 itself. Visual Basic .NET supports procedural types through the `Delegate` class. Delegates maintain the addresses of procedures used as callback procedures. When referring to a procedural type, think of a variable declaration whose type happens to be the signature of a procedure. *Procedural type* is the generic term that has been in existence in other languages for years; in Visual Basic .NET, procedural types are specifically referred to as *delegates*.

Because delegates are classes in Visual Basic .NET, we have extended capabilities beyond one instance of a `Delegate`—procedural type—containing a single address of one procedure. Delegates are implemented to support a list of addresses referred to as an *invocation list*. Delegates that contain multiple procedure addresses are referred to as *multicast delegates*. Multicast delegates support a single event having multiple respondents.

> **Note**
>
> VB6 required a control array if you wanted one event handler to handle events for multiple controls. Visual Basic .NET introduces the `Delegate` class to keep track of event handlers. Visual Basic .NET supports multiple event handler respondents for a single control event and supports multiple controls being associated with a single event handler.

In Chapter 9, you will learn all about defining, declaring, and invoking delegates. Additionally, I will demonstrate how delegates can be used as procedure arguments to support dynamic behavior. We will begin coverage of delegates in this chapter by looking at one of the most common pre-existing delegates, `EventHandler`.

Using the `EventHandler` Delegate

The most common delegate is `EventHandler`. A delegate is defined by preceding the name and signature of a procedure with the keyword `Delegate`. Applying this to what we know about the `EventHandler` delegate, we see that in Visual Basic .NET we can write a statement similar to the following:

```
Delegate Sub EventHandler(sender As Object, e As System.EventArgs)
```

This statement identifies a type name `EventHandler` as a delegate that takes an `Object` and `System.EventArgs` parameters. (If you've written or seen a function pointer in C/C++ or defined a procedural type in Object Pascal, this syntax will appear similar to you.) The delegate `EventHandler` is a type. Variables of type `EventHandler` can be the `AddressOf` any subroutine that has the same signature as the `EventHandler` delegate; specifically, the address of any subroutine that takes an `Object` and `System.EventArgs` parameters, in that order, can be assigned to an instance of an `EventHandler` delegate. We will come back to defining delegates and declaring instances of delegates in upcoming sections. For now, because `EventHandler` is so prevalent, let's take a look at how we can employ its generic arguments.

> **Tip**
>
> Delegates can be initialized with subroutines or functions.

Using the `EventHandler` Object Argument

The generic signature of the `EventHandler` `Delegate` wasn't picked by accident. From other architectures, specifically Delphi, a common ancestry has proven to be effective in implementing event handlers for controls like buttons and forms.

Many controls, for example, support a click event. To respond to an event, it's often helpful to know the originator of the event. For example, when a button is clicked, it's often helpful to be able to use the button object itself. The same may be true for forms or pictureboxes; you may want to respond to a click event. Without a common ancestry, an event handler would have to be defined specifically for each of these controls. An event handler for a picturebox would take a `PictureBox` argument, a form handler a `Form` argument, and so on. All of these variations of event handlers would cause any implementation supporting dynamic event handlers to swell up and complicate using the event handlers.

Consider a better alternative. A click event really just needs the object that invoked the event. Assuming a common ancestry—which is what we have in Visual Basic .NET—we can define one type of event handler and allow polymorphism to support specific behaviors for subclasses of Object.

This is exactly what we have in Visual Basic .NET. Object is the common ancestor for classes, ValueTypes (like Integer), and structures. Roughly, this means that anything can be passed to satisfy the Object argument, and dynamic type-checking through the TypeOf operator can be used to determine the specific subclass passed to satisfy that argument.

> **Note**
>
> Let's pause for a minute and examine the need for a generic object reference. It begs the question: If a generic object parameter is so important, why are we just now getting an implementation of event handling that supports it?
>
> The direct answer is that previous versions of VB had some shortcomings. Delegates are one of the reasons Microsoft can market Visual Basic .NET as a first-class language. VB6 supported a weaker style of programming event handlers.
>
> In VB6, we would implement an event handler and refer to the specific object in the event-handling code, for example:
>
> ```
> Sub Command1_Click()
>   MsgBox Command1.Name
> End Sub
> ```
>
> Unfortunately, this style of programming tightly couples the event handler with a single control. In VB6, this worked moderately well, because in the absence of a control array, only one control would be using this code. However, this code would break if you changed the name of the control. Visual Basic .NET supports the event handler as a property of the control. Consequently, if the control name changes, the property value doesn't, and the event handler still works correctly.
>
> Additionally, Visual Basic .NET supports assigning multiple control events to a single handler. Thus the exact same handler may be invoked by many objects. Attempting the latter would break the VB6 model for event handlers. From the preceding fragment, the equivalent of Command1_Click may not have been invoked by the Command control.
>
> Delegates and a stronger event-programming model required that event handlers have arguments, and sanity justified a polymorphic means of implementing event handlers.

Another factor may be that Distinguished Architect Anders Hejlsberg was instrumental in implementing Delphi event handlers this way and Microsoft needed something that worked.

The benefit of a generically defined event-handling `Delegate` means that multiple controls, supporting semantically similar operations, can be assigned to exactly the same event handler without using control arrays or specific references to controls.

Multiple Event Respondents

Suppose we have a main form with two metaphors for closing the application. For argument's sake, suppose that a File, Exit menu closes the application by closing the main form, as does a button with the text Quit. Each metaphor for closing the application performs semantically the same operation—to run the `End` statement. Clearly, one procedure should be able to handle this operation no matter how it is invoked.

The solution `EventHandlerDelegate.sln` on this book's CD-ROM contains the code for this example. The form is implemented by adding a `MainMenu` control from the Windows Forms tab of the toolbox and a `Button` to a `Form`. Add a File menu with an Exit submenu by clicking and typing in the menu designer on the form (see Figure 9.1), and modify the Text property of `Button`, adding the text Quit.

FIGURE 9.1

MainMenu control editing can be performed directly on the Form Designer as shown.

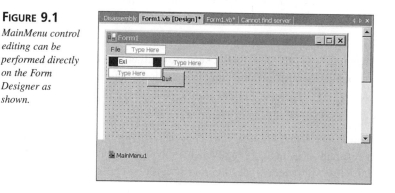

Double-click on the Exit submenu to generate the event handler procedure body (shown in Listing 9.1). Add the Quit button to the `Handles` clause. In this example, the default control names were maintained, so you'll see `Handles MenuItem2.Click, Button1. Click` in the listing.

LISTING 9.1   An event handler responding to similar events for two separate controls

```
Private Sub MenuItem2_Click(ByVal sender As System.Object, _
  ByVal e As System.EventArgs) Handles MenuItem2.Click, Button1.Click
    End
End Sub
```

The code is simple. It calls End to terminate the application. What is important is that MenuItem2 and Button1 are two disparate controls with semantically identical events, allowing one event handler to respond to an event raised by either control. Handles MenuItem2.Click and the event handler were added by double-clicking on the Exit menu item. The Button1.Click predicate was added manually.

In Listing 9.1, the code doesn't make use of either the Object or System.EventArgs argument. Sometimes, as in the example, you won't need these arguments. However, if the response is dependent on the type of the argument, you will need to type-check the sender argument to determine which action to take.

Type-Checking the Object Argument

Suppose in the example described in the previous section, you wanted to perform one of two slightly different operations based on which metaphor was used to invoke the operation. For example, Quit might prompt the user to make sure they wanted to exit not only the current context but the entire program, whereas the more deliberate File, Exit might suggest that the user is clear about his or her intentions and definitely wants to exit the application.

We could perform dynamic type checking on the sender argument in this instance, still using the same event handler and performing similar operations—quitting—but the Quit menu would ask the user to verify his or her intentions. You can type-check the sender argument by using the TypeOf operator.

From the implementation statement, after the user chooses the Quit button, the application exits if the user responds affirmatively to a verification prompt; otherwise, the application does not end. Listing 9.2 demonstrates the revision to Listing 9.1.

LISTING 9.2   Revised code from Listing 9.1, which dynamically type-checks the sender argument

```
1: Private Sub MenuItem2_Click(ByVal sender As System.Object, _
2:   ByVal e As System.EventArgs) Handles MenuItem2.Click, Button1.Click
3:
4:   If (TypeOf sender Is Button) Then
```

LISTING 9.2   continued

```
 5:     If (MsgBox("Are you sure?", MsgBoxStyle.YesNo, "Exit Application") _
 6:        = MsgBoxResult.No) Then
 7:
 8:         Exit Sub
 9:
10:     End If
11:   End If
12:
13:   End
14:
15: End Sub
```

The revised code is defined on lines 4 through 11. Lines 4 through 11 test the negative case. If sender is a button and the user answers No to the MsgBox prompt, the subroutine exits; otherwise, the application is terminated on line 13. The type of the sender argument is checked on line 4 with the TypeOf operator. In the next subsection, we will use this operator to determine the type of the sender argument and cast the Object type to a specific type.

Refactoring and Algorithmic Decomposition

Let's take a moment to address stylistic issues. Some programmers may object to multiple exit points, but other than some programmers finding the code a little confusing, there is no prohibition against multiple exit points. The alternative is to test the positive case:

```
If sender is button type then
  If user wants to quit is True then
    End
  else (user doesn't want to quit) Exit Sub
else (sender is menu item) End
```

Testing the positive case results in needing the end statement to appear twice.

As a matter of taste, I would prefer one exit point and a simpler event handler. In this event handler, all I want to know is whether the application can terminate. How termination is decided adds too much complexity to the event handler. Essentially the algorithm is "If CanQuit is True Then End" and this reflects what the code should say. Listing 9.3 demonstrates the revision using the more precise version of the algorithm.

LISTING 9.3   A more precise implementation of the dual-metaphor application termination event handler

```
1: Private Sub MenuItem2_Click(ByVal sender As System.Object, _
2:   ByVal e As System.EventArgs) Handles MenuItem2.Click, Button1.Click
```

9

UNDERSTANDING
DELEGATES

LISTING 9.3 continued

```
3:
4:     If (CanQuit(sender)) Then End
5:
6: End Sub
```

At this point the event handler is run, and the code now only asks "Can I quit?" If the answer is yes, the application terminates. (This is the singular level of complexity I strive for in my code.) Now the only problem is to implement CanQuit. Just as the event handler is a singular procedure now, so will CanQuit be. This singular division of labor plays to the short-term memory and problem-solving capability of the human mind and is supported by the concept of refactoring.

To implement the revision to Listing 9.3 from Listing 9.2, the refactoring "Extract Method" (introduced in Chapter 8) can be used twice to factor the prompt "are you sure?" and the test to determine whether sender is a button. Alternatively, you can decompose the problem as an algorithm and then implement each of the supporting pieces of the algorithm. CanQuit is decomposed as "sender is a button and prompt response is yes" or "sender isn't a button."

Choosing refactoring or algorithmic decomposition depends on where you are in development of the code. If the code is already written, use the refactoring; if you are writing the code for the first time, state the algorithm and decompose it into its supporting pieces. Refactoring implies revision after the fact, versus decomposition, which is revision before the fact. Because the long version was introduced first, I will demonstrate the Extract Method refactorings in the bulleted list that follows. (Use Listing 9.4 to follow along with the bulleted list of steps.)

- Factor out the MsgBox statement to a Function Quit that displays the message box prompt. Quit returns True if the user clicks Yes in response to the message box.

- Replace the literal call to MsgBox in Listing 9.2 with the call to Quit() testing for False, that is, Quit() = False.

- Replace the dynamic type check of sender with a function IsButton taking a sender As Object argument. (I am performing this refactoring for clarity here, but probably wouldn't in production code).

- Replace the dynamic type-check with the call to IsButton, passing sender in Listing 9.2. If codified, this change would yield:

```
If( IsButton(sender)) Then
  If( Quit() = False ) Then
    Exit Sub
```

```
    End If
  End IF
  End
```

- Define a `Function CanQuit()`, which returns a Boolean. Perform the positive test in `CanQuit` to return a Boolean True if `sender` is a button and the response to `Quit` is True or `sender` isn't a button. `CanQuit` is implemented using the `IsButton` and the `Quit` methods defined thus far. `CanQuit()` is shown in Listing 9.4.

LISTING 9.4 Revision of the code from Listing 9.3 using the refactoring Extract Method

```
 1: Private Function Quit() As Boolean
 2:   Const Prompt As String = "Are you sure?"
 3:   Return MsgBox(Prompt, MsgBoxStyle.YesNo,
 4:    "Exit Application") = MsgBoxResult.Yes
 5: End Function
 6:
 7: Private Function IsButton(ByVal sender As Object) As Boolean
 8:   Return TypeOf sender Is Button
 9: End Function
10:
11: Private Function CanQuit(ByVal sender As Object) As Boolean
12:   Return (IsButton(sender) AndAlso Quit()) Or Not IsButton(sender)
13: End Function
14:
15: Private Sub MenuItem2_Click(ByVal sender As System.Object, _
16:   ByVal e As System.EventArgs) Handles MenuItem2.Click, Button1.Click
17:
18:     If (CanQuit(sender)) Then End
19:
20: End Sub
```

Listing 9.4 is longer than Listing 9.2, the original implementation. In fact, refactoring may result in temporarily longer fragments of code but shorter, more reusable algorithms and fewer lines of code in an overall system. Each algorithm in Listing 9.4 is expressive and very easy to understand.

9

UNDERSTANDING DELEGATES

> **Note**
>
> I have met many people who don't understand the style of code in Listing 9.4. Simplistically, it seems as if I have traded one longer procedure for many shorter ones. A counter argument on the benefit side is that whereas the reader had to remember one slightly longer procedure, now the reader has to remember several, although short, procedures.

In very short examples, the use of many short procedures to replace a few longer ones seems to make very little sense. Instead of remembering what lines do, you have to figure out what functions do. Keep in mind that this argument only makes sense in individual examples, not systems. Using the strategies—decomposition or refactoring—discussed in this section results in more legible code, the need for fewer comments, procedures that are easier to understand and debug, and a greater number of reusable procedures. Time and experience bear these assertions out and the adoption of refactoring as a methodology supports the argument for singular, factored procedures.

Admittedly none of the methods in Listing 9.4 can be used again, but it's the overall strategy of factoring code to make individual pieces very easy to understand and more likely to be reused that we are striving for. Further, we are unlikely to know what a candidate for reuse is at the moment we are implementing a particular procedure. Consequently, refactoring provides us with an avenue for extracting code when potential reuse is identified.

Note

The preceding paragraph referring to reusable code is our justification for an architectural model. Without models it becomes increasingly difficult to realize optimal code reuse because developers lose track of available classes and procedures.

Perhaps the absence of models is the reason the industry is not realizing the full potential of object-oriented development. (The last statement is based on personal experience. Only one in 30 projects that I have worked on was actively building an architectural model prior to my participation.)

Typecasting the Object Argument

If you use the `sender` argument of an `EventHandler Delegate` as is, you will only be able to use the members of the `Object` class. To use members of the specific instance, you will need to determine the actual type of the `sender` argument and cast `sender` to that type. The preceding section demonstrated the `TypeOf` and `Is` operators. To cast a base class to a specific subclass, use the `CType` function.

Alan Cooper, in his book *The Inmates Are Running the Asylum*, addresses confirmation dialog boxes in the opening sentence of the chapter "Software Won't Take Responsibility." "Confirmation dialog boxes are one of the most ubiquitous examples of bad design; the ones that ask us '*are we sure*' that we want to take some action." (p. 67) Cooper goes on to suggest that the "are you sure" dialog box was designed to absolve the programmer of responsibility. Instead of prompting "are you sure," Cooper suggests that the user should be presumed sure but be able to change her mind later, and that it's the programmer's responsibility to make sure that the user can change her mind (that is, undo an action).

> **Note**
>
> Alan Cooper is the original inventor of Visual Basic, although he hasn't been active in its implementation or design for many years. When I asked Mr. Cooper by e-mail about his book Inmates, I suggested that he had some interesting ideas, and asked if he thought they would be generally adopted. He was kind enough to answer, stating something to the effect that he wanted to make money.
>
> I understood this to mean that perhaps his software would be more people-friendly and would represent its own compelling selling proposition. Contrarily, I think that the WinTel model is ubiquitous and a tremendous upheaval would occur if software were to change radically.

For the example in this section, we will take the middle road. We will assume that the user doesn't want to be prompted to verify any action but the option is a user-configurable option. (Perhaps in tutorial mode, the verification prompts would be presented.)

> **Caution**
>
> A production system must replace the verification screens with an undo capability. For example, deleting a record from a database needs to be undoable, especially if the user isn't prompted simply because this represents a significant departure from many implementations.
>
> Although Cooper condemns abdicating responsibility to the user, writing software that is smarter—for example, can undo a delete record—is significantly more challenging than writing software that displays a verification dialog box.

The metaphor used to implement the configurable behavior is represented by a menu option and a checkbox. In a production system, you might represent this behavior with an Options dialog box and persist the choice to a user options table of the Registry. (Keep in mind that the purpose of this example is to demonstrate dynamic typecasting.) To try the example, open `DynamicTypeCast.sln` from this book's CD-ROM or create a Windows application and add a MainMenu with a Tools, Prompt On Close menu item and a checkbox. Complete the following steps to re-create the example:

1. Create a Windows application.

2. Add a MainMenu with a Tools, Prompt On Close menu item.

3. Add a Checkbox control to the form.

4. Double-click on the Prompt On Close menu item to generate the Click event handler (shown in Listing 9.5).

5. Add `CheckBox1.CheckedChanged` to the `Handles` clause of the event handler.

Complete the numbered steps and add the code as shown in Listing 9.5. A synopsis of the code follows the listing.

LISTING 9.5   A single event handler maintaining the state of a user-configurable option

```
 1: Private FClosePrompt As Boolean = False
 2:
 3: Property ClosePrompt() As Boolean
 4:    Get
 5:       Return FClosePrompt
 6:    End Get
 7:    Set(ByVal Value As Boolean)
 8:       FClosePrompt = Value
 9:       Changed(Value)
10:    End Set
11: End Property
12:
13: Private Sub Changed(ByVal Checked As Boolean)
14:    MenuItem4.Checked = Checked
15:    CheckBox1.Checked = Checked
16: End Sub
17:
18: Private Sub MenuItem4_Click(ByVal sender As System.Object, _
19:    ByVal e As System.EventArgs) _
20:    Handles MenuItem4.Click, CheckBox1.CheckedChanged
21:    Static semaphore As Boolean = False
22:    If (semaphore) Then Exit Sub
23:    semaphore = True
24:
```

LISTING **9.5**   continued

```
25:    Try
26:
27:       If (TypeOf sender Is MenuItem) Then
28:          ClosePrompt = Not CType(sender, MenuItem).Checked
29:       Else
30:          ClosePrompt = CType(sender, CheckBox).Checked
31:       End If
32:
33:    Finally
34:       semaphore = False
35:    End Try
36:
37: End Sub
```

Note that the Handles clause on line 19 indicates that MenuItem4_Click handles MenuItem4.Click and CheckBox1.CheckedChanged events. Because both events have the same Delegate type, the single handler can handle both types of events. The Private field FClosePrompt on line 1 maintains the state, and by default is initialized to False. The property ClosePrompt is defined on lines 3 through 11. Line 8 stores the new ClosePrompt state and line 9 calls the Changed method, which synchronizes both controls' Checked states. Line 18 through 37 define the single event handler.

Line 21 defines a variable named semaphore. This variable is Static to ensure that the event handler maintains the state of the semaphore between calls. It will be apparent soon why the semaphore is used. Line 22 exits if semaphore is True, and line 23 sets semaphore to True. Line 25 starts a Try Finally block with the Finally setting semaphore to False.

The If condition on lines 27 through 31 sets the value of ClosePrompt depending on whether sender is the MenuItem or CheckBox. If sender is a MenuItem, the Checked property is toggled with a Not statement; otherwise, the Checked property of the CheckBox already has the correct state. Setting ClosePrompt takes care of synchronizing the controls.

What does the semaphore do? The MenuItem part of the If statement updates ClosePrompt, which effectively changes the value of the CheckBox.Checked state. Changing this state causes the event handler to be called recursively, halfway through. The semaphore prevents the code from being executed a second time unnecessarily by making the event handler behave like an empty subroutine until the handler has completely finished the first time.

9

UNDERSTANDING
DELEGATES

> **Tip**
>
> IntelliSense can provide member information to typecast objects at design time.

It's important to note that the CType function takes an Object and a class. The Object is cast to the type of the class. If the Object doesn't represent the class, a System. InvalidCastException occurs. For example, line 28 casts sender as a MenuItem; however, if sender is actually a Checkbox, this line would cause a System. InvalidCastException. After sender is cast, the members of the cast type can be used.

Using the `EventHandler` `System.EventArgs` Argument

The EventHandler is defined to pass a second argument, System.EventArgs. For generic events like Click, the EventArgs argument does not play a big role. However, it does act as a placeholder for more advanced events, like Paint. Paint uses a subclass of EventArgs to pass an instance of the device context wrapped in the Graphics class to the paint event handler.

Reviewing Delegate Members

Languages like C++ and Object Pascal support function pointers (also referred to as procedural types in Pascal) as simple types. Delegates were subclassed from the Object class and were implemented to support dynamic programming using procedure addresses to implement event handlers. Delegate is a subclass of Object in Visual Basic .NET. Table 9.1 lists and describes public members of Delegate.

TABLE 9.1 Delegate Members

Member	Description
	Shared Methods
Combine	Combines the delegate invocation lists
CreateDelegate	Creates a delegate of the indicated type
Remove	Removes the delegate from the invocation list
	Shared Operators
op_Equality	Tests for equality
op_Inequality	Test for inequality

TABLE 9.1 continued

Member	Description
	Instance Properties
Method	Returns the signature of the procedural type represented by the delegate
Target	Gets the class instance that created the delegate
	Instance Methods
Clone	Returns a shallow copy of the delegate
Invoke	Invokes the procedure referred to by the delegate
DynamicInvoke	Invokes the Delegate method
Equals	Returns True of Instance and single-cast Delegate share the same Target, Method, and invocation list
GetHashCode	Returns the hash code representing the instance
GetInvocationList	Returns the invocation list
GetObjectData	Returns information needed to serialize the Delegate
GetType	Returns the type of the instance
ToString	Returns a string representing the Delegate

Note

Table 9.1 contains two strangely named methods: op_Equality and op_Inequality. Visual Basic .NET does not currently support operator overloading, but C# does. Because both languages share the same CLR and C# supports operator overloading, there has to be an intermediate form of the overloaded operator for equality and inequality.

It is an exceptionally good practice to implement overloaded operators as regular methods first and implement the overloaded operators in terms of the method. The existence of methods like op_Equality suggests that Visual Basic .NET will support operator overloading soon.

9

UNDERSTANDING DELEGATES

Combine and Remove are commonly used to manage multicast delegates. For the most part, other than Combine and Remove, you will probably be using delegates as procedural types and event handlers. However, for exposure to the behavior of the Delegate methods, a brief example subroutine that demonstrates some of the Delegate methods is defined in Listing 9.6.

LISTING 9.6   Delegate methods example

```
 1: Private Sub Button1_Click(ByVal sender As System.Object, _
 2:     ByVal e As System.EventArgs) Handles Button1.Click
 3:
 4:     Dim Handler As EventHandler
 5:     Handler = AddressOf Form1_Load
 6:     Handler.Invoke(sender, e)
 7:     Debug.WriteLine(Handler.Method().ToString())
 8:     Debug.WriteLine(Handler.Target.ToString)
 9:     Debug.WriteLine(Handler.ToString)
10:
11:     Dim Handler2 As EventHandler
12:     Handler2 = AddressOf Form1_Load
13:     Debug.WriteLine(EventHandler.op_Equality(Handler, Handler2))
14:
15: End Sub
```

Listing 9.6 demonstrates a few `Delegate` members. Line 4 declares `Handler` as the Delegate `EventHandler`. Line 5 initializes `Handler` to the `Form1_Load` subroutine (which can be created by double-clicking on the form). Line 6 manually invokes the handler. In the example, line 6 causes the program to run the `Form1_Load` method. Line 7 prints the static `Delegate` method, resulting in the following line:

```
Void Form1_Load(System.Object, System.EventArgs)
```

This is the signature of the method. (The signature shown here is actually very similar to a C-style procedure declaration.) Line 8 shows the class containing the `Delegate`. In the example the default form, `Form1`, is the owner of this `Delegate`. Line 9 calls the `ToString` method. `ToString` is defined to display the class name, so `System.EventHandler` is displayed. Lines 11 and 12 declare and initialize a second `Delegate` to the address of `Form1_Load`, resulting in the `op_Equality` test to yield True.

Defining Delegates

The procedure for defining new delegates is very similar to declaring subroutines and functions, except without the function and subroutine body. The key to defining delegates is to decide whether you need a function or a subroutine and what information you want to pass to the handler procedure.

From the signature of the existing `EventHandler` delegate, we can derive the `EventHandler` declaration as stated previously:

```
Delegate Sub EventHandler( ByVal sender As Object, _
  e As System.EventArgs )
```

Suppose you wanted a delegate that defined a function taking two string arguments and returning a Boolean. Perhaps you would use this to define comparison behavior; you would define the delegate as follows:

```
Delegate Function Compare(ByVal Str1 As String, _
  ByVal Str2 As String ) As Boolean
```

After you have determined the signature of the Delegate type and declared the delegate, it's simply a matter of defining procedures matching those signatures and assigning the address of those procedures to Delegate instances.

Declaring Procedures That Match Delegate Signatures

Continuing our example from the beginning of this section, the values of Delegates are the addresses of procedures. Using the Delegate Compare as a further example, any function taking two string arguments and returning a Boolean could be assigned to compare delegates:

```
Function Ascending( ByVal Str1 As String, _
  ByVal Str2 As String ) As Boolean
    Return Str1 > Str2
End Function
```

The rule is that the signature must match. The signature is made up of the type of procedure—function or subroutine, the argument-passing convention and types, and the return type for functions. As demonstrated by the function Ascending, the function name can be anything. Although not demonstrated here, the argument names can be anything as long as their types, order, number, and passing conventions are identical.

Initializing a Delegate

Delegates are initialized by assigning the address of a suitable procedure to a Delegate instance. Continuing our example, a Delegate of type Compare would be declared as follows:

```
Dim MyCompare As Compare
```

To initialize MyCompare (we could have done it on the same line as the Dim statement), we can assign it to the address of the Ascending function:

```
MyCompare = Addressof Ascending
```

After we have the Delegate initialized, we can invoke the referenced procedure by treating the delegate as if it were the procedure. MyCompare("one", "two") returns False because the string "one" isn't greater than the string "two".

9

UNDERSTANDING
DELEGATES

Motivation for Using Delegates

If this and the previous chapter are your first exposure to events and procedural types, you might be wondering why we would do any of these things. For example, why not simply call the `Ascending` function directly? The answer is easy. At the time we write the code, we may have more than one procedure that makes sense based on the state of the program which is only known at runtime.

Consider the sorting example again. Suppose the user wants to sort a list in ascending order. We could write conditional code that reads algorithmically *if user wants an ascending sort, call the ascending sort function, else call the descending sort function.* Notice, however, that this implies two functions. We really only want one function. Hence, someone might suggest that we add an `If` conditional and a flag. Revising the algorithm to accommodate the flag and conditional code, we have: *if ascending, then set ascending flag, else set descending flag. For each element, if ascending, then compare ascending, else compare descending.* The second implementation complicates the logic, and we would pay performance penalties for the `If` conditional check. Finally, if we simply pass the `Compare` procedure to the sort algorithm, whichever type of compare we need is the one that is used. Passing the address of the comparison function (as one example) means we have one function and no conditional code. Read the next section for an example of a sorting algorithm with dynamic comparison arguments.

That's all fine and good. A reasonable person might ask, "Do we have any other motivation for using delegates?" The answer is a resounding yes. Any time we can anticipate needing a procedural respondent, but we won't know until runtime what will need a respondent, we need delegates. Consider the case where you are adding controls to your forms at runtime. These controls will need event handlers. You may be able to define the event handler while you are coding, but the object to which event it will be assigned won't exist until the program is running. You will need delegates to manage this scenario.

Granted, passing procedural types and dynamically creating components aren't things you will do every day, but you are likely to create classes and controls that define events. Someone will be defining event handlers for those classes and controls, and they will need to assign the handlers to the `Delegate` properties.

Using procedural types is an advanced aspect of programming that you may not use every day. However, when you need delegates, they will be there, and sometimes will be the best way to solve problems that can be solved no other way. Experience and practice will ultimately be your best guides.

Passing Delegates as Arguments

The classic example of procedural types is to pass the address of functions to sorting algorithms. As in the "Hello World!" examples, it's almost tradition to demonstrate procedural types using sort algorithms. In this section, I will demonstrate three sort algorithms that use one of two comparison functions to alternate between ascending and descending sort order.

To demonstrate passing `Delegate` arguments, I will guide you through the construction of `SortAlgorithms.sln` (contained on this book's CD-ROM, and shown in Figure 9.2). To complete the sample program, we will define a `Compare Delegate` that compares two integers. To perform comparisons based on a user preference of ascending or descending order, we will define two compare procedures suitably named `Greater` and `Less`. Listing 9.7 shows just the `Delegate` definition and two function definitions. Listing 9.8 contains the complete `SortAlgorithms.sln` listing (except for the Windows Form Designer-generated code).

FIGURE 9.2

The SortAlgorithms application showing BubbleSort swaps in progress.

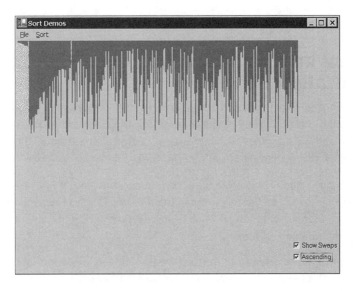

LISTING 9.7   The `Delegate` definition and two suitable functions for instances of the `Compare Delegate`

```
1: Delegate Function Compare(ByVal Height1 As Integer, _
2:    ByVal Height2 As Integer) As Boolean
3:
4: Public Function Greater(ByVal H1 As Integer, _
5:    ByVal H2 As Integer) As Boolean
```

LISTING 9.7 continued

```
 6:    Return H1 > H2
 7: End Function
 8:
 9: Public Function Less(ByVal H1 As Integer, _
10:    ByVal H2 As Integer) As Boolean
11:    Return H1 < H2
12: End Function
```

Notice that the Delegate procedural value is defined as a function that takes two integers and returns a Boolean. The signatures of Greater and Less precisely match the definition of the Delegate. To declare and initialize an instance of the Compare Delegate, do so in a Dim statement such as this:

```
Dim LessCompare As Compare = AddressOf Less
```

Referring to Figure 9.2, the sort order is indicated by the state of the Ascending checkbox shown in the lower-right corner of the main form in Figure 9.2. If the box is checked, the address of the Less function will be passed to the algorithm; otherwise, the address of the Greater function will be passed to the sort algorithm.

Reviewing the Sort Algorithms and Demo Application Behavior

The basics of sorting algorithms are the mechanisms for iterating, comparing, and swapping the elements of a group of similar data. For the sample program, I added a slight twist: We will iterate, sort, and swap rectangles drawn on a form to allow the user to see the effect of a particular algorithm (and for fun).

The SortAlgorithms application initializes a System.Array of Rectangles with random heights along the top of the form containing the code. The Random generator is invoked on Form_Load (refer to Listing 9.7) and can be regenerated with the Sort, Randomize menu in the sample program.

Based on the sort selected from the Sort menu—Bubble, Selection, or Quick—a specific sort is run. The iteration algorithms for the sorts are based on classic implementations of these algorithms.

The Compare algorithms compare heights of the rectangles only and swap the actual rectangles and rectangle heights because all other coordinates of the rectangles are relative to the top-left corner of the form. See Listing 9.8 for the complete implementation.

Sort Algorithms

The three sort algorithms were chosen because they are quite common. The Bubble sort uses a nested For loop, comparing and swapping each element where the ith element is less than or greater than the ith + n element, depending on the order of the sort. A Bubble sort performs n^2 comparisons and possibly the same number of swaps (see BubbleSort in Listing 9.8).

The Selection sort is essentially a Bubble sort. Slightly better performance characteristics are achieved because the Selection sort only performs n-swaps (see SelectionSort in Listing 9.8).

The Quick sort has Log_2n, or logarithmic, performance characteristics. Performance decay of a Quick sort occurs very slowly, making the Quick sort a good general-purpose, fast sort. Quick sort performance decays in highly ordered sets, with results on ordered sets decaying to those of a Selection sort (refer to QuickSort in Listing 9.8).

Walking Through the SortAlgorithms Demo Application

We have covered the basic steps in defining the SortAlgorithms application. Listing 9.8 contains the complete listing of demo application. A synopsis follows the listing, elaborating on some of the other examples of using delegates contained in the actual solution.

LISTING 9.8 The SortAlgorithms demo application uses procedural type arguments with rectangles and sorting algorithms for context

```
 1: Public Class Form1
 2:   Inherits System.Windows.Forms.Form
 3:
 4: [ Windows Form Designer generated code ]
 5:
 6:   Private Rectangles(300) As Rectangle
 7:   Private FSortOrder As Boolean
 8:   Private CompareProcs() As Compare = _
 9:     {AddressOf Less, AddressOf Greater}
10:
11:   Delegate Function Compare(ByVal Height1 As Integer, _
12:     ByVal Height2 As Integer) As Boolean
13:
14:   Private Function GetCompareProc(ByVal Value _
15:     As Boolean) As Compare
16:     Return CompareProcs(Math.Abs(CInt(Value)))
17:   End Function
18:
```

LISTING 9.8 continued

```
19:  Private Sub DrawRandomBars()
20:
21:    Array.Clear(Rectangles, 0, _
22:      Rectangles.GetUpperBound(0))
23:
24:    Dim I As Integer
25:
26:    For I = Rectangles.GetLowerBound(0) To _
27:      Rectangles.GetUpperBound(0)
28:        Rectangles(I) = New Rectangle(I * 2, 0, 1, Rnd() * 200)
29:    Next
30:
31:    Invalidate()
32:  End Sub
33:
34:  Private Sub ConditionalInvalidate()
35:    If (Not CheckBoxShowSwaps.Checked) Then _
36:        Invalidate()
37:  End Sub
38:
39:  Private Sub DrawRectangle(ByVal Rect As Rectangle, _
40:    ByVal APen As Pen)
41:    CreateGraphics.DrawRectangle(APen, Rect)
42:  End Sub
43:
44:  Private Sub Form1_Paint(ByVal sender As System.Object, _
45:    ByVal e As System.Windows.Forms.PaintEventArgs) _
46:    Handles MyBase.Paint
47:
48:    Dim Graphics As System.Drawing.Graphics = CreateGraphics()
49:    Graphics.DrawRectangles(Pens.Green, Rectangles)
50:
51:  End Sub
52:
53:  Public Function Greater(ByVal H1 As Integer, _
54:    ByVal H2 As Integer) As Boolean
55:
56:    Return H1 > H2
57:
58:  End Function
59:
60:  Public Function Less(ByVal H1 As Integer, _
61:    ByVal H2 As Integer) As Boolean
62:
63:    Return H1 < H2
64:
65:  End Function
66:
67:  Public Sub EraseOld(ByVal Rects() As Rectangle, _
```

LISTING 9.8 continued

```
68:     ByVal I As Integer, ByVal J As Integer)
69:
70:     If (Not CheckBoxShowSwaps.Checked) Then Exit Sub
71:     DrawRectangle(Rects(I), Pens.LightGray)
72:     DrawRectangle(Rects(J), Pens.LightGray)
73:
74:   End Sub
75:
76:   Public Sub DrawNew(ByVal Rects() As Rectangle, _
77:     ByVal I As Integer, ByVal J As Integer)
78:
79:     If (Not CheckBoxShowSwaps.Checked) Then Exit Sub
80:     DrawRectangle(Rects(I), Pens.Green)
81:     DrawRectangle(Rects(J), Pens.Green)
82:
83:   End Sub
84:
85:   Public Sub Swap(ByVal Rects() As Rectangle, _
86:     ByVal I As Integer, ByVal J As Integer)
87:
88:     EraseOld(Rects, I, J)
89:
90:     Dim R As Rectangle
91:     R = Rects(I)
92:     Rects(I) = Rects(J)
93:     Rects(J) = R
94:
95:     Dim X As Integer = Rects(I).X
96:     Rects(I).X = Rects(J).X
97:     Rects(J).X = X
98:
99:     DrawNew(Rects, I, J)
100:  End Sub
101:
102:  Public Sub BubbleSort(ByVal Rects() As Rectangle, _
103:    ByVal CompareProc As Compare)
104:
105:    Dim I, J As Integer
106:    For I = 0 To Rects.GetUpperBound(0) - 1
107:
108:      For J = I + 1 To Rects.GetUpperBound(0)
109:        Application.DoEvents()
110:
111:        If (CompareProc(Rects(I).Height, _
112:         Rects(J).Height)) Then
113:
114:          Swap(Rects, I, J)
115:
116:        End If
```

9

UNDERSTANDING
DELEGATES

LISTING 9.8 continued

```
117:        Next
118:     Next
119:
120:     End Sub
121:
122:     Public Sub SelectionSort(ByVal Rects() As Rectangle, _
123:       ByVal CompareProc As Compare)
124:
125:       Dim I, J, SwapIndex As Integer
126:
127:       For I = 0 To Rects.GetUpperBound(0) - 1
128:         SwapIndex = I
129:
130:         For J = I + 1 To Rects.GetUpperBound(0)
131:           If (CompareProc(Rects(SwapIndex).Height, _
132:             Rects(J).Height)) Then
133:
134:             SwapIndex = J
135:
136:           End If
137:         Next
138:
139:         Swap(Rects, I, SwapIndex)
140:       Next
141:
142:     End Sub
143:
144:     Public Sub QuickSort(ByVal Rects() As Rectangle, _
145:       ByVal Left As Integer, ByVal Right As Integer, _
146:       ByVal Comp1 As Compare, ByVal Comp2 As Compare)
147:
148:       Dim I, J As Integer
149:       Dim Rect As Rectangle
150:
151:       If (Right > Left) Then
152:         Rect = Rects(Right)
153:         I = Left - 1
154:         J = Right
155:
156:         Do While (True)
157:           Do
158:             I += 1
159:           Loop While (Comp1(Rects(I).Height, Rect.Height))
160:
161:           Do
162:             J = J - 1
163:             If (J < Rects.GetLowerBound(0)) Then Exit Do
164:           Loop While (Comp2(Rects(J).Height, Rect.Height))
165:
```

LISTING 9.8   continued

```
166:        If (I >= J) Then Exit Do
167:
168:          Swap(Rects, I, J)
169:        Loop
170:
171:        Swap(Rects, I, Right)
172:        QuickSort(Rects, Left, I - 1, Comp1, Comp2)
173:        QuickSort(Rects, I + 1, Right, Comp1, Comp2)
174:
175:
176:      End If
177:
178:    End Sub
179:
180:    Private Sub Form1_Load(ByVal sender As System.Object, _
181:      ByVal e As System.EventArgs) Handles MyBase.Load
182:
183:      DrawRandomBars()
184:
185:    End Sub
186:
187:    Private Sub MenuExit_Click(ByVal sender As System.Object, _
188:      ByVal e As System.EventArgs) Handles MenuExit.Click
189:
190:      End
191:
192:    End Sub
193:
194:    Private Sub MenuRandomize_Click(ByVal sender As System.Object, _
195:      ByVal e As System.EventArgs) Handles MenuRandomize.Click
196:
197:      DrawRandomBars()
198:
199:    End Sub
200:
201:    Private Sub MenuSelection_Click(ByVal sender As System.Object, _
202:      ByVal e As System.EventArgs) Handles MenuSelection.Click
203:
204:      SelectionSort(Rectangles, _
205:        GetCompareProc(CheckBoxAscending.Checked))
206:
207:      ConditionalInvalidate()
208:    End Sub
209:
210:    Private Sub MenuBubble_Click(ByVal sender As System.Object, _
211:      ByVal e As System.EventArgs) Handles MenuBubble.Click
212:
213:      BubbleSort(Rectangles, _
214:        GetCompareProc(CheckBoxAscending.Checked))
```

9

UNDERSTANDING DELEGATES

LISTING 9.8 continued

```
215:
216:    ConditionalInvalidate()
217:  End Sub
218:
219:  Private Sub menuQuick_Click(ByVal sender As System.Object, _
220:    ByVal e As System.EventArgs) Handles menuQuick.Click
221:
222:    QuickSort(Rectangles, Rectangles.GetLowerBound(0), _
223:      Rectangles.GetUpperBound(0), _
224:      GetCompareProc(Not CheckBoxAscending.Checked), _
225:      GetCompareProc(CheckBoxAscending.Checked))
226:
227:    ConditionalInvalidate()
228:  End Sub
229:
230: End Class
```

> **Note**
>
> All of the source code for this book is contained on the accompanying CD-ROM. For that reason, in general, long listings will be avoided. However, Listing 9.8 demonstrates several programming techniques in context, so it was listed in its entirety to facilitate discussion.

The three sort subroutines—BubbleSort, SelectionSort, and QuickSort—are defined on lines 102 to 178. From the listing, it's apparent that both the Bubble and Selection sorts use a nested For loop. The biggest difference is the point at which swaps are made. The Bubble sort swaps in the inner For loop, and the Selection sort swaps at the end of the outer loop. Important to our discussion is the use of the Delegate Compare as the last argument to each subroutine. This argument is satisfied by passing either AddressOf Greater or AddressOf Less to the CompareProc parameter.

The SortAlgorithms demo passes the sort ordered based on the state of the CheckBoxAscending.Checked property. In the MenuBubble_Click handler, such code might be written as follows:

```
If( CheckBoxAscending.Checked ) Then
  BubbleSort( Rectangles, AddressOf Greater )
Else
  BubbleSort( Rectangles, AddressOf Less )
End If
```

To yield a more concise implementation, as opposed to repeating the If conditional code, an array of procedural types was used. The resultant event handler was implemented as follows:

```
BubbleSort( Rectangles, GetCompareProc( CheckBoxAscending.Checked ))
```

GetCompareProc is defined as a function that uses a Boolean to index an array of the initialized Delegates. The initialized array of Delegates is defined on lines 8 and 9:

```
Private CompareProcs() As Compare = _{AddressOf Less, AddressOf Greater}
```

> ### Tip
>
> Sometimes using arrays of objects, like the Delegate array on lines 8 and 9 of Listing 9.7, can be a bit esoteric. The use of the wrapper function GetCompareProc may help clear up confusion and provide a convenient place for a block comment, letting less experienced developers in on the secret.

The array CompareProcs is an array of the Delegate Compare initialized to the AddressOf the Less and Greater functions. (Using an array instead of If-conditional code generally leads to more concise machine instructions, but this wasn't verified with respect to Visual Basic .NET.) The array of Delegates does demonstrate that it is possible to have an array of complex types, including Delegates. Such an array is a more concise, reasonable alternative to using long If-conditional statements or case statements.

The Quick sort—lines 144 to 178—takes two comparisons; it chunks the subset of elements roughly in half recursively, ordering successively smaller subsets of elements. The two delegates are used to switch the order of the sort. Based on the state of the CheckBoxAscending.Checked property, the Compare procedures are flip-flopped in the order in which they are passed. Line 159 uses the argument Comp1 and line 164 uses Comp2. Less is passed to Comp1 if the checkbox is Checked and Greater to Comp2. The argument values are switched if the checkbox is unchecked. This swapping of delegates is demonstrated on lines 224 and 225.

Illustrating an Alternative to Procedural Types

The EraseOld subroutine erases an existing rectangle by drawing a masking rectangle over the existing rectangle. The DrawNew subroutine draws the rectangle in its new position. The EraseOld and DrawNew subroutines demonstrate an alternative to procedural arguments. EraseOld and DrawNew are always called in the Swap algorithm; however, the code in them is only run based on the state. Because the state of the CheckBoxShowSwaps.Checked property is checked potentially thousands of times each time Swap is called, EraseOld and DrawNew add to a sort algorithm's decay based on the number of swaps. The two methods demonstrate how conditional behavior has always been handled in the absence of procedural types: Check the conditional value each time.

Delegates used to implement dynamic behavior allow you to write code that evaluates a condition one time and then act on that state condition until the state condition changes. Using the delegates, your code only has to evaluate the desired sort order one time, prior to calling a sort algorithm. Use the conditional code without the delegates and, as is the case with the Bubble sort, your code will evaluate the state condition possibly millions of times. In a production system, a couple of million extra conditional checks will make a big difference.

Multicasting Delegates

All instances of Delegate are MulticastDelegates, a subclass of the Delegate class. Specifically, multicasting refers to a delegate having more than one procedure address in its invocation list.

When you define multiple event handlers for a single event, when the event occurs, each event handler is called. (This behavior is probably implemented internally by iterating through the invocation list—accessible by the method GetInvocationList—and calling each method in the list, passing the required arguments. Suppose you have a Button control named Button1. Defining two methods with the Handles Button1.Click clause would cause the Button1.Click event to multicast the event to both methods with the Handles Button1.Click clause. Procedures are invoked in the order they appear in the invocation list. If you write the event handlers at design time, they are added to the invocation list in the order they appear in the code.

> **Caution**
>
> Avoid writing event handlers in such a way as to depend on their invocation order.

Listing 9.9 demonstrates two event handlers responding to a single click event. The first event handler, Button1_Click, was generated by double-clicking on the button control.

The second event handler was added explicitly by defining a subroutine that matched the signature of the `EventHandler` and typing the `Handles` clause manually.

LISTING 9.9   Two event handlers for the same event

```
 1: Private Sub Button_Click(ByVal sender As System.Object, _
 2:   ByVal e As System.EventArgs) Handles Button1.Click
 3:
 4:   MsgBox("Button click added manually")
 5:
 6: End Sub
 7:
 8: Private Sub Button1_Click(ByVal sender As System.Object, _
 9:   ByVal e As System.EventArgs) Handles Button1.Click
10:
11:   MsgBox("Button1_Click added by the form designer")
12:
13: End Sub
```

Lines 8 through 13 were added by the Form designer when I double-clicked on the button. Lines 1 through 6 were typed. The `Handles Button1.Click` clause is all that distinguishes these two methods from being regular methods and makes them event handlers for Button1's `Click` event. (You can call `Button_Click` and `Button1_Click` directly, too.)

The `Handles` clause is used to define event handlers at code-time. When your program is running, you need to use `AddHandler` and `RemoveHandler` to add and remove additional procedures to or from a Delegate's invocation list. The form of the call is `AddHandler Object As Event, Object As Delegate` where the first parameter is an event object and the second parameter is a reference to a `Delegate` (see Listing 9.10 for an example).

9

UNDERSTANDING
DELEGATES

> **Note**
>
> I asked a couple of the .NET programmers about the absence of parentheses for the `AddHandler` and `RemoveHandler` statements. (Recall that everything else uses the parentheses in Visual Basic .NET.) No concise answer was offered. For consistency, perhaps parentheses will ultimately be required for `AddHandler` and `RemoveHandler`.
>
> Better than adding parentheses to `AddHandler` and `RemoveHandler`, if operator overloading were supported, you could write *delegate = addressOf procedure*, which is much more intuitive.

LISTING 9.10   Adding and removing a handler from an invocation list

```
 1: Private Sub Button_Click(ByVal sender As System.Object, _
 2:   ByVal e As System.EventArgs) Handles Button1.Click
 3:
 4:   MsgBox("Button click added manually")
 5:
 6: End Sub
 7:
 8: Private Sub Button1_Click(ByVal sender As System.Object, _
 9:   ByVal e As System.EventArgs) Handles Button1.Click
10:
11:   MsgBox("Button1_Click added by the form designer")
12:
13: End Sub
14:
15: Private Sub RemoveDelegate()
16:
17:   Dim ADelegate As EventHandler = AddressOf Button_Click
18:   RemoveHandler Button1.Click, ADelegate
19:
20: End Sub
```

Lines 1 through 13 represent the static code typed at design time. Line 17 declares a
Delegate and initializes it to the address of Button_Click. RemoveHandler instructs
the application to remove the delegate whose address is equal to Button_Click from
the Click Delegate—or Event—Object. In other words, Click is a Delegate and
Button_Click is removed from Click's invocation list. If we wanted to add
Button_Click back to Click's invocation list, we would write AddHandler
Button1.Click, ADelegate.

Using the Combine Method

An alternative way to add procedure addresses to a Multicast Delegate is to use the
Combine method. Combine is overloaded so it can be called with two different parameter
signatures, either an array of Delegate or two individual instances of Delegate. In either
case it returns a Delegate whose invocation list contains all of the delegates passed to it
(all delegates in the array or the two individual delegates). Assume that you have
Delegate instances D1, D2, and D3 defined as EventHandler Delegates as follows:

```
Dim D1, D2, D3 As EventHandler
```

Also, assume that you initialized D2 and D3 to the address of a suitable subroutine.
Calling the Combine method passing D2 and D3 as arguments would return a Delegate

whose invocation list contained the procedural address of D2's and D3's combined invocation lists:

```
D1 = System.Delegate.Combine(D2, D3)
```

If D2 and D3 each contained one procedure in their invocation lists, D1 would contain the sum of the number of elements, or two in this instance. Keep in mind that a Delegate is a class, but it basically represents a procedural type. To manually invoke all of the procedures in the invocation list of D1, write D1 as if you were calling a procedure:

```
D1( Nothing, Nothing )
```

In this example Nothing, Nothing represents passing nothing for both the Object and EventArgs parameters of an EventHandler Delegate. To remove a Delegate from the invocation list, call the Shared method Remove. For example, to remove the D3 methods from D1's invocation list write:

```
D1 = System.Delegate.Remove( D1, D3 )
```

D1 now contains only the procedures in D2's invocation list. Calling Remove with Delegates not previously combined performs no action and doesn't raise an error.

Using Multicast Delegates

Multicast delegates support adding the address of one or more procedures to the invocation list of a delegate. For example, you might have behaviors that are only invoked when an application is in a specific state. In such a state, you can invoke several procedures when a single event occurs. With multicasting capability, you can layer in or remove code that responds to an event from an invocation list, much as a symphony conductor layers in musical instruments.

You are more likely to singlecast regularly than you are to multicast, but multicasting is available to you if you need it. In addition to thinking of multicasting delegates as a means of responding to events, you can also think of delegates as a way to define a list of procedures that all operate on the same object. You have one object and many operations; none, some, or all of which are invoked on the object depending on the program's state. A delegate can be used to begin each step in processing an object's event and the steps taken are regulated by adding or removing additional delegates to the invocation list.

9

UNDERSTANDING
DELEGATES

Using Delegates Across Project Boundaries

Events can be defined and used across project boundaries. An event defined in a class library can be handled in an application making reference to that class and having defined an event handler for the class library event. The net result is that classes don't have to be defined within your application to take advantage of the event mechanism.

Complete the numbered steps.

1. Create a new blank Windows application project.

2. Using the Solution Explorer, add a new Class Library project named RaisesEvent to the Windows application solution started in step 1.

3. Name the class library file `RaisesEvent.vb` and the class `RaiseTest`.

4. Declare an Event attribute by typing `Public Event SendString( ByVal Str As String )`.

5. Add a method test that raises the event with the statement `RaiseEvent SendString("RaisesEvent")`.

6. In the Form Designer of the Windows application, add a button control. Double-click the button control to generate the `Click` event handler for the button.

7. Outside the `Button1_Click` event handler, declare the statement `WithEvents R As RaisesEvent.RaiseTest`, where `RaisesEvent` is the class library and `RaiseTest` is the name of the class.

8. Within the `Button1_Click` event handler, create an instance of `RaiseTest` and assign it to `R`, the name in the `WithEvents` statement in step 7, and call the `Test` method with `Obj.Test()`.

9. Select the name `R` from the objects list and `R_SendString` from the procedure list to generate the event handler in the form.

10. Add the statement `MsgBox(Str)` to the `R_SendString` event handler.

After completing steps 1 through 10, run the Windows application part of the solution and click the button. You should get a message with the string of text sent from the event in the `RaisesEvent` class library. Listing 9.11 contains the complete code listing for the Windows application (this listing demonstrates a Windows `Form` class responding to an event raised in a class library). (The class library is in Listing 9.12).

LISTING 9.11   Handle an event across project boundaries

```
 1: Public Class Form1
 2:     Inherits System.Windows.Forms.Form
 3:
 4: [ Windows Form Designer Code ]
 5:
 6:     WithEvents R As RaisesEvent.RaiseTest
 7:
 8:     Private Sub Button1_Click(ByVal sender As System.Object, _
 9:       ByVal e As System.EventArgs) Handles Button1.Click
10:
11:         Dim Obj As New RaisesEvent.RaiseTest()
12:         R = Obj
13:         Obj.Test()
14:
15:     End Sub
16:
17:     Private Sub R_SendString(ByVal Str As String) Handles R.SendString
18:         MsgBox(Str)
19:     End Sub
20:
21: End Class
```

The `WithEvents` statement sets up the event-handling capability for the `RaiseTest` class.
`Button1_Click` creates a `RaiseTest` object and calls the `Test` method.
`RaisesEvent.Test` raises the `SendString` event, which is handled on lines 17 through 21
of Listing 9.11.

Listing 9.12 demonstrates declaring the event and raising it.

LISTING 9.12   Declare and raise an event in a class. The event can be handled in the
same or external project

```
1: Public Class RaiseTest
2:
3:     Public Event SendString(ByVal Str As String)
4:
5:     Public Sub Test()
6:         RaiseEvent SendString("RaisesEvent.Test")
7:     End Sub
8:
9: End Class
```

This is identical to the code you would write if `RaiseTest` and `Form1` were defined
within the same project. The implied difference is that delegates are working behind the
scenes to support this event interaction.

When you define a statement such as the one on line 3 of Listing 9.12, you are implicitly declaring a Delegate. The WithEvents statement is creating the necessary connection piece that allows you to express the relationship between event and handler. This relationship could have been explicitly defined, as demonstrated in the revised code in Listings 9.13 and 9.14.

LISTING 9.13 Revision of the code from Listing 9.12, defining the form using delegates explicitly

```
 1: Public Class Form1
 2:     Inherits System.Windows.Forms.Form
 3:
 4: [  Windows Form Designer generated code  ]
 5:
 6:     Private Sub Button1_Click(ByVal sender As System.Object, _
 7:       ByVal e As System.EventArgs) Handles Button1.Click
 8:
 9:         Dim Obj As New RaisesEvent.RaiseTest()
10:         Obj.D = AddressOf SendString
11:         Obj.Test()
12:
13:     End Sub
14:
15:     Private Sub SendString(ByVal Str As String)
16:         MsgBox(Str)
17:     End Sub
18:
19: End Class
```

Note the absence of the WithEvents statement. Line 10 takes care of assigning the AddressOf the handler SendString to the Delegate member RaisesEvent.D. Look at Listing 9.14 for the revised implementation of the event and its invocation.

LISTING 9.14 Revised implementation of RaiseTest from Listing 9.12, using Delegates instead of RaiseEvent

```
 1: Public Class RaiseTest
 2:
 3:     Public Delegate Sub Sender(ByVal Str As String)
 4:     Public D As Sender
 5:
 6:     Public Sub Test()
 7:         D("RaisesEvent.Test")
 8:     End Sub
 9:
10:     Public Sub HandleClick(ByVal sender As System.Object, _
11:       ByVal e As System.EventArgs)
```

LISTING 9.14   continued

```
12:        MsgBox("RaisesEvent.Click")
13:    End Sub
14: End Class
```

In Listing 9.14, the `Delegate` is explicitly defined on line 3. Line 4 declares a public attribute named `D`, representing an instance of the `Delegate Sender`. Line 7 calls all of the procedures in `D`'s invocation list oblivious to whether there are any procedures or not. The revised version performs exactly like its predecessor in Listing 9.12, without the `Event` and `RaiseEvent` statements.

> **Note**
>
> The reverse of the behavior supported by Listings 9.11 and 9.12 or 9.13 and 9.14 can be implemented also. That is, you could define an event in `Form1` and the handler in the `RaiseTest` class (or any class). Try this operation by creating a `RaiseEvent` object in the `Form1` class. In `Form1_Load` use `AddHandler Button1.Click, AddressOf Obj.Handler` to add a procedure named `Handler`, defined in `RaiseTest`, to `Button1`'s Click invocation list. When `Button1` is clicked, `RaiseTest`'s `Handler` event handler will respond. The code is defined in `InterProjectEvent.sln` along with the code from Listings 9.11 through 9.14.

Using `Delegates` explicitly may take a little getting used to if you were accustomed to using the `WithEvents`, `RaiseEvent`, and `Event` statements. However, calling the event using the same notation as a procedure is a little cleaner implementation.

Summary

Chapter 9 demonstrated the fundamentals of singlecast and multicast delegates. Delegates support a dynamic event programming model as well as passing procedural types as arguments. In addition to learning how to declare and define `Delegate` types, you learned how to respond to events across project boundaries.

Events are an essential part of Windows programming. You will probably write event handlers to respond to user activity. However, when you are defining custom controls and new classes, you will need to define events, and the delegates that respond to those events will contain the list of responses.

Going forward, you will see many examples of events and delegates in use. New information relating to how an event or delegate was employed will be imparted in the chapter in which it's introduced.

9

UNDERSTANDING DELEGATES

Inheritance and Polymorphism

Visual Basic .NET supports inheritance. VB6 did not. VB6 supported interface implementation, which is a facility of the Component Object Model (COM). Why Microsoft chose to implement COM and interfaces before classes and inheritance is anybody's guess, but Visual Basic .NET supports both interfaces and inheritance. The net result is that Visual Basic .NET is significantly more powerful and has features and capabilities consistent with the most advanced languages available today.

Through version 6, we said that Visual Basic was object-based rather than object-oriented. The primary missing ingredient was inheritance. Visual Basic .NET rectifies this deficit.

Chapter 10 demonstrates how to use inheritance in Visual Basic .NET, as well as the new capabilities associated with inheritance relationships. Additionally there are revisions to the way interfaces are supported in Visual Basic .NET. Chapter 10 will demonstrate inheritance, virtual abstract classes, final classes, polymorphic behavior, dynamic type-casting, and how to define and implement interfaces in Visual Basic .NET.

Inheritance Basics

Interfaces contain declarations only. Classes can contain both declarations and definitions. Classes can implement interfaces as well as inherit from a single parent class. Interfaces use the keyword `Interface`, and classes use the keyword `Class` in Visual Basic .NET.

The difference between an `interface` and a `class` is that classes provide implementations for their members and interfaces define members without implementations. Both classes and interfaces support inheritance. A class may inherit from a single parent and implement zero or more interfaces, and interfaces support multiple interface inheritance but provide no implementation. (We will return to interfaces later in this chapter. For now let's focus on what classes offer.) Even if your understanding of inheritance is expert, you are encouraged to read the remainder of this section simply to see the grammar used to support class inheritance in Visual Basic .NET.

What Is Inheritance?

Recall that classes contain fields, properties, events, and methods. Inheritance implies at least two classes: one class plays the role of parent and the second class plays the role of child. (Occasionally we refer to sibling classes, those descended from the same parent. Seldom do we refer to a grandparent; generally when we discuss any ancestor beyond an immediate parent, we use the term *ancestor*.)

> **Note**
>
> A parent class is also referred to as a *superclass*, and a child class is also referred to as a *subclass*.
>
> Remember that the same class can be parent or child, depending on your perspective. For example, you are the parent of your children but the child of your parents. If you combine the parent-child relationship with the interchangeable parent/superclass and child/subclass vernacular, and mix in a few people talking about classes and objects as if they were the same things, a discussion can become quite confusing.
>
> We can dispel one concept completely. Classes are not objects. A class is a definition and an object is an instance of a definition. If a discussion becomes confused, consider sticking to one pair of terms, parent and child, and using class to mean only definition and object to mean only instance.

When we say inheritance in Visual Basic .NET, we mean that a child gets a copy of everything found in a parent plus anything we add to that child. Technically, a child gets a copy of the data and access to a methods table, but for simplicity we think of child classes as getting their own copy of everything. This does not mean that a child can directly access every member inherited from the parent; access rules still apply. The child gets a copy of everything, but can only directly access public, protected, and friend members of a parent. Because private members represent implementation details, a child class is usually interacting with private members indirectly via public, protected, or friend members.

The simplest representation of the parent-child relationship is that of union from mathematics (see Figure 10.1). (I always wondered where it would be necessary to use those union and intersection diagrams from elementary school.)

FIGURE 10.1

Inheritance can be appropriately represented as the union of parent and child.

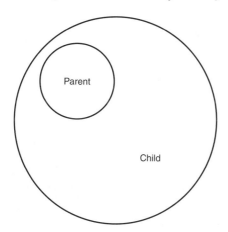

Parent

Child

A reasonable representation of inheritance access is represented by an intersection relationship (see Figure 10.2).

FIGURE 10.2
Inheritance access is represented by an intersection relationship.

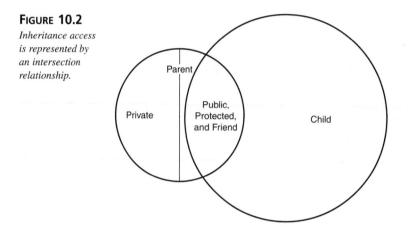

The child class shown in Figure 10.1 is a replica, plus something additional, of its parent. Information hiding and complexity management is represented by Figure 10.2. From the child-as-consumer perspective, the child in Figure 10.2 is only concerned with the members not in the `Private` section of the parent class.

Basic Inheritance Statement

Fortunately the grammatical complexity of inheritance relationships is miniscule. Given two classes, one playing parent and the other child, all you need to do is add a single statement to indicate inheritance in Visual Basic .NET. Listing 10.1 demonstrates the statement for indicating inheritance.

LISTING 10.1 The simplest inheritance relationship.

```
Public Class Parent

End Class

Public Class Child
   Inherits Parent
End Class
```

From the listing you can see that `Inherits Parent` is all that we must add to indicate inheritance of child from parent. The grammar is the easy part. Choosing what to expose in a parent and what to add to a child is the very subjective part of object-oriented programming that trips some programmers up.

There are no good general rules dictating what to inherit or how many members to add to a child class or override from a parent class. What are available are platitudes like "subjective good taste" and "reasonable and sufficient." What these statements mean is that inheritance is like flying or surgery: You have to land dozens of times or carve up numerous cadavers before you fly with passengers or operate on real people.

Having read thousands of pages and written tens of thousands of lines of code spanning two decades, I can tell you that I am seldom happy with my first attempt. The rest of this book provides many examples of inheritance; here I can offer a few basic guidelines that will get you started:

- Make methods protected and virtual unless you are reasonably sure they should not be.

- When you have a class that works and needs new behavior, create a child class and add the behavior to the child. You will not break existing code by modifying an existing class. You will have the old and new behavior and two classes to draw from.

- When defining reference parameters, define parameters to be parents reasonably high up in the architecture. You can always pass an instance of a child and typecast the parameter.

- Keep the number of public members to about a half-dozen.

- Keep methods and property methods very short and singular.

- Name methods using good verbs and properties using good nouns. Don't scrimp by using nonstandard abbreviations; use whole words.

- Try to maintain a balance between breadth and depth in your architecture, not too deep or wide.

- Refactor. Refactor. Refactor.

For every rule in the bulleted list, there is an exception, almost. In a large number of cases these rules will keep you in safe territory. The only one that shouldn't be optional is refactoring.

Inheritance by Example

The best way to gain experience with inheritance is to write and read a lot of code that involves inheritance. If most of your programming experience has been in Visual Basic—not in languages like C++, Java, and Object Pascal—you have not had much experience in defining inheritance relationships. The code in this book uses inheritance a lot, and several examples of inheritance follow in this section. Each example is followed by a brief synopsis. Consider this code:

```
Public Class Form1
  Inherits System.Windows.Forms.Form
End Class
```

Every form in a Windows applications inherits from the base form class defined in `System.Windows.Forms`. You will see this statement every time you design a new form in a Windows application:

```
Public Class WebForm1
  Inherits System.Web.UI.page
End Class
```

This fragment demonstrates a Web form that inherits from `System.Web.UI.page`. When you create an ASP.NET Web application in Visual Basic .NET, your Web forms will inherit from the `page` class.

Here's another type of inheritance example:

```
Private Class RedLight
  Inherits Light
End Class
```

The `Private` nested class `RedLight` inherits from `Light`. This is an example from Chapter 7 that demonstrates how to implement a private nested class and inherit from it.

Look at the next example:

```
Public Class IndexedException
  Inherits ApplicationException
End Class
```

When you extend the exception architecture, you can inherit from `ApplicationException` to implement custom exception classes. (This is also an example from Chapter 7.)

As demonstrated, the inheritance statement is always the same. The exact details about a parent class you want to modify and extend in a child class determine what code you will write in that child.

Implementing Properties, Events, and Methods in the Code Editor

When you inherit from a class, the Method Name combo box at the top-right side of the code editor will contain a hierarchical sublist of properties, events, and methods that can be implemented in a child class. For example, when you add a new form to a Windows application, you can pick from a list of members that are inherited, a list of overridable members, and a list of events.

Applying the behavior of the code editor to responses to the inputs during design time, if you double-click on a form, you will get a generated event handler for the Load event. The empty event handler represents an event handler for the base class event Load (see Figure 10.3).

```
Private Sub Form1_Load(ByVal sender As Object, _
   ByVal e As System.EventArgs) Handles MyBase.Load

End Sub
```

FIGURE 10.3

Events are organized in the code editor by (Base Class Events) *in the Class Name list, shown open in the figure.*

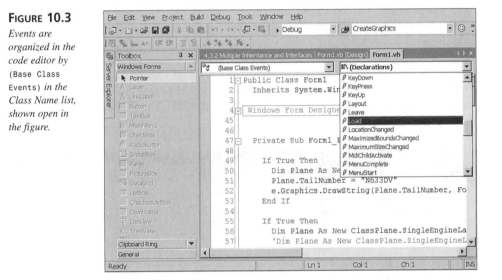

However, if you select the (Overrides) sublist, you can override the method that invokes the Load event.

```
Protected Overrides Sub OnLoad(ByVal e As System.EventArgs)

End Sub
```

Note

If you have Form_Load and OnLoad implemented in the same class, Form_Load will only be called if you call the base class method or raise the event yourself.

The event handler is related to the method that raises the event. In the Form parent class, it is the OnLoad event that raises the event your code is responding to in Form1_Load. Because events are not polymorphic directly, events can be made polymorphic indirectly by raising them via a method that can be overridden. (Refer to the section "Polymorphism" later in this chapter.)

If you want to respond to the OnLoad event, implement the Form_Load event handler. If you want to modify the OnLoad response in a subclass, you can override the OnLoad subroutine in a child. The default OnLoad method raises the event. An overridden OnLoad method can elect to perform the default behavior—that is, raise the event—or some new behavior.

Using MyBase

If you override a parent behavior in a child class, you can then call the parent behavior, or not call the parent behavior and perform some additional operation before or after invoking the parent behavior.

You only need to override a parent method if you want to extend or replace the parent method. Applied to our OnLoad versus Form_Load scenario, only implement OnLoad if the default behavior that raises the event is insufficient.

Tip

MyBase is a keyword like Me. Whereas Me refers to self, MyBase refers to the immediate ancestor of self.

If you want to perform the behavior of the parent, call MyBase.*parentmethod*. For example, MyBase.OnLoad will call the parent class behavior in the OnLoad method, and you can add other behavior before or after calling the parent behavior. An OnLoad method that produces behavior identical to the default Form.OnLoad method follows:

```
Protected Overrides Sub OnLoad(ByVal e As System.EventArgs)
   MyBase.OnLoad
End Sub
```

Overloading the Form.OnLoad Method

Suppose you wanted to add an entry into the Windows Event Log (see Figure 10.4) during testing every time a form was loaded. You could overload the OnLoad method and add the code to write the event log entry after the default behavior is performed, as demonstrated in Listing 10.2.

> **Tip**
>
> If you want to perform some behavior on an event, implement an event handler. If you want to change the way, order, or timing of the event handler, overload the On... method that raises the event.

LISTING 10.2   By convention, events are raised by methods prefixed with On; overload these methods to alter the behavior, order, or timing of an event invocation.

```
1: Protected Overrides Sub OnLoad(ByVal e As System.EventArgs)
2:   MyBase.OnLoad
3:   EventLog.WriteEntry("Form1", "OnLoad method called")
4: End Sub
```

Line 2 calls the parent class's method, which raises the Load event, and line 3 performs the additional behavior of adding an entry to the Application event log (shown in Figure 10.4).

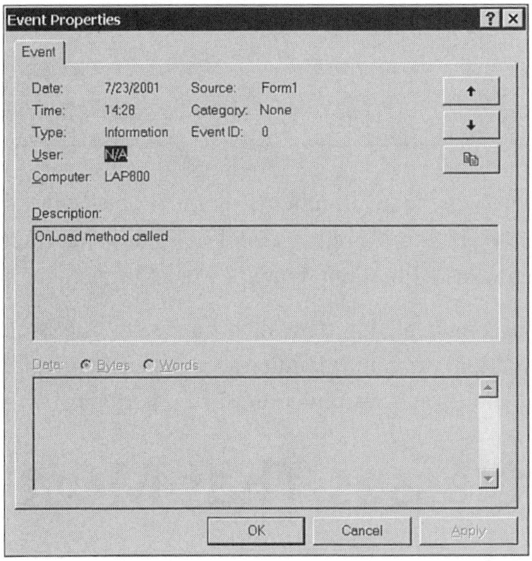

FIGURE 10.4

A logged application event using the Shared *method* EventLog. WriteEntry.

Single Inheritance Versus Multiple Inheritance

Visual Basic .NET does not support multiple class inheritance. Visual Basic .NET does support multiple interface derivation (discussed later), but then you are not inheriting the members. When a class agrees to implement multiple interfaces, the contract between class and interface is that the class implements all members of all interfaces.

> **Note**
>
> Multiple inheritance is demonstrated by a class that has more than one parent class. For example, you have physical attributes that can be described as having been inherited from mother and father.
>
> Visual Basic .NET supports single class inheritance and multiple interface inheritance.

You will encounter Inherits statements that look like multiple inheritance but are actually indicating interface inheritance. That is, an interface can be described as an aggregate of more than one interface using the Inherits keyword (refer to Listing 10.3).

LISTING 10.3   Multiple interface inheritance is supported in Visual Basic .NET.

```
Public Interface I1
End Interface

Public Interface I2
End Interface

Public Interface I3
  Inherits I1, I2
End Interface
```

Listing 10.3 indicates that Interface I3 inherits the interface described by I2 and I1. I3 does not get the members of I2 and I3; rather I3 defines a new interface that is made up of I1's and I2's interfaces. Classes that implement I3 must implement all of I1 and I2.

Visual Basic .NET supports multiple interface inheritance but only single class inheritance. A new interface that inherits multiple interfaces is perfectly valid. Interface I3 in the preceding example demonstrates multiple interface inheritance.

Defining Classes That Must Be Subclassed

A class that cannot be instantiated and must be inherited is referred to generically as a *virtual abstract class*. Such classes in Visual Basic .NET are indicated by the presence of the MustInherit class modifier.

Virtual abstract classes were defined in C++ before COM interfaces. Virtual abstract classes are the closest thing to pure COM interfaces. When you define a class with the

MustInherit modifier, you are communicating to consumers that all child classes of the virtual abstract class must implement all of the members marked with the MustOverride modifier in the parent class. If a child only implements some of the virtual abstract members in the parent, the child also is virtual and abstract.

MustInherit classes have at least one MustOverride member. Methods and property methods that have the MustOverride modifier are referred to as *virtual abstract methods*. In addition to the MustOverride directive, virtual abstract members have no method body. (Method properties have no property body either.)

A MustInherit class where all members are MustOverride members is a pretty good approximation of an interface.

Chapter 7 defines a virtual abstract Light class that is part of a traffic signal class. Each of the three traffic lamps must override and provide an implementation of the Brush property used to constrain the color of the lamp for each traffic signal. The subsection that follows demonstrates another example for aircraft.

Virtual Abstract Class Example

Planes in the U.S. have a call sign designator that begins with an N-prefix. For example, N633DV is a call sign on a Cessna 172 parked at Austin-Bergstrom. If we were representing planes, perhaps for an inventory-tracking application for a reseller, we would probably want to ensure that the tail number is a member of our plane class.

To ensure that all aircraft that needed a tail number had one, we could define an interface or an abstract virtual (MustInherit) class that had a TailNumber property. Listing 10.4 demonstrates using an interface and Listing 10.5 demonstrates using an abstract class.

LISTING 10.4   Using an Interface to describe planes as having a required tail number.

```
 1: Namespace InterfacePlane
 2:    Public Interface Plane
 3:      Property TailNumber() As String
 4:    End Interface
 5:
 6:    Public Class SingleEngineLand
 7:      Implements Plane
 8:
 9:      Private FTailNumber As String
10:      Public Property TailNumber() As String Implements Plane.TailNumber
11:        Get
```

LISTING 10.4   continued

```
12:         Return FTailNumber
13:       End Get
14:       Set(ByVal Value As String)
15:         FTailNumber = Value
16:       End Set
17:     End Property
18:   End Class
19:
20: End Namespace
```

Line 1 begins a new namespace, InterfacePlane. The example plane.sln defines the name Plane name twice; in the example, separating the same name, Plane, with a namespace is a notational convenience. Lines 2 through 4 define the Plane interface as having a TailNumber property. Line 7 indicates that the SingleEngineLand category of plane implements the Plane interface, and line 10 satisfies the contract between interface and class by implementing the Plane.TailNumber property. (The Implements clause is tagged to the end of the property statement on line 10.)

LISTING 10.5   Using an abstract virtual class to describe planes as having a required tail number.

```
 1: Namespace ClassPlane
 2:
 3:   Public MustInherit Class Plane
 4:     Public MustOverride Property TailNumber() As String
 5:   End Class
 6:
 7:   Public Class SingleEngineLand
 8:     Inherits Plane
 9:     Private FTailNumber As String
10:
11:     Public Overrides Property TailNumber() As String
12:       Get
13:         Return FTailNumber
14:       End Get
15:       Set(ByVal Value As String)
16:         FTailNumber = Value
17:       End Set
18:     End Property
19:
20:   End Class
21:
22: End Namespace
```

Listing 10.5 employs the `MustInherit` modifier on line 3 to define an abstract `Plane` class. Line 8 indicates that `SingleEngineLand` inherits from `Plane`, and the contract between abstract class and child class is fulfilled by the `Overrides Property` statement that defines a `TailNumber` property.

The `InterfacePlane.SingleEngineLand` and `ClassPlane.SingleEngineLand` interface and class are very similar in a technical sense. There are a few pragmatic considerations to help you choose between using an interface or an abstract class:

- Child classes that inherit from abstract classes get a copy of the defined methods, properties, and events and have to define the abstract members. If you think you will be creating multiple versions of a class, use abstract classes. Revisions in the abstract base class will be inherited by child classes.

- If the capabilities will be useful across disparate kinds of classes, use an interface. Abstract classes are generally used for classes that are closely related. For example, a Skyhawk is a kind of plane; hence we are talking about an inheritance relationship. Alternatively, we might implement a throttle interface in a plane and a car. A throttle is not a kind of car or plane, and both planes and cars would probably implement throttles but differently.

- Think of an interface as an attachment to a class that allows you to access a concise set of capabilities externally, like a portal. Think of a class as being a fundamental identifier. For example, a home receiver and car radio are kinds of radios, clearly defining a class relationship. The ability to attenuate volume can be applied to a microphone, megaphone, or radio; attenuating volume describes concise capability, and thus can serve as an interface.

- If you need partial implementation and some abstract aspects, use an abstract class and inheritance. Interfaces provide no implementation.

C++ and Object Pascal programmers have been aware of the absence of inheritance and abstract classes in VB (if they thought of VB at all). If you have only programmed in VB, you may be comfortable with interfaces, but from now on, when you want to inherit partial implementation and some abstraction, bear in mind that abstract classes are perfect.

Defining Classes That Cannot Be Subclassed

When a branch of your class hierarchy comes to a point and you want to ensure that no further inheritance occurs, you can define a final class.

A *final class* is a class that has the NotInheritable modifier in the class statement. For example, if we wanted to indicate that no child class can be derived from the SingleEngineLand plane, we could introduce the NotInheritable keyword, revising the class statement as follows:

```
Public NotInheritable Class SingleEngineLand
```

With that done, consumers can no longer subclass SingleEngineLand planes.

Using modifiers like NotInheritable or MustInherit is like using access specifiers Public, Private, Protected, or Friend, in that you can elect not to use them. Make everything public and avoid modifiers altogether if you want to, but the end result is code that is less explicit and controlled. Explicit controlled code is more likely to yield manageable, less complex code.

Polymorphism

Polymorphism is a facility supported by Visual Basic .NET. Polymorphic behavior occurs when you declare a parent type and instantiate a child type. The compiler adds code to resolve the actual method that needs to be called by the instance of the object.

Continuing the plane example, we could add a MultiEngineLand plane to our plane class. Operations that use the same code to work with both kinds of plane could be written in one procedure. If we defined the parameters to the procedure to take a Plane, we could pass any subclass of plane to the procedure.

Polymorphic behavior is generally needed when you see code that takes an action based on a case statement evaluating a type code. Let's step back and look at polymorphism relative to our Plane class.

Suppose we only had one Plane class and a type code indicating two kinds of planes: single-engine and multi-engine planes. If we had a method Start() and used a type code to determine plane type, single- or multi-engine, we would implement Start() using a Select Case statement, as demonstrated in Listing 10.6.

LISTING 10.6 Case statements are often indicative of a flat class that needs subclasses with polymorphic methods.

```
1: Namespace NeedsPolymorphism
2:    Public Enum PlaneType
3:       SingleEngineLand
4:       MultiEngineLand
5:    End Enum
6:
```

LISTING 10.6 continued

```
 7:    Public Class Plane
 8:      Private FType As PlaneType
 9:
10:      Public Sub New(ByVal Type As PlaneType)
11:        MyBase.New()
12:        FType = Type
13:      End Sub
14:
15:      Public Sub Start()
16:        Select Case FType
17:          Case PlaneType.SingleEngineLand
18:            ' start engine 1
19:          Case PlaneType.MultiEngineLand
20:            ' start engines 1 and 2
21:        End Select
22:      End Sub
23:
24:    End Class
25: End Namespace
```

`Plane` contains an enumeration `PlaneType` that is used to decide how many engines to start, lines 15 to 22. However, this is a bad implementation. Single-engine planes do not actually have two engines, one of which we choose not to start. A single-engine plane has one engine that we start, and a multi-engine plane has more than one engine that we start. Clearly, there are two classes here. This is the exact kind of scenario that inheritance and polymorphism were designed to solve. By defining two subclasses of the abstract class `Plane`, we offload the `case` statement to the compiler (see Listing 10.7).

> **Note**
>
> Generally, polymorphism is implemented using a *virtual methods table*—an array of method pointers—and a `case` statement based on type is replaced with an index into the method table.
>
> The benefit to you is that you do not have to write and maintain `if` conditional or `case` statements every time you add a new type. In effect, the compiler manages the virtual methods table and resolves the call to the method based on type automatically.

LISTING 10.7   By subclassing `Plane`, we can offload the `case` statement to the compiler.

```
 1: Namespace ClassPlane
 2:
 3:    Public MustInherit Class Plane
 4:       [...]
 5:       Public MustOverride Sub Start()
 6:    End Class
 7:
 8:    Public NotInheritable Class SingleEngineLand
 9:       Inherits Plane
10:       [...]
11:       Public Overrides Sub Start()
12:          ' start 1
13:       End Sub
14:    End Class
15:
16:    Public NotInheritable Class MultiEngineLand
17:       Inherits Plane
18:       [...]
19:       Public Overrides Sub Start()
20:          ' start 1 and 2
21:       End Sub
22:
23:    End Class
24:
25: End Namespace
```

Notice that Listing 10.7 requires no `case` statement. You will not require a `case` statement anywhere else in your code either. The correct `Start` method will be called based on the type of plane you create, `SingleEngineLand` or `MultiEngineLand`. Further, if you add additional kinds of planes, you will not need to create or extend a `case` statement either. Simply implement the `Start` method for each kind of plane, and the compiler will resolve the method call via a virtual methods table.

Understanding the Three Kinds of Polymorphism

Polymorphic behavior can be implemented for properties and methods. (Keep in mind that property statements are really methods, as demonstrated by the call—not shown—and the stack frame management and `ret` statement in the disassembly shown in Figure 10.5.) Polymorphic behavior can also be contrived relative to events by raising the event in an overridable procedure.

FIGURE 10.5

Property methods have all of the aspects of a method as shown in the disassembly.

```
Plane - Microsoft Visual Basic.NET [break] - Disassembly

File  Edit  View  Project  Build  Debug  Tools  Window  Help

                                          Debug          Display(

Program [1512] Plane.exe      Thread [1508] <No Name    Stack Frame  Plane.exe!Plane.InterfacePlane

Object Browser | Form1.vb [Design] | Form1.vb | AssemblyInfo.vb | Disassembly

Address  Plane.InterfacePlane.SingleEngineLar

              Set(ByVal Value As String)
    00000000  push       ebp
    00000001  mov        ebp,esp
    00000003  sub        esp,8
    00000006  mov        eax,edx
    00000008  nop
              FTailNumber = Value
    00000009  lea        edx,[ecx+4]
    0000000c  call       5D5820B8
          End Set
    00000011  nop
    00000012  mov        esp,ebp
    00000014  pop        ebp
    00000015  ret

Ready
```

Visual Basic .NET supports three kinds of polymorphism in comparison to VB6's one kind of polymorphism. Visual Basic .NET supports interface, inheritance, and abstract polymorphism. Each kind of polymorphism is described in the following subsections.

Interface Polymorphism

Interface polymorphism is the kind of polymorphic behavior carried over from VB6. Interface polymorphism means that multiple classes can implement an interface, or a single class can implement many interfaces.

The interface itself provides no implementation. The implementation is up to the user implementing that interface.

Define parameters as interface types and any object of any type that implements that interface can be passed as the argument for the parameter. The code behaves polymorphically based on the actual object passed and the way that object implements the interface.

Inheritance Polymorphism

Inheritance polymorphism supports multiple child classes inheriting from a single parent class. All child classes get a copy of everything in the parent class and can extend the parent by implementing additional members in the child class or overriding members in the base class.

> **Note**
>
> You can invoke parent behavior from a child using the `MyBase` reference from the child method.

If you want to layer behavior on a member in a parent class, override the member and call `MyBase.member` in the child class and add the new behavior after the call to the parent behavior.

Child methods that override a parent method generally call the parent method first, followed by new behavior, but you are not obligated to do so.

Abstract Polymorphism

Abstract virtual methods must be implemented by a child class or the child class itself will be abstract. Abstract classes cannot be instantiated.

> **Note**
>
> Some languages allow you to instantiate classes containing abstract methods, but calling the abstract method results in an exception.
>
> Delphi's Object Pascal is an example of a language that supports creating instances of abstract classes; Visual Basic .NET does not support creating instances of abstract classes (that is, classes with the `MustInherit` modifier).

If you attempt to call an abstract method in a base class using `MyBase`, you will get an error similar to "The method 'Public MustOverride Property PropertyName() As String' is declared with 'MustOverride' and so cannot be called with 'MyBase'."

Implemented virtual methods are inherited from abstract base classes, and you must provide an implementation of abstract methods if you want to create instances of your child class.

Calling Inherited Methods

Methods inherited from a parent class are invoked using the `MyBase` reference. When you encounter `MyBase.name`, the code is invoking a method or property of the immediate ancestor of the class containing the call.

If you want to find out type information about the immediate ancestor, call `MyBase.GetType`. `Debug.WriteLine(MyBase.GetType.Name)` will write the name of the immediate ancestor to the Output Window.

Another internal reference is `MyClass`. `MyClass` is similar to `Me` but disregards the runtime type of the object. If you invoke a method using `Me`, the method invocation will behave polymorphically. `MyClass` does not behave polymorphically; `MyClass` calls the method defined in the actual class of the object when it was declared, not when it was instantiated.

Assume for debugging purposes that every type of plane needs the ability to write its tail number to the Output window. Because the behavior is the same and only the tail number query is polymorphic, we only need one implementation of `WriteTailNumber` in the base class `Plane`.

```
Public MustInherit Class Plane
  Public MustOverride Property TailNumber() As String
  Public MustOverride Sub Start()

  Public Sub WriteTailNumber()
   Debug.WriteLine(Me.TailNumber)
  End Sub
End Class
```

`Me.TailNumber` gets the correct tail number based on the runtime type of `Me`. If we changed the invocation to `MyClass.TailNumber`, Visual Basic .NET would attempt to read `Plane.TailNumber`, which is an abstract method and would result in a compiler error.

Use `MyBase` when you want to refer to the parent. Refer to `MyClass` when you want to refer to the containing class's reference to self, and `Me` when you need to refer to the actual instance, rather than the containing class.

Overriding a Parent Class Method

To designate a method as a virtual method, add the `Overridable` keyword to the procedure in the parent class. To override an overridable method defined in a parent class, define the method with an identical signature in the child class and add the `Overrides` modifier to the child class method.

Virtual Methods

For example, if we want to make `WriteTailNumber` virtual, we can revise the implementation in the `Plane` class, adding the `Overridable` modifier to the implementation.

```
Public Overridable Sub WriteTailNumber()
  Debug.WriteLine(TailNumber)
End Class
```

To override the method in a child class, reimplement the method, changing the modifier to Overrides:

```
Public Overrides Sub WriteTailNumber()
  ' New Code!
End Sub
```

> **Tip**
>
> You are not obligated to override virtual Overridable methods.

If you are satisfied with the implementation of a virtual method in a parent class, do not override the method in a child class.

Shadow Methods

As an alternative, suppose you have a method in a parent class and you want to reintroduce new behavior in a child class. Instead of making the consumer remember a new name for the same semantic operation, shadow the method.

You can use the Shadows modifier—placed in the same location as the Overrides or Overridable modifiers—to conceal a method with the same signature in an ancestor. To completely replace the WriteTailNumber method in a child class, reimplement the method as follows:

```
Public Shadows Sub WriteTailNumber()
  ' New Implementation!
End Sub
```

There are several facts you need to know in addition to the grammar:

- Shadows is required if you introduce a method in a child class with the same signature as a nonvirtual method in a parent.
- Shadowed methods do not behave polymorphically. If you declare a reference as type parent and instantiate a child type, when you call the nonvirtual method you will not get the new method. The parent class method will be called. To call the shadowed method, the reference must be declared as a child class type.
- Shadowed methods are not removed. You can invoke shadowed behavior using the MyBase reference.

Shadowed methods are not polymorphic. The Shadows modifier allows you to reintroduce behavior for nonvirtual methods and will avoid a compiler error, but shadowed method calls are not resolved in a polymorphic way.

Shadowing Classes

The Shadows modifier will most often be used to reintroduce individual methods, but you can use the Shadows modifier to reintroduce nested classes.

From Chapter 7, we know that a nested class is a class defined within a class. If a parent has a nested class, you can redefine that nested class in a child. Listing 10.8 demonstrates the mechanics of shadowing nested classes.

LISTING 10.8   Shadowing nested classes.

```
 1:  Public Class ParentClass
 2:    Protected Class NestedClass
 3:      Public Shared Name As String = "Parent.NestedClass"
 4:    End Class
 5:
 6:    Public Shared Function GetName() As String
 7:      Return NestedClass.Name
 8:    End Function
 9:  End Class
10:
11: Public Class ChildClass
12:    Inherits ParentClass
13:
14:    Protected Shadows Class NestedClass
15:      Public Shared Name As String = "Child.NestedClass"
16:    End Class
17:
18:    Public Shared Shadows Function GetName() As String
19:      Return NestedClass.Name
20:    End Function
21: End Class
```

ParentClass contains a nested class, NestedClass. ChildClass inherits from ParentClass and reintroduces NestedClass by adding the Shadows modifier to the nested class definition in ChildClass (refer to lines 14 through 16).

Dynamic Typecasting

VB6 supported variant types and it was common to see code that depended on late bound objects.

VB6 and Visual Basic .NET support two kinds of reference use, early bound and late bound. *Early bound* references are references where the type of the object is known or resolved programmatically. *Late bound* references are resolved at runtime. Code like the following example relies on late binding:

```
Private Sub TextBox1_TextChanged(ByVal sender As System.Object, _
    ByVal e As System.EventArgs) _
    Handles TextBox1.TextChanged

  MessageBox.Show(sender.Text)
End Sub
```

Clearly, `sender` is an `Object` type and `Object` does not have `Text` member. Because the `Handles TextBox1.TextChanged` clause indicates that the event handler responds to a `Changed` event for `TextBox1`, this code is reasonable. To revise this example to demonstrate early binding, we use the `CType` method to cast the type of `sender` to the correct type:

```
Private Sub TextBox1_TextChanged(ByVal sender As System.Object, _
    ByVal e As System.EventArgs) _
    Handles TextBox1.TextChanged

  MessageBox.Show(CType(sender, TextBox).Text)
End Sub
```

Now the compiler can check to make sure that `Text` is a member of the target type, `TextBox`.

You are encouraged to use early binding in Visual Basic .NET. You can enforce early binding with `Option Strict On`. Using early binding means that you will have to use the more verbose form of the call, performing dynamic type casting. Using `Option Strict On` will ensure that inappropriate member usage will be caught at compile time and you will get a trappable `System.InvalidCastException` when you attempt to cast a generic type to a specific type and the instance is not an instance of the specific type (see Figure 10.6).

FIGURE 10.6

Casting to an invalid type will result in a catchable exception.

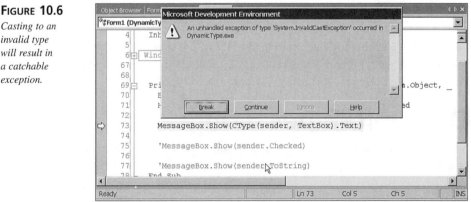

> **Note**
>
> Visual Basic .NET supports late binding to public methods only. You may not perform late binding on nonpublic methods or interface methods.

Verbose explicit code is preferable in Visual Basic .NET. Set `Option Strict On` and use the `CType` function to dynamically cast a more general type to a specific type.

Defining Interfaces

A Visual Basic .NET interface is neither a Visual Basic .NET class nor a COM class. The Component Object Model (COM) is language-neutral. Although Visual Basic .NET interfaces are also language-neutral, they represent an evolutionary progression from COM and ActiveX. Visual Basic .NET interfaces are managed code and COM is considered unmanaged code, meaning there is not a 1:1 mapping between COM and .NET interfaces. For now, suffice it to say that COM interfaces are not .NET interfaces. COM interop allows COM objects and .NET interfaces to interoperate; the subject of interoperation is discussed in Chapter 14, ".NET Framework." In this section we will be looking at how to define and implement Visual Basic .NET interfaces and comparing .NET interfaces to .NET classes.

Interfaces Compared to Classes

Interfaces in Visual Basic .NET define an interface only. Although Visual Basic .NET interfaces provide no implementation, classes can provide both an interface and an implementation. Visual Basic .NET classes provide an interface through abstract methods and an implementation through nonabstract methods.

There are only a few basic differences between interface and class grammar, as follows:

- Interface members are public and class members can use any access specifier.
- Interfaces use interface block and classes are defined in a class block.
- Interfaces are implemented in classes as members tagged with the `implements` clause; class members use no special suffix clause.
- Interfaces support multiple interface inheritance; classes support single inheritance only, but a single class may implement multiple interfaces.
- Classes can inherit from one class and implement one or more interfaces in the same class; interfaces provide no implementation.

To keep the differences between interfaces and classes distinct in your mind, think of a class as describing a thing and an interface as describing a capabilities-adapter for a thing. For example, television is a good concept captured by a class. A cigarette lighter adapter for a television is a reasonable interface. A better interface for a television would be the capabilities of turning the television on and off and changing channels. The controls physically on the outside of the television could implement the control interface, as well as a remote control device implementing the control interface. The television and the remote control are two disparate things, but they both implement the interface necessary to control a television: `TurnOn`, `TurnOff`, `ChangeChannel`, and perhaps a method for selecting a specific channel.

The subsections that follow demonstrate how to define and implement an interface by implementing a television class and a control interface, and implementing the controls on both the television class and a remote control class.

Defining an Interface

The example consists of a `Television` class, a `RemoteControl` class, and a `Control` interface. Both the `Television` and `RemoteControl` classes implement the `Control` interface. The `RemoteControl` is initialized with a reference to a TV instance, simulating the infrared communication between TV and remote. The visual displays simulating the TV and remote are implemented using the Windows Media Player and Button controls (shown in Figure 10.7).

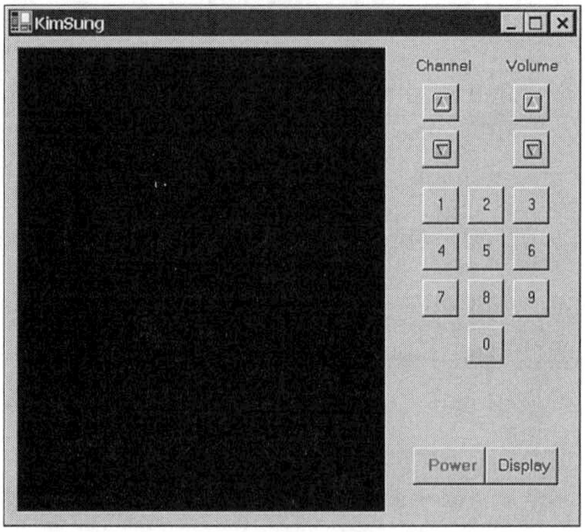

FIGURE **10.7**

The form representing the television and remote control.

The purpose of this section is to demonstrate interfaces in Visual Basic .NET, so we will emphasize the `Control` interface in this section.

LISTING 10.8 The `Control` interface listing.

```
1: Public Interface Control
2:    Sub Power()
3:    Sub VolumeUp()
4:    Sub VolumeDown()
5:    Sub ChannelUp()
6:    Sub ChannelDown()
7:    Sub SelectChannel(ByVal Value As String)
8:    Property Channel() As String
9:    Sub Display()
10:   Event PowerChange(ByVal IsOn As Boolean)
11: End Interface
```

The `Control` interface demonstrates that interfaces are definitions without implementations. Every class that implements the `Control` interface must implement all of the interface members. Notice that there are no access specifiers; every member of an interface is public.

Implementing an Interface

A remote control passes requests from a TV viewer to the television. For our purposes a reasonable implementation is to implement the control interface and send the user-request to the TV (simulating an infrared signal). Listing 10.9 demonstrates the `RemoteControl` class, which implements the `Control` interface.

LISTING 10.9 The `RemoteControl` class implements the `Control` interface.

```
1: Public Class RemoteControl
2:    Implements Control
3:    Private FTV As Television
4:
5:    Public Event PowerChange(ByVal IsOn As Boolean) _
6:       Implements Control.PowerChange
7:
8:    Protected Overridable Sub OnPowerChange()
9:       RaiseEvent PowerChange(FTV.IsOn)
10:   End Sub
11:
12:   Public Sub New(ByVal TV As Television)
13:      MyBase.New()
14:      FTV = TV
15:   End Sub
```

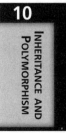

LISTING 10.9 continued

```
16:
17:    Public Sub ChannelDown() Implements Control.ChannelDown
18:        FTV.ChannelDown()
19:    End Sub
20:
21:    Public Sub ChannelUp() Implements Control.ChannelUp
22:        FTV.ChannelUp()
23:    End Sub
24:
25:    Public Sub VolumeDown() Implements Control.VolumeDown
26:        FTV.VolumeDown()
27:    End Sub
28:
29:    Public Sub VolumeUp() Implements Control.VolumeUp
30:        FTV.VolumeUp()
31:    End Sub
32:
33:    Public Sub SelectChannel(ByVal Value As String) _
34:        Implements Control.SelectChannel
35:        FTV.SelectChannel(Value)
36:    End Sub
37:
38:    Public Property Channel() As String Implements Control.Channel
39:        Get
40:           Return FTV.Channel
41:        End Get
42:        Set(ByVal Value As String)
43:           FTV.Channel = Value
44:        End Set
45:    End Property
46:
47:    Public Sub Display() Implements Control.Display
48:        FTV.Display()
49:    End Sub
50:
51:    Public Sub Power() Implements Control.Power
52:        FTV.Power()
53:        OnPowerChange()
54:    End Sub
55: End Class
```

Line 2 indicates that RemoteControl is going to implement all of the members of the Control interface. Line 3 maintains a reference to the television set simulating infrared communication. (We could add an infrared transmitter and receiver if it suited our needs; we do not need to go that far to demonstrate interfaces, though.) If you compare the number of methods that have Implements clauses, you will see that there is a one-to-one relationship between interface members in the Control interface and methods with

`Implements` clauses in the `RemoteControl` class. You must implement every member of an interface.

> **Note**
>
> Notice that methods that implement an interface are public in Visual Basic .NET. You can call interface methods from consumers in Visual Basic .NET. For example, you could create an instance of the `RemoteControl` class and call the interface methods directly or access the interface methods via a reference to the interface type.
>
> In VB6, implemented interface methods were private and consumers could not call them directly.

Notice that we can define and implement interfaces with methods, properties, and events. The `Control` interface contains several methods, the `Channel` property, and a `PowerChange` event.

The most significant difference between interface definitions and implementations—refer to Listings 10.8 and 10.9—is that interfaces do not contain implementations of members.

Interface Inheritance

Interfaces support inheritance too. You can define an interface and define a second interface that inherits from the original interface. By adding new interface members to the new interface, you can extend the definition of an interface or inherit from multiple interfaces.

Any class that implements an interface must implement all of the members of the interface. Refer back to Listing 10.3, which demonstrated the syntax for multiple interface inheritance.

Summary

Visual Basic .NET supports inheritance. In addition to defining and implementing interfaces, Visual Basic .NET supports class inheritance. Because of the incorporation of class inheritance in Visual Basic .NET, you now have three kinds of polymorphism to choose from: interface polymorphism, inheritance polymorphism, and abstract polymorphism.

10

INHERITANCE AND
POLYMORPHISM

Use inheritance to support subclassing when you want to generalize an existing class, and use interface polymorphism when you need to support similar capabilities across disparate classes. Abstract classes allow you to combine constraining an interface with inheritance. When you are defining classes, keep an eye out for conditional behavior or select case statements. Type codes that are used to determine dynamic behavior usually suggest code that can benefit from a refinement in the class definitions and polymorphic behavior.

Visual Basic .NET supports single class inheritance and multiple interface inheritance. Classes and interfaces can be combined in whatever manner suits your needs. If a class describes a specialized type of an existing class, use inheritance. Alternatively, if you need to create an adapter that provides access to a concise set of capabilities, implement an interface.

Shared Members

CHAPTER 11

Shared members in Visual Basic .NET are equivalent to Object Pascal class members and C++ and Java static members. The term *member* refers to anything that is part of a class or structure, which includes fields, properties, methods, and events. The designator Shared means that you can access the member without creating an instance—or declaring a variable—of the class or structure. Using the Shared designation means that the member is a metaclass member; that is, shared members are accessible from the class (and from objects).

Until Visual Basic .NET, shared members haven't been supported in Visual Basic. In this chapter, you will discover that there are many shared members in existing Visual Basic .NET code and the CLR, and that you can implement some advanced idioms using shared members. Chapter 11 demonstrates how to declare and use shared fields, properties, methods, constructors, overloaded members, and events. In addition to explaining shared members, Chapter 11 will demonstrate idioms, such as how to implement factory methods.

Declaring Shared Fields

Fields are variables defined in classes and structures. (Effectively, the use of data in modules is roughly equivalent to the use of shared fields in structures and classes.)

To define a shared field, precede the field declaration with the desired access specifier, the Shared keyword, the variable name, and the data type. Include an initializer if it's appropriate to do so. The following statement demonstrates declaring a shared integer:

```
Public Shared Counter As Long = 0
```

No matter how few or how many instances of the objects there are containing the preceding statement, there will only ever be exactly one Counter field for that class. Contained in a class, Counter may appear this way:

```
Public Class SharedInteger
  Public Shared Counter As Integer = 0
End Class
```

Counter can be accessed using the class name:

```
SharedInteger.Counter = 1
```

Counter also can be accessed through an instance of the class:

```
Dim Instance As SharedInteger
Instance.Counter = 1
```

In both examples, .Counter refers to the same Counter field, yet the first fragment accesses Counter using the class and the second example refers to Counter through the object named `Instance`. If we were able to evaluate the address of `Counter` in both examples, the address of `SharedInteger.Counter` would be equal to the address of `Instance.Counter`.

Shared fields have been used for reference counting. For example, COM uses reference counting to determine when to release an object. Each time an object is created, the code increments the counter. When an object is released, the counter is decreased. Memory allocated in the object is released only when the reference count is decreased to zero. (Keep in mind that the garbage collector takes care of releasing memory in Visual Basic .NET; reference counting is used for COM objects and historically for languages that haven't implemented garbage collection.)

In new code, you might want to implement shared fields to store data that doesn't change regardless of the state of a particular instance. Practical examples of shared fields include the `Math.Pi` and `Math.E` values representing the ratio of a circle's circumference to diameter and the natural logarithmic base, respectively.

Defining Shared Properties

As a general rule, fields are declared as private members. You can declare shared fields as private members too and use shared properties to provide access to shared fields.

A property is a special kind of method that is used like data but calls getter and setter methods, which for all intents and purposes are methods. The relationship is that fields are private and properties provide a public means of accessing data through implicit calls to property methods with the ease of using data. Thus you would use shared fields and properties in pairs just as you would use instance fields and properties in pairs. To define shared properties, you will need to place the `Shared` keyword between the access specifier and the keyword property.

If you are going to implement validation procedures for shared properties, the validation procedures need to be shared too. Any shared fields, properties, and methods that interact must interact with shared methods. Listing 11.1 defines a structure and class with examples of shared fields and shared properties.

LISTING 11.1 Shared fields and properties defined in a class and structure

```
1: Public Class PropertyExamples
2:    Private Shared FInt As Integer
3:
4:    Public Shared Property Int() As Integer
5:      Get
6:        Return FInt
```

LISTING 11.1   continued

```
 7:     End Get
 8:     Set(ByVal Value As Integer)
 9:       FInt = Value
10:     End Set
11:   End Property
12:
13:   Public Shared ReadOnly Property Name() As String
14:     Get
15:       Return "SharedStructureProperties"
16:     End Get
17:   End Property
18:
19:   Private Shared FReference As Date
20:   Public Shared WriteOnly Property Reference() As Date
21:     Set(ByVal Value As Date)
22:       FReference = Value
23:     End Set
24:   End Property
25:
26: End Class
27:
28: Public Structure SharedStructureProperties
29:   Public Dummy As Integer
30:
31:   Private Shared FInt As Integer
32:
33:   Public Shared Property Int() As Integer
34:     Get
35:       Return FInt
36:     End Get
37:     Set(ByVal Value As Integer)
38:       FInt = Value
39:     End Set
40:   End Property
41:
42:   Public Shared ReadOnly Property Name() As String
43:     Get
44:       Return "SharedStructureProperties"
45:     End Get
46:   End Property
47:
48:   Private Shared FReference As Date
49:   Public Shared WriteOnly Property Reference() As Date
50:     Set(ByVal Value As Date)
51:       FReference = Value
52:     End Set
53:   End Property
54:
55: End Structure
```

Listing 11.1 defines shared fields and properties for syntactical demonstration rather than utility. Most importantly, notice that the shared elements in both the class and structure use an identical syntax (and, in fact, are identical). The class defines a private field `FInt` on line 2 represented by the shared property `Int` on lines 4 through 11. Note the exact same implementation in the structure on lines 31 through 40. Lines 13 through 17 define a shared `ReadOnly` property `Name` that returns a literal string containing the name of the structure. Properties with the `ReadOnly` modifier can only be used as a right-hand side value in statements. Lines 19 through 24 implement a `WriteOnly` shared property `Reference`, which is defined as a `Date` and is written to the `FReference` field.

Listing 11.1 duplicates the members of the class in the structure to demonstrate that identical syntax for shared fields and properties. The only difference between the structure and class is that the structure must have at least one nonshared member.

Tip

Structures require at least one nonshared member, hence the `Public Dummy As Integer` member on line 29 of Listing 11.1 in the structure `SharedStructureProperties`.

Other than the `Shared` keywords, shared property and field declarations are identical to nonshared members. Listing 11.2 demonstrates the aggregate types defined in Listing 11.1.

LISTING 11.2 Using shared properties of structures and fields

```
1: PropertyExamples.Int = 10
2: Debug.WriteLine(PropertyExamples.Int)
3: Debug.WriteLine(PropertyExamples.Name)
4: PropertyExamples.Reference = Now
5:
6: SharedStructureProperties.Int = 13
7: Dim Struct As SharedStructureProperties
8: Debug.WriteLine(Struct.Int)
9: Struct.Int = -1
10: Debug.WriteLine(SharedStructureProperties.Int)
11:
12: Debug.WriteLine(SharedStructureProperties.Name)
13: SharedStructureProperties.Reference = Now
14:
15: Debug.WriteLine(Struct.Name = SharedStructureProperties.Name)
```

Line 1 of Listing 11.2 uses the Shared Int property of the PropertyExamples class. Line 3 demonstrates using the ReadOnly Name property of the same class, and line 4 assigns the current date and time to the PropertyExamples.Reference property. It's important to note that all references to properties on lines 1 through 4 are successfully accomplished using the class in the form *class.property.*

Line 6 assigns the value 13 to the shared property of the structure named SharedStructureProperties. Line 7 declares a structure instance and line 8 writes the value of the Int property using the instance Struct. If you guessed that 13 is written to the Output window, you're getting the hang of shared fields and properties. Line 9 assigns -1 to the Int property. The result of the assignment on line 9 is that every instance of SharedStructureProperties will have the value -1 assigned to the field FInt, including instances not yet in existence. The remaining lines demonstrate that values assigned to the properties through the instance are reflected in the property accessed by the structure. The output from Listing 11.2 is listed next (without the symbol loading information):

```
10

SharedStructureProperties
13
-1
SharedStructureProperties
True
```

Tip

You can save the contents of the Output window to a file by selecting the Output window and clicking File, Save in the development environment.

Shared fields and properties aren't used heavily; on occasion you might encounter them or contrive a use that makes sense to you. If you encounter them in code, you will know what they are and have some ideas as to how the author of the code might be using the shared fields and properties. Listing 11.3 implements a class with all shared members that describe a self-contained counter. I commonly need a unique number or test data when developing applications; the following examples preclude the need to declare a local integer and write the code to increment the counter.

LISTING 11.3   A self-contained counter using shared members

```
 1: Public Class Counter2
 2:    Private Shared FValue As Long
 3:
 4:    Public Shared Sub Reset()
 5:      FValue = -1
 6:    End Sub
 7:
 8:    Public Shared ReadOnly Property Value() As Long
 9:      Get
10:        FValue += 1
11:        Return FValue
12:      End Get
13:    End Property
14:
15: End Class
```

The shared field `FValue` stores the count. The shared method `Reset` initializes the field value to `-1` and the shared property `Value` increments the field and returns the field value. The field value is initialized to `-1`, and the increment is performed first because the `Return` statement in Visual Basic .NET actually causes the code to branch out of the block on the line of code containing the `Return` statement (see line 11). To use the code in Listing 11.3, simply call `Counter2.Reset()` to initialize the counter and write `Counter2.Value` to increment and return the current counter value.

Shared methods are more commonly employed than shared fields and properties. But, if the value of a shared method needs to be stored, you will encounter shared fields and properties along with shared methods. Let's take a look at shared methods next.

Using Shared Methods

Shared members are prevalent in Visual Basic .NET. Many of the classes in the CLR and all the methods in the base class `Object` are shared. Shared members are commonly employed in utility classes where it's not important to capture state. For example, you don't need to store the state of an integer to calculate the absolute value of an integer.

Classes containing all shared methods are implemented for organizational purposes more than anything. It's easy and convenient to define shared members in a class in an effort to ensure that code is more manageable. The `Reset` method in Listing 11.3 on lines 4 through 6 demonstrates a shared method.

Shared methods can be added to structures and classes, and it's reasonable to think of a module as a special class containing all shared methods. Expanding the concept of the counter as a means of implementing a self-contained counting mechanism or a way of contriving unique values, the Counter class in Listing 11.4 demonstrates a counter that returns a unique integer, string made up of digits, or a string made up of alphabetic characters.

LISTING 11.4 The Counter class uses shared members to return a unique integer, or string of digits or alphabetic characters

```
 1: Public Class Counter
 2:
 3:   Public Shared Function Value(Optional ByVal Reset As Boolean = False, _
 4:     Optional ByVal Seed As Long = -1) As Long
 5:
 6:     Static I As Long = Seed
 7:     If (Reset) Then
 8:       I = Seed
 9:     Else
10:       I += 1
11:     End If
12:
13:     Return I
14:   End Function
15:
16:   Public Shared Function Str(Optional ByVal Reset As Boolean = False, _
17:     Optional ByVal Length As Long = 1) As String
18:
19:     Static S As String = New System.String("A", Length)
20:     If (Reset) Then
21:       S = New System.String("A", Length)
22:     Else
23:       S = Roll(S, "A", "Z")
24:     End If
25:
26:     Return S
27:   End Function
28:
29:   Private Shared Function Chunk(ByVal Str As String) As String
30:     Return Right(Str, Str.Length() - 1)
31:   End Function
32:
33:   Private Shared Function Roll(ByVal S As String, ByVal Low As Char, _
34:     ByVal High As Char) As String
35:     If (S.Length() = 0) Then
36:       S = Low
37:     ElseIf (S.Chars(0) < High) Then
38:       S = Chr(Asc(S) + 1) + Chunk(S)
39:     Else
40:       S = Low + Roll(Chunk(S), Low, High)
41:     End If
```

LISTING 11.4 continued

```
42:
43:      Return S
44:    End Function
45:
46:    Public Shared Function Digits(Optional ByVal Reset As Boolean = False, _
47:      Optional ByVal Length As Long = 1) As String
48:
49:      Static D As String = New System.String("0", Length)
50:      If (Reset) Then
51:        D = New System.String("0", Length)
52:      Else
53:        D = Roll(D, "0", "9")
54:      End If
55:
56:      Return D
57:    End Function
58:
59: End Class
```

The `Value` function on lines 3 through 14 implements the same behavior as the `Counter2` example in Listing 11.3. In addition, you can use optional parameters to reset the value (defined as a static variable in `Value`), and the optional parameter seed can be used to start counting at an arbitrary. Suppose for example that you wanted a unique identifier for rows in a table. After you closed the table, you could find the highest identifier and start incrementing during the next session from the highest value plus one. Lines 16 through 27 implement a unique string of alphabetic characters from A to Z. Each time the first character reaches A, another character is appended to the string, resulting in a sequence A, B, C, ..., Z, AA, BA, CA, ..., ZA, AB, up to a string of about two billion alphabetic characters. Lines 46 through 57 implement an equivalent form of the random string generator using the digits 0 through 9. The `Chunk` and `Roll` private functions are reused for the public `Str` and `Digits` shared methods.

To use the `Str` function, call `Counter.Str(True)` to initialize the static string `S` to a one-character length string, "A". Each successive call to `Counter.Str()` returns the next string in the succession.

In production applications, you are likely to encounter classes and structures that have a combination of shared and nonshared methods, as well as utility classes that contain only shared methods.

Listing 11.5 contains the complete listing for the form and the Rects class.

LISTING 11.5 Shared utility methods in a Rects class and a form that uses GDI+ to display random rectangle subdivisions

```
 1: Public Class Form1
 2:   Inherits System.Windows.Forms.Form
 3:
 4: [ Windows Form Designer generated code ]
 5:
 6:   Private Sub MenuItem2_Click(ByVal sender As System.Object, _
 7:     ByVal e As System.EventArgs) Handles MenuItem2.Click
 8:     Application.Exit()
 9:   End Sub
10:
11:   Public Shared Function GetAboutText() As String
12:     Return "Rectangles Demo" & vbCrLf & _
13:         "Copyright  2001. Paul Kimmel." & vbCrLf & _
14:         "Visual Basic.NET Unleased"
15:   End Function
16:
17:   Private Sub MenuItem6_Click(ByVal sender As System.Object, _
18:     ByVal e As System.EventArgs) Handles MenuItem6.Click
19:     MsgBox(GetAboutText(), MsgBoxStyle.Information, "About Rectangles")
20:   End Sub
21:
22:   Private Function RandomPens() As Pen
23:
24:     Randomize()
25:
26:     Select Case Rnd() * 6
27:       Case Is < 1 : Return Pens.AliceBlue
28:       Case Is < 2 : Return Pens.Red
29:       Case Is < 3 : Return Pens.Bisque
30:       Case Is < 4 : Return Pens.Blue
31:       Case Is < 5 : Return Pens.Plum
32:       Case Else
33:          Return Pens.DarkGoldenrod
34:     End Select
35:
36:   End Function
37:
38:   Private Sub MenuItem4_Click(ByVal sender As System.Object, _
39:     ByVal e As System.EventArgs) Handles MenuItem4.Click
40:
41:     Dim I As Integer
42:     Dim G As System.Drawing.Graphics = CreateGraphics()
```

11

LISTING **11.5**   continued

```
43:
44:      Refresh()
45:
46:      Dim Segments As Integer
47:      For I = 0 To 25
48:        Randomize()
49:        Segments = CInt(Rnd() * 100)
50:
51:        G.DrawRectangle(RandomPens(), _
52:          Rects.RandomRectangle(ClientRectangle, Rnd() * Segments, _
53:          Segments + 1))
54:      Next I
55:
56:    End Sub
57:
58: End Class
59:
60: ' Rectangle.vb - Defines several rectangle sub-division shared methods
61: ' Copyright  2001. All Rights Reserved.
62: ' By Paul Kimmel. pkimmel@softconcepts.com
63:
64: Imports System.Drawing
65:
66: Public Class Rects
67:
68:    Public Shared Function RandomRectangle(ByVal Rect As Rectangle, _
69:      ByVal Index As Integer, ByVal Segments As Integer) As Rectangle
70:
71:      If (Index Mod 3 = 0) Then
72:        Return RectangleSector(Rect, Index, Index / 2, Segments)
73:      ElseIf (Index Mod 2 = 0) Then
74:        Return VerticalRectangle(Rect, Index, Segments)
75:      Else
76:        Return HorizontalRectangle(Rect, Index, Segments)
77:      End If
78:
79:    End Function
80:
81:    Public Shared Function RectangleSector(ByVal Rect As Rectangle, _
82:      ByVal X As Integer, ByVal Y As Integer, _
83:      ByVal Segments As Integer) As Rectangle84:    Dim R As Rectangle
85:      R = VerticalRectangle(Rect, Y, Segments)
86:      R = HorizontalRectangle(R, X, Segments)
87:      Return R
88:
89:    End Function
90:
91:    Public Shared Function VerticalRectangle(ByVal Rect As Rectangle, _
92:      ByVal Index As Integer, ByVal Segments As Integer) As Rectangle
```

LISTING 11.5   continued

```
93:
94:     Return New Rectangle(Rect.Left, NewTop(Rect, Index, Segments), _
95:        Rect.Width, NewBottom(Rect, Index, Segments))
96:
97:   End Function
98:
99:   Public Shared Function HorizontalRectangle(ByVal Rect As Rectangle, _
100:     ByVal Index As Integer, ByVal Segments As Integer) As Rectangle
101:
102:     Return New Rectangle(NewLeft(Rect, Index, Segments), Rect.Top, _
103:        NewRight(Rect, Index, Segments), Rect.Bottom)
104:
105:   End Function
106:
107:   Public Shared Function NewTop(ByVal Rect As Rectangle, _
108:     ByVal Index As Integer, ByVal Segments As Integer) As Integer
109:
110:     Return (Rect.Top + (Index / Segments) * Rect.Height)
111:
112:   End Function
113:
114:   Public Shared Function NewBottom(ByVal Rect As Rectangle, _
115:     ByVal Index As Integer, ByVal Segments As Integer) As Integer
116:
117:     Return NewTop(Rect, Index, Segments) + (Rect.Height / Segments)
118:
119:   End Function
120:
121:   Public Shared Function NewLeft(ByVal Rect As Rectangle, _
122:     ByVal Index As Integer, ByVal Segments As Integer) As Integer
123:
124:     Return Rect.Left + (Index / Segments) * Rect.Width
125:
126:   End Function
127:
128:   Public Shared Function NewRight(ByVal Rect As Rectangle, _
129:     ByVal Index As Integer, ByVal Segments As Integer) As Integer
130:
131:     Return NewLeft(Rect, Index, Segments) + Rect.Width / Segments
132:
133:   End Function
134:
135: End Class
```

To shorten the listing, the 135 lines of code shown in Listing 11.5 conceal the generated code. Listing 11.5 demonstrates the interplay between an application (although a trivial one) and shared methods in a class. The code shows two units, Form1.vb and

`Rectangles.vb`. `Rectangles.vb` begins on line 60 and continues to line 135. As you can determine from the listing, the class `Rects` in `Rectangles.vb` maintains no state; `Rects` simply calculates subdivisions of rectangles. The methods were originally implemented with creating custom components. The rectangles were used to calculate bounding regions for complex visual controls. In the example, each time the user presses F5, the program draws 26 rectangles on `Form1` (see lines 46 through 54). The example also provides further examples of using a `Graphics` object (lines 42 and 51) from GDI+, the global `Pens` class, which contains shared `Pen` objects (beginning on line 22),and several examples of shared methods. (Refer to Chapter 17, "Programming with GDI+," for more information on graphics programming.)

Defining Shared Constructors

Visual Basic .NET implements constructors as `Sub New`. By prefixing a constructor with the `Shared` modifier, you can implement a shared constructor.

Shared constructors are used to initialize shared members to their default values implicitly and can be implemented to perform additional initialization of shared members. Shared constructors are run implicitly after your program loads and are guaranteed to run only once before any instances of a type containing a shared constructor are created and before any shared members are accessed. Shared constructors are also run before derived types are used.

You can't overload shared members. Shared constructors cannot call other constructors, cannot take parameters, and cannot be used to overload instance constructors. The declaration of a shared constructor is always in the following format:

```
Shared Sub New()
End Sub
```

Implicitly, this is a public member. The shared constructor in the preceding fragment is distinct from an instance constructor:

```
Sub New()
End Sub
```

The implicit nature of shared constructors makes them excellent devices for initializing shared members and simulating `Singleton` objects by using class methods and a shared constructor.

Shared Constructors and Singletons

A `Singleton` object is an object that is only created once. There are certain resources of which you generally only need one when a program is running and of which only one is accessible to the running program. A good candidate for a `Singleton` object is the registry.

Programs generally update the registry to persist state information about an application, such as paths for data files, login information, last Web site visited, or file opened. The registry is a good place to store this information. And, a good strategy for implementing a mechanism to store state information is to wrap the `Registry` class that ships with .NET in a class that exposes named state properties. In this way, the state information is accessible anywhere in your program, including an `Options` form, and is easy to access and modify. The alternative is to create, initialize, and release the object each time you want to modify the state information.

Tip

A further benefit of encapsulating the registry in a class is that you change how and where state information is saved without having to modify the code that uses it. Define an interface that allows users to get and set state information, and you can change the underlying implementation at any time. This is useful during development. Sometimes it's easier to save state information to an INI file while you're developing the code and switch to the registry before releasing your product. Using a wrapper class insulates the rest of your code from this strategy.

Because there is only one registry, the registry is a good example of something that can be treated as a `Singleton` object. Making the registry even easier to use can be accomplished via a shared constructor in a class that encapsulates a registry object and has shared setters and getters (property methods) for reading and writing registry information. The next section contains an example.

Shared Constructor Example

Shared constructors can be used to emulate `Singleton` objects. `Singleton` objects are generally implemented via a shared method that ensures that only one instance of the object is created. This is accomplished by making the constructor private. A private constructor means that consumers can't create instances of the class. However, if there is a public shared method of the same class, it can call the private constructor and subsequently create instances. Using a `Static` counter or a shared field, the public shared method can ensure that only one instance of the `Singleton` exists.

Singletons are used when it's beneficial or important that only one instance of an object exists. The technique is also used for convenience. What better way to simplify code than to inhibit the unnecessary creation of objects?

Using a shared constructor and a `Private` constructor to prevent consumers from creating unnecessary objects, Listing 11.6 demonstrates two kinds of persistency in the limited context of the text editor; one half of the code demonstrates using the Registry and the other half demonstrates using a `HybridDictionary` object. (The text editor itself is intentionally only partially complete. The example solution is on this book's Web site (see `www.samspublishing.com`) in DualModeStateExample.sln).

> **Note**
>
> The `Registry` class will be used when the `DualModeStateExample.exe` is distributed, and a `HybridDictionary` will be used during development. (Refer to the code listing for the implementation of the persisted `HybridDictionary`.)

The `Options` class uses the Registry to save state information if we aren't configured for DEBUG mode, and uses a persisted `HybridDictionary` class if we are still testing.

LISTING 11.6   Both implementations of persisted application options

```
 1: ' Options.vb - Implements dual mode state persistency using
 2: '    a shared constructor and properties
 3: ' Copyright  2001. All Rights Reserved.
 4: ' Written by Paul Kimmel. pkimmel@softconcepts.com
 5:
 6: Imports Microsoft.Win32, System.Collections.Specialized, System.IO
 7:
 8: #If DEBUG = False Then
 9:
10: Public Class Options
11:
12:   Private Sub New()
13:   End Sub
14:
15:   Private Enum Keys
16:     LastFileName
17:   End Enum
18:
19:   Public Shared Property LastFileName() As String
20:     Get
21:       Return ReadString(Keys.LastFileName.ToString)
22:     End Get
```

LISTING **11.6**   continued

```
23:        Set(ByVal Value As String)
24:           WriteString(Keys.LastFileName.ToString, Value)
25:        End Set
26:     End Property
27:
28:     Private Shared Function Subkey() As String
29:        Return "Software\" & "VB.NET UNLEASHED"
30:     End Function
31:
32:     Private Shared Function OpenKey() As RegistryKey
33:
34:        Return Registry.LocalMachine.OpenSubKey(Subkey(), True)
35:
36:     End Function
37:
38:     Private Shared Function ReadString(ByVal Key As String, _
39:        Optional ByVal Value As String = "") As String
40:        Try
41:           Return OpenKey().GetValue(Key, Value)
42:        Catch
43:           Return Value
44:        End Try
45:     End Function
46:
47:     Private Shared Sub WriteString(ByVal Key As String, _
48:        ByVal Value As String)
49:        Try
50:           OpenKey().SetValue(Key, Value)
51:        Catch
52:           Registry.LocalMachine.CreateSubKey(Subkey())
53:           OpenKey().SetValue(Key, Value)
54:        End Try
55:     End Sub
56:
57:
58: End Class
59:
60: #Else
61:
62: Public Class Options
63:
64:     Private Sub New()
65:
66:     End Sub
67:
68:     Private Enum Keys
69:        LastFileName
70:     End Enum
71:
```

LISTING 11.6 continued

```
72:  Private Shared Loading As Boolean
73:  Private Shared FDictionary As HybridDictionary
74:
75:  Shared Sub New()
76:    FDictionary = New HybridDictionary()
77:    LoadDictionary()
78:  End Sub
79:
80:  Public Shared Property LastFileName() As String
81:    Get
82:      Return ReadString(Keys.LastFileName.ToString)
83:    End Get
84:    Set(ByVal Value As String)
85:      WriteString(Keys.LastFileName.ToString, Value)
86:    End Set
87:  End Property
88:
89:
90:  Private Shared Function ReadString(ByVal Key As String, _
91:    Optional ByVal Value As String = "")
92:
93:    If (FDictionary.Item(Key) Is Nothing) Then Return Value
94:    Return FDictionary.Item(Key)
95:
96:  End Function
97:
98:  Private Shared Sub WriteString(ByVal Key As String, _
99:    ByVal Value As String)
100:   FDictionary.Remove(Key)
101:   FDictionary.Add(Key, Value)
102:   SaveDictionary()
103: End Sub
104:
105: Private Shared Function GetOptionsFile() As String
106:   Return Application.StartupPath & "\options.ini"
107: End Function
108:
109: Private Shared Sub SaveDictionary()
110:   If (Loading) Then Exit Sub
111:   Dim Writer As StreamWriter = _
112:     File.CreateText(GetOptionsFile())
113:   Try
114:     Writer.WriteLine(Keys.LastFileName.ToString & "=" & _
115:       FDictionary.Item(Keys.LastFileName.ToString))
116:   Finally
117:     Writer.Close()
118:   End Try
119: End Sub
120:
```

LISTING **11.6**   continued

```
121:    Private Shared Sub LoadDictionary()
122:        If (Not File.Exists(GetOptionsFile())) Then Exit Sub
123:
124:        Dim Reader As StreamReader = _
125:            File.OpenText(GetOptionsFile())
126:
127:        Try
128:            Loading = True
129:            Dim Line As String = Reader.ReadLine()
130:            LastFileName = Mid(Line, InStr(Line, "=") + 1)
131:
132:        Finally
133:            Reader.Close()
134:            Loading = False
135:        End Try
136:
137:    End Sub
138:
139: End Class
140:
141: #End If
```

Listing 11.6 implements two versions of the Options class. Both versions have the exact same interface, so consumers aren't affected adversely when the Configuration information changes and we switch from persisting application settings to an OPTIONS.INI file versus the registry. Using an OPTIONS.INI file is a safer alternative and is more convenient when doing initial development.

Each version of the Options class uses a Private constructor, ensuring that consumers don't create instances. The classes are defined in such a manner as not to require instances, that is, all members are shared. (Unless mentioned, further discussion of the Options class applies to both examples.) Options uses an enumeration to make reading and writing keys easy to follow. Although the class only persists the LastFileName value, implementing additional state information simply requires adding enumerated values to the Keys enum and implementing the shared properties. LastFileName is a suitable model for any shared state information. Each shared property delegates reading and writing to the ReadString and WriteString methods. Because everything except the property is private, this class will be easy for consumers to use even though it required a little extra effort to write.

The biggest difference between the two versions of Options is that the registry version has to create and open registry keys. It's assumed that the registry information exists unless an exception occurs (starting at line 51); in the event of an exception, the key is created and the write is attempted again.

The HybridDictionary (defined in the System.Collections.Specialized namespace) example stores the keys in name/value pairs and uses the File, StreamReader, and StreamWriter classes defined in System.IO to manage file persistence. Only the HybridDictionary version requires a shared constructor (lines 75 to 78), which is responsible for creating an instance of the dictionary. Keep in mind that you never have to call the Shared constructor, and the compiler will generate code guaranteeing that the Shared constructor is called before any other code uses the class.

Listing 11.7 demonstrates a consumer that uses the Options class. The consumer is indifferent to which Options class is used. Switching back and forth between implementations of the Options class based on configuration settings has no impact or revisionary requirements on the consumer.

LISTING 11.7 Form1 represents a consumer of the Options class

```
1: Public Class Form1
2:   Inherits System.Windows.Forms.Form
3:
4:   [ Windows Foprm Designer generated code ]
5:
6:   Private Sub MenuItem5_Click(ByVal sender As System.Object, _
7:           ByVal e As System.EventArgs) Handles MenuItem5.Click
8:     Application.Exit()
9:   End Sub
10:
11:   Private Sub MenuItem2_Click(ByVal sender As System.Object, _
12:           ByVal e As System.EventArgs) Handles MenuItem2.Click
13:     ShowOpenFile()
14:   End Sub
15:
16:   Private Sub AddRecentFile(ByVal FileName As String)
17:     Options.LastFileName = FileName
18:     AddSubMenu(FileName)
19:   End Sub
20:
21:   Private Sub OnOpen(ByVal sender As Object, ByVal e As System.EventArgs)
22:     DoOpenFile(CType(sender, MenuItem).Text)
23:   End Sub
24:
25:   Private Sub AddSubMenu(ByVal RecentFile As String)
26:     MenuItemRecent.MenuItems.Add(RecentFile, AddressOf OnOpen)
27:   End Sub
28:
29:   Private Sub DoOpenFile(ByVal FileName As String)
30:     RichTextBox1.LoadFile(FileName, _
31:       RichTextBoxStreamType.PlainText)
32:   End Sub
```

LISTING 11.7   continued

```
33:
34:    Private Sub OpenFile(ByVal FileName As String)
35:       DoOpenFile(FileName)
36:       AddRecentFile(OpenFileDialog1.FileName)
37:    End Sub
38:
39:    Private Sub ShowOpenFile()
40:       OpenFileDialog1.Filter = "Plain Text (*.txt)|*.txt"
41:       OpenFileDialog1.InitialDirectory = "C:\"
42:
43:       If (OpenFileDialog1.ShowDialog() <> DialogResult.OK) Then _
44:          Exit Sub
45:
46:       OpenFile(OpenFileDialog1.FileName)
47:    End Sub
48:
49:    Protected Overrides Sub OnLoad(ByVal e As System.EventArgs)
50:       If (Options.LastFileName = "") Then Exit Sub
51:       AddSubMenu(Options.LastFileName)
52:
53:    End Sub
54: End Class
```

Listing 11.7 defines a form (with the generated code hidden) that implements a simple text editor. The application allows the user to open a file. The file is loaded into a RichTextBox control. The Recent menu is dynamically updated to contain submenus referring to previously opened files, and Options.LastFileName is updated. On subsequent runs, LastFileName is added to the Recent menu when the program is started (refer to the OnLoad method on lines 49 to 53).

The very short functions demonstrate optimum reuse. AddSubMenu is reused in AddRecentFile and OnLoad, and DoOpenFile (which loads the file into the RichTextBox) is reused in the OpenFile method and OnOpen event handler.

Listing 11.7 demonstrates several techniques that you might find practical. Line 26 demonstrates how to add submenus dynamically and associate event handlers with those menus. Line 22 demonstrates an example of using a dynamic menu caption as an argument to a method and dynamic type conversion. Lines 30 and 31 demonstrate how to load the contents of a file into a RichTextBox control; you could create the text editor by using additional properties defined in the RichTextBox control, like SaveFile. And, there are several examples of the refactoring "Extract Method," reducing the code listing considerably. An example of refactoring was extracting DoOpenFile from OpenFile on lines 29–37.

Implementing Factory Methods

A subject indirectly related to `Singleton` objects is the use of factory methods. From the last chapter, you know that the `Singleton` idiom is implemented by using a shared method to ensure the creation of one object, and defining a private constructor to ensure external consumers can't create objects without the help method. These helper methods are often referred to as factory methods.

A factory method is a shared method whose job it is to create instances of objects. Factory methods are used to instantiate `Singleton` objects, and are used to orchestrate object construction to facilitate the proper initialization of objects. A perfect example of a factory method is the `CreateGraphics` method. You can't instantiate a GDI+ `Graphics` object; you must request one from the `CreateGraphics` method (see Listing 11.5). (In the case of the `Graphics` object, a factory method was probably used because graphics are a limited and expensive resource.)

Factory methods don't have to be shared members of a class. In fact, in VB6 they couldn't be because we had no equivalent of the `Shared` modifier. In VB6, factory methods had to be defined as regular functions in a module. Visual Basic .NET supports shared members, allowing us to implement the factory method idiom as a member of a global function.

Martin Fowler's book *Refactoring: Improving the Design of Existing Code* provides a general motivation for the refactoring "Replace Constructor with Factory Method." However, in general, you can use a factory method whenever you find yourself repeatedly writing the same couple of lines that create and initialize an object.

A factory method is a function that takes the necessary arguments to initialize an object. The factory method creates the designated object and uses passed parameters to initialize the object, returning the instance of the properly constructed object in the `Return` statement.

To compel a consumer to use a factory method, you can define a constructor as protected or private and make the factory method shared and public. As a consequence, the only way to create an object would be to call the factory method and pass the correct arguments. Sometimes you can accomplish the same thing by introducing a parameterized constructor; however, if the class in question can't be subclassed, you can use a factory method to ensure proper initialization.

Listing 11.8 defines two factory methods that hide the details of initializing an `ADODB.Recordset` and an `ADODB.Connection`. The example demonstrates an alternative solution for storing application configuration options in a text file by using an Access database.

LISTING 11.8 Two factory methods for creating and initializing a Connection and Recordset object

```
 1: Private Function ConnectionString() As String
 2:     Return "Provider=Microsoft.Jet.OLEDB.4.0;Data Source=" & _
 3:     Application.StartupPath & "\Options.mdb"
 4: End Function
 5:
 6: Private Function Connection() As ADODB.Connection
 7:
 8:     Dim C As New ADODB.Connection()
 9:     C.ConnectionString = ConnectionString()
10:     C.Open()
11:     Return C
12:
13: End Function
14:
15: Private Function Recordset(ByVal AConnection As _
16:     ADODB.Connection) As ADODB.Recordset
17:
18:     Dim R As New ADODB.Recordset()
19:     R.Open("Options", AConnection, _
20:       ADODB.CursorTypeEnum.adOpenDynamic, _
21:       ADODB.LockTypeEnum.adLockOptimistic)
22:
23:     Return R
24: End Function
25:
26: Private Sub DoAddOption(ByVal R As ADODB.Recordset, _
27:     ByVal C As ADODB.Connection, _
28:     ByVal Key As String, ByVal Value As String)
29:
30:     R.AddNew()
31:     R.Fields("Key").Value = Key
32:     R.Fields("Value").Value = Value
33:     R.Update()
34:     R.Close()
35:     C.Close()
36:
37: End Sub
38:
39: Private Sub AddOption(ByVal C As ADODB.Connection, _
40:     ByVal Key As String, ByVal Value As String)
41:
42:     DoAddOption(Recordset, C, Key, Value)
43:
44: End Sub
45:
46: Private Sub Button1_Click(ByVal sender As System.Object, _
47:     ByVal e As System.EventArgs) Handles Button1.Click
48:
```

LISTING 11.8   continued

```
49:     AddOption(Connection(), "LastFileName", "file.txt")
50:
51:   End Sub
```

The factory methods are the `Connection` and `Recordset` functions started on lines 6 and 15, respectively. Each factory method declares an initialized instance of its respective objects. If you define a factory method as a member of a class, and that method returns an instance of the containing class, the method will be more useful if it's a shared method. Suppose, for example, that we defined the `Options` class from Listing 11.6 to be used by instances, and then we could define a factory class method to return an instance of the `Options` class as follows:

```
Public Class Options
  Public Shared Function CreateOptions() As Options
    Return New Options
  End Function
  ...
End Class
```

The preceding example could be called as an initializer: `Dim MyOptions As Options = Options.CreateOptions`. This statement demonstrates using the factory method, and roughly approximates the behavior of a constructor call. The benefit derived from a factory method is attained when you include necessary, additional initialization before returning the object, as demonstrated in Listing 11.8.

Overloading Shared Members

Chapter 7 introduced basic object-oriented concepts related to defining classes and members, and Chapter 10 introduced overloading, overriding, and shadowing. Overloading rules for instance methods apply to shared methods.

Overloading `Shared` members refers to two or more procedures that have the same name, use the `Overloads Shared` modifiers for properties and methods, and rigorously adhere to differentiating requirements. Specifically, the compiler must be able to use key aspects of the signature of the method call to determine which method (or property) is meant to be called by the user.

Specifically, overloaded shared members

- Can't be differentiated only by the argument modifiers `ByVal` or `ByRef`.
- Can't be differentiated only by the names of the arguments.
- Can't be differentiated only by return types.

- Can't be differentiated because one version is a subroutine and a second is a function. (Think of subroutines as functions that return the C/C++ void type; hence a subroutine and function differ by return types, violating the preceding rule.)

Recall from Chapter 10 that the motivation for using overloaded members is to define two or more members with semantically similar behavior—for example, two methods that print a value—but operate on different data types. The motivation is the same for shared members: semantically similar operations performed on different numbers and types of data with the added benefit or working at the class level.

Unlike C++ and Object Pascal, Visual Basic .NET allows you to overload types in the same family (see Listing 11.9). C++ and Object Pascal don't support overloading on, for example, an integer versus a long type, because it might be impossible to determine by the argument which overloaded method invocation is desired. Visual Basic .NET does allow this, as demonstrated in Listing 11.9.

LISTING 11.9 Overloaded shared members are employed for the same motivations as overloaded instance members and have the same restrictions

```
1: Public Class Form1
2:    Inherits System.Windows.Forms.Form
3:
4: [ Windows Form Designer generated code ]
5:
6:    Private Sub Button1_Click(ByVal sender As System.Object, _
7:      ByVal e As System.EventArgs) Handles Button1.Click
8:
9:      HasOverloaded.Print("Hello World!")
10:     HasOverloaded.Print(43L)
11:
12:   End Sub
13: End Class
14:
15: Public Class HasOverloaded
16:
17:   Overloads Shared Sub Print(ByVal Text As String)
18:     Debug.WriteLine(Text)
19:   End Sub
20:
21:   Overloads Shared Sub Print(ByVal Ch As Char)
22:     Debug.WriteLine(Ch)
23:   End Sub
24:
25:   Overloads Shared Sub Print(ByVal ALong As Long)
26:     Debug.WriteLine(ALong)
27:   End Sub
28:
```

LISTING 11.9 continued

```
29:    Overloads Shared Sub Print(ByVal Int As Integer)
30:      Debug.WriteLine(Int)
31:    End Sub
32:
33: #If False Then
34:    Overloads Shared Sub Foo()
35:
36:    End Sub
37:
38:    Overloads Shared Function Foo() As Integer
39:
40:    End Function
41: #End If
42:
43: End Class
```

Button1_Click calls overloaded shared Print methods defined in the class HasOverloaded defined on lines 15 through 43. Line 9 calls the Print subroutine that accepts a string on line 17. Line 10 calls the Print subroutine on line 25 that accepts a Long argument. Notice the Print subroutine that accepts an Integer. If we were to remove the L, type-designator on line 10, the Print subroutine that accepts integers (line 29) would be called. Lines 33 through 41 define two improperly overloaded methods, overloaded on the return type. The syntax checker catches this error at design time and reports Foo conflicts with a function by the same name defined in HasOverloaded in the Task List.

Raising Shared Events

Chapters 8 and 9 explained dynamic programming afforded to us by events and event handlers, all falling under the auspices of the Delegate class.

Keep in mind that RaiseEvent incurs no penalty if there are no respondents. If you write your code to invoke a specific method, at runtime you are stuck with the behavior described by that respondent. However, if you define an event and raise the event, any respondent can answer the event. Consider the revised code from Listing 11.9, shown in Listing 11.10, that demonstrates using a fixed respondent to indicate to the consumer of HasOverloaded that a Print method was invoked. (Parts of the original code from Listing 11.9 were concealed with code outlining to shorten the listing.)

Caution

Listing 11.10 demonstrates code that is too dependent on the existence of a specific form, Form1. Avoid writing code that relies on a specific object instance.

LISTING 11.10   A shared method talking to an instance of a form

```
 1: Public Class Form1
 2:    Inherits System.Windows.Forms.Form
 3:
 4: [ Windows Form Designer generated code ]
 5:
 6:    Private Sub Button1_Click(ByVal sender As System.Object, _
 7:      ByVal e As System.EventArgs) Handles Button1.Click
 8:
 9:      HasOverloaded.Print("Hello World!")
10: [...]
11:
12:    End Sub
13:
14:    Public Sub Print(ByVal Value As Object)
15:      Text = "Print: " & Value
16:    End Sub
17:
18:    Private Sub Form1_Load(ByVal sender As System.Object, _
19:      ByVal e As System.EventArgs) Handles MyBase.Load
20:
21:      HasOverloaded.AForm = Me
22:
23:    End Sub
24:
25: End Class
26:
27: Public Class HasOverloaded
28:
29:    Public Shared AForm As Form1
30:
31:    Overloads Shared Sub Print(ByVal Text As String)
32:      AForm.Print(Text)
33:      Debug.WriteLine(Text)
34:    End Sub
35:
36: [...]
37:
38: End Class
```

HasOverloaded uses a shared field, AForm on line 29, to obtain a reference to an instance of Form1. Form1's OnLoad event handler, defined on lines 18 through 23, initializes the shared reference in HasOverloaded. Functionally, and to a limited degree, this code works, but as a rule it's considered bad form. Although aggregation, inheritance, and references are a good thing in general, the reference to Form1 makes HasOverloaded brittle. In essence, the instance of the form breaches the invisible bubble of encapsulation, which should be avoided. Consider what happens to HasOverloaded if Form1 is destroyed. The Print method on line 31 is no longer valid. Again, what happens if Form1 is given a better name? Again, HasOverloaded.Print (line 31) is invalid.

A preferable alternative in this instance is to use a shared event to promote the interaction to the class interface level. The end result (shown in Listing 11.11) is valid code regardless of whether or not Form1 exists or is renamed because the interaction happens at the class interface—along the edges described by the public members—instead of inside the methods.

LISTING 11.11 Using a shared event to facilitate interactions with class methods

```
 1: Public Class Form1
 2:    Inherits System.Windows.Forms.Form
 3:
 4: [ Windows Form Designer generated code ]
 5:
 6:    Private Sub Button1_Click(ByVal sender As System.Object, _
 7:      ByVal e As System.EventArgs) Handles Button1.Click
 8:
 9:      HasOverloaded.Print("Hello World!")
10: [...]
11:
12:    End Sub
13:
14:    Private Sub OnPrint(ByVal Value As Object)
15:      Text = "OnPrint: " & Value
16:    End Sub
17:
18:    Private Sub Form1_Load(ByVal sender As System.Object, _
19:      ByVal e As System.EventArgs) Handles MyBase.Load
20:
21:      AddHandler HasOverloaded.OnPrint, AddressOf OnPrint
22:
23:    End Sub
24:
25: End Class
26:
27: Public Class HasOverloaded
28:
29:    Public Shared Event OnPrint(ByVal Value As Object)
```

LISTING 11.11 continued

```
30:
31:    Overloads Shared Sub Print(ByVal Text As String)
32:       RaiseEvent OnPrint(Text)
33:       Debug.WriteLine(Text)
34:    End Sub
35:
36: [...]
37:
38: End Class
```

The revised listing adds the handler Form1.OnPrint to the implicit Delegate defined by the shared event on line 29 in the HasOverloaded class. Line 32 simply raises the event and is indifferent to the specific recipients, or even if there are recipients. What you don't see is that the RaiseEvent statement on line 32 checks an invocation list and sends the event to respondents, but it works correctly whether there are respondents or not.

An additional benefit of using the public Shared event is that other objects can implement OnPrint handlers and add themselves to the invocation list of the Delegate in HasOverloaded. This minor revision might seem trivial, but these small changes in implementation mean the difference between flexible, robust, and loosely coupled code (as in Listing 11.11) and brittle, unmanageable, and tightly coupled code (as in Listing 11.10). That is all the difference in the world.

Summary

Shared members allow you to perform operations, and shared fields and properties allow you to maintain state information when only one instance of the information is needed. The general class and object relationship supports maintaining individuated state between objects. Most of the time you need an object, and some of the time it's simply more convenient not to have to create an instance of an object. A utility class such as the Math class is a perfect example of a stateless class that uses shared members.

In addition to learning about shared fields, properties, and methods, Chapter 11 introduced shared events and overloaded shared members. You probably won't need these idioms on a routine basis, but if and when you do need them, they will be sorely missed.

Some techniques, like linking instances by a shared field, allow you to write more expressive code. If what we can think about is limited by our language, the more expressive a language is, the more flexibility we have in expression. Visual Basic .NET is a much more expressive language than its predecessors, allowing us to implement more advanced idioms.

Defining Attributes

CHAPTER 12

Earlier in the book we mentioned that the sweeping changes in .NET required sweeping changes to the Visual Basic language. When you define, code, and compile a project in Visual Studio .NET, you are creating an assembly. Only part of that assembly is an executable. Another significant part of an assembly is the self-describing metadata.

Metadata, or additional declarative information, was added to combat "DLL Hell." Until now, Windows applications were coded and compiled, and additional information was stored in the registry separately from those compiled applications. Applications such as regtool5.dll or `GetSetting` and `SaveSetting` in VB6 were used to read the extra data an application needed to function correctly. This extra data included the location and registration of dependent files, About information, and application settings. The problem was that the extra information an application needed did not travel with the application. Further, DLLs were registered based on filename. A newer file with the same name as a predecessor would overwrite registry settings, breaking existing applications.

Metadata travels with an application in .NET, binding the application to its supporting data in an assembly. Additionally, application uniqueness is not based on just filename. Application uniqueness is based on the name, a strong name, version, and locale, allowing assemblies with the same name to coexist.

The role attributes play is that of providing a means of specifying that metadata. Attributes allow you to provide simple application and About information as well as provide advanced control over code and request security permissions.

Historically, Windows programming required that developers specify extra data in a variety of places like the registry, .INI files, and setup script files. The .NET Framework binds that metadata to the assembly, which also contains the executable. The combination of an assembly storing metadata and the executable eliminates "DLL Hell." This combination of metadata and executable supports xcopy deployment, too.

> **Note**
>
> The `xcopy.exe` command-line tool originally shipped with the MS-DOS operating system. (It was B.A.S.I.C. that made Microsoft a very profitable company, but it was MS-DOS that led to desktop domination and tremendous profitability.) The `xcopy.exe` program is a tool (still in Windows XP) that allows you to copy files and folders with a single command.
>
> By *xcopy deployment*, Microsoft means that you can deploy your applications by copying them. The term implies that you can deploy your .NET applications without complicated installation scripts or tools, and you won't need to register DLLs.

> This is not exactly true. Add-ins, wizards, and applications that use COM will still need to register GUIDs, and consequently have more complicated deployment models. This requirement will go away if COM goes away.
>
> You may still need to persist external application settings and the registry is still a convenient place to do this.

In this chapter you will learn how to define assembly and type and member attributes. You will learn how to subclass attributes in order to define custom attributes, and how to discover information about an assembly using the IL disassembler and reflection.

Understanding the Role of Attributes

Attributes are used to add metadata to an assembly. From the introduction we know that attributes provide information such as the vendor or author information, but attributes provide much more.

Attributes describe how data is serialized—written as a stream of bytes for transmission, security models, limiting optimizations for the Just-In-Time compiler (or JITter), and runtime behavior. This section examines the role of attributes, demonstrating how these different uses for attributes are applied.

What Is Metadata?

Metadata is binary data that describes your application. The metadata can be stored in memory or as part of a *portable executable* (PE).

Metadata describes the elements of your application in a multilanguage format. This allows a JIT compiler that can read the assembly metadata to translate the multilanguage information into an executable for a specific platform.

Microsoft believes that metadata is essentially a simpler application building model. Metadata accomplishes the following:

- Eliminates the need for separate Interface Definition Language (IDL) files
- Combines definition and implementation into a single file
- Ensures that files are self-describing
- Enables custom attributes, thus providing extensibility

Metadata Eliminates IDL Files

IDL is that cryptic language used to define interfaces in support of COM. Listing 12.1 contains the IDL code for ATL.IDL, the Abstract Template Library IDL file. (Don't worry—you will not need to fully understand or work with this file.)

LISTING 12.1   An example of IDL code from ATL.IDL

```
#include <olectl.h>
// atl.idl : IDL source for atl.dll
//

// This file will be processed by the MIDL tool to
// produce the type library (atl.tlb) and marshalling code.
import "oaidl.idl";
import "atliface.idl";
import  "ocidl.idl";

[
    uuid(44EC0535-400F-11D0-9DCD-00A0C90391D3),
    version(1.0),
    helpstring("ATL 2.0 Type Library")
]
library ATLLib
{
    importlib("stdole32.tlb");
    importlib("stdole2.tlb");

    interface IDocHostUIHandlerDispatch;
    interface IAxWinAmbientDispatch;
};
```

Fortunately, as Visual Basic developers we never had to worry much about IDL and in .NET, metadata eliminates the need for it.

Metadata Combines Definition and Implementation

Listing 12.1 contains references to other .idl files as well as an olectl.h file. Files with a .h extension are C++ header files. The C++ programming language uses .h files to describe classes and .cpp files to implement those classes.

The need for separate definition and implementation files has been eliminated by metadata. This benefit will be less noticeable to VB developers but represents one of the problems metadata redresses.

Metadata Makes Assemblies Self-Describing

Metadata makes assemblies self-describing in a multilanguage way. The benefit of this capability is that the additional information travels with the executable, and the multilanguage implementation of the metadata allows for seamless integration between assemblies written in disparate .NET languages.

Listing 12.2 demonstrates the seamlessness of .NET languages. This listing shows two modules from separate assemblies. One is a class library implemented in C# (C Sharp), and the other is a simple Windows application written in Visual Basic .NET.

LISTING 12.2   Two modules from separate assemblies, each implemented in a different .NET language

```
 1:    ' C# Module
 2:    using System;
 3:
 4:    namespace CSharpLibrary
 5:    {
 6:       /// <summary>
 7:       /// Summary description for Class1.
 8:       /// </summary>
 9:       public class MyMath
10:       {
11:          static public double Add( double lhs, double rhs)
12:       {
13:         return lhs + rhs;
14:       }
15:       }
16:    }
17:
18:    ' VB .NET Module
19:    Public Class Form1
20:       Inherits System.Windows.Forms.Form
21:
22:    [ Windows Form Designer generated code ]
23:
24:       Private Function DoConvertError(ByVal E As Exception, _
25:         ByVal Control As TextBox)
26:
27:       Const Message As String = _
28:         "'{0}' cannot is not a valid number"
29:       MsgBox(String.Format(Message, Control.Text), MsgBoxStyle.Exclamation)
30:       Control.Focus()
31:       Throw E
32:    End Function
33:
34:       Private Function ToDouble(ByVal Control As TextBox) As Double
```

LISTING 12.2   continued

```
35:        Try
36:            Return CDbl(Control.Text)
37:        Catch E As InvalidCastException
38:            DoConvertError(E, Control)
39:        End Try
40:    End Function
41:
42:    Private ReadOnly Property LeftHandSide() As Double
43:        Get
44:            Return ToDouble(TextBox1)
45:        End Get
46:    End Property
47:
48:    Private ReadOnly Property RightHandSide() As Double
49:        Get
50:            Return ToDouble(TextBox2)
51:        End Get
52:    End Property
53:
54:    Private Sub UpdateSum()
55:        Try
56:            TextBox3.Text = _
57:                CSharpLibrary.MyMath.Add(LeftHandSide, RightHandSide)
58:        Catch
59:        End Try
60:    End Sub
61:
62:    Private Sub Button1_Click(ByVal sender As System.Object, _
63:        ByVal e As System.EventArgs) Handles Button1.Click
64:        UpdateSum()
65:    End Sub
66: End Class
```

The first 16 lines hold the code from the .cs (C#) module extracted from the class library implemented in C#. The rest of the code is from a .vb module excerpted from the Windows application implemented in Visual Basic .NET. The example is quite straightforward. The Windows application accepts two doubles and returns the sum of the two doubles by calling the static—equivalent to shared in Visual Basic .NET—method Add on line 57, in the C# class library.

Both of the projects reside in the same solution (on the www.samspublishing.com Web site). VS .NET allows you to easily step from the Visual Basic .NET code right into the C# code and back without any special effort.

Previously, if you wanted to use DLLs implemented in other languages, you had to be intimately aware of the language the library was implemented in, how to load those libraries, and what the calling convention of the library's language was. For instance, you had to know if the arguments to methods were called in reverse order or in order and indicate this knowledge by using calling convention specifiers like cdecl. Even if you knew intimate details about the external library, it was often difficult if not impossible to trace from your application into the source code of the library.

The .NET world allows you to reference an assembly, import the namespace of interest, and go. You can step into and out of code implemented in various .NET languages, as well as use object-oriented idioms between languages. For example, a Visual Basic .NET class can inherit from a C# class or implement an interface defined in C# and vice versa.

This interchangeability between .NET languages, the similarities between languages, and commonality of the CLR are reasons that Microsoft says that the language you choose is more of a lifestyle choice than a technical choice, at least as far as .NET is concerned. Technically, you could hire C# and Visual Basic .NET developers and have them work on the same project quite easily. The class listing in Listing 12.3 demonstrates a revision to the earlier code. The MyMath class is subclassed and extended in the VB .NET code.

LISTING 12.3 A VB .NET class that subclasses and extends a C# class, all facilitated by metadata

```
1:  Public Class VBMyMath
2:      Inherits CSharpLibrary.MyMath
3:
4:      Public Shared Function Divide( _
5:        ByVal lhs As Double, ByVal rhs As Double) As Double
6:        Return Decimal.op_Division(lhs, rhs)
7:      End Function
8:
9:  End Class
```

Note that the code listing is VB .NET code. Clearly the VBMyMath class inherits CSharpLibrary.MyMath. The VBMyMath class extends the C# class by adding a divide method.

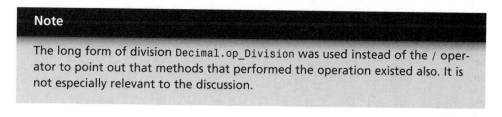

Note

The long form of division Decimal.op_Division was used instead of the / operator to point out that methods that performed the operation existed also. It is not especially relevant to the discussion.

VBMyMath contains two shared methods now: Add and Divide. Just for fun, some additional oddities were implemented. Listing 12.4 contains a revised listing to the Windows application to illustrate some of the advanced idioms available in VB .NET code.

LISTING 12.4 Language aerobics

```
 1:  Public Class Form1
 2:    Inherits System.Windows.Forms.Form
 3:
 4:  [ Windows Form Designer generated code ]
 5:
 6:    Private Function DoConvertError(ByVal E As Exception, _
 7:      ByVal Control As TextBox)
 8:
 9:      Const Message As String = _
10:        "'{0}' cannot is not a valid number"
11:      MsgBox(String.Format(Message, Control.Text), MsgBoxStyle.Exclamation)
12:      Control.Focus()
13:      Throw E
14:    End Function
15:
16:    Private Function ToDouble(ByVal Control As TextBox) As Double
17:      Try
18:        Return CDbl(Control.Text)
19:      Catch E As InvalidCastException
20:        DoConvertError(E, Control)
21:      End Try
22:    End Function
23:
24:    Private ReadOnly Property LeftHandSide() As Double
25:      Get
26:        Return ToDouble(TextBox1)
27:      End Get
28:    End Property
29:
30:    Private ReadOnly Property RightHandSide() As Double
31:      Get
32:        Return ToDouble(TextBox2)
33:      End Get
34:    End Property
35:
36:    Private Overloads Sub UpdateSum()
37:      Try
38:        TextBox3.Text = _
39:          CSharpLibrary.MyMath.Add(LeftHandSide, RightHandSide)
40:      Catch
41:      End Try
42:    End Sub
43:
```

LISTING 12.4   continued

```
44:    ' Just for fun!
45:    Private Delegate Function Procedure(ByVal lhs As Double, _
46:      ByVal rhs As Double) As Double
47:
48:    Private Overloads Sub UpdateSum(ByVal Proc As Procedure)
49:      Try
50:        TextBox3.Text = Proc(LeftHandSide, RightHandSide)
51:      Catch
52:      End Try
53:    End Sub
54:
55:    Private Sub Button1_Click(ByVal sender As System.Object, _
56:      ByVal e As System.EventArgs) Handles Button1.Click
57:
58:      UpdateSum(AddressOf VBMyMath.Add)
59:
60:    End Sub
61:
62:    Private Sub Button2_Click(ByVal sender As System.Object, _
63:      ByVal e As System.EventArgs) Handles Button2.Click
64:      UpdateSum(AddressOf VBMyMath.Divide)
65:    End Sub
66: End Class
```

12

DEFINING ATTRIBUTES

> **Note**
>
> Listing 12.4 demonstrates some advanced idioms for fun. Clearly we would not write production code to perform arithmetic like this, but the listing does illustrate the newfound expressiveness in Visual Basic that previously was only available in C++ and Object Pascal.
>
> Download MultilanguageDemo.sln from the `www.samspublishing.com` Web site, or create a Windows Application and add three textbox controls and two buttons to the default form.

The listing introduces a `Delegate` on lines 45 and 46. Instances of the delegate will contain functions that take two doubles and return a double. Using the `Delegate`, we can overload the `UpdateSum` method to accept an argument of type `Procedure`, the name of the `Delegate`. The overloaded version is defined on lines 48 through 53. The new `UpdateSum` looks almost identical to the old `UpdateSum` except for the addition of the `Delegate` argument and the fact that the `Delegate` argument is used to invoke the behavior. Finally the two button-click events invoke the `Add` or `Divide` behavior.

It is interesting to note that we are able to leverage the error-handling and field-handling code for the TextBox controls and had to write very little GUI code using these highly refactored methods.

Attributes Support Extensibility

Attributes support extensibility. Attribute is a class in the CLR that can be inherited from and extended. Because attributes provide you with a way to add additional metadata, you can extend and customize the IDE using attributes. (Refer to the section "Creating Custom Attributes" later in this chapter for examples.)

Attribute Naming

Attributes are classes. By convention they are named with the word Attribute attached as a suffix. Attributes are applied using a special metatag notation and do not require the full name when applied.

Attribute tags generally have a syntax that looks similar to a method call where the attribute name is the method and you pass any parameters needed by the attribute in parentheses. Attribute tags are placed before the method inside metatag brackets <>. The following syntax example demonstrates attribute usage in general:

```
<attributename( [args0, args1..argsn] )> ProcedureHeader
```

AttributeName is the name of the attribute with or without the Attribute suffix. Attribute constructors can be overloaded, allowing you to select the specific overloaded version and pass the arguments you need to.

A single example of an attribute class is System.ObsoleteAttribute. The Obsolete attribute can be used to mark obsolete code that you might intend to remove in future versions of your application. You can look up the ObsoleteAttribute class and find out information about its constructors, properties, and methods in the help file.

There are three versions of the ObsoleteAttribute.New method. One version accepts a message string and a Boolean indicating whether using the method will cause a compiler error or not. Let's revisit Listing 12.4. Suppose that we want to encourage users of the code not to call the old UpdateSum method on line 36; we would rather have them use the new version that takes a Delegate. We could mark the old UpdateSum method with the Obsolete tag, discouraging developers from using it. Listing 12.5 demonstrates the technical aspects.

LISTING 12.5 `System.ObsoleteAttribute` demonstrates the technical application of attributes

```
<Obsolete("This method is going to be removed", True)> _
Private Overloads Sub UpdateSum()
  Try
    TextBox3.Text = _
      CSharpLibrary.MyMath.Add(LeftHandSide, RightHandSide)
  Catch
  End Try
End Sub
```

The excerpt from Listing 12.4 has been modified to use the `Obsolete` attribute. When the application is compiled, a compiler error will be indicated displaying the text message "This method is going to be removed". If we had passed False, the application would compile without a failure because of the `Obsolete` attribute.

Things That Attributes Describe

Attributes are used to describe a wide variety of things. Attributes describe how data is serialized, specify assembly security, limit JIT compiler optimizations, control the visibility of members, prevent the debugger from stepping into specific methods, and define runtime behavior.

Because attributes are an extensible part of VS .NET, you will discover that the pool of attributes will grow over time.

Describing an Assembly

A common use for attributes is to describe the assembly. These attributes are assembly-level attributes and are placed in the assemblyinfo.vb file and tagged with the `Assembly` keyword.

Assembly attributes provide Title, Description, Company, Product, Copyright, Trademark, and CLS compliance information. You will also find version information and a GUID that is used in case the assembly is exposed to COM, such as an add-in.

To modify attributes providing assembly information, open the assemblyinfo.vb file from the Solution Explorer and enter the assembly-level information using the code editor. Listing 12.6 contains the assemblyinfo.vb file from the MultilanguageDemo.vbproj project.

LISTING 12.6   A typical assemblyinfo.vb file containing assembly-level information

```
 1: Imports System.Reflection
 2: Imports System.Runtime.InteropServices
 3:
 4: ' General Information about an assembly
 5: ' is controlled through the following
 6: ' set of attributes. Change these attribute
 7: ' values to modify the information
 8: ' associated with an assembly.
 9:
10: ' Review the values of the assembly attributes
11:
12: <Assembly: AssemblyTitle("")>
13: <Assembly: AssemblyDescription("")>
14: <Assembly: AssemblyCompany("")>
15: <Assembly: AssemblyProduct("")>
16: <Assembly: AssemblyCopyright("")>
17: <Assembly: AssemblyTrademark("")>
18: <Assembly: CLSCompliant(True)>
19:
20: 'The following GUID is for the ID of the
21: 'typelib if this project is exposed to COM
22: <Assembly: Guid("A5AC547D-3C13-4C7F-A917-BE076B3331C6")>
23:
24: ' Version information for an assembly
25: ' consists of the following four values:
26: '
27: '       Major Version
28: '       Minor Version
29: '       Build Number
30: '       Revision
31: '
32: ' You can specify all the values or you
33: ' can default the Build and Revision Numbers
34: ' by using the '*' as shown below:
35:
36: <Assembly: AssemblyVersion("1.0.*")>
```

Using the code editor, we can type in a view-friendly application title between the double quotation marks after AssemblyTitle. The same is true for each of the attributes describing the assembly.

Assembly attributes are also referred to as *global attributes*. There are four categories of global attributes, including: identity attributes, information attributes, manifest attributes, and strong name attributes. The categories of attributes are briefly described in the subsections that follow.

Identity Attributes

The identity attributes are `AssemblyVersionAttribute`, `AssemblyCultureAttribute`, and `AssemblyFlagsAttribute`. Listing 12.6 demonstrates the `AssemblyVersionAttribute`. (Recall that the full class name is not required and not used by convention. This yields the actual application of the attribute as `AssemblyVersion`.)

Identity and strong name attributes uniquely identify an assembly. This is an evolutionary distinction from earlier versions where the filename was used to distinguish one application from another.

Informational Attributes

Informational attributes are used to provide About information, who you and your company are and what your product is all about. These attributes are

```
AssemblyProductAttribute

AssemblyTrademarkAttribute

AssemblyInformationalVersionAttribute

AssemblyCompanyAttribute

AssemblyCopyrightAttribute

AssemblyFileVersionAttribute
```

You can find examples of these attributes in Listing 12.6.

Manifest Attributes

Assembly manifest attributes are used to provide information in the assembly's manifest. Manifest attributes provide title, description, configuration, and default alias information. These attributes are: `AssemblyTitleAttribute`, `DescriptionAttribute`, `ConfigurationAttribute`, and `DefaultAliasAttribute`.

To view manifest information, use the ildasm.exe application that ships with the framework SDK.

Strong Name Attributes

Strong name attributes define the strong name key file, which is used in conjunction with identity attributes to uniquely identify assemblies. Strong name attributes are: `AssemblyDelaySignAttribute`, `AssemblyKeyFileAttribute`, and `AssemblyKeyNameAttribute`.

Annotating Types and Members

Thus far we have covered the general benefits of attributes and explored global attributes. Attributes can be applied at the type, method, property, and field levels, too.

The general syntax for applying attributes at a lower level of granularity is similar to using global attributes. Non-global attributes do not use the `Assembly:` prefix. Let's take a look at some specific attributes that can be applied to types (like classes) and members of types.

Adding Type Attributes

Attributes can be applied to types as well as members of types. The `AttributeUsageAttribute` is used to define an attribute class and the `AttributeTargets` enumeration flag passed to that attribute determines how a particular attribute can be used and what it can be applied to. For example, to use a particular attribute on a class, that attribute must have been tagged with the `<AttributeUsage(AttributeTargets.All)>` or `<AttributeUsage(AttributeTargets.Class)>` attribute when the attribute was defined. (Refer to the section "Creating Custom Attributes" later in this chapter for more information.)

The application of an attribute is the same regardless of whether that attribute is applied to a type, property, method, field, or assembly. Whether you can use an attribute on a particular code element or not depends on the `AttributeTargets` enumerations applied to that attribute. If an attribute cannot be applied to a code element, you will get an error in the Task List. For instance, if you apply the `<DebuggerHidden()>` attribute on a form class, you will get the following error:

```
'DebuggerHiddenAttribute' cannot be applied to 'Form1' because the attribute
is not valid on this declaration type.
```

If an attribute is suitable, the syntax and requirements of a particular attribute are the same whether the attribute is applied to a type or some other declaration type.

Basic Attribute Statement

The basic attribute statement uses the enclosing <> brackets with the attribute class name written as a method call followed by parentheses. Here is a syntactical example: `<attributename()>`.

> **Caution**
>
> The `HelpAttribute` class is not part of the CLR. The sample class is demonstrated in the VS .NET help files and a close variation is defined later in this chapter in the section "Creating Custom Attributes."

Borrowing the custom `HelpAttribute` class from the VS .NET help files (see `ms-help://MS.VSCC/MS.MSDNVS/vbls7/html/vblrfVBSpec4_10.htm`), we can apply a variation of the `HelpAttribute` class that has an `Optional` constructor argument.

For our purposes, we will assume that `HelpAttribute` can be applied with no flags or parameters of any kind. Perhaps the default behavior is to point at your company's Web site. To apply `HelpAttribute` to a form class, we must add a reference to the assembly (think DLL!) containing the attribute class and add an `imports` statement or use the full name of the attribute class, including the namespace. To apply `HelpAttribute` to a class, assuming that we have added a reference to the assembly containing the attribute, use the following code as a guide.

```
Imports MyHelpAttribute
<Help()> Public Class Form1
...
```

The `Imports` statement imports the namespace containing the attribute class `HelpAttribute`, and `<Help()>` applies the attribute to the `Form1` class in the example. (Recall that we can use the complete name of the attribute class—which for the example would be `HelpAttribute`—but we drop the attribute suffix by convention.)

Using Positional Parameters

When you add an attribute tag like `<Help()>`, you are actually constructing an instance of the `HelpAttribute` class, which is discernible by examining the disassembled IL (refer to the section "Viewing Attributes with the MSIL Disassembler").

I also indicated that the `HelpAttribute` class was defined to have an optional parameter. The `HelpAttribute` is defined as follows:

```
Public Sub New(Optional ByVal AUrn As String = "Add Help Reference Here")
   FUrn = AUrn
End Sub
```

The implication is that you can pass a substitute argument to the optional parameter. Parameters passed between the attribute parentheses to supply information for constructor arguments are referred to as positional parameters. We could redefine the application of the `HelpAttribute` class by supplying an argument for the first (and only, in this instance) positional parameter.

```
Imports MyHelpAttribute
<Help("http://www.softconcepts.com")> Public Class Form1
...
```

In this example the `FUrn` field will contain the reference to `http://www.softconcepts.com`. Positional parameters are matched by position and type, identical to supplying parameters for any other methods.

Using Named Arguments

You can supply named arguments when you apply an attribute. Named arguments initialize public fields or public readable and writable properties. Suppose we have an additional field named `Topic` that is not expressed as an argument to the constructor. To initialize public fields or properties when you apply an attribute, append the name argument using the following syntax:

```
Name:=Value
```

Initializing the `Topic` field for the `HelpAttribute` using the named argument syntax, the `HelpAttribute` applied to the `Form1` class would be revised as follows:

```
Imports MyHelpAttribute
<Help("http://www.softconcepts.com"), Topic:="AttributeDemo"> Public Class Form1
...
```

The word `Help` is understood to invoke the `HelpAttribute`. The first argument is the positional argument passed to the constructor, and the `Topic:="AttributeDemo"` argument is a named argument that would initialize the `Topic` field.

If you need multiple named arguments, type additional arguments in the form `Name:=Value`, separating each named argument by inserting a comma between arguments.

Applying Multiple Attributes

Consider the case where you want to apply more than one attribute. Additional attributes applied to a single code element are inserted between the <> brackets, separating each attribute statement with a comma.

Thus, if you applied a `DescriptionAttribute` in conjunction with the default `HelpAttribute`, the attribute statement would be written as demonstrated.

```
<Help(), Description("This is my description.")>
```

The benefit of using attributes is to provide additional data, or metadata, that is beneficial to other developers or to support extensions to VS .NET.

Adding Method Attributes

After reading the previous section, you are aware of the general syntax for applying attributes. You know how to apply singular and multiple attributes and how to provide positional and named arguments. The technical application of attributes to other code elements is identical to their use as applied to classes. For this reason we will take a look at a couple of useful attributes that you can apply to methods.

Using `DebuggerHiddenAttribute`

The `DebuggerHiddenAttribute` class is used to hide methods from the debugger. This attribute requires no positional or named arguments and is defined in the `System.Diagnostics` namespace.

Suppose you have debugged code thoroughly and want to avoid stepping through tested code as your system evolves. You can add the `<DebuggerHidden()>` attribute to specific methods to skip over them as you are stepping and tracing your application. Skipping long or tested methods can be beneficial in speeding up white box—tracing and stepping through code in the IDE—testing.

Using `ConditionalAttribute`

`ConditionalAttribute` can be used to allow code to be emitted to IL or not based on the value of the positional argument passed to `ConditionalAttribute`.

VB6 supported operations similar to this using conditional compiler code. Consider the example where you want to write entries to the event log during testing and disable event logging when you have finished testing. Listing 12.7 demonstrates a reasonable technique for VB6.

LISTING 12.7   Conditional code and event logging in VB6

```
1:  Private Sub Log(ByVal Message As String)
2:     #Const DebugMode = 1
3:     #If DebugMode Then
4:       Call App.LogEvent(Message, vbLogEventTypeInformation)
5:     #End If
6:  End Sub
7:
8:  Private Sub Command1_Click()
9:     Call Log("Command1_Click")
10: End Sub
```

Implementing the log procedure shown in the listing, we can wrap the VB6 call `App.LogEvent` in VB6 between the conditional compiler directives and use the pragma `DebugMode` to enable or disable logging. (Logging is enabled in the listing. As a result, all of our logging code can remain in place, allowing us to quickly turn on logging when we go into maintenance mode.)

Unfortunately, this technique is not wholly suitable. If `#DebugMode = 0`, logging will not occur, but we will have potentially dozens of empty procedure calls to `Log`.

`ConditionalAttribute` in Visual Basic .NET yields a better result. If we apply `ConditionalAttribute` to a method, the method and all statements calling it are removed if the conditional string variable is passed the name of a pragma variable that is equivalent to False. Listing 12.8 demonstrates using `ConditionalAttribute` with code equivalent to that in Listing 12.7.

LISTING 12.8   Using the VB .NET `ConditionalAttribute` and the `EventLog` component

```
1:  Public Class Form1
2:      Inherits System.Windows.Forms.Form
3:
4:  [ Windows Form Designer generated code ]
5:
6:  #Const LogMode = True
7:
8:    <Conditional("LogMode")> _
9:    Private Sub Log(ByVal Message As String)
10:      EventLog1.WriteEntry("Application", Message)
11:    End Sub
12:
13:    Private Sub Button1_Click(ByVal sender As System.Object, _
14:      ByVal e As System.EventArgs) Handles Button1.Click
15:      Log("Button1_Click")
16:    End Sub
17: End Class
```

Line 6 defines the pragma constant `LogMode` and initializes it to True. (You can set the value of custom constants on the Build Property Page of the project's properties.) The `Conditional` on line 8 passes the name of the constant to the attribute. `LogMode` evaluates to True; consequently, the `Log` procedure is included in the emitted IL. Unlike what would happen in VB6, the statement on line 15 is omitted, too. Running the sample program, we can view the logged entry (see Figure 12.1).

Event Viewer
Action View
Tree
Application Log 1 event(s)
Event Viewer (Local)
Application Log
Security Log
System Log
Custom
Type
Date
Time
Source
Informati... 9/21/2001 2:39:5... Application None

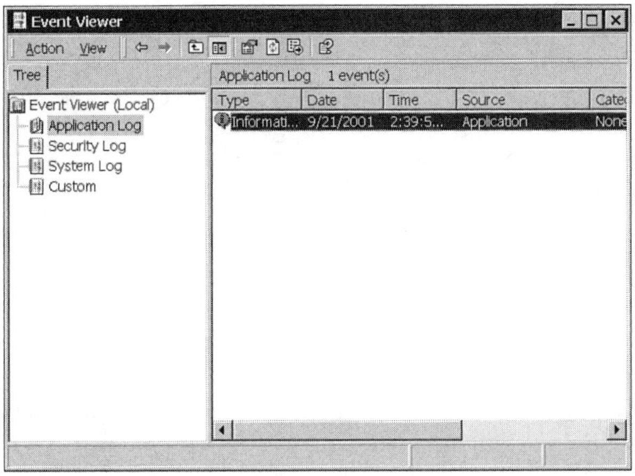

FIGURE 12.1
The Event Viewer in Windows 2000 showing the logged event using the `EventLog` *component.*

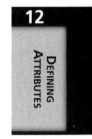

If we change the `LogMode` constant to False, we can view the IL code and clearly note that all calls to the `Conditional Log` method have been removed from the IL. (Figure 12.2 shows the IL with `LogMode = True` and `LogMode = False` respectively.) Visual Basic .NET eliminates the overhead of empty method calls.

LogMode = True - VS.NET emits IL with the call to Log (see IL_0007)
Form1::Button1_Click : void(object,class [mscorlib]System.EventArgs)
.method private instance void Button1_Click(object sender,
class [mscorlib]System.EventArgs e) cil mana
{
// Code size 15 (0xf)
.maxstack 8
IL_0000: nop
IL_0001: ldarg.0
IL_0002: ldstr "Button1_Click"
IL_0007: callvirt instance void ConditionalAttributeDemo.Form1::Log(string)
IL_000c: nop
IL_000d: nop
IL_000e: ret
} // end of method Form1::Button1_Click
LogMode = False - VS.NET emits IL with no-op (nop) effectively stripping the Conditional method invocation for us
Form1::Button1_Click : void(object,class [mscorlib]System.EventArgs)
.method private instance void Button1_Click(object sender,
class [mscorlib]System.Ev
{
// Code size 3 (0x3)
.maxstack 8
IL_0000: nop
IL_0001: nop
IL_0002: ret
} // end of method Form1::Button1_Click

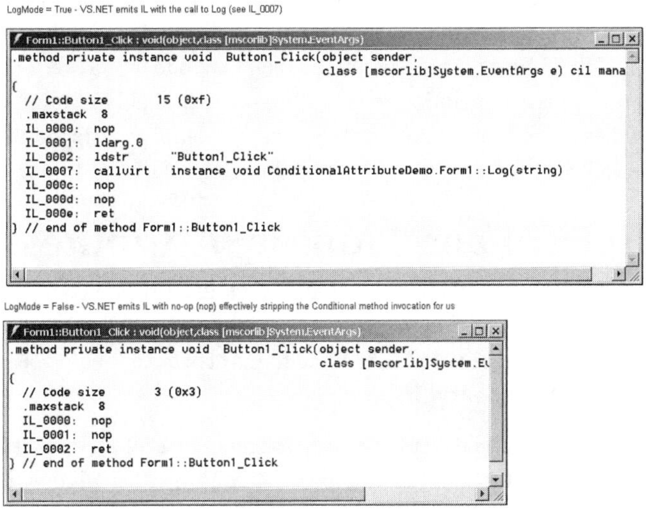

FIGURE 12.2
Emitted IL showing the "before and after" pictures when employing the `Conditional Attribute`.

> **Note**
>
> Looking at IL code can provide interesting clues as to how idioms are implemented in .NET. (It is too bad we cannot get the complete CLR source code for our edification.) From the IL in Figure 12.2, it looks as if IL is similar to assembly language, and it also looks as if the compiler has a distinct C# slant on the way code is treated. `Instance void`
> `ConditionalAttributeDemo::Form1::Log(string)` looks suspiciously like C++ code.
>
> A final note: the IL_0007 instruction `callvirt` sounds like a virtual method invocation, suggesting that `ConditionalAttribute` may use a pointer to a virtual methods table to implement `ConditionalAttribute`. Point at a specific method if the conditional argument is True and a null table entry if the conditional is False. This last part is supposition, but examining other developers' code provides insight.

You do not have to know how to read IL to program in .NET. However, if you can read a little assembly language, IL is similar, and you can tell what is going on. In the top half of Figure 12.2, you can see that `LogMode = True`. As a result, everywhere the call to `Log` occurs, IL will be emitted—notice that instruction IL_0007 calls the `Log` method. The bottom half of the figure is the IL emitted when `LogMode = False`. The `nop` (no-op) instruction performs no operation; `nop` is filler code, probably to align code instruction boundaries. The important thing to note is that the compiler stripped the calls out for us, allowing us to leave our valuable, conditional code in place for future use.

Adding Field and Property Attributes

We already know that attributes are attributes regardless of the code elements they are applied to. In order to apply an attribute to a field or property, that attribute must have been defined with `AttributeTargets` including `AttributeTargets.Field` and `AttributeTargets.Property` flags.

`DescriptionAttribute` and `CategoryAttribute` are useful for organizing component properties and events (the latter only appear in the Properties window in C#). `DescriptionAttribute` allows you to provide a brief description for a property, and `CategoryAttribute` facilitates categorical grouping of properties and events. When a property is selected in the Properties window, the value provided to the `Description` attribute is displayed at the bottom of the Properties window (see Figure 12.3). When the Categorized button is clicked in the Properties window, properties are organized by category.

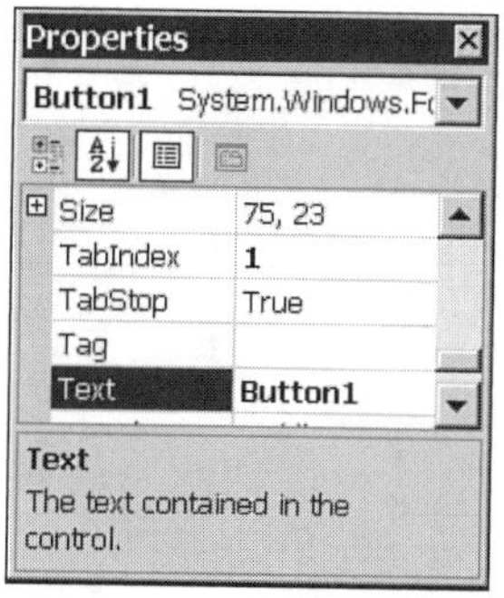

FIGURE 12.3

Description Attribute is read to display a description of component properties, as demonstrated for the `Button.Text` *property.*

To demonstrate using `DescriptionAttribute` and `CategoryAttribute`, we will take a slightly circuitous route. I will quickly demonstrate how to create a component, enabling you to see the end result: the description and categorization capabilities supported by the Properties window. (We will return to component building in Chapter 16, "Designing User Interfaces.")

Creating a Custom Component

Custom components are class library projects. To create the project for the custom component, select the Class Library project from the New Project dialog box.

The component we will create is a label that displays shadowy text. The effect is created by painting the text twice with a slightly offset contrast color. The component will need an additional color property, reflecting the contrasting color of the shadow.

To create the effect, we can overload the `Paint` method of a label control, painting the label's text at a slightly offset position using the shadow color. Listing 12.9 demonstrates how to subclass the `System.Windows.Forms.Label` control, adding the `ShadowColor` and the overloaded `Paint` method.

LISTING 12.9 A custom control used to demonstrate `DescriptionAttribute`

```
1:  Imports System.Windows.Forms
2:  Imports System.Drawing
3:  Imports System.ComponentModel
4:
5:  Public Class EffectsLabel
6:     Inherits Label
7:
8:     Private FShadowColor As Color = Color.WhiteSmoke
9:
10:    Private Const sDescription As String =
➥"Background color used to create the shadow effect."
```

LISTING 12.9 continued

```
11:    Private Const sCategory As String = "Appearance"
12:
13:
14:    Public Property ShadowColor() As Color
15:      Get
16:        Return FShadowColor
17:      End Get
18:      Set(ByVal Value As Color)
19:        If (Value.Equals(FShadowColor)) Then Exit Property
20:        FShadowColor = Value
21:        Invalidate()
22:      End Set
23:    End Property
24:
25:    Private Function ShadowBrush() As Brush
26:      Return New SolidBrush(FShadowColor)
27:    End Function
28:
29:    Protected Overrides Sub OnPaint( _
30:      ByVal e As PaintEventArgs)
31:
32:      Dim Rect As New RectangleF(-2, -2, Width, Height)
33:
34:      e.Graphics.DrawString(Text, Font, _
35:        ShadowBrush(), Rect, FormatObject())
36:
37:      MyBase.OnPaint(e)
38:
39:    End Sub
40:
41: #Region "These functions are monolithic. Replace with a better algorithm."
42:
43:    Private Function FormatObject() As StringFormat
44:      ' Note: Uses the function name as a temporary variable name!
45:      FormatObject = New StringFormat()
46:      SetLineAlignment(FormatObject)
47:      SetAlignment(FormatObject)
48:
49:      If (RightToLeft) Then
50:        FormatObject.FormatFlags = FormatObject.FormatFlags Or _
51:          StringFormatFlags.DirectionRightToLeft
52:      End If
53:    End Function
54:
55:    Private Sub SetLineAlignment(ByVal FormatObject As StringFormat)
56:      Select Case TextAlign ' Hideous algorithm!
57:        Case ContentAlignment.BottomLeft To _
58:          ContentAlignment.BottomRight
59:
```

LISTING 12.9 continued

```
60:          FormatObject.LineAlignment = StringAlignment.Far
61:
62:        Case ContentAlignment.MiddleLeft To _
63:          ContentAlignment.MiddleRight
64:
65:          FormatObject.LineAlignment = StringAlignment.Center
66:
67:        Case ContentAlignment.TopLeft To _
68:          ContentAlignment.TopRight
69:
70:          FormatObject.LineAlignment = StringAlignment.Near
71:      End Select
72:    End Sub
73:
74:    Private Sub SetAlignment(ByVal FormatObject As StringFormat)
75:      Select Case TextAlign ' Hideous algorithm!
76:        Case ContentAlignment.BottomLeft, _
77:          ContentAlignment.TopLeft, _
78:          ContentAlignment.MiddleLeft
79:
80:          FormatObject.Alignment = StringAlignment.Near
81:
82:        Case ContentAlignment.MiddleCenter, _
83:          ContentAlignment.BottomCenter, _
84:          ContentAlignment.TopCenter
85:
86:          FormatObject.Alignment = StringAlignment.Center
87:
88:        Case ContentAlignment.TopRight, _
89:          ContentAlignment.BottomRight, _
90:          ContentAlignment.MiddleRight
91:
92:          FormatObject.Alignment = StringAlignment.Far
93:      End Select
94:    End Sub
95:
96: #End Region
97:
98: End Class
```

The listing seems a little long; however, for the most part Listing 12.9 only introduces an overloaded Paint method and the ShadowColor property. ShadowColor is used to paint the background text. Unfortunately, lines 41 through 98 contain monolithic code to convert a ContentAlignment enumeration property describing both of the label's horizontal and vertical offsets to the individual horizontal StringFormat.Alignment and the vertical StringFormat.LineAlignment properties because a more convenient algorithm was not discovered.

The `Paint` method creates an offsetting rectangle on line 32. The rectangle and the `StringFormat` object returned by the `FormatObject` function on lines 43 to 53 are used as arguments to `DrawString` on lines 34 and 35. The call to `Graphics.DrawString` draws the string in the `ShadowColor` and then invokes the base method—`MyBase.OnPaint`, on line 37—to draw the foreground label text.

Applying the Description and Category Attribute

You can apply the `DescriptionAttribute` to properties and events. Because events do not show up in the Properties window in Visual Basic .NET (they do in Visual C#), we will add a `DescriptionAttribute` to our only property, `ShadowColor`.

Modify line 13 which was blank in Listing 12.9 to apply the `DescriptionAttribute` to the `ShadowColor` property. The `CategoryAttribute` was used to enable categorical organization of the property.

Tip

The attribute statement is actually part of the property statement. Either add attributes to the same thing to which they are applied or add attributes on a preceding line and include the line continuation character, the underscore.

```
<Description(sDescription), Category(sCategory)> _
```

Notice that the attributes are followed by the line continuation character (_), which allows you to break long lines of code for formatting purposes. Attributes are required to be on the same line as the entity they describe.

Adding the Custom Component to the Toolbox

The component can be added to the Toolbox by compiling the Class Library project. When you have compiled the component's assembly (.DLL file), create a new Windows application to test the component.

Follow the numbered steps to add the control to the Toolbox and test the control.

1. Select the default form's design view.
2. Select the Windows Forms Toolbox page, and click Customize Toolbox from the Toolbox's context menu.
3. With the Customize Toolbox open, select the .Net Framework Components tab.
4. Click the Browse button, and find the new component's assembly (the .DLL file).

5. When the assembly is added to the list of components, click the checkbox. (This step will add the control to the Toolbox.)

6. Close the Customize Toolbox dialog box.

Select the component from the Windows Forms Toolbox page and drop it on the form. The default effect should be an `EffectLabel` named `EffectLabel1` by default. Press F4 to display the Properties window. Select the `ShadowColor` property and verify that the description is displayed (see Figure 12.4).

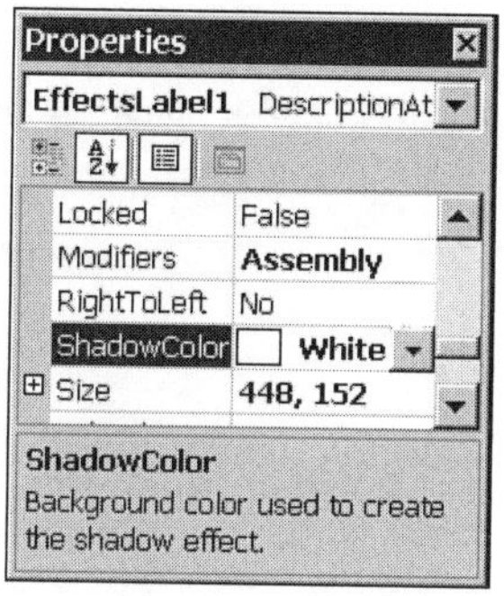

FIGURE 12.4
The result of adding `Description` `Attribute` *to a component's property.*

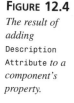

Viewing Attributes with the MSIL Disassembler

The MSIL Disassembler is an application that ships with the Framework SDK. The application name is ildasm.exe. By default this application is installed when you install the .NET framework into the \Program Files\Microsoft.NET\FrameworkSDK\Bin directory.

The ildasm.exe utility allows you to view an assembly's manifest and IL information. Part of this information is the attribute information applied to entities. Refer to Figure 12.2 for an example showing the `ConditionalAttribute` emitted to IL.

Extracting Attributes Using Reflection

You can discover and respond to attribute information programmatically using reflection. Chapter 6, "Reflection," provides an example demonstrating how to use reflection to extract attributes programmatically. Many of the reflection capabilities for managing attributes are also covered in Chapter 6. In this section I have included a brief example that demonstrates how to extract the URN associated with entities that use the `HelpAttribute` introduced earlier in this chapter.

Suppose you elected to extract `Help` attributes programmatically to facilitate displaying help information from a central repository. You could write generic code that read `HelpAttribute` URNs on demand and displayed the content referenced by the URN. Listing 12.10 demonstrates how to use reflection to extract the `URN` and `Topic` information programmatically.

LISTING 12.10 Using reflection to extract attribute information

```
1:    Private Overloads Sub DisplayAttribute(ByVal Obj As Object)
2:       Dim TypeInfo As Type = Obj.GetType
3:       Dim Attributes() As Object = _
4:         TypeInfo.GetCustomAttributes(GetType(HelpAttribute), False)
5:
6:       If (Attributes.Length > 0) Then
7:         Dim Help As HelpAttribute = _
8:            CType(Attributes(0), HelpAttribute)
9:         DisplayContent(Help.Urn)
10:      End If
11:   End Sub
12:
13:   Private Sub DisplayContent(ByVal URN As String)
14:      AxWebBrowser1.Navigate2(URN)
15:   End Sub
```

The code is an excerpt from HelpAttributeDemo.sln located on this book's Web site. The code is written to take a generic `Object` as a parameter to the `DisplayAttribute` method. `DisplayAttribute` retrieves type information for the `Obj` on line 2. From the `TypeInfo` object we are able to retrieve an array of attributes by calling `GetCustomAttribute`. Because this code was written to extract only `HelpAttribute` information, the type of attribute is expressed literally on line 4. If there are any attributes— line 6—the first generic attribute object returned by the `GetCustomAttributes` is typecast to a `HelpAttribute` object. When we have a `HelpAttribute` object, we can access the `Urn` property. (The example employs the Internet Explorer ActiveX control defined in the shdocvw.dll. Yes, this is a COM control.)

The two methods extract a URN added using a custom attribute and navigate to a Web document in 15 lines of code. Assuming that the application is on a LAN, the user is connected to the Internet, or the Help content ships with your application, you could use this technique to integrate help content into code that is not made up of components, just as VS .NET does. Tools like RoboHelp make it very easy to create rich HTML help content, but you could use a word processor such as Word or WordPerfect, or an HTML editing program such as FrontPage or Dreamweaver.

Creating Custom Attributes

First and foremost, attributes are classes that are subclassed from the `System.Attribute` class. The implication is that all the skills you have acquired can be used to generalize the `Attribute` class and define custom attributes.

Custom attributes allow third parties to participate in extending the .NET framework. To demonstrate creating custom attributes, I will walk you through creating the `HelpAttribute` introduced in the VS .NET documentation. Let's review a couple of guidelines for creating custom attributes first.

- Add the `Attribute` suffix to the attribute class name.
- Apply the `AttributeUsageAttribute` to the custom attribute class, indicating intended usage.
- Use positional arguments for required information.
- Use named parameters for optional information.
- Arguments should not be both named and positional.
- Use read-only properties for positional properties. (You can use the F prefix for the field and drop the F for the property name.)
- Include a readable and writable property for named arguments.

These guidelines are provided to facilitate custom attribute implementation and keep you out of trouble. Like any guidelines, they exist for your benefit, but you can experiment with slight variations and deviate from the guidelines if you have a good reason.

Implementing the `HelpAttribute`

The `HelpAttribute` sample class defined in this section was borrowed from the VS .NET help documentation. The original reference is located at `ms-help://MS.VSCC/MS.MSDNVS/cpguide/html/cpconwritingcustomattributes.htm#cpconcustomattributeexample`.

You can reference that document to find additional information on creating custom attributes. The specific requirements for creating custom attributes are covered here.

Declaring the Attribute Class

Attributes are used by other applications and effectively extend VS .NET resources. You will need to create a Class Library project to end up with a .DLL assembly. By default a Class Library template adds a .vb module with a class defined in it. This is what we need.

After you create the new Class Library, rename the project MyHelpAttribute and rename the class HelpAttribute. The result is a .vb module with the following lines of code:

```
Public Class HelpAttribute
End Class
```

The rest is almost as easy if you know what each step is and the role of each part of the process.

Specifying `AttributeUsage`

The next step is to indicate what entities the attribute will be used to describe. We want to allow developers to associate help with any code entity; hence we will indicate this information in AttributeUsageAttribute.

AttributeUsageAttribute defines one positional argument and supports two named arguments. The positional argument indicates the AttributeTargets, and the two named arguments are AllowMultiple and Inherited.

Using the `AttributeTargets` Argument

AttributeTargets describes the entities that the attribute can be applied to. AttributeTargets is an enumeration. (You can look it up in the help documentation for specifics, but the enumerations are just the names of kinds of code entities: Class, Property, Assembly, Enum, and so forth.)

To indicate that our attribute is suitable for all targets we can add AttributeUsageAttribute to our code, which evolves as follows:

```
<AttributeUsage(AttributeTargets.All)> Public Class HelpAttribute
End Class
```

Remember that by convention the Attribute suffix is dropped when applied.

Using the `AllowMultiple` Argument

AllowMultiple is a named argument. From the earlier guidelines, we know that named arguments are used for optional arguments. AllowMultiple is False by default; it indicates whether a given attribute can be applied more than once to the same entity. For our purposes, each entity only needs one help reference.

Attributes that are defined with `AllowMultiple:=True` are referred to as *multiuse attributes*. When `AllowMultiple:=False`, you have a *single-use attribute*.

Using the `Inherited` Argument

`Inherited` is a named argument. Recall that named arguments are passed using the `Name:=Value` syntax between the parentheses and after the positional arguments.

The `Inherited` named argument is False by default. `Inherited` indicates whether or not the attribute can be subclassed.

Inheriting from `System.Attribute`

After we have specified attribute usage, we need to indicate that we are generalizing, or subclassing, the attribute class. The attribute class we are developing evolves as shown.

```
<AttributeUsage(AttributeTargets.All)> Public Class HelpAttribute
  Inherits System.Attribute
End Class
```

Implementing the Constructor

We determined that the URN is a positional argument. That is, the URN is a required argument. Consequently this choice guides the implementation of our constructor. We also need a field to store the value in and a read-only property to provide public access to the underlying field.

Applying these choices, we can update the class:

```
<AttributeUsage(AttributeTargets.All)> Public Class HelpAttribute
  Inherits System.Attribute

  Private FUrn As String
  Public ReadOnly Property Urn() As String
    Get
      Return FUrn
    End Get
  End Property

  Public Sub New(ByVal AUrn As String)
    FUrn = AUrn
  End Sub

End Class
```

The revision adds the private field, using our F-prefix convention. The read-only property provides public access to the private field, also a convention we employ in object-oriented programming. Finally, the constructor specifies the required positional argument used to initialize the URN, or location, of the help content.

Adding Named Arguments

Finally, we can add named arguments to our attribute class. Named arguments are public fields or private fields represented by public readable and writable properties. (Notice that named arguments are writable.)

Generally, we use private fields and public properties. However, in this case we will deviate and simply add a public field to represent our named argument, `Topic`. As a final touch, I elected to make the positional argument optional and have `HelpAttribute` default to my Web site. (In your application you could have this attribute default to your root help document.) Listing 12.11 shows the completed attribute class.

LISTING 12.11 A completed `HelpAttribute` attribute class

```
 1: Imports System
 2:
 3: <AttributeUsage(AttributeTargets.All)> _
 4: Public Class HelpAttribute
 5:   Inherits Attribute
 6:
 7:   Private FUrn As String
 8:   Public Topic As String
 9:
10:   Public ReadOnly Property Urn() As String
11:     Get
12:       Return FUrn
13:     End Get
14:   End Property
15:
16:   Public Sub New(Optional ByVal AUrn As String _
17:     = "http://www.softconcepts.com")
18:     FUrn = AUrn
19:   End Sub
20:
21: End Class
```

The completed class is quite short, but the attribute allows us to tag any elements of code we choose with any documentation we want.

Component Attributes

There are dozens of attributes that we have not covered yet. You already know how to use attributes in general. The only thing you have to do is discover the attribute's name, determine its purpose and its positional and named arguments, and you will be able to subclass or employ those attributes.

To provide you with a starting point, several attributes that you might see in other sections of this book are listed by name.

There are several component attributes. These include the following:

BindableAttribute	DescriptionAttribute
BrowsableAttribute	DesignerAttribute
CategoryAttribute	DesignerSerializableAttribute
DefaultEventAttribute	EditorAttribute
DefaultPropertyAttribute	LocalizableAttribute
DefaultValueAttribute	TypeConverterAttribute

`DescriptionAttribute` and `CategoryAttribute` were demonstrated earlier in this chapter, and you can read Chapter 16, "Designing User Interfaces," for more examples of component building.

COM Interop Attributes

There are a dozen or so attributes that support COM interop. *COM interop* is the general name used to refer to the namespaces that support using COM in .NET and .NET assemblies in COM.

Summary

Chapter 12 should have made it clear that Visual Basic .NET is a significantly advanced version of its predecessor. There are analogies for many of the fundamental idioms between VB6 and Visual Basic .NET. Even attributes have analogies in VB6. If you ever opened a .frm or .cls file in VB6 in a text editor, you might have seen text like the following: `Attribute VB_PredeclaredId = True`. If you change this attribute manually to True in a .cls file, you end up with an autocreated class. Clearly this suggests that VB6 had precursors to .NET attributes. The difference is that Visual Basic .NET makes them intentionally accessible.

In addition to being accessible, attributes are greatly enhanced in .NET. Attributes provide users with a way to add metadata that is included with the emitted IL code and ships with the assembly. The attribute idiom enables individual developers to incorporate additional information and capabilities into the .NET framework.

12

DEFINING ATTRIBUTES

User Interface Design

IN THIS PART

Creating a Console Application

A console application is an executable program that runs in a command window. Although console applications are decreasing in popularity, you might still have occasion to write a standalone, formless executable that runs at a command prompt. With the incorporation of multithreading in Visual Basic .NET, a console application may be more useful than ever for writing utilities or unattended applications.

In many circumstances, you might want to write an NT Service, a Windows application without a user interface, or a .DLL service that can be managed by an application controller. Console applications are easy to implement because there is no user interface to design. A reasonable use for a console application might be to test code that will ultimately reside in a Windows application.

Chapter 13 provides you with an opportunity to experiment purely with code without forms. Chapter 13 describes features available for building console applications in Visual Basic .NET by implementing a file-sorting utility that—by the end of the chapter—is capable of sorting multiple text files at a time using a thread for each file.

This chapter will demonstrate how to define and implement a console application, use the `Console` namespace, and implement the `IComparer` interface to define customized sorting behavior. It will also provide more examples of multithreading.

Console Application Basics

Like VB6 Windows applications, a console application needs a `Sub Main` as the starting point for the application. In Visual Basic .NET, console applications have no graphical user interface (GUI), so there is no form to designate as the main form. Also different from Windows applications is the means by which a console application gets input from the operator. Generally,console applications are not interactive, so a console application is generally a linear application. The operator starts the program passing the name of a file or files or command-line arguments to the console application, and it runs from beginning to end without interrupt.

You certainly could define user interaction with a console application by using `Console.ReadLine` and `Console.Writeline`, but if you need much more than initial input values, you might want to implement a Windows application. We won't talk about interactive input and output in this chapter. All of the input will be derived from the command line. Let's begin by implementing a simple console application's `Sub Main` procedure.

Implementing Sub Main in a Module

You can select the Console Application template from the New Project dialog box as shown in Figure 13.1. When you select the Console Application template, provide a name for the project. The name you enter will be the namespace for the application. Click OK to generate the template solution containing a module containing a default Sub Main, References, and the AssemblyInfo.vb file (see Figure 13.2).

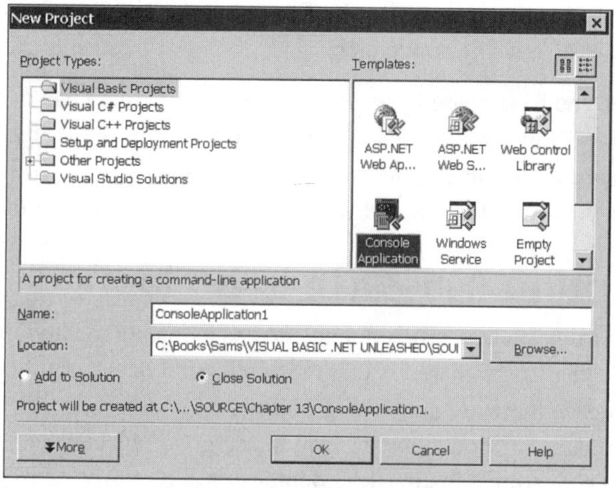

FIGURE 13.1

Select the Console Application template applet to start a formless, standalone executable project.

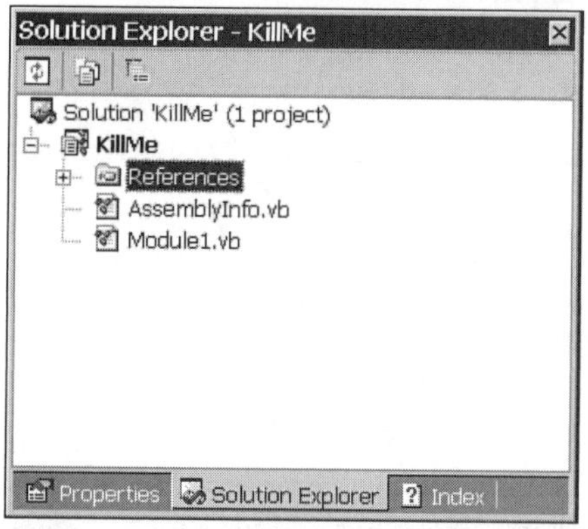

FIGURE 13.2

Basic elements of a console application include a default Module1.vb file containing the starting point, Sub Main.

The default module, named Module1.vb, contains a single module definition with one procedure, Sub Main.

```
Module Module1

  Sub Main()
```

```
    End Sub

End Module
```

When your console application runs, it begins by executing the first line of code after the line Sub Main().

Modules exist for familiarity in Visual Basic .NET. Essentially, a module is a class where all of the members are implicitly defined as Shared members. Add Console. WriteLine("Hello World!") between the Sub Main and End Sub lines and press F5 to define and run a basic console application.

Fortunately, after you have started your console application, you can add as much or as little as necessary to solve your problem. Two added benefits are that you can define and implement classes and use inheritance in console applications, and you can implement the starting point for your console application in a class rather than a module.

Implementing Sub Main in a Class

The Sub Main starting point can be implemented as a Shared method in a class. The reason that Sub Main has to be shared is that the application begins running at Sub Main and as a consequence there are no existing objects. Of course, you can create an object from the Shared Main method, allowing you to use good object-oriented programming even in console applications. Listing 13.1 demonstrates a revised console application that uses a Shared Sub Main as the application starting point.

LISTING 13.1   Define a class with a Shared Sub Main() to start console execution in a class

```
1:  Public Class Main
2:
3:    Public Shared Sub Main()
4:       Console.WriteLine("Hello Console World!")
5:       Threading.Thread.Sleep(2500)
6:    End Sub
7:
8:  End Class
```

Note

The call to Thread.Sleep in line 5 of Listing 13.1 was added to provide time to observe output. There is no additional benefit of Thread.Sleep here.

The very short program defines a `Shared` procedure named `Main` in a class with the same name. Before the application will begin executing in `Main.Main`, we will need to tell the IDE that `Main` is our startup object. To make `Main.Main` our startup object, open the Solution Explorer as shown in Figure 13.2. Right-click on the project name and select Properties from the context menu. In the Property Pages dialog box (see Figure 13.3), select the General page. Pick the `Main` class as the startup object as shown in the figure.

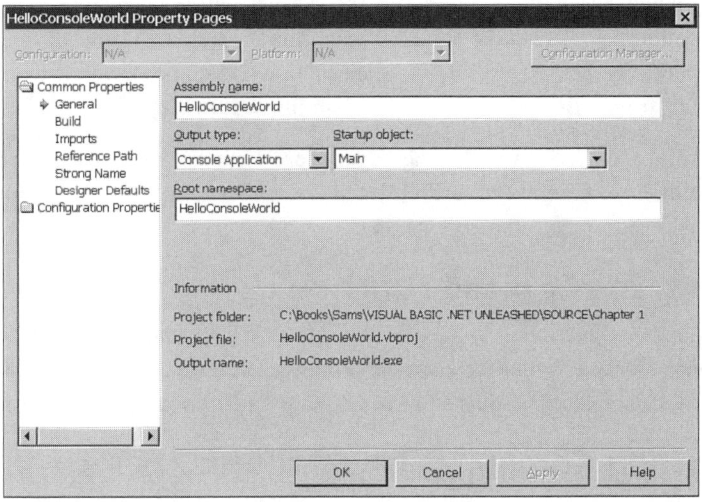

FIGURE 13.3
Use the General page of the Project Property Pages to indicate the startup object in a console application.

Now when you run the demo application, the program will begin executing in `Main.Main`. Keep a few things in mind at this point. First, the startup point for the program is a shared method in the class. There is no instance of `Main` when the startup procedure is running. You can elect to create an instance of the `Main` class if the class contains primary capabilities, or you can create an instance of any other class defining your application's primary capabilities. Second, the procedure must be a procedure named main having no parameters, and the procedure may be in a module or a shared procedure in a class. Finally, command-line arguments can be retrieved by calling the `Command` function.

Overloading `Sub Main`

If you implement the startup code in a class, you can overload the `Sub Main`. Add the `Overload` directive and any parameters you want to distinguish to the overloaded `Main` procedure. An empty procedure overloading the `Main` method in Listing 13.1 is defined as follows:

```
Sub Overloads Shared Sub Main( ByVal Message As String )
End Sub
```

If you added the Shared procedure to the Main class from Listing 13.1, you would need to add the Overloads modifier to the original startup procedure, too. You will not be able to designate the new Main as the startup procedure, but you could call the overload Main that takes a string parameter from the parameterless Main.

Retrieving Command-Line Arguments

Some languages allow you to define the startup routine in such a way as to indicate that command-line values are passed to the startup procedure. Visual Basic .NET returns command-line values via the Command function. If you are familiar with the Command$ function from VB6, this section will seem familiar to you.

Command in VB6 returns a String ValueType, which provides us with some additional capabilities you might find useful. Read the remainder of the section for a demonstration of parsing command-line arguments.

Using the Command Function

The Command function is defined in the Microsoft.VisualBasic namespace. The important thing to note is that the Command function returns a String, which means that you can use the capabilities of the String class to manipulate command-line arguments.

Splitting Command-Line Arguments into an Array

Often when you are creating a console application, you will read one or more arguments from the command line. Because the Command function returns the command-line arguments as a String object, we'll use String methods to manage command-line arguments rather than handcrafting custom command-line management tools.

In our sample application—FileSort.sln, not listed yet—we will be retrieving a list of files containing text to sort. In advance we will designate a comma as the file delimiter for the command line and use the String.Split method to split each comma-delimited filename passed by the user. Listing 13.2 demonstrates the Main startup procedure and the code that processes the command-line arguments.

LISTING 13.2 Using the String.Split method to parse the command-line arguments

```
 9:    Private Shared Sub ProcessEach(ByVal CommandLine As String)
10:
11:      Dim Files() As String = CommandLine.Split(",")
12:      Dim Enumerator As IEnumerator = Files.GetEnumerator
13:      While (Enumerator.MoveNext())
14:        If (ValidCommandLine(Enumerator.Current)) Then
```

LISTING 13.2   continued

```
15:          Sorter.Sort(Enumerator.Current)
16:        End If
17:      End While
18:
19:    End Sub
20:
21:    Public Shared Sub Process(ByVal CommandLine As String)
22:      If (Help.WantsHelp(CommandLine)) Then
23:        Help.Show()
24:
25:      Else
26:        ProcessEach(CommandLine)
27:      End If
28:
29:    End Sub
30:
31:    Public Shared Sub Main()
32:      Process(Command())
33:    End Sub
34:
35: End Class
```

Listing 13.2 is an excerpt from FileSort.sln and is listed using the line numbers in the order they appeared in the original listing before the revisions in Listing 13.3. Lines 31 to 32 define the Main procedure; keeping Main short is a convention employed in many languages and tools. In the listing, Main delegates processing to a procedure named Process, passing the command-line arguments as a string. Process is defined to scan the CommandLine argument to see if the user wants the help information. (Providing command-line help is not a requirement of any system, but you will see it employed via the -?, -h, or -help command-line arguments in many console applications. If the user does not want help (implementation of the help class is not shown), ProcessEach takes over and processes each argument in the command line.

13

CREATING A
CONSOLE
APPLICATION

> **Note**
>
> From the section "Employ Refactoring: Replace Temp with Query" in Chapter 3, "Basic Programming in Visual Basic .NET," you know that it is a good idea to replace the temporary Files in Listing 13.2 with a query. Because String.Split plays the role of query, we can and should consolidate lines 11 and 12 of Listing 13.2 to Dim Enumerator As IEnumerator = CommandLine.Split(",").GetEnumerator.

> After we have compiled and retested the code with the refactoring, we can remove the temporary Files.
>
> The code was listed in its verbose form for clarity during presentation but the refactored version is preferable.

ProcessEach is defined on lines 9 to 19. ProcessEach calls String.Split on line 11 to parse the CommandLine string into an array of strings, passing the command (,) character as the delimiter. Line 12 requests an IEnumerator from the array returned by Split. Line 11 creates a temporary array, Files, and line 12 returns the Enumerator from the array.

Lines 13 to 17 use the Enumerator and after making sure each argument is valid for the FileSort.exe, Sorter.Sort is called for each filename passed to the command-line.

Working with Delimited Arguments

The FileSort.exe application anticipates the command line to take the following form: FileSort text1.txt,text2.txt,text3.txt. However, for practical applications, you can reasonably anticipate a desire for more flexibility. When building practical applications, you have a couple of choices: try to strangle the user into a perfect syntax, or relax the syntax requirement to make the application easier to use.

If you are the only user and are writing a utility for yourself, you may be aware of the syntax, and the cost of adding flexibility outweighs the benefit. In this case, write the simplest implementation possible. A real user might not appreciate having to provide a perfect syntax, though. If you are writing for other users, add some flexibility.

What would happen if the user typed something like FileSort text1.txt, text2.txt, text3.txt? (Note just the reasonable introduction of spaces after the comma.) The ProcessEach method would pass " text2.txt" to the Sorter.Sort method; that is, the filename would be preceded with a space and might not be a valid filename. To resolve this problem, you could trim the filename when it is passed to the ValidCommandLine and Sort methods. As an alternative, you could refine the call to Split, indicating that spaces might reasonably be in the command line.

Condensing and refining the call to Split from Listing 13.2 yields a replacement for lines 11 and 12:

```
11: Dim Enumerator As IEnumerator = _
12:   CommandLine.Split(", ".ToCharArray()).GetEnumerator()
```

Keep in mind that the literal ", " is converted to an implicit String object. ToCharArray() is being invoked on the implicit String created from the literal, and

GetEnumerator is being invoked on the array of strings returned by Split. The new statement resolves the problem of additional delimiters, but the code is verbose and might be difficult to maintain because it is not very readable. Instead of removing the verbose code, introducing a lot of temporaries, or adding lengthy comments, we can introduce a query method that indicates what the code does and means. Query methods are preferable to monolithic code, temporary variables, and comments. Listing 13.3 demonstrates a revision that wraps the monolithic code in a method and removes all temporaries.

LISTING 13.3   A revision of Listing 13.2 that removes temporaries and wraps monolithic statements into a well-named function method

```
9:    Private Shared Function GetEnumerator(ByVal CommandLine As String)
➡As IEnumerator
10:     Return Command.Split(", ".ToCharArray()).GetEnumerator
11:   End Function
12:
13:   Private Overloads Shared Sub ProcessEach(ByVal CommandLine As String)
14:     ProcessEach(GetEnumerator(CommandLine))
15:   End Sub
16:
17:   Private Overloads Shared Sub ProcessEach(ByVal Enumerator As IEnumerator)
18:     While (Enumerator.MoveNext())
19:       If (ValidCommandLine(Enumerator.Current)) Then
20:         Sorter.Sort(Enumerator.Current)
21:       End If
22:     End While
23:   End Sub
24:
25:   Public Shared Sub Process(ByVal CommandLine As String)
26:     If (Help.WantsHelp(CommandLine)) Then
27:       Help.Show()
28:
29:     Else
30:       ProcessEach(CommandLine)
31:     End If
32:
33:   End Sub
34:
35:   Public Shared Sub Main()
36:     Process(Command())
37:   End Sub
```

Listing 13.3 introduces a query method that clearly indicates we are deriving an IEnumerator from the CommandLine. GetEnumerator is a private method. Producers will be the only ones modifying private methods; any producer that wants to modify

GetEnumerator can determine its behavior from the name and parameter and can take some initiative in understanding how it works. Lines 13 to 15 and 17 to 23 provide two overloaded methods (ProcessEach) for processing each command-line argument. Process is unmodified and Sub Main remains unmodified.

Keep in mind that we could have used temporaries, comments, or left the verbose statement (line 10) in a single ProcessEach method. Our motivation for choosing a query method is straightforward: no temporaries, no comments, and the verbose statement is commented by the encapsulating query method. The final benefit of the query method GetEnumerator is that methods are reusable, but statements, comments, and temporaries are not.

There is no enforcing body that requires you to program in a way consistent with Listing 13.3, but there are supporting reasons for doing so. Until there is a standards body enforcing how code is written, you can write code any way that you want. (Such an enforcement body might ultimately base qualitative assessments on refactorings.) In the absence of an enforcement body, you are protecting yourself from digititis or carpal tunnel syndrome by writing less code and more reusable code.

Using the `Console` Class

When you are creating a console application, the Console class in the System namespace contains several shared properties and methods that facilitate working with the standard input and output device, generally the keyboard and console window. Table 13.1 lists the members of the Console class.

TABLE 13.1 Members of the System.Console Class

Member	*Description*
Shared Properties	
Error	The standard error output stream
In	The standard input stream
Out	The standard output stream
Shared Methods	
OpenStandardError	Acquires the error stream
OpenStandardInput	Acquires the input stream
OpenStandardOutput	Acquires the output stream
Read	Reads the next character in the input stream
ReadLine	Reads the next line from the input stream

TABLE 13.1 continued

Member	Description
Shared Methods	
SetError	Assigns an output stream to the error property
SetIn	Assigns an input stream to the In property
SetOut	Assigns an output stream to the Out property
Write	Writes information to the output stream
WriteLine	Writes the specified data to the output stream followed by the line terminator

Notice that the members of the Console class are all shared. The console generally consists of the keyboard and display screen (although other devices can be assigned as the standard input and output devices), and for practical purposes, there is only one console. Consequently, the Console class behaves like a Singleton; that is, because there is only one console and the console does not maintain any state, all of the members are shared.

Reading from and Writing to the Standard Input/Output Devices

The easiest way to implement line-based input and output from a console application is to use the Console.ReadLine method for input and Console.WriteLine for output.

By default, ReadLine returns a line of text from the keyboard after the user presses the Enter key, and WriteLine adds a carriage-return/linefeed pair after the line of text sent to the display device. Listing 13.4 is a console application in Console.sln on this book's Web site that provides you with some console code to experiment with that demonstrates reading and writing to the standard devices.

LISTING 13.4 Command-line sorting

```
1:  Imports System.Threading
2:
3:  Public Class Sort
4:
5:  #Region " Public Methods "
6:     Public Sub New(ByVal Args() As String)
7:        Data = Args
8:     End Sub
9:
10:    Public Sub BubbleSort()
11:       Dim I, J As Integer
```

LISTING 13.4 continued

```
12:
13:    For I = Data.GetLowerBound(0) To Data.GetUpperBound(0) - 1
14:      For J = I + 1 To Data.GetUpperBound(0)
15:        If (Data(I) > Data(J)) Then
16:          Dim Temp As Object
17:          Temp = Data(I)
18:          Data(I) = Data(J)
19:          Data(J) = Temp
20:        End If
21:      Next
22:    Next
23:   End Sub
24:
25:   Public Shared Sub Run()
26:     Sort.DoCommand(GetInput().Split(", ".ToCharArray()))
27:   End Sub
28:
29:   Public Shared Sub DoCommand(ByVal Args() As String)
30:     Dim Sorter As New Sort(Args)
31:     Dim NewThread As New Thread(AddressOf Sorter.Process)
32:     NewThread.Start()
33:   End Sub
34:
35: #End Region
36:
37: #Region " Private Methods "
38:   Private Data() As String
39:
40:   Private Sub Process()
41:     BubbleSort()
42:     Display()
43:   End Sub
44:
45:   Private Sub Display()
46:     Dim Enumerator As IEnumerator = Data.GetEnumerator
47:     While Enumerator.MoveNext
48:       System.Console.WriteLine(Enumerator.Current)
49:     End While
50:   End Sub
51:
52:   Private Shared Sub Prompt()
53:     Const Text As String = _
54:       "Enter comma delimited list to sort:  "
55:     System.Console.Write(Text)
56:   End Sub
57:
58:   Private Shared Function GetInput() As String
59:     If (Command() = vbNullString) Then
60:       Prompt()
```

LISTING 13.4   continued

```
61:        Return System.Console.ReadLine()
62:      Else
63:        Return Command()
64:      End If
65:    End Function
66: #End Region
67:
68: End Class
69:
70: Module Module1
71:
72:    Sub Main()
73:      Sort.Run()
74:      Thread.Sleep(2500)
75:    End Sub
76:
77: End Module
```

The entire application is contained to Module1.vb. The module file contains a Module containing a very short startup Main procedure. Main invokes the shared method Sort. Run. The Public methods are defined in the Region between lines 5 and 35. There are only four public methods, making the class—also defined in the Module1.vb file—relatively easy to use. Run calls GetInput, which returns the command-line argument if there is one or prompts the user for input if the Command function returns a vbNullString. The returned input, whether from the command line or returned from the ReadLine method, is parsed using the String.Split method and passed to the shared method DoCommand. DoCommand constructs an instance of the Sort class and sorts the input on its own thread. After the BubbleSort is called, the string-sorted input is written to the standard output device using an IEnumerator and Console.WriteLine. The sample program demonstrates using ReadLine, WriteLine, and Write.

13

CREATING A
CONSOLE
APPLICATION

> **Note**
>
> It is not necessary to write your own sort. System.Array implements a shared Sort method. Pass an array to the System.Array.Sort shared method, replacing the call to BubbleSort, to sort the array of strings referenced by Data in Listing 13.4.

A final note on the code in Listing 13.4. When shared members of the Console class were used, notice that the System namespace was prefixed to the class name Console. This was done to avoid ambiguity between the namespace given to the sample application when it was created as Console.sln and the `Console` class in the `System` namespace. You can use the fully qualified namespace statement to clarify references to classes with the same name residing in different namespaces.

Writing to the Error Device

The `Error` device (see Table 13.1) by default is the same device as the default `Out` device, the display adapter. If you use the `Console.Error` shared property to differentiate writing output versus writing error messages, you can elect to change the default `Out` or `Error` device. Listing 13.5 demonstrates a revision to Console.sln that writes an error message to the standard error device.

LISTING 13.5 Writing an error message to the `Error` device

```
1:  Private Shared Sub Validate(ByVal Input As String)
2:
3:     Const Text As String = "Syntax: console 1,2,3,4,...,n"
4:
5:     If (Input = vbNullString) Then
6:        System.Console.Error.WriteLine(Text)
7:        End
8:     End If
9:
10: End Sub
11:
12: Private Shared Function GetInput() As String
13:    If (Command() = vbNullString) Then
14:      Prompt()
15:      GetInput = System.Console.ReadLine()
16:    Else
17:      GetInput = Command()
18:    End If
19:
20:    Validate(GetInput)
21:    Return GetInput
22: End Function
```

Tip

Use the function name if you really need a temporary variable, for example, for validation.

The revised code performs validation on the input. If `Validate` determines that `Input` is a `vbNullString`, the `Error` property—a `TextWriter` object—is used to write a syntax example to the error device and the application is terminated. Validate is defined on lines 1 through 10.

If you need a temporary variable to hold a calculated return value, as demonstrated in GetInput, you can use the function name as a temporary instead of introducing a new temporary. The function will not return until the end of the procedure or execution reaches a Return statement.

Changing the Error Device

The Console.Error property is a TextWriter object. By assigning an instance of a System.IO.TextWriter to the Error property, you can redirect error output from the default error device, the console, to an alternate instance of a TextWriter. (TextWriter is an abstract class, so you must choose a subclass of TextWriter.) Listing 13.6 demonstrates assigning the Error property to an instance of the System.IO.StreamWriter class that encapsulates a file stream. As a result, error output is written to a file rather than the console, allowing the behavior of your code to change without changing your code.

LISTING 13.6   Redirecting error output to a file stream, System.IO.StreamWriter

```
1:  Module Module1
2:
3:     Private NewError As System.IO.StreamWriter
4:
5:     Sub SetErrorDevice()
6:       NewError = New System.IO.StreamWriter("error.log")
7:       NewError.AutoFlush = True
8:       System.Console.SetError(NewError)
9:     End Sub
10:
11:    Sub Main()
12:      SetErrorDevice()
13:      Sort.Run()
14:      Thread.Sleep(2500)
15:    End Sub
16:
17: End Module
```

Tip

One requirement necessary to allow Console redirection is to have UnmanagedCode permissions. Refer to Chapter 12, "Defining Attributes," for more on security permissions and attributes.

Revising Listing 13.4's `Module1`, we add a procedure called `SetErrorDevice`. The new procedure creates an instance of the `StreamWriter` class and calls the constructor with a suitable filename. `AutoFlush` is set to `True` to ensure that the stream is automatically flushed, that is, written to the file. If you forget to set `AutoFlush` to `True`, the file will be created on line 6, but there may be no data written to disk.

The `Console.Error` property is `ReadOnly`, so we must use the `SetError` method to intentionally redirect the `Error` device output to an alternate stream. (If you want to redirect the `Console.In`, `Console.Out`, and `Console.Error` devices to an alternate device, you have to explicitly call `SetIn`, `SetOut`, and `SetError`. This explicit method call was probably designed intentionally to avoid accidental console redirection.)

Defining the `FileSort` Demo

Console applications these days are typically simple utility applications. Dynamic link libraries and executables with interfaces are probably better candidates for more complicated applications, although no limitation is imposed by the language except for the absence of graphical interface controls. With the addition of multithreading, the complexity and variety of console applications is likely to increase rather than the opposite. However, in keeping with the utility theme, we will create a multithreaded sort utility application.

The sample application adds an additional twist you might find helpful. There is a lot of legacy data still in existence. Big corporations with demanding data needs are working with data that is moved back and forth between mainframes with older data formats and newer client/server systems. Whether this is the best way to manage the data stored in legacy systems or not is questionable; it is a practical problem. The solution assumes that it may be beneficial to provide a flexible modus for defining how the data is sorted.

The FileSort.sln sample application allows you to pass multiple files at the command line and sort each file on its own thread. In addition to sorting the files on individual threads and avoiding shorter files waiting on longer files, the sample application demonstrates how to implement a comparator apart from the core solution.

Using `TextReader`

FileSort.sln validates multiple files passed to the application on the command line. For each valid file, `FileSort` reads the file contents into an `ArrayList` and uses the shared `Sort` method of `System.Array` to sort the data. It is reasonable to assume that you might want to perform different kinds of comparisons on the data and order the data in ascending or descending order based on predetermined criteria. It is the comparison process that guides the ordering of data, so we will use the `IComparer` interface rather than implementing alternate sorts to manage the sort order.

To get data into the `ArrayList`, we will assume that the data is represented by lines of text, and we will use the methods of the `ArrayList` and `TextReader` classes to read and cache data in text files. The complete solution to the FileSort.sln is shown in Listing 13.7, and excerpts describing the various aspects of the solution are described in the subsections that follow.

LISTING 13.7   The complete listing to the multithreaded FileSort.sln sample program, demonstrating sorting lines of text and implementing the `IComparer` interface

```
1:  Imports System.IO
2:
3:  Public Class Main
4:
5:    Private Overloads Shared Function ValidCommandLine( _
6:      ByVal CommandLine As String) As Boolean
7:      Return Sorter.Valid(CommandLine)
8:    End Function
9:
10:   Private Shared Function GetEnumerator( _
11:     ByVal CommandLine As String) As IEnumerator
12:     Return Command.Split(", ".ToCharArray()).GetEnumerator
13:   End Function
14:
15:   Private Overloads Shared Sub ProcessEach( _
16:    ByVal CommandLine As String)
17:     ProcessEach(GetEnumerator(CommandLine))
18:   End Sub
19:
20:   Private Overloads Shared Sub ProcessEach( _
21:     ByVal Enumerator As IEnumerator)
22:     While (Enumerator.MoveNext())
23:       If (ValidCommandLine(Enumerator.Current)) Then
24:         Sorter.Sort(Enumerator.Current)
25:       End If
26:     End While
27:   End Sub
28:
29:   Public Shared Sub Process(ByVal CommandLine As String)
30:     If (Help.WantsHelp(CommandLine)) Then
31:       Help.Show()
32:     Else
33:       ProcessEach(CommandLine)
34:     End If
35:   End Sub
36:
```

LISTING 13.7 continued

```
37:    Public Shared Sub Main()
38:       Process(Command())
39:    End Sub
40: End Class
41:
42: Public Class Sorter
43:    Private FFileName As String
44:    Private FData As ArrayList
45:
46:    Public Property FileName() As String
47:      Get
48:         Return FFileName
49:      End Get
50:      Set(ByVal Value As String)
51:         FFileName = Value
52:      End Set
53:    End Property
54:
55:    Public Sub New(ByVal AFileName As String)
56:      FData = New ArrayList()
57:      FFileName = AFileName
58:    End Sub
59:
60:    Public Sub Read()
61:      Dim Reader As TextReader = File.OpenText(FFileName)
62:
63:      Try
64:        While Reader.Peek <> -1
65:          FData.Add(Reader.ReadLine)
66:        End While
67:
68:      Finally
69:         Reader.Close()
70:      End Try
71:
72:    End Sub
73:
74:    Private Sub WriteElapsedTime(ByVal Elapsed As Double)
75:      Debug.WriteLine(String.Format("Elapsed milliseconds: {0} ", Elapsed))
76:    End Sub
77:
78:    Public Sub TimedSort()
79:      Dim Start As Double = Timer
80:      Sort()
81:      WriteElapsedTime(Timer - Start)
82:    End Sub
83:
84:    Public Sub Sort()
85:      FData.Sort(New StringComparer())
```

LISTING **13.7**   continued

```
86:    End Sub
87:
88:    Private Function TempFileName() As String
89:      Return "..\" & Path.GetFileName(Path.GetTempFileName)
90:    End Function
91:
92:    Public Sub Write()
93:      Dim Writer As TextWriter = File.CreateText(TempFileName())
94:      Dim Enumerator As IEnumerator = FData.GetEnumerator
95:
96:      Try
97:        While Enumerator.MoveNext
98:          Writer.WriteLine(Enumerator.Current)
99:        End While
100:
101:      Finally
102:        Writer.Close()
103:      End Try
104:
105:    End Sub
106:
107:    Private Sub Run()
108:      Read()
109:      TimedSort()
110:      Write()
111:    End Sub
112:
113:    Public Shared Sub Sort(ByVal FileName As String)
114:      Dim Instance As New Sorter(FileName)
115:      Dim Thread As New Threading.Thread(AddressOf Instance.Run)
116:      Thread.Start()
117:    End Sub
118:
119:    Public Shared Function Valid(ByVal CommandLine As String) As Boolean
120:      Return System.IO.File.Exists(CommandLine)
121:    End Function
122:
123: End Class
124:
125: Public Class Help
126:    Private Shared Function ContainsHelpSwitch( _
127:      ByVal CommandLine As String) As Boolean
128:
129:      Return CommandLine.IndexOf("-?") > -1 Or _
130:        CommandLine.ToUpper.IndexOf("-H") > -1 Or _
131:        CommandLine.ToUpper.IndexOf("-HELP") > -1 Or CommandLine = ""
132:
133:    End Function
134:
```

LISTING **13.7**   continued

```
135:   Public Shared Function WantsHelp(ByVal CommandLine As String) As Boolean
136:      Return ContainsHelpSwitch(CommandLine)
137:   End Function
138:
139:   Public Shared Function Usage() As String
140:      Return _
141:        "Usage: filesort filename.txt | [-h,-?-help] " & vbCrLf & _
142:        "Sorts lines of text in file" & vbCrLf & _
143:        "-h|-?-help - Displays the help message" & vbCrLf
144:   End Function
145:
146:   Public Shared Sub Show()
147:      Console.WriteLine(Usage())
148:   End Sub
149: End Class
150:
151: Public Class StringComparer
152:   Implements IComparer
153:
154:   Public Function Compare(ByVal x As Object, _
155:     ByVal y As Object) As Integer _
156:     Implements System.Collections.IComparer.Compare
157:     Try
158:       Return String.Compare(x.ToString.Substring(0, 3), _
159:          y.ToString.Substring(0, 3))
160:     Catch
161:       Return String.Compare(x.ToString, y.ToString)
162:     End Try
163:   End Function
164: End Class
```

Tip

If you type this code from scratch, remember to make a public, shared subroutine named Main the startup subroutine. Visual Studio .NET should prompt you for this information.

The Read method is an instance method that assumes that FFileName contains a valid filename and creates an instance of a TextReader initializing the TextReader with the FFileName field value. The resource protection block, represented by the Try.. Finally..End Try block on lines 62 to 70, ensures that the reader is closed. In the listing, we are using the Finally clause to ensure that the TextReader—the file—is closed; see line 69. The While..End While loop ensures that we read all lines. Reader.Peek <> -1 checks for the end of the file. `Peek` returns the next character in the stream; when `Peek` returns `-1`, we have reached the end of the file. The `ReadLine` method reads a single line of text and `FData.Add` inserts the line into the `ArrayList` object represented by the name `FData`.

Lines 60 through 72 demonstrate one means of reading an entire text file. For practical solutions you might need to devise a cleverer means of caching, sorting, and managing text data. The sample solution shown worked reasonably well on a 250MB file, containing approximately 2.7 million rows of exported data on a PC with 256MB of RAM.

There are several shared members in the `System.IO.File` class. The online help documentation and experimentation will allow you to discover several of these methods. The shared method `File.OpenText` returns a `TextReader` instance. To write the sorted file back to disk, we will use an instance of `TextWriter`.

Using `TextWriter`

`System.IO.File.CreateText` returns an instance of the `TextWriter` class. `TextWriter` objects are used to write text to disk files. The `TextWriter` class is an abstract class—has the `MustInherit` modifier—and `CreateText` returns an instance of a subclass of `TextWriter`, `StreamWriter`.

```
92:    Public Sub Write()
93:       Dim Writer As TextWriter = File.CreateText(TempFileName())
94:       Dim Enumerator As IEnumerator = FData.GetEnumerator
95:
96:       Try
97:          While Enumerator.MoveNext
98:             Writer.WriteLine(Enumerator.Current)
99:          End While
100:
101:       Finally
102:          Writer.Close()
103:       End Try
104:
105:    End Sub
```

Writing the sorted file back to disk is the reverse of the read process. An excerpt from Listing 13.7 on lines 92 to 105 retrieves an instance of a `TextWriter` by calling the shared method `File.CreateText` and calling the `System.IO.Path.GetTempFilename` to ensure that we create a unique output file. The enumerator returned by `ArrayList.GetEnumerator` is used to iterate each element of the `ArrayList` and the `TextWriter.WriteLine` method is used to write the line of text to the new output file. The result is that we have the original file and the new sorted file.

Getting a Temporary File

The System.IO.Path class contains the GetTempFileName method that returns a unique filename. Like many methods in .NET, the CLR implements capabilities that used to be accessed by API calls as members of classes defined in suitable namespaces. The Path class defines several shared methods described in Table 13.2.

TABLE 13.2   Shared Members of the System.IO.Path Class

Member	Description
Shared Fields	
AltDirectorySeparatorChar	Platform-specific alternate directory separator
DirectorySeparatorChar	Platform-specific directory separator
InvalidPathChars	Platform-specific list of invalid path characters
PathSeparator	Platform-specific directory separator
VolumeSeparatorChar	Platform-specific volume separator
Shared Methods	
ChangeExtension	Changes the file extension
Combine	Combines two file paths
GetDirectoryName	Returns path without the filename
GetExtension	Returns a file extension
GetFileName	Returns the filename, including the extension
GetFileNameWithoutExtension	Returns a filename without the extension
GetFullPath	Expands the path argument to the full path
GetPathRoot	Returns the root of the path
GetTempFileName	Returns a unique filename and creates an empty file on the disk
GetTempPath	Returns the path to your system temporary directory
HasExtension	Indicates if the path contains a file extension
IsPathRooted	Indicates if the path contains the root

As demonstrated by the members in Table 13.2, the CLR plays the role that Windows API declarations play in VB6. If you are looking for a method that you used to include using an API method, check namespaces and classes in the CLR.

Using the `IEnumerator` Interface

The section "Using Array Methods" in Chapter 3 introduced the `IEnumerator` interface. The `IEnumerator` interface introduces three members, `MoveNext`, `Current`, and `Reset`, that offer a consistent interface for iterating the elements of a class that contains multiple objects, like the `ArrayList`.

Any class that implements the `IEnumerator` class can be passed to methods that expect an `IEnumerator` and can be used in a loop (see lines 22 to 26 and 97 to 99 in Listing 13.7) consistent with the examples in Listing 13.7. Additionally, it is important to remember that methods and classes are reusable, whereas statements are not. Any class that implements the `IEnumerator` interface can be passed as a value to a method that has an `IEnumerator` parameter.

Sorting an `ArrayList`

The `ArrayList` implements an instance `Sort` method. You can sort the entire array, a subsection of the array, or pass an `IComparer` object to describe how the comparison works. The three overloaded `ArrayList.Sort` procedure headers follow:

```
Overloads Overridable Public Sub Sort()
Overloads Overridable Sub Sort(IComparer)
Overloads Overridable Public Sort(Integer, Integer, IComparer)
```

The `Sort` method implements the quick sort algorithm, which has $O(n \log_2 n)$ characteristics. The value n represents the number of elements and the order-of-magnitude is a mathematical description of the performance of the algorithm. Simplistically, a quick sort takes n multiplied by the log base 2 of n units of time. Quick sorts decay to roughly the performance characteristics of a bubble sort, which is $O(n^2)$, or n-squared, if the elements are already sorted.

The first implementation of `Sort` uses the default implementation of the `IComparer` interface in each element in the `ArrayList`. The second implementation allows you to pass an object that implements `IComparer`, and the third method allows you to selectively sort a range of elements using a custom class that implements `IComparer`.

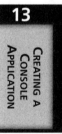

13

CREATING A
CONSOLE
APPLICATION

Implementing the `IComparer` Interface

Listing 13.7 uses a custom class `StringComparer` that implements the `IComparer` interface to sort the lines of text based on field offsets. The only method in the `IComparer` interface is a `Compare` function that returns a negative number to indicate if argument x is less than argument y, 0 if the arguments are equal, and a positive number if argument x is greater than y. However, you can implement the comparison any way you want to. In

Listing 13.7, an exception block is used to prevent failure. The first three characters are compared as a string. If either x or y represents a string less than three characters long, a straight string comparison is performed. Lines 158 and 159 demonstrate how to compare a substring.

Keep in mind that x and y can represent any kind of data. Listing 13.7 is designed with the foreknowledge that the class will be comparing strings. Line 85 of Listing 13.7 demonstrates how to construct an instance of the StringComparer class and pass it to the ArrayList.Sort method.

Console Application Namespaces

When you create a new console application, the Console Application template includes the System, System.Data, and System.XML namespaces by default. You do not get System.Window.Forms, precluding access to classes that allow you to define a GUI and the Application class.

System.Data includes classes in the ADO.NET architecture, allowing you to access data. System.XML offers classes for processing XML, and the System namespace is a core namespace in the CLR and includes access to classes like the Console class used throughout this chapter.

Note

To clearly show where some capabilities came from, Listing 13.7 uses the complete path at a couple of locations. Line 120 uses the complete path to the shared methods Exists. We could have skipped the System.IO portion of the namespace because we imported that namespace at the top of the module. Line 156 uses the complete System.Collections.IComparer.Compare path to indicate that StringComparer implements the Compare interface.

Tip

Other languages in .NET do not support including a class or interface name in an Imports statement. C# (C-sharp) requires that an Imports statement only include namespaces.

If you need additional capabilities, you can add an `Imports` statement at the top of the module that needs a particular namespace or add the namespace on the Imports page of the Property Pages dialog box. Listing 13.7 imports the `System.IO` namespace.

Multithreading a Console Application

The `FileSort` application is a utility application that sorts the contents of text files. The intent is that the text files contain fixed-length records, each record represented by a line of text, and we want to sort the lines of text by some subfields in the line of text. Perhaps the text file is an exported table from a legacy database.

The example presumes that there might be very large and very small files and some further processing—like loading the rows into a relational database—will be performed on the data. To ensure that shorter files do not get stuck behind longer files, we elected to allow the user to specify several files on the command line and thread the sort process. Each file is sorted on its own thread.

From Listing 13.7, we can determine that the `Main.ProcessEach` is defined to enumerate the list of command-line arguments and process each argument that represents a valid command line argument. (For our purposes, `ValidCommandLine` ensures that the argument is an existing file. Refer to lines 5 through 8 and lines 119 through 121 of Listing 13.7 for the implementation of command-line validation.) If an element of the command line is an existing file, the shared method `Sorter.Sort` is called.

```
20:    Private Overloads Shared Sub ProcessEach( _
21:      ByVal Enumerator As IEnumerator)
22:      While (Enumerator.MoveNext())
23:        If (ValidCommandLine(Enumerator.Current)) Then
24:          Sorter.Sort(Enumerator.Current)
25:        End If
26:      End While
27:    End Sub
```

The preceding fragment from Listing 13.7 calls the shared method in the `Sorter` class. `Sorter` creates an instance of itself and creates and starts a thread to perform the actual sorting (see Listing 13.8).

LISTING 13.8 The `Sorter` class performs the file sort on a separate thread as demonstrated

```
42: Public Class Sorter
43:    Private FFileName As String
```

LISTING 13.8   continued

```
44:   Private FData As ArrayList
45:
46:   Public Property FileName() As String
47:     Get
48:       Return FFileName
49:     End Get
50:     Set(ByVal Value As String)
51:       FFileName = Value
52:     End Set
53:   End Property
54:
55:   Public Sub New(ByVal AFileName As String)
56:     FData = New ArrayList()
57:     FFileName = AFileName
58:   End Sub
59:
60:   Public Sub Read()
61:     Dim Reader As TextReader = File.OpenText(FFileName)
62:
63:     Try
64:       While Reader.Peek <> -1
65:         FData.Add(Reader.ReadLine)
66:       End While
67:
68:       Finally
69:         Reader.Close()
70:     End Try
71:
72:   End Sub
73:
74:   Private Sub WriteElapsedTime(ByVal Elapsed As Double)
75:     Debug.WriteLine(String.Format("Elapsed milliseconds: {0} ", Elapsed))
76:   End Sub
77:
78:   Public Sub TimedSort()
79:     Dim Start As Double = Timer
80:     Sort()
81:     WriteElapsedTime(Timer - Start)
82:   End Sub
83:
84:   Public Sub Sort()
85:     FData.Sort(New StringComparer())
86:   End Sub
87:
88:   Private Function TempFileName() As String
89:     Return "..\" & Path.GetFileName(Path.GetTempFileName)
```

LISTING 13.8 continued

```
 90:   End Function
 91:
 92:   Public Sub Write()
 93:     Dim Writer As TextWriter = File.CreateText(TempFileName())
 94:     Dim Enumerator As IEnumerator = FData.GetEnumerator
 95:
 96:     Try
 97:       While Enumerator.MoveNext
 98:         Writer.WriteLine(Enumerator.Current)
 99:       End While
100:
101:     Finally
102:       Writer.Close()
103:     End Try
104:
105:   End Sub
106:
107:   Private Sub Run()
108:     Read()
109:     TimedSort()
110:     Write()
111:   End Sub
112:
113:   Public Shared Sub Sort(ByVal FileName As String)
114:     Dim Instance As New Sorter(FileName)
115:     Dim Thread As New Threading.Thread(AddressOf Instance.Run)
116:     Thread.Start()
117:   End Sub
118:
119:   Public Shared Function Valid(ByVal CommandLine As String) As Boolean
120:     Return System.IO.File.Exists(CommandLine)
121:   End Function
122:
123: End Class
```

The shared Sort method takes a FileName argument (lines 113 to 117) and creates an instance of the Sorter class, initializing the FFileName field. Fulfilling the requirements of threading (refer to Chapter 14, "Multithreaded Applications," for more on writing multithreaded VB applications), we must create an instance of the Thread class, passing a Delegate. Line 115 creates the thread and passes the address of the Instance.Run method. Run will be the starting point for the new thread. Line 116 starts the thread; at line 116 control branches to Instance.Run.

13

CREATING A
CONSOLE
APPLICATION

> **Note**
>
> As a general strategy, you might want to consider adding timing code to algorithms that might be processor- or time-intensive. It is reasonable to assume that empirical data reflecting how long key processes are taking will be beneficial at some point during development. The `TimedSort` method in Listing 13.8 demonstrates an example using the `Timer` function.

`Run` is very short. `Run` calls `Read` to load the file into the `ArrayList FData`, calls `TimedSort`, and writes the results to a new file. (`Run` is defined on lines 107 to 111. We covered `Read` and `Write` in the earlier sections "Using a TextReader" and "Using a TextWriter," respectively.) `TimedSort` is implemented to call the `ArrayList.Sort` method wrapped by code that gets a relative start and stop time and writes the results to the Output window.

Debugging Console Applications

Console applications can be debugged in the IDE just as you would debug Windows applications, controls, or Web applications. There are a couple of extra considerations you might want to consider when debugging console applications, and we will cover those briefly in this section.

Specifying Command-Line Arguments in the IDE

Console applications are typically run from the `Cmd` window. While debugging, you might want to start the application from the Visual Studio IDE. If your application needs command-line parameters, as `FileSort` does, you can indicate those command-line arguments in the Debugging page of the application's Property Pages (see Figure 13.4). To set command-line arguments, select the project name in the Solution Explorer and press Shift+F4.

Attaching Visual Studio to a Running Application

As an alternative to debugging in the IDE, you might have a tester performing black box testing on your application and the application appears to hang. Instead of shutting down the application and trying to reproduce the problem, you might consider attaching to the already running application. After you have attached to the application, you might more readily be able to figure out what has broken.

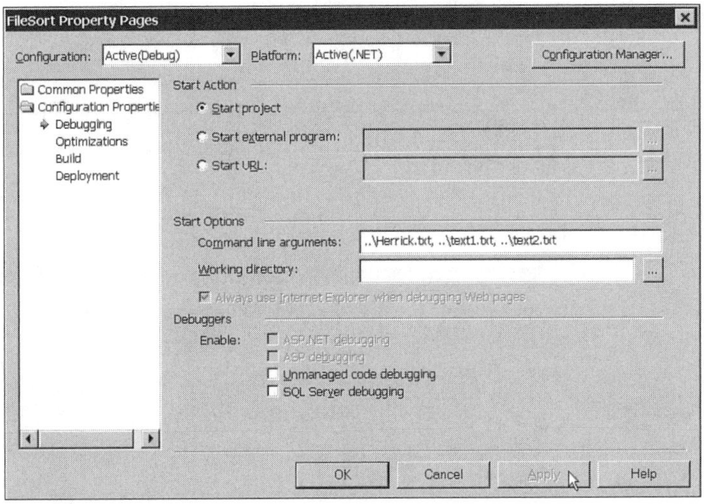

13

CREATING A
CONSOLE
APPLICATION

FIGURE 13.4

Set command-line arguments for a console application in the Start Options section of the Debugging page.

Starting the Application from the Command Prompt

To recreate a hung application scenario, open the InfiniteLoop.sln on this book's Web site. To ensure that the application does not quit before we can attach to it, the Main procedure contains an intentional infinite loop.

InfiniteLoop.sln is compiled and then started from the command line. To attach to the running program and begin debugging it, we will need to start Visual Studio .NET, and open the InfiniteLoop.sln. The next section describes the steps for attaching to the running process.

Attaching Visual Studio

InfiniteLoop.exe is running and appears to be hung. Because we are running outside of the IDE, we need to start an instance of Visual Studio .NET and open the Processes window. From the list of available processes (see Figure 13.5), find the process that you want to attach to, select the process, and click Attach. In the Attach To Process dialog box, check Common Language Runtime process type, uncheck the Native process type, and click OK.

Tip

If you want to terminate the running process, you can do so by clicking the Terminate button after you have attached to a process. The Task Manager can be used to achieve this result, too.

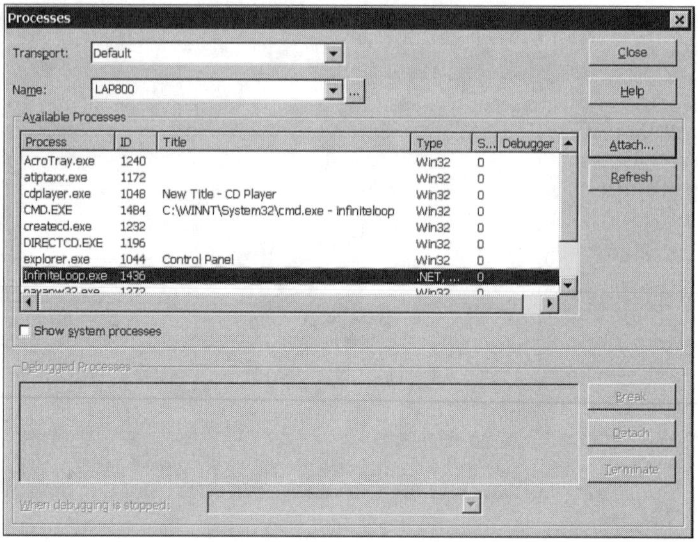

FIGURE 13.5

Attach to a running process to debug a process that is running outside of the IDE.

The Processes dialog box will be updated to show the selected process in the Debugged Processes pane (see Figure 13.6). Click Close. The code view in focus should be the process being debugged (see Figure 13.7).

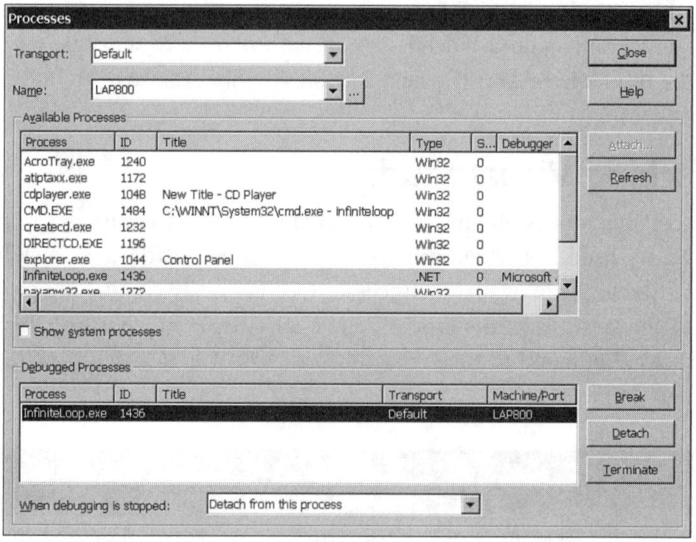

FIGURE 13.6

The selected process in the Processes pane.

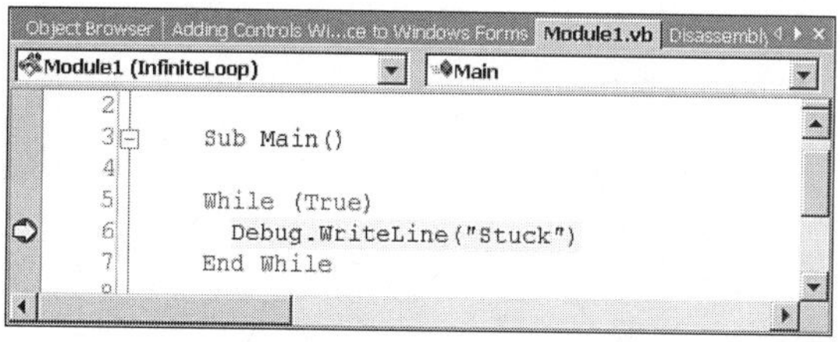

FIGURE 13.7

The `InfiniteLoop.exe` *process stopped at a breakpoint inserted after we attached to it.*

```
Object Browser | Adding Controls Wi...ce to Windows Forms | Module1.vb | Disassembl\ ◀ ▶ ×
Module1 (InfiniteLoop)               ▼    Main                         ▼
    2
    3       Sub Main()
    4
    5       While (True)
    6          Debug.WriteLine("Stuck")
    7       End While
    8
```

Tip

If you want the process to stop when you stop debugging the attached process, select Terminate This Process from the combo box labeled When Debugging Is Stopped in the Processes dialog box.

The execution point is easy to find in our sample application because it was planted. Fortunately, the Visual Studio IDE makes it easy to find the execution point even when it is not contrived. Simply press Ctrl+Break and the IDE will suspend execution and show the current execution point. Having a grasp of where the problem resides, you can add conditional breakpoints to begin figuring out the problem.

Debugging on a Remote Machine

Perhaps the tester is at a remote site or does not have Visual Studio installed in the testing machine (which is a likely scenario). In this instance you may want to attach to and debug a process running on a remote machine from your development machine. You can select a remote machine name from the combo box labeled Name in the Processes dialog box.

Visual Studio defaults to using DCOM to debug applications on remote machines, or you can choose Native-only TCP/IP if you are debugging remotely and cannot use DCOM.

Detaching from a Native Process

If you attach Visual Studio to a Native process, you will need the `dbgproxy.exe` service installed and running on your machine before running a Native process, or you will not be able to detach from the process. You can install `dbgproxy.exe` by entering

```
dbgproxy.exe –install
```

13

CREATING A
CONSOLE
APPLICATION

at the command prompt. You can start the dbgproxy application from the Services applet or the command line. The commands for starting and stopping the debug proxy application are

```
net start dbgproxy
```

and

```
net stop dbgproxy
```

If you are attaching to CLR applications written in Visual Basic .NET, you do not need to install and run the dbgproxy service.

Keeping Track of the File System

Some processes might require the presence or arrival of a file. For example, you might want to sort a file when it shows up on the machine running the sort process, or you might want to be notified when the sort has completed and the sorted file is available for further processing. Visual Basic .NET allows you to use the `FileSystemWatcher` component to dynamically track changes to the file system.

You can add a `FileSystemWatcher` to the component tray at the bottom of the form's designer or programmatically. Because `FileSort` is a console application, the component tray is not available. Therefore, we will add a `FileSystemWatcher` to the FileSort.sln programmatically and use it to notify us when the .tmp file containing the sorted data has been created (Listing 13.9 contains the new code added to the FileSort.sln sample program).

LISTING 13.9   Programmatically adding a `FileSystemWatcher` component to a console application

```
1:  #Region " FileSystemWatcher Example "
2:     Private Watcher As FileSystemWatcher
3:
4:     Private Sub OnCreated(ByVal sender As Object, _
5:       ByVal e As System.IO.FileSystemEventArgs)
6:       Console.WriteLine("Created: " & e.FullPath)
7:     End Sub
8:
9:     Private Sub AddWatcher()
10:      Watcher = New FileSystemWatcher("..\", "*.tmp")
11:      Watcher.EnableRaisingEvents = True
12:      AddHandler Watcher.Created, AddressOf OnCreated
13:    End Sub
14: #End Region
15:
```

LISTING 13.9 continued

```
16:    Public Sub New(ByVal AFileName As String)
17:      FData = New ArrayList()
18:      FFileName = AFileName
19:      AddWatcher()
20:    End Sub
```

The code region tagged " FileSystemWatcher Example " was added to the FileSort.sln sample program. The FileSystemWatcher is created in AddWatcher called by the New constructor on lines 16 to 20. Line 10 creates an instance of the FileSystemWatcher indicating the directory—"..\" representing the executable's parent directory—to watch. The second parameter, "*.tmp", indicates that the watcher should watch changes to files in the executable's parent directory having a .tmp extension.

Line 11 indicates that the watcher should be raising events and line 12 establishes the OnCreated method as an event handler that will respond when .tmp files are created in the watcher's directory. The event handler is defined in lines 4 to 7; the watcher's event handler simply displays the full path of created files. Line 2 defines a reference variable named Watcher that will be used to reference the watcher component.

Whenever a .tmp file is created in the parent directory containing the executable, the watcher will display the complete path to that file. The FileSort.sln on this book's Web site contains the complete revised listing of the sample program.

Summary

Console applications aren't used as widely today as they were just 5 or 10 years ago. Many users expect a GUI, which console applications do not support. As a consequence, console applications are practically limited to the utility category. However, if you are writing an application used by other processes or as part of a batch process, a console application might be perfect.

Visual Basic .NET supports multithreading, providing you with a greater variety when it comes to implementing Visual Basic applications, including console applications.

When implementing console applications, keep in mind that input and output are generally derived from very rudimentary sources like the keyboard and monitor, but the Console class does support IO redirection. For example, you can redirect console error information to a file rather than the default error device, the CRT.

Combine multithreading, command-line parsing, and file system watching with your console applications, and you can implement fairly powerful solutions without the expense of designing and testing complex user interfaces.

CHAPTER 14

Multithreaded Applications

A lot of excitement has been generated over the discussion of multithreading capability being added to Visual Basic .NET. We know that it is possible to write professional applications without multithreading. The next year will demonstrate the impact, positive or negative, that multithreading will have on Visual Basic .NET applications. It remains to be seen what productivity gains might be attained and what the added costs of development might be.

As you know, you can solve many day-to-day problems without using multiple threads, but you might find threads useful at times, such as if you need an advanced algorithm. Threads can make your applications more responsive, but they will also probably make your applications more difficult to test and debug.

Chapter 14 is designed to help guide you to using threads safely when you need them. Keep in mind, though, that Windows Forms are not considered thread-safe (although I hope Windows Forms controls will be thread-safe in the very near future). You need to anticipate that using threads might introduce some pernicious bugs that are very difficult to find. Draw on your years of experience and be willing to seek the guidance of those who have been writing multithreaded applications in other languages for years. Remember, even those people will have limited threading experience with .NET, and things that may be true in general may not be true about .NET and threads.

Consider solving problems that can be solved without threads without them, but don't be afraid of or completely avoid using multiple threads. Share your experiences with the general user community, look at the examples in the Microsoft Quickstarts, and check out newsletters. Best practices for threading in .NET will probably evolve over time.

There are basically three kinds of ways you can perform asynchronous tasks in Visual Basic .NET, and you should consider each before committing to any one. You can use a timer or the application idle event for quick-and-dirty lightweight tasks. (You already know how to use timers from VB6.) You can use the thread pool for multithreaded tasks; the thread pool simplifies thread management significantly. Finally, you can create an instance of the `Thread` class and manage the threaded task completely. This chapter demonstrates all three variations of asynchronous processing in Visual Basic .NET.

Asynchronous Processing without Threads

This section is short because you probably already know how to use a timer. Visual Basic .NET supports an `Application` object, similar to the VB6 `App` object. The VB .NET `Application` object implements an `Idle` event. You can assign a delegate to the `Application.Idle` event and achieve asynchronous capabilities too.

Using a Timer

The Timer is implemented as a control. A crystal oscillates at a certain frequency in your PC and this known oscillating frequency is used to clock your PC. At a very low level, the BIOS supports implementing an interrupt event handler that is notified when the internal hardware timer ticks. After 10 years or so, the low-level capabilities inherent in the average PC were wrapped in a control.

The Timer control supports your indicating a number of milliseconds to wait before the timer raises an event. When the indicated milliseconds elapse, the Timer control raises a Tick event in VB .NET.

A common task for which the timer is used is to display a clock on the status bar. The following code fragment demonstrates what this might look like in .NET:

```
Private Sub Timer1_Tick(ByVal sender As System.Object, _
  ByVal e As System.EventArgs) Handles Timer1.Tick

  StatusBar1.Text = Now
End Sub
```

The fragment assumes that you have a Windows Form with a Timer control added to the component tray, and perhaps you clicked the control to generate the event handler.

The timer tick operates asynchronously, but the event is still on the same thread as the form. This means that it is safe to interact directly with Windows Forms controls in a timer event handler, but you do not want the timer to fire a second time while you are still processing a previous request.

Asynchronous timer tasks should be concise. A reasonable amount of work is similar to that performed when updating a viewable clock. Much more than that, and you should consider using a different approach.

Using the Application Idle Event

Applications spend a significant amount of time idle. Just look in Windows Task Manager and you can see that processor utilization peaks occasionally, but most processes sit around waiting most of the time. Visual Basic .NET supports adding an event handler to respond to the application idle event.

Currently, Application is not represented as a control. You just have to know it is there. The Application class is defined in System.Windows.Forms, making it available to Windows applications but not console or Web applications.

To use the `Idle` event, you will need to define a method in your application, preferably the main form that is always open, and use `AddHandler` to associate the method-as-delegate to the `Idle` event. Listing 14.1 demonstrates very brief code that does exactly this.

LISTING 14.1 Assigning an event handler to the `Application.Idle` event

```
 1: Public Class Form1
 2:     Inherits System.Windows.Forms.Form
 3:
 4: [ Windows Form Designer generated code ]
 5:
 6:     Private Sub OnIdle(ByVal sender As Object, ByVal e As EventArgs)
 7:       Text = Now
 8:     End Sub
 9:
10:     Private Sub Form1_Load(ByVal sender As System.Object, _
11:       ByVal e As System.EventArgs) Handles MyBase.Load
12:
13:       AddHandler Application.Idle, AddressOf OnIdle
14:
15:     End Sub
16: End Class
```

The `Idle` event property is defined as an `EventHandler` delegate. From Chapters 8 and 9, you know that `EventHandler` is initialized with the address of a subroutine that has `Object` and `EventArgs` parameters, as does `OnIdle` defined on lines 6 through 8. The `Application.Idle` event is associated with the `OnIdle` method in the form's `Load` event.

Note

Line 13 effectively associates an event handler with an event (in the preceding example, the `Idle` event). What the `AddressOf` actually does is construct an instance of a delegate. The statement on line 13 is identical to `AddHandler Application.Idle, New EventHandler(AddressOf OnIdle)`.

Examining the verbose form of the call, it is clear that `EventHandler` is a class. In fact, it's a delegate class. It is also clear that we are initializing the class with the address of a procedure, a function pointer.

Personally I think it would be clearer to write `Application.Idle = AddressOf OnIdle`. When I asked some folks at Microsoft why it wasn't implemented using assignment, the response I got had to do with overloading the assignment (=) operator to work with delegate objects. Regardless, it is worth noting that `AddressOf` implicitly constructs a delegate object, and .NET supports the verbose form of delegate construction, which you are likely to encounter.

The code updates the time as the form's caption but does so at irregular intervals. The Timer is better for a clock. Like the Timer control, the Application.Idle event is suitable for short processes. Unlike the Timer control, Application.Idle is more suited for tasks that can run at irregular intervals; if they don't run, they will not have a deleterious impact on your application.

The Timer control and the Application object are useful, but that's not why we're here. One final word on these two ways of performing asynchronous processes: They are easy to use and less likely to introduce bugs, so don't completely overlook them. Now on to meatier subjects.

Lightweight Threading with Thread Pools

Visiting the Microsoft campus in Redmond, Washington in August, I asked a couple of developers what the difference is between using the thread class and using the thread pool. The answer I got was that there is no real difference. The thread pool is easier because it manages thread objects for you; when you create a thread object, you have to manage it yourself.

Using threads in the ThreadPool was referred to as "lightweight" threading, and creating an instance of the Thread class was referred to as "heavyweight" threading. The adjectives did not refer to their capability but rather to ease of use. The thread pool is easier to use, but when using the thread pool, you are multithreading just as assuredly as you are when creating instances of the Thread class. One developer said something to the effect of "Why wouldn't you always use the thread pool?"

In effect, identical end results can be achieved with lightweight threading or heavyweight threading. It's easy to use the thread pool, and a little harder to use the Thread class.

What Is the Thread Pool?

The thread pool is a class defined in the System.Threading namespace. The class is ThreadPool. What the ThreadPool class does is manage a few threads that are available for you to request work. If the pool has available threads, the work is completed on an available thread. If no thread is available in the pool, the thread pool creates another task or may wait for a thread to become available. For the most part, you do not care exactly how it proceeds.

Very simply, the thread pool uses an available thread or creates a new one, manages starting the task on the thread, and cleans up. The thread pool is a thread manager.

A consequence is that if you use the thread pool, you do not need to create and keep track of individual thread objects, but you get the same benefit as if you had.

How Does the Thread Pool Work?

The thread pool works in much the same manner as creating and using an instance of the Thread class. You have a thread and you give it work by passing the thread a delegate. In the case of the thread pool, you give the pool a delegate and the pool manager assigns the work represented by the delegate to a thread. The result is the same.

Using the Thread Pool

You are familiar with keeping track of the time in a Windows application, so we will start there. (When you have the basics down, we will progress to more interesting tasks.)

There are three things we will need to use the thread pool in a Windows Form to implement a clock. We will need to define a procedure that interacts with the Windows Form on the same thread as the form. We will need to define a procedure that represents work occurring on a separate thread than the form, and we will need to request that the thread pool perform the work. Listing 14.2 demonstrates how straightforward this is.

LISTING 14.2   Implementing a clock on a separate thread

```
1:  Imports System.Threading
2:
3:  Public Class Form1
4:     Inherits System.Windows.Forms.Form
5:
6:  [ Windows Form Designer generated code ]
7:
8:     Private Sub UpdateTime()
9:       SyncLock Me.Name
10:         Text = Now
11:       End SyncLock
12:    End Sub
13:
14:    Private Sub TrackTime(ByVal State As Object)
15:
16:      While (True)
17:        Try
18:          'Invoke(New MethodInvoker(AddressOf UpdateTime))
19:          Invoke(CType(AddressOf UpdateTime, MethodInvoker))
20:        Catch
21:
22:        End Try
23:        Thread.CurrentThread.Sleep(500)
```

LISTING 14.2 continued

```
24:      End While
25:
26:   End Sub
27:
28:   Private Sub Form1_Load(ByVal sender As System.Object, _
29:      ByVal e As System.EventArgs) Handles MyBase.Load
30:
31:      ThreadPool.QueueUserWorkItem(AddressOf TrackTime)
32:
33:   End Sub
34: End Class
```

UpdateTime on lines 8 through 12 updates the form's caption—Text property—to display the current time. (We have dispensed with the StatusBar because it isn't relevant to the discussion.) We use SyncLock and End SyncLock to block any other thread from trying to update the text property, but what makes the code safe is that UpdateTime occurs on the same thread that the form is on. (We will inspect this hypothesis in a minute.)

TrackTime has the signature of a WaitCallback delegate. WaitCallback is initialized with a subroutine that takes a single Object argument. Line 16 begins an infinite loop. We know from experience, of course, that an infinite loop in our main thread would spell death in the form of unresponsiveness to our application. Because TrackTime runs on its own thread, infinite-loop death does not occur. Lines 18 and 19 are effectively identical. Lines 18 and 19 use the Invoke method (which all controls have), which allows you to invoke a process. Calling Invoke bumps the work over to the thread that the control is on. On line 18 we are indicating that we want to invoke the UpdateMethod on the form's thread. Implicit in the call on lines 18 and 19 is the Me object reference.

Finally, line 31 calls the shared method ThreadPool.QueueUserWorkItem passing a delegate returned by the AddressOf statement as the work item. Line 31 will place TrackTime on its own thread. Figures 14.1 through 14.3 show the threads running and the changing of contexts as the code runs. A brief explanation follows each figure.

Figure 14.1 shows the debugger stopped on line 63 on the statement Thread.CurrentThread.Sleep(500). From the Threads window—which you can open by choosing Debug, Windows, Threads in the Visual Studio .NET IDE—you can see that the TrackTime method is running on thread 2460. We use the Step Into shortcut until the debugger reaches line 57 in the TrackTime method. We use Debug, Step Into twice more until the debugger reaches line 60, which contains an Invoke method call.

14

MULTITHREADED
APPLICATIONS

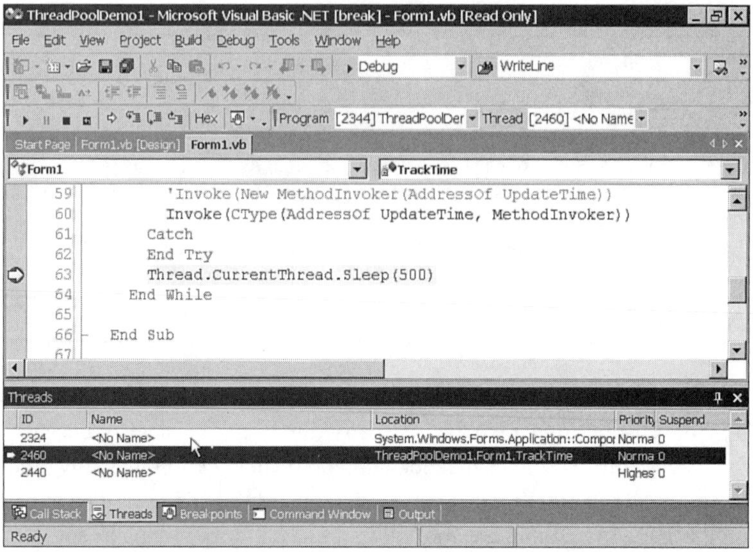

FIGURE **14.1**

Form1.TrackTime
shown on a sepa-
rate thread, thread
ID 2460.

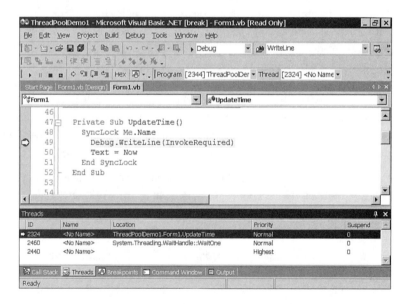

FIGURE **14.2**

Form1.UpdateTime
shown on the
same thread as
the Form itself,
thread 2324.

From Figure 14.2, you can see that the Invoke method caused the debugger to switch threads. UpdateTime is running on thread 2324. If we continue stepping to the end of UpdateTime, we see that the thread switches back to 2460 after the debugger returns from UpdateTime (see Figure 14.3).

FIGURE 14.3

Form1.TrackTime *shown after returning from* UpdateTime *and back on thread* 2460.

```
                    Invoke(CType(AddressOf UpdateTime, MethodInvoker))
 61          Catch
 62          End Try
 63          Thread.CurrentThread.Sleep(500)
 64       End While
 65
 66     End Sub
 67
 68     Private Sub Form1 Load(ByVal sender As System.Object,
```

ID	Name	Location	Priority	Suspend
2324	<No Name>	System.Windows.Forms.ScrollableControl::WndProc	Normal	0
2460	<No Name>	ThreadPoolDemo1.Form1.TrackTime	Normal	0
2440	<No Name>		Highest	0

But how do we know we are on the same thread as the form? There are two ways we can determine that UpdateTime is on the same thread as the form. When the Form.Load event occurs, we can use the QuickWatch window, accessed by pressing Shift+F9 and invoking the AppDomain.GetCurrentThreadID shared method. This method will indicate the form's thread, and we can visually compare it to the thread ID in the Threads window when UpdateTime is processing. The second way we can know if the UpdateTime is on the form's thread is by calling Control.InvokeRequired.

Each control implements InvokeRequired. Calling InvokeRequired compares the control's thread with the thread on which the InvokeRequired method was called. If the threads are identical, InvokeRequired returns False.

Problems

There is a problem with the code example in Listing 14.2. What if the form is shutting down or disposed of and the code calls the form's Invoke method on line 18? Although the help indicates that Invoke is safe to call from any thread, you still can't call a method on an object that has been disposed of. You could write to check to see if the form is Disposing, but if the form is already disposed of, this will fail.

You could check the IsDisposed property. This property will return True if the form is disposed of, but the garbage collector has not cleaned up the memory yet. However, if the GC has cleaned up the form, you will still get an exception.

14

MULTITHREADED
APPLICATIONS

You could use a flag in the form that indicates that the form is being closed, but the `Invoke` method could be called after the flag is checked.

Resolutions

For this example, I would make one of three decisions based on the importance of the task. One choice would be to consider the task simplistic enough that a silent exception handler around the `Invoke` call would catch calls after the form had been destroyed.

```
Try
  Invoke(CType(AddressOf UpdateTime, MethodInvoker))
Catch
End Try
```

Where the form has been disposed of, this silent exception handler would provide blanket protection. Because there is nothing to corrupt here, this is a reasonable solution. I am not a big fan of silent exceptions, but I do use them on rare occasions. The relatively low importance of keeping time might warrant such an approach.

A second choice would be to create the thread myself and keep track of the thread, shutting down and disposing of the thread when the application shuts down. This solution is clean and demonstrates an instance when owning the thread helps.

A third choice would be to consider the relatively low importance of the task and use a timer to get asynchronous background behavior. In a real-world application where the timer is simply providing a clock, this is the choice I would make.

Using a `WaitHandle` and Synchronizing Behavior

The `WaitHandle` class is a base class used to implement synchronization objects. `AutoResetEvent`, `ManualResetEvent`, and `Mutex` are subclassed from `WaitHandle` and define methods to block access to shared resources.

To demonstrate blocking and synchronization of shared resources, I will implement a class named `Dice`. Each `Dice` instance rolls on its own thread, but the total score of all of the dice cannot be obtained until all of the dice have finished rolling. `WaitHandle` objects are used in conjunction with the thread pool, so we will roll the dice using the threads in the pool.

Listing 14.3 implements `Dice` and `DiceGraphic` classes. The `Dice` class represents a single die and the `DiceGraphic` class supports painting the graphical view of one face of a die. Listing 14.3 contains the code that runs on a unique thread, contains the shared `WaitHandle`, and uses synchronization to determine when all dice have finished rolling.

Listing 14.4 lists the form that contains the graphical representation of five dice. A synopsis of the code follows each listing.

LISTING 14.3 Contains the threaded behavior, `WaitHandle`, and synchronized behavior

```
1:  Imports System.Threading
2:  Imports System.Drawing
3:
4:  Public Class Dice
5:
6:    Private FValue As Integer = 1
7:    Private Shared FRolling As Integer = 0
8:    Private FColor As Color
9:    Private FRect As Rectangle
10:   Public Shared Done As New AutoResetEvent(False)
11:
12:   Public Shared ReadOnly Property IsRolling() As Boolean
13:     Get
14:       Return FRolling > 0
15:     End Get
16:   End Property
17:
18:   Public Sub New()
19:     MyClass.New(New Rectangle(10, 10, 50, 50), Color.White)
20:   End Sub
21:
22:   Public Sub New(ByVal Rect As Rectangle, ByVal color As Color)
23:     MyBase.New()
24:     FRect = Rect
25:     FColor = color
26:   End Sub
27:
28:   Public ReadOnly Property Value() As Integer
29:     Get
30:       Return FValue
31:     End Get
32:   End Property
33:
34:   Public Sub Roll(ByVal State As Object)
35:
36:     Interlocked.Increment(FRolling)
37:     Try
38:       DoRoll(CType(State, Graphics))
39:     Finally
40:       If (Interlocked.Decrement(FRolling) = 0) Then
41:         Done.Set()
42:       End If
43:     End Try
44:
```

LISTING 14.3 continued

```
45:    End Sub
46:
47:    Public Sub Draw(ByVal Graphic As Graphics)
48:      DiceGraphic.Draw(Graphic, FValue, FRect, FColor)
49:    End Sub
50:
51:    Private Sub DoRoll(ByVal Graphic As Graphics)
52:      Dim I As Integer = GetRandomNumber()
53:      While (I > 0)
54:        FValue = GetRandomDie()
55:        Draw(Graphic)
56:        Beep()
57:        I -= 1
58:        Thread.CurrentThread.Sleep(50)
59:      End While
60:    End Sub
61:
62:    Private Shared Random As New Random()
63:
64:    Private Shared Function GetRandomNumber() As Integer
65:      Return Random.Next(30, 50)
66:    End Function
67:
68:    Protected Shared Function GetRandomDie() As Integer
69:      Return Random.Next(1, 7)
70:    End Function
71: End Class
72:
73: Public Class DiceGraphic
74:
75:    Public Shared Sub Draw(ByVal Graphic As Graphics, _
76:      ByVal Value As Integer, _
77:      ByVal Rect As Rectangle, ByVal Color As Color)
78:
79:      Graphic.FillRectangle(New SolidBrush(Color), Rect)
80:      Graphic.DrawRectangle(Pens.Black, Rect)
81:      DrawDots(Graphic, GetRects(Value, Rect))
82:
83:    End Sub
84:
85:
86:    Private Shared Function GetRects(ByVal Value As Integer, _
87:      ByVal Rect As Rectangle) As Rectangle()
88:
89:      Dim One() As Rectangle = {GetRectangle(Rect, 1, 1)}
90:      Dim Two() As Rectangle = {GetRectangle(Rect, 0, 2), _
91:      GetRectangle(Rect, 2, 0)}
92:
93:      Dim Three() As Rectangle = {GetRectangle(Rect, 0, 2), _
```

LISTING 14.3 continued

```
 94:     GetRectangle(Rect, 1, 1), GetRectangle(Rect, 2, 0)}
 95:
 96:     Dim Four() As Rectangle = {GetRectangle(Rect, 0, 0), _
 97:       GetRectangle(Rect, 0, 2), GetRectangle(Rect, 2, 0), _
 98:       GetRectangle(Rect, 2, 2)}
 99:
100:     Dim Five() As Rectangle = {GetRectangle(Rect, 0, 0), _
101:       GetRectangle(Rect, 1, 1), GetRectangle(Rect, 0, 2), _
102:       GetRectangle(Rect, 2, 0), GetRectangle(Rect, 2, 2)}
103:
104:     Dim Six() As Rectangle = {GetRectangle(Rect, 0, 0), _
105:       GetRectangle(Rect, 0, 1), GetRectangle(Rect, 0, 2), _
106:       GetRectangle(Rect, 2, 0), GetRectangle(Rect, 2, 1), _
107:       GetRectangle(Rect, 2, 2)}
108:
109:     Dim Rects As Rectangle()() = _
110:       {One, Two, Three, Four, Five, Six}
111:
112:     Return Rects(Value - 1)
113:
114:   End Function
115:
116:   Protected Shared Function GetRectangle(ByVal Rect As Rectangle, _
117:     ByVal X As Integer, ByVal Y As Integer) As Rectangle
118:
119:     Return New Rectangle(Rect.X + _
120:       (Rect.Width * X / 3), _
121:       Rect.Y + (Rect.Height * Y / 3), _
122:       GetDotSize(Rect).Width, GetDotSize(Rect).Height)
123:   End Function
124:
125:
126:   Protected Shared Function GetDotSize( _
127:     ByVal Rect As Rectangle) As Size
128:
129:     Return New Size(Rect.Width / 3, Rect.Height / 3)
130:   End Function
131:
132:   Private Shared Sub DrawDot(ByVal Graphic As Graphics, _
133:     ByVal Rect As Rectangle)
134:
135:     Graphic.SmoothingMode = _
136:       Drawing.Drawing2D.SmoothingMode.AntiAlias
137:
138:     Rect.Inflate(-3, -3)
139:     Graphic.FillEllipse(New SolidBrush(Color.Black), Rect)
140:
141:   End Sub
142:
```

14

**MULTITHREADED
APPLICATIONS**

LISTING 14.3   continued

```
143:    Private Shared Sub DrawDots(ByVal Graphic As Graphics, _
144:    ByVal Rects() As Rectangle)
145:
146:      Dim I As Integer
147:      For I = 0 To Rects.Length - 1
148:        DrawDot(Graphic, Rects(I))
149:      Next
150:
151:    End Sub
152:
153: End Class
```

Listing 14.3 implements the Dice class as a class that rotates a random number of times through the values 1 through 6. During each roll (see lines 51 through 60), a random value for the dice is obtained, Beep is used to simulate the sound of rolling dice, and the die is drawn. The drawing of the die's face is managed by the DiceGraphic class using GDI+ (see Chapter 17, "Programming with GDI+," for more information on using the Graphics object).

Transitioning to the topic of our discussion, the rolling behavior is run on its own thread invoked by an external source. Lines 34 through 45 implement the rolling behavior. Line 36 calls the shared Interlocked.Increment(FRolling) method to perform an atomic increment of the shared FRolling field. Dice are rolling when FRolling > 0, as implemented by the shared IsRolling property of the Dice class. A resource protection block is used to ensure that the FRolling property is decremented. The rolling behavior is called on line 38. From the typecast on line 38—CType(State, Graphics)—it is apparent that we will be passing in the Graphics object each time we roll the dice, because GDI+ is stateless. The Graphics object represents the device context, or canvas, of the control we are painting on, and its stateless implementation simply means that we do not cache Graphics objects. The Finally block ensures that the FRolling field is decremented, again using an atomic shared method Interlocked.Decrement. The new value of FRolling is evaluated. If FRolling = 0 after it has been decremented, all dice have stopped rolling and we can signal the WaitHandle that we are finished.

Done is instantiated on line 10 as an AutoResetEvent. AutoResetEvent is subclassed from WaitHandle, and it is created in an unsignaled state, represented by the False argument. Done is shared because one WaitHandle is shared by all instances of Dice. In summary, each Dice instance increments the shared FRolling field and decrements it when it is finished rolling. When FRolling is 0 again, we notify whoever is waiting that all dice are finished rolling. Listing 14.4 demonstrates a client that shows the dice (see Figure 14.4).

FIGURE 14.4

The threaded dice after they have been rolled on their own threads.

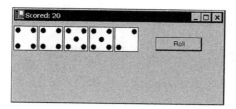

LISTING 14.4   Each die rolls on its own thread, while waiting for all dice before scoring the roll

```
1:   Option Explicit On
2:   Option Strict On
3:
4:   Imports System.Threading
5:
6:   Public Class Form1
7:     Inherits System.Windows.Forms.Form
8:
9:   [ Windows Form Designer generated code ]
10:
11:    Private FDice(4) As Dice
12:
13:    Private Sub Form1_Load(ByVal sender As System.Object, _
14:      ByVal e As System.EventArgs) Handles MyBase.Load
15:
16:      Dim I As Integer
17:      For I = 0 To FDice.Length - 1
18:        FDice(I) = New Dice(New Rectangle(54 * I, 10, 50, 50), _
19:          Color.Ivory)
20:      Next
21:    End Sub
22:
23:    Private Sub RollDice()
24:      Dim I As Integer
25:      For I = 0 To FDice.Length() - 1
26:        ThreadPool.QueueUserWorkItem(AddressOf FDice(I).Roll, CreateGraphics)
27:      Next
28:
29:      Dice.Done.WaitOne()
30:    End Sub
31:
32:    Private Sub Score()
33:      Dim I, Sum As Integer
34:      For I = 0 To FDice.Length() - 1
35:        Sum += FDice(I).Value
36:      Next
37:
38:      Text = String.Format("Scored: {0}", Sum)
39:    End Sub
```

14

MULTITHREADED
APPLICATIONS

LISTING 14.4   continued

```
40:
41:    Private Sub Button1_Click(ByVal sender As System.Object, _
42:      ByVal e As System.EventArgs) Handles Button1.Click
43:
44:      RollDice()
45:      Score()
46:
47:    End Sub
48:
49:    Private Sub Form1_Paint(ByVal sender As Object, _
50:      ByVal e As System.Windows.Forms.PaintEventArgs) _
51:      Handles MyBase.Paint
52:
53:      Dim I As Integer
54:      For I = 0 To FDice.Length - 1
55:        FDice(I).Draw(CreateGraphics)
56:      Next
57:
58:    End Sub
59:
60: End Class
```

> **Note**
>
> The threaded rolling behavior is cool, but it is worth noting that it took me
> about five times longer to write a threaded version of the rolling dice and get it
> to work correctly than simply rolling all dice on the same thread as the form.

Most of the code in Listing 14.4 is straightforward, so I won't itemize all of it. To review, the form is created. Five Dice are constructed in the form's Load event. The form's Paint event ensures that the dice are repainted if the form is repainted. (If the dice were user controls, they would receive their own paint message.) When the user clicks the button labeled Roll (refer to Figure 14.4), the RollDice and Score methods are called. The Score method simply sums the Value of each die. The interesting bit happens in the RollDice method.

The RollDice method on lines 23 through 30 iterates over each Dice in the FDice array declared on line 11. The Roll method of each Dice object is treated as the WaitCallback argument of the shared ThreadPool.QueueUserWorkItem method. Dice.Roll represents the work. The second argument is a Graphics object returned by the CreateGraphics factory method. After the loop exits, each dice is rolling on its own thread in the ThreadPool.

Resynchronizing occurs on line 29. The shared `AutoResetEvent` object is used to wait for all of the dice to stop rolling. Recall that the code does not call `AutoResetEvent.Set` until `IsRolling` is False, that is, until all dice have stopped rolling. By implementing the code this way, the message queue is filling up with input but not responding until `AutoResetEvent.WaitOne` (represented on line 29 by `Done.WaitOne`) returns.

> **Note**
>
> The first time you roll the dice, there is a brief delay between when the first die begins rolling and each subsequent die. This reflects the time it takes for the thread pool to construct additional thread objects. Subsequent rolls appear to start almost concurrently.

If you try to close the form, for example, the application will wait until the dice have stopped rolling before responding to an application shutdown. If you try to roll a second time before an ongoing roll is over, the application will respond after `WaitOne` returns. You would not want to be using the `Graphics` object passed to each die if the form object were being destroyed. Finally, because each die paints itself, you get a smooth graphic result without repainting the entire form, which would result in flicker.

ManualResetEvent

The `ManualResetEvent` is a `WaitHandle` that remains signaled until the `Reset` method is called, and remains unsignaled until the `Set` method is called.

Mutex

`Mutex` is a synchronization primitive that provides synchronized access to a shared resource. If one thread acquires a mutex, subsequent threads are blocked until the first thread releases its mutex.

Synchronization with the `Monitor` Class

Synchronizing critical sections of your code is essential when you may have multiple threads accessing a shared section of your code. For general synchronization, you can use the `SyncLock...End SyncLock` construct.

The `SyncLock...End SyncLock` construct is implemented using the `Monitor` class. You cannot create an instance of `Monitor`; all of the methods are shared anyway. Invoking `Monitor.Enter(object)` and `Monitor.Exit(object)` is identical to using the `SyncLock...End SyncLock` construct.

Monitor also contains methods `Pulse`, `PulseAll`, `TryEnter`, and `Wait`. `Pulse` notifies a single object in the waiting queue of a state change in the locked object. `PulseAll` notifies all waiting threads of a state change, and `Wait` releases the lock and waits until it reacquires the lock. The `TryEnter` method attempts to acquire an exclusive lock on an object.

Listing 14.5 demonstrates how to use the `Monitor` class to switch back and forth between two threads interacting with the same object.

LISTING 14.5 Using the `Monitor` class

```
1:  Option Explicit On
2:  Option Strict On
3:
4:  Imports System
5:  Imports System.Threading
6:
7:  Class MonitorDemo
8:
9:    Private Integers() As Integer
10:   Private MAX As Integer = 1000
11:
12:   Private I, J As Integer
13:
14:   Public Sub FillArray()
15:     Dim I As Integer
16:     ReDim Integers(MAX)
17:     Dim R As New Random()
18:
19:     For I = 0 To Integers.Length - 1
20:       Integers(I) = Integers.Length - 1 - I
21:     Next
22:   End Sub
23:
24:   Public Sub SortArray(ByVal State As Object)
25:     Monitor.Enter(Integers)
26:
27:     For I = 0 To Integers.Length - 1
28:       For J = I + 1 To Integers.Length - 1
29:         If (Integers(I) > Integers(J)) Then
30:           Dim T As Integer = Integers(I)
31:           Integers(I) = Integers(J)
32:           Integers(J) = T
33:         End If
34:       Next
35:
36:     Monitor.Wait(Integers)
37:     Console.Write("Sorted: ")
38:     Monitor.Pulse(Integers)
```

LISTING 14.5   continued

```
39:      Next
40:
41:      Monitor.Exit(Integers)
42:    End Sub
43:
44:    Public Sub PrintArray(ByVal State As Object)
45:      Static K As Integer = 0
46:
47:      Monitor.Enter(Integers)
48:      Monitor.Pulse(Integers)
49:
50:      While (Monitor.Wait(Integers, 1000))
51:
52:        If (K <= I) Then
53:          Console.WriteLine(Integers(K))
54:          K += 1
55:        End If
56:
57:        Monitor.Pulse(Integers)
58:      End While
59:
60:      Monitor.Exit(Integers)
61:    End Sub
62:
63:    Public Shared Sub Main()
64:
65:      Dim Demo As New MonitorDemo()
66:      Demo.FillArray()
67:
68:      ThreadPool.QueueUserWorkItem(AddressOf Demo.SortArray)
69:      ThreadPool.QueueUserWorkItem(AddressOf Demo.PrintArray)
70:
71:      Console.ReadLine()
72:
73:    End Sub
74:
75: End Class
```

Listing 14.5 uses `Monitor.Enter` and `Monitor.Exit` on lines 25 and 41 and again on lines 47 and 60. We would get the same result if we used the `SyncLock...End SyncLock` construct.

The `Main` subroutine is the starting point for this console application. An instance of the `MonitorDemo` class is created on line 65 and an array is filled with a thousand integers in reverse order. The `ThreadPool` is used on lines 68 and 69 requesting work from the `SortArray` and `PrintArray` methods. `SortArray` sorts the array of integers and `PrintArray` prints the integers in the array.

After each complete pass through the inner loop of the bubble sort, `Monitor.Wait` is called on line 36, giving the `PrintArray` method a chance to print the ordered *i*th element. Line 57 calls `Monitor.Pulse` notifying the `SortArray` method that the state has changed and allowing `SortArray` to reacquire the lock. The `Monitor.Wait` call on line 50 blocks the loop until the `PrintArray` method can reacquire the lock on the `Integers` object or one thousand milliseconds have elapsed. In summary, the code sorts each *i*th element and then prints the newly sorted element at the *i*th position.

Heavyweight Threading

Thus far all the examples could have been accomplished by creating an instance or instances of the `Thread` class and managing the thread directly. It is easiest to implement asynchronous behavior using the `Timer` control and the `Application.Idle` event, and easier to use threads in the thread pool. Using `Thread` objects is not significantly more difficult, but you do have to actively manage the threaded behavior and the thread objects. When you're writing code for money, the more difficult something is, the more it will cost. Unfortunately, that extra cost is seldom linear.

Creating and Using Threads

The basic steps for using the `Thread` class are an expansion of using the thread pool. The mechanics of using the `Thread` class include creating an instance of the `Thread` class, passing a worker method in the form of a delegate to the `Thread` constructor, setting `Thread.IsBackground = True`, and cleaning up when the thread is finished. In between you will have to contrive ways to synchronize the thread's interaction with shared resources; you can use several of the ways already discussed, including the `SyncLock..End SyncLock` construct, `WaitHandle` objects, and the `Monitor` class.

Table 14.1 lists some of the basic members of the `Thread` class that are available to facilitate thread management.

TABLE 14.1 Members of the `Thread` Class

Member Name	Description
	Instance Property
`ApartmentState`	Gets or sets the thread apartment model, either single-threaded apartment (STA) or multithreaded apartment (MTA).
`CurrentThread`	Returns the currently running thread.

TABLE 14.1 continued

Member Name	Description
	Instance Property
IsAlive	Returns True unless the thread state is Unstarted, Stopped, or Aborted.
IsBackground	True if the thread is a background thread; does not prevent a process from terminating.
Priority	Sets or gets the ThreadPriority, which is Normal, Lowest, Highest, BelowNormal, or AboveNormal.
ThreadState	Returns one value from the ThreadState enumeration.
	Instance Methods
Abort	Usually terminates the thread after raising a ThreadAbortException.
Interrupt	Interrupts a thread in the WaitSleepJoin state.
Join	Blocks the calling thread until it terminates.
Resume	Resumes a thread that has been suspended.
Start	Starts the thread.
Suspend	Suspends the thread (has no effect on a suspended thread).
	Shared Methods
GetDomain	Returns the AppDomain that the current thread is running on; for example, an AppDomain can be used to get the thread ID.
Sleep	Blocks the current thread for a specified number of milliseconds.
SpinWait	Causes a thread to wait a specified number of iterations.

Thread Demo

You already have some experience with the Dice demo. An updated copy of the Dice demo is in ThreadRollDice2 for you to compare to the first version that uses ThreadPool. A much shorter demonstration can be completed using the Monitor example from the section "Synchronization with the Monitor Class" and still demonstrate the salient differences between threading with ThreadPool and with the Thread class.

The revised complete application is defined on this book's Web site in the MonitorDemo2 folder. Listing 14.6 only contains the revised shared Sub Main from Listing 14.5 because that is pretty much all we have to change to use Thread objects.

LISTING 14.6   Using instances of the Thread class

```
1:  Public Shared Sub Main()
2:
3:      Dim Demo As New MonitorDemo()
4:      Demo.FillArray()
5:      Dim SortThread As New Thread(AddressOf Demo.SortArray)
6:      SortThread.IsBackground = True
7:
8:      Dim PrintThread As New Thread(AddressOf Demo.PrintArray)
9:      PrintThread.IsBackground = True
10:
11:      SortThread.Start()
12:      PrintThread.Start()
13:
14:      SortThread.Join()
15:      PrintThread.Join()
16:
17:      Console.ReadLine()
18:
19:  End Sub
```

As you recall from the earlier listing, the complete sample is a console application that uses the Monitor class to swap between two threads that sort and print an array. After each complete set of inner loop comparisons, the sorted *i*th element is printed on the second thread. In the original listing, ThreadPool was used. Here we use Thread objects that we create.

Lines 5–6 and 8–9 each create a Thread object and set its IsBackground property to True. If you forget to set IsBackground to True and forget to stop the thread, your application will mysteriously seem to hang after you exit, while any running foreground threads unwind. Notice that just as with ThreadPool, we are assigning work to the thread in the form of a delegate. The delegate used to construct a Thread object is a ThreadStart delegate, which is essentially the address of a subroutine that takes no arguments. (Recall that the ThreadPool.QueueUserWorkItem method takes a WaitCallBack delegate that requires a single Object argument.)

The two threads are started on lines 11 and 12, and each thread is blocked in turn until each exits. The Console.ReadLine call is provided to suspend closing the console until you have had a chance to review the results.

Applying the `ThreadStatic` Attribute

The `ThreadStatic` attribute can be applied to a shared field. Normally if a field is `Shared`, that field is accessible to an instance of the class as well as through the class itself.

The `ThreadStatic` attribute ensures that each instance of a class gets a unique copy of shared fields in those instances. Listing 14.7 demonstrates the `ThreadStatic` attribute.

LISTING 14.7 Using the `ThreadStatic` attribute

```
1: Imports System.Threading
2:
3: Public Class ThreadStaticDemo
4:   <ThreadStatic()> Private Shared I As Integer = 0
5:   Private Count As Integer = 0
6:
7:   Private Sub WriteCount()
8:
9:     Console.WriteLine( _
10:       String.Format("Thread {0} added {1} to count", _
11:       Thread.CurrentThread.GetDomain.GetCurrentThreadId(), _
12:       Count))
13:
14:   End Sub
15:
16:   Public Sub Increment()
17:
18:     While (Interlocked.Increment(I) < 1000000)
19:       Count += 1
20:     End While
21:
22:     WriteCount()
23:
24:   End Sub
25:
26:   Public Shared Function Instance() As ThreadStaticDemo
27:     Return New ThreadStaticDemo()
28:   End Function
29:
30: End Class
31:
32:
33: Module Module1
34:
35:
```

14

MULTITHREADED APPLICATIONS

LISTING 14.7 continued

```
36:    Sub Main()
37:
38:      Dim Threads(10) As Thread
39:      Dim I As Integer
40:      For I = 0 To Threads.Length - 1
41:        Threads(I) = New Thread( _
42:          AddressOf ThreadStaticDemo.Instance.Increment)
43:
44:        Threads(I).IsBackground = True
45:        Threads(I).Start()
46:      Next
47:
48:      For I = 0 To Threads.Length - 1
49:        Threads(I).Join()
50:      Next
51:
52:      Console.ReadLine()
53:
54:    End Sub
55:
56: End Module
```

Listing 14.7 defines a class `ThreadStaticDemo` and a module `Module1`. `Module1.Main` creates 11 `Thread` objects, and each one increments a shared variable `I` some number of times until `I` is equal to one million.

Notice the use of the `ThreadStatic` attribute on line 4. Line 4 as it is in the listing ensures that each instance of `ThreadStaticDemo` works with its own unique copy of `I`. With the `ThreadStatic` attribute, each thread increments its own `I` as reported by the `WriteCount` procedure. Remove the `ThreadStatic` attribute, and each thread works with the same `I`, and each thread performs only part of the total work. (See Figures 14.5 and 14.6.)

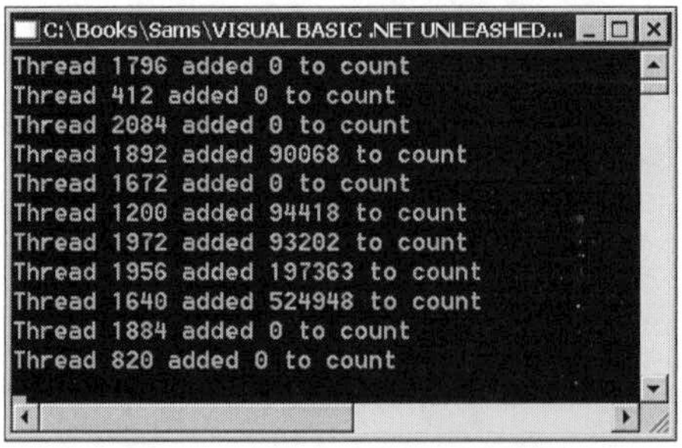

FIGURE 14.5

The results from Listing 14.7 without the `ThreadStatic` *attribute.*

```
C:\Books\Sams\VISUAL BASIC .NET UNLEASHED...
Thread 1796 added 0 to count
Thread 412 added 0 to count
Thread 2084 added 0 to count
Thread 1892 added 90068 to count
Thread 1672 added 0 to count
Thread 1200 added 94418 to count
Thread 1972 added 93202 to count
Thread 1956 added 197363 to count
Thread 1640 added 524948 to count
Thread 1884 added 0 to count
Thread 820 added 0 to count
```

```
C:\Books\Sams\VISUAL BASIC .NET UNLEASHED...
Thread 1892 added 999999 to count
Thread 1972 added 999999 to count
Thread 412 added 999999 to count
Thread 1884 added 999999 to count
Thread 1200 added 999999 to count
Thread 2084 added 999999 to count
Thread 1672 added 999999 to count
Thread 820 added 999999 to count
Thread 1956 added 999999 to count
Thread 1592 added 999999 to count
Thread 1640 added 999999 to count
```

Figure 14.5 shows the output from the console application without the ThreadStatic
attribute where the workload is somewhat distributed, and Figure 14.6 shows the output
from the example with the ThreadStatic attribute where each thread performs the same
amount of work.

Multithreading in Windows Forms

> **Tip**
>
> This section assumes that you have a certain comfort level working with
> Windows Forms, and delves directly into the topic of multithreading with forms.
> If you need basic information on how to design and construct Windows Forms,
> turn to Chapter 15, "Using Windows Forms," for coverage from the ground up.

Windows controls are not thread-safe. You are going to hear this a lot as you begin to
explore Visual Basic .NET, participate in user discussions, and read technical materials.
All of the implications of this statement remain to be determined except by perhaps a very
small minority at Microsoft. I know this from having several discussions with program
managers and a few developers, and reading the opinions of other developer-writers.

> **Note**
>
> One of the best discussions on the risks of using threads in VB .NET can be
> found in *Moving to VB.NET: Strategies, Concepts, and Code, Beta 2* (Appleman,
> 2001). Appleman's approach is somewhat conservative—probably derived from
> years of learning the hard way.

14

**MULTITHREADED
APPLICATIONS**

Software is difficult enough to write well; throw in multithreading and it can get downright tricky. My approach is somewhat less conservative. Threads exist for a reason, and limitations regarding the CLR—specifically, Windows Forms—are problems for Microsoft to solve. Other frameworks have breached this threshold, as I am sure Microsoft will.

Know what you are getting into. Use threads sparingly. Anticipate trickier bugs. Don't hesitate to ask for experienced help, and don't blow deadlines striving for anticipated multithreading performance gains. If you are adding threading for performance reasons, consider making the revisions after you have established proof that performance tuning is needed, and ensure that you have a rollback plan in case threads break your application. Potential problems can be further mitigated by writing refactored code, isolating the multithreaded code as much as possible, and having a backup plan in case your threaded code fails catastrophically.

Multithreaded Strategies for Windows Forms

The purpose of using threads with Windows Forms will generally be that you want some action and a visual representation of a result to be displayed on a form. The most common approach to this problem is to write the thread, having the thread update a field that you have added to the form, and then have a timer at regular intervals read the value and update the form.

The reason for this is that you are not directly interacting with Windows Forms across thread boundaries if you are writing to a field you added, and the timer `Tick` event will be running on the same thread as the form. In essence, the thread updates the data and the timer updates the form.

The second approach that is often mentioned is to use the `Control.Invoke` method implemented in every control. You can call `Control.InvokeRequired` first, but when you're working with Windows Forms controls, assume that it is required. `Control.Invoke` takes a `MethodInvoker` delegate argument and calls the method referenced by the delegate on the same thread as the form. Listing 15.6 in the "Region Class" section of Chapter 15 demonstrates using the `ThreadPool` and the `Invoke` method, combined with the `Form.Opacity` property to fade in a form.

Both the `Timer` and the `Control.Invoke` have worked reliably for me when using threads in conjunction with Windows Forms. The bigger problem has been determining when to allow the user to update the form or control based on completion of the thread or threads.

This problem can be resolved using synchronization techniques explained earlier in this chapter.

As you will quickly determine from many of the Quickstarts samples provided by Microsoft, many of the sample threading applications are console applications. However, the form fade-in example in Chapter 15 and the dice example in this chapter are not; they both interact with Windows forms and seem to do so reliably.

Synchronous Calls with `Invoke`

Windows Forms are based on Win32, which uses the single-threaded apartment model. This means that a window can be created on any thread but cannot switch threads. Consequently, you must call methods of a window on the same thread that the window is on. The CLR supports synchronous calls using `Invoke` and asynchronous calls using `BeginInvoke` and `EndInvoke`. (We'll return to asynchronous calls in a moment.)

You have already used the synchronous `Invoke` in this chapter. To recap, `Invoke` takes a `MethodInvoker` delegate—essentially, the `AddressOf` a subroutine with no parameters—calls the delegate on the same thread as the control calling `Invoke` and waits for the `Invoke` method to return. That's the synchronous part.

All Windows Forms controls implement `Invoke`, `BeginInvoke`, and `EndInvoke` because these methods are introduced in the `Control` class.

Asynchronous Calls with `BeginInvoke` and `EndInvoke`

`BeginInvoke` effectively performs the same task as `Invoke` but does so asynchronously. That is, `BeginInvoke` does not sit around and wait for the invoked method to return. As a result, you need another mechanism to respond at a later time when the asynchronous call returns. This is the `EndInvoke` method.

Calling `BeginInvoke`

`BeginInvoke` is introduced in the `Control` class. `BeginInvoke` is safe to call from any thread and marshals a call via a delegate onto the thread that the control's handle is on. `BeginInvoke` is a lightweight means of introducing asynchronous behavior into your Windows Forms-based applications.

`BeginInvoke` has two versions. The first version takes a delegate and the second (overloaded) version takes a delegate and an array of objects representing the parameters to the delegate method. Because the first parameter in both versions of `BeginInvoke` takes a `System.Delegate`, you can define any delegate with any number of parameters and

invoke a method asynchronously using methods that match the signature of the delegate. The two signatures for BeginInvoke follow.

```
Overloads Public Function BeginInvoke(Delegate) As IAsyncResult
Overloads NotOverridable Public Function BeginInvoke(Delegate, _
  Object()) As IAsyncResult Implements ISynchronizeInvoke.BeginInvoke
```

Although BeginInvoke runs on the same thread as the calling control, it does so asynchronously much the same way any event would run. You get behavior similar to starting a process on a Timer tick. Listing 14.8 demonstrates using the asynchronous behavior of BeginInvoke to initialize a ListBox when an application loads while letting the form's Load event complete.

LISTING 14.8   Using BeginInvoke for lightweight asynchronous processing

```
 1:  Imports System.Threading
 2:
 3:  Public Class Form1
 4:      Inherits System.Windows.Forms.Form
 5:
 6:  [ Windows Form Designer generated code ]
 7:
 8:      Private Delegate Sub Invoker(ByVal Count As Integer)
 9:
10:      Private Sub LoadListBox(ByVal Count As Integer)
11:        Dim I As Integer
12:        For I = 0 To Count
13:          ListBox1.Items.Add(I)
14:        Next
15:      End Sub
16:
17:      Private Sub Form1_Load(ByVal sender As System.Object, _
18:       ByVal e As System.EventArgs) Handles MyBase.Load
19:
20:        Dim AsynchResult As IAsyncResult
21:        Dim Count As Integer = 100000
22:        AsynchResult = BeginInvoke(New Invoker(AddressOf LoadListBox), _
23:          New Object() {Count})
24:
25:      End Sub
26:
27: End Class
```

This listing simulates a labor-intensive form initialization process by adding 100,000 elements to a ListBox. With synchronous behavior, the ListBox would delay the appearance of the form and completion of the form's Load event. As a result of invoking the ListBox initialization process with BeginInvoke, the ListBox loads asynchronously, allowing the Load event to finish and mitigating the need for a thread for such a simple task.

The delegate Invoker is defined as a subroutine taking a single integer argument. The method LoadListBox matches the signature of the delegate and is used as the first argument for BeginInvoke on line 22. (Notice that the verbose construction of the Invoker delegate was employed.) The second argument to BeginInvoke is an array of objects. The way this array is created and initialized may look a little strange.

The second argument to BeginInvoke demonstrates an inline construction of an Object initialized as an array. The value of Count on line 23 becomes the value passed to the Count parameter in the LoadListBox method. If you need to pass additional arguments to your delegate, add them to the array initializer, delimiting each argument with a comma. The verbose form demonstrating construction of an array of objects initialized by an array of value types follows.

```
Dim O() As Object = {Count}
Dim O As Object() = {Count}
Dim O() As Object = New Object() {Count}
Dim O As Object() = New Object() {Count}
```

All four versions construct the same object. (You might encounter any of the four types depending on the inclinations of individual programmers.) Versions 1 and 2 declare an array of Object and initialize the array to a single-element array containing the value Count. The first version uses the array descriptor on the variable name and the second uses the array descriptor on the type. The third and fourth versions vary the position of the array descriptor as well as employ the verbose version of object construction and initialization using the New keyword to invoke the constructor.

IAsyncResult Interface and EndInvoke

The object implementing the IAsyncResult interface returned by BeginInvoke implements four public properties, providing you with a variety of ways to manage the asynchronous process. These properties are AsyncState, AsyncWaitHandle, CompletedSynchronously, and IsCompleted. Table 14.2 briefly describes the uses for these properties.

14

MULTITHREADED APPLICATIONS

TABLE 14.2 IAsyncResult Public Properties

Property Name	Description
AsyncState	Gets user-defined information about an asynchronous process
AsyncWaitHandle	A WaitHandle that can be used to wait for the asynchronous process

TABLE 14.2   continued

Property Name	Description
CompletedSynchronously	Returns a Boolean indicating if the asynchronous process returned synchronously
IsCompleted	A Boolean indicating that the process has completed

The `EndInvoke` method takes a specific `IAsyncResult` object returned by `BeginInvoke` and blocks until the asynchronous behavior returns. Upon return, the `IAsyncResult` object contains information about the state of the asynchronous process, and `EndInvoke` returns an object representing the return value of the invoked method.

If you add the following code to the example in Listing 14.8, the code will block until the `ListBox` is loaded and display the results of the asynchronous process.

```
EndInvoke(AsynchResult)
MsgBox(AsynchResult.IsCompleted)
```

Insert the preceding two lines of code at line 24 of Listing 14.8. The `EndInvoke` method will block and the `MsgBox` statement will display a Boolean value indicating whether or not the process finished.

Summary

The CLR supports asynchronous processing, lightweight threading using `ThreadPool`, and heavyweight threading by constructing instances of the `Thread` class. You are not limited to an all-or-nothing approach when implementing asynchronous or threaded behavior.

Choose the `Timer` control or `Application.Idle` event or `BeginInvoke` and `EndInvoke` for lightweight asynchronous behavior in Windows Forms. Consider using `ThreadPool` for many everyday multithreading tasks, and pull out the big gun—the `Thread` class—if you need absolute control. Of course, when using the `Thread` class, you have to take complete ownership of the behavior of the thread, including creating, starting, and stopping the thread.

The CLR, and consequently Visual Basic .NET, support asynchronous and multithreaded behavior as well as a whole complement of synchronization and shared resource management by using the `WaitHandle` or `Monitor` classes. Consider all of the available resources for asynchronous and threaded behavior before selecting a particular implementation strategy.

CHAPTER 15

Using Windows Forms

The `System.Windows.Forms` namespace provides a diverse hierarchy of classes, structures, delegates, and events for creating a rich graphical user interface. The `Forms` namespace contains the `Form` class as well as controls that can be used and subclassed for Windows applications.

Chapter 15 explores the `System.Windows.Forms` namespace, demonstrating some of the controls that you will commonly employ to design and implement graphical user interfaces. In this chapter, we will take a tour of the `Forms` namespace, demonstrate how to implement the various aspects of a form in .NET, and look at custom form shaping and painting afforded by GDI+.

Reviewing the `Forms` Namespace

This section offers an overview of some of the members of the `System.Windows.Forms` namespace—as opposed to those in the `System.Web` namespace, commonly referred to as WebForms—that you will use frequently to design Windows applications.

> **Note**
>
> Visual Basic .NET allows you to write an `Imports` statement that includes the class name. For example, `Imports System.Windows.Forms.Form` is valid in Visual Basic .NET, but you can't use the class, `Form`, in C# (C Sharp).

A discussion of all the members of the `System.Windows.Forms` namespace and their respective elements would require a book of its own. Hence, we will limit our discussion to a sampling of the classes and other elements of the `Forms` namespace. For a complete reference, check out the `System.Windows.Forms` namespace help topic. (Throughout the rest of this section, we will refer to the `System.Windows.Forms` namespace as the `Forms` namespace for brevity.)

Classes in the `Forms` Namespace

There are dozens of classes in the `Forms` namespace. In this section we will cover a few of them and demonstrate some interesting characteristics or uses for each of the classes covered. (Keep in mind that the list isn't comprehensive.)

Application Class

The `Application` class is similar to the VB6 `App` object. In Visual Basic .NET, the application class is defined to contain all shared members; an alternative would be to implement the `Application` object as a singleton instance.

Only one instance of a *singleton* class is created. Singleton objects are created implicitly or on demand and often represent a single physical object. For example, a `Printer` object might represent the notion of the single printer in use at any given time.

ExecutablePath

The `Application` class contains shared methods and events that allow you to manage a Windows application. The `Application` class represents a single Windows application. You can use the shared `ExecutablePath` property to get the path of the executable that started the application.

DoEvents

The `DoEvents` method has been moved to the `Application` class. `DoEvents` processes all messages in the message queue. Just as in VB6, you will want to call `Application.DoEvents` when you are performing loop-intensive processes like loading a file, filling a list, or processing a custom sort; if you don't, your application may appear to be sluggish when it comes to repainting or responding to user feedback.

> ### Caution
>
> DoEvents can cause code such as event handlers to be re-entrant.

Exit and ExitThread

The `Application.Exit` method causes all message queues to shut down and closes all forms. The `Exit` method doesn't force the application to shut down but does cause the `Application.Run` method to return.

If you want to exit the current thread only, call `Application.ExitThread`. Keep in mind that Visual Basic .NET supports multiple threading, so exiting a thread may become a common occurrence.

Idle Event

Applications tend to have a tremendous amount of idle time. To get background tasks to process, we implemented `Timer` event handlers in VB6 and we can use the `Idle` event in Visual Basic .NET.

The `Idle` event is raised when your application isn't actively processing. Idle processor time may be less prevalent with multithreaded Visual Basic .NET, but is likely to still exist. Use the `Idle` event to perform short, staccato tasks that won't adversely affect your

15

application's performance if it's not called occasionally. Listing 15.1 demonstrates using the `Idle` event to update a clock on a status bar.

LISTING 15.1   Using the `Application.Idle` event to perform lightweight background processing

```
 1: Private Sub OnIdle(ByVal sender As Object, _
 2:   ByVal e As System.EventArgs)
 3:
 4:   StatusBarPanelClock.Text = TimeOfDay
 5:
 6: End Sub
 7:
 8: Private Sub Form1_Load(ByVal sender As System.Object, _
 9:   ByVal e As System.EventArgs) Handles MyBase.Load
10:
11:   AddHandler Application.Idle, AddressOf OnIdle
12:
13: End Sub
```

The `Application.Idle` event requires an `EventHandler` delegate; that is, it requires the address of a procedure that has two parameters: `Object` and `System.EventArgs`. The `OnIdle` procedure was added manually and the delegate was created and associated with the `Application.Idle` event on line 11 of Listing 15.1. (You can also define a `WithEvents` statement and add the `Handles` clause to the `OnIdle` event handler, as demonstrated in Chapter 8, "Adding Events.")

The `StatusBar` was added from the Windows Forms tab of the toolbox and the panel `StatusBarPanelClock` was added using the `Panels` collection in the Properties window. (Also, set the `StatusBar.ShowPanels` property to True.)

If you need lightweight processing, use the `Idle` event of the `Application` object. If you need serious processing power, the best way to get it is to create a new thread, instead of using a `Timer` or the `Idle` event.

ContextMenu Class

Context menus are all those menus that pop up when you right-click over controls that have a menu associated with them. Context menus are also referred to as pop-ups, speed menus, or right-click menus. The `ContextMenu` control is added to the component tray, as shown in Figure 15.1.

FIGURE 15.1

Nonvisual controls are added to the component tray as shown.

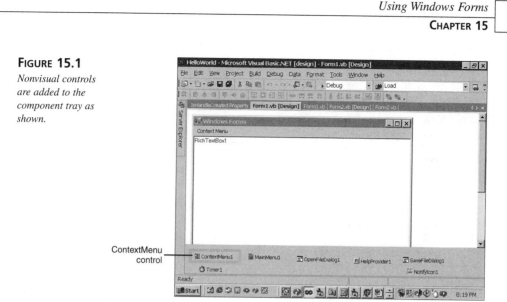

ContextMenu control

Context menus work by adding menu items, implementing event handlers to respond to menu clicks, and associating the context menu with one or more controls. Essentially, a ContextMenu control is designed like any menu (see the section on the Menu class coming up) and is associated with a second control's ContextMenu property. For example, to have ContextMenu1 (shown in Figure 15.1) pop up when the user right-clicks over the form shown in the figure, assign Form1's ContextMenu property to ContextMenu1 (see Figure 15.2).

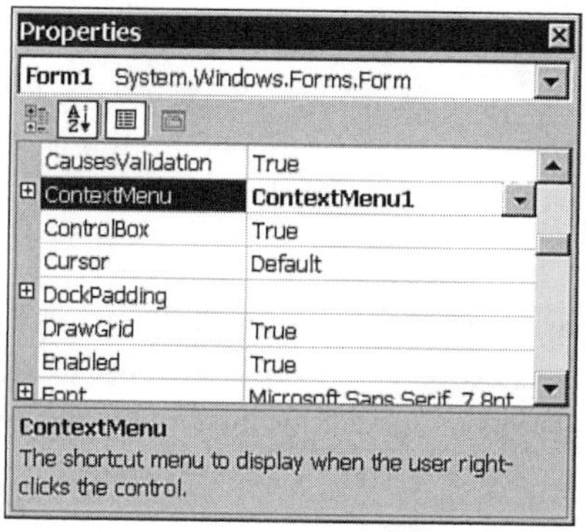

FIGURE 15.2

Associating a ContextMenu *with a control via the* ContextMenu *property.*

Cursor Class

The Cursor class represents the iconic pointing device. There is a collection of cursors that you can choose from to indicate what is occurring internally in your application. For example, if you have a long startup process, you might want to display the AppStarting

15

USING WINDOWS FORMS

cursor. The Load event demonstrated earlier isn't particularly long, but we will use it to demonstrate how to change cursors.

LISTING 15.2   Displaying the AppStarting cursor and using a resource protection block to make sure the cursor is reset

```
 1: Private Sub Form1_Load(ByVal sender As System.Object,
 2:    ByVal e As System.EventArgs) Handles MyBase.Load
 3:
 4:    Cursor = Cursors.AppStarting
 5:    Try
 6:      AddHandler Application.Idle, AddressOf OnIdle
 7:    Finally
 8:      Cursor = Cursors.Default
 9:    End Try
10:
11: End Sub
```

> **Tip**
>
> Use a Try..Finally block to ensure that resources, like the Cursor, are managed.

Listing 15.2 displays the AppStarting cursor while the application is loading (line 4) and uses a resource protection block—represented by the Try..Finally..End Try block—to ensure that the cursor is reset to the default cursor. There is nothing more confusing than an inappropriate cursor.

The Cursors class contains all shared properties, each representing a specific cursor object. In Listing 15.2, the Cursors.AppStarting and the Cursors.Default properties are demonstrated.

The Cursors class contains methods for hiding and showing the cursor, changing the position, and customizing the appearance of the cursor. For example, you can call Cursor.DrawStretched to make a small image fill up the cursor image space.

FileDialog Class

The FileDialog class is an abstract class. FileDialog is the base class for the OpenFileDialog and SaveFileDialog controls. OpenFileDialog and SaveFileDialog replace the CommonDialog from VB6 and allow you to navigate through the file system to open and save files respectively.

The easiest way to use the `FileDialog` controls is to add one each to a form and call the `ShowDialog` method. Comparing the return value of `ShowDialog` to one of the `DialogResult` enumerations will allow you to determine user feedback.

`FileDialog` controls display the same dialog boxes you see when you are interacting with Windows (see Figure 15.3).

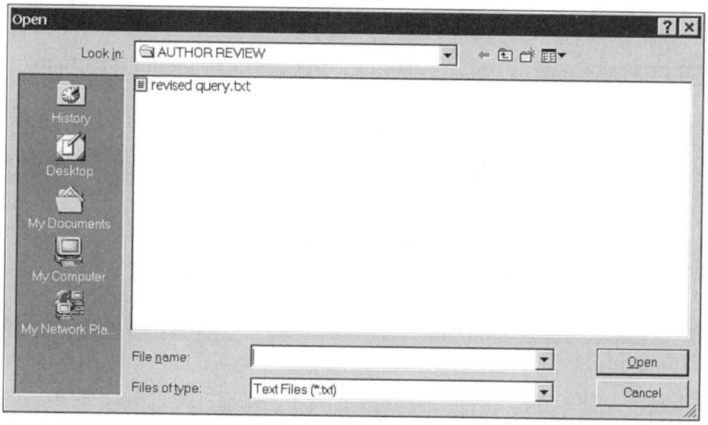

FIGURE 15.3

`OpenFileDialog` *displays the same dialog box used by the Windows Explorer.*

The `HelloWorld.sln` demonstrates several capabilities of the `RichTextBox` control, including the ability to load and save rich text or plain text files. To load the contents of a text file into a `RichTextBox` control, call `RichTextBox.LoadFile(path)`. An overloaded version allows you to indicate what kind of text is in the file. By default, the `RichTextBox` control attempts to load the file as rich text. If the file contains plain text, an exception is raised. To indicate that you want to load a plain text file, call the file as follows:

```
RichTextBox.LoadFile(FileName, RichTextBoxStreamType.PlainText)
```

Passing the enumerated value `PlainText` indicates the type of contents.

Similar to the `CommonDialog` in VB6, it's helpful to specify a value for the `Filter` property to help constrain the type of files returned in the list. (The `Filter` property is applicable to the `SaveFileDialog` and `OpenFileDialog`. Assuming that you have an `OpenFileDialog1` control added to your application, the following statement would add filters to the Files of Type list (shown in Figure 15.3).

```
OpenFileDialog1.Filter = "Text Files (*.txt)|*.txt" & _
  "|Rich Text (*.rtf)|*.rtf|All Files(*.*)|*.*"
```

The same filter would work adequately for a SaveFileDialog, too. The following code fragment demonstrates how to initialize the filter, show the Open dialog box, and load the value of a file into a RichTextBox.

```
OpenFileDialog1.Filter = "Text Files (*.txt)|*.txt" & _
  "|Rich Text (*.rtf)|*.rtf|All Files(*.*)|*.*"
If (OpenFileDialog1.ShowDialog() = DialogResult.OK) Then
  RichTextBox.LoadFile(FileName, RichTextBoxStreamType.PlainText)
End If
```

Similar code could be used to save the contents of the RichTextBox.

Form Class

Forms are full-fledged classes in Visual Basic .NET with no hinky stuff going on in the background. Form classes have constructors and destructors and can be created and used like any other class. Distinct from VB6, too, is the fact that forms are contained in a .vb file as a class, and the file can contain more than one class, structure, or module.

The visual description of a form is contained in a file with a .resx extension. All the code is contained in a file with a matching name and a .vb extension.

Because this chapter is about using Windows Forms as well as the Forms namespace, we will look at how to take full advantage of the Form class after we finish a tour of the Forms namespace.

Help Class

The Help class encapsulates the HTML Help 1.0 Engine. You can't create an instance of the Help class. You will need to add a HelpProvider control to your application and call the static methods Help.ShowHelp and Help.ShowHelpIndex.

To show the help index, call the shared method Help.ShowHelpIndex. If you want to associate an HTML help file with controls on your form, use the HelpProvider control. The code fragment that follows demonstrates how to display the demo help file index created with RoboHelp HTML:

```
Help.ShowHelpIndex(Me, "..\..\Help\DemoHelp\DemoHelp.chm")
```

The help window is shown in Figure 15.4.

> **Note**
>
> RoboHelp is a product developed by Blue Sky Software. Discussions of RoboHelp are beyond the scope of this book, but RoboHelp HTML is very easy and intuitive to use.

FIGURE 15.4

The DemoHelp *file created for the* HelloWorld, *Windows Forms sample application.*

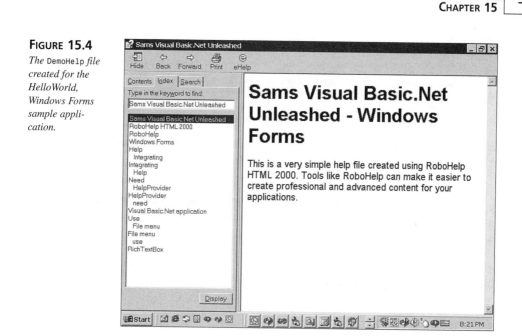

The example uses a relative file path. Alternatively, the HelpNamespace property of a HelpProvider could be used to satisfy the url argument containing the help file.

Menu Class

The Menu class is the abstract base class for menus in Visual Basic. NET. The sample HelloWorld application demonstrates using the MainMenu and MenuItems controls.

Unlike menus in VB6, menus are classes in Visual Basic .NET. You can add a MainMenu control to the component tray, and the menu design process is WYSIWYG. Visual Basic .NET doesn't use a separate dialog box for menus. To create the sample menu demonstrated in the HelloWorld.sln for Chapter 15, follow these steps:

1. With a Windows Form in the foreground, select the MainMenu control from the Windows Forms tab of the toolbox.

2. With the MainMenu selected, click the component tray beneath the visible form. (Alternatively, you can double-click the MainMenu control and the IDE will place the control in the tray for you.)

3. Click the MainMenu in the tray to give it the focus. At the top of the form you will see an outlined box with the words "Type Here" in a gray-colored font.

4. Click the box and begin typing the menu name, preceding the key you want to be the hotkey with an ampersand (&). (This part works just like VB6.)

5. You can provide a better name later using the Properties window. For now, the menu designer will provide the control with a default name similar to `MenuItem1`, where each subsequent menu item has a suffix, which is the next number in the sequence.

6. Double-click the menu item to generate an event handler.

Notice that when you select a menu with text, a child and sibling position (with the text "Type Here") are added automatically.

To insert child or sibling menus, select the child or sibling at the insertion point and press the Insert key. Use the same technique to delete child or sibling menus. With any menu item selected, you can also use the context menu in the IDE for managing menus, but you probably won't need to.

The `MainMenu` and all `MenuItems` are objects. You can refer to the main menu or its items directly by name, or you can access menu items through the `MainMenu.MenuItems` collection. The following statement shows the text property of the first menu's submenu:

```
MsgBox(MainMenu1.MenuItems(0).MenuItems(0).Text)
```

In the `HelloWorld.sln` example, the message box will display the text `"&New"`.

MessageBox Class

The `MessageBox` class has one practical, shared, overloaded method named `Show`. `MessageBox.Show` displays a dialog box identical to the `MsgBox` function from VB6. More than likely, the `MsgBox` function in Visual Basic .NET is implemented in terms of the `MessageBox` class.

The `MsgBox` function is introduced in the `Microsoft.VisualBasic` namespace and isn't part of the CLR. You can still use the `MsgBox` function if you would like to, but it's the `MessageBox` class in `Systems.Windows.Forms` that's part of the CLR. There are 12 overloaded `Show` methods in the `MessageBox` class; for the most part, you will use `MessageBox.Show` just as you would the old `MsgBox` function.

```
MessageBox.Show("Hello World!")
```

The preceding text yields the same visual result as `MsgBox("Hello World!")`. IntelliSense is a quick way to identify acceptable variations of methods and other class members as you are developing your code. When you type the `Show` method and then type its opening parenthesis, for example, IntelliSense displays a scrollable list of all 12 versions of the `Show` method.

MouseEventArgs Class

The MouseEventArgs class encapsulates the information necessary to determine the mouse state when a mouse event occurs. When you create a mouse event handler, you will get a MouseEventArgs parameter as the second argument of the event handler.

Fundamental members of the MouseEventArgs class include the Button, Clicks, Delta, X, and Y properties. Button indicates which mouse button was clicked. Clicks indicates the number of times the button was clicked. Delta indicates the number of detents the mouse wheel was rotated as a signed value (*detents* are the notches on the internal mouse wheel). Delta is signed. A positive number indicates a mouse wheel forward movement, and a negative number indicates backward movement. X and Y indicate the x and y offsets of the mouse position. The top-left corner of a control is 0, 0 and the lower-right corner is width, height.

NativeWindow Class

The NativeWindow class provides a low-level encapsulation of the WndProc and window Handle. NativeWindow implements AssignHandle, CreateHandle, DestroyHandle, and the WndProc procedure.

> ### Tip
>
> The WindowTarget property allows you to assign OnMessage and OnHandleChange delegates to a window control, providing you with low-level message access and handle change notification.

Assigning the WindowTarget property of a window control to a NativeWindow variable provides you with direct access to the underlying native Windows handle and window procedures of a control. IntelliSense provides no clue that WindowTarget exists, suggesting that WindowTarget has little pedestrian use.

> ### Note
>
> Some members are considered *advanced members* by Microsoft developers. If you choose Tools, Options, and choose the Basic folder of the Text Editor Options, you can uncheck Hide Advanced Members. Unchecking this option allows IntelliSense to show advanced members, but WindowTarget and NativeWindow still will not be displayed.

Only Microsoft knows the reasoning here, which is one reason why many people are pushing for them to release all of the CLR code to developers. An excellent way to learn is by examining the code that supports the framework. Having access to the CLR code beats the pants off guesswork.

NotifyIcon Class

The NotifyIcon control is placed in the component tray. NotifyIcon allows you to associate an icon and ContextMenu with the control and shows the icon in the system tray (the rectangular area on the lower-right side of the taskbar).

Generally, system tray icons are used to access background applications. Figure 15.5 shows the U.S. flag in the system tray for the HelloWorld.sln.

FIGURE 15.5

Use the NotifyIcon control to add an icon and ContextMenu to the system tray shown.

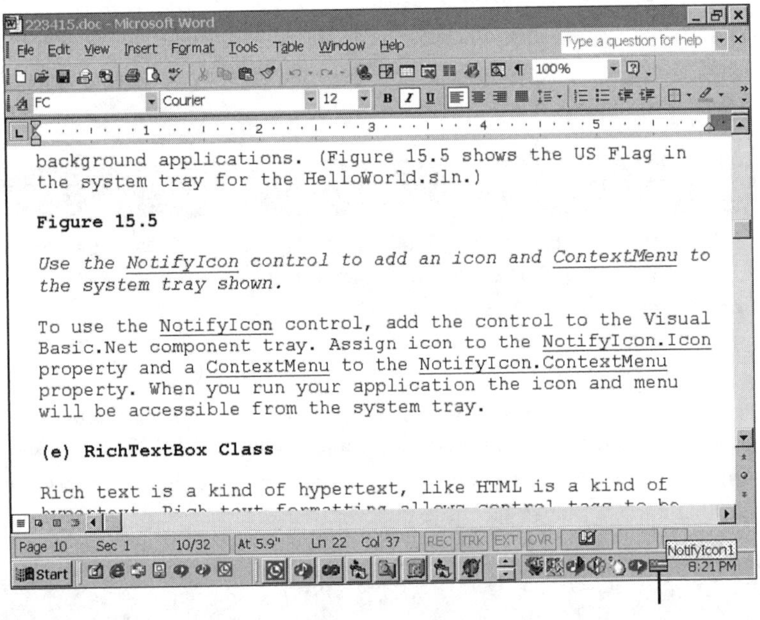

To use the NotifyIcon control, add the control to the Visual Basic .NET component tray. Assign an icon to the NotifyIcon.Icon property and a ContextMenu to the NotifyIcon. ContextMenu property. When you run your application, the icon and menu will be accessible from the system tray.

RichTextBox Class

Rich text is a type of hypertext, just as HTML is a type of hypertext. Rich text formatting allows control tags to be embedded in plain text, and a rich text control can evaluate the text to determine how to display the content. Rich text uses tags and was the precursor to HTML, WML, and XML.

> **Note**
>
> HTML refers to *hypertext markup language*. WML refers to *wireless markup language*, and XML refers to *extensible markup language*. Markup languages generally are plain text with embedded tags that are interpreted and used to display the text in the format we specify.

The RichTextBox control makes it easy to load and save text and facilitates text formatting and searching. Sample code earlier in the chapter demonstrates how to load and retrieve text using a combination of the RichTextBox and dialog controls.

Splitter Class

The Splitter control is a visual control used to manage graphical real estate between nested window controls. Applied to the HelloWorld sample program, you might choose to display two text controls. One control shows the formatted rich text, and the second shows the raw text. By placing the splitter control between the two TextBoxBase-based controls, you allow the end user to visually apportion screen real estate.

StatusBar Class

The StatusBar control is used to create a displayable text region at the bottom of forms. Generally, status bars are used to provide textual indicators of what is going on in your application. (In the HelloWorld sample application, the system time is displayed.)

The new StatusBar is object oriented. When you use the Panels property to create subpanels on the StatusBar, the panels themselves are generated as independent controls. The result is that you can refer to individual panels through the StatusBar.Panels collection or directly using the StatusBarPanel control (refer to Listing 15.1 for an example).

Timer Class

You are familiar with the `Timer` control from VB6. Use the `Timer` control when you want some lightweight processing to occur at regular intervals.

Of course, Visual Basic .NET supports multithreading, but you should avoid rampant thread usage. Consider using the `Application.Idle` event or the `Timer` control for simple background processing and use an additional thread if you have some processor-intensive process that can run suitably in the background.

> **Tip**
>
> The `Timer` control is located on the `Windows Forms` tab of the toolbox.

To use the `Timer`, add a `Timer` control to the component tray and double-click the control to generate the `Tick` event handler. Earlier in the chapter, we used the `Idle` event of the `Application` object to update the clock in the `StatusBar` of the `HelloWorld.sln`. Alternately, we could use a timer to ensure the clock was updated at regular intervals, rather than the sporadic intervals of the `Idle` event.

Interfaces in the `Forms` Namespace

As you can determine from the preceding sampling of some of the classes in the `Forms` namespace, `Forms` has a lot of good stuff in it. As you might expect, all the common controls for building Windows applications—such as combo boxes, text boxes, and labels—are in the Windows Forms namespace, in addition to several new interfaces.

This section provides a sampling of interfaces in the `Forms` namespace; however, as we have already discussed, you will need to explore the .NET Framework to find out more.

`IButtonControl` Interface

The `Button` and `LinkLabel` control implement this interface. The `IButtonControl` introduces the `DialogResult` property and the `NotifyDefault` and `PerformClick` methods. Implement this interface for controls that behave like buttons.

`DialogResult` returns an enumeration indicating the value returned to a parent form when the button is clicked. `NotifyDefault` notifies a control that it's the default control, and `PerformClick` invokes the click behavior of the control.

IMessageFilter Interface

The Splitter control is the only control that implements the IMessageFilter interface. The only instance method you have to implement for this interface is the PreFilterMessage method. PreFilterMessage allows controls that implement this interface to filter the message. PreFilterMessage is a function; if it returns True, the control doesn't receive the message.

Call Application.AddMessageFilter to your class that implements IMessageFilter to add a message filter to the application message queue. Listing 15.3 demonstrates how to implement the IMessageFilter.

LISTING 15.3 Implementing the IMessageFilter and viewing all messages processed in the application queue

```
 1: Public Class Form1
 2:    Inherits System.Windows.Forms.Form
 3:    Implements IMessageFilter
 4:
 5:    Private Function PreFilterMessage(ByRef m As Message) _
 6:      As Boolean Implements IMessageFilter.PreFilterMessage
 7:
 8:      Try
 9:        RichTextBox1.Text &= m.ToString & vbCrLf
10:      Catch
11:        RichTextBox1.Text = vbNullString
12:      End Try
13:
14:      Return False
15:    End Function
16:
17: [ Windows Form Designer generated code ]
18:
19:    Private Sub Form1_Load(ByVal sender As System.Object, _
20:      ByVal e As System.EventArgs) Handles MyBase.Load
21:
22:      RichTextBox1.Clear()
23:      Application.AddMessageFilter(Me)
24:    End Sub
25: End Class
```

Caution

Filtering messages can cause sluggish application performance.

15

USING WINDOWS FORMS

Listing 15.3 implements the IMessageFilter on line 3. Lines 5 through 15 implement the only required interface method. The PreFilterMessage method writes the message to a RichTextBox. By returning False, the application gets all messages (line 14). You could provide conditional logic and selectively filter messages by returning True. Line 23 adds the Form—using the reference to self, Me—as a recipient of messages from the application's message queue.

IWin32Window Interface

The IWin32Window interface is implemented in the class Control. This interface provides access to a single property, Handle, enabling you to access the window handle of the control.

Structures in the Forms Namespace

In Chapter 4, "Macros and Visual Studio Extensibility," you learned that the Visual Basic .NET Structure replaces the VB6 Type but is more closely related to the C++ struct; Visual Basic .NET structures support methods, properties, and constructors. (Read Chapter 4 for a complete discussion of the Structure idiom in Visual Basic .NET.)

There are just a couple of ValueType definitions in the Forms namespace, including the most essential one, Message, and the LinkArea structure.

Message Structure

The Message structure implements the Windows messages. To create an instance of a Windows message structure, use the Create method. Two important members of the Message structure include the handle represented by the HWnd property and the Msg property.

LinkArea Structure

The LinkArea structure represents the hyperlink portion of the LinkLabel control.

Delegates in the Forms Namespace

Delegates encapsulate function pointers to event handlers. A subclass of the Delegate class is the multicast delegate. There are several Delegate subclasses in the Forms namespace to facilitate the needs of handling specific kinds of device-related events. Keyboard handlers need key information. Mouse handlers need mouse state information, different from keyboard state information, and paint messages need a Graphics object indicating the paint surface.

This section covers some of the specific delegates necessary to make the rich graphical user interface environment work interactively.

ControlEventHandler Delegate

The ControlEventHandler is used to respond to ControlAdded and ControlRemoved events. These two events fire when a control is added to or removed from a control's Controls collection.

> **Tip**
>
> The ControlEventHandler for ControlAdded and ControlRemoved events combined provides behavior similar to the Object Pascal Notification method. (If you are familiar with Delphi, this information will be useful.)

The event handler has the following form:

```
Sub eventhandlername(ByVal sender As Object, ByVal e As ControlEventArgs)
```

The second parameter contains a reference to the control being added or removed. These events are especially useful when you are adding and removing controls dynamically (as Visual Studio .NET does when you are designing in the IDE) and are maintaining references to those controls. The following code fragment demonstrates a scenario in which the ControlAdded event would be raised:

```
Dim AButton As New Button()
AButton.Text = "Click"
AButton.Name = "AButton"
AButton.Top = 0 : AButton.Left = 0
Controls.Add(AButton)
AddHandler AButton.Click, AddressOf MyClick
```

The first line creates the control, followed by lines that add a caption, name the control, and define a top-left corner position. The line Controls.Add(AButton) adds the button to the Controls collection and consequently raises the ControlAdd event. The last line demonstrates how to dynamically add an event handler for the button itself.

KeyEventHandler Delegate

KeyEventHandler delegates describe method pointers that respond to KeyUp and KeyDown events. The second parameter is a KeyEventArgs class that contains the key that was pressed and any key modifiers like Ctrl, Alt, or Shift.

15

USING WINDOWS FORMS

KeyPressHandler Delegate

The KeyPressHandler responds to key-press events, passing a KeyPressEventArgs object to the event handler. The KeyPressEventArgs object contains a KeyChar property, which represents the value of the key including the modifiers. For example, pressing Shift+P raises key-down, key-press, and key-up events in that order. KeyDown and KeyUp get the raw key and modifier Shift and KeyPress would receive a capital P as the value of the KeyChar property.

MouseEventHandler Delegate

The MouseEventHandler receives a MouseEventArgs object that contains the mouse state information as described in the earlier section "MouseEventArgs Class" in this chapter.

PaintEventHandler Delegate

The PaintEventHandler receives a PaintEventArgs object that contains a Graphics object representing the graphics device context of the control that needs to respond to a paint event. (See the section later in this chapter, "Overriding the OnPaint Method," for an example of using the Graphics object.)

Enumerations in the Forms Namespace

You will find that enumerations make your code more comprehensible than literal integral values. There are a few in the Forms namespace that you will find useful.

BootMode Enumeration

The BootMode enumeration indicates the mode that the computer was booted in. The enumerations include FailSafe, FailSafeWithNetwork, and Normal.

> **Tip**
>
> FailSafe BootMode is commonly referred to as *safe mode.*

FailSafe mode indicates that the computer was started with basic files and drivers only. FailSafeWithNetwork includes the FailSafe mode and network drivers sufficient to enable networking. Normal mode is self-explanatory: It starts your computer with everything you would normally expect to start, load, and run.

CharacterCasing Enumeration

CharacterCasing is the enumeration used to indicate the case of characters displayed in the TextBox control. The three enumerated values are Lower, Normal, and Upper.

Day Enumeration

The Day enumeration is used by the MonthCalendar. Day defines the days of the week in whole-word form: Sunday, Monday, Tuesday, Wednesday, Thursday, Friday, and Saturday. In addition, the Day enumeration contains a Default enumerated element, which is equivalent to 7.

Keys Enumeration

The System.Windows.Forms.Keys enumeration contains a huge list of enumerated elements representing individual keys like the letter S, CapsLock, BrowserForward, and HanguelMode to facilitate the symbolic processing of keyboard input.

Reviewing the System.Drawing Namespace

The System.Drawing (GDI+) namespace is one of those great features that will allow you to exercise precise control over custom drawing and your graphical user interface in Windows Forms. (You can use the classes in System.Drawing for WebForms, too.)

This section provides an overview of the System.Drawing namespace with some brief examples. For an extensive review and additional examples of GDI+, see Chapter 17, "Programming with GDI+."

Classes in the System.Drawing Namespace

There are several key classes in the Drawing namespace that are part of GDI+. Important classes include those that represent brushes, fonts, pens, drawing regions, and the Graphics class. Together these classes will allow you to create basic line art and font-based graphics output as well as advanced graphics rendering.

Brushes Class

The Brushes class contains a long list of static properties that return system brushes—Brush objects. A Brush object is used to define objects for filling the interior of graphical objects like rectangles and ellipses.

You can create an instance of a Brush object or use one of the many predefined brush objects in the Brushes class. Listing 15.4 demonstrates using Reflection to load a combo box with the names of all available brushes; this solution is more extensible and less painful than typing the brush names manually. When you select the brush represented by the name of its color in the demo application (DrawingDemo.sln), the name of the brush is displayed to the right of the combo box.

LISTING 15.4 Using Reflection to list and display all brushes

```
 1: Imports System.Drawing
 2:
 3: Public Class Form1
 4:    Inherits System.Windows.Forms.Form
 5:
 6: [ Windows Form Designer generated code]
 7:
 8:    Private Sub Initialize()
 9:      Dim Information() As System.Reflection.PropertyInfo _
10:        = GetType(Brushes).GetProperties()
11:
12:      Dim I As Integer
13:      For I = 0 To Information.Length - 1
14:        ComboBox1.Items.Add(Information(I).Name)
15:      Next
16:
17:    End Sub
18:
19:    Private Sub Form1_Load(ByVal sender As System.Object, _
20:      ByVal e As System.EventArgs) Handles MyBase.Load
21:      Initialize()
22:    End Sub
23:
24:    Private Function GetLeft() As Single
25:      Return ComboBox1.Left + ComboBox1.Width + 10
26:    End Function
27:
28:    Private Function GetTop() As Single
29:      Return Label1.Top
30:    End Function
31:
32:    Private Function GetBrush() As Brush
33:      Return New SolidBrush(Color.FromName(ComboBox1.Text))
34:    End Function
35:
36:    Private Function GetText() As String
37:      Return ComboBox1.Text
38:    End Function
39:
40:    Private Sub ComboBox1_SelectedIndexChanged( _
```

LISTING 15.4 continued

```
41:      ByVal sender As System.Object, ByVal e As System.EventArgs) _
42:      Handles ComboBox1.SelectedIndexChanged
43:
44:      Invalidate()
45:    End Sub
46:
47:    Private Sub Form1_Paint(ByVal sender As Object, _
48:      ByVal e As System.Windows.Forms.PaintEventArgs) _
49:      Handles MyBase.Paint
50:
51:      If (GetText() = vbNullString) Then Exit Sub
52:
53:      e.Graphics.DrawString(GetText(), _
54:        New Font("Courier", 16), GetBrush(), GetLeft(), GetTop())
55:
56:    End Sub
57: End Class
```

There are a few interesting aspects to the demo application. Initialize, beginning on line 8, uses the `Reflection.PropertyInfo` class to dynamically return the array of property information about the `Brushes` class. The names of the properties are written to `ComboBox1`. Because every property in `Brushes` consists only of `Brush` objects and includes all system brushes, the combo box will contain the names of all system `Brush` objects.

Lines 32 through 34 construct a `SolidBrush` object, initializing the color of the brush with the shared method `Color.FromName`. The names of the system brushes happen to be the names of the system colors, too. The `Form.Paint` handler tests to see if a brush is picked. If you select a brush, the `Graphics` argument representing the device context (DC) passed in the `PaintEventArgs` object is used to render the name of the brush to the right of the combo box. (The methods `GetLeft` and `GetTop` are refactored query methods that return offsets relative to adjacent controls.)

Font Class

When you are writing text directly to a canvas, you can use an existing font object from the control containing the DC or you can create a new `Font` object.

Listing 15.4 demonstrates a simple way to create a new `Font` object on line 54. The Visual Basic .NET garbage collector (GC) will destroy the `Font` object when it's no longer needed, so it's perfectly acceptable to create the object inline. In fact, it's preferable to create the font object inline rather than introducing a temporary.

15

USING WINDOWS FORMS

Suppose we wanted to display the brush using an italicized font. We could call an overloaded version of the `Font` constructor, passing the `FontStyle` to the constructor inline:

```
New Font("Garamond", 16, FontStyle.Italic)
```

The statement creates a font using the Garamond font family and the enumerated `FontStyle.Italic` style. If you want to combine font styles, use an *or* operation to combine styles. `FontStyle.Italic Or FontStyle.Bold` will display a bold and italicized font.

Pens Class

`Brush` objects are used to define fill color and patterns for shapes, and `Pen` objects are used to define line colors and styles.

We can use exactly the same technique to fill a combo box with the names of `Pens`. `Pens`, like `Brushes`, use the system color for the display name of the system pens in the `Pens` collection. Again, just as with the `Brushes` collection, `Pens` contains shared properties representing system `Pen` objects. Listing 15.5 demonstrates how to draw an ellipse using `Graphics`, `Pen`, and `RectangleF` objects.

LISTING 15.5   Using `Graphics`, `Pen`, and `RectangleF` objects

```
 1: Private Function RandomRect( _
 2:    Optional ByVal Max As Integer = 36) As RectangleF
 3:
 4:    Static Count As Integer = 0
 5:    Count += 1 : If (Count >= Max) Then Count = 0
 6:    Return New RectangleF( _
 7:      (Panel1.ClientRectangle.Width - (Count*10))/2, 10, Count*10, 300)
 8:
 9: End Function
10:
11: Private Sub Panel1_Paint(ByVal sender As Object, _
12:    ByVal e As System.Windows.Forms.PaintEventArgs) _
13:    Handles Panel1.Paint
14:
15:    Const Max As Integer = 36
16:    Dim I As Integer
17:    For I = 1 To Max
18:      e.Graphics.DrawEllipse(Pens.Blue, RandomRect(Max))
19:    Next
20:
21: End Sub
```

Listing 15.5 creates some basic nested elliptical shapes. Pens are used to define lines. The listing uses a `for` loop and draws `Max` ellipses with a blue `Pen` and `Max` number of ellipses constrained by a bounding rectangle, all with the same center (see Figure 15.6).

FIGURE 15.6

Ellipses drawn using a blue Pen *and bounding rectangles with the same center.*

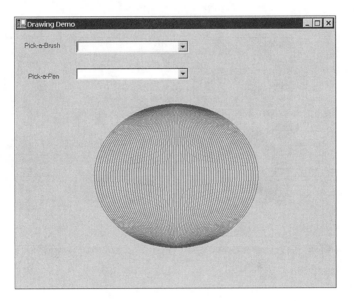

Region Class

The `Region` class is used to define clipping regions in Visual Basic .NET. One humorous use for the `Region` was to create the dashboard for `Donkey.Net`, the game marking the 10-year anniversary of Visual Basic that Bill Gates played during his keynote address at TechEd 2001.

> impressive VB capabilities, including Web Services, threads, and the `Region` class, among others.
>
> Last time I checked, you could download the source for `Donkey.Net`—and run over evil bunnies or pirates—from MSDN at `http://msdn.microsoft.com/vbasic/donkey.asp`.

The `Region` class provides several capabilities for clipping text. (We will discuss GDI+ in greater detail in Chapter 17.) Figure 15.7 demonstrates the `Region` and `GraphicsPath` objects being used to create a clipped form region from a string.

FIGURE 15.7

The `Region` class can be used to create shaped forms, as shown.

Listing 15.6 contains the verbose form of the code—unrefactored code, using temporary variables—demonstrating a `GraphicsPath` and `Region` that produce the string-shaped form shown in Figure 15.7.

LISTING 15.6   Regions, Opacity, `GraphicsPath`, and `Threads`. Oh my!

```
 1: Imports System.Threading
 2: Public Class Form1
 3:   Inherits System.Windows.Forms.Form
 4:
 5: [ Windows Form Designer generated code ]
 6:
 7:   Private Sub Form1_Load(ByVal sender As System.Object, _
 8:     ByVal e As System.EventArgs) Handles MyBase.Load
 9:
10:     Dim AGraphicsPath As New Drawing2D.GraphicsPath()
11:     Dim AFontFamily As New FontFamily("Haettenschweiler")
12:     Dim APointF As New PointF(10, 10)
13:     Dim AStringFormat As _
14:       New StringFormat(StringFormatFlags.NoWrap)
15:
```

Listing 15.6   continued

```
16:     Const Text As String = "Visual Basic .NET" & vbCrLf & "  Unleashed"
17:
18:     AGraphicsPath.AddString(Text, AFontFamily, _
19:        FontStyle.Bold, 100, APointF, AStringFormat)
20:
21:     Region = New Region(AGraphicsPath)
22:     Opacity = 0
23:
24:     ThreadPool.QueueUserWorkItem( _
25:        CType(AddressOf FadeIn, WaitCallback))
26:
27:   End Sub
28:   Private Done As Boolean = False
29:   Private Sub FadeIn(ByVal State As Object)
30:      While (Not Done)
31:         Invoke(CType(AddressOf SynchOpacity, MethodInvoker))
32:      End While
33:   End Sub
34:
35:   Private Sub SynchOpacity()
36:      Opacity += 0.1
37:      Done = Opacity >= 1
38:   End Sub
39:
40: End Class
```

Lines 10 through 21 demonstrate how to use the `Region` and `GraphicsPath` to create Figure 15.7. In short, you will need to construct a `GraphicsPath` object, construct a `Region` object, initializing the `Region` with the `GraphicsPath` object, and assign the new `Region` object to the Form's `Region` property.

Initializing the `GraphicsPath` Object

The `GraphicsPath` class is defined in the `System.Drawing.Drawing2D` namespace. Line 10 of Listing 15.6 constructs an instance of the `GraphicsPath` object, and lines 18 and 19 demonstrate using the `GraphicsPath.AddString` method to constrain the graphics path by the string. The `FontFamily`, `PointF`, `StringFormat`, and `String` objects created on lines 11 to 16 are used as arguments for the `GraphicsPath.AddString` method. (The `FontStyle` enumeration is used on lines 18 and 19, too.)

Basically, each of these arguments results in the creation of the image shown in Figure 15.7. `FontFamily` defines the font; Haettenschweiler is used in the example. `PointF` defines the starting top-left offset of the string-based `GraphicsPath`. `StringFormat` constrains the behavior of the string, `String` contains the text `Visual Basic .NET Unleashed`, and `FontStyle.Bold` describes the style of font to use.

Initializing the `Region` Object

The `Region` object constrains the clipping region based on the manner in which the `GraphicsPath` is initialized. There are several overloaded versions of the `Region` constructor, including a version that allows you to constrain the clipping region by a much simpler rectangle. The following code demonstrates a simple rectangular clipping region.

```
Region = New Region(New RectangleF(10, 10, 500, 100))
```

Replace lines 10 through 21 with the preceding single line, and you get a similar effect but a rectangular clipped region.

Using the `ThreadPool`

Line 24 demonstrates an easy way to use threads in Visual Basic .NET. The `ThreadPool` is a collection of threads managed by the CLR. Using the `ThreadPool` allows you to skip over the relatively expensive cost of creating a thread object, ensuring that it's initialized correctly, and writing your own thread pool. By queuing a work item, the `ThreadPool` will place the task described by the delegate (line 25) in a queue and the `ThreadPool` will process the task defined by the delegate procedure on a separate thread. The result is relatively easy multithreading.

The argument `CType(AddressOf FadeIn, WaitCallback)` is simply converting the delegate returned by `AddressOf FadeIn` to a `WaitCallBack` delegate. Alternatively, you could declare a `WaitCallBack` delegate and initialize it with the address of the `FadeIn` method, which has the correct signature.

The `FadeIn` method continues until the form's `Opacity` is 100%, or 1. The `Opacity` itself is actually changed on the same thread as the form. Because Windows `Forms` controls aren't thread safe, you have to use the `Invoke` method and a delegate to modify or interact with controls across thread boundaries. Again, on line 31 we are coercing the delegate returned by `AddressOf SynchOpacity` to a `MethodInvoker` delegate rather than explicitly declaring a `MethodInvoker` variable.

`Control.Invoke` essentially places interactions with Windows `Forms` controls in the same message queue on the same thread as the one on which the control resides. Rewriting the `FadeIn` procedure as follows might work, but isn't recommended and will likely result in sporadic and unreliable behavior:

```
29:    Private Sub FadeIn(ByVal State As Object)
30:       While (Opacity < 1)
31:          Opacity += .1
```

```
32:     End While
33:  End Sub
```

To determine whether interthread access requires you to use the method invocation form of the call, you can call `Control.InvokeRequired`. `InvokeRequired` returns `False` if the thread on which you called the method is the same one on which the control resides. If `InvokeRequired` returns `True`, you need to call `Invoke` as demonstrated in Listing 15.6.

Graphics Class

The `Graphics` class contains a Windows Device Context, also referred to as DC or sometimes the canvas. `Graphics` objects are returned by calling a control's `CreateGraphics` method or as one of the properties of the `PaintEventArgs` object passed to the `Paint` event handler.

Call `CreateGraphics` when you need a `Graphics` object and don't cache the object when you get it. You can't construct instances of `Graphics` objects manually; you must use the factory method `CreateGraphics`. The `Graphics` class is defined in the `System.Drawing` namespace. We will cover `Graphics` in detail in Chapter 17.

Structures in the `System.Drawing` Namespace

There are a couple of straightforward structures defined in the `System.Drawing` namespace, including `Point`, `Rectangle`, and `Size`. `Point` encapsulates a Cartesian X,Y location; `Rectangle` and `RectangleF` encapsulate the `X`, `Y`, `Width`, and `Height` properties for defining a rectangle, and `Size` represents the size of a rectangular region.

We will cover other interesting `System.Drawing` namespaces and elements of those namespaces in Chapter 17.

Using the Form Class

The `Form` class in `System.Windows.Forms` is the control that you will use to design graphical user interfaces. The `Form` class is a bona fide class in Visual Basic .NET, rather than something slightly different, as it was in VB6.

> **Note**
>
> In Visual Basic 6, it's the `Attribute VB_PredeclaredId = True` statement that you don't see in a VB6 form that instructs the VB6 compiler to create an autoinstance of a VB6 form. In fact, if you open a VB6 .CLS file with a text editor and modify this `Attribute`, VB6 will autocreate your classes too.

The project settings stored in the .vbproj file—`StartupObject = "ShapedForm.Form1"`—define the object or class that will be autocreated in Visual Basic .NET. You will have to write a slightly modified version of the code you wrote in VB6 to work with multiform Windows applications. In this section, we will take a look at how to construct instances of forms and some of the useful features of the `Form` class and how the new IDE helps you work more efficiently. (Chapter 16, "Defining User Interfaces," will cover advanced topics on interface design.)

Creating an Instance of a Form

Assume that you have a two-form application in VB6. Also, assume that `Form1` is the startup form, and `Form2` is the second form. VB6 allowed you to write `Form2.Show` when you wanted to display `Form2` as a modal dialog box; all you had to do was call `Form2.Show vbModal`. (You could optionally pass an `owner` argument as a second argument to `Show`.)

Visual Basic .NET doesn't support this autocreated use of forms. In VB6, again, if you want to create a second or third instance of a form, you need to declare a variable of the form type, invoke a new instance, load the form, and then show it. Listing 15.7 contains an example demonstrating both styles of showing VB6 forms.

LISTING 15.7 Visual Basic 6 allowed you to use an autocreated instance of a form or create a new instance

```
 1: Private Sub CommandShow_Click()
 2:    Dim F As Form2
 3:    Set F = New Form2
 4:    Load F
 5:    F.Show
 6: End Sub
 7:
 8: Private Sub CommandShowModal_Click()
 9:    Call Form2.Show(vbModal)
10: End Sub
```

Note

Visual Basic .NET doesn't support autocreated forms. You will have to use the create, use, and release modality for forms in Visual Basic .NET.

> **Tip**
>
> You don't have to show a form to use the methods and properties on that form.

The `CommandShowModal_Click` event from Listing 15.7 demonstrates reliance on an autocreated `Form2`. The `CommandShow_Click` handler demonstrates how to explicitly create a new instance of `Form2`, and then load and show that new instance. It's the latter explicit creation of a form and showing it that you will have to do in Visual Basic .NET.

The code for creating a form is very similar to VB6 but much abbreviated: `Dim AForm As New Form2()` is equivalent to the `Dim`, `New`, and `Load` form used in VB6.

Showing Forms

Instead of passing parameters to a form in Visual Basic .NET, you can call one of two methods to show a form. `Show` takes no parameters and displays a modeless form. `ShowDialog` has two versions. The first version requires no arguments, and the second takes an argument that implements the `IWin32Window` interface—a form being an example of a class that implements `IWin32Window`—and returns a `System.Windows.Forms.DialogResult` enumerated value indicating the action taken to close the form. The following two examples demonstrate creating a form and showing both modeless and modal.

```
Dim F As New Form2
F.Show()

Dim F1 As New Form2()
If (F1.ShowDialog() = DialogResult.Cancel) Then
  MsgBox(DialogResult.Cancel.ToString)
End If
```

The first two statements create and show `Form2` using an object named `F`. The last four statements create a second instance of `Form2`, named `F1` and show the dialog modally. (The `ShowDialog()` method used is the overloaded instance that requires no arguments.) If the user clicks the `Cancel` button, the enumerated `Cancel` value is displayed in a message box.

Getting the Modal Result

The modal result when you call `ShowDialog` is one of the enumerated values in the `DialogResult` enumeration. Return values are contrived by placing buttons on the form or some other control that returns a modal result when the form is closed.

For example, if you want to create a standard dialog box with an OK button, add a Button control to the form and set the Button.DialogResult property to OK in the properties window. If the form was displayed using ShowDialog, when the user clicks OK, the form will close and ShowDialog will return DialogResult.OK.

Designing the User Interface

User interfaces are easier to design in Visual Basic .NET for many reasons. We will go into greater detail in Chapter 16, but here are a few highlights.

Painting Controls on a Form

Painting controls is the process of dragging controls from the toolbox onto a form. Visual Basic .NET supports double-clicking a control in the toolbox, which causes the IDE to add the control to the form, and simply clicking on the control and once on the form.

If you click a control in VB6 and then click the form once, nothing happens. In Visual Basic .NET, when you click the form, the control is painted using the default size described by the control's constructor; now you get an intuitive behavior. And, of course, as is true with VB6, you can drag the control to any size and position as you are painting the control on the form.

Docking Controls on a Form

Many controls in Visual Basic .NET have a Dock property. Click the drop-down button in the Properties window and the visual dock guide is displayed. Click a button in the Dock editor, and the control will be docked, or aligned, relative to the organization shown in the Dock editor (see Figure 15.8).

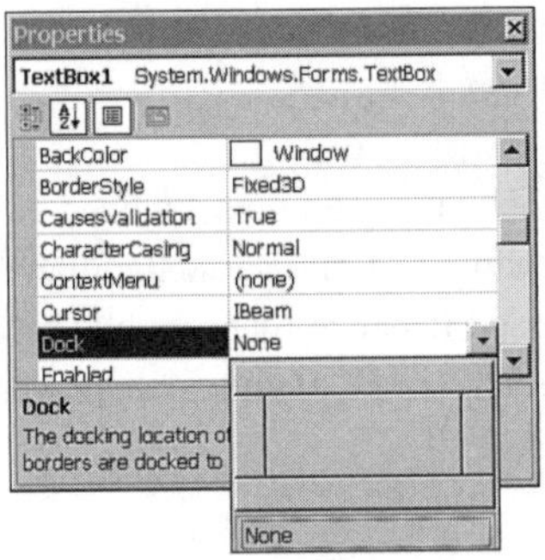

FIGURE 15.8

The Dock property editor allows you to visually control the placement of controls in Visual Basic .NET.

Use the Dock property rather than code to control the location and alignment of controls on Windows Forms.

Managing Controls on a Form

This version of Visual Basic doesn't require you to create a control array. When you copy and paste a control, you get a new instance of the control with cloned properties, with a few differences. The most important difference is that the copied control is an independent object.

> **Tip**
>
> You won't be prompted to create a control array in Visual Basic .NET, nor do you need one.

In effect, all controls on a form—or on the parent control, like a `Panel`—have a `Controls` collection property. When you paint a control, a reference is added to the `Control` collection and Windows Forms uses these object references to manage the controls and propagate messages to the controls.

If you create controls at runtime with code, you will need to add those dynamic controls to the owning control's `Controls` collection before the dynamic control will be painted.

Creating Controls Dynamically

Creating a control at runtime is identical to creating any other object: Declare an instance and invoke the constructor. The biggest difference where controls are concerned is that you need to insert the control into the parenting control's `Controls` collection. Listing 15.8 demonstrates how to dynamically create a button on a form.

LISTING 15.8   Dynamically create a button with code

```
 1: Private Function UniqueName() As String
 2:    Static I As Integer = Controls.Count + 1
 3:    I += 1
 4:    Return String.Format("Button{0}", I)
 5: End Function
 6:
 7: Private Sub CreateButton(ByVal ButtonToCopy As Button)
 8:    Dim B As New Button()
 9:
10:    B.Size = ButtonToCopy.Size
11:    B.Location = ButtonToCopy.Location
12:    ButtonToCopy.Dispose()
13:
14:    B.Name = UniqueName()
15:    B.Text = String.Format("{0} ({1})", _
```

15

USING WINDOWS FORMS

Listing 15.8   continued

```
16:     "Create Button", B.Name)
17:
18:    AddHandler B.Click, AddressOf Button2_Click
19:    Controls.Add(B)
20: End Sub
21:
22: Private Sub Button2_Click(ByVal sender As System.Object, _
23:    ByVal e As System.EventArgs) Handles Button2.Click
24:
25:    CreateButton(sender)
26: End Sub
```

The refactored code in the listing calls a method `CreateButton` when the `Button2_Click` event occurs (line 25). Instead of writing the code to perform the type conversion from the `sender` `Object` to a `Button`, use a method call and perform the conversion implicitly. (This is safe if you know that the event `sender` object is a specific type.) In addition to avoiding the `CType` conversion call, there is a well-named method in its place, `CreateButton`.

`CreateButton` creates a new `Button` control and copies the original button's `Size` and `Location`, and then disposes of the original button. A query method, `UniqueName`, is used to provide a well-named method to assist in getting a unique control name. `UniqueName` uses a `Static` variable and begins incrementing beyond the highest-numbered control. (This isn't a perfect method, but works in the example.) The name of the button is added to the button's caption, the `Text` property, to illustrate that we have a new control object. The handler that invoked this method is added to the new button's `Click` event, and the control is added to the form's `Controls` collection.

Each time you click the button in the sample program, it's replaced with a new one with the same functionality and in the same location.

Assigning Event Handlers to Dynamic Controls

The `WithEvents` statement is used to associate an event handler to an object at compile time. When you are adding event handlers at runtime, use the `AddHandler` and `RemoveHandler` statements to associate event handlers with objects. Keep in mind that a single event is a multicast delegate, meaning that an event can invoke more than one handler per event. (Read Chapters 8 and 9, "Understanding Delegates," for more on event handlers.)

Finding the Active Form

Every form has an `ActiveForm` property. This property will return a reference to the form that has the focus or `Nothing` if no form is active.

> **Note**
>
> You might have noticed that a lot of code listings don't use the Form's reference to self, Me. Me is implied but if you aren't sure of the members of a form, type the Me reference and IntelliSense will display the members of the Form class.

When you have a modal dialog box displayed, that will be the active form. However, modeless and MDI forms allow you to show and switch between forms with one or more forms remaining open. If you are executing code in one form and need to find the active form, use the `Form.ActiveForm` property.

Adding Code to Forms

When you add a new form to your project, you are adding a class. A class is a class is a class, in Visual Basic .NET. This means that you can add the same elements to your form classes that you would add to any other class.

The purpose of a form is to support a graphical metaphor for the behavior supported by that form. However, this doesn't mean that all behavior should be defined in the form class. It's important and beneficial to separate the classes in the solution domain between those that describe the behaviors of the form and those that provide the underlying solution. (Refer to Chapter 16 for more on user interface and form design.) For more on the mechanics of adding events, properties, fields, structures, enumerations, and methods to classes, read Chapter 7, "Creating Classes."

Custom Form Painting with GDI+

GDI+ represented by the `System.Drawing` namespace makes advanced form painting and creating custom views ever easier. From the earlier example, it was demonstrated that the `Region` and `GraphicsPath` class can be used to create shaped forms.

For simple painting jobs, you can implement a `Paint` handler for your form or inherit from and override the `Paint` method for a particular control. The `PaintEventArgs` object passed to the `Paint` event contains a reference to the device context, represented by the

15

USING WINDOWS FORMS

`Graphics` object. There are several examples of using the `Graphics` object earlier in this book, and Chapter 17 provides comprehensive coverage of this subject.

Summary

There is a lot just in the Windows `Forms` namespace. At last check, there were three gigabytes of information in the MSDN help files. This chapter's quick overview of the framework will help you know where to look when solving new problems; learning all that's in there is impossible.

Chapter 15 provided you with an overview of some of the things in the Windows `Forms` namespace, including how to create shaped forms, a multithreaded example, and dynamic control creation. Chapter 16 builds from here, demonstrating how you can apply advanced subjects, like GDI+, to create world class interfaces.

Designing User Interfaces

CHAPTER

16

Many of you have been designing user interfaces for years. If you started using Visual Basic for DOS or the BASIC programming language before Visual Basic, you have 10 or more years of experience in developing the presentation layer of applications.

Even if you are completely new to visual programming, it is intuitive. Click a control from the toolbox and drop it on a form or Web form, and then tie the necessary code to that control. Even nonprogrammers understand the metaphor for visual programming; this is what makes visual programming tools so powerful.

Chapter 16 demonstrates what might not be intuitive about assembling and designing a graphical user interface (GUI) using Visual Basic .NET. I will also demonstrate how to do things that earlier tools were incapable of doing. In this chapter we will look at the new designer tools for implementing menus and how to add menus on the fly. We will take a quick look at new features for managing control layout, and we will spend considerable time on component building. Components are essential to GUIs, so we will spend a predominant amount of time in this chapter building components. If you can easily build components, you will surely be able to use them. The rest is aesthetics.

Managing Control Layout

My version of what constitutes a visually pleasing interface is likely to be very different from yours, and a lot different than Alan Cooper's. In *About Face* and *The Inmates Are Running the Asylum*, Cooper writes at length about interface design and departs from the kind of interfaces that are part of his legacy as the original VB implementer. However, whether you are creating a vanilla Windows application or something that radically departs from the basic Windows metaphor, you will more than likely need to spend some time on symmetry and components.

If you are building an application that has the basic Windows look and feel, you can work with Windows Forms controls or Web Forms controls (refer to Chapter 19, "ASP .NET Web Programming," for more information on Web Controls) for Web applications. If you are contriving something radically new—perhaps a kiosk application for shopping malls or software to run on something other than a PC—you might need to build your own components.

> **Note**
>
> A couple of additional books on general design are Jerry Hirshberg's *The Creative Priority: Putting Innovation to Work in Your Business* and Donald Norman's *The Design of Everyday Things*.

Whether you use standard components or custom components, you will need to manage the layout of those components in almost every instance. (So far there are no amorphous interfaces.) To this end, Windows Forms controls provide some basic properties for managing control layout, including: Anchor, Dock, DockPadding, Location, and Size.

Anchoring Controls

The Control class is the base class for Windows Forms controls. Because inheritance has been introduced into Visual Basic .NET, it is important to begin thinking of behaviors that are introduced somewhere in a component's ancestral chain. One such property is the Anchor property.

The Control class introduces the Anchor property, which is defined as an AnchorStyles enumerated value. Acceptable values of the Anchor property are Bottom, Left, Right, Top, and None. You can use combinations of these enumerated values to specify where a control is logically attached to its parent control.

Anchoring a control ensures that it maintains the same relative relationship to its parent control at the anchor point when the parent control changes size. Figure 16.1 shows the Anchor property editor modified to anchor a MonthCalendar by its relative top-right position.

FIGURE 16.1

Anchored controls will maintain their relative position when the form changes size.

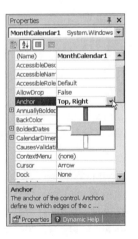

Docking Controls

The Dock property is used to indicate which edge of a parent control a contained control is aligned to. The Dock property allows you to align controls without writing runtime code to help them maintain their edge alignment.

Padding Docked Controls

A direct descendant of the `Control` class is the `ScrollableControl` class. The `ScrollableControl` class introduces the `DockPadding` property.

Scrollable controls support expressing the amount of padding between any of the edges of the contained control and its container. Use the `DockPadding` property (see Figure 16.2) to indicate the amount of space between the edge of a control and its dock location.

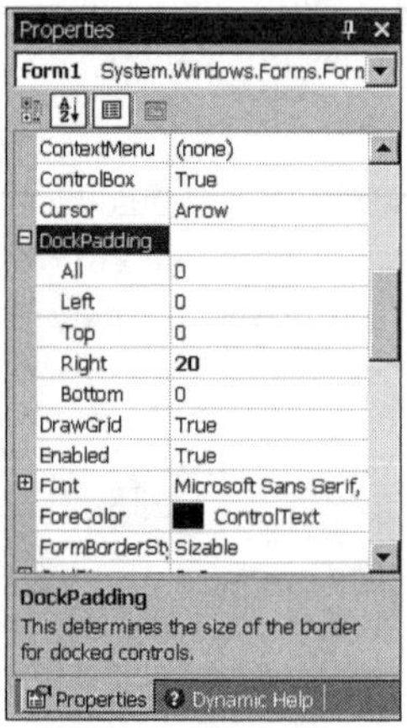

FIGURE 16.2

`ScrollableControl` *classes support* `DockPadding`.

Managing Location and Size

`Control` introduces `Location` and `Size` properties. Both `Location` and `Size` are defined as `Point` structures having an `X` and a `Y` property.

In the Properties window, use `Location.X` where you would have used `Left`, and use `Location.Y` where you would have used `Top` in VB6. `Size.Width` and `Size.Height` replace `Width` and `Height` respectively.

You have a couple of options when sizing controls with code. You can directly manipulate `Left`, `Top`, `Width`, and `Height` properties programmatically, or you can assign a new `Size` structure to the `Size` property and a `Point` structure to the `Location` property. The following statements demonstrate resizing and relocating a `Panel` control in Visual Basic .NET.

```
Panel1.Size = New Size(200, 300)
Panel1.Location = New Point(10, 10)
```

The preceding code is equivalent to the same code using the individual location and size properties:

```
Panel1.Left = 10
Panel1.Top = 10
Panel1.Width = 200
Panel1.Height = 300
```

You cannot, however, modify members of the `Size` or `Location` properties directly. The following code is invalid:

```
Panel1.Location.X = 10
Panel1.Location.Y = 10
Panel1.Size.Width = 200
Panel1.Size.Height = 300
```

It might be a little unclear why the preceding is invalid code. Both `Location` and `Size` are value types. When you reference their property methods, the getter returns a copy of the structure because structures are value types; you don't get a reference. As a result, the `.X` and `.Y` and `.Width` and `.Height` properties are effectively read-only.

Working with Menus

VB6 had cobbled support for menus. Menus were managed through the IDE's menu editor. Menus were not full-fledged components, controllable at runtime. Visual Basic .NET introduces the `MainMenu` and `ContextMenu` components.

These two components come replete with design-time and runtime capabilities. You can easily add menu items at design time using the menu editors, and at runtime using the methods and properties of these two subclasses of the `Menu` component.

I will briefly describe how to use the redefined Menu Designer and proceed to the technical steps for programmatically adding menu items at runtime.

Defining a `MainMenu` or `ContextMenu`

Most of the steps for implementing either `MainMenu` or `ContextMenu` are identical. I will present the `MainMenu` steps in this section and point out the few differences between `MainMenu` and `ContextMenu` at the end of this subsection.

The `MainMenu` is a component. You have to select the `MainMenu` component from the Windows Forms toolbox and drop it onto the form. The component is actually placed into the component tray beneath the form, but the Menu Designer adds a box region where you would expect a menu at the top-left corner of the form. The text has the words "Type Here". To design a menu, that is exactly what you do. Type the text for the menu in place of the words `Type Here`, adding an ampersand immediately before any letter that is meant to be a hot key.

When you begin typing the menu caption, a submenu is added beneath the menu and a sibling menu is added to the right of the menu. Right-clicking over a menu item displays a context menu on which you can click Insert New to add submenus or nested submenus. In this manner you visually design the menu system by adding submenus and typing menu captions. Use the Properties window to modify properties like the menu name.

Adding Supporting Menu Code

Menus are event-driven components. There is one crucial event for menus, the `Click` event. If you double-click on the menu item itself in the designer, the designer will generate the `Click` event handler for you. There are four other `MenuItem` events that you might want to use: `DrawItem`, `MeasureItem`, `Popup`, and `Select`. We will return to these events in a moment.

`MenuItem` is actually a component that is also generalized from the `Menu` component. The relationship between `MenuItem` objects and a `Menu` is that a `Menu` has 0 to many `MenuItem` objects. The subsection "Adding Menu Items Dynamically" goes into more detail about working with `MenuItem` objects in code.

When you have created a `Click` event handler, the result is that the menu designer will generate an `EventHandler` delegate method for you. (Recall that the signature of an `EventHandler` delegate method is a subroutine that has an `Object` parameter named `sender` and a `System.EventArgs` parameter named e.) When the menu is clicked, the `sender` object will be the specific `MenuItem` and the `EventArgs` argument will contain benign data.

If you need a reference to the specific `MenuItem`, you can dynamically cast the `sender` object to a `MenuItem` with the following code:

```
CType(sender, MenuItem)
```

As a good general rule, the `Click` event handler should simply invoke a method of the `Form` rather than having code in the event handler. This is a good rule because it allows you to document what the event handler does by providing a good procedure name, and that implementation procedure can be used in some other context besides the `Click` event.

Of course, you can ignore this general rule if the `Click` event contains very simple code like the following:

```
Private Sub MenuItem4_Click(ByVal sender As System.Object, _
    ByVal e As System.EventArgs) Handles MenuItem4.Click

    Application.Exit()

End Sub
```

When you have designed the menu, implementing click event handlers is very similar to implementing menu event handlers in VB6.

DrawItem and MeasureItem Events

The menu DrawItem and MeasureItem events work hand in hand. When you set the MenuItem.OwnerDraw property to True, the DrawItem and the MeasureItem events are raised. MeasureItem is raised first, allowing you to express the size of the displayed menu. The DrawItem event is raised second, allowing you to render the menu item.

MeasureItem is passed an object, e, that is a MeasureItemEventArgs type. The properties ItemHeight and ItemWidth are used to express the dimension of the custom-drawn menu. The following code demonstrates how to establish the size of an owner-drawn menu item:

```
Private Sub MenuItemRectangle_MeasureItem(ByVal sender As Object, _
    ByVal e As System.Windows.Forms.MeasureItemEventArgs) _
    Handles MenuItemRectangle.MeasureItem

    e.ItemHeight = 20
    e.ItemWidth = 60
End Sub
```

Tip

To implement the DrawItem menu, in the code editor, select the specific MenuItem from the Class Name list and the DrawItem event from the Method Name list.

After the size of the custom menu is established, you can draw the menu using the Graphics object passed as a property of the DrawItem event argument DrawItemEventArgs. The second argument of the DrawItem event contains a Graphics object representing the device context of the menu item that raised the event.

Suppose you have a drawing application, and you elect to use a visual metaphor for menu operations rather than text. When the user selects a menu item to insert a rectangle, for example, he or she can click a menu with a rectangle on it instead of the text Rectangle. By combining the MeasureItem and DrawItem events, you can achieve the result shown in Figure 16.3. The code for both events is shown in Listing 16.1.

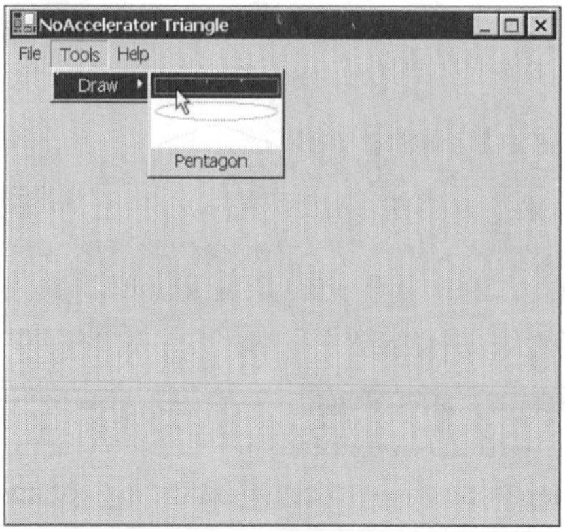

FIGURE 16.3

Custom-drawn menu item.

LISTING 16.1 Combining the `OwnerDraw` property with `DrawItem` and `MeasureItem` events to create custom menu items

```
1:  Private Sub MenuItemRectangle_MeasureItem(ByVal sender As Object, _
2:      ByVal e As System.Windows.Forms.MeasureItemEventArgs) _
3:      Handles MenuItemRectangle.MeasureItem
4:
5:      e.ItemHeight = 20
6:      e.ItemWidth = 60
7:    End Sub
8:
9:  Private Sub MenuItemRectangle_DrawItem(ByVal sender As Object, _
10:     ByVal e As System.Windows.Forms.DrawItemEventArgs) _
11:     Handles MenuItemRectangle.DrawItem
12:
13:     e.DrawBackground()
14:     Dim R As Rectangle = e.Bounds
15:     R.Inflate(-3, -4)
16:     e.Graphics.DrawRectangle(Pens.Red, R)
17:
18: End Sub
```

`MeasureItem` sets the width and height of the menu item. `DrawItem` draws the background, which will show the selected menu item background, copies the bounds of the rectangle to a local variable, and shrinks the rectangle a bit. This allows the visual metaphor to fit within the space available to the menu item.

Popup Event

The `MenuItem.Popup` event occurs before a menu's submenu items are displayed. This event allows you to insert custom behavior before menu items are available to the user.

Select Event

The `MenuItem.Select` event occurs when the user places the mouse over a menu item. You could insert custom effects associated with the menu to respond when the user hovers over a menu item.

Differences between `MainMenu` and `ContextMenu`

The differences between `MainMenu` and `ContextMenu` are few from the application developer's point of view. Both menus can contain submenus and nested submenus. Both menus contain a collection of `MenuItem` objects that can be customized by setting `OwnerDraw` equal to True and implementing the `MeasureItem` and `DrawItem` events.

The one difference you will note is when you visually describe the menu items. `MainMenu` supports adding a top-level `MenuItem`, but `ContextMenu` does not. Additionally, you can implement as many `ContextMenu` objects as you see fit.

The `Control` class introduces the `ContextMenu` property. Any subclass of the `Control` class supports associating a `ContextMenu` with the control by selecting `ContextMenu` from a drop-down list in the Properties window.

Only forms support `MainMenu`. You can implement multiple `MainMenu` objects and assign a particular `MainMenu` control to the `Form.Menu` property based on the state of your application; this is useful, for example, to sometimes show a complete menu but other times show a partial menu.

Adding Menu Items Dynamically

A powerful feature of the `Menu` class is the capability to dynamically add and remove menus programmatically at runtime and associate delegates with those menus' events.

Generally you will need to write the code to support dynamic menus at design time, but you can easily devise a means of determining when to show those menus and wire them up. For example, suppose you have both professional and enterprise versions of your software. If a DLL is present, its presence indicates that the user has the enterprise features and associated menus should be displayed.

The code in Listing 16.2 demonstrates the technical aspects of adding a dynamic menu item to the MenuDemo.sln available for download. Listing 16.3 demonstrates an approach to dynamically adding behaviors defined in an external assembly.

LISTING 16.2   The basics of creating a dynamic menu option

```
1:   Private Sub DoAbout(ByVal sender As Object, _
2:     ByVal e As System.EventArgs)
3:
4:     Const Message As String = _
5:       "Menu Demo" & vbCrLf & _
6:       "Sams VB .NET Unleashed" & vbCrLf & _
7:       "Written by Paul Kimmel. Copyright (c) 2001."
8:
9:     MsgBox(Message, MsgBoxStyle.Information, "About")
10:
11:  End Sub
12:
13:  Private Sub Form1_Load(ByVal sender As System.Object, _
14:    ByVal e As System.EventArgs) Handles MyBase.Load
15:
16:    Dim About As New MenuItem("About")
17:    AddHandler About.Click, AddressOf DoABout
18:    MenuItemHelp.MenuItems.Add(About)
19:
20:  End Sub
```

The Load event creates a MenuItem named About and associates the subroutine DoAbout with the MenuItem.Click delegate. In the last step, the menu is added to the MenuItems collection of the menu that will play the role of parent menu. The DoClick event handler performs the behavior you would reasonably expect for an About menu.

Listing 16.3 demonstrates the scenario introduced near the beginning of this section, a pluggable extension to the application.

LISTING 16.3   Plugging a class library into a Windows application using dynamic menus

```
1:   Imports System.Windows.Forms
2:   Imports System.Drawing
3:
4:   Public Class AdvancedShape
5:
6:     Implements PluggableShape
7:
8:     Public Function GetMenuItem(ByVal Click As EventHandler) _
9:       As MenuItem Implements PluggableShape.GetMenuItem
10:
11:      Dim MenuItem As New MenuItem("Pentagon")
12:      AddHandler MenuItem.Click, Click
13:
14:      Return MenuItem
```

LISTING 16.3 continued

```
15:    End Function
16:
17:    Public Function GetPoints(ByVal Rect As Rectangle) As Point()
18:      Dim p1 As New Point(Rect.X + Rect.Width / 2, Rect.Y)
19:      Dim p2 As New Point(Rect.X, Rect.Y + Rect.Height / 3)
20:      Dim p3 As New Point(Rect.X + Rect.Width / 4, _
21:        Rect.Y + Rect.Height)
22:      Dim p4 As New Point(Rect.X + Rect.Width * 3 / 4, _
23:        Rect.Y + Rect.Height)
24:      Dim p5 As New Point(Rect.X + Rect.Width, _
25:        Rect.Y + Rect.Height / 3)
26:
27:      Return New Point() {p1, p2, p3, p4, p5}
28:    End Function
29:
30:    Public Sub Draw(ByVal Graphics As Graphics, _
31:      ByVal Rect As Rectangle) _
32:      Implements PluggableShape.Draw
33:
34:      Graphics.DrawPolygon(Pens.Red, GetPoints(Rect))
35:    End Sub
36:
37: End Class
38:
39: Public Interface PluggableShape
40:
41:    Function GetMenuItem(ByVal Click As EventHandler) As MenuItem
42:    Sub Draw(ByVal Graphics As Graphics, _
43:      ByVal Rect As Rectangle)
44:
45: End Interface
```

Listing 16.3 uses a generic interface named PluggableShape to allow consumers a non-specific means of incorporating PluggableShape objects into a client application. Lines 4 to 37 contain the class AdvancedShape, which implements PluggableShape.

AdvancedShape returns a MenuItem and implements a Draw method that draws the actual shape based on a bounding rectangle and the device context of the control the shape is to be drawn on. Draw is implemented on lines 30 to 35. The shape is defined by the array of points returned by GetPoints. (The shape drawn is a pentagon.) By using a generic interface, we could feasibly implement many advanced shapes and dynamically plug them into our application.

Listing 16.4 demonstrates using the PluggableShape interface to plug the AdvancedShape capability into our Windows application.

LISTING 16.4   Plugging in a `MenuItem` and additional behavior supported in a class library

```
1:    Private FPlug As PluggableShape
2:
3:    Private Sub Plugin(ByVal Plug As Drawing.PluggableShape)
4:      Try
5:        FPlug = Plug
6:        MenuItemDraw.MenuItems.Add( _
7:          FPlug.GetMenuItem(AddressOf DoClick))
8:      Catch
9:        FPlug = Nothing
10:     End Try
11:   End Sub
12:
13:   Private Sub Form1_Load(ByVal sender As System.Object, _
14:     ByVal e As System.EventArgs) Handles MyBase.Load
15:
16:     Plugin(New AdvancedShape())
17:
18:   End Sub
```

> **Note**
>
> Chapter 6, "Reflection," demonstrates the technical aspects of reflection. You could use reflection to dynamically discover classes implementing the `PluggableShape` interface in any assembly and make the code completely generic. As it stands, Listing 16.4 would require you to change line 16 to plug in a new shape library.

There is nothing special about the actual code. Add a reference to the class library containing `AdvancedShape` to the Windows application that will use the custom feature. Add an `Imports` statement to the Windows Form that will use the behavior of the shape—the form that will display the menu—and initialize the menu when the form loads. Notice that everything in `Form1` references the generic interface `PluggableShape` rather than a specific class; in this way, any object implementing the interface `PluggableShape` could be plugged into the client without significant changes.

Advanced Form Techniques

Windows Forms support several advanced techniques for creating form-based effects by modifying properties, as well as more advanced techniques supported through GDI+.

By setting a form's Opacity property to 100%, you get a normal-looking form. As you decrease Opacity toward 0%, the form becomes transparent. In addition, the Transparency property allows you to specify a transparent color. For example, if White is your Transparent color, all regions of the form that are White will be transparent. (These are simple property settings, so no example is provided here. Chapter 15, "Using Windows Forms," contains an example of using the Opacity method in the section titled "Region Class.")

Creating shaped forms is a simplified by-product of GDI+. Refer to Chapter 17, "Programming with GDI+," and the section titled "Shaped Forms" for an example of implementing a shaped form using GDI+.

In addition to shaped and transparent forms, there are some additional capabilities inherent in forms that resolve problems related to scrolling and scaling.

Form.AutoScale Property

The Form.AutoScale property solves the problem that occurs when a user changes the size of fonts. Historically, when the font size was changed by the user, controls were clipped inappropriately, resulting in a choppy-looking GUI. By default Form.AutoScale is True.

Autoscrolling the Device Context

The Form.AutoScroll property is False by default. If you place controls on a form that has AutoScroll = False and the control's bounds are outside of the form's bounds, the control is clipped. If AutoScroll is True, a scrollbar is added to the form automatically when a control is placed beyond the visible bounds of the form. Autoscrolling allows you to expand the virtual boundary of the control. The visible real estate used remains the same as it would without scrolling, but the virtual real estate is much larger. Figure 16.4 shows a TextBox clipped when AutoScroll is False, and Figure 16.5 shows the improved behavior when AutoScroll is True.

FIGURE 16.4
When AutoScroll is False, controls are clipped to the visible region of the parent.

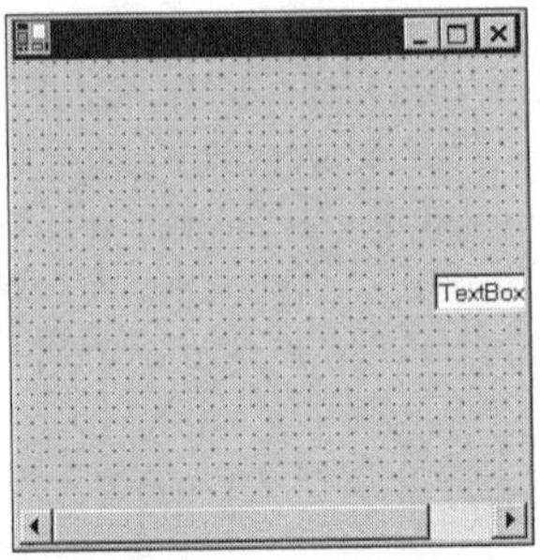

FIGURE 16.5

When AutoScroll *is True, controls are not clipped and a scrollbar is used to extend the virtual real estate held by the parent control.*

AutoScrollMargin Size

The Form.AutoScrollMargin property is a Size structure; it contains Width and Height properties that describe how much space to add between controls falling outside the bounding region when AutoScroll is True.

By default the value of Form.AutoScrollMargin is 0, 0. This means that if you place a control outside of the visible bounding rectangle, the scrollbar added by AutoScroll (as you saw in Figure 16.5) will allow you to scroll to the very edge of the clipped control. If AutoScrollMargin is non-zero, you will be able to scroll to the edge of the control plus the additional margin amount.

Using Custom CreateParams

Classes in the CLR hide the murky world of Windows API programming, but Windows hasn't gone anywhere. Nowhere is this more apparent than when you use the CreateParams class and override the ReadOnly property CreateParams.

CreateParams effectively adds values to the CREATESTRUCT API record that tell the Windows operating system what kind of window to create. The reason you might want to override CreateParams is to add something extra to a window control (controls that have an HWND, or window handle, field).

Although customizing a basic Windows Forms control by modifying the CreateParams values is not something you will do every day, it is something you might want to do at some point. Unfortunately, when working with CreateParams, you will be poking around in the world of Or'd integers with cryptic numbers that define window styles. You will need a good book on Windows API programming, such as *Dan Appleman's Visual Basic Programmer's Guide to the Win32 API,* by Dan Appleman, or a lot of experimentation and patience.

Believe it or not, the control shown in Figure 16.6 is a customized Windows Forms
`Button` control that has simply overridden its `CreateParams` property. Listing 16.5
demonstrates the technical aspects of overriding `CreateParams`.

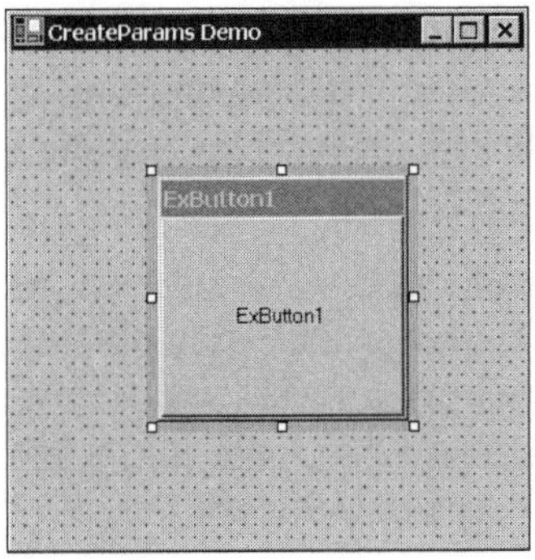

FIGURE 16.6

A custom `Button`
*with a caption and
dialog-style bor-
der implemented
by overriding*
`CreateParams`.

LISTING 16.5 Subclass the `Button` control and override the `CreateParams` property
for custom Windows styles

```
1:  Imports System.Windows.Forms
2:
3:  Public Class ExButton
4:
5:    Inherits System.Windows.Forms.Button
6:
7:    Protected Overrides ReadOnly Property CreateParams() _
8:      As CreateParams
9:      Get
10:       Dim Params As CreateParams = MyBase.CreateParams()
11:       Params.Style = Params.Style Or &HC00000
12:       Params.ExStyle = Params.ExStyle Or &H100
13:
14:       Return Params
15:     End Get
16:   End Property
17:
18: End Class
```

Line 11 uses the value of the WS_CAPTION style to add the caption to the button, and
the value of the WS_EX_WINDOWEDGE constant to create the raised-edge border, both
shown in Figure 16.6.

What Do the Component and Control Classes Do for Us?

Frameworks provide us with a hierarchy of relationships. It is beneficial to understand different branches in a framework like the CLR. Understanding the relationships and knowing where the branches are is beneficial to finding opportunistic points to extend a framework into your application.

When it comes to building graphical user interfaces in Visual Basic .NET for Windows applications, the essential first two branches occur at the Component and Control classes. The Component class introduces the notion of visually designable objects. The Control class, which inherits from Component, introduces the notion of a Control that receives messages, can have the input focus, and maintains a Windows handle for these purposes.

Nonvisual components will inherit directly from the Component class, and components that are manipulated visually and have a visual representation on a Windows Form are derived from the Control class.

Component Class

The Component class inherits from MarshalByRefObject, which in turn inherits directly from the root class, Object. Component is the base class for all components in the CLR. Component implements the IComponent interface, which supports the notion of designable objects, and maintains a list of event handlers containing the delegates for a particular component.

IComponent Interface

Component inherits the MarshalByRefObject class. MarshalByRefObject implements the IComponent interface, which allows components to be shared across application boundaries.

> **Note**
>
> Marshaling interapplication communication between objects falls under the auspices of .NET remoting. Basically, Remoting is the capability that replaces DCOM. All of this marshaling messages through object proxies is invisible and automatic while we are designing user interfaces. The first place object marshaling probably occurs is between the assembly that implements the component and Visual Studio .NET designers.

For our purposes we do not need to explore Remoting further, but if you are building distributed applications, the subject of Remoting will be of direct interest to you.

MarshalByRefObject allows messages to be sent across application boundaries using proxies. MarshalByRefObject objects are accessed within the local application domain, as contrasted to MarshalByValueComponent objects, which send a copy of the component to the remote application.

Events

The notion of events supports the Windows operating system's event-driven model. The class EventHandler is a base class for event handlers, and the Component.Events property is an EventHandlerList that maintains a list of events that a particular component will respond to.

DesignMode

The Component.DesignMode property indicates whether the component is currently being manipulated in design mode. This is necessary to support behaviors that are only necessary in the designer, like drawing a focus rectangle around a control that has the focus.

If you want a nonvisual control, you can inherit from the Component class to obtain the minimal capabilities necessary to support design-time manipulation.

Control Class

The Control class represents controls that users interact with directly. The Control class encapsulates the WndProc—the Grand Central Station of Windows messages. You can override the WndProc method to receive any Windows message, but Control classes are capable of handling most Windows messages.

Windows messages are sent to controls because each control has an HWND (window handle) encapsulated by a Handle property, introduced in the Control class.

Because a Control object has a visual presence, Control also makes the canvas (or device context) available through a call to the factory method CreateGraphics.

All of these features combined in the Control class result in controls being able to receive input focus, respond to Windows messages, and support default as well as custom painting.

Finally, Windows Forms controls are not thread-safe but introduce five thread-safe members. The `Control` class introduces `Invoke, InvokeRequired, BeginInvoke, EndInvoke,` and `CreateGraphics`. These thread-safe methods support synchronous and asynchronous control interaction by using delegates to perform work on a control's thread. (Read Chapter 14, "Multithreaded Applications," for more on using these five thread-safe methods.)

Adding Controls Dynamically

Adding controls dynamically allows you complete flexibility over your user interface. VB6 supported dynamic control addition, but the addition of controls was inconsistent with the model of declaring an object, creating a new instance of the object, and adding that object to a parent container.

VB6 supported adding controls to a form using a syntax that is more consistent with late-binding COM syntax than an object creation syntax (see Listing 16.7 for a VB6 example). Dynamic control creation in Visual Basic .NET is close enough that you should be able to make the transition easily enough (see Listing 16.8).

LISTING 16.7   Dynamic control creation in VB6

```
 1: Option Explicit
 2:
 3: Private WithEvents Button As CommandButton
 4:
 5: Private Sub Button_Click()
 6:    MsgBox "Hello"
 7: End Sub
 8:
 9: Private Sub Form_Load()
10:    Set Button = _
11:      Form1.Controls.Add("VB.CommandButton", "Dynamic")
12:    Button.Left = 100
13:    Button.Top = 100
14:    Button.Visible = True
15:    Button.Caption = "Dynamic"
16: End Sub
```

Lines 9 through 16 create and add the dynamic control in VB6. Line 11 both creates and adds a `CommandButton` using the *library.controlname* syntax, and returns the dynamic object to the `Button` variable. Lines 12 through 15 locate and name the control. A limitation here is wiring the control up to an event handler; the programmer must declare the `WithEvents` statement at design time. Requiring the `WithEvents` statement at design time limits dynamic control creation to some extent; this is necessary because there is no pro-grammable equivalent to delegates in VB6.

LISTING 16.8   Dynamic control creation in Visual Basic .NET

```
 1:  Private Sub Form1_Load(ByVal sender As System.Object, _
 2:    ByVal e As System.EventArgs) Handles MyBase.Load
 3:
 4:    Dim Button As New Button()
 5:    Button.Text = "Dynamic"
 6:    Button.Location = New Point(10, _
 7:      Controls.Count * Button.Height)
 8:    AddHandler Button.Click, AddressOf Form1_Load
 9:    Controls.Add(Button)
10:
11:  End Sub
```

Listing 16.8 creates a new Button on line 4, and assigns the Button object to a variable named Button. The button's caption is added on line 5, and the Button.Location prop-erty is established on lines 6 and 7. Line 8 adds the event handler dynamically, and the Button is added to the form's Controls array on line 9.

When the dynamic control is added to the form's Controls collection on line 9, the Button control will receive messages, including a paint message to display the control.

Notice that you still have to have code—in the case of the Button, an EventHandler—to respond to user inputs. Everything else about the code is completely dynamic.

The steps are identical for adding any controls to your applications at runtime. You can dynamically create as many controls as you need, all you have to do is ensure that you have somewhere to wire them to.

Creating Custom UserControls

Essential to creating powerful user interfaces and cutting down on redundant work is creating custom controls. Whenever you contrive a partial solution that can be used more than one time, create a control.

The easiest way to create a control is to add a UserControl to your project. The UserControl acts as a drawing surface that you can paint a variety of controls onto and reuse that control. To create a user control and add it to the toolbox, follow these steps:

1. Create a new Windows Control Library.
2. From the Visual Studio .NET main menu, click Project, Add User Control.

3. Add the controls, code, and events to describe the behavior supported by your user control.

4. Compile the Class Library containing your user control.

5. Drag the UserControl.vb file from the Solution Explorer to the toolbox.

User controls in Visual Basic .NET are subclassed from `System.Windows.Forms.UserControl`. Their power is in their ease of use, and the ability to visually design them using the same technique you would use if you were designing a form.

Adding Controls to a `UserControl`

There are no differences between adding controls to a form and adding them to a `UserControl`. If a control can be added to a `UserControl`, that control will be enabled in the Windows Forms toolbox when the `UserControl` designer has the focus.

Some controls, like a `MainMenu` control, cannot be supported for `UserControl` objects.

Adding Events to a `UserControl`

The custom `UserControl` shown in Figure 16.7 demonstrates a control that implements an Open Picture dialog box. The control allows the user to preview various kinds of images, and to select a particular image by clicking the Open button (see Listing 16.9).

FIGURE 16.7

The `OpenPictureDialog` *custom* `UserControl`.

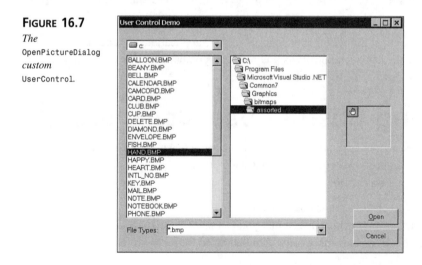

LISTING 16.9 A custom `UserControl` that allows the user to preview images

```
 1: Imports System.Windows.Forms
 2: Imports System.Drawing
 3: Imports Microsoft.VisualBasic
 4:
 5: Public Class OpenPictureDialog
 6:   Inherits System.Windows.Forms.UserControl
 7:
 8: [ Windows Form Designer generated code ]
 9:
10:   Public Sub UpdateFilePath(ByVal Path As String)
11:     FileListBox1.Path = Path
12:   End Sub
13:
14:   Public ReadOnly Property FullName() As String
15:     Get
16:       Return GetFullName()
17:     End Get
18:   End Property
19:
20:   Public Overloads Function GetFullName() As String
21:     Return FileListBox1.Path & "\" & FileListBox1.FileName
22:   End Function
23:
24:   Public Sub UpdatePictureBox(ByVal PictureName As String)
25:     Try
26:       PictureBox1.Image = Image.FromFile(PictureName)
27:     Catch
28:       Beep()
29:     End Try
30:   End Sub
31:
32:   Public Sub UpdateDirectory(ByVal DriveName As String)
33:
34:     Try
35:       DirListBox1.Path = DriveName
36:     Catch x As Exception
37:       MsgBox(x.Message, MsgBoxStyle.Exclamation)
38:     End Try
39:
40:   End Sub
41:
42:   Public Sub UpdateFilePattern(ByVal Pattern As String)
43:     FileListBox1.Pattern = Pattern
44:   End Sub
45:
46:   Private Sub DirListBox1_Change(ByVal sender As Object, _
47:     ByVal e As System.EventArgs) Handles DirListBox1.Change
48:     UpdateFilePath(DirListBox1.Path)
49:   End Sub
```

LISTING 16.9 continued

```
50:
51:
52:    Private Sub FileListBox1_SelectedValueChanged( _
53:      ByVal sender As Object, ByVal e As System.EventArgs) _
54:      Handles FileListBox1.SelectedValueChanged
55:
56:      UpdatePictureBox(FullName)
57:    End Sub
58:
59:    Private Sub DriveListBox1_SelectionChangeCommitted( _
60:      ByVal sender As Object, ByVal e As System.EventArgs) _
61:      Handles DriveListBox1.SelectionChangeCommitted
62:
63:      UpdateDirectory(DriveListBox1.Drive)
64:
65:    End Sub
66:
67:    Private Sub ComboBox1_SelectedValueChanged( _
68:      ByVal sender As Object, ByVal e As System.EventArgs) _
69:      Handles ComboBox1.SelectedValueChanged
70:
71:      UpdateFilePattern(ComboBox1.Text)
72:
73:    End Sub
74: End Class
```

The UserControl has a DriveListBox, FileListBox, and DirListBox all available in the Microsoft.VisualBasic namespace. (The fact that these are legacy controls is not relevant to our discussion; any control is fair game.) The controls were all painted on the canvas of the UserControl in the same manner you would paint them on a form.

Several public methods are added to allow a consumer to modify the state of any aspect of the UserControl programmatically without interacting with specific controls. This choice would allow you to change the controls used without adversely affecting consumers.

You can easily add events when working with a user control in the control designer or the code editor. If you double-click on the control, the default event will be generated for that control. Alternatively, if you select the Class Name and Method Name in the code editor, you can implement any event, again, just as you would generate events for controls on a form.

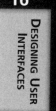

Adding Code to a `UserControl`

A class is a class is a class. One of the benefits of Visual Basic .NET is that the language is more consistent. If an entity is a class, you can interact with that class as you would any other class. You can generalize the class and add new elements to the class. You can create instances of the class and use properties, fields, events, and methods.

Adding a `UserControl` to Visual Studio .NET

When you have tested your `UserControl`, you can compile the library containing the control. To add the control to Visual Studio .NET, you can drag the control from the Solution Explorer by dragging the .vbproj file to the toolbox, or through the toolbox context menu.

To add the control to the toolbox using the toolbox context menu, follow these steps:

1. Right-click over the Windows Forms toolbox.
2. Click the Customize Toolbox menu item.
3. In the Customize Toolbox dialog box, click the .NET Framework Components tab.
4. Click the Browse button and navigate to the .DLL assembly containing your component or components.
5. When you have selected the component, ensure that the checkbox in the Name column of the Customize Toolbox dialog box is checked.

The component will show up in the toolbox, and you can drag and drop it onto any suitable container, like a form (see Figure 16.8).

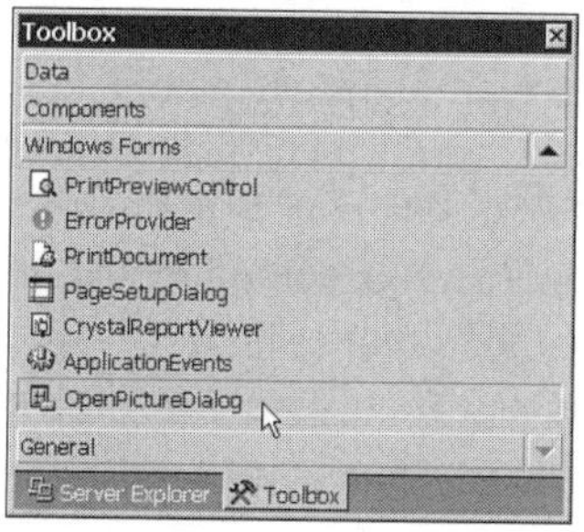

FIGURE 16.8

The `OpenPictureDialog` control added to the Windows Forms toolbox.

Associating a Toolbox Bitmap with Your Control

You can associate a custom bitmap with your control by adding the `ToolboxBitmapAttribute` to your control's class definition. You can type the literal name of the .bmp file, including the path, or use the `Type` information of an existing type.

To associate the bitmap used for the `OpenFileDialog` with our `OpenPictureDialog` control, add the following attribute statement before the class statement before line 5 in Listing 16.9:

```
<ToolboxBitmap(GetType(OpenFileDialog))> _
```

The constructor for the `ToolboxBitmapAttribute` class is overloaded and supports using the path information, too.

```
<ToolboxBitmap("c:\myimage.bmp")> _
```

Recall that by convention we drop the `Attribute` suffix for attribute classes.

Creating Custom Controls

What is the difference between a `UserControl` and a custom control? Not much. The `UserControl` jumpstarts creating custom controls because it provides you with a form-like canvas to paint controls on. However, if you want to extend the behavior of an existing control, rather than starting from scratch, you want to implement a custom control.

The most significant difference is that when you define a custom control, you will modify the `Inherits` statement to inherit from a specific existing control. When you inherit from an existing control, you get all of the behaviors and attributes of that existing control and anything else you add. The section "Creating a Custom Component" in Chapter 12, "Defining Attributes," demonstrates creating a custom label.

In other respects, creating a custom component is identical to creating a `UserControl`, except for having the `UserControl` designer to draw components on.

Several additional factors apply to controls in general. You do not need to implement a class library or Windows control library to create a custom control. You can create the control in a Windows application; this is a reasonable approach if the control will only be used in that application. You can also start a custom control as a `UserControl` and change your mind, making the same control a custom control by changing the `Inherits` statement. To effect the conversion, simply modify the `Inherits` `System.Windows.Forms.UserControl` to inherit from some other specific control, for example, `Inherits System.Windows.Forms.Button`.

The class library and Windows control library projects are there to help you get started but are not required aspects of creating controls. Keep in mind that controls are classes, and you can introduce them anywhere and at any time in your application where it makes sense to do so.

Creating a Nonvisual Component

There are several instances of user and custom controls throughout this book that demonstrate the mechanics of creating components. For this reason I have added an example of a nonvisual component in this section.

A nonvisual component is a component that generalizes the Component class. An example is the familiar Timer component. The component in Listing 16.10 wraps the events of the Application object, representing a Windows Forms application. By wrapping the events in the ApplicationEvents class, it becomes much easier to associate event handlers with Application events.

LISTING 16.10   Wrapping the application object events in a component

```
1:  Imports System.Threading
2:  Imports System.Windows.Forms
3:  Imports System.ComponentModel
4:
5:
6:  Public Class ApplicationEvents
7:    Inherits System.ComponentModel.Component
8:
9:    Public Event ApplicationExit As EventHandler
10:   Public Event Idle As EventHandler
11:   Public Event ThreadException As ThreadExceptionEventHandler
12:   Public Event ThreadExit As EventHandler
13:
14:   Public Sub New()
15:     AddHandler Application.ApplicationExit, _
16:       AddressOf DoApplicationExit
17:     AddHandler Application.Idle, _
18:       AddressOf DoIdle
19:
20:     AddHandler Application.ThreadException, _
21:         AddressOf DoThreadException
22:     AddHandler Application.ThreadExit, _
23:         AddressOf DoThreadExit
24:   End Sub
25:
26:   Private Sub DoApplicationExit(ByVal sender As Object, _
27:     ByVal e As System.EventArgs)
28:     RaiseEvent ApplicationExit(sender, e)
29:   End Sub
30:
31:   Private Sub DoIdle(ByVal sender As Object, _
32:     ByVal e As System.EventArgs)
33:
34:     RaiseEvent Idle(sender, e)
```

LISTING 16.10   continued

```
35:    End Sub
36:
37:    Private Sub DoThreadException(ByVal sender As Object, _
38:      ByVal e As ThreadExceptionEventArgs)
39:
40:      RaiseEvent ThreadException(sender, e)
41:
42:    End Sub
43:
44:    Public Sub DoThreadExit(ByVal sender As Object, _
45:      ByVal e As System.EventArgs)
46:
47:      RaiseEvent ThreadExit(sender, e)
48:
49:    End Sub
50: End Class
```

The ApplicationEvents component in Listing 16.10 inherits from Component. When you add it to a form, it will actually be added to the component tray. There are four events on lines 9 through 12 that exactly mirror the four Application events. The constructor on lines 14 to 24 adds the ApplicationEvents handlers to the Application events. When Application raises any of these events, the ApplicationEvents component receives the event and re-raises it, passing the event notification to the respondent.

We add a very modest procedural indirection by layering in a component, but we obtain maximum ease of use.

Test the ApplicationEvents component by installing the component and adding code to handle the individual events.

Specifying the Default Event

When you click on a form or a button, have you gotten around to wondering how a default event handler is selected and generated? Wonder no more. The System. ComponentModel.DefaultEventAttribute accepts the name of the event that is designated as the default event. If you add the following statement on line 5 of Listing 16.10, it will designate the Idle event as the default event for the ApplicationEvents class.

```
<DefaultEvent("Idle")> _
```

Recompile ApplicationEvents.vbproj. Now when you click the ApplicationEvents component, an Idle event handler will be generated by default. Of course, you can still pick individual events in the code designer, and the method bodies for those will be generated, too.

Summary

Components represented the biggest shift in the object-oriented paradigm and made rapid application development tools powerful and possible. More than likely, whole books will be written on this subject alone.

In this chapter you learned that the same techniques you use for implementing any class can be used to implement custom controls. Generalize the UserControl for simplified control creation, and generalize a specific control to extend the behavior of an existing control without reproducing available code.

Visual Studio .NET makes incorporating components a straightforward process. Compile a class library assembly and use the Customize Toolbox dialog box to add your custom controls to the toolbox.

Inheritance means that you are likely to find more custom, third-party components than ever before because building components in Visual Basic .NET is easier than ever before.

Programming with GDI+

IN THIS CHAPTER

The biggest gain that an object-oriented framework gives us is productivity. It's not necessarily that we can accomplish a greater variety of things with Graphics Device Interface (GDI+); rather, it's that we can be more productive in a shorter period of time. This productivity increase is provided to the framework developers too, resulting in a growing productivity for them as well.

You can walk from New York to Los Angeles, but you can get there a lot faster by car, or fastest of all by plane. Think of the 5-hour trip by plane from LaGuardia to LAX as a productivity gain of about 40 hours. (I am guessing here because I have made the trip from Michigan to Los Angeles and Michigan to New York several times but never coast to coast. I know with authority that you can listen to 30 hours of Ken Follett's *The Pillars of the Earth* while traveling from Las Vegas to Lansing by car.)

Is a 40-hour productivity gain valuable? Let me rephrase that. Is a 90% reduction in travel time—from 45 hours to 5—worth the effort it takes to get that savings? You better believe it. A good object-oriented framework may not provide any more technical opportunities than assembly language does, but a good framework will provide a significant productivity gain. A big productivity gain is what Visual Basic .NET and GDI+ do for us.

GDI+ wraps API calls into tidy namespaces and classes and makes it easier to work with what is euphemistically referred to as a *canvas,* the *device context (DC).* Instead of requiring the individual developer to carefully manage the DC, the `Graphics` object provided by GDI+ is stateless and is easier to use than disjointed API calls. In this chapter you will find out how much easier it is to perform custom painting and drawing and create shaped and opaque forms, and how the GDI+ namespaces make it easier to render graphics on other objects like printers.

GDI+ Basics

GDI+ is supported in the CLR by the `System.Drawing` namespace and subordinate elements. GDI+ includes classes representing the DC, brushes, pens, fonts, and basic shape-drawing capabilities, as well as support for imaging and rendering graphics on devices in addition to Windows Forms.

Support for drawing in Windows Forms is supported at the API level. GDI+ is a framework within the CLR that provides us with refined metaphors that make what we have always been able to do easier.

Using Graphics Objects

The `Graphics` class is the metaphor that represents the API device context. Methods, fields, and properties in the `Graphics` class conceal working with handles and `HRESULT` return values.

Generally, you have access to a `Graphics` object when you explicitly call `CreateGraphics` or as a member of the `PaintEventArgs Paint` event argument. Because the `Graphics` object is stateless, you should not cache a `Graphics` object; you should request a `Graphics` object each time you need to perform a graphics operation. Additionally, the `Graphics` object represents a valuable system resource; thus, following advice earlier in this book, we should call `Dispose` when we are done with any `Graphics` object.

17

PROGRAMMING
WITH GDI+

Tip

Any object you are going to create and destroy should be wrapped in a resource protection block using the `Try..Finally` idiom introduced in VB .NET.

As with any resource, if you want to ensure that the `Dispose` method is called, wrap the call to `CreateGraphics` and `Dispose` in a resource protection block.

Creating a Graphics Object

Classes in Visual Basic .NET support constructors instead of the `Finalize` event called internally. The availability of constructors allows additional idioms to be employed. One such idiom is to devise a factory method and make the constructor protected or private. The `Graphics` class uses this technique, with the end result being that you might only create instances via the factory method.

The reason for employing a factory method is usually to ensure that a construction and initialization order occurs reliably. `Graphics` objects are associated by the *handle of a device context (hDC)* for a specific control.

As with any other object, when you have an instance, you can invoke any of the instance methods or properties. To create an instance of a `Graphics` object, call `Control.CreateGraphics` where `Control` is the instance of the control whose DC, or canvas, you want to draw on. The following code demonstrates how to get an instance of a `Graphics` object for a `Form`:

```
Dim G As Graphics = CreateGraphics()
```

> **Note**
>
> You can create `Graphics` objects from static methods of the `Graphics` class by passing the `HWnd`, or windows handle, using the `Handle` property. There are several other shared `Graphics` methods that allow you to create instances, but the constructor is `Private`.
>
> Unless there are exigent circumstances, you should use the `Control.CreateGraphics` method.

Do not cache `Graphics` objects. `Graphics` objects are defined to be stateless. As a consequence of their statelessness, if you cache a `Graphics` object for a form and the form is resized, the cached `Graphics` object will not render the output correctly. Each time you need a `Graphics` object to paint a particular control, call `CreateGraphics`. You can use a single `Graphics` instance within a single method and called methods; when the method that created the `Graphics` object exits, call `Dispose`.

Custom Graphics in the `Paint` Event

Another way you get a `Graphics` object is when you write an event handler for a control's `Paint` event. The first argument in the `Paint` event is the `Object` parameter and the second is a `PaintEventArgs` object. The parameter e contains a property that is an instance of the `Graphics` object for the control that raised the `Paint` event. Listing 17.1 demonstrates a shadowed text effect created in a form's `Paint` event.

LISTING 17.1 Simple graphic effects, like shadowed text, require very little effort using GDI+

```
1:   Private Sub ShadowText(ByVal G As Graphics, _
2:     ByVal Text As String, ByVal X As Integer, _
3:     ByVal Y As Integer)
4:
5:     G.DrawString(Text, _
6:       New Font("Times New Roman", 16, FontStyle.Bold), _
7:       Brushes.Silver, X - 3, Y - 3)
8:
9:     G.DrawString(Text, _
10:      New Font("Times New Roman", 16, FontStyle.Bold), _
11:      Brushes.Black, X, Y)
12:
13:  End Sub
14:
15:  Private Sub Form1_Paint(ByVal sender As Object, _
16:    ByVal e As System.Windows.Forms.PaintEventArgs) _
```

LISTING 17.1   continued

```
17:     Handles MyBase.Paint
18:
19:     ShadowText(e.Graphics, "GOTDOTNET", 11, 11)
20:   End Sub
```

Line 19 calls a well-named method, passing basic information to create a shadowed-text effect. The `Graphics.DrawString` method is called on lines 5 and 9. The first time the text is drawn, the X and Y values are offset and the text is drawn using a `Silver` brush. The foreground text is drawn at the X and Y positions using a darker, contrasting foreground brush color.

> **Note**
>
> You could create custom text in VB6. There are, however, some distinct differences between VB6 and VB .NET. In VB6 you probably had to import API methods, like `WriteText` and `GetDC`. Also, in VB6 many controls did not raise a `Paint` event.
>
> With Visual Basic .NET, more controls implement the `Paint` method and raise a `Paint` event, enabling you to perform custom painting on a wider variety of Windows Forms controls.

Using variations of offsetting values, you can create embossed, shadowed, engraved, or outlined text with the code demonstrated in the listing.

Basic Drawing Classes

The `System.Drawing` namespace contains fundamental classes for drawing. GDI+ is a stateless implementation. The result is that you will need to pass in instances of fonts, colors, brushes, pens, and shapes depending on the needs of the class and methods each time you invoke a drawing operation.

There are collections, such as `Brushes`, that contain dozens of properties that return predefined items (such as brushes), making the task of acquiring a brush (color, pen, and so on) easier.

Color Class

The `Color` class implements about 50 `Shared` properties that return a specific color value. (The list is extensive enough to include colors like `AliceBlue`.) Use the class and refer to the color property by name to get an instance of that color. For example,

`Color.AliceBlue` returns an instance of a `Color` object that is the color `AliceBlue`. (I wonder what `Color.AliceCooper` would return?)

The `Color` class also allows you to manually initialize a `Color` object and define the color by specifying the `A`, `R`, `G`, and `B` values. `R`, `G`, and `B` are the red, green, and blue percentages, and `A` is the alpha component of the color. (The alpha part of color has to do with the transparency of a color relative to the background.)

Additionally, you can create a `Color` by calling the shared methods `FromArgb` or `FromName`. For example, `BackColor = Color.FromName("PapayaWhip")` will turn the background color of a form to a salmony-beige color. If you are comfortable with or want to experiment with RGB colors—or know a color by name—you can get `Color` objects using these two shared methods.

Brushes Class

The `Brushes` class is similar to the `Color` class in the members it contains. `Brushes` contains shared properties defined by the color of the brush and has properties with the same names as the color properties. Keep in mind that `Brushes` returns an instance of a `Brush` object, not a color.

It would have been consistent if there were simply a `Brush` class with the shared properties that returned brushes, but if you need an instance of a custom `Brush`, you have to construct an instance of the `Brush` class, not `Brushes`. (There is no `Colors` equivalent.)

A `Brush` is used to describe how the interiors of shapes are filled, including the color component. (See Listing 17.1 for an example of how to use the `Brushes` class in context.)

Pens Class

The `Pens` class is analogous to the `Brushes` class. There are shared properties named by the color of the pen that you can access to quickly get a `Pen` object. Pens are used to define the color of lines and curves. If you need to manually create an instance of a `Pen`, you will need to construct a `Pen`, rather than a `Pens` object. (See the section on the `Rectangle` class for an example of using the `Pens` class.)

Simple GDI+ Operation

Using the simple primitives, you can provide the appropriate arguments necessary to satisfy the stateless behavior of GDI+. Listing 17.2 demonstrates using the `Pens`, `Graphics`, and `RectangleF` classes to perform some basic architectural drawing.

LISTING 17.2 Basic graphics example using `Pens`, `Graphics`, and `RectangleF`

```
1:  Private Sub DrawArc(ByVal G As Graphics)
2:     Const Max As Integer = 36
3:     Dim I As Integer
4:     For I = 1 To Max
5:        G.DrawArc(Pens.Red, RandomRect(Max), 0, 180)
6:     Next
7:  End Sub
8:
9:  Private Function RandomRect( _
10:    Optional ByVal Max As Integer = 36) As RectangleF
11:
12:    Static Count As Integer = 0
13:    If (Count >= Max) Then Count = 0
14:    Count += 1
15:
16:    Return New RectangleF( _
17:      (ClientRectangle.Width - (Count * 10)) / 2, _
18:      10, Count * 10, 300)
19:
20: End Function
```

The `DrawArc` procedure beginning on line 1 is passed an instance of a `Graphics` object and draws 36 arcs using the `Red` pen property from the `Pens` class. The last two parameters of `DrawArc` express the start angle and sweep. The parameters 0 and 180 draw the bottom half of an ellipse. The `RectangleF` object returned by `RandomRect` defines a rectangle that acts as the constraining boundary of the ellipse. (See the upcoming sections on `DrawArc` and `Rectangle` for some additional information.)

Drawing Shapes and Text

Using the primitives for pens, colors, brushes, and fonts, GDI+ provides methods for drawing shapes, text, and graphics, like icons.

Rectangle and RectangleF Structures

There seems to be little comparative difference between the `ValueType` structures `RectangleF` and `Rectangle`. Some methods seem to require the `RectangleF` and others the `Rectangle`. Rectangles are structures that define a rectangular area by tracking the `X` and `Y` ordered pair and `Width` and `Height` properties.

> **Note**
>
> The difference between structures like `Rectangle` and `RectangleF` is that the suffix indicates that the fields are floating-point rather than integer fields.
>
> There are overloaded versions of methods that take both integer and floating-point versions of similar structures. Why this difference exists is presumed to be related to the range of possible values supported by each type.

Recall that you do not have to use the `New` keyword when declaring a `ValueType` variable; however, if you want to call a parameterized constructor for a `ValueType`, declare the variable with the `New` keyword. For example, the following line declares a variable `R` that is a ready-to-use `Rectangle`:

```
Dim R As Rectangle
```

If you want to initialize the `Rectangle` with the `X`, `Y` and `Width`, `Height` arguments, use the parameterized constructor version with the `New` keyword:

```
Dim R As New Rectangle(1,1, 10,10)
```

The Cartesian quadrant in Windows Forms is quadrant II, where the origin 0, 0 is the upper-left corner of the `Form` (or control).

If you need more advanced region management than provided by the `Rectangle` or `RectangleF` structures, use the `Region` class. `Region` is covered in the section titled, "Advanced Drawing." (For additional code samples demonstrating `Region`, refer to Chapter 15, "Using Windows Forms.")

Point and PointF Structures

`Point` and `PointF` are `ValueTypes` that represent an X,Y ordered-pair in the Cartesian plane. Points are used to represent a position in a two-dimensional drawing surface, a Windows Form.

DrawArc

The `Graphics.DrawArc` method is used to draw arcs (see Figure 17.1), or part or all of an ellipse. If you want a closed arc, call `DrawEllipse`. If you want an open arc, use `DrawArc`.

FIGURE 17.1

The Graphics.
DrawArc *method
employs a* Pen,
a bounding
Rectangle, *a start
angle, and the
sweep of the arc.*

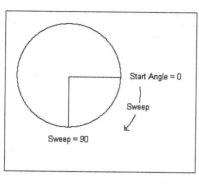

There are four versions of DrawArc. Essentially an arc requires a Pen, a bounding Rectangle, a start angle, and the sweep of the arc. A start angle of 0 is the right-horizontal from the center of the arc, and the sweep proceeds clockwise. For example, a start angle of 0 and a sweep of 360 would draw a closed arc. Figure 17.1 illustrates the 0-angle and direction and relative position of a 90-degree sweep.

DrawEllipse

The Graphics.DrawEllipse method draws a closed arc, so it does not need the angle and sweep parameters. The Pen argument describes the color of the line used to draw the ellipse, and the Rectangle parameter defines the bounding region.

Calling Graphics.DrawEllipse(Pens.Blue, New RectangleF(10, 10, 100, 50) yields the same result as Graphics.Draw(Pens.Blue, New RectangleF(10, 10, 100, 50), 0, 360). Replace the call to DrawArc on line 5 of Listing 17.2, losing the angle and sweep arguments to create the visual effect of a 3D sphere.

DrawRectangle

Graphics.DrawRectangle has three overloaded versions that take a Pen and a Rectangle object or the four coordinates of a rectangle.

DrawPolygon

Polygons are many-sided shapes whose edges are defined by connecting points. Graphics.DrawPolygon takes a Pen argument and an array of points. The first point is the last point; consequently, you do not have to repeat the first point to close the polygon. The number of sides in the polygon will be equal to the number of points, although if you define only two points, the polygon will appear to be a line.

Listing 17.3 demonstrates an array of five points that roughly define a pentagon.

Listing 17.3 Using `Graphics.DrawPolygon` to draw a pentagon

```
1:  Private Sub DrawPolygon(ByVal G As Graphics)
2:
3:      Dim Points() As Point = {New Point(10, 30), _
4:        New Point(100, 10), New Point(150, 75), _
5:        New Point(100, 150), New Point(10, 130)}
6:
7:      G.DrawPolygon(Pens.Purple, Points)
8:
9:  End Sub
```

The `Point` type is a `ValueType`; however, to use the overloaded, parameterized constructor of a `ValueType`, we need to use the `New` keyword. `Points` defines an array of five point structures. `DrawPolygon`, on line 7, draws the polygon defined by the array of points. `DrawPolygon` closes the polygon defined by the points, mitigating the need for specifying a last point matching the first point.

DrawPie

The `Graphics.DrawPie` method works similarly to the `DrawArc` method. `DrawPie` takes a bounding rectangle, a start angle, and a sweep. The distinction between `DrawArc` and `DrawPie` is that the latter closes the arc with line segments. Listing 17.4 demonstrates the `DrawPie` method, using a `TextureBrush`, to fill a wedge of the pie (see Figure 17.2).

Listing 17.4 Calling the `Graphics.DrawPie` method and a `Brush` subclass, `TextureBrush` to fill a pie wedge

```
1:  Private Sub DrawPie(ByVal G As Graphics)
2:    Dim R As Rectangle = New Rectangle(50, 50, 125, 150)
3:    Dim B As New TextureBrush(Icon.ToBitmap)
4:
5:    G.FillPie(B, R, 0, 90)
6:    G.DrawPie(Pens.Black, R, 0, 270)
7:  End Sub
```

Line 2 calls the parameterized constructor for the `Rectangle ValueType`, so we must invoke the constructor using `New`. Line 3 creates a subclass of `Brush`—`TextureBrush`—using the form's `Icon` to create the texture. (`TextureBrush` is overloaded and takes a `Bitmap`; to satisfy the overloaded `TextureBrush` constructor, we call `Icon.ToBitmap` to convert the icon to a bitmap.) Line 5 creates the wedge first using the texture brush and line 6 draws the pie, outlining the wedges.

FIGURE 17.2

A TextureBrush *filled pie wedge using methods of the* Graphics *object.*

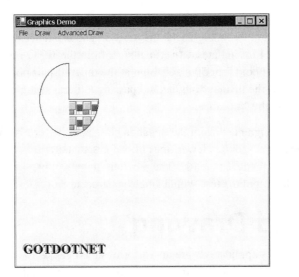

DrawString

As demonstrated in this chapter's examples so far, rendering graphics-based images is much easier in Visual Basic .NET. You can also use some of the techniques demonstrated thus far to create some neat string-drawing effects.

The basic Graphics.DrawString method takes a string, font, brush, and an ordered-pair indicating the starting left-top position of the text. The color of the string is determined by the font argument, and the fill characteristics are determined by the brush. For example, if you pass a textured brush, you can get some unique-looking strings. Listing 17.5 demonstrates using a textured brush that uses the JPEG image of this book's jacket to create some fiery text.

LISTING 17.5   Employs a textured brush to create some unique-looking text

```
1:  Private Sub DrawText(ByVal G As Graphics)
2:    Dim Image As New Bitmap("..\..\Images\VBNET.jpg")
3:
4:    Dim ATextureBrush As New TextureBrush(Image)
5:    Dim AFont As New Font("Garamond", 50, _
6:      FontStyle.Bold, GraphicsUnit.Pixel, 0)
7:
8:    G.DrawString("Unleashed!", AFont, ATextureBrush, 10, 10)
9:  End Sub
```

Line 2 creates a `Bitmap` object from a JPEG file, which provides for high levels of compression. (You might want to double-check the location and existence of the image file in production code.) Line 4 instantiates a `TextureBrush` from the JPEG image. Line 5 instantiates a Garamond bold font 50 pixels high at the ordered-pair position X = 10 and Y = 10. Line 8 invokes the `DrawString` method passing a literal string message, the font and brush objects, and the X,Y offset.

You could use an existing `Brush` from the `Brushes` class and the form's `Font`, resulting in a simpler appearance that requires fewer lines of code: `G.DrawString("Unleashed!"`, `50, Font, Brushes.Orange, 10, 10)`. The previous statement uses an existing font and brush and would output the text with a single statement.

Advanced Drawing

Truly advanced graphics applications are an art form. Video games like *Half Life* that render moving, jumping, and running images in a 3D world are excellent examples of the result of graphics programming in the hands of talented craftsmen.

Whether Visual Basic .NET will be used to write multiplayer Internet games remains to be seen. At TechEd the game Donkey.Net demonstrated that advanced 3D imagery could be created in VB. (Donkey.Net used the Revolution3D graphics engine implemented in VB6, but the game is actually implemented in VB .NET.) At the time of this writing you could still download Donkey.Net from the Microsoft Web site.

This section will not teach you how to create visually complex results as demonstrated by games like *Quake* or *Half Life*, but you will learn more about GDI+ features in the `System.Drawing.Drawing2D` namespace that are available to help you get started. You will probably find some of these capabilities helpful in business programming, too.

Drawing Curves

The `Graphics` object defines a method for drawing curves based on multiple points. The `DrawBezier` and `DrawBeziers` methods take four points and an array of `Points`, respectively, including a starting and ending point and points in between that define the shape of the curve.

The Bézier drawing capabilities allow you to draw elaborate curves as long as you can define the points that describe the curve.

17

PROGRAMMING
WITH GDI+

Note

Bézier curves, or splines, were invented by Pierre Bézier for applications in the automotive industry. Bézier splines are curves based on four points and have found widespread use in CAD systems and defining the outline of fonts.

For our purposes, Bézier curves are curves defined by points.

Drawing Complex Curves, or Bézier Curves

Instead of contriving random curves to demonstrate the curve drawing capabilities of the `Graphics` class, the example in this section copies points described by a `GraphicsPath` and uses those points to render the image using `DrawBeziers`. Listing 17.6 demonstrates code that draws the curve shown in Figure 17.3. An overview follows the listing. (The `GraphicsPath` is covered in the next section.)

FIGURE 17.3

A Bézier curve drawn from a `GraphicsPath` *initialized with* `Chr(174).`

```
Graphics Demo                                    _ □ x
File   Draw   Advanced Draw




   ®








                   GOTDOTNET
```

LISTING 17.6   A complex array of points used to draw a moderately complex Bézier curve based on the ® symbol

```
1:    Private Overloads Function GetAdjustedCount( _
2:      ByVal Size As Integer) As Integer
3:
4:      While ((Size - 4) Mod 3 <> 0)
5:        Size -= 1
6:      End While
7:
```

LISTING 17.6 continued

```
 8:        Return Size
 9:     End Function
10:
11:     Private Overloads Function GetAdjustedCount( _
12:        ByVal Source() As PointF) As Integer
13:        Return GetAdjustedCount(Source.GetUpperBound(0))
14:     End Function
15:
16:     Private Sub CopyPoints(ByVal Source() As PointF, _
17:        ByRef Target() As PointF)
18:
19:        ReDim Target(GetAdjustedCount(Source) - 1)
20:        Array.Copy(Source, Target, Target.Length)
21:     End Sub
22:
23:     Private Function GetPath2() As Drawing2D.GraphicsPath
24:        GetPath2 = New Drawing2D.GraphicsPath()
25:        GetPath2.AddString(Chr(174), FontFamily.GenericSerif, _
26:            FontStyle.Bold, 100, New PointF(50, 50), _
27:            StringFormat.GenericDefault)
28:     End Function
29:
30:     Private Sub DrawBezier(ByVal G As Graphics)
31:        Dim Points() As PointF
32:        CopyPoints(GetPath2.PathPoints, Points)
33:        G.DrawBeziers(Pens.Red, Points)
34:     End Sub
```

DrawBeziers draws multiple curves. If you call Graphics.DrawBezier (singular), you will need to pass four points. If you call Graphics.DrawBeziers (plural), you will need to pass four points plus an additional number of points evenly divisible by 3 or you will get a System.ArgumentException error.

> **Note**
>
> Depending on your keyboard's character set, you can get different results. If the code seems to work correctly but you get a blank screen, replace the Chr(174) with some alternate random numbers.

The first overloaded GetAdjustedCount method in Listing 17.6 drops a few points to make the equation (points - 4) Mod 3 = True. The second overloaded GetAdjustedCount method takes an array of points and passes the size of the array to the original method on lines 1 to 9. (Having two GetAdjustedCount methods simply makes it more convenient to ask for the correct count in the main method, DrawBezier in lines 30 to 34.)

> **Tip**
>
> If you do need a temporary variable that is the same type as a function's return type, you can use the function name instead of introducing a new temporary variable (see the function GetPath2 from Listing 17.6).

CopyPoints copies the Source points into the Target points; Target points are passed ByRef because CopyPoints modifies the array on line 19. If we changed only the elements of the array, Target, we could pass the array ByVal. GetPath2 creates a GraphicsPath object and initializes it with the ASCII character 174. (We will discuss GraphicsPath in the next section.) Finally, my DrawBezier method creates an array of points, copies the points from the GraphicsPath.PathPoints, and uses the adjusted points to draw the curve in Figure 17.3.

GraphicsPath Class

The graphics engine maintains graphics as coordinates of geometric shapes in world-space. The GraphicsPath class is responsible for maintaining the coordinates describing the figures described by the GraphicsPath.

Paths are used to draw outlines, fill shapes, and create clipping regions. A path can contain any number of figures, referred to as subpaths. New figures are started when you create a GraphicsPath, call CloseFigure or Graphics.FillPath, or you explicitly call StartFigure.

As demonstrated in the preceding section, strings can be used to initialize graphics paths (see line 25 of Listing 17.6). Additionally, Bézier curves, simple curves, polygons, rectangles, ellipses, lines, and pies can be added to a GraphicsPath. When you've created a GraphicsPath object, you can get the points that describe the path or you can perform other operations on the image.

PathPoints

The PathPoints property is a read-only property that returns an array of PointF structures. Line 32 of Listing 17.6 uses the points returned from GraphicsPath.PathPoints to draw the Bézier curve shown in Figure 17.3.

PointCount

The PointCount property is a read-only property that indicates the number of points in the GraphicsPath. You can also get the number of points from the Array.GetUpperBound method from the array PathPoints.

Reverse

GraphicsPath.Reverse reverses the order of the points in the PathPoints array. Using reversed PathPoints to draw a Bézier curve does not result in a mirror image; rather, the points are drawn in reverse order. Listing 17.7 is excerpted from a C# example in the MSDN help files. The example reverses the path points for a line, ellipse, and arc and displays all of the path points in initial order and again after they have been reversed.

LISTING 17.7 Reversing the order of PathPoints

```
 1:  Private Sub Reverse(ByVal G As Graphics)
 2:    Dim Path As New Drawing2D.GraphicsPath()
 3:    Path.AddLine(New Point(0, 0), New Point(100, 100))
 4:    Path.AddEllipse(100, 100, 200, 250)
 5:    Path.AddArc(300, 250, 100, 100, 0, 90)
 6:
 7:    DrawPoints(G, Path.PathPoints, 20)
 8:    Path.Reverse()
 9:    DrawPoints(G, Path.PathPoints, 150)
10:  End Sub
11:
12:  Private Sub DrawPoints(ByVal G As Graphics, _
13:    ByVal Points() As PointF, ByVal Offset As Integer)
14:
15:    Dim Y As Integer = 20
16:    Dim I As Integer
17:    Dim AFont As New Font("Arial", 8)
18:
19:    For I = 0 To Points.Length - 1
20:      G.DrawString(Points(I).X.ToString & _
21:      ", " & Points(I).Y.ToString, AFont, _
22:      Brushes.Black, Offset, Y)
23:      Y += 20
24:    Next
25:  End Sub
```

> **Note**
>
> The sample code was ported from a C# example in the help files. The code was translated line for line, demonstrating the very close match in capability

between C# and Visual Basic .NET. Choosing Visual Basic over C#, or vice versa, is referred to as a lifestyle choice. The implication is that there are no practical technical reasons for choosing C# over VB .NET; program in the language you like.

The listing adds a line, ellipse, and arc to the graphics path on lines 2 through 5. Lines 7, 8, and 9 draw the point values, reverse the order of the points, and draw the point values in their new order. Call `Graphics.DrawBezier` to see that the same image results before and after the point order is changed.

Transform

The `GraphicsPath.Transform` method applies a matrix transform to the `GraphicsPath` and can be used to rotate, translate, skew, or scale a `GraphicsPath`.

To transform a `GraphicsPath`, create an instance of a `Matrix` object (found in the `System.Drawing.Drawing2D` namespace), invoke one of the transformation methods on the `Matrix`, and then call `GraphicsPath.Transform(Matrix)`.

Creating a Matrix

The `Matrix` class has a default constructor that allows you to create an instance of the matrix without any parameters, or, you can constrain the matrix to a specific region by passing a rectangle and an array of points.

The following code demonstrates default construction of a `Matrix`.

```
Dim MyMatrix As New Matrix
```

With the `Matrix` object, we can invoke methods to describe the impact the matrix will have on the `GraphicsPath` when the matrix is passed to the `Transform` method.

Scaling

Using the object from the preceding section, `MyMatrix.Scale( 2, 2 )` scales the matrix object by the X,Y vectors where X = 2 and Y = 2. Modifying `DrawBezier` from Listing 17.6 to incorporate the scale transform yields the code shown in Listing 17.8.

LISTING 17.8   An excerpt from Listing 17.6 in which we modified `DrawBezier` to scale the Bézier by the vector 2, 2

```
1:   Private Sub DrawBezier(ByVal G As Graphics)
2:
3:       Dim Points() As PointF
```

LISTING 17.8 continued

```
 4:      Dim Path As Drawing2D.GraphicsPath = GetPath2()
 5:      Dim AMatrix As New Drawing2D.Matrix()
 6:
 7:      AMatrix.Scale(2, 2)
 8:      Path.Transform(AMatrix)
 9:      CopyPoints(Path.PathPoints, Points)
10:      G.DrawBeziers(Pens.Red, Points)
11:
12: End Sub
```

The only modification from Listing 17.6, lines 30 through 34, is the introduction of a temporary `Path` to store the `GraphicsPath` object, allowing us to invoke the `Transform` method, the instantiation of the new matrix. Lines 7 and 8 scale the matrix and apply the matrix transform to the `GraphicsPath` object `Path`.

The end result of this subtle change is that the registered trademark symbol (®) will be displayed roughly twice as large as the original shown in Figure 17.3.

Translating

`Matrix.Translate( X, Y )` applies the translation vector defined by X and Y to a `GraphicsPath`. The net result is that the world-space position of the graphics is moved. (Replace `Scale` on line 7 of Listing 17.8 with `Translate` to demonstrate the difference between scaling and translating.)

Inverting

The `Matrix.Invert` method will invert a `Matrix` transform if the matrix is invertible. You can call `Matrix.IsInvertible` to determine whether a particular matrix instance is invertible.

Inserting `AMatrix.Invert()` between lines 7 and 8 of Listing 17.8 will invert the doubling in size of the matrix and halve the matrix instead, resulting in an image that is smaller than the original.

Rotating

Rotating a matrix results in a clockwise rotation around the origin. For example, `AMatrix.Rotate(10)` will rotate the `GraphicsPath` object 10 degrees in a clockwise position around the origin.

To visualize the result, draw an imaginary line from 0, 0 (the upper-left corner) of the control that will display the image. Then, draw a vector 10 degrees down from the first line and move the center of the image to a point along the new vector a radial distance equal to the distance from the origin to the image's current location. The effect is an orbital path around the origin.

Warp

The GraphicsPath.Warp method applies a warp transform described by a parallelogram and a rectangle. Warp causes the effect that results from leaving vinyl LPs in the sun too long. (You remember LPs, don't you? They're the Long Playing records that predate audio cassettes and CDs.) Listing 17.9 draws a GraphicsPath object with a warped appearance.

LISTING 17.9   Applying a warp transform to a GraphicsPath

```
1:  Private Sub DrawBezier(ByVal G As Graphics)
2:
3:      Dim Points() As PointF
4:      Dim Path As Drawing2D.GraphicsPath = GetPath2()
5:      Dim AMatrix As New Drawing2D.Matrix()
6:
7:      Dim ARectangle = New RectangleF(0, 0, 100, 200)
8:      Dim AParallelogram() As PointF = {New PointF(200, 200), _
9:        New PointF(400, 250), New PointF(220, 400)}
10:
11:     Path.Warp(AParallelogram, ARectangle, AMatrix, _
12:        Drawing2D.WarpMode.Perspective, 0.5)
13:
14:     CopyPoints(Path.PathPoints, Points)
15:
16:     G.DrawBeziers(Pens.Red, Points)
17:
18: End Sub
```

DrawBezier in the example is again taken from the original in Listing 17.6. In the preceding example, a parallelogram defined by the three points on lines 8 and 9 and the rectangle on line 7 are used to define the warp. (If you omit the fourth point of the parallelogram, it is implied by the first three points.) The parallelogram, rectangle, and matrix are all passed to the GraphicsPath.Warp method resulting in a warped or stretched effect.

Widen

The GraphicsPath.Widen method takes a Pen or a Pen and a Matrix and adds an additional outline to the GraphicsPath.

Region Class

The Region class is a more powerful version of its cousin the Rectangle. Regions are composed of the interior part of a graphic described by paths and rectangles. Like GraphicsPath, regions are defined in world-space coordinates, making them scalable.

Regions, not rectangles, are used to define the drawing area of a window and are used to perform hit-testing. By assigning a Region object to the Region property, you can define shaped forms that are described by GraphicsPath objects. (The ShapedForm.sln from Chapter 15 demonstrates using a Region to create a custom shaped form, and the next section explores the topic of shaped forms in further detail.)

Shaped Forms

John Percival demonstrates how to use the API to create shaped forms in an article "Creating Odd Shaped Forms" published on www.vbworld.com by creating a form in the shape of a smiley face. To Mr. Percival's credit, the project imports a dozen or so API methods and completes the task in an additional 50 to 100 lines of code, an example of mental gymnastics.

What a good object-oriented framework does for us is introduce new things and make old things easier. By incorporating spurious API features into a coherent framework, capabilities are organized by utility and consequently easier to use.

Listing 17.10 demonstrates code that creates a smiley face form (see Figure 17.4). The form is similar to the example in the vbworld.com example by John Percival. In the VB6 example, when the API functions are included, the code is all about drawing the shapes and defining the regions that describe the form. For this reason the code in the VB6 example (not provided, but available online at www.vbworld.com) is similar to the VB .NET example in Listing 17.10. The biggest difference is in the tenor of the code.

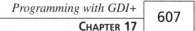

FIGURE 17.4

A smiley face form uses clipping regions to define the boundaries of the form.

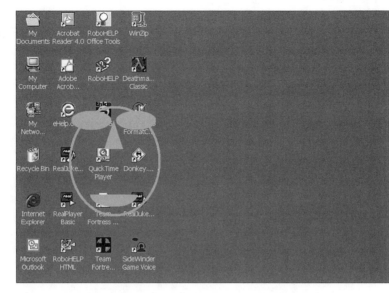

LISTING 17.10 A form based on simple line, curve, and polygon regions

```
1:  Public Class Form1
2:    Inherits System.Windows.Forms.Form
3:
4:  [Windows Form Designer generated code]
5:
6:    Private Sub AddOutline(ByVal Face As Region)
7:
8:      Dim OutlinePath As New Drawing2D.GraphicsPath()
9:      OutlinePath.AddEllipse(5, 90, 195, 230)
10:     Dim Outline As New Region(OutlinePath)
11:
12:     Dim InlinePath As New Drawing2D.GraphicsPath()
13:     InlinePath.AddEllipse(10, 95, 185, 220)
14:     Dim Inline As New Region(InlinePath)
15:
16:     Dim Ring As New Region()
17:     Outline.Xor(Inline)
18:     Face.Intersect(Outline)
19:
20:   End Sub
21:
22:   Private Sub AddEyes(ByVal Face As Region)
23:
```

LISTING 17.10 continued

```
24:     Dim LeftEyePath As New Drawing2D.GraphicsPath()
25:     LeftEyePath.AddEllipse(10, 100, 85, 40)
26:
27:     Dim RightEyePath As New Drawing2D.GraphicsPath()
28:     RightEyePath.AddEllipse(105, 100, 85, 40)
29:
30:     Dim LeftEye As New Region(LeftEyePath)
31:     Dim RightEye As New Region(RightEyePath)
32:     Face.Union(LeftEye)
33:     Face.Union(RightEye)
34:
35:   End Sub
36:
37:   Private Sub AddNose(ByVal Face As Region)
38:     Dim Nose(2) As PointF
39:     Nose(0).X = 100
40:     Nose(0).Y = 120
41:     Nose(1).X = 80
42:     Nose(1).Y = 180
43:     Nose(2).X = 120
44:     Nose(2).Y = 180
45:
46:     Dim NoseRegionPath As New Drawing2D.GraphicsPath()
47:     NoseRegionPath.AddPolygon(Nose)
48:     Dim NoseRegion As New Region(NoseRegionPath)
49:     Face.Union(NoseRegion)
50:
51:   End Sub
52:
53:   Private Sub AddLips(ByVal Face As Region)
54:
55:     Dim TopLipPath As New Drawing2D.GraphicsPath()
56:     TopLipPath.AddArc(50, 250, 100, 50, 0, 180)
57:     Dim TopLip As New Region(TopLipPath)
58:     Face.Union(TopLip)
59:
60:   End Sub
61:
62:   Private Sub DrawFace()
63:     Dim Face As New Region()
64:     AddOutline(Face)
65:     AddEyes(Face)
66:     AddNose(Face)
67:     AddLips(Face)
68:     Region = Face
69:   End Sub
70:
71:   Private Sub Form1_Load(ByVal sender As System.Object, _
72:     ByVal e As System.EventArgs) Handles MyBase.Load
```

LISTING 17.10 continued

```
73:     BackColor = Color.Salmon
74:     DrawFace()
75:   End Sub
76:
77:   Private Sub MenuItem1_Click(ByVal sender As System.Object, _
78:     ByVal e As System.EventArgs) Handles MenuItem1.Click
79:     Application.Exit()
80:   End Sub
81:
82: End Class
```

> **Note**
>
> No special technique was used to contrive the regions. Percival's code was used as a starting point reference for the general appearance, and trial and error was used to create the image shown in Figure 17.4. For advanced images, a more advanced approach needs to be devised.

When the main form loads, the BackColor is set to Color.Salmon and DrawFace is called. The application does more than draw the face; the form actually *is* the face. Thus if you click on a visible part of the face (see Figure 17.4), you are interacting with the form; otherwise, you are interacting with whatever appears behind the form.

The DrawFace method adds an outline region, eyes, nose, and lips to a Region object, using variations of unions and intersections. The basic process is to create a GraphicsPath, add some points to the path, and construct a Region, adding the GraphicsPath object to the Region. For example, AddNose on lines 37 to 51 creates a GraphicsPath object and adds a polygon describing the nose and adds the polygon to the nose region. The NoseRegion is then added to the Region for the entire Face with a Union operation, Face.Union(NoseRegion).

To demonstrate that the face is now the form, a ContextMenu is associated with the form's ContextMenu property. If you right-click over a filled-in area of the smiley face, the context menu is displayed. Click anywhere else and you are clicking on something unrelated to the form.

Icon Class

The Icon class is in the System.Drawing namespace. Icon makes it easier to load an icon from an external file, a stream, or use an existing icon as a template. Dim AnIcon

As New Icon("my.ico") will create an instance of a new icon and load it from a file named my.ico in the current directory.

Icon has properties that are self-explanatory: Width, Height, Size, and Handle. Additional useful methods include Save, which allows you to save the icon to a Stream, and ToBitmap, which converts the icon to a Bitmap object.

Imaging Namespace

The System.Drawing.Imaging namespace contains classes for managing pixel-based pages, such as JPEG and BMP files that might not be suitable for representation using vector-based graphics.

The System.Drawing namespace contains classes for managing primitives, like lines, curves, and figures, as we have seen. The System.Drawing.Imaging namespace contains classes for managing images that cannot be represented using vector-based primitives, such as photographs.

Listing 17.11 demonstrates how various bitmapped images can be loaded and displayed using the System.Drawing.Imaging.Bitmap class. The images demonstrated include ICO, WMF, JPG, BMP, GIF, and EMF files.

LISTING 17.11   Bitmapped images supported by classes in the System.Drawing. Imaging namespace

```
1:  Imports System.Drawing.Drawing2D
2:  Imports System.Drawing.Imaging
3:
4:  Public Class Form1
5:    Inherits System.Windows.Forms.Form
6:
7:  [Windows Form Designer generated code]
8:
9:    Private AnImage As Bitmap
10:
11:   Private Sub Form1_Paint(ByVal sender As Object, _
12:     ByVal e As System.Windows.Forms.PaintEventArgs) _
13:     Handles MyBase.Paint
14:
15:     If (AnImage Is Nothing) Then Exit Sub
16:     e.Graphics.DrawImage(AnImage, 10, 10)
17:
18:   End Sub
19:
20:
21:   Private Sub Form1_Load(ByVal sender As System.Object, _
22:     ByVal e As System.EventArgs) Handles MyBase.Load
```

LISTING 17.11   continued

```
23:
24:     ComboBox1.Text = vbNullString
25:     Dim Files As New IO.DirectoryInfo("..\Images\")
26:     Dim FileInfos() As IO.FileInfo = Files.GetFiles("*.*")
27:
28:     Dim Info As IO.FileInfo
29:
30:     For Each Info In FileInfos
31:        ComboBox1.Items.Add(Info.FullName)
32:     Next
33:  End Sub
34:
35:  Private Sub ComboBox1_SelectedIndexChanged( _
36:     ByVal sender As System.Object, _
37:     ByVal e As System.EventArgs) _
38:     Handles ComboBox1.SelectedIndexChanged
39:
40:     Try
41:        AnImage = New Bitmap(ComboBox1.Text)
42:        Invalidate()
43:     Catch Except As System.Exception
44:        MsgBox(Except.Message)
45:     End Try
46:  End Sub
47:
48:  Private Sub Button1_Click(ByVal sender As System.Object, _
49:     ByVal e As System.EventArgs) Handles Button1.Click
50:
51:     If (AnImage Is Nothing) Then Exit Sub
52:     AnImage.RotateFlip(RotateFlipType.Rotate90FlipX)
53:     Invalidate()
54:  End Sub
55: End Class
```

The example is straightforward. The Load event loads all of the files in the Images subdirectory into the combo box using System.IO capabilities (lines 21 to 33). Each time the user selects an image file from the combo box, the image is updated, the form is invalidated, and the new image is painted on the form.

The sample images demonstrate that the Bitmap class is capable of working with a wide variety of images; notice that there is no special code for managing any particular kind of compressed image.

Further, VB .NET provides support for managing custom images via the Encoder and Decoder classes. You can use the Encoder and Decoder objects to extend GDI+ to support custom image formats.

Custom Drawing in Windows Forms

When you need to perform custom painting in Windows Forms, implement an event handler for the Paint event for Windows Forms controls. The Paint event is passed an object indicating which event raised the event and a second argument, PaintEventArgs. PaintEventArgs has a Graphics object property that is the Graphics object of the control that raised the event.

Listing 17.1 demonstrates an example where a form's Paint event is used to create a shadow effect for a string. If you find yourself writing a paint event handler to create custom effects, consider subclassing a control to make those custom paint effects permanent. (Refer to Chapter 16, "Designing User Interfaces," for advanced topics.)

Additionally, Listing 17.11 demonstrates painting the selected Bitmap in the Paint event. When a bitmap is painted directly to the form without a control, we need to paint the image in the Paint event to ensure that the Bitmap is repainted when the form is invalidated. If the Bitmap were rendered in a control, the control would receive a WM_PAINT message when its owning form was invalidated and would repaint itself.

Graphics Printing

Just a few years ago, if you wanted to provide print preview and printer behavior, you had to write a lot of custom code for the preview device and the printer device. GDI+ insulates us from writing significantly different code even when we are targeting different devices for our graphics output.

In Visual Basic .NET, code targeted at a Windows Form is almost identical to code to produce the same result on a printer device. Because of the similarities between printing on a form versus a printer, we will not rehash the GDI+ features we have covered. Assume that scaling, translating, rotating, and other vector-based and imaging graphics capabilities just work, even when the target device is a printer. Listing 17.12 demonstrates code similar to earlier examples, but targeted at a printer. (The printer used to test the code was a Hewlett-Packard LaserJet 4.)

LISTING 17.12   Vector-based graphics sent directly to the printer

```
1:  Imports System.Drawing.Printing
2:
3:  Public Class Form1
4:     Inherits System.Windows.Forms.Form
```

LISTING 17.12 continued

```
 5:
 6:    [Windows Form Designer generated code]
 7:
 8:    Private Sub Button1_Click(ByVal sender As System.Object, _
 9:       ByVal e As System.EventArgs) Handles Button1.Click
10:       PrintDocument1.Print()
11:    End Sub
12:
13:    Private Sub PrintDocument1_PrintPage(ByVal sender As Object, _
14:       ByVal e As System.Drawing.Printing.PrintPageEventArgs) _
15:       Handles PrintDocument1.PrintPage
16:
17:       Dim AnImage As Image = Image.FromFile("..\images\jacket.jpg")
18:       Dim M As New Drawing2D.Matrix()
19:       M.Scale(2, 2)
20:       e.Graphics.Transform = M
21:       e.Graphics.DrawImage(AnImage, 0, 0)
22:
23:    End Sub
24: End Class
```

17

PROGRAMMING
WITH GDI+

To prepare the example, add the Imports System.Drawing.Printing namespace as demonstrated on line 1 of Listing 17.12. The easiest means of accessing the default printer is to add a PrinterDocument control to the form. (The PrinterDocument control will be added to the component tray.) The code example shows that the default name PrinterDocument1 was kept.

The sample program, PrinterDemo.sln, calls PrintDocument1.Print when Button1_ Click is raised. The real work begins in the PrintPage event handler. One of the properties of the PrintPageEventArgs parameter is a Graphics object. After you have the Graphics object representing the canvas of the printer, you can write your graphics code as if you were displaying the output to a Windows Form.

The code example—beginning on line 17—loads an image from a JPG file. Line 18 creates a Matrix object, and line 19 scales the matrix, M.Scale(2, 2). The Matrix transform is applied to the Graphics object representing the printer's canvas, and DrawImage is called. If you compare Listing 17.12 to Listing 17.8, you will see that the code for displaying graphics on the printer is consistent with code for displaying graphics on a form. In fact, if you literally copy and paste the code from the PrintPage event to the forms Paint event handler, the precise code will display the graphic on the form, too.

Frameworks help organize code into logically associated bits. An object-oriented framework both organizes code and makes it behave in a polymorphic way. In the example, the exact same code displays the graphic on a printed page or a form because the actual

`Graphics` object behaves in a polymorphic way depending on whether the object represents the form's DC or the printer's.

Use the code in earlier examples throughout this chapter to experiment with vector-based printing and bitmapped printing.

Summary

The Graphics Device Interface plus (GDI+) provides all of the power and functionality of the API and more. GDI+ enables you to create custom graphics, create shaped forms, and manage imaging tasks across a broad and extensible range of bitmapped image types.

In this chapter you learned how to create text effects, implement shaped Windows Forms, and work with vector-based graphics using classes in the `System.Drawing` namespace.

You will find vector graphics useful in small portions for spicing up your GUI forms, as well as for writing graphics to printer devices, creating pies and charts, and for imaging. Examples of tools that currently support graphics and imaging, and that might provide you with ideas as to how GDI+ might be employed, include Crystal Reports, Adobe Photoshop, and Microsoft Excel.

Building Web Services

PART
IV

Using and Implementing Web Services

The advent of Web Services has introduced a plethora of acronyms. I will try to avoid going into detail about new Web-related acronyms like UDDI, SOAP, XML, XSLT, XSI, and WSDL. However, Web Services represent one of the most exciting features of Visual Basic .NET programming and it will be important for you to have a basic grasp of the facets of Web Services, so you can decide which to focus on and which to ignore.

The introductory material will provide you with a brief overview of the acronym-laden technologies supporting Web Services and a brief review of what Web Services do for us. The bulk of the chapter will focus on the essential mechanics of building and using Web Services.

Web Services in Review

Personally, I believe that Web Services move us closer to a microkernel operating system. Basically, a microkernel operating system means that your computer has basic operating system services and everything else comes from a central, shared repository. With the widespread adoption of the World Wide Web, direct movement toward microkernels seemed to be placed on a back burner. Now that we can download widely distributed Web Services from the Web, we may be heading back toward a microkernel operating system in a circuitous fashion. A microkernel operating system can contain the BIOS, a bootstrap program, and networking drivers to get your computer connected to the Web, and then individual services can be run from a centralized cluster of computers somewhere on the Web. The benefits of such a system might be immediate power-on and power-off, pay-only-for-what-you-use software, and automatic upgrades—no more CD-ROMs and patches.

Right now, whether we are intently moving towards a microkernel or not remains to be seen. What we are definitely doing is trying to make digital services more widely and readily available.

Until recently the model of software development for Windows and much of the Internet was COM, HTML, and ASP. A programmer builds a COM component and one or more developers share that component as part of a framework for a single system. The deficits of this model are that everyone cannot easily share those COM objects, and COM is proprietary.

Web Services were invented to solve issues related to shareability and making a protocol that is more palatable by using open standards. This brought in all of the acronyms mentioned in the chapter's opening paragraph and more.

The Web Services technology is based primarily on a basic Hyper Text Transfer Protocol (HTTP) connection, SOAP, and Extensible Markup Language (XML). HTTP is the most generic Internet connection that uses dotted IP addresses to locate and share information between computers, usually on port 80 in each computer. SOAP used to be an acronym for Simple Object Access Protocol but is now just SOAP. SOAP is a protocol based on XML that is used to describe how requests and responses and user-defined data types are shared across a network. XML is an evolution of HTML (see the note).

> **Note**
>
> XML is a metalanguage—a language used to describe language—that supports creating or extending markup languages. XML was originally invented to support the exchange of documents on the Internet. XML was written in Standard Generalized Markup Language (SGML), a standardized language for describing the structure of a computer document.
>
> XML is an industry standard that is simple and customizable. Because it is a general standard rather than a proprietary protocol owned by Microsoft, it has a greater likelihood of being palatable to the computer industry as a whole when used in the context of a new technology.
>
> Because XML is text, it is easy and convenient to send over a network using any TCP/IP protocol, like HTTP. An industry standard that is easy to transmit over a network and already available is a good choice to base new technologies on, like Web Services.

18

What Web Services do for us is hide the fact that when you use an object that happens to be residing in an assembly across a network, Web Services are converting the request to a SOAP-based XML request. The XML text is sent to the server. The server packages the XML back into an object, and the server responds. The server responds in the same manner as the client. The server uses Web Services to package everything up into XML, sends it across the wire as XML text, and Web Services on the client side convert the XML back into an object.

The easiest way to grasp what is going on is that the client and server objects are serialized into a standard format, XML, while they are going back and forth across a network. When our code actually sees the information, it has been repackaged into an object. All of this marshaling of objects to XML and XML to objects happens behind the scenes. The concepts are similar to DCOM, but instead of using a proprietary intermediate form of the object, XML is used.

What does this mean for developers? On the surface, it means that we can ignore XML and SOAP and focus on the code. What it will ultimately mean has probably not been determined yet. All of this is reasonably new technology that is intended to replace a lot of existing technology. And, Microsoft is betting that by using an industry standard, XML, Web Services will be palatable to more than just Windows programmers. The other thing it means for developers is that you can write Web Services for Windows and Web applications, and have the possibility of building a whole new customer base, dependent on your universally available Web Services.

The rest of this chapter focuses on finding, using, and implementing Web Services in Visual Basic .NET. Where you may be interested in knowing more about specific protocols throughout the chapter, I have included references to the Requests for Comments (RFCs) that describe what a specific protocol is.

Finding Web Services with UDDI

The amount of information on the Web is growing tremendously every day. Although a lot of this information might be rubbish, an equally significant chunk consists of beneficial goods and services. Unfortunately, those useful goods and services may be hard to find among the trillions of bytes of data. This is where UDDI enters from stage right.

Universal Description, Discovery, and Information (UDDI) is a service spearheaded by Microsoft. In essence, UDDI refers to both a directory and a means of using information in that directory. There is the `http://uddi.microsoft.com` Web site where businesses are encouraged to register and share Web Services, and there is UDDI in the sense of the tools and capabilities that support finding and using Web Services. (There is even a UDDI SDK. New programmers are going to choke on acronyms.)

The idea is that you can go out to `uddi.microsoft.com` and shop for Web Services by industry or business. What else it might mean, probably even Microsoft doesn't know yet. This is leading-edge stuff, and it is impossible to predict how far this technology will take us.

> **Note**
>
> I am not picking on Microsoft about UDDI. I think it's too new, and there are just too few Web Services yet for everyone to know what to build, whom to build Web Services for, and how to make money in this arena.
>
> Checking the Microsoft UDDI site in October 2001, I found a link to "A Beckmann Inn and Carriage House Bed and Breakfast." Either the folks at

Beckmann Inn are building leading Web Services or they were just happy to find a place to list themselves on a Microsoft site. So far, no actual Web Services appear to be available from the bed and breakfast.

I certainly don't want to suggest that this technology is so new that it is unstable. The opposite is true, in fact. Because the Web Services technology is based on HTTP, SOAP, and XML—basically hypertext—it is nearly perfect in its simplicity. Web Services are ready for prime time already. What is probably true, however, is that everyone will be caught off guard for a short period of time, and it may not settle in that new, powerful possibilities exist.

Forget sharing and registering COM objects. Sure, this technology will exist for a while, but Web Services do not have to be downloaded. Web Services do not have to be installed, and there is no "DLL Hell" when it comes to Web Services. Web Services are reference-and-go solutions.

uddi.microsoft.com

In the previous section I related the story about the bed and breakfast. Ultimately, there will probably be thousands of Web Services at uddi.microsoft.com. Prior to the release of .NET, most of the registered companies seemed to be registry services, and actual Web Services were a little hard to find.

The model I envision is that great Web Services will spread by word of mouth and e-mail, and developers will be told to use a specific Web Service or will probably recommend them to their bosses. Those Web Services that solve practical business problems will probably be the second wave of services. The first wave will probably be entertainment, travel, and pornography. (I'm not making this pattern up; it's historically the way the Web has progressed.)

Slowly but surely, business will figure out how to use this technology to make money. Early adopters, like Scandinavian Airlines, already have Web Services, but it may be several more months before the average programmer is using Web Services as readily as we now use off-the-shelf components.

Keep checking on uddi.microsoft.com for Web Services, and I encourage you to register your company and Web Services on the UDDI site when appropriate. Even if you don't think anyone would be interested, sharing Web Services will be important in the early phases of this new technology. (At least the Beckmann Inn thinks so.)

Local Web Services

You will have to install the .NET Framework and register your server with a directory service to share Web Services. The installation of the .NET Framework on mission-critical Web servers may be the biggest stumbling block to quick adoption and use of Web Services. However, you do not have to wait for your company to install the .NET Framework to build and test Web Services.

> **Tip**
>
> If you plan on building and testing Web Services on your PC, install IIS 5.0 before installing the .NET Framework.

All that is required to build and test Web Services is a PC, Windows 2000 or Windows XP, the .NET Framework, Visual Studio .NET, and IIS 5.0 or greater. IIS 5.0 comes with Windows 2000 and Windows XP.

If you intend to build and test Web Services on your PC, you will be prompted to install IIS on your PC before the Windows Component Update part of the installation process occurs. (Even if you don't intend to build Web Services initially, you should install IIS. IIS is an excellent way to create team intranets, and you will ultimately want to work with Web Services.)

By default, when you build Web Services on your PC, a project will be added to your local IIS directory. By default this directory is `c:\inetpub\wwwroot` and the URL is `localhost` or IP `127.0.0.1`. The IP `127.0.0.1` is the loopback IP address that is a computer's TCP/IP reference to itself. The loopback IP is in addition to the IP associated with your network interface card (NIC).

Your NIC IP, `localhost`, `127.0.0.1`, and your machine name all refer to the same physical box. If you are running IIS on your PC, any of these values will allow you to browse to the pages served by your PC. (By the way, running IIS and adding content is all you need to do to create an intranet site on your PC.)

Four Facets of Web Services

There are four facets to Web Services. These are directory, discovery, description, and wire format. The following list briefly describes each of the facets.

- The UDDI directory exists to aid in registering and locating Web Services.
- Discovery is supported by the .vsdisco files that are created as part of an ASP.NET and Web Service application.

- The description of Web Services is supported by the Web Services Description Language (WSDL, pronounced *whiz-dul*).
- The wire format can be SOAP and XML, HTTP GET and HTTP POST, or a proprietary format like DCOM.

You can specifically request the service description by invoking the Web Service with the **?WSDL** query. For example, assuming a Web Service named service1.asmx on the localHost, the following query will return the service description:

```
http://localhost/service1.asmx?WSDL
```

Because Microsoft is using or trying to establish open standards, a lot of information is available regarding these various specifications. You can read more about the WSDL specification at `http://www.w3.org/TR/wsdl/` and more about the SOAP specification at `http://www.w3.org/TR/soap/`.

At this point we won't digress any further into these specifications. We will proceed with our discussion of using and implementing Web Services. If you need to know more about SOAP, UDDI, or WSDL (or any other protocols), you will have to do some independent exploration.

Calling Web Services

The benefit of open standards is that other language and tool vendors can and probably will support Web Services. Because Visual Basic .NET hides much of the marshaling between client and server in the background, you can use Web Services as if they were local objects.

Taking a hint from the "Four Facets of Web Services" from the preceding section, the first thing you will need to do to use a Web Service is to look in a directory for the Web Service. (There are several Web Service examples on this book's Web site, and we will cover how you can use and experiment with those later in this chapter.)

Adding a Web Reference

To use a Web Service, you need to add a reference to the service. The Reference folder in the Solution Explorer has a context menu that has two menu items (see Figure 18.1). The first menu item supports adding references to .NET assemblies, COM objects, and Visual Studio .NET projects. The second menu is used to add Web references, that is, references to Web Services.

FIGURE 18.1

Adding Web references to a project.

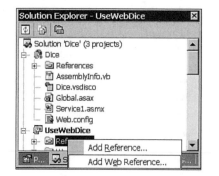

When you choose Add Web Reference, the Add Web Reference dialog box (see Figure 18.2) is displayed. This dialog box provides links to the Microsoft UDDI Directory, a Test Microsoft UDDI Directory, and Web References on Local Server. We will use the latter for our initial demonstration.

FIGURE 18.2

The Add Web References dialog box.

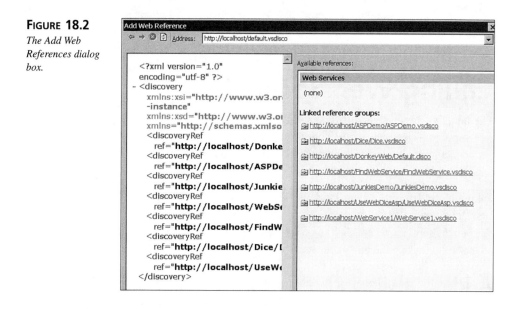

To add a Web reference to a project, follow these steps:

1. Create a Windows application.
2. Click View, Solution Explorer to open the Solution Explorer.
3. Right-click over the References folder in the Solution Explorer and choose Add Web Reference.

4. In the Add Web Reference dialog box, choose Web References on Local Server.

5. If there are any .vsdisco files on your local IIS server, a list of available Web Services will be displayed in the available references list. For our purposes we will assume that WebService1.vsdisco exists.

6. Choose the WebService1.vsdisco file and click the Add Reference button. This will add a Web References folder to the Solution Explorer (see Figure 18.3).

FIGURE 18.3

The Solution Explorer after a Web reference has been added.

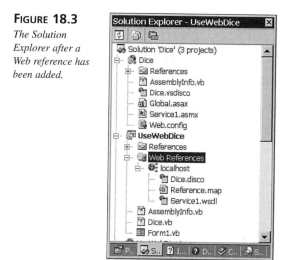

When a Web Service is compiled, a .DLL is created. After you have added the Web Reference, you are ready to use any Web Services defined. Using the Web Service DLL is like using any other DLL after the reference has been added. You can declare instances of classes defined in the Web Service DLL just as you would any classes defined in a vanilla class library.

Using Windows Forms Applications

Web Services can be used for Windows or Web development. Although it is assumed that a Web application will have a connection to the Internet, the implication is that a Windows application calling a Web Service will be connected too.

WebService1.dll added in the preceding section contains a single WebService instance named Service1. There is only one public WebMethod in the class, named HelloWorld.

After the service has been added, we can declare an instance of the WebService class, Service1, and invoke any methods that have the WebMethodAttribute. Using our example WebService and WebMethod, Listing 18.1 demonstrates creating the WebService and invoking the WebMethod.

LISTING 18.1 Instantiating a WebService and invoking a WebMethod from a Windows application

```
1:  Public Class Form1
2:    Inherits System.Windows.Forms.Form
3:
4:  [ Windows Form Designer generated code ]
5:
6:    Private Sub Button1_Click(ByVal sender As System.Object, _
7:      ByVal e As System.EventArgs) Handles Button1.Click
8:
9:      Dim Service As New localhost.Service1()
10:     MsgBox(Service.HelloWorld())
11:
12:   End Sub
13: End Class
```

As you can determine from line 2 of the listing, the code resides in a Windows Form. Lines 6 through 12 implement a Button.Click event handler. Line 9 instantiates the WebService, and line 10 invokes the WebMethod HelloWorld.

We will look at implementing WebService and WebMethod later in this chapter.

Using Web Forms Applications

Roughly the equivalent solution can be contrived using the same Web Service in an ASP.NET (or Web) application. To use a Web Service in an ASP.NET application, create a new ASP.NET application in Visual Studio .NET. Add a Web reference to the ASP.NET application pointing to the same Web Service, WebService1.

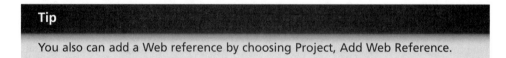

Tip

You also can add a Web reference by choosing Project, Add Web Reference.

The demo application, FindWebService.vbproj, contains a single WebForm with a Button painted from the Web Forms page of the toolbox. (Refer to Chapter 19, "ASP.NET Web Programming," for more on ASP.NET and Web Forms.) The Button control was double-clicked to add a Click event handler. Just as in Listing 18.1, an instance of the Web Service was created and used in the Click event handler. Listing 18.2 demonstrates using the Web Service from an ASP.NET page, and Figure 18.4 shows the page in a browser.

FIGURE 18.4

ASP.NET application demonstrating a simple Web Service.

LISTING 18.2   Instantiating and calling a Web Service from an ASP.NET application

```
1:  Public Class WebForm1
2:    Inherits System.Web.UI.Page
3:    Protected WithEvents Button1 As System.Web.UI.WebControls.Button
4:
5:  [ Web Form Designer Generated Code ]
6:
7:    Private Sub Button1_Click(ByVal sender As System.Object, _
8:      ByVal e As System.EventArgs) Handles Button1.Click
9:
10:     Dim Service As New localhost.Service1()
11:     Response.Write("<i>" & Service.HelloWorld() & "</i>")
12:
13:   End Sub
14: End Class
```

Notice the striking similarities between the Visual Basic .NET in the Windows application in Listing 18.1 and the Visual Basic .NET in the ASP.NET application in Listing 18.2. We can't show a modal dialog using MsgBox in Internet Explorer, so the output from WebForm1 is rendered using HTML.

The Response object is implemented using the Request and Response pattern (that exists in at least two development tools, Delphi and Visual Basic .NET). For now, just think of the Response object as roughly the equivalent of the Console object for console applications. The Response object is a public property of WebForm and is used to send information back to the Web server; we will cover Response in greater detail in Chapter 19.

> **Tip**
>
> The WebForm class is subclassed from System.Web.UI.Page. Look in the Page class for more information on Web Forms.

18

USING AND
IMPLEMENTING
WEB SERVICES

The HTML is easy. The `<i>` and `</i>` tags italicize the text between the tags. Combined, the `Response.Write` statement yields the text portion of the Web page shown in the browser in Figure 18.4.

Implementing Web Services

Web Services are Web application DLLs that contain classes generalized from the `System.Web.Services.WebService` class. Web methods are methods in a `WebService` that are tagged with the `WebMethodAttribute`. The easiest way to create a `WebService` is to select an ASP.NET Web Service template from the New Project dialog box. The ASP.NET Web Service template will prepare the project for you, including creating the global.asax file, adding an .asmx file that contains the ASP code that will be your Web Service, creating the web.config file and the .vsdisco file.

We will cover the role of each of these files and wrap up this section with the .asmx file and implementing the Web Service.

global.asax File

The global.asax file is the entry point for your `HttpApplication`, the Web Service application. global.asax contains a class named `Global` that provides an empty module containing empty application-level event handlers that you can write code to respond to.

The ASP.NET Web Service template creates a global.asax module automatically. However, if you were to start your Web Service with the empty Web application template, no global.asax file would be generated. If no global.asax file exists, .NET assumes that you are not handling application-level events. Table 18.1 contains the list of application-level events.

TABLE 18.1   Application Events Defined in the global.asax Module

Event Name	Description
Application_Start	Raised when the application starts
Session_Start	Raised when a session starts
Application_BeginRequest	Raised when a request begins
Application_AuthenticationRequest	Raised when authentication is attempted
Application_Error	Raised when an application error occurs
Session_End	Raised when a session ends
Application_End	Raised when the application ends

Write handling code for these methods if you determine that some custom response is needed. The global.asax file is a module, containing a class derived from System.Web.HttApplication. There are several methods, properties, and additional events that you can use to manage the way that the application containing your Web Service behaves.

web.config File

The web.config file resides in the application root directory containing your Web Service. Listing 18.3 contains a sample web.config file generated for the Web Service example, WebService1.dll, used until now.

LISTING 18.3   A sample web.config file

```
1:  <?xml version="1.0" encoding="utf-8" ?>
2:  <configuration>
3:
4:    <system.web>
5:
6:      <compilation defaultLanguage="vb" debug="true" />
7:
8:      <customErrors mode="RemoteOnly" />
9:
10:     <authentication mode="Windows" />
11:
12:     <authorization>
13:        <allow users="*" />
14:     </authorization>
15:
16:     <trace enabled="false" requestLimit="10"
➡pageOutput="false" traceMode="SortByTime" localOnly="true" />
17:
18:     <sessionState
19:        mode="InProc"
20:        stateConnectionString="tcpip=127.0.0.1:42424"
21:        sqlConnectionString="data source=127.0.0.1;user id=sa;password="
22:        cookieless="false"
23:        timeout="20"
24:     />
25:
26:     <globalization requestEncoding="utf-8" responseEncoding="utf-8" />
27:
28:    </system.web>
29:
30: </configuration>
```

The web.config file contains well-formed, nested XML tags. XML tags are case sensitive. Tag names and attributes are camel-cased (the first character is lowercase, and the first character of concatenated words is uppercase). For example, `requestLimit` is an example of an attribute. Attribute values are Pascal-cased (the first character of each word is uppercased). For example, `RemoteOnly` is an example of an attribute value.

Line 1 defines the XML version and UTF-8 encoding means that the file contains Unicode characters.

Lines 2 and 30 are the `<configuration>` and `</configuration>` tags that define the beginning and end of the configuration information.

Lines 4 and 28—`<system.web>` and `</system.web>`—are tags that indicate that these configuration options are for ASP.NET Web applications.

The compilation tag on line 6 defines the language and debugging mode. If debugging mode is True, extra symbolic debugging information is added to the Web Service and a .pdb file is created to facilitate debugging. You should only leave the `debug="true"` value until you are ready to deploy your service. The .asmx file is compiled by the JITter and the debug attribute is used to include symbolic debug information or not.

Set the `customErrors` mode to "On" or "RemoteOnly" to enable custom error messages (see line 8). "Off" will disable custom error messages. Add `<error>` tags to indicate each error that you want to handle.

Line 10 describes the authentication mode. You can choose between `Windows`, `Forms`, `Passport`, and `None`. Use `Windows` authentication when you are using any form of IIS authentication. `Forms` authentication uses ASP.NET forms-based authentication. Passport authentication is a forms-based authentication model that uses Triple DES encryption to encrypt and decrypt query strings. Passport is a centralized, secure authentication service provided by Microsoft; you will have to register to use this service. Use `None` to support anonymous users.

The block on lines 12 through 14 allows you to specify allowed or denied users or roles. The wildcard "*" means applies to everyone, and "?" means applies to anonymous users. Line 13 allows all users to use the Web Service associated with the web.config file in Listing 18.3.

Line 16 specifies application tracing. If `trace="true"`, application tracing occurs. Each time the Web Service is requested, an entry is written to the trace.axd file. You can view the trace file information by browsing to the trace.axd file for a Web Service. Assuming that we are still using WebService.dll on a PC, the trace file (see Figure 18.5) can be viewed by browsing to the following URL:

```
http://localhost/WebService1/trace.axd
```

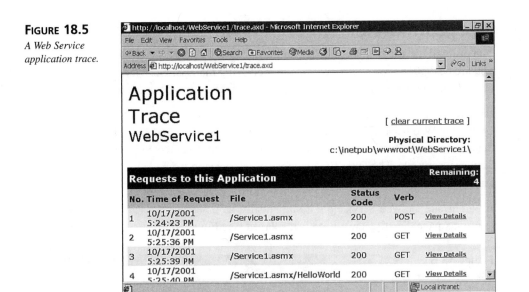

FIGURE **18.5**

*A Web Service
application trace.*

The sessionState tag on lines 18 to 24 indicates whether cookies will be used to maintain state and stores information about the TCP/IP connection and SQL connection data. The sessionState mode attribute can be InProc, Off, SQLServer, or StateServer. InProc, or In-Process, is the default. SQLServer is an example of an out-of-process state information store. The StateServer is a service that can be started and stopped by typing **net start aspnet_state** and **net stop aspnet_state**, respectively. The ASP.NET State Server is an out-of-process state manager too.

The globalization tag on line 26 contains information about the request and response encoding. requestEncoding and responseEncoding of utf-8 indicates that the Web Service will use Unicode encoding.

The Disco File

The .vsdisco file contains discovery information about the Web Service. You can invoke the Web Service with the query string Disco to display a copy of the XML discovery information, for example:

```
http://localhost/WebService1/Service1.asmx?Disco
```

Disco information is used to find Web Services and support a directory service maintaining references to Web Services.

The .asmx File

The .asmx file contains the ASP.NET code generated by your Web Service class. When you are designing a Web Service, you are modifying the Designer view of the .asmx.vb file. When you write code, you are adding the code directly to the .asmx.vb file.

For example, a `WebService` class named `Service1` would consist of a Service1.resx file containing Web resource information in XSD (XML Schema and Data) format, a Service1.asmx.vb file containing your Visual Basic .NET source code, and a Service1.asmx file. The latter file maintains a reference to the code behind the page that is JITted when the page is requested.

If you invoke the Web Service programmatically, an object is returned. If you navigate to the .asmx page directly, a test page is displayed (see Figure 18.6).

FIGURE 18.6

A Web Service test page that allows you to invoke Web methods.

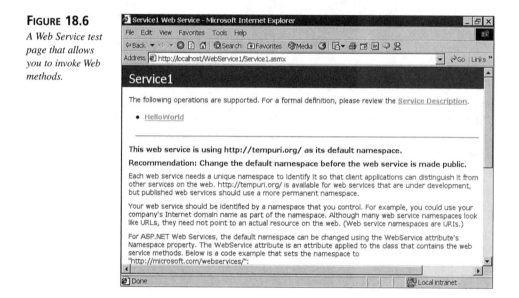

Near the top of the page shown is a hyperlink to the `WebMethod` defined by this service. Click the hyperlink and a test page for that service is displayed (see Figure 18.7). Click the Invoke button (see Figure 18.7) and the `WebMethod` is invoked. When a `WebMethod` is invoked directly through this test page, appropriate XML is returned. In the example shown in Figure 18.8, the value returned by the `HelloWorld` Web method is returned.

FIGURE **18.7**

Test page displayed when you navigate directly to a Web Service.

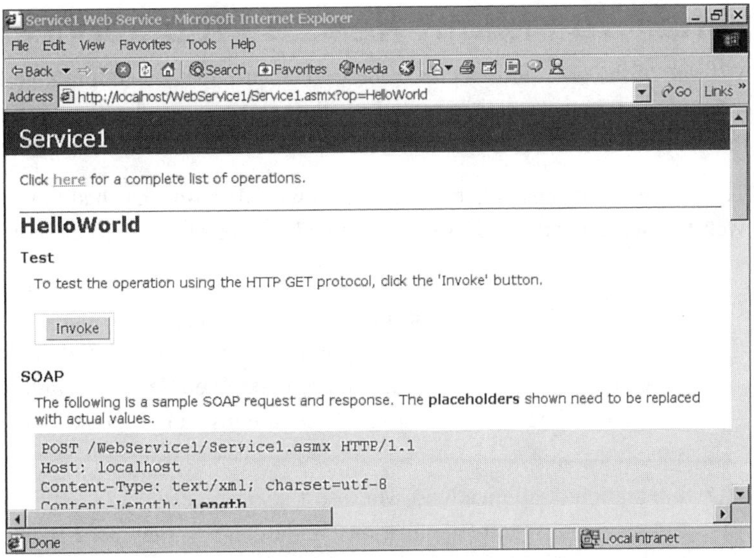

FIGURE **18.8**

XML response returned from the HelloWorld *Web method.*

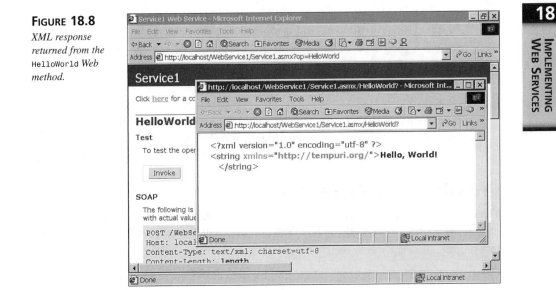

Clearly, if these rudimentary test pages were the only way to test Web Services, you would quickly find testing to be tedious. Fortunately, Web Services are implemented in Visual Studio .NET, and we can use the IDE's integrated debugger to test and debug Web Services just as we would any other code. Doing so is discussed later in the chapter.

When You Might Need a Web Service

With all of the possibilities that Web Services provide, it is impossible to predetermine most of the things developers will do with Web Services. There are some basic scenarios that suggest a need for a Web Service.

The scenarios suggested here are not my own. Microsoft has had longer to think about Web Services, and the scenarios presented here are gleaned from the help file text.

- Core business solutions. Build a Web Service to represent a core business solution. If you're building software for an airline, perhaps you'll build an itinerary manager. If you are a software toolsmith, you might specialize in building tools for other developers. Maybe Amazon.com will make Web Services available so that participating Web sites can offer a search engine instead of a link to the Amazon.com site.

- Integration of applications. Microsoft also suggests that Web Services can be used to integrate disparate applications. Although you may need to build Web Services for each application, and modify those applications to interact with the Web Services, this solution sounds better than rewriting several applications to create an Enterprise solution. Suppose you work for an insurance company, and your company has a good underwriting system. Now suppose that you can buy an off-the-shelf claims system. Rather than rewriting one or the other application to integrate them, you might choose to expose some of their functionality through Web Services.

- Distribution applications. To some extent, consider using Web Services where you would have used DCOM and HTTP in the past. Web Services are not based on proprietary protocols, and make writing distributed applications easier.

Creating a Web Service

The most direct way to build a Web Service is to select the ASP.NET Web Service template from the New Project dialog box. The template will add all of the pieces you need to a project, allowing you to focus on the code.

Central to the Web Service is the .asmx file. By default the .asmx file will be named Service1.asmx for the first file, incrementing the numeric suffix for each successive file.

You interact with an .asmx file much as you would with a UserControl. There is a designer for adding controls, and you can press F7 to switch to the code editor and Shift+F7 to switch back to Designer view.

Inheriting from `WebService`

Web Services inherit from the `System.Web.Services.WebService` class. All the basic information necessary to compile and build a Web Service is provided by inheriting from `WebService`. To add capabilities you will need to define methods. To expose those capabilities to users, you will need to define methods that use `WebMethodAttribute`.

We will return to Web methods in a moment.

Applying the `WebService` Attribute

Optionally, you can apply the `WebServiceAttribute` to a Web Service class. This enables you to provide additional information about your Web Service by initializing the properties of the `WebServiceAttribute` class.

The `WebServiceAttribute` class has no positional arguments but introduces three new named arguments: `Description`, `Name`, and `Namespace`. `Description` allows you to provide a text description for your `WebService`. `Description` supports adding a helpful description when the description documents for a Web Service are generated (see Figure 18.6). `Name` gets or sets the name of the XML Web Service, and `Namespace` allows you to specify a namespace in the form of a URL.

18

USING AND
IMPLEMENTING
WEB SERVICES

> **Tip**
>
> Keep in mind that when attributes are employed, the `Attribute` suffix is dropped by convention.

The following example demonstrates using the `WebServiceAttribute` and the named arguments `Namespace` and `Description`.

```
<WebService(Description:="Represents a user-defined number of Dice,
➥with random roll values.", _
Namespace:="http://www.softconcepts.com/")> _
```

When the description page is shown, the value of the `Description` field will be displayed, and the URL `Namespace` helps uniquely identify the Web Service.

Implementing Web Methods

When you have created the ASP.NET Web Service project, you automatically get the module containing the `WebService` class. Adding `WebServiceAttribute` is optional.

At this juncture, implementing `WebService` is a matter of implementing methods and choosing those that will make up the interface of your service by applying the

WebMethodAttribute. Web methods must actually be procedures, but you can implement all of the other elements of a class. Users simply won't be able to directly invoke anything that is not a procedure and doesn't have WebMethodAttribute applied.

There are five overloaded versions of the WebMethodAttribute constructor. These represent the positional arguments. And, there are six additional properties that can be initialized using the positional argument syntax. (Refer to Chapter 12, "Defining Attributes," for more information on attributes, including information about using named and positional arguments.) Table 18.2 describes each of the positional arguments that can be initialized when applying WebMethodAttribute.

TABLE 18.1 WebMethodAttribute Positional Arguments

Property Name	*Description*
BufferResponse	Indicating whether the response to a request is buffered. Default is False.
CacheDuration	An integer indicating the number of seconds a response should be buffered. Default is 0, or no cache support.
Description	A string describing the WebMethod. The default is an empty string.
EnableSession	A Boolean indicating whether session state is enabled for a WebMethod. The default is False.
MessageName	The name used for the method when passed to and from the Web Service. (The most common use is to provide an alias for polymorphic methods.)
TransactionOption	An enumeration indicating the transaction support. The default is Disabled.

The basic application of WebMethodAttribute has the following form:

```
<WebMethod()> _
Public Sub SomeProcedure()...
```

If you use the basic form, the default values for the properties of the WebMethodAttribute attribute will be used. Listing 18.4 demonstrates a WebService and the WebMethod attribute in a Web Service that returns a random roll of dice.

LISTING 18.4 A WebService that returns randomly generated six-sided dice values

```
1:  Imports System.Web.Services
2:
3:  <WebService( _
```

LISTING 18.4 continued

```
4:    Description:="Represents a random six-sided Dice roller.", _
5:    Name:="Dice", Namespace:="http://www.softconcepts.com/")> _
6: Public Class Service1
7:    Inherits System.Web.Services.WebService
8:
9: [ Web Services Designer Generated Code ]
10:
11:    <WebMethod( _
12:    Description:="Returns random values representing six-sided dice.")> _
13:    Public Function Roll(ByVal HowMany As Integer) As Integer()
14:      Dim DiceValues(HowMany) As Integer
15:      Dim R As New Random()
16:
17:      Dim I As Integer
18:      For I = 0 To DiceValues.Length - 1
19:        DiceValues(I) = R.Next(1, 7)
20:      Next
21:
22:      Return DiceValues
23:    End Function
24:
25: End Class
```

> **Note**
>
> The Roll Web Method rolls HowMany + 1 dice because arrays are zero-based. It is
> a simple matter to adjust the number of dice to account for the extra, zero-
> indexed Die in this implementation.

Milton Bradley executives aren't going to lose any sleep, but it does demonstrate that game developers working in collaboration could create common objects shared by many games. Every online game could use the random Dice-roll generator.

Lines 3, 4, and 5 demonstrate the WebServiceAttribute and named values for the Description, Name, and Namespace. Line 7 demonstrates inheritance from the WebService class. Lines 11 and 12 demonstrate applying the WebMethodAttribute to a public method to designate it as a Web Method.

The number of dice is passed to the Roll Web Method, which in turn uses the Random class to generate numbers between 1 and 6 for each die. (The upper bound value of the Random.Next method is not inclusive.) Listing 18.5 shows the code from a Windows application that uses the WebService and the Dice.vb module from Chapter 14, "Multithreaded Applications."

LISTING 18.5 A Windows application that uses the random Dice Web Service

```
1:  Imports UseWebDice
2:
3:  Public Class Form1
4:    Inherits System.Windows.Forms.Form
5:
6:  [ Windows Form Designer generated code ]
7:
8:    Private FDice() As Dice = _
9:       {New Dice(New Rectangle(10, 10, 50, 50), Color.Red), _
10:      New Dice(New Rectangle(70, 10, 50, 50), Color.Blue)}
11:
12:   Private Sub Button1_Click(ByVal sender As System.Object, _
13:      ByVal e As System.EventArgs) Handles Button1.Click
14:
15:
16:      Dim Dice As New localhost.Dice()
17:      Dim FValues() As Integer = Dice.Roll(2)
18:
19:      Dim I As Integer
20:      For I = 0 To FDice.Length - 1
21:        If (I < FValues.Length) Then
22:          FDice(I).Value = FValues(I)
23:          FDice(I).Draw(CreateGraphics)
24:        End If
25:      Next
26:
27:   End Sub
28:
29:   Private Sub Form1_Paint(ByVal sender As Object, _
30:      ByVal e As System.Windows.Forms.PaintEventArgs) _
31:    Handles MyBase.Paint
32:
33:      Dim I As Integer
34:      For I = 0 To FDice.Length - 1
35:        FDice(I).Draw(CreateGraphics)
36:      Next I
37:
38:   End Sub
39:
40:   Private Sub Timer1_Tick(ByVal sender As System.Object, _
41:      ByVal e As System.EventArgs) Handles Timer1.Tick
42:      Button1_Click(sender, e)
43:   End Sub
44: End Class
```

Each time a button is clicked on the form, the Dice object from the Web Service is created and the random roll of the Dice is returned. The returned values are used to specify the value of each `Die` and the `Die` is drawn. (The `Timer` was added—on lines 40 to 44 to roll the `Dice` on auto-pilot.)

Choosing Web Access Methods

Web access methods indicate how Web Services are made available across a network. There are two options to choose from: File-share access and FrontPage Server Extensions Access. The Web Settings page of the Property Pages (see Figure 18.9) is used to indicate Web access.

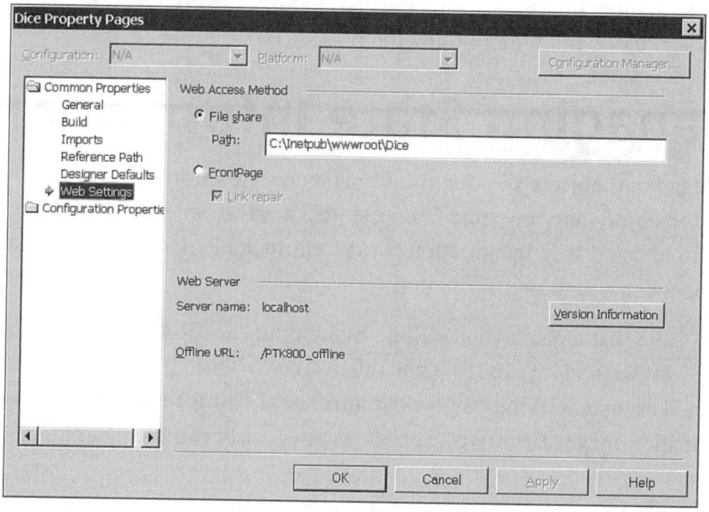

FIGURE 18.9

Specifying the Web Access Method is accomplished in the Property Pages as shown.

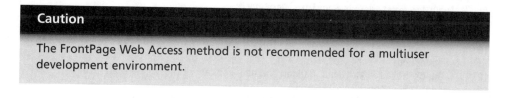

The File-share access method uses Windows-based file management commands, and the FrontPage Server Extensions access uses FrontPage Server Extensions and the HTTP protocol. There are two considerations you need to resolve before choosing a Web access method: the location of the Web Service and whether or not you are using Source Control.

Caution

The FrontPage Web Access method is not recommended for a multiuser development environment.

File-share access is appropriate for Web Services that will reside on a local intranet— your own desktop, for example—and for Web Servers shared over the Internet, use FrontPage Server Extensions. However, there are limiting factors related to FrontPage source control. When you're using FrontPage, only one copy of the project exists and all developers are working on a single copy of the project. Further, if you use FrontPage Server Extensions, those projects can only be opened under FrontPage control. The file-share Web access method is recommended for a multiuser development environment.

Although it is recommended that you select the access method before creating a project, you can switch the Web access method after the project is created. To change the Web Access Method after a project is created, modify the Web Access method in the Property Pages and close and then re-open the project.

Managing State Information

There are two objects you can use to manage state information. The `Application` and `Session` objects are inherited from the `WebService` class. The `Application` object is used to manage state information for the entire application. The `Session` object is used to manage per-session information.

To indicate that a `WebMethod` will be maintaining session information, we need to initialize the `WebMethodAttribute.EnableSession` to True. This is accomplished by providing a named argument to the `WebMethod` attribute. Listing 18.6 demonstrates maintaining roll information for the `Dice` Web Service created earlier in the chapter.

LISTING 18.6   Extends the code from Listing 18.4 to include the sum, roll-count, and average roll of the dice, demonstrating session state information

```
 1:  Imports System.Web.Services
 2:
 3:  <WebService( _
 4:    Description:="Represents random Dice roll values.", _
 5:    Name:="Dice", Namespace:="http://www.softconcepts.com/")> _
 6:  Public Class Service1
 7:    Inherits System.Web.Services.WebService
 8:
 9:  [ Web Services Designer Generated Code ]
10:
11:    <WebMethod( _
12:      Description:="Returns random values representing six-sided dice.", _
13:      EnableSession:=True)> _
14:    Public Function Roll(ByVal HowMany As Integer) As Integer()
15:      Dim DiceValues(HowMany) As Integer
16:      Dim R As New Random()
```

Listing 18.6 continued

```
17:
18:     Dim I As Integer
19:     For I = 0 To DiceValues.Length - 1
20:       DiceValues(I) = R.Next(1, 7)
21:     Next
22:
23:     UpdateAverage(DiceValues)
24:
25:     Return DiceValues
26:   End Function
27:
28:   <WebMethod(EnableSession:=True)> _
29:   Public Function GetCount() As Integer
30:     Return Count
31:   End Function
32:
33:   <WebMethod(EnableSession:=True)> _
34:   Public Function GetSum() As Integer
35:     Return Sum
36:   End Function
37:
38:   Private Property Count() As Integer
39:     Get
40:       Return CInt(Session("Count"))
41:     End Get
42:
43:     Set(ByVal Value As Integer)
44:       Session("Count") = Value
45:     End Set
46:
47:   End Property
48:
49:   Private Property Sum() As Integer
50:     Get
51:       Return CInt(Session("Sum"))
52:     End Get
53:     Set(ByVal Value As Integer)
54:       Session("Sum") = Value
55:     End Set
56:   End Property
57:
58:   <WebMethod(EnableSession:=True)> _
59:   Private Sub UpdateAverage(ByVal Values() As Integer)
60:     Count += 1
61:
62:     Dim I As Integer
63:     For I = 0 To Values.Length - 1
64:       Sum += Values(I)
65:     Next
```

LISTING 18.6 continued

```
66:
67:    End Sub
68:
69:    <WebMethod(EnableSession:=True)> _
70:    Public Function AverageRoll() As Integer
71:
72:       Try
73:          Return Sum \ Count
74:       Catch
75:          Return 0
76:       End Try
77:    End Function
78:
79: End Class
```

The Roll, GetCount, GetSum, and AverageRoll methods all demonstrate WebMethod procedures that use the EnableSession named argument. The key to storing session information is storing the session state information in the Session object. Session is an instance of the HttpSessionState class, and maintains a collection of session information that you explicitly add to the Session object.

The properties Count and Sum—on lines 38 through 56—simplify using the Session object by wrapping the storing and retrieving of the session state information. The Session object stores information as plain objects, so we have to convert the value to a specific value when retrieving information back from the Session object, as demonstrated on lines 40 and 51.

The initial values for the two Session variables are provided in the global.asax module, in the Session_Start event. The following fragment demonstrates the implementation of that method.

```
Sub Session_Start(ByVal sender As Object, ByVal e As EventArgs)
   Session("Sum") = 0
   Session("Count") = 0
End Sub
```

We still have to use the exception handler beginning on line 72 and ending on line 76 to catch the divide-by-zero exception that will occur if the roll count is zero.

Handling and Throwing Exceptions in Web Services

Exception handling between Web Services and clients uses the same mechanics as exception handling in Windows Forms, for example.

You can use a `Try...Catch...End Try` block to catch any exception within the Web Service. However, if you propagate, or allow an exception to be propagated, across a Web Service boundary, the exception is serialized as an XML `<Fault>`. When it gets to your client application, it arrives as a `SoapException` or `SoapHeaderException`.

For example, if we did not catch a `DivideByZeroException` on line 73 of Listing 18.6, a `DivideByZeroException` would occur in the Web Service, but ASP.NET would propagate this as a `SoapException` in the client application. To catch an exception raised by an ASP.NET Web Service, you can write a generic exception handler or catch one of the two SOAP exceptions.

```
Try
  ' Some Web Service Code
Catch
  ' Do something to recover
End Try
```

or

```
Try
  ' Some Web Service Code
Catch x As SoapException
  ' Do Something to recover
End Try
```

Either version would allow you to catch a Web Service exception in the client application. However, if you wrote a specific exception handler to catch the `DivideByZeroException` thrown by the scenario described at the beginning of this section, the `Catch` block would not catch the exception because your `Catch` block would contain the wrong type.

The `SoapException.Message` property will contain the text of the original exception. Figure 18.10 shows the `Message` value of a `DivideByZeroException` originating in the `Dice` Web Service as received by an ASP.NET Web application.

18

USING AND IMPLEMENTING WEB SERVICES

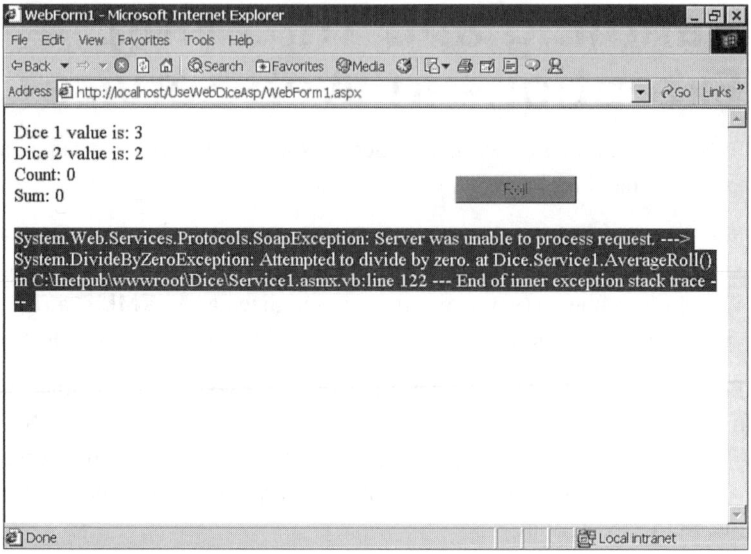

FIGURE 18.10

*An exception
thrown in a Web
Service is serial-
ized and sent to
a client as a*
`SoapException,`
as shown.

Debugging Web Services

You can build and run your Web Service in one of three ways:

- Set the Web Service as the Startup Project in the Solution Explorer and press F5.
- Choose Debug, Start Without Debugging (or use the Ctrl+F5 shortcut).
- Build your Web Service and browse to it.

Integrated Debugging

Web Services can be debugged in the Visual Studio .NET IDE. To debug in the IDE, make a Web Service the startup project. This can be accomplished from the Project menu of the Solution Explorer. Press F5 to run the application.

When you run the application in the debugger, the Service Description page is shown. This page will provide a list of Web methods that you can invoke. To debug a specific method, manage breakpoints in the IDE and invoke the methods from the Service Description page.

When the IDE encounters a breakpoint, Visual Studio .NET will focus the Code Designer and you can debug your code as you would any other application. When you are performing integrated debugging, IIS plays the role of host application and the Service Description plays the role of client.

When you have debugged the basic behaviors of your Web Service using the Service Description, you can incorporate the Web Service as part of a whole solution. If the Web Service is referenced by an ASP.NET Web application, you can use the integrated debugger to step between your ASP.NET Web application and your Web Service. To do so, specify an ASP.NET application as the startup project. (The ASP.NET Web application must have a reference to the Web Service.) Press F5 to begin debugging or F8 to begin stepping. The Visual Studio .NET IDE will step into the Web Service or stop on breakpoints in the Web Service.

Start Without Debugging

If you choose Debug, Start Without Debugging, you will be able to invoke methods using the Service Description page, but the IDE will not break into the Code Designer view. This is equivalent to a form of white-box testing where the Service Description plays the role of thin client.

Build and Browse

The final way to test your application is to build the application, open the browser, and browse to the .asmx page representing the Service Description—a thin-client application—that you can use to invoke Web methods.

Compiling and Deploying Web Projects

When you have finished testing and debugging your Web Service you are ready to compile and deploy it. Open the Configuration Manager for the Web Service and change the configuration from Debug to Release. Rebuild the Web Service.

> **Caution**
>
> If you leave the Configuration Manager configured to Debug when you build, a .pdb debug file is created and symbolic information remains in your Web Service. This extra overhead may make your Web Service a bit sluggish.

Visual Studio .NET saves all files before compiling. During compilation the .asmx, .vb, and global.asax files are compiled into the Web Service DLL. For example, our dice example is compiled into Dice.dll.

To deploy the application, you can add a Web Setup Project from the Add New Project dialog box, or you can simply copy the necessary files to the target Web server. (If the development server is the target Web server, you are finished.)

The ability to copy a Web Service is a matter of copying the folder containing the project files to your Web server's root directory, or if you want to get just the minimum files then use the Project, Copy Project menu. To deploy a Web Service using the Copy Project menu item, follow these steps (use Figure 18.11 as a guide):

1. Choose View, Solution Explorer to open the Solution Explorer view.

2. Click on the Web Service project.

3. Choose the Project, Copy Project menu.

4. In the Copy Project dialog box, specify the target Web server, the Web access method, and the Copy mode. (Select the option labeled Only Files Needed to Run This Application unless you have a specific reason for choosing one of the other options.)

5. Click OK.

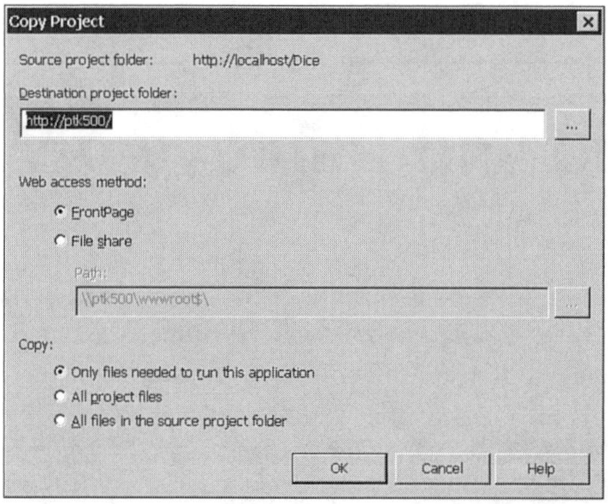

FIGURE 18.11

Use the Copy Project dialog box to deploy a Web Service.

When you have completed step 5, the Web Service will be copied to the Bin folder in the Web directory and the web.config, .asmx, and global.asax files will be copied to your root folder. If you want the Web Service copied to a subfolder, specify the subfolder in the Copy Project dialog box.

That is all there is to it. Copy deployment is significantly easier than registering COM DLLs and coping with "DLL Hell." Your team or your customers are ready to begin using your Web Service.

Summary

Visual Studio .NET is one of the most tangible products since the original Visual Basic. Web Services constitute the secret weapon in the .NET initiative. What developers ultimately will do with them is the great unknown. One thing for sure is that Web Services are flexible, powerful, and will change the landscape of Web applications and tools development significantly.

Chapter 18 demonstrated how to use the technologies surrounding Web Services to find, implement, and deploy Web Services. There are many tangential subjects that we did not have space to explore. Hopefully, the main message you take away from this chapter is that Web Services are accessible. You do not have to be a SOAP, WSDL, XSD, XML, or HTTP expert to build and use Web Services.

Granted, for very advanced problems you probably will need further exploration and you are encouraged to explore the help documentation and acquire additional books on specialized, tangential topics.

ASP.NET Web Programming

From the perspective of someone who loves object-oriented code, I am not a big fan of ASP. Relative to pure Visual Basic, ASP produces spaghetti code because it is a heterogeneous mixture of HTML and script. Fortunately, this is one of the challenges undertaken by the ASP.NET developers: clean up ASP.

ASP.NET aims squarely at providing a rich user interface for multiple browsers, separation of client and server, stateless execution, simplifying data access, and enhancing scalability. ASP.NET does all of these things nicely. In addition to making the ASP.NET experience more like programming, developers benefit from the .NET Framework object model, having access to all of the CLR. ASP.NET is an event-driven programming environment. Although you do not have as many events in Web Forms as in Windows Forms, ASP.NET supports a rich, interactive, event-driven model. ASP.NET renders browser-independent applications by dynamically generating HTML based on the manufacturer and version of the browser. ASP.NET provides intuitive state management mechanisms, security, and scalable performance.

Chapter 19 introduces you to some of the aspects of ASP.NET from the Visual Basic .NET programmer's perspective. If you are intent on ASP.NET development, consider buying and reading either of these books from Sams Publishing: *ASP.NET: Tips, Tutorials, and Code* by Doug Seven et al. or *Programming Data-Driven Web Applications with ASP.NET*, by Donny Mack and Doug Seven. These authors maintain a Web site at `www.dotnetjunkies.com`.

In this chapter, we will take a look at creating ASP.NET applications using Web Forms, caching, and state management, and creating server controls.

Web Forms

Web Forms are one of the new, exciting features in Microsoft's .NET initiative. Web Forms are instances of the `System.Web.UI.Page` class. The benefit is that Web Forms support WYSIWYG user interface design and your favorite .NET programming language as the code behind the form. The result is that programming in ASP.NET is a lot like programming Windows Forms.

ASP.NET takes the design view in the .aspx, combined with the code behind the form in the .aspx.vb module, and automatically renders HTML. The automatically rendered HTML is browser-agnostic for styles and layout, or you can target a specific browser and version.

Web Forms Designer

The Web Forms Designer has two views: the design view and the raw HTML format view. You can toggle between views by clicking the tabs at the bottom of the designer (see Figure 19.1).

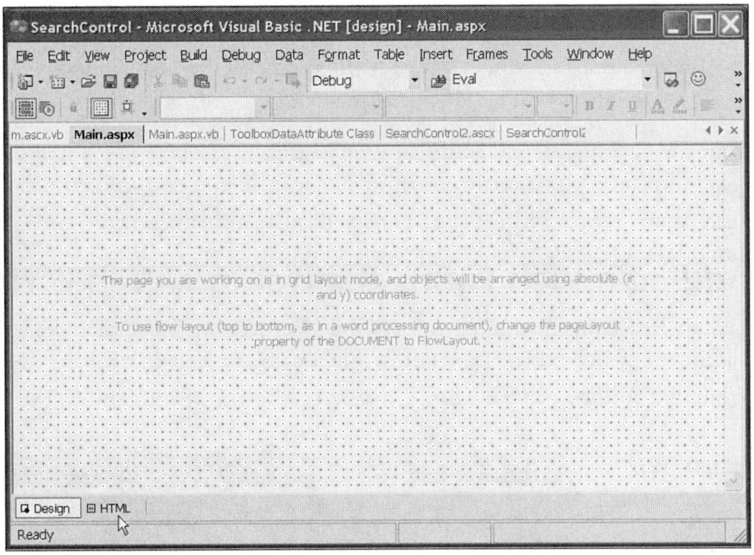

FIGURE 19.1

Switch between the WYSIWYG design view and the raw HTML format.

![Screenshot of SearchControl - Microsoft Visual Basic .NET [design] - Main.aspx showing the Web Forms Designer with Design and HTML tabs at the bottom. The design surface displays grid layout dots and the message: "The page you are working on is in grid layout mode, and objects will be arranged using absolute (x and y) coordinates. To use flow layout (top to bottom, as in a word processing document), change the pageLayout property of the DOCUMENT to FlowLayout."]

You can perform as much design as you want in either format. For Visual Basic programmers, the design view may be more intuitive than the HTML view, but in the latter you can manually enter code in raw HTML format. Alternatively, the .aspx file may contain XML, WML, HTML, and ECMAScript (JScript and JavaScript). Thus far I have found that a combination of the design and HTML views allows me to achieve the greatest ease of use and flexibility.

Choosing Grid or Flow Control Mode

You can toggle the `Page.PageLayout` property between `GridLayout` and `FlowLayout`. The `GridLayout` will be familiar to Visual Basic developers. `GridLayout` paints dots on the page during design mode, making it easy to place controls in precise locations. Although you can place controls anywhere on a page by dragging and dropping in `GridLayout` mode, you cannot directly enter text.

> **Tip**
>
> Page properties are modified by selecting the DOCUMENT object in the Properties window.

If you want to directly enter text on the page, you need to switch to FlowLayout mode. In FlowLayout mode you can type text directly on the page, but any Web Forms controls or HTML controls will be left-justified.

You can switch back and forth between GridLayout and FlowLayout at any time during design. As an alternative to switching to FlowLayout mode to add text to a page, you can elect to use a Web Forms Label control to place text on a page.

Adding a Web Forms Control to a Web Form

Listing 19.1 contains the obligatory Hello World example application, which is available on this book's Web site. The HelloAspDotNet.sln contains a single Web Forms button. When the button is clicked, text is written to the page (see Figure 19.2).

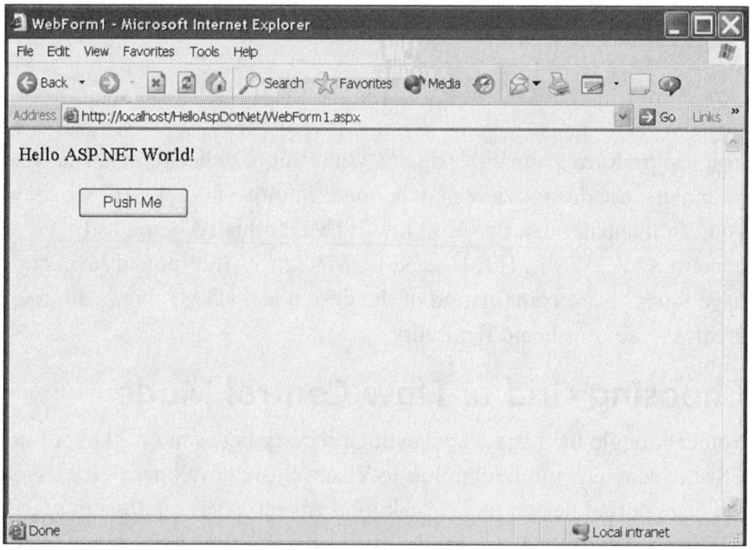

FIGURE 19.2

HelloAspDotNet. sln demonstrates basic Web Forms design.

To create the Web application shown in Figure 19.2, follow these steps:

1. Ensure that you have IIS 5.0 or greater available on your PC or network. You will need IIS 5.0 running to create and run the Web application.

2. Run Visual Studio .NET. Choose File, New, Project. In the New Project dialog box, select ASP.NET Web Application. The application will be created on your PC's IIS server by default (see Figure 19.3).

3. Click OK. An ASP.NET project will be created in your root directory. For example, if IIS is running on your PC, the default directory will be `c:\inetpub\wwwroot\` [`web application`], where *web application* is the folder containing your ASP.NET application files.

4. In the toolbox, click the Web Forms tab and drag a `Button` control to the design view of the .aspx page.

FIGURE 19.3

Creating an ASP.NET Web application.

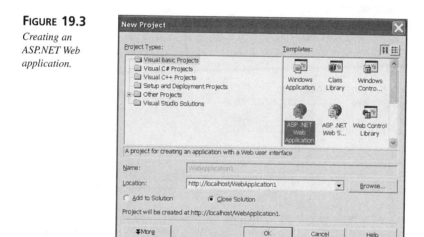

Web Forms Code Behind the Form

Just as you would when designing a Windows application, you can double-click controls in the Web Forms designer to generate event handlers. We want to add code that displays the "Hello ASP.NET World!" text as shown in Figure 19.2.

Listing 19.1 shows the code behind the Web Form, and Listing 19.2 shows the raw HTML code generated by the designer after the button is placed on the page.

LISTING 19.1 The code behind a Web Forms Page

```
1:  Public Class WebForm1
2:      Inherits System.Web.UI.Page
3:    Protected WithEvents Button1 As System.Web.UI.WebControls.Button
4:
5:  #Region " Web Form Designer Generated Code "
```

LISTING 19.1 continued

```
 6:
 7:        'This call is required by the Web Form Designer.
 8:        <System.Diagnostics.DebuggerStepThrough()> _
 9:        Private Sub InitializeComponent()
10:
11:    End Sub
12:
13:      Private Sub Page_Init(ByVal sender As System.Object, _
14:        ByVal e As System.EventArgs) Handles MyBase.Init
15:          'CODEGEN: This method call is required by the Web Form Designer
16:          'Do not modify it using the code editor.
17:          InitializeComponent()
18:      End Sub
19:
20: #End Region
21:
22:
23:      Private Sub Button1_Click(ByVal sender As System.Object, _
24:        ByVal e As System.EventArgs) Handles Button1.Click
25:
26:        Response.Write("Hello ASP.NET World!")
27:
28:      End Sub
29:
30: End Class
```

A quick glance at the listing and you will note many similarities between Windows Forms code and Web Forms code. Both Windows and Web applications use common object-oriented idioms. For example, both are implemented as classes. Both Windows and Web applications have designer-generated code, including the use of attributes and initialization code. Both kinds of applications use event handlers. If you look closely at line 23, you will see that a Button.Click event handler in an ASP.NET page is identical to the signature of a click handler in a Windows Forms application.

The code in ASP.NET applications is CLR code. You might not use all of the same classes when building Web Forms as when building Windows Forms, but the language is exactly the same. ASP.NET provides all of the benefits of the .NET Framework, including inheritance, managed code, and visual design.

LISTING 19.2 Raw HTML generated by the designer

```
1:   <%@ Page Language="vb" AutoEventWireup="false"
2:     Codebehind="WebForm1.aspx.vb" Inherits="HelloAspDotNet.WebForm1"%>
3:   <!DOCTYPE HTML PUBLIC "-//W3C//DTD HTML 4.0 Transitional//EN">
4:   <HTML>
```

LISTING 19.2 continued

```
 5:    <HEAD>
 6:      <title>WebForm1</title>
 7:      <meta name="GENERATOR" content="Microsoft Visual Studio.NET 7.0">
 8:      <meta name="CODE_LANGUAGE" content="Visual Basic 7.0">
 9:      <meta name="vs_defaultClientScript" content="JavaScript">
10:      <meta name="vs_targetSchema"
➥content="http://schemas.microsoft.com/intellisense/ie5">
11:    </HEAD>
12:    <body MS_POSITIONING="GridLayout">
13:      <form id="Form1" method="post" runat="server">
14:        <asp:Button id="Button1" style="Z-INDEX: 101;
➥LEFT: 75px; POSITION: absolute; TOP: 60px"
15:          runat="server" Text="Push Me" Width="119px"
➥Height="32px"></asp:Button>
16:      </form>
17:    </body>
18:  </HTML>
```

When you are visually designing your Web Forms, the designer is generating the HTML code for you. The benefit is that you do not have to type the terse HTML code; the Web Forms Designer takes care of this for you.

If you have worked with HTML or ASP in the past, you might recognize many of the elements in Listing 19.2. The <HTML></HTML> tags define the content of the HTML document on lines 4 and 18. A <HEAD></HEAD> section is defined on line 5 through 11, and the body of the document is defined on lines 12 through 17.

Lines 13 through 16 represent the page—bounded by the <form> tag—and the button is rendered as the <asp:Button> tag on lines 14 and 15. Clearly, it is easier to drag a button on the design view of the form than it is to remember this code.

The Codebehind attribute on line 2 indicates the file that contains the code behind the form (see Listing 19.1).

Building and Running the ASP.NET Application

When you build the ASP.NET application, all of the source files are compiled into a .DLL. In the example, HelloAspDotNet.dll is compiled, and consists of .aspx, .aspx.vb, and global.asax files.

You can run the application by pressing F5 or browsing to the .aspx file in your browser. Enter **http://localhost/HelloAspDotNet/WebForm1.aspx** in the Address field of your browser to run the Web application.

Using Request and Response

ASP.NET is a redesigned and re-engineered evolution of ASP. Several metaphors from ASP were carried over to ASP.NET (although their implementations might be vastly different). Two such objects are the `Request` and `Response` introduced in the `System.Web.UI.UserControl` class.

These objects also exist in the `System.Web.UI.Page` class. The `Request` object is an instance of the `HttpRequest` class, and the `Response` object is an instance of the `HttpResponse` class. Basically, `Request` represents the HTTP values sent by the client, and `Response` represents the information sent by the server application back to the client.

We use the `Request` and `Response` relative to the properties and methods their classes expose and their respective roles. When you need specific information about a client request in your code, get that information from the `Request` object. The parallel is true for the `Response` object. From Listing 19.1 it is apparent that we can use the `Response.Write` method to render HTML directly on the page (see line 26 of Listing 19.1).

ASP.NET and ADO.NET

You might have noticed that a significant portion of new technology is considered stateless or connectionless. For example, GDI+ is stateless, meaning you have to pass in font, color, brush, and pen information each time you interact with a GDI+ device context.

ADO.NET is connectionless. What this means to you is that you do not have a live cursor when you get data from a database using ADO.NET. In fact, the `DataSet` component actually grabs a copy of the data and caches it locally. This means that you will want to reconsider those `SELECT * FROM` *tablename* queries and be more circumspect about how and what you request. On a positive note, working with ADO.NET is easier than ADO, and data-enabling an ASP.NET Web application is straightforward (after someone shows you the ropes).

There are two basic components you need to know about when working with ADO.NET. Forget about the `Recordset` and think about the `DataSet` and the `DataReader`. The new `DataSet` component is used for connectionless forward and backward, editable data and `DataReaders` are for read-only, forward-only data—the kind of navigability you need when you are querying for values. There are also two flavors of the `DataSet` and

`DataReader`, the OLEDB flavor and the Sql flavor. The Sql flavor is designed and optimized for SQL Server 7.0 and higher and bypasses OLEDB, and the OLEDB flavor is for everything else, MS Access included. Thus if you are working with SQL Server 7.0 or higher, you will use classes that are prefixed with Sql, like `SqlDataReader`. If you are working with Access, Paradox, Sybase, or Oracle, you will use the `OleDbDataReader`.

One means of getting data from a database to a Web page is to establish a connection, define a command that describes your result set, and bind that data to a page. There are several classes you can use to accomplish this feat. I will demonstrate the code here, and of course, you are welcome to supplant the literal code for components on your own to speed things up.

Browsing a Code Database

What better example in a programming book than to implement a code database? The example in this section makes a database containing procedures and classes available for other developers available on the Web. (This is an idea I am playing with to make it easier for me to reuse my own code when I travel to customer's sites. Instead of taking code with me, I will just make it available on the Web.)

The sample database contains just a few examples of code, enough to demonstrate the steps for getting our database connected. (A better example would be to put all of the code in this book in a similar database—now, if I ever get around to it.)

The schema for the code database is pretty straightforward. There is a lookup table describing the `Language` the code is in to help browsers filter their searches. There is a `Submitter` table, perhaps to allow users to submit code and log in, and there is the `Source` table that contains the actual code listing and some description fields. (I won't go into detail about the schema here. You can open the table and look at it for yourself.)

In this first pass at a code database application, we will use the `DataGrid` component and bind the code listings to the `DataGrid`. The Web interface won't be fancy, but it will allow us to examine the basic steps for data-enabling Web pages.

Most of the page is created using code. To create the basic application, you will need the CodeDatabase.mdb (Access database), available from the `samspublishing.com` Web site, and you will need to create an ASP.NET Web application with a Web Forms `DataGrid` control dropped on the form. The rest of the application, shown in Figure 19.4, is implemented as code (provided in Listing 19.3).

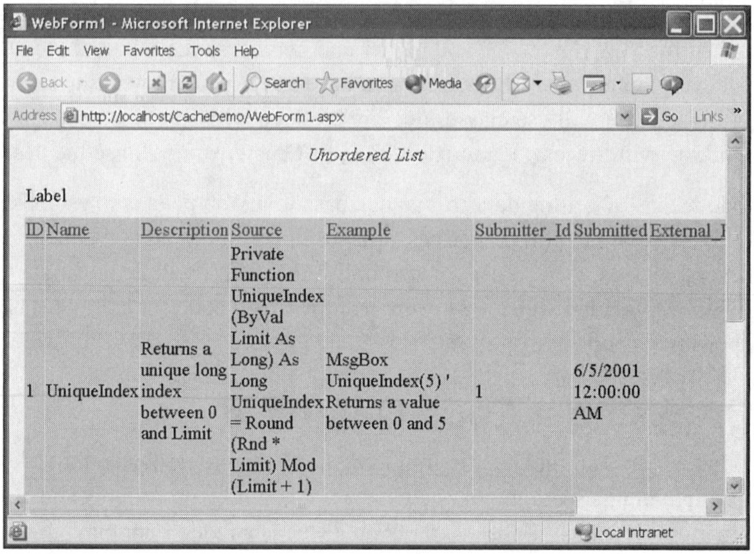

FIGURE **19.4**

The CacheDemo *sample application, demonstrating basic ADO.NET.*

ID	Name	Description	Source	Example	Submitter_Id	Submitted	External_I
1	UniqueIndex	Returns a unique long index between 0 and Limit	Private Function UniqueIndex (ByVal Limit As Long) As Long UniqueIndex = Round (Rnd * Limit) Mod (Limit + 1)	MsgBox UniqueIndex(5) ' Returns a value between 0 and 5	1	6/5/2001 12:00:00 AM	

LISTING **19.3** A data-aware ASP.NET Web application

```
1:  Imports System.Data.OleDb
2:
3:  Public Class WebForm1
4:    Inherits System.Web.UI.Page
5:
6:    Protected WithEvents DataGrid1 As _
7:      System.Web.UI.WebControls.DataGrid
8:
9:  [ Web Form Designer Generated Code ]
10:
11:   Private Function ConnectionString() As String
12:     Return "Provider=Microsoft.Jet.OLEDB.4.0;" & _
13:       "Data Source=c:\inetpub\wwwroot\" & _
14:       "CodeDatabase\data\CodeDatabase.mdb"
15:   End Function
16:
17:   Private Function Query() As String
18:     Return "SELECT * FROM SOURCE"
19:   End Function
20:
21:   Private Sub Page_Load(ByVal sender As System.Object, _
22:     ByVal e As System.EventArgs) Handles MyBase.Load
23:     'Put user code to initialize the page here
24:
25:     If (IsPostBack()) Then Exit Sub
26:     BindData(Query())
```

LISTING 19.3   continued

```
27:
28:    End Sub
29:
30:    Private Sub BindData(ByVal SQL As String)
31:       Dim Adapter As New _
32:          OleDbDataAdapter(SQL, ConnectionString())
33:       Dim DataSet As New DataSet()
34:       Adapter.Fill(DataSet, "Source")
35:       DataGrid1.DataSource = DataSet.Tables("Source")
36:       DataGrid1.DataBind()
37:    End Sub
38:
39: End Class
```

Line 1 imports the System.Data.OleDb. Because this sample uses Access, we need to use OleDb components instead of Sql components. Lines 3 and 4 indicate that this class is a Web Form—a subclass of the System.Web.UI.Page class. Lines 6 and 7 were added by the designer when a DataGrid was dragged from the Web Forms page of the toolbox onto the .aspx page.

Lines 11 to 15 implement a query method that returns a connection string. ADO.NET connection strings are consistent with ADO connection strings. (I prefer to use a query method to ensure that one convenient place contains all of that very specific text.) The connection string uses the Microsoft.Jet.OLEDB.4.0 provider.

The method Query on lines 17 to 19 is implemented as a query method, too. SQL littered all over your application will uglify code. Using a query method makes the code—see line 26—look a bit tidier. All of the code to line 20 should not be new to you at this point. Lines 21 to 39 represent the new information.

Lines 21 to 26 implement a Page.Load event handler. ASP.NET is written as Visual Basic .NET (or any other .NET language), which means you can use all of the language features supported by Visual Basic .NET when implementing ASP.NET applications. Lines 25 and 26 represent new code. Line 25 checks to see if this event is being invoked because of an HTTP-Post form operation. If we are loading because of a Post, we don't need to run the query again. The sentinel short-circuits the method on line 25. Otherwise, we call BindData(Query()), passing the SQL string to the BindData method. It is the databinding that is the real workhorse here.

My implementation of BindData creates an OleDbDataAdapter object. An OleDbDataAdapter can be instantiated with SQL and a connection string. The adapter will in turn create an OleDBConnection object and an OleDbCommand object for you. (As an alternative, you could create the connection and command object; using an

19

ASP.NET WEB
PROGRAMMING

adapter is more convenient.) The `OleDbAdapter` is used to populate the `DataSet` object with the specified table (see lines 33 and 34). Finally, the `DataSet.Tables`, which returns a `DataTable`, is used as the `DataSource` for the `DataGrid`, and `DataGrid.DataBind` populates the table.

To summarize, the `OleDbAdapter` creates an `OleDbCommand` and `OleDbConnection`. The connection represents the connection to the database, and the command represents the SQL. The adapter uses the connection and command to populate a `DataTable` maintained in the `DataSet.Tables` collection. The `DataTable` object provides data to the `DataGrid`. It is important to keep in mind that we don't have a cursor or an open connection at this point. A copy of the data has been copied over to the requesting client.

Sorting Data in a Web Form

Another reasonable operation you might want to allow consumers to perform is to sort the data on a Web page. The `DataGrid` facilitates this, too. You probably know how to sort a result set by using the `ORDER BY` clause of a SQL statement. The `DataGrid` provides an `AllowSorting` property. If you make the value of `AllowSorting` equal to True, the `DataGrid` will add hyperlinks to the column headers. When a user clicks on a column header, the `DataGrid.CommandSort` event will be raised.

By rerunning your query using the selected column header as the sort field, you can reorganize the result set and bind the sorted result set to the `DataGrid`. Essentially you are performing all of the steps demonstrated in Listing 19.3 with a revised query. Before you try the code in Listing 19.4, make sure that you set the `AllowSorting` property to True.

LISTING 19.4   Supporting dynamic sorting using the `DataGrid`

```
 1:  Imports System.Data.OleDb
 2:
 3:  Public Class WebForm1
 4:    Inherits System.Web.UI.Page
 5:
 6:    Protected WithEvents DataGrid1 As _
 7:      System.Web.UI.WebControls.DataGrid
 8:
 9:  [ Web Form Designer Generated Code ]
10:
11:    Private Function ConnectionString() As String
12:      Return "Provider=Microsoft.Jet.OLEDB.4.0;" & _
13:        "Data Source=c:\inetpub\wwwroot\CodeDatabase\data\CodeDatabase.mdb"
14:    End Function
15:
16:    Private Function Query() As String
17:      Return "SELECT * FROM SOURCE"
```

LISTING 19.4   continued

```
18:    End Function
19:
20:    Private Function OrderBy(ByVal SortColumn As String) As String
21:      If (SortColumn = "") Then
22:        Return ""
23:      Else
24:        Return " ORDER BY " & SortColumn
25:      End If
26:    End Function
27:
28:    Private Function Query(ByVal SortColumn As String) As String
29:      Return Query() & OrderBy(SortColumn)
30:    End Function
31:
32:    Private Sub Page_Load(ByVal sender As System.Object, _
33:      ByVal e As System.EventArgs) Handles MyBase.Load
34:      'Put user code to initialize the page here
35:
36:      If (IsPostBack()) Then Exit Sub
37:      BindData(Query())
38:
39:    End Sub
40:
41:    Private Sub BindData(ByVal SQL As String)
42:      Dim Adapter As New _
43:        OleDbDataAdapter(SQL, ConnectionString())
44:      Dim DataSet As New DataSet()
45:      Adapter.Fill(DataSet, "Source")
46:      DataGrid1.DataSource = DataSet.Tables("Source")
47:      DataGrid1.DataBind()
48:    End Sub
49:
50:
51:    'Private Sub DataGrid1_PageIndexChanged(ByVal source As Object, _
52:    '  ByVal e As System.Web.UI. _
53:    '  WebControls.DataGridPageChangedEventArgs) _
54:    '  Handles DataGrid1.PageIndexChanged
55:
56:    '  DataGrid1.CurrentPageIndex = e.NewPageIndex
57:    '  BindData(Query(FSortColumn))
58:
59:    'End Sub
60:
61:    Private FSortColumn As String = ""
62:    Private Property SortColumn() As String
63:      Get
64:        Return FSortColumn
65:      End Get
66:      Set(ByVal Value As String)
```

19

ASP.NET WEB
PROGRAMMING

LISTING 19.4   continued

```
67:        FSortColumn = Value
68:        Changed()
69:     End Set
70:  End Property
71:
72:
73:  Private Sub Changed()
74:     BindData(Query(FSortColumn))
75:  End Sub
76:
77:  Private Sub DataGrid1_SortCommand(ByVal source As Object, _
78:     ByVal e As System.Web.UI. _
79:     WebControls.DataGridSortCommandEventArgs) _
80:     Handles DataGrid1.SortCommand
81:
82:     SortColumn = e.SortExpression
83:  End Sub
84: End Class
```

We won't cover the code discussed earlier in the context of Listing 19.3, just the revisions. Listing 19.4 adds the `DataGrid1_SortCommand` event handler. When the event is raised, we can determine the column clicked from the `DataGridSortCommandEventArgs`. `SortExpression`. (The value represented by `e.SortExpression` will be the name of one of the columns.)

Line 82 calls the setter property method of a property named `SortColumn`, defined on lines 66 through 69. Line 68 calls the `Changed` method, which requests an updated query based on the `FSortColumn` field and binds the new `DataTable` to the `DataGrid`. (The balance of the changes were added to facilitate reuse and simplicity. For example, the `OrderBy` function determines a suitable `ORDER BY` clause depending on whether `FSortColumn` contains a value or not.)

To recap, the basic mechanics are to create an `OldDbConnection`, `OleDbCommand`, a `DataSet`, and bind a `DataTable` from the `DataSet` to the `DataGrid` control. As an alternative, you can substitute an `OleDbDataAdapter` for the connection and command; the adapter will create a connection-and-command object for you.)

Paging Using the `DataGrid`

Suppose you have too much data to show in a single Web page. A user might not want to wait for a huge result set; however, that same user might want all of the information accessible eventually. The `DataGrid` is a flexible control that automatically supports paging, too.

If you set the `DataGrid.AllowPaging` to True, ASP.NET will display basic paging controls and raise the `DataGrid.PageIndexChanged` event (see the commented handler in Listing 19.4, lines 51 to 57). The `DataGridPageChangedEventArgs` supplies the `NewPageIndex` property, containing the newly requested page index. Assign the event argument to the `DataGrid.PageIndexChanged` property and rebind the data to the page. The result is paging á la carte.

The last two sections demonstrated some reasonably powerful capabilities supported by very little code. With some experimentation, you can modify the properties to create some advance presentations.

Output Caching

Web Forms—the `Page` class—define a `Cache` property. `Cache` functions like a data dictionary of name and values. By associating a key with an object in the cache, you can store processor-intensive data the first time you request it.

The ease with which you can use the cache is part of what makes it so powerful. Assume that you run a query on the code database that returns a `DataTable` of source code. You can store that `DataTable` in the cache. You can manipulate the data in the cache instead of requerying the database. If you modify data in the cache, you can update the database from the cache.

This is especially useful for CPU-intensive processes like sorting database queries. Instead of a thousand users all hitting the database, when the first user requests the data, it is cached with the application on the server, resulting in lower traffic between the Web application and the database.

The `Page` class contains a `Cache` property. The `Cache` works like a data dictionary (or collection). Include a bit of code to see if an item needs to be added to or is available in the cache, and you have a Web application that caches data. Listing 19.5 adds caching to the code database `DataGrid` browser, caching sorts to avoid requesting a particular sort from the database more than once. (The whole application is listed here to facilitate your understanding of the necessary changes.)

LISTING 19.5   Caching processor-intensive tasks, like requesting sorted data from a database

```
1:  Imports System.Data.OleDb
2:
3:  Public Class WebForm1
4:      Inherits System.Web.UI.Page
5:
```

LISTING 19.5   continued

```
 6:
 7:   [ Web Form Designer Generated Code ]
 8:
 9:     Private Function ConnectionString() As String
10:       Return "Provider=Microsoft.Jet.OLEDB.4.0;" & _
11:         "Data Source=c:\inetpub\wwwroot\CodeDatabase\data\CodeDatabase.mdb"
12:     End Function
13:
14:     Private Function Query() As String
15:       Return "SELECT * FROM SOURCE"
16:     End Function
17:
18:     Private Function OrderBy(ByVal SortColumn As String) As String
19:       If (SortColumn = "") Then
20:         Return ""
21:       Else
22:         Return " ORDER BY " & SortColumn
23:       End If
24:     End Function
25:
26:     Private Function Query(ByVal SortColumn As String) As String
27:       Return Query() & OrderBy(SortColumn)
28:     End Function
29:
30:     Private Sub Page_Load(ByVal sender As System.Object, _
31:       ByVal e As System.EventArgs) Handles MyBase.Load
32:       'Put user code to initialize the page here
33:
34:       If (IsPostBack()) Then Exit Sub
35:       BindData(Query())
36:
37:     End Sub
38:
39:     Private Sub DataGrid1_PageIndexChanged( _
40:       ByVal source As System.Object, _
41:       ByVal e As System.Web.UI.WebControls. _
42:       DataGridPageChangedEventArgs)
43:
44:       DataGrid1.CurrentPageIndex = e.NewPageIndex
45:       BindData(Query(FSortColumn))
46:
47:     End Sub
48:
49:     Protected WithEvents DataGrid1 As _
50:       System.Web.UI.WebControls.DataGrid
51:     Protected WithEvents Label1 As _
52:       System.Web.UI.WebControls.Label
53:
54:     Private FSortColumn As String = ""
```

LISTING 19.5 continued

```
55:    Private Property SortColumn() As String
56:      Get
57:        Return FSortColumn
58:      End Get
59:      Set(ByVal Value As String)
60:        FSortColumn = Value
61:        Changed()
62:      End Set
63:    End Property
64:
65:    Private Overloads Sub BindData(ByVal SQL As String)
66:      Dim Adapter As New _
67:        OleDbDataAdapter(SQL, ConnectionString())
68:      Dim DataSet As New DataSet()
69:      Adapter.Fill(DataSet, "Source")
70:      BindData(DataSet.Tables("Source"))
71:      AddToCache(FSortColumn, DataSet.Tables("Source"))
72:    End Sub
73:
74:    Private Overloads Sub BindData(ByVal Table As DataTable)
75:      DataGrid1.DataSource = Table
76:      DataGrid1.DataBind()
77:    End Sub
78:
79:    Private Sub AddToCache(ByVal Column As String, ByVal Table As DataTable)
80:      If Not (CachedTable(Column) Is Nothing) Then Exit Sub
81:      CachedTable(Column) = Table
82:    End Sub
83:
84:    Private Property CachedTable(ByVal Column As String) As DataTable
85:      Get
86:        Return CType(Cache(Column), DataTable)
87:      End Get
88:      Set(ByVal Value As DataTable)
89:        If (Column = "") Or (Value Is Nothing) Then Exit Property
90:        Cache.Insert(Column, Value)
91:      End Set
92:    End Property
93:
94:    Private Sub Changed()
95:
96:      If (CachedTable(FSortColumn) Is Nothing) Then
97:        BindData(Query(FSortColumn))
98:        Label1.Text = "Ran Query"
99:      Else
100:       BindData(CachedTable(FSortColumn))
101:       Label1.Text = "From Cache"
102:     End If
103:
```

19

ASP.NET WEB PROGRAMMING

LISTING 19.5 continued

```
104:    End Sub
105:
106:    Private Sub DataGrid1_SortCommand( _
107:      ByVal source As Object, ByVal e As _
108:      System.Web.UI.WebControls.DataGridSortCommandEventArgs) _
109:      Handles DataGrid1.SortCommand
110:
111:      SortColumn = e.SortExpression
112:    End Sub
113: End Class
```

The bulk of the revisions occur between lines 65 and 104. An overloaded version of
BindData was implemented to separate binding from SQL and binding from a
DataTable. When we bind from SQL, we add the DataTable to the Cache (see line 71).
The biggest change occurs in the Change method. If the sorted column was previously
requested, the binding occurs from the cache rather than creating the adapter, running
the query, creating the dataset, and binding from the DataSet's Tables collection.

> **Note**
>
> Listing 19.5 wraps the Cache access in a property method; you don't have to do
> that. As a matter of technique, though, adding a property wrapper around the
> cache access allows us to add any additional constraints transparently. For exam-
> ple, in the listing, we don't try to add anything to the cache if the key or object
> is null.

There are a few salient points about general technique and the specific mechanics of
caching that you should be aware of. The CachedTable property on lines 84 to 92
demonstrates an indexed property. Line 86 demonstrates how to retrieve an object
from the page's cache and cast it to the type of the object we stored in the cache, a
DataTable. Line 96 demonstrates how to inspect the cache using the key-value. If there
is no cached DataTable for a specific column, we call BindData; our BindData accesses
the database. On the other hand, if the cache contains a DataTable for a particular column, we bind the data from the cache (see line 100).

Adding and Removing Cached Items

The System.Web.Caching.Cache class allows you to Add and Insert items into the
cache. Insert supports four overloaded methods of varying degrees of difficulty. The
Add method is not overloaded. The basic parameters of the two methods depend on

which version of `Insert` or `Add` you call. IntelliSense and the help files will ably assist you on a case-by-case basis.

The following example shows the syntax of the `Add` method. Each argument (or return value) is described in Table 19.1.

```
Public Function Add( _
    ByVal key As String, _
    ByVal value As Object, _
    ByVal dependencies As CacheDependency, _
    ByVal absoluteExpiration As DateTime, _
    ByVal slidingExpiration As TimeSpan, _
    ByVal priority As CacheItemPriority, _
    ByVal onRemoveCallback As CacheItemRemovedCallback _
) As Object
```

TABLE 19.1 Arguments You Need to Supply to `Cache.Add` or `Cache.Insert`

Argument	*Description*
Key	The string value used to index the cache.
Value	The object to be cached.
Dependencies	`CacheDependency` used to determine validity of cached object.
AbsoluteExpiration	`DateTime` indicates expiration of cached object.
SlidingExpiration	Expiration interval from last access (see next subsection for an example).
Priority	`CacheItemPriority` enumeration.
Object	Return value. Equivalent to the `Value` argument passed to the `Add` method.
OnRemoveCallback	Optional callback that will be raised when the item is removed from the cache.

The biggest difference between `Add` and `Insert` is that `Insert` replaces items with the same key and `Add` does not replace the item.

Setting an Expiration Time for Cached Items

The `Cache` class allows you to proactively manage the amount of data that ends up in the cache. As you might imagine, storing data tables for dozens or hundreds of users can become resource-intensive. By passing `AbsoluteExpiration` or `SlidingExpiration` arguments, you can control how long an object lives in the cache.

`AbsoluteExpiration` indicates how long an item can remain in the cache before it is removed. `SlidingExpiration` determines how long since the last access something can stay in the cache. For example, an `AbsoluteExpiration` of five minutes means that an item will be removed after five minutes has expired. A `SlidingExpiration` of five minutes means that the item will remain in the cache as long as someone accesses it within each five-minute interval or until the `AbsoluteExpiration` interval expires.

Performance Considerations

The help topic "Developing High-Performance ASP.NET Applications" (available at `ms-help://MS.VSCC/MS.MSDNVS/cpguide/html/cpcondevelopinghigh-performanceaspnetapplications.htm`) provides options that are worth exploring. I won't repeat that information in its entirety, but the list that follows is provided for quick reference.

- Disable the session state unless you are using it. Add the `enableSessionState="false"` attribute to the page directive to disable the session state.

- You can store session information in a variety of in-process and out-of-process providers. An example of an in-process provider is the `Session` object; an example of an out-of-process provider is SQL Server. Choose your session information provider accordingly. Small data that you need quick access to can be stored with an in-process provider. If the state must be maintained even in the event of a crash, you need an out-of-process provider like SQL Server.

- Use `Page.IsPostBack` to keep the number of round trips to the server to a minimum.

- Use server controls appropriately. The `Page` attribute `EnableViewState` allows server controls to repopulate their values without your having to write code, but this feature incurs a performance penalty.

- Multiple calls to `Response.Write` can concatenate strings faster than performing concatenation and having a single call to `Response.Write`.

- Avoid using exceptions to control the flow of control. If you can handle an anticipated error condition, use conditional statements, but don't avoid using exceptions.

- Declare all variables explicitly, avoiding late binding. `Option Strict On` will enforce this constraint.

- Port COM components to .NET (although COM interop supports using COM components in .NET).

- Use stored procedures for scalable data access and the `SqlReader` for forward-only fast data access.

- Use output caching when possible.

- Enable Web gardening on multiprocessor computers.

- Build your application with debugging off before deploying it.

Rendering Controls

The `WebControl` class introduces the `Render` method. You can override the `Render` method to perform custom HTML rendering via the `System.Web.UI.HtmlTextWriter` object passed to the `Render` method.

`HtmlTextWriter` allows you to add HTML directly to a Web page through generic and specific methods both designed for this purpose. `Render` is commonly used by server controls to update their presentation on the client.

The `HtmlTextWriter` object and the `Render` method can be used to create dynamic pages that are made up of programmatically derived HTML elements. You can write raw HTML or use methods like `HTMLTextWriter.WriteBeginTag` and `HtmlTextWriter.WriteEndTag` to simplify rendering the HTML (and probably reduce the likelihood of HTML syntax errors). Refer to Listing 19.6 for an example of dynamically rendered HTML.

LISTING 19.6 Dynamically rendered HTML that adds a header to the code database listing

```
 1:    Private ReadOnly Property FormattedColumn() As String
 2:      Get
 3:        If (FSortColumn = "") Then
 4:          Return "Unordered List"
 5:        Else
 6:          Return "Ordered List by " & FSortColumn
 7:        End If
 8:      End Get
 9:    End Property
10:
11:   Protected Overrides Sub Render( _
12:      ByVal writer As System.Web.UI.HtmlTextWriter)
13:
14:      MyBase.Render(writer)
15:      writer.WriteBeginTag("center") :
➥writer.Write(HtmlTextWriter.TagRightChar)
16:
```

LISTING 19.6 continued

```
17:     writer.WriteBeginTag("i") :
➡writer.Write(HtmlTextWriter.TagRightChar)
18:     writer.Write(FormattedColumn)
19:     writer.WriteEndTag("i")
20:
21:     writer.WriteEndTag("center")
22:
23:   End Sub
```

The listing was added to the CacheDemo.sln from Listing 19.5 to render a title for the DataGrid containing the source code from the code database. Line 14 calls the inherited Render method; otherwise, only the dynamic code will be displayed in the form. Lines 15 and 21 write the begin and end tags for centering text, respectively.

```
<center></center>
```

Some tags require additional parameter information. For this reason, the right tag character is not rendered on the begin tag. You have to invoke the HtmlTextWriter.TagRightChar to render the right tag character for beginning tags explicitly. This is demonstrated on lines 15 and 17.

Inside the center tag is the italics tag (<i></i>). The result is HTML that centers and italicizes the text. The formatted output is derived from the property method, followed by the closing tags. Listing 19.6 renders the HTML shown next (assuming the HTML source is examined before performing a sort):

```
<center><i>Unordered List</i></center>
```

Dynamically Adding Controls to a Page

ASP.NET supports dynamic control creation, and as a result, dynamic Web applications. You can use Repeater, DataList, or the DataGrid controls, or render dynamic HTML for a considerable degree of dynamic customization.

When you need complete customization, you can dynamically add programmatically created controls to a page. The controls must be added to a container control. You can use the PlaceHolder or Panel controls as containers or access the HtmlForm control through the page's Controls collection. The rest of the effort is just VB code.

Programmatically Adding Static Text to a Page

If you want to add static text dynamically to a page, you can create an instance of the `Label` control and place it on a container residing on a page (see Listing 19.7). To add the `Label` control, follow these steps:

1. Write code that declares an instance of a `System.Web.UI.WebControls.Label` control.

2. Assign a text value for the label control's `Text` property.

3. Add the control to the container's `Controls` property using the `Add` method.

LISTING 19.7 Dynamically adding a `Label` control to a Web Form

```
 1:  Private Function GetForm() As HtmlForm
 2:      Return CType(FindControl("Form1"), HtmlForm)
 3:  End Function
 4:
 5:  Private Sub Button1_Click(ByVal sender As System.Object, _
 6:    ByVal e As System.EventArgs) Handles Button1.Click
 7:
 8:  Dim Label As New Label()
 9:    Label.Text = "Label"
10:    GetForm().Controls.Add(Label)
11:
12: End Sub
```

Line 8 creates an instance of the `Label` control. Line 9 assigns some arbitrary text to the `Label.Text` property. The `GetForm` query method returns the `HtmlForm` object, which plays the role of container in this example. Line 10 uses the `HtmlForm.Controls` collection to add the `Label` to the page.

Modifying Control Properties Using the Attributes Collection

In the preceding section, we modified the `Label.Text` property directly. You can also modify properties using the control's `Attributes` collection. For example, you might want to set the `Name` attribute of the `Label`; however, there is no matching `Name` property. The only way to modify this property programmatically is to use the attributes collection.

By adding the revision to the code from Listing 19.7, Listing 19.8 demonstrates how to modify attributes directly.

LISTING 19.8   Modifying attributes directly

```
 1:  Private Sub Button1_Click(ByVal sender As System.Object, _
 2:      ByVal e As System.EventArgs) Handles Button1.Click
 3:
 4:      Dim Label As New Label()
 5:      Label.Text = "Label"
 6:      Label.Attributes.Add("Id", Label.Text)
 7:      Label.Attributes.Add("Name", Label.Text)
 8:      GetForm().Controls.Add(Label)
 9:
10:  End Sub
```

Lines 6 and 7 demonstrate code that sets the Id and Name attributes of the Label control. (Alternately, you can modify the Id attribute directly using the Label.Id property as follows: Label.Id = "text".)

The Label control is rendered as a <span> tag. The HTML for the code in Listing 19.8 follows:

```
<span Id="Label" Name="Label">Label</span>
```

Use the properties when they are available, but remember that you can modify the attributes for the rendered HTML by name.

Programmatically Adding a LiteralControl to a Page

LiteralControl objects are those tags and elements that don't require processing on the server, like the line-break <br> tag. Notably, HTML elements that don't use or need the runat="server" attribute can be implemented as LiteralControl instances.

To assist in positioning controls like the Label from the last section, we can use LiteralControls—HTML—to programmatically position the Label. Listing 19.9 demonstrates the revision to Listing 19.8 that adds a paragraph before the Label and a line-break after it.

LISTING 19.9   Using LiteralControl objects

```
 1:  Private Sub Button1_Click(ByVal sender As System.Object, _
 2:      ByVal e As System.EventArgs) Handles Button1.Click
 3:
 4:      Dim Label As New Label()
 5:      Label.Text = "Label" & (GetForm().Controls.Count).ToString()
 6:      Label.Text = "Label"
 7:      Label.Attributes.Add("Id", Label.Text)
```

LISTING 19.9   continued

```
 8:      Label.Attributes.Add("Name", Label.Text)
 9:      GetForm().Controls.Add(New LiteralControl("<p>"))
10:     GetForm().Controls.Add(Label)
11:     GetForm().Controls.Add(New LiteralControl("<br>"))
12:
13: End Sub
```

> **Note**
>
> Notice that the `LiteralControl` objects are created as parameters to the `Controls.Add` method. This is done for convenience. You're welcome to declare a variable and assign the instance to the variable before passing the literal control to the `Add` method.

Lines 9 and 11 define two instances of `LiteralControl` objects. The objects are represented by the literal HTML tags passed to the constructors.

Adding a Control Using the `PlaceHolder`

The previous listings demonstrated how to walk the page's `Controls` collection to find the `HtmlForm` and use that form as the container for dynamic controls. An easier operation is to add a `PlaceHolder` or `Panel` control to the page and place dynamic controls on the `PlaceHolder` control.

The technique for adding controls to a `PlaceHolder` is the same as adding dynamic controls to any other container:

1. Define a control instance and create a new instance programmatically.

2. Modify any properties or attributes.

3. Add the dynamic control to the `PlaceHolder.Control` collection.

You can add and arrange controls on the `PlaceHolder` just as you would on an `HtmlForm` or `Panel`. The next section demonstrates creating a dynamic, data-bound control using the `PlaceHolder` control as the container, including a code listing.

Programmatically Adding a Databound Control to a Page

Programmatically adding a databound control combines two of the techniques we have discussed in this chapter: dynamically creating a control and binding a control to a data source. To review, the numbered list that follows summarizes all of the steps to create a DropDownList control and bind it to the code database. This time we will use an OleDbConnection and an OleDbCommand instead of the OleDbDataAdapter, as shown in Listing 19.10.

1. Create an instance of OleDbConnection, initializing the connection with a connection string. (If you are using SQL Server 7.0 or greater, use the Sql-prefixed versions of these objects.)

2. Create an instance of OleDbCommand, initializing it with the SQL string defining the result set we want.

3. Open the connection.

4. Define an OleDbDataReader and initialize the reader by calling OleDbCommand. ExecuteReader.

5. Initialize the control, and assign the control's DataSource property to the OleDbDataReader.

6. Remember to call *control*.Databind, where *control* is the name of the instance of the control.

LISTING 19.10 An example of code that creates a control and binds it to data, programmatically

```
1:    Private Sub CreateAndBind()
2:
3:      Dim Connection As New _
4:        OleDbConnection(ConnectionString())
5:      Dim Command As New _
6:        OleDbCommand("SELECT ID, Name FROM SOURCE", Connection)
7:
8:      Connection.Open()
9:      Dim Reader As OleDbDataReader = _
10:       Command.ExecuteReader(CommandBehavior.Default)
11:
12:     Dim List As New DropDownList()
13:     List.DataTextField = "Name"
14:     List.DataSource = Reader
15:
16:     Response.Write(CType(Controls(1), HtmlForm).Name)
17:
18:     PlaceHolder1.Controls.Add(List)
19:     List.DataBind()
20:   End Sub
```

Lines 1 through 20 demonstrate a more verbose variation of creating a connection and command instead of an adapter. Because we are only browsing the data in the `DropDownList`, we can use the `OleDbDataReader`, which provides unidirectional reading from the database. Lines 13 and 14 bind the `DataTextField` to a column in our result set and assigns the `OleDbDataReader` to the `DataSource`. When the code runs, it creates the `DropDownList` shown (expanded) in Figure 19.5.

FIGURE 19.5

A programmati-cally created and bound `DropDownList`.

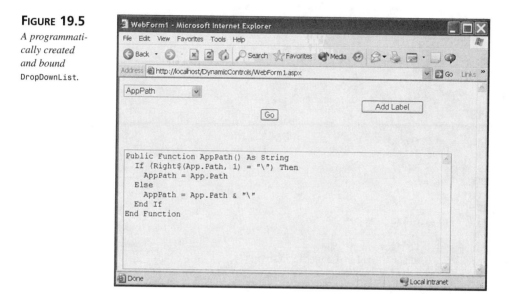

Wiring Dynamic Controls to an Event Handler

Controls that don't respond to user feedback are not any more useful in Web Forms than they are in Window Forms. Now that you know how to programmatically add controls to a Web Form, you need to know how to wire them up.

Would you be surprised if I said this process was identical to wiring controls up in Windows Forms? That's right. All you need is a procedure, a delegate, and the `AddHandler` method. I can't say this enough: This kind of consistency is the hallmark of a "first-class" language and tools. A class is a class is a class (see Listing 19.11 for an example that adds an event handler). The fact that Microsoft has extended this consistency to ASP.NET via Visual Basic .NET means that when you learn how to work with objects in VB .NET, you know how to work with them in ASP.NET.

LISTING 19.11   Hooking an event handler to the dynamic `DropDownList`

```
 1:    Private Sub SelectedIndexChanged(ByVal Sender As Object, _
 2:      ByVal e As System.EventArgs)
 3:
 4:      Dim Connection As New OleDbConnection(ConnectionString)
 5:
 6:      Dim Command As New _
 7:        OleDbCommand(BuildQuery( _
 8:        CType(Sender, DropDownList).SelectedItem.Text), _
 9:        Connection)
10:
11:    Connection.Open()
12:
13:    Dim Reader As OleDbDataReader = _
14:        Command.ExecuteReader()
15:
16:    If (Reader.Read()) Then
17:      TextBox1.Text = Reader.GetString(0)
18:    End If
19:
20:  End Sub
21:
22:
23:    Private Sub CreateAndBind()
24:
25:      Dim Connection As New _
26:        OleDbConnection(ConnectionString())
27:      Dim Command As New _
28:        OleDbCommand("SELECT ID, Name FROM SOURCE", Connection)
29:
30:      Connection.Open()
31:      Dim Reader As OleDbDataReader = _
32:        Command.ExecuteReader(CommandBehavior.Default)
33:
34:      Dim List As New DropDownList()
35:      List.DataTextField = "Name"
36:      List.DataSource = Reader
37:
38:      PlaceHolder1.Controls.Add(List)
39:
40:      AddHandler List.SelectedIndexChanged, _
41:        AddressOf SelectedIndexChanged
42:
43:      List.DataBind()
44:
45:    End Sub
```

Lines 23 through 45 borrow from `CreateAndBind` in Listing 19.10. The additional code is the association of the event handler to the dynamic list box on lines 40 and 41. If you change the selected element in the list, the event handler `SelectedIndexChanged` will be invoked when the form is posted. Lines 1 through 20 implement the event handler.

`SelectedIndexChanged` creates an `OleDbConnection`, `OleDbCommand`, `OleDbDataReader`, and uses the value returned by the query to display the code in a textbox control. All of this code works dynamically because the handler is associated with the `DropDownList.SelectedIndexChanged` event on lines 40 and 41.

Creating Custom Web Controls

There are a few basic ways to create custom controls for ASP.NET Web applications. Essentially, creating controls for the Web involves similar processes to creating controls for Windows Forms. You can create a control derived from a `UserControl` or create a Web Control Library project and generalize an existing Web Server Control.

There is a third way to create user controls that involves removing code more than writing code. This third way is to use the design view to visually design a Web page, add the code to the page, and then save the page as a server control.

We'll cover these three ways of creating user controls and custom controls, as well as demonstrating a couple of interesting solutions using these controls.

Saving a Web Page as a Server Control

A server control created by chopping out some HTML tags is easy to create and has some attractors and detractors.

If you want to create a server control from a Web page, you have all of the benefits of the Visual Studio Designer when creating the initial page. Hence, you can drag and drop controls onto the page and add the code behind the form. Unfortunately, when you are prepared to use the control you have, there is limited support for manipulating the page-with-control after it has been converted to a control.

The result is that controls contrived from pages are relatively easier to design and create but are most useful for specific solutions within a single application. (Don't worry, you can create custom controls that are very portable with other techniques. We'll get to those in a moment.)

19

ASP.NET WEB PROGRAMMING

To create a control from a Web page, you will need to design the page and follow these numbered steps:

1. After you have the Web page designed, you need to remove all of the beginning and ending <HTML>, <FORM>, <BODY>, and <HEAD> tags from the HTML source.

2. The raw HTML contains an @ Page directive. Change the @ Page directive to an @ Control directive, and get rid of attributes that are not supported by the @ Control directive. (Look in the help documentation for supported attributes.)

3. Change the extension of the .aspx file to .ascx and the .aspx.vb (code-behind) file to .ascx.vb.

4. Change the extension of the code-behind attribute in the Raw HTML file to reflect the change to the code-behind file extension.

5. Change the Inherits statement in the code-behind from Inherits System.Web.UI.Page to Inherits System.Web.UI.UserControl.

After you have saved the new .ascx (control files), you can drag and drop the .ascx file from the Solution Explorer to a new Web page, to use the control.

The next two listings show the before and after changes to the raw HTML text. The first, Listing 19.12, shows the HTML (in the .aspx file); the page contains a DropDownList, a Button, and a TextBox. The second, Listing 19.13, shows the .ascx file with all of the necessary revisions.

LISTING 19.12   A Web page before it is converted to a control

```
 1: <%@ Page Language="vb" AutoEventWireup="false"
 2:     Codebehind="BeforeAndAfter.aspx.vb"
 3:     Inherits="SearchControl.BeforeAndAfter"%>
 4:
 5: <!DOCTYPE HTML PUBLIC "-//W3C//DTD HTML 4.0 Transitional//EN">
 6: <HTML>
 7:   <HEAD>
 8:     <title>BeforeAndAfter</title>
 9:     <meta name="GENERATOR"
10:         content="Microsoft Visual Studio.NET 7.0">
11:
12:     <meta name="CODE_LANGUAGE"
13:         content="Visual Basic 7.0">
14:
15:     <meta name="vs_defaultClientScript"
16:         content="JavaScript">
17:
18:     <meta name="vs_targetSchema"
➥content="http://schemas.microsoft.com/intellisense/ie5">
19:
```

LISTING 19.12   continued

```
20:    </HEAD>
21:    <body MS_POSITIONING="GridLayout">
22:      <form id="Form1" method="post" runat="server">
23:
24:        <asp:DropDownList id="DropDownList1"
25:            style="Z-INDEX: 101; LEFT: 23px;
26:            POSITION: absolute; TOP: 22px"
27:            runat="server" Width="376px" Height="29px">
28:        </asp:DropDownList>
29:
30:        <asp:Button id="Button1" style="Z-INDEX: 102;
31:            LEFT: 413px; POSITION: absolute;
32:            TOP: 26px" runat="server" Width="39px"
33:            Height="27px" Text="Button">
34:        </asp:Button>
35:
36:        <asp:TextBox id="TextBox1" style="Z-INDEX: 103;
37:            LEFT: 29px; POSITION: absolute; TOP: 64px"
38:            runat="server" Width="610px" Height="345px"
39:            TextMode="MultiLine">
40:        </asp:TextBox>
41:      </form>
42:    </body>
43: </HTML>
```

I will point out the elements we need to modify after you have a chance to look at the revised page converted to a control.

LISTING 19.13   The code from Listing 19.12 converted from a page to a control

```
 1:  <%@ Control Language="vb" AutoEventWireup="false"
 2:      Codebehind="BeforeAndAfter.ascx.vb"
 3:      Inherits="SearchControl.BeforeAndAfter"%>
 4:  <asp:DropDownList id="DropDownList1"
 5:      style="Z-INDEX: 101; LEFT: 23px;
 6:      POSITION: absolute; TOP: 22px"
 7:      runat="server" Width="376px" Height="29px">
 8:  </asp:DropDownList>
 9:  <asp:Button id="Button1" style="Z-INDEX: 102;
10:      LEFT: 413px; POSITION: absolute;
11:      TOP: 26px" runat="server" Width="39px"
12:      Height="27px" Text="Button">
13:  </asp:Button>
14:  <asp:TextBox id="TextBox1" style="Z-INDEX: 103;
15:      LEFT: 29px; POSITION: absolute; TOP: 64px"
16:      runat="server" Width="610px" Height="345px"
17:      TextMode="MultiLine">
18:  </asp:TextBox>
```

19

ASP.NET WEB PROGRAMMING

Comparing Listing 19.12 to Listing 19.13, you can determine that lines 4 through 23 were removed. Lines 41, 42, and 43 were also removed. This takes care of step 1. Step 2 indicates that we have to change the @ `Page` directive. This directive is on line 1. Change `Page` to `Control` leaving the space between the `At` (@) and the directive word. The attributes used for the `Page` directive apply to the `Control` directive, so we will leave those in place.

Step 3 indicates that we need to change the .aspx and .aspx.vb extensions. If you simply rename the .aspx file extension to .ascx in the Solution Explorer, Visual Studio will change the .aspx.vb file to .ascx.vb and modify the code-behind directive too (see line 2). This takes care of step 4 automatically.

The fifth and final step indicates to change the inheritance from `Page` to `UserControl`. Just edit the code. You will get a runtime exception reminding you that @ `Control` classes must inherit from `System.Web.UI.UserControl` if you forget.

Adding the User Control to a Web Page

Using a user control is straightforward. Drag the control from the Solution Explorer to the Web page. If you ever have to perform this step manually, here is what Visual Studio .NET does for you.

When you drag a user control from the Solution Explorer to a Web Form, Visual Studio .NET adds an @ `Register` directive to the HTML code and includes the HTML that describes the control instance.

```
<%@ Register tagPrefix="uc1" tagName="BeforeAndAfter"
➥src="BeforeAndAfter.ascx" %>
```

The register directive associates aliases with namespaces and classes. The `tagPrefix` attribute is to associate an alias with a namespace. The `tagName` is an alias to associate with a class. The `src` is the location of the user control. The `assembly` attribute (not shown) is the name of the assembly containing the user control. The `nameSpace` (not shown) is the namespace associated with the `tagPrefix`.

When you drag the control onto a Web page, the HTML describing the control is added to the form. The HTML is started with a beginning tag in the form *tagprefix:tagname* and ends with the </*tagprefix:tagname*> tag. Between the beginning and ending tag are the attributes to initialize the control.

Figure 19.6 shows a search user control specifically designed to search order information in the Northwind.mdb database. The user control HTML is provided in Listing 19.14 and the Visual Basic .NET code is provided in Listing 19.15.

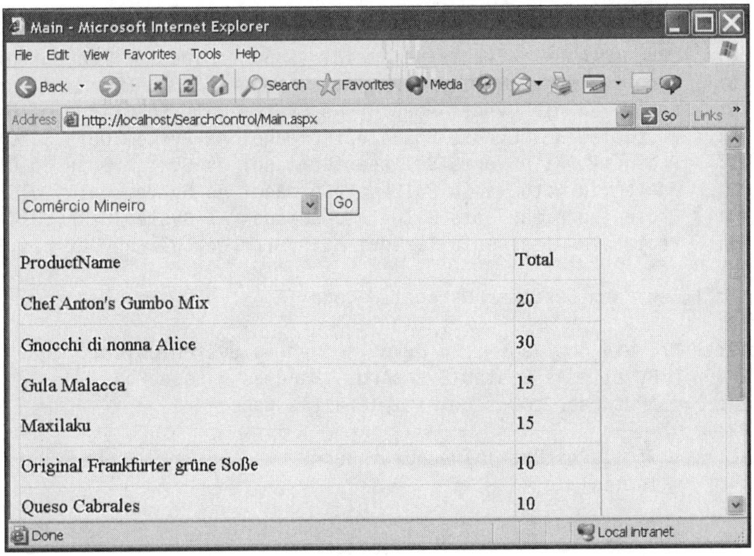

FIGURE 19.6

A user control that searches a database using a stored procedure.

LISTING 19.14   HTML code for the `SearchControl` user control

```
<%@ Control Language="vb"
AutoEventWireup="false"
Codebehind="SearchForm.ascx.vb"
Inherits="SearchControl.SearchControl"%>
<P>
  <asp:DropDownList id="DropDownList1" runat="server"
➥Width="323px" Height="265px"></asp:DropDownList>
  <asp:Button id="Button1" runat="server"
➥Width="37px" Text="Go"></asp:Button>
</P>
<P>
  <asp:DataGrid id="DataGrid1" Height="424px"
➥Width="622px" runat="server"></asp:DataGrid>
</P>
```

LISTING 19.15   Visual Basic .NET code that implements the user control

```
1:  Imports System.Data.SqlClient
2:
3:
4:  Public Class SearchControl
5:    Inherits System.Web.UI.UserControl
6:    Protected WithEvents DropDownList1 As
➥System.Web.UI.WebControls.DropDownList
7:    Protected WithEvents TextBox1 As System.Web.UI.WebControls.TextBox
```

LISTING **19.15**   continued

```
 8:    Protected WithEvents DataGrid1 As System.Web.UI.WebControls.DataGrid
 9:    Protected WithEvents SqlConnection1 As System.Data.SqlClient.SqlConnection
10:   Protected WithEvents Adapter As System.Data.SqlClient.SqlDataAdapter
11:   Protected WithEvents SqlSelectCommand1 As System.Data.SqlClient.SqlCommand
12:   Protected WithEvents SqlInsertCommand1 As System.Data.SqlClient.SqlCommand
13:   Protected WithEvents SqlUpdateCommand1 As System.Data.SqlClient.SqlCommand
14:   Protected WithEvents SqlDeleteCommand1 As System.Data.SqlClient.SqlCommand
15:   Protected WithEvents Button1 As System.Web.UI.WebControls.Button
16:
17: [ Web Form Designer Generated Code ]
18:
19:   Private Sub Page_Load(ByVal sender As System.Object, _
20:     ByVal e As System.EventArgs) Handles MyBase.Load
21:     'Put user code to initialize the page here
22:
23:     If (IsPostBack) Then Exit Sub
24:     Initialize()
25:
26:   End Sub
27:
28:   Private Sub Initialize()
29:
30:     SqlConnection1.Open()
31:     Dim Table As New DataSet()
32:     Adapter.Fill(Table)
33:
34:     DropDownList1.DataSource = Table
35:     DropDownList1.DataTextField = "CompanyName"
36:     DropDownList1.DataValueField = "CustomerID"
37:     DropDownList1.DataBind()
38:
39:     SqlConnection1.Close()
40:
41:   End Sub
42:
43:   Private Function GetQuery(ByVal Key As String)
44:     Const SQL As String = _
45:       "SELECT * FROM Orders O, [Order Details] D " & _
46:       "WHERE O.OrderID = D.OrderID " & _
47:       "AND CustomerID = '{0}'"
48:
49:     Return String.Format(SQL, Key)
50:   End Function
51:
52:   Private Sub ShowOrders(ByVal Key As String)
53:
54:     Dim Command As New SqlCommand("CustOrderHist", SqlConnection1)
55:     Command.CommandType = CommandType.StoredProcedure
56:     Command.Parameters.Add(New SqlParameter("@CustomerID", Key))
57:
```

LISTING 19.15   continued

```
58:      SqlConnection1.Open()
59:      Dim Reader As SqlDataReader = _
60:         Command.ExecuteReader(CommandBehavior.Default)
61:
62:      DataGrid1.DataSource = Reader
63:      DataGrid1.DataBind()
64:
65:      SqlConnection1.Close()
66:   End Sub
67:
68:   Private Sub DropDownList1_SelectedIndexChanged( _
69:      ByVal sender As System.Object,  ByVal e As System.EventArgs) _
70:      Handles DropDownList1.SelectedIndexChanged
71:
72:      ShowOrders(CType(sender, DropDownList).SelectedItem.Value)
73:
74:   End Sub
75: End Class
```

Most of this code you have seen earlier in this chapter. There are a couple of revisions. A `SqlDataAdapter` and `SqlConnection` were used and configured automatically by dragging the Customers table from the Server window (see Figure 19.7) to the component tray, and `ShowOrders` demonstrates the revisions necessary to call a stored procedure. The stored procedure performs roughly the same task as the SQL returned by the `GetQuery` method beginning on line 43.

FIGURE 19.7

Drag and drop elements from the Server window for automatic database connectivity.

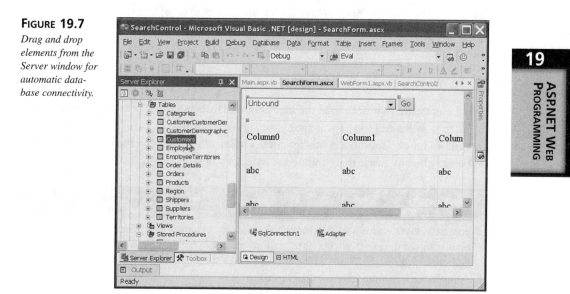

19

ASP.NET WEB
PROGRAMMING

Tip

Use stored procedures when possible for optimal performance and application scalability.

Line 54 initializes the `SqlCommand` object with the name of a pre-existing stored procedure in the Northwind database. Line 55 changes the command type to `CommandType.StoredProcedure`, and line 56 creates and passes the `SqlParameter` object to the `SqlCommand` object before requesting the `SQlDataReader`.

Creating the User Control Programmatically

To create a user control programmatically (see Listing 19.16), you will need to include the @ `Register` directive at design time. After the user control has been registered in your application, you can create an instance of it by calling the `Page.LoadControl` method.

LISTING 19.16 Dynamically loading a user control

```
 1:    Private Sub Page_Load(ByVal sender As System.Object, _
 2:       ByVal e As System.EventArgs) Handles MyBase.Load
 3:       'Put user code to initialize the page here
 4:
 5:       Dim Control As UserControl = LoadControl("SearchForm.ascx")
 6:       Dim I As Integer
 7:       For I = 0 To Controls.Count - 1
 8:         If (Controls(I).GetType() Is GetType(HtmlForm)) Then
 9:           CType(Controls(I), HtmlForm).Controls.Add(Control)
10:         End If
11:      Next
12:
13:    End Sub
```

Line 5 demonstrates how to load the user control. Declare a `UserControl` reference and initialize it with a call to `LoadControl`, passing the name of the .ascx file containing the control. Add the control to a container control. (Recall that you can use a `PlaceHolder` or `Panel`, which is easier than finding the `HtmlForm` object.)

Caution

You can rewrite line 5 as `Dim Control As New SearchControl`, although this results in some uninitialized data and an object reference error on line 97 of SearchForm.ascx.vb. This may be a bug in ASP.NET. `LoadControl` seems to work reliably for dynamic user control creation.

Creating a Custom User Control

The fastest way to create a user control is to choose Project, Add Web User Control in Visual Studio .NET. Similar to building user controls for Windows Forms, this approach will provide you with RAD design-time support and coding.

Add code and controls to the UserControl just as you would to a Web Form, and you can use the control by dragging it onto a form or loading it dynamically (see the previous section).

Creating a Web Control Library

Custom, or composite, controls are moderately more difficult to create but offer a different set of advantages than creating user controls. Table 19.2 compares the advantages and costs of creating composite controls in a Web Control Library to those of creating user controls. Consider your objectives before deciding which kind of control to create.

TABLE 19.2   A comparison between composite and user controls

Composite Control	*User Control*
Minimum design-time support	Full, RAD design-time support
Creating by writing code	Creating by dragging and dropping controls and adding code-behind modules or using script
Compiled into a .DLL assembly	Persisted as an .ascx text file with optional code-behind file, .ascx.vb
Good for creating redistributable controls	Good for specific application solutions
Complete design-time control support and can be added to the toolbox	Very little design-time support when using the user control

The best reason to build a composite control in a Web Control Library is that you want to build a redistributable, generic control bundled in a tidy .DLL assembly. If you just need a control that will be reused a couple of times in the same application, a user control is easier to create.

The general steps for creating a Web Control Library follow:

1. Create a Web Control Library Project. This will create a Web Control project with a generic class inheriting from System.Web.UI.WebControl. (The control will have a default text property.)

2. Modify the inheritance statement to inherit from a subclass of WebControl that has the closest behavior to the control you want to create. (To create a brand-new control, inherit from WebControl. To extend an existing WebControl, inherit from the existing control.)

3. Define properties and methods for the control.

4. Override the Render method to define the presentation of the control. (Refer to Listing 19.17 for the module code created by the Web Control Library template.)

LISTING 19.17 Contains the default code generated by the Web Control Library template

```
1:  Imports System.ComponentModel
2:  Imports System.Web.UI
3:
4:  <DefaultProperty("Text"), ToolboxData("<{0}:WebCustomControl1
➡runat=server> _
5:  </{0}:WebCustomControl1>")> Public Class WebCustomControl1
6:      Inherits System.Web.UI.WebControls.WebControl
7:
8:      Dim _text As String
9:
10:     <Bindable(True), Category("Appearance"), DefaultValue("")> _
11:     Property [Text]() As String
12:         Get
13:             Return _text
14:         End Get
15:
16:         Set(ByVal Value As String)
17:             _text = Value
18:         End Set
19:     End Property
20:
21:     Protected Overrides Sub Render( _
22:      ByVal output As System.Web.UI.HtmlTextWriter)
23:         output.Write([Text])
24:     End Sub
25:
26: End Class
```

After 19 chapters, I'm tempted to say you know what all of these elements are and how to use them. In case you skipped ahead to this chapter, I will review this code because it looks a little strange with all of the attribute information.

If you look at lines 5 and 26, you will see that this is just a class. If you look at lines 11 and 19, you will see that Text is just a property.

The `DefaultProperty` attribute comes from the `ComponentModel` namespace and tells the compiler which property is the default property.

Normally the HTML tag for a control is an empty tag. The `ToolboxData` attribute allows you to specify attributes for the designer-generated HTML tag representing the control. The `ToolboxDataAttribute` on line 4 provides a format string for the tag and includes the `runat="server"` attribute, indicating this control is a server control.

The `BindableAttribute` indicates whether a particular property is bindable at design time. The `CategoryAttribute` is used to categorize the property in the Properties window, and `DefaultValueAttribute` enables you to indicate a default value for the property.

In the example, this control is rendered as the value of its text property.

Summary

Chapter 19 has covered some fundamentals of ASP.NET programming. The most important thing to keep in mind is that when you create ASP.NET applications and controls, you are writing VB code; the programming model is the same.

ASP.NET applications can be implemented in any .NET language. Because we are using Visual Basic .NET, all of the CLR is available to us. This means that you can define structures, define classes, and add properties, methods, and events. Some classes in the CLR aren't appropriate for ASP.NET programming and some aren't appropriate for Windows applications, but the syntax is the same and the CLR is the same whether you are creating a Windows or a Web application. (I haven't figured out how to create shaped forms in ASP.NET, though.)

Most of the programming skills you have acquired in the first 18 chapters of this book can be applied to ASP.NET programming. The biggest differences are the notion of rendering controls versus painting them, the stateless behavior of Web applications, and the fact that your application can be run by anyone, anywhere in the world.

19

ASP.NET WEB PROGRAMMING

CHAPTER 20

Writing to the Event Log

IN THIS CHAPTER

A common technique employed before integrated debuggers were popularized was to write application trace information to the console. An evolution of this process was to write application information to a text file. This is a strategy still employed today. Windows NT 4.0, 5.0 (2000), and XP use an event log to track significant system, security, and application information.

Visual Basic .NET supports a general logging strategy based on the Windows 2000 EventLog. An event log is a file with a .evt extension. The three common event logs used in the Event Viewer are Application, System, and Security. (These files can be found on your computer as AppEvent.evt, SecEvent.evt, and SysEvent.evt.)

You can use the EventLog class in the Common Language Runtime from Visual Basic .NET to write significant application information and a custom event log for tracing of debugging messages during development. It's not a recommended practice to write line items to existing logs, like the Application log, but you can employ a custom event log during development and testing. Using EventLog is a superior approach to logging application and debugging information relative to creating a custom solution.

This chapter demonstrates how to use the enhanced capabilities of the EventLog class, and how to use the EventLogTraceListener. The EventLogTraceListener allows you to make the EventLog and a custom log source a recipient of Trace messages.

Caution

Before experimenting with the examples in this chapter, run the Registry Editor (regedit.exe or regedt32.exe) and export a copy of your registry. If you run into any problems, you can use the exported registry to restore your settings.

Managing an Event Source

The EventLog class is a component in the System.Diagnostics namespace. You can add an EventLog object to your application by using an Imports System.Diagnostics statement in your module (or the Imports view of the project's Properties Pages) and instantiating an instance of the EventLog class, or you can pick the EventLog component from the Components tab of the toolbox (see Figure 20.1).

When creating an EventLog object, you will need to register your application as an event source. Registering your application as the source allows you to manage entries using the source name as a key to identifying entries made by your application. By convention, the event source name is the name of your application.

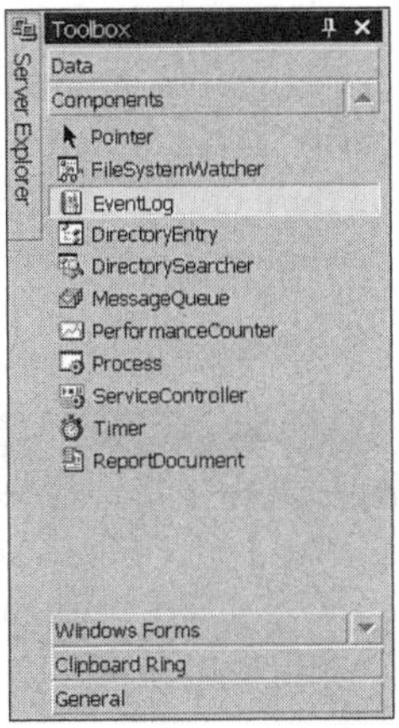

FIGURE 20.1

Selecting the EventLog component from the Components tab of the toolbox.

Creating an Event Source

You only need to create an event source once. If you call `EventLog.CreateEventSource`, your event source—your application's name by convention—is listed in the registry in HKEY_LOCAL_MACHINE\SYSTEM\Services\EventLog as an originator of logged messages.

> **Note**
>
> The significance of registered sources is probably one of hierarchical organization more than anything else. The `EventLog` is organized to key entries by a source name, much as a relational database might use a unique field value to identify rows in a table.
>
> If you try to create a source that already exists, you will get a `System.ArgumentException`. If you try to write to an unregistered source, `WriteEntry` will create the specified source for you.

The following code fragment demonstrates how to create an `EventLog` source and to check for an existing source. Both `CreateEventSource` and `SourceExists` are shared methods, so you don't have to create an instance of `EventLog` to verify that your source is available.

`CreateEventSource` is an overloaded shared method that has two forms:

```
Overloads Public Shared Sub CreateEventSource(source As String, _
  logName As String)
Overloads Public Shared Sub CreateEventSource(source As String, _
  logName As String, machineName As String)
```

The source argument is the name of the originator of the log entries. Your application's name is a suitable value for the source argument. The logName argument can be one of the existing logs ("Application," "System," or "Security") or a custom log name. The second overloaded form of CreateEventSource takes a third argument, a string specifying the machine name. You can log events to a remote computer (see "Using a Remote Event Log"). The "." supplied for the MachineName argument represents the local machine.

> **Tip**
>
> You aren't required to create an event source. If you specify an event source that doesn't exist in the WriteEntry, the source is created automatically. If you don't specify a log name, the entry defaults to the Application log.

The SourceExists method is an overloaded method that has two forms:

```
Overloads Public Shared Function SourceExists(logName As String) As Boolean
Overloads Public Shared Function SourceExists(logName As String, _
  machineName As String) As Boolean
```

The first version checks on the local machine and the second version checks on a remote machine. Calling SourceExists(*logName*, ".") is equivalent to calling the first version of the method. The following code procedure demonstrates checking for an existing source and creating the source if it doesn't exist.

```
Private Const EventSourceName As String = "AAA"
Private Sub CheckEventSource()
  If (Not EventLog.SourceExists(EventSourceName)) Then
    EventLog.CreateEventSource(EventSourceName, "Application")
  End If
End Sub
```

Try running the code and then checking the registry for the source entry, as shown in Figure 20.2.

Deleting an Event Source

Suppose you create an event source for debugging purposes only. Your application has a self-test mode. When the application is in self-test mode, a custom log and an associated event source are defined. When you turn off self-test mode, you elect to clean up the event source. You can use the overloaded shared method DeleteEventSource to clean up event sources you have finished with.

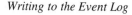

FIGURE 20.2

The AAA application `EventSource` *registry entry.*

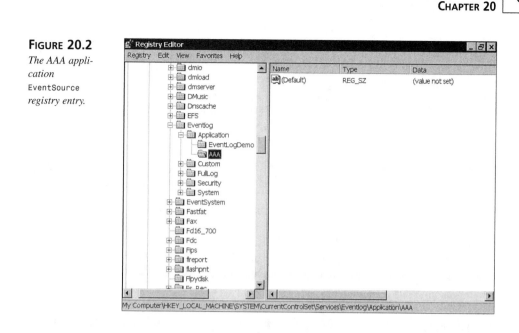

```
Private Sub DeleteEventSource()
  If (SourceExists()) Then
    EventLog.DeleteEventSource(EventSourceName)
  End If
End Sub
```

Note

For our example thus far we have been creating an event source in the "Application" log. Windows 2000 won't create a new .evt event log file. We will only get a new event log file if we specify a custom log name when the event source is created.

The Windows 2000 Registry Editor (regedt32.exe) contains menu options for backing up and restoring your registry.

The preceding procedure performs the symmetric operation to the `CreateEventSource` procedure in the previous subsection. Two versions of `DeleteEventSource` exist to allow you to pass a remote machine name containing the event source.

Retrieving an Array of Event Logs

You can get an array containing all of the event logs on a particular machine by calling the `EventLog.GetEventLogs` shared method. Using a loop or an enumerator, you can

20

WRITING TO THE EVENT LOG

perform operations on each instance of an event log or on an individual log. The following fragment demonstrates getting an array of event logs and iterating over each log.

```
Public Shared Sub IterateLogs()
  Dim Logs() As EventLog = EventLog.GetEventLogs()
  Dim Enumerator As IEnumerator = Logs.GetEnumerator

  While Enumerator.MoveNext

    Debug.WriteLine(CType(Enumerator.Current, _
      EventLog).LogDisplayName)

  End While
End Sub
```

The listing calls the `Event.GetEventLogs` shared method, which returns an array of `EventLog` objects. The `Logs` array is derived from `System.Array` and implements the `IEnumerator` interface, allowing us to iterate through each of the logs in the array using an enumerator. The code displays the user-friendly display name of the log.

Finding the Log Name from the Source Name

If you have the source name but not the log name, you can query the `EventLog` for the log name. The `EventLog.LogNameFromSourceName` shared method will return the log that the `source` argument is writing to. You can use the log name to remove the log. You should avoid deleting the default logs: Application, Security, and System.

`EventLog.LogNameFromSourceName("myApp", ".")` returns the log name that `myApp` is writing to on the local machine.

Deleting a Log

You can manage the system or custom logs. The `Exists` and `Delete` shared methods allow you to determine whether a log exists and delete the log. The following statement demonstrates this:

```
If( EventLog.Exists(logname)) Then
  EventLog.Delete(logname)
End If
```

Caution

Avoid deleting the System, Security, or Application logs. Even if you re-create these logs at a later date, you may not be able to re-create the individual application keys. Without the source keys, applications won't be able to write information to the event log.

In addition to passing the log name, you can indicate a machine name as the second parameter. Be careful when using the EventLog.Delete method; this method will allow you to delete the System, Security, and Application logs. Avoid deleting the default logs because the associated .evt files and the registry keys will be deleted too.

Writing Events to an Existing Log

If you examine the event log, you will notice that it's not crammed full of procedural-level statements indicating everything your application is or isn't doing. The event log does contain significant information about applications that were unable to start, services that failed, perhaps unavailable database connections, and other application, system, or security information that is essential to the proper initialization of your system or an application. This doesn't mean, however, that you cannot use the event log for application line items at a more granular level. What it does suggest is that you shouldn't use the existing Application, System, or Security logs for this purpose.

You will find it beneficial to ship your applications with some logging. When a subsystem is unable to start, perhaps because an Internet connection or database is unavailable, you may want to log that information to the Application log to help users troubleshoot. Logging subsystem failures will point troubleshooters to specific problems and help guide them to a specific resolution.

Generally the hardware or operating system writes entries to the System log. The Security log is read-only. This leaves the Application log or a custom log as the recipient for your application's critical event information. To log application information to the Application log, you need to set a log source, call WriteEntry, and close the log when you are finished.

You only need to create the event source once. You can check to see if the event source exists when your application starts. If it doesn't exist, create it. After the event source exists, you can write entries to the indicated log using shared or instance versions of WriteEntry. When your application shuts down, you can call the Close instance method. If you have used the shared form of EventLog.WriteEntry, you don't have to explicitly call Close.

```
Private Sub Form1_Load(ByVal sender As Object, _
  ByVal e As System.EventArgs) Handles MyBase.Load
  If (Not EventLog.SourceExists("Application")) Then
    EventLog.CreateEventSource("EventLogDemo", "Application")
  End If
End Sub
```

The fragment demonstrates initializing the source and log in the OnLoad event of a form. The main form is a good candidate for creating the source. Adding the WriteEntry statement to the Except block of an exception handler is a reasonable place to write event log entries. The simplest form is the shared WriteEntry(*string*) method. There are five overloaded shared versions of WriteEntry. (Check out the help file for details on each version.) The following statement adds an entry to the "EventLogDemo" source, indicating that the source was created. Several forms of WriteEntry allow you to indicate the event log entry type.

```
EventLog.WriteEntry("EventLogDemo", "Created Source", _

 EventLogEntryType.Information)
```

EventLogEntryType is an enumeration that determines the icon that is displayed with the log entry (see Figure 20.3). Valid entry types are Error, FailureAudit, Information, SuccessAudit, and Warning.

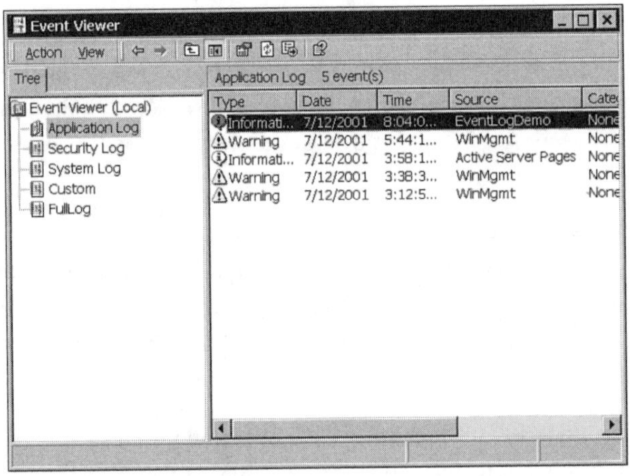

FIGURE 20.3

Windows 2000 Event Viewer.

The EventLog.Close method requires an instance and takes no parameters.

Writing to the event log is a time-consuming process. Microsoft recommends that you only write event information in error-handling blocks to reduce the overhead of writing to the event log.

Writing to a Custom Event Log

The EventLog service is an excellent component to reuse. By reusing the EventLog service, you avoid the work involved in creating a custom process for logging critical events, and you provide your user community with a reliable, consistent, and anticipated location to check for application problems.

A second benefit of the `EventLog` service is that you can choose to create a custom log and use it during the development, testing, and debugging of procedural-level details in your application. For example, you can use it to ensure that you handle the possibility of a full event log (see Figure 20.4).

FIGURE 20.4

Your application should be defined to handle a full event log, as shown.

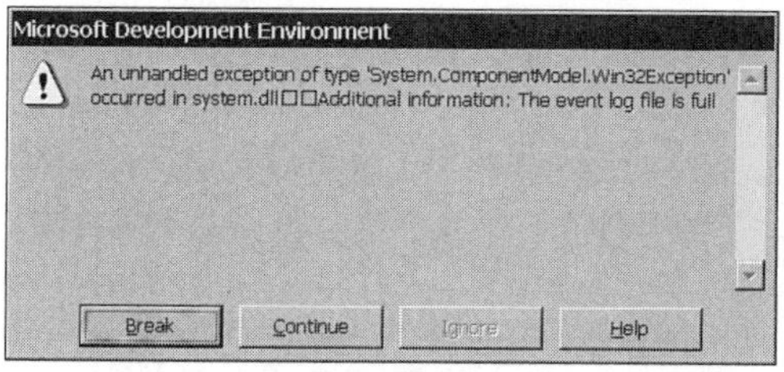

The code for using a custom event log is almost identical to that for using an existing log. When you create the custom log, specify a new log name when you create the event source. `EventLog.CreateEventSource( sourcename, logname )` will create a custom log file, adding a key to the registry and leaf node to the Event Viewer (see Figure 20.5).

FIGURE 20.5

A custom log, FullLog, shown in the Event Viewer.

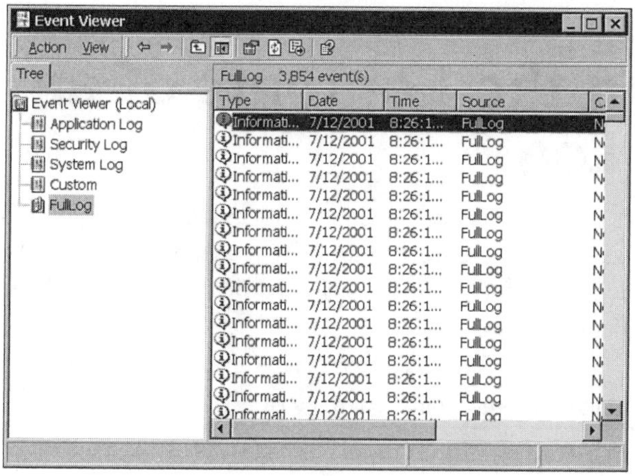

Choosing Action, Properties in the Event Viewer allows you to customize individual event logs. If you change the Log Size property to Overwrite Events as Needed, you will avoid exceptions because of full event logs. However, overwriting entries too frequently may make it hard to sift through the log and determine what caused the system to fail (see Figure 20.6 for a view of the log properties).

20

WRITING TO THE
EVENT LOG

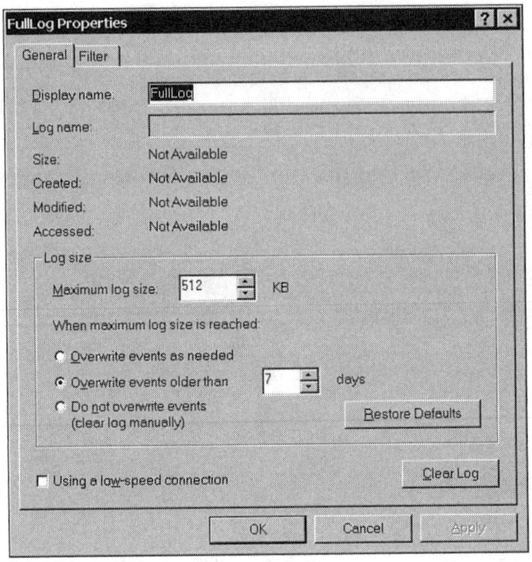

FIGURE 20.6

The FullLog *Properties Page allows you to change the event log's maximum size and control log overwriting.*

Source names may only be used once across all logs. For example, if the source "FullLog" exists in a custom log, you may not create a "FullLog" source in some other log. Check out the EventLogDemo for many examples using the EventLog class and component.

Getting the Contents of an Event Log

Event log entries can be obtained individually for evaluation by your program. The EventLog.Entries property returns an array of EventLogEntry objects. You can iterate through the array to look for specific kinds of entries or just print all entries, as the code in Listing 20.1 demonstrates.

LISTING 20.1 Iterating over EventLogEntry objects

```
1:    Private Sub DisplayEntries(ByVal LogName As String)
2:
3:      If (Not EventLog.Exists(LogName)) Then Exit Sub
4:
5:      TextBox1.Clear()
6:      Dim Log As New EventLog(LogName)
7:      Try
8:
9:        Dim Entry As EventLogEntry
```

LISTING 20.1 continued

```
10:        For Each Entry In Log.Entries
11:            TextBox1.Text = TextBox1.Text & Entry.Message & _
12:                vbCrLf
13:        Next
14:
15:      Finally
16:        Log = Nothing
17:      End Try
18:
19:  End Sub
```

The `Entries` array is an instance property. Line 6 creates an instance of an `EventLog` that refers to a specific log. The `For Each` constructor iterates over each `EventLogEntry` and adds the `EventLogEntry.Message` value to a `TextBox` control. The resource protection block `Try..Finally` sets the `Log` instance to `Nothing`. The `EventLogEntry` type properties are shown in Table 20.1.

TABLE 20.1 `EventLogEntry` Access Properties

Member Name	Description
Category	Returns the text associated with the `CategoryNumber`
CategoryNumber	Returns the category number for this application
Container	Returns the `IContainer` interface
Data	Returns the binary entry data
EntryType	Returns the `EventLogEntryType`
EventID	Returns the event identifier
Index	Returns the index for an entry
MachineName	Returns the name of the machine that generated the entry
Message	Returns the text for the entry
ReplacementStrings	Returns the replacement string-values for an entry
Site	Gets or sets the component site
Source	The source (usually the application) that generated the entry
TimeGenerated	Returns the time the event was generated
TimeWritten	Returns the time the entry was written
UserName	Returns the user originating the event

20

WRITING TO THE EVENT LOG

Clearing an Event Log

You can use the `EventLog.Clear` instance method to clear an event log. You are likely to want to do this when writing a custom event log, where a lot of procedural-level entries might fill up the log. The following fragment demonstrates how to clear a specific log:

```
Dim Log As New EventLog("Application")
Log.Clear()
```

`Log.Clear` requires no parameters because it's an instance method. The `EventLog` instance knows which log it's associated with.

Receiving Event Notifications

You can define an `OnEntryWritten` event handler for an instance of an `EventLog` component. If you add an `EventLog` component from the Component tab of the toolbox, you can double-click the `EventLog` component (shown in the component tray in Figure 20.7) to generate the event. An example of an `OnEntryWritten` event handler is shown next.

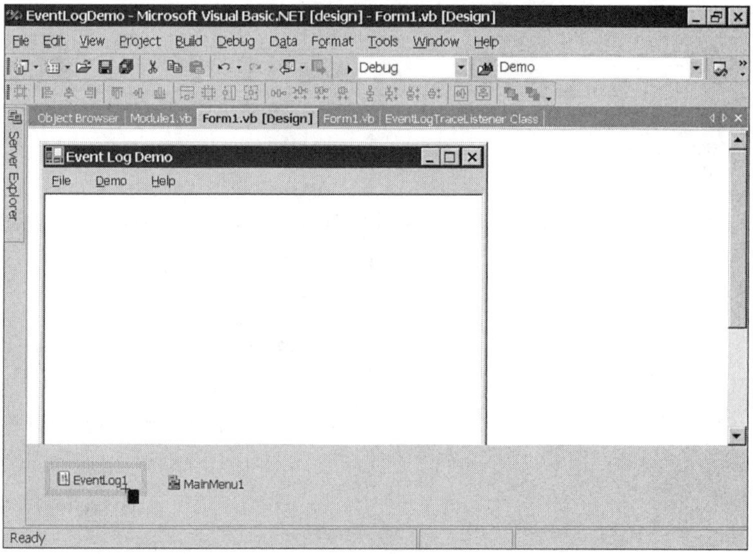

FIGURE 20.7

Nonvisual components like the EventLog *component are managed in the component tray.*

```
Private Sub EventLog1_EntryWritten(ByVal sender As System.Object, _
    ByVal e As System.Diagnostics.EntryWrittenEventArgs) _
    Handles EventLog1.EntryWritten

    MsgBox("Log Written")

End Sub
```

The OnEntryWritten event is an EntryWrittenEventHandler delegate. The first argument is an Object argument, which if invoked by the EventLog, is an EventLog object. The second argument is an EntryWrittenEventArgs object. A significant property of the e parameter is an EventLogEntry, Entry. The Entry property allows you to evaluate entry objects as they are being added.

Unlike many events, the OnEntryWritten event isn't raised automatically. You must set the EnableRaisingEvents property to True before your application will receive entry event notification. EnableRaisingEvents is a dynamic property that can be set from the Dynamic Properties dialog box (see Figure 20.8) or by using an external configuration file.

FIGURE 20.8

Check the EnableRaising Properties *value in the Dynamic Properties dialog box.*

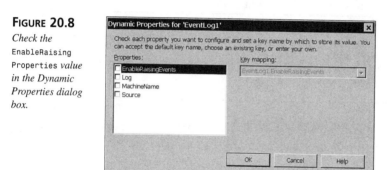

Dynamic configuration files can be used to manage dynamic properties with XML in a .config file. You can use .config files to manage the state of properties without rebuilding your applications. For example, the configuration file can be used to turn entry events on or off externally.

Using a Remote Event Log

The MachineName property defaults to ".", representing the local machine. If you enter a remote machine name, your application can write logs to a remote machine and manage those logs across a network.

Using EventLogTraceListener

Visual Basic .NET (and the CLR) define and implement listener interfaces. *Listeners* are classes that can receive information written using the System.Diagnostics.Trace and System.Diagnostics.Debug objects. Debug and Trace provide advanced debugging capabilities and can broadcast messages to all of the listeners associated with the Trace or Debug objects. For example, if you write Debug.WriteLine, the text passed to WriteLine is sent to all listeners.

The EventLogTraceListener allows you to associate an EventLog with the Trace object. As a result, when you write Trace statements in your application for debugging and testing purposes, those statements will be written to the event log.

Listing 20.2 demonstrates how to associate a specific EventLog object via an EventLogTraceListener with the Trace object.

LISTING 20.2   Associate an instance of an EventLog with the Trace object to automatically log Trace statements to an event log

```
1:  Sub Main()
2:    Dim EventLog As New EventLog("Application", ".", "WriteToEventLog")
3:    Dim Listener As New EventLogTraceListener(EventLog)
4:    Trace.Listeners.Add(Listener)
5:    Trace.WriteLine(Command())
6:  End Sub
```

The EventLogTraceListener is constructed with an instance of an EventLog object. The EventLogTraceListener implements the TraceListener interface and takes the responsibility of writing to the event log (created on line 2). The Trace object knows how to communicate with objects that implement the TraceListener interface. The Trace object will send information passed to methods like WriteLine to all the listeners that have been added to the Trace.Listeners collection. Line 5 demonstrates obtaining command-line arguments using the Command function. When line 5 runs, the text returned by the Command function is written to the Application event log.

Summary

Employing the EventLog component saves you a lot of time that might otherwise be spent implementing a mechanism for logging critical problems in your application, or a tracing utility that can be used during development, testing, and debugging. The more such prebuilt components you can use to support your development efforts, the more time you can spend solving the primary problem.

Writing to the event log was available to us as VB6 developers, but the EventLog and the TraceListener interface make it easier than ever to manage logs and sources on local or remote machines. This chapter demonstrated most of the capabilities of the EventLog component.

VB6 Programming Element Changes in VB .NET

IN THIS APPENDIX

Many elements of Visual Basic 6 have changed in Visual Basic .NET. Individual grammar, declaration, procedure, and user-defined type changes are discussed in context throughout this book; they are consolidated and covered in context in this appendix for reference. If you find yourself needing to know about a specific language change in Visual Basic .NET, you are in the right place.

Discontinued Programming Elements

Table A.1 lists programming elements that are no longer supported or that are supported differently. The first column lists elements from VB6 that have changed in Visual Basic .NET, and the second column helps you find the section in this appendix that covers that changed element.

TABLE A.1 Discontinued Programming Elements

Discontinued Element	Explanatory Section
As Any	Declaration and Grammar Changes
Atn	Replaced Programming Elements
Calendar	Programming Elements Supported Differently
Circle	Replaced Programming Elements
Currency	Changes to Data Types
Date	Programming Elements Supported Differently
Date$	Programming Elements Supported Differently
Debug.Assert	Replaced Programming Elements
Debug.Print	Replaced Programming Elements
DefType	Changes to Data Types
DoEvents	Replaced Programming Elements
Empty	Programming Elements Supported Differently
Eqv	Changes to Operators
GoSub	Changes to Flow Control
Imp	Changes to Operators
Initialize	Changes to Classes and Interfaces
Instancing	Changes to Classes and Interfaces
IsEmpty	Programming Elements Supported Differently
IsMissing	Changes to Procedure Declarations

TABLE A.1 continued

Discontinued Element	Explanatory Section
IsNull	Replaced Programming Elements
IsObject	Replaced Programming Elements
Let	Changes to Properties
Line	Replaced Programming Elements
Lset	Replaced Programming Elements
MsgBox	Replaced Programming Elements
Now	Programming Elements Supported Differently
Null	Programming Elements Supported Differently
On..GoSub	Changes to Flow Control
On..GoTo	Changes to Flow Control
Option Base	Changes to Array Bounds
Option Private Module	Changes to Classes and Interfaces
Property Get	Changes to Properties
Property Let	Changes to Properties
Property Set	Changes to Properties
Pset	Programming Elements Supported Differently
Rnd	Programming Elements Supported Differently
Round	Programming Elements Supported Differently
Rset	Replaced Programming Elements
Scale	Programming Elements Supported Differently
Set	Changes to Properties
Sgn	Programming Elements Supported Differently
Sqr	Programming Elements Supported Differently
String	Programming Elements Supported Differently
Terminate	Changes to Classes and Interfaces
Time	Programming Elements Supported Differently
Time$	Programming Elements Supported Differently
Timer	Programming Elements Supported Differently
Type	Changes to Data Types
Variant	Replace Variant with Object
VarType	Programming Elements Supported Differently
Wend	Replaced Programming Elements

A

PROGRAMMING
ELEMENT CHANGES

Declaration and Grammar Changes

This section describes changes to variable declarations in Visual Basic .NET.

As Any

VB6 supported the As Any clause used for Declare statements. As Any suppresses type checking and allows you to pass any data type to the library procedure, as demonstrated.

```
Private Declare Sub Sleep Lib "kernel32" _
  (ByVal Milliseconds As Any)

Private Sub Command1_Click()

  Call MsgBox("Press [OK] to sleep")
  Dim WaitFor As Long
  WaitFor = 1000
  Call Sleep(WaitFor)
  Call MsgBox("Awake!")
End Sub
```

The first statement declares the API procedure Sleep. The type is declared as an As Any type. The API procedure still requires a valid argument, but if the parameter is invalid, we are not aware of it until we use File, Make or actually run and invoke the procedure. (We could also call Sleep(1000&), using the ampersand to coerce the integer 1000 to a long type.)

As Any is a weak construct anyway. When we are writing code, we want to be notified of errors as early as possible. The sooner we are aware of errors, the earlier we can reconcile them.

In Visual Basic .NET, you must specifically declare the data type of the arguments.

Variable Declaration

Visual Basic 6 supported comma-delimited, multivariable declarations.

```
Dim I, J, K As Integer
```

Unfortunately, the variables I and J are Variant types, which can lead to confusing code like the following:

```
Dim I, J, K As Integer
I = "This is not an integer!"
MsgBox I, vbExclamation
```

The message box displays the text "This is not an integer!" However, if you examine the variable declaration, you might infer that the author intended for I and J to be integers, but in actuality I and J are Variants and the code compiles and runs. Using Variant types results in weaker code that is more likely to behave in an unruly manner.

Visual Basic .NET provides for a more intuitive understanding. In Visual Basic .NET, Dim I, J, K As Integer interprets the intent intuitively and makes I, J, and K all integer types. You can also mix types in a single statement:

```
Dim I As Integer, D As Double
```

And, statements such as Dim O, where no explicit data type is used, are implemented as Object types. The Variant type is not supported. Refer to the section "Replace Variant with Object" at the end of this appendix.

Using Line Numbers

VB6 supported line numbers directly in your code. For example, we could have written the fragment from the last section as

```
1 Dim I, J, K As Integer
2 I = "This is not an integer!"
3 MsgBox I, vbExclamation
```

resulting in some strange-looking code. And, of course, if you change code at line 150 and have a thousand more lines of code after 150, you would have the pleasure of renumbering 850 lines of code. In addition, VB6 did not require that the line numbers be sequential or even unique.

Visual Basic .NET still supports line numbers added directly to your code text, but you must follow the line number with a semicolon.

You do not need internal line numbers for reference. The property page, which you can access by choosing Tools, Options, Text Editor, All Languages, has a Line Numbers check box and will add and maintain line number references for you automatically. If you choose File, Page Setup in Visual Studio .NET and check Line Numbers (see Figure A.1), Visual Studio .NET will print the line numbers for you (see Figure A.2).

Letting the IDE manage line numbers for you is much more convenient in Visual Studio .NET.

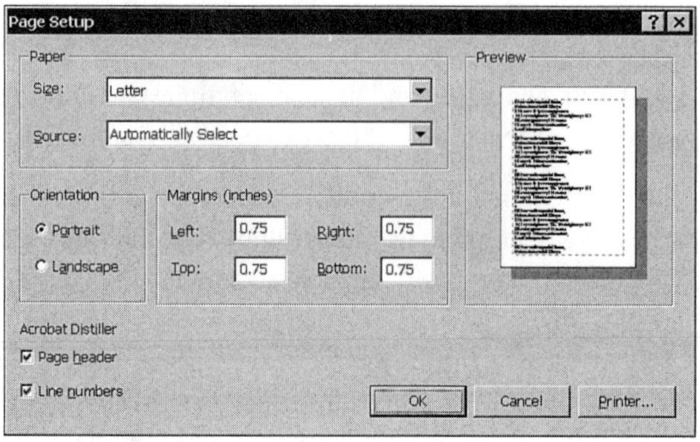

FIGURE A.1

Printing line numbers for code listings in Visual Studio .NET from the Page Setup dialog box.

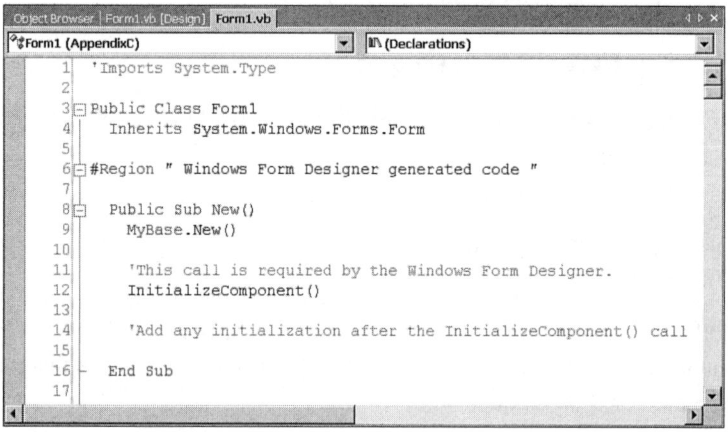

FIGURE A.2

Line numbers maintained automatically and displayed in Visual Studio .NET.

Variable Scope Changes

Block scope has been added to Visual Basic .NET. If you declared a variable in a block like a loop construct in VB6, that variable was also visible in the outer, containing scope. The following code fragment from VB6 demonstrates.

```
Private Sub Command3_Click()
  If True Then
    Dim I As Integer
    I = 5
  End If
  MsgBox I
End Sub
```

The variable I is declared inside the If..Then block terminated by the End If clause. In Visual Basic 6, the preceding code was valid and the message box would display the value of I, which is 5.

Visual Basic .NET supports block level scope. This means that the variable I in the example fragment is not visible outside the If Then..End If block. The code fragment would incur an error, "The name 'I' is not declared," in Visual Basic .NET on the line containing MsgBox I.

Changes to Procedure Declarations

Many procedures are no longer supported in Visual Basic .NET. The fact that Visual Basic .NET is strongly typed makes the procedures or the constructs irrelevant; thus irrelevant procedures were removed or retasked in Visual Basic .NET.

IsMissing Is Missing

The IsMissing function checks for Optional Variant parameters that may not have a value. VB6 allowed Optional arguments to be declared without a default value.

> **Tip**
>
> Many of the constructs that have changed or been removed are demonstrated in the VB6 sample code, Grammar.vbp, on this book's Web site at www. samspublishing.com.

```
Private Sub HasOptional(Optional ByVal Value As Variant)
  MsgBox IsMissing(Value)
End Sub
```

If the caller invokes the HasOptional procedure without a value, the missing flag in the Variant type is set to True; in VB6 the IsMissing function could be used to test for an uninitialized Variant parameter. (IsMissing does not work on native data types.)

IsMissing is counterintuitive to the purpose of Optional parameters. An Optional parameter is defined when there is a value that supports the general case of the procedure. In such a general case, there is a default value that makes sense. If there is no default value, do not use an Optional parameter. Visual Basic .NET requires that all Optional parameters have a default value. The default value is appended as a suffix to the end of the parameter, as in: Private Sub HasOptional(Optional ByVal MyParam As Boolean = True). IsMissing is not supported in Visual Basic .NET.

Providing a default value tells consumers what the general case is and allows you to get rid of code checking to see if there is a valid value for the parameters. Parameters should always have a valid value. A good technique is to use the `Debug.Assert` method to ensure that every consumer passes a valid value for each parameter.

Procedure Invocation

Use parentheses in Visual Basic .NET. If you type a procedure with an empty parameters list in Visual Basic .NET, the IDE will insert the empty parameter list represented by empty parentheses for you. You can precede procedure calls with the `Call` keyword, but it is no longer required. An empty procedure call looks like the following:

```
MyProcedure()
```

The `Return` statement has been retasked and has a new meaning. Read the next subsection for revisions to the use of the `Return` keyword.

Using Return

The `Return` keyword was used to return from a `GoSub` branch statement. `GoSub` is not supported in Visual Basic .NET. (See the section on "Changes to Flow" control for more on `GoSub`.) The `Return` keyword has been retasked; Visual Basic .NET uses `Return` to immediately return from a subroutine or function.

When used with a subroutine, `Return` requires no modifiers. By default, when execution reaches the `End Sub` line, the code returns to the calling procedure. You can, however, use `Return` to exit from a subroutine. When used in this manner, `Return` behaves exactly like the `Exit Sub` statement, branching immediately out of the current procedure.

When used with a function, the `Return` statement must return a value of the type specific in the `As` *datatype* clause in the function statement:

```
Function CalledFunction() As Integer
   CalledFunction = 43
End Function

Function CalledFunction() As Integer
   Return 43
End Function
```

The fragment shows the older and newer styles of returning a value from a function. Visual Basic .NET still supports assigning the return value from a function to the function name, but the `Return` statement is the preferred method and the older style of returning values from functions is likely to disappear in future versions of Visual Basic.

Passing Properties by Reference

If you pass a `Property` by reference (using the `ByRef` modifier), VB6 does not reflect the modified property value when the procedure returns. In essence the `ByRef Property` behaves like a value argument.

```
Private Sub ByRefProperty(ByRef AHeight As Integer)
  AHeight = 10
End Sub

Private Sub Command5_Click()
  Call ByRefProperty(Me.Height)
End Sub
```

A reader might presume that the height of the object represented by `Me` (a form in the example) is modified and has a new value of 10 when the procedure `ByRefProperty` returns. In VB6 the code had no effect on the height of the form. In Visual Basic .NET the equivalent code is actually modifying the height property of the form. Here is the equivalent code in Visual Basic .NET:

```
Private Sub ByRefProperty(ByRef AHeight As Integer)
  AHeight = 10
End Sub

Private Sub Form1_Load(ByVal sender As System.Object, _
  ByVal e As System.EventArgs) Handles MyBase.Load

  ByRefProperty(Me.Height)
End Sub
```

After the equivalent Visual Basic .NET code runs, the object represented by `Me` has been resized to a `Height` of 10 `twips`. Be careful when you are passing properties; if you want the change to a property reflected back to the consumer, pass the property `ByRef`. If you want the property changes to be local to the called procedure, define the parameter as a `ByVal` parameter.

Argument Modifiers Default to `ByVal`

Visual Basic 6 defaults argument modifiers to `ByRef`. Visual Basic .NET defaults to `ByVal`. If you do not explicitly type a modifier for an argument, the IDE will add `ByVal` for you.

It is a good practice to always explicitly indicate your intent; this rule applies to argument modifiers, too.

ParamArray Arguments Are Always Passed ByVal

Arguments defined using the ParamArray modifier are always passed ByVal in Visual Basic .NET. Additionally, all of the arguments stored in the parameter array must be of the type declared in the As clause of the parameter array declaration.

VB6 allowed you to declare Variant type parameter arrays. You cannot use the modifiers ByVal, ByRef, or Optional with ParamArray arguments. In VB6, ParamArray arguments were always implicitly optional and passed ByRef. The following code demonstrates the ParamArray in VB6 and why the behavior is risky.

```
Private Sub HasParamArray(ParamArray Data() As Variant)
  Dim I As Integer
  For I = LBound(Data) To UBound(Data)
3    Debug.Print Data(I)
    Data(I) = "Changed"
  Next I
End Sub

Private Sub Command6_Click()
  Dim A, B, C As Variant
  A = 1
  B = "B"
  C = Now
  Call HasParamArray(A, B, C)
  Call HasParamArray(A, B, C)
End Sub
```

In the fragment, HasParamArray is called with three different kinds of arguments: an integer, a string, and a date and time value, a double. HasParamArray displays each value in the parameter array data and then modifies the element. When HasParamArray is called a second time, each value of the array is "Changed". Code like the preceding is difficult to debug and maintain because you would probably have to write a lot of error-handling and runtime type-checking code to determine what to do with the elements of the ParamArray. In Visual Basic .NET, the elements of the ParamArray are immutable from the caller's perspective, and every element is the same data type.

Using the Static Modifier

Static variables maintain their value between successive calls to the procedure. Visual Basic 6 allows you to add the Static modifier in the procedure definition, for example, Private Static Sub ProcName(). When used in this manner, the Static modifier caused every local variable in the procedure to be static.

```
Private Static Sub HasStatic()
  Dim I As Integer
```

```
   I = I + 1
   Dim S As String
   S = S & I
   Debug.Print I & " " & S
End Sub
```

Each successive call to `HasStatic` increments `I` and concatenates the value of `I` to the string `S`. After the first call, the Immediate Window contains 1 1; the output to the Immediate Window progresses to 2 12, 3 123, 4 1234, 5 12345, and so on.

Visual Basic .NET does not support the `Static` modifier in the procedure heading that begins a subroutine or function block. Visual Basic .NET does support static local variables, but you must use the `Static` keyword explicitly for every local variable you want to be static. Identical code in Visual Basic .NET would look like the following procedure.

```
Private Sub HasStatic()
   Static I As Integer
   I += 1
   Static S As String
   S &= I
   Debug.WriteLine(String.Format("{0} {1}", I, S))
End Sub
```

In the revised listing for Visual Basic .NET, both `I` and `S` are defined as `Static` variables. The local variable `I` is incremented with the new increment operator (+=), and `I` is appended to the string `S` using the concatenate operator (&=). `Debug.WriteLine` displays the result in the Output window using the class method `String.Format` to format the output.

Changes to Properties

Properties have been modified in Visual Basic .NET to use a unified approach to ensure that modifiers to property methods are applied uniformly to the getter and setter methods. Whereas VB6 implemented the property getter and setter as two separate property methods, Visual Basic .NET groups properties into a single block with the getter and setter as nested elements.

Unified Property Statement in Visual Basic .NET

The basic, unified property statement in Visual Basic .NET has an outer property block and an inner `Get` and `Set` block.

```
Private Property Dummy() As Integer
   Get
```

```
    End Get
    Set(ByVal Value As Integer)

    End Set
End Property
```

The As clause in the property header defines the property's data type. Dummy is an Integer property. Treat the Get and End Get block as the property getter; it returns the underlying field value. Treat the Set block as the property setter; it sets the underlying field value. The argument passed to a property when the property is used as an l-value is the parameter Value. (Notice that you do not have to indicate the set parameter between the parentheses in the property header, represented by the empty parentheses.)

Property Let Is Not Supported

You do not need to distinguish between value type and reference type assignment in Visual Basic .NET. The result is that all assignments are accomplished with the assignment operator (=) and Set is never required. Set only appears in a property setter block in Visual Basic .NET.

Because there is no distinction between reference type and value type assignment, the Let keyword is no longer needed and is not supported in Visual Basic .NET.

Default Properties Cannot Be Shared or Private

Visual Basic .NET requires that Default properties must not be Shared or Private members.

Default Properties Must Take Arguments

Any property could be a Default property in VB6. Because the Set keyword was used for object assignment in VB6, VB6 could distinguish between default property usage and object assignment by the presence or absence of the keyword Set.

Because Set is not supported in an assignment operation, Visual Basic .NET requires an alternate queue indicating when the user wants to use a default property and when they mean object assignment. The new visual queue is the use of parentheses and a parameter, in conjunction with the property name. Listing A.1 demonstrates an example of a default property. (Refer to Figure A.3, illustrating how IntelliSense technology helps you use the default property.)

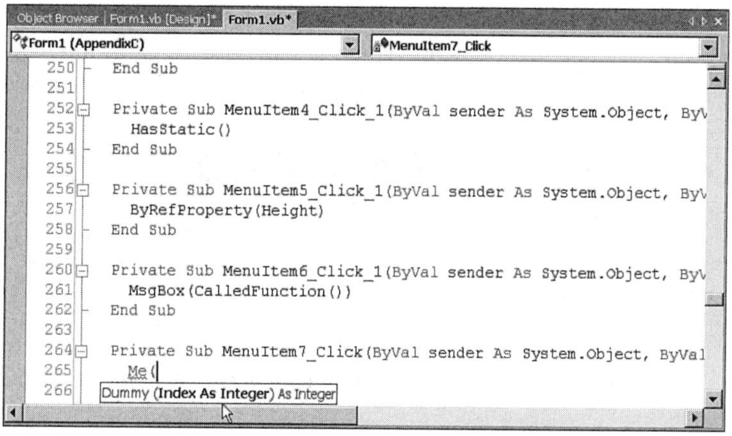

FIGURE A.3

When we add parentheses after the reference to self, Me, IntelliSense displays the default property syntax example as shown.

LISTING A.1   A basic, parameterized default property

```
1: Default Public Property Dummy(ByVal Index As Integer) As Integer
2:    Get
3:       MsgBox(Index)
4:    End Get
5:    Set(ByVal Value As Integer)
6:       MsgBox(Index)
7:    End Set
8: End Property
```

`Default` properties must be parameterized. Generally the parameter plays the role of index to some underlying collection. In the property header the parameter is represented by the `Index` argument, and the keyword `Default` indicates that `Dummy` is the default property. The `Dummy` property is invoked in the following manner: *Object(index)* = *IntegerValue* or *IntegerValue* = *Object(index)*. The first example uses `Dummy` as an l-value, invoking the property setter, and the second example uses the `Dummy` as an r-value, invoking the property getter. (Refer to the section on "Using Default Properties," in Chapter 7, "Creating Classes," for an extensive discussion of the default property idiom.)

Property Arguments Cannot Be Passed `ByRef`

Visual Basic .NET allows properties to be passed to methods `ByRef`, enabling a property to be changed within the called procedure (refer to "Passing Properties by Reference" earlier in this appendix).

Allowing arguments to properties to be passed `ByRef` would allow the property methods to change the argument, resulting in quirky behavior. Property arguments are immutable from the view of the caller.

Changes to Array Bounds

Array bounds have gone through several revisions in Visual Basic .NET. Several books based on Beta versions of Visual Basic .NET covered this topic incorrectly because array implementation evolved in response to outcry from some developers who apparently had Microsoft's ear.

By Beta 2 build 9254, the array behavior had reached its final form, but the Visual Basic .NET help still reported incorrect information as indicated by the following quote from the help topic "Array Bound Changes in Visual Basic":

> *The number you specify for each dimension in the declaration is the initial element count. The upper bound is equal to that count minus one.*

`Option Base` is not supported in Visual Basic .NET. The array bounds are from 0 to n, meaning that every array has $n + 1$ elements. The best way to write code that is independent of such revisions is to use methods that dynamically return the upper and lower bounds of arrays:

```
Dim A(10) As Integer
Dim I As Integer
For I = A.GetLowerBound(0) To A.GetUpperBound(0)
  ' some code
Next I
```

`GetLowerBound` and `GetUpperBound` are methods of `System.Array`. The argument to these two methods indicates the dimension of the array whose bound you want to know. A one-dimensional array is referenced by dimension 0. (Refer to the section "Using Arrays" in Chapter 3, "Basic Programming in VB.NET," for more on `System.Array` in Visual Basic .NET.)

Array Size Can Change but the Number of Dimensions Is Fixed

You can not initially declare an array with the `ReDim` statement in Visual Basic .NET. All arrays are dynamic in Visual Basic .NET and must initially be declared with a `Dim` statement in Visual Basic .NET. And, although you size the number of elements, the number of dimensions is fixed in Visual Basic .NET. This is a departure from the way arrays were declared and behaved in VB6. The following statements demonstrate some basic array declarations.

```
Dim a(10) As Integer
Dim a() As Integer = New Integer(10){}
Dim a() As Integer = {0,1,2,3,4,5,6,7,8,9,10}
```

The first statement declares an array containing 11 elements, indexable from 0 to 10. The array is uninitialized. The second statement uses the long form of array declaration, initializing an array capable of containing 11 integers. The final statement uses the array initializer syntax and creates an array containing 11 elements indexed from 0 to 10, containing the values 0 to 10.

Changes to Data Types

Several changes to data types and user-defined types have evolved in Visual Basic .NET. Those changes are described in this section.

Currency Data Type

The `Currency` type has been replaced by the `Decimal` type. Changes to value types are described in the section on "Data Types" in Chapter 2, "Out with the Old, In with the New."

Def*Type* Is Not Supported

Visual Basic 6 allowed you to add a Def*Type* statement at the module level. For example, `DefBool B` indicates that all variables that are introduced without a variable type and begin with the letter *B* default to a Boolean data type.

VB6 supported `DefBool`, `DefByte`, `DefCur`, `DefDate`, `DefDbl`, `DefDec`, `DefInt`, `DefLng`, `DefObj`, `DefSng`, `DefStr`, and `DefVar`, followed by a range of letters; all non-type-specified variables beginning with one of the letters in the range defaulted to the Def*Type* type. Visual Basic .NET does not support Def*Type*.

User-Defined `Type` Construct Is Replaced with `Structure`

The user-defined `Type` block has been replaced with a more powerful `Structure` block. Chapters 3 and 5, "Subroutines, Functions, and Structures," explain using the new `Structure` construct. `Type` is not supported in Visual Basic .NET.

Fixed-Length Strings Are Not Supported in Visual Basic .NET

Visual Basic 6 allowed you to define a fixed-length string. By following the `String` data type with the asterisk and a number, you could indicate a fixed-length string in VB6.

```
Dim S As String * 10
```

> **Note**
>
> The MSDN help for .NET suggests that appending the string identifier ($) to any identifier forces it to the string data type.
>
> I found no instance in which the $ type identifier was necessary to perform the conversion, and in fact, in all instances tested, appending $ to an identifier resulted in an error. The reason for this is probably that all types inherit from `Object`, which implements a `ToString` method. In most cases this method is probably called implicitly in situations where nonstring types are used when a string is expected.
>
> ```
> Dim S As String = 3.1459
> ```
>
> The preceding statement implicitly constructs a `Double` from 3.1459 and invokes the `Double.ToString()` method. (Although this cannot be verified because Microsoft hasn't released the source code for the CLR, it is a reasonable inference from the behavior of the code.)
>
> Try the following statement to verify the implicitly `ValueType` creation for the literal 3.1459.
>
> ```
> MsgBox((3.1459).GetType.Name())
> ```
>
> Although the statement looks strange, it does display the word `Double` in the message box.

The fixed-length string is not supported in Visual Basic .NET. All strings in Visual Basic .NET are variable length. The length of the string is updated when you assign a string to the reference. Strings in Visual Basic .NET can be up to approximately two billion Unicode characters in length.

Changes to Integer Types

Integer types have been modified as we converge on 64-bit processors. You have a wider array of integral types to choose from in Visual Basic .NET (refer to Table A.2), but

32-bit systems process 32-bit integers better than 16-bit or 64-bit integers. Table A.2 describes the revisions made to integral data types in .NET.

TABLE A.2 Revisions to Integer Data Types

Size	VB6 Type	Visual Basic .NET Type	CLR Type
8 bits	(none)	(none)	System.SByte
16 bits	Integer	Short	System.Int16
32 bits	Long	Integer	System.Int32
64 bits	(none)	Long	System.Int64

The first column indicates the number of bits used to store values for each type. The number of bits used as an exponent of 2 indicates the number of possible values. For example, a 32-bit integer is 2^{32} or 4,294,967,296, which means that integers can store approximately 4 billion possible values. Integers are signed in Visual Basic .NET, so an integer can store values up to about plus or minus 2 billion.

From Table A.2, you can see that 8-bit types are not supported in VB directly but are supported in the CLR. The optimal integral type to use for 32-bit systems is the Integer type, which should be the type you use for integral values unless you have very specific needs. (Refer to Chapter 2 for specific information on the capacity of specific data types in Visual Basic .NET.)

Changes to Operators

Operators have undergone some changes in Visual Basic .NET, too. This section describes some changes to existing operators and the introduction of a few new operators in Visual Basic .NET.

Equivalence and Implication Operators

The equivalence operator Eqv and the implication operator Imp are not supported in Visual Basic .NET. Where you would have used Eqv operations in VB6, replace the Eqv operator with the equals operator =. Where implication operations made sense in VB6, substitute Imp operations with Not and Or combined.

Implication is equivalent to (Not A) Or B. That is, negate proposition A and Or the result with proposition B.

And, Or, Xor, and Not

Early Beta builds of Visual Basic .NET had removed the bitwise behavior of `And`, `Or`, `Xor`, and `Not` in Visual Basic .NET. You may have heard that bitwise behavior in `And`, `Or`, `Xor`, and `Not` had been removed, leaving only logical operator behavior. By Beta 2, build 9254, Microsoft had restored bitwise behavior in `And`, `Or`, `Xor`, and `Not` and removed the planned operators `BitAnd`, `BitOr`, `BitXor`, and `BitNot`.

According to Microsoft's Ari Bixhorn, VB6 bitwise and logical operations were restored to `And`, `Or`, `Xor`, and `Not` and will be there when you get your copy of Visual Studio .NET. This means that the four operators will perform bitwise operations on integral types and logical (or Boolean) operations on logical predicates.

As a reminder, Boolean operations evaluate predicates to determine whether a proposition is True or False. Bitwise operations evaluate the individual bits of each operand. `True Or False` is an example of Boolean evaluation, and `1 And 2` is an example of a bitwise operation.

Short-Circuit Evaluations

Another planned change was rolled back as of Beta 2. Microsoft had planned to short-circuit Boolean evaluations, resulting in more efficient code. However, because of some influential customers, short-circuiting was rolled back and two new operators were added: `AndAlso` and `OrElse`.

A short-circuited evaluation is one that stops evaluating as soon as the result of the proposition can be determined. For example, `False And anything` yields False regardless of the value of the second predicate. Short-circuiting can safely yield False without evaluating the second predicate.

Some programmers write evaluations that have side effects. A side effect usually happens as a result of one or more predicates being the result of a function that performs some action too. If the Boolean operation short-circuits, the side effect may not occur, breaking code that uses side effects. Refer to the example in the section "Boolean Evaluations Are Not Short-Circuited" in Chapter 2 for a discussion of the impact short-circuited evaluations can have on the behavior of code.

If you want to write `And` or `Or` operations that do short-circuit, and produce more efficient code, use `AndAlso` where you would use `And` and `OrElse` where you would use `Or`. `AndAlso` and `OrElse` were introduced when short-circuiting was removed from logical evaluations.

Changes to Flow Control

Several flow control statements were removed in Visual Basic .NET. I didn't think any-one was still using these statements, but apparently at least one developer was disap-pointed, perhaps even upset, that GoSub is no longer supported in Visual Basic .NET.

The fact is that GoSubs result in spaghetti code and should not be used anyway. (The last time I wrote one was in GW-BASIC.) Several flow control features have been revised from VB6 to Visual Basic .NET.

Replace GoSub with Function Call

The GoSub is no longer supported. Where you employed a GoSub in your VB6 code, Visual Basic .NET requires that you replace the GoSub with a function call. The following Command button event handler demonstrates a GoSub in VB6.

```
Private Sub Command1_Click()
  GoSub RetroCode
  MsgBox "I'm dizzy!"
  Exit Sub
RetroCode:
  Return
End Sub
```

When I opened the VB6 project GoSubDemo.vbp in Visual Basic .NET, the migration wizard kicked in and modified the code. The first thing I looked at was the Upgrade Report (shown in Figure A.4). The report clearly indicates that GoSub is no longer sup-ported and the Return keyword has been reassigned. (The report and the upgraded GoSubDemo project are contained on this book's Web site.)

FIGURE A.4

The migration wizard will modify code and create an upgrade report helping you resolve unsup-ported problems like anachronistic GoSub statements.

Object Browser | Form1.vb [Design] | Form1.vb | **Browse - GoSubD...p Upgrade Report**

Upgrade Report for GoSubDemo.vbp

Time of Upgrade: 7/18/2001 1:09 PM

List of Project Files

New Filename	Original Filename	File Type	Status	Errors	Warnings	Total Issues
⊟ (Global Issues)				0	0	0
Global update issues:						
None						
⊟ Form1.vb	Form1.frm	Form	Upgraded with issues	1	1	2
Upgrade Issues for Form1.frm:						

# Severity	Location	Object Type	Object Name	Property	Description
1 Compile Error	Command1_Click				GoSub statement is not supported.
2 Runtime Warning	Command1_Click				Return has a new behavior.

The migration wizard was unable to resolve the code; a comment suggesting a resolution and resource material was provided instead.

```
Private Sub Command1_Click(ByVal eventSender As System.Object, _
    ByVal eventArgs As System.EventArgs) Handles Command1.Click

    'UPGRADE_ISSUE: GoSub statement is not supported.
    'Click for more: ms-help://MS.MSDNVS/vbcon/html/vbup1014.htm
    GoSub RetroCode

    MsgBox("I'm dizzy!")

    Exit Sub

RetroCode:
    'UPGRADE_WARNING: Return has a new behavior.
    'Click for more: ms-help://MS.MSDNVS/vbcon/html/vbup1041.htm
    Return
End Sub
```

As you can quickly determine, the migrated code is almost identical to the VB6 code but will not compile. In the migrated code you will have to manually resolve the `GoSub` problem. If your procedures are short, manually resolving these kinds of problems will not be too difficult. To fix the problem, we need to replace the `GoSub` subroutine with a function or subroutine. In this case a subroutine is fine for our do-nothing block:

```
Private Sub Command1_Click(ByVal eventSender As System.Object, _
    ByVal eventArgs As System.EventArgs) Handles Command1.Click

    RetroCode()
    MsgBox("I'm dizzy!")

End Sub

Private Sub RetroCode()

End Sub
```

A good place to start if you are having trouble unraveling code is Martin Fowler's book *Refactoring: Improving the Design of Existing Code*.

On..GoSub and On..Goto Are Not Supported

The computed `On..GoSub` and `On..GoTo` are not supported in Visual Basic .NET. You can replace these constructs with `Select Case` statements in Visual Basic .NET. The following examples demonstrate an `On..GoSub` statement (Listing A.2) followed by a Visual Basic .NET revision (Listing A.3) that uses the `Select Case` instead.

LISTING A.2   A computed On..GoSub

```
Private Sub Form_Click()
  Dim Value As Integer
  Value = 1
  On Value GoSub RetroCode
  MsgBox "I'm dizzy again!"
  Exit Sub
RetroCode:
  MsgBox "Retro": Return
End Sub
```

LISTING A.3   Replacing computed On..GoSub and On..Goto statements with a Select Case statement in Visual Basic .NET

```
Private Sub Form1_Click(ByVal sender As Object, _
  ByVal e As System.EventArgs) Handles MyBase.Click

  Dim Value As Integer = 1
  Select Case Value
    Case 1 : MsgBox("Retro")
  End Select

  MsgBox("I'm dizzy again!")
End Sub
```

The Select Case statement clause performs the evaluation and branches to the Case block containing the suitable matching value.

Changes to Classes and Interfaces

VB6 used the Initialize and Terminate methods that are implemented as Class_Initialize and Class_Terminate in VB6. The VB6 Initialize method has been replaced with the constructor Sub New in Visual Basic .NET.

Object destruction is indeterminate in Visual Basic .NET. Objects are destroyed whenever the Garbage Collector (GC) gets around to it. By convention you can implement a Public Dispose subroutine that releases limited resources, like file handles and record sets, and you can overload a Protected Finalize destructor. Just keep in mind that object destruction does not necessarily happen immediately. (Read Chapter 7 for more information on constructors and destructors.)

Parameterized Constructors

Visual Basic .NET supports parameterless and parameterized constructors. When you needed initial values for objects in VB6, you might have implemented an `Initialize` subroutine. Visual Basic .NET supports parameterized constructors, which means you can pass initial values when you create objects.

```
Dim TextFile As _
  New System.IO.FileStream("c:\temp\test.txt", IO.FileMode.Create)
```

The statement demonstrates constructing a `FileStream` object in the `System.IO` namespace. The constructor parameters are the filename and mode. (Refer to Chapter 7 for more on constructors and parameterized constructors.)

Option Private Module Is Not Supported

Visual Basic 6 supported the `Option Private Module` statement, which makes all of the members in a module private. Use the access modifier `Private` on every member in the module to create the same result in Visual Basic .NET. `Option Private Module` is not supported in Visual Basic .NET.

Changes to Interfaces

Every VB6 class is a COM class. When you define a class in VB6, all you have to do to implement the public methods in the class is to add a statement `Implements` *classname* in a second module. The result is that the second module becomes an implementation of the first module. The first module is the interface, and the second module is the implementation.

When you add the `Implements` statement to a module, you can select the interface name from the `Objects` list in the code view and select each of the public interface methods from the procedures list. VB6 generates the interface method automatically.

> **Tip**
>
> You can select an interface from the Class Name list and the interface method from the Method Name list (in the code editor), and Visual Basic .NET will generate the interface method body automatically, too.

Visual Basic .NET requires that you add the `Implements` statement to the class definition, and an `Implements` clause is added as a suffix to the end of the procedure header.

(Chapter 7 discusses the grammar for implementing interfaces in Visual Basic .NET.) Listing A.4, excerpted from Chapter 7, demonstrates an example of an implementation of the IDisposable.Dispose interface.

LISTING A.4   An excerpt from Chapter 7, demonstrating how to implement interface methods in Visual Basic .NET

```
Public Sub Dispose() Implements IDisposable.Dispose
  If (FDisposed) Then Exit Sub
  FDisposed = True
  Close()
  FArrayList = Nothing
End Sub
```

The subroutine is a member of a class that implements IDisposable. VB6 (as shown in Listing A.5) would generate a private subroutine prefixed with the interface name.

LISTING A.5   VB6 generated a private method with the interface name prefixed to the procedure name

```
Private Sub IDisposable_Dispose()
  If (FDisposed) Then Exit Sub
  FDisposed = True
  Close()
  FArrayList = Nothing
End Sub
```

The biggest difference between the VB6 and Visual Basic .NET interface methods is the syntax for indicating that a method or property implements an interface.

Replaced Programming Elements

Several programming elements have been moved, refined, or removed in Visual Basic .NET. This section covers in alphabetical order general programming elements that have changed in some minor way.

Arctangent (Atn)

The arctangent function Atn has been relocated to the System.Math namespace and is called ATan in Visual Basic .NET.

Circle

The Circle statement from VB6 has been refined in the DrawEllipse method defined in the System.Drawing.Graphics namespace.

Debug Printing and Asserting

The debug tools Debug.Assert and Debug.Print have been moved and revised in Visual Basic .NET. Debugging tools exist in the System.Diagnostics namespace and have increased in number and power. Basic asserting and printing are supported in the System.Diagnostics namespace as Debug.Assert and Debug.WriteLine.

DoEvents

If your VB6 application performed many processor-intensive instructions in a loop, you might have called DoEvents after each pass of the loop to ensure that other processes did not become CPU-starved.

DoEvents plays the same role in Visual Basic .NET and has been moved to the System.Windows.Forms.Application namespace.

IsNull

IsNull was used in VB6 to determine whether a variant type contains a value initialized to Null. Comparisons directly to Null evaluate to False. For example, you might think that If(Val = Null) Or If(Val <> Null) is True, either Val is Null or it is not. VB6 evaluates the preceding Or condition and returns Null.

IsNull from VB6 has been removed, and IsDBNull has been added to Visual Basic .NET. IsDBNull evaluates an Object and determines whether the object contains missing or nonexistent data; that is, if the object evaluates to DBNull. Just like IsNull, direct comparisons to DBNull yield DBNull rather than True or False.

As the name IsDBNull suggests, IsDBNull can be used with null data fields and can be written in expressions in the same way you would have used IsNull in VB6.

IsObject

IsObject from VB6 has been replaced with IsReference in Visual Basic .NET. IsReference returns True if an expression returns an object reference with instance assigned to it.

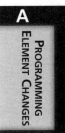

Line

The Line statement from VB6 has been replaced with the Graphics.DrawLine method in the System.Drawing namespace.

```
CreateGraphics.DrawLine(Pens.Salmon, 0, 0, Width, Height)
```

You can get a Graphics object by calling CreateGraphics. With the Graphics object you can call one of four overloaded DrawLine methods. (The example uses a salmon-colored pen from the Pens collection and draws a diagonal line from the top left to the bottom right of the containing control.) Refer to Chapter 17, "Programming with GDI+," for more on custom drawing and painting in Visual Basic .NET.

LSet and RSet

LSet and RSet from VB6 have been replaced with PadLeft and PadRight, instance methods of the String class. Each method has two versions: one version pads the string with spaces and the second allows you to specify the padding character.

PadLeft inserts padding on the left side of the string and PadRight inserts padding on the right side of the string. Debug.WriteLine("Welcome to Valhalla Tower Material Defender".PadLeft(100)) invokes the PadLeft method of the String object represented by the literal string and inserts the string into a space 100 characters wide. All of the padding occurs to the left of the literal string; the length of the padding is the total width minus the string length.

MsgBox

The MsgBox behavior from VB6 has been supported by the MessageBox.Show method in the System.Windows.Forms namespace. MsgBox is supported by the Microsoft.VisualBasic compatibility namespace.

Tip

The Microsoft.VisualBasic.Interaction namespace contains interactive functions like MsgBox, InputBox, and IIf, carried over from VB6. They are carried over from VB6 but are not part of the CLR and probably will disappear over time.

The Microsoft.VisualBasic namespace is automatically included in Windows form-based applications, and you will see MsgBox (and some examples of MessageBox.Show) used extensively in the demo listings in this book.

Wend

The abbreviated `Wend` from VB6 has been replaced with the more symmetric `End While` to terminate a `While` loop block in Visual Basic .NET.

Programming Elements Supported Differently

Several programming elements are supported differently in Visual Basic .NET than they were in VB6. This section highlights existing functions and what-nots that are still supported, but some fundamental aspect of their behavior or value has been modified for .NET.

Calendar

The `Calendar` class is an abstract class defined in the `System.Globalization` namespace. There are several subclasses derived from `Calendar`, supporting current and historic calendars like the Gregorian calendar.

The `Calendar` class contains methods for managing time, including adding increments of time, cultural information, and functions like `IsLeapYear`. The following example creates an example of a `JulianCalendar`, used in the West and in Western Europe, and asks whether 1966 is a leap year.

```
Dim Calendar As New System.Globalization.JulianCalendar()
MessageBox.Show(Calendar.IsLeapYear(1966))
```

The fragment uses the fully qualified namespace because the sample program did not import the `System.Globalization` namespace. The `MessageBox.Show` method displays False; 1966 was not a leap year.

Date

Several aspects of dates have changed in Visual Basic .NET. The `Date` function has been replaced with the `Today` function for getting and setting the system date.

Date types are no longer implemented as `Double` precision numbers where the whole number represents the date and the fraction represents the time. In Visual Basic .NET, date and time values are implemented as a `ValueType` structure. You can use the procedure shared method `Convert.ToDouble` to convert a `DateTime` value in Visual Basic .NET to a `Double` and existing Visual Basic for Applications (VBA) double-dates can be converted to Visual Basic .NET `DateTime` values by calling the `Shared` method

FromOADate. (FromOADate is shorthand for *From Office Automation Date*, or the old double-style date still used in VBA.)

Date$ has been replaced by DateString in Visual Basic .NET. DateString can be used to get the system date as a string or set the system date from a string.

Empty Has Been Replaced with Nothing

Visual Basic 6 supported the notion of null values with Empty, Null, "", and Nothing. Fewer variations representing nothingness exist in Visual Basic .NET; Empty and Null have been replaced with Nothing. Where you would have used Empty and Null in VB6, replace them with a comparison to Nothing.

The IsEmpty and IsNull functions are not supported in Visual Basic .NET.

Now

Now and Timer are ReadOnly Shared properties in Visual Basic .NET that return the current date and time and the seconds and milliseconds since midnight, respectively. Get a value from the Now property by using the DateTime structure or a DateTime instance. The Timer property is defined in the Microsoft.VisualBasic namespace. (There are also Timer classes defined in the System.Timers and System.Windows.Forms namespaces.)

You can get the current date and time by calling DateTime.Now. You can use the Timer property to cache a reference time, and then compare the reference time to a future time (see Figure A.5).

```
Dim Start As Double = Timer
System.Threading.Thread.Sleep(1500)
MsgBox(Format("Elapsed time is {0}", Timer - Start))
```

FIGURE A.5

The MsgBox showing the value of the elapsed time after the thread sleeps for 1.5 seconds.

AppendixC

1.50216000000364

OK

The fragment declares a Double and uses the Timer property to cache a reference number of milliseconds. The shared method Sleep puts the current thread to sleep for 1500 milliseconds and then displays the elapsed time.

Rnd and Round

The random function (Rnd) and the Round function, like many things in Visual Basic
.NET, have been relocated to the System namespace in the Math class as Shared members. Rnd returns a random number, and Round performs rounding on floating-point numbers. The System namespace is automatically imported into your applications; just
remember that these methods are shared members of the Math class.

Instead of the Rnd function, you can use the new Random class to generate random numbers in a more organized manner. The following code fragment demonstrates how to construct a Random object, passing the random number generator seed to the constructor.

```
Dim R As New Random(100)
Dim I As Integer
For I = 0 To 9
  Debug.WriteLine(R.Next(100))
Next
```

The first statement constructs an instance of Random with a seed of 100. Random numbers are floating-point numbers between 0.0 and 1.0. In VB6 we multiplied these small
decimal numbers by a scalar to generate random numbers within a particular range of
numbers; for example, Rnd * 100 generated random numbers from 0.0 to 100.0. The
statement R.Next(100) employs one of the overloaded Random methods that returns a
number less than or equal to max value.

PSet and Scale Are Not Supported in Visual Basic .NET

PSet allows you to set a single pixel in VB6, and Scale allows you to define the coordinate system of forms and various other controls. These procedures have no direct support
in Visual Basic .NET. Refer to the System.Drawing and System.Drawing.Design namespaces for graphics support in .NET. (Chapter 17 covers graphics programming in Visual
Basic .NET.)

Sgn and Sqr Have New Home and Name in Visual Basic .NET

Like the Atn procedure, Sgn and Sqr are supported in Visual Basic .NET, but they have a
new home and the names have been refined to make them more readable.

Math routines are defined in the System namespace in the Math class as shared methods
Sign and Sqrt, respectively. Sign returns -1 if the value is less than 0, 0 if the value is 0,
and 1 if the value is greater than 0. Sqrt returns the square root of a number.

String Class

Strings are immutable instances of the `String` class in Visual Basic .NET. When you modify a string, you are actually implicitly creating a new instance of a string, initialized with the new value.

`String` is derived directly from `Object`. You can declare string variables as you did in VB6, treating a string like a value type, or you can use the object-creation syntax and pass parameters to the string class. Strings behave like `ValueType` structures but are reference types.

In most cases, you will use Visual Basic .NET strings just as you would VB6 strings.

```
Dim S As String
S = "Some Text!"
```

The `String` class is worth examining because it contains many new capabilities. Refer to Chapter 2's section "String Type" for more on strings in Visual Basic .NET.

Time

The `Time` function has been replaced with the `DateTime.TimeOfDay` property in Visual Basic .NET. The `TimeOfDay` property can be used to get and set the system time.

As with the `Date$` function, the `Time$` function has been replaced with the `Microsoft.VisualBasic.TimString` property. `TimeString` can be used to get the system time as a string or set the system time from a string.

VarType

The VB6 `VarType` function that returned an enumerated value indicating the type of data stored in a variant has been replaced with the `Value__` field of `System.TypeCode`. To retrieve an enumerated representation of a type, access the `Value__` property of the `TypeCode` enumeration. The following statement prints the `Value__` of the `sender` object passed to an event handler.

```
MsgBox(sender.GetType.GetTypeCode(sender.GetType).value__)
```

IntelliSense does not provide a hint indicating the presence of the `Value__` attribute of the `TypeCode` enumeration; you just have to know it is there. Keep in mind that code that is written based on underlying values of types is not very portable and should be avoided.

Replace `Variant` with `Object`

The `Variant` type was implemented in VB6 to support COM. Variant types have been replaced with `Object` types in Visual Basic .NET. Where you would have used a `Variant` in VB6, use an `Object` in Visual Basic .NET.

> **Tip**
>
> When you type the word **Variant** as a data type, Visual Studio .NET—the code editor—replaces it with the `Object` type.

There are several other noteworthy facts regarding `Variant` types. The `Variant` keyword still exists in Visual Basic .NET, but it is a do-nothing reserved word that has no meaning. And, finally, in VB6, if you performed arithmetic that resulted in a number too big for a data type—for instance, adding two integers whose sum was greater than the maximum value for integers—VB6 converted the result to a `Variant`. This situation is referred to as *overflow*. Visual Basic .NET indicates that an overflow condition exists in the task list and refers you to the help documentation indicating the acceptable values for specific data types.

Bibliography

Appleman, Dan. *Moving to VB.NET: Strategies, Concepts, and Code (Beta 2)*. Berkeley, CA: APress, 2001.

Booch, Grady. *Object-Oriented Analysis and Design with Applications*. Reading, MA: Addison-Wesley, 1994.

Booch, Grady. *Object Solutions: Managing the Object-Oriented Project*. Reading, MA: Addison-Wesley, 1995.

Cooper, Alan. *The Inmates Are Running the Asylum: Why High-Tech Products Drive Us Crazy and How To Restore the Sanity*. Indianapolis, IN: Sams Publishing, 1999.

Coplien, James O. *Advanced C++ Programming Styles and Idioms*. Reading, MA: Addison-Wesley, 1991.

Fowler, Martin. *Refactoring: Improving the Design of Existing Code*. Reading, MA.: Addison-Wesley, 1999.

Hirshberg, Jerry. *The Creative Priority: Putting Innovation to Work in Your Business*. New York, NY: HarperBusiness, 1999.

Hollis, Billy, et al. *VB.NET Programming with the Public Beta*. Burmingham, UK: Wrox Press, 2001.

Kimmel, Paul. *Sams Teach Yourself Microsoft Access 2002 Programming in 24 Hours*. Indianapolis, IN.: Sams Publishing, 2001.

Mack, Donny and Doug Seven. *Programming Data-Driven Web Applications with ASP.NET*. Indianapolis, IN: Sams Publishing, 2002.

Michaelis, Mark, and Philip Spokas. *C# Developer's Headstart*. Berkeley, CA: Osborne McGraw-Hill, 2001.

Norman, Donald A. *The Design of Everyday Things*. New York, NY: Doubleday, 1988.

Patton, Ron. *Software Testing*. Indianapolis, IN: Sams Publishing, 2000.

Platt, David. *Introducing Microsoft .NET*. Redmond, WA: Microsoft Press, 2001.

Sedgewick, Robert. *Algorithms in C++*. 1st ed. Reading, MA.: Addison-Wesley, 1992.

Stroustrup, Bjarne. *The Design and Evolution of C++*. Reading, MA: Addison-Wesley, 1994.

Thai, Thuan, and Hoang Lam. *.NET Framework Essentials*. Sebastopol, CA: O'Reilly & Associates, 2001.

Utley, Craig. *A Programmer's Introduction to Visual Basic.NET*. Indianapolis, IN: Sams Publishing, 2001.

Zuboff, Shoshana. *In the Age of the Smart Machine: The Future of Work and Power*. New York, NY: Basic Books, 1988.

INDEX

M